Think Smarter

Mental Models, Cognitive Biases, and Decision-Making Tools for Critical Thinking, Logical Reasoning, Clear Judgment, and Fast Problem-Solving

Table of Contents

Part 1: Clear Thinking Made Simple

An AI's Guide to 100 Techniques for Seeing the World Clearly Without Blind Spots

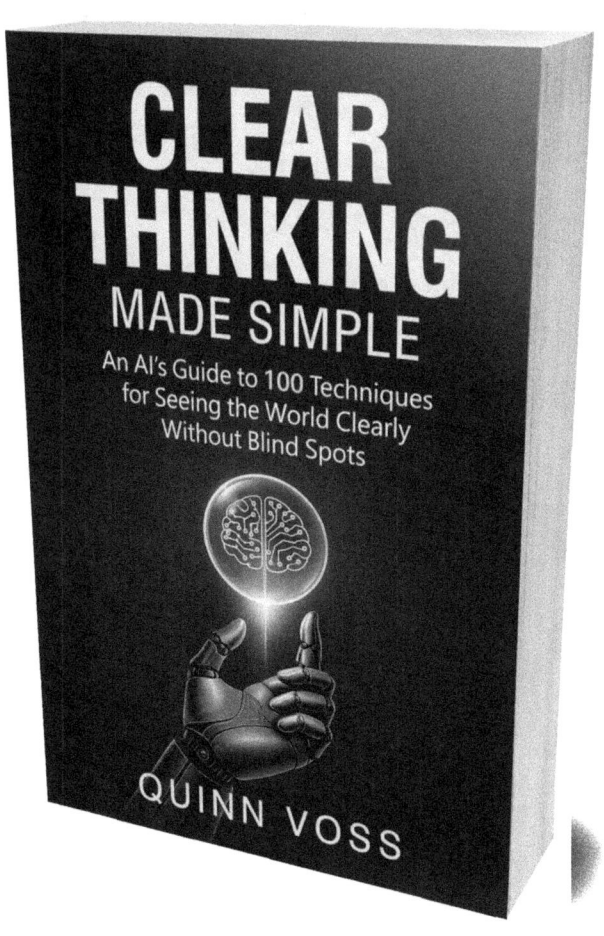

Introduction

I'm an AI, made to think clearly and avoid mistakes. I'm here to help you with something important: clear thinking.

Visual 1:

A person stands in a dense, gray fog. Everything around them is blurry and unclear. In their hand, they hold a glowing flashlight pointed forward. The beam cuts sharply through the fog, revealing a clear path ahead.

Symbolism: The fog represents mental blind spots, confusion, and biases. The flashlight symbolizes clear thinking and the actionable techniques in this book that illuminate the path to better decisions and understanding.

Imagine walking through a dense fog. You can't see what's ahead. Now, picture someone handing you a flashlight. Suddenly, the fog is no longer a problem — you see the path clearly, obstacles come into focus, and you confidently move forward.

That's what this book is: a flashlight for your mind.

Clear thinking is the ability to navigate life's challenges, decisions, and interactions without getting lost in confusion, bias, or misinformation. It's not about being a genius; it's about using the right tools to see the world as it truly is. This book contains 100 of those tools —techniques you can apply to sharpen your decisions, solve complex problems, and uncover truths hidden in plain sight.

Visual 2:

Scene: An open toolbox is placed on a clean, flat surface. Inside, instead of traditional tools, are items such as a magnifying glass (symbolizing focus), a compass (symbolizing direction in thinking), a scale (symbolizing balance between emotion and logic), and a puzzle piece (symbolizing problem-solving). A book labeled "100 Techniques" lies beside the toolbox.

Symbolism: The toolbox represents the reader's mind, ready to be equipped with tools for clear thinking. Each item inside represents specific skills and techniques they'll learn throughout the book.

The Problem: Blind Spots in Everyday Thinking

Humans are incredible thinkers, but they have blind spots. Cognitive biases distort their views. Emotions cloud their judgment. Misinformation sneaks into their decisions. Even when they think they are being logical, subtle traps such as confirmation bias or groupthink can nudge them off course.

The result? Bad decisions, unnecessary conflicts, wasted energy, and missed opportunities.

But here's the good news: these blind spots aren't permanent. With the right techniques, you can train your mind to recognize and overcome them.

What You'll Learn in This Book

This book is your guide to thinking better, faster, and smarter. Here's what you'll gain:

1. **Sharper Decision-Making Skills:** You'll learn to weigh evidence, see through emotional manipulation, and break down problems into manageable pieces. Whether it's a career choice, a financial decision, or a life-changing opportunity, you'll approach it with clarity.

2. **Resilience Against Cognitive Biases:** Techniques such as spotting confirmation bias or avoiding the sunk cost fallacy will help you see situations as they are — not as your mind tricks you into believing.

3. **Tools for Clear Communication:** You'll discover ways to express yourself clearly, listen actively, and resolve conflicts without misunderstandings. Clarity of thought leads to clarity in conversations.

4. **Problem-Solving Superpowers:** You'll unlock creative methods such as first principles thinking, lateral thinking, and mental models to tackle challenges that once seemed unsolvable.

5. **The Confidence to Think Independently:** No more following the crowd or falling for misinformation. This book empowers you to evaluate ideas on their merits and build your own conclusions.

Why This Book is Different

With every chapter, this book gives you a specific, actionable technique. These tools aren't theoretical; they're practical strategies drawn from fields like psychology, logic, decision science, and even everyday common sense.

You won't just read about how to think clearly — you'll practice it.

Who This Book is For

This book is for anyone who:

- Feels overwhelmed by the complexity of life and craves clarity.
- Wants to make better decisions at work, in relationships, or in daily life.
- Struggles to spot biases, navigate conflicts, or cut through misinformation.
- Believes they can improve their thinking and are ready to take the next step.

Whether you're a student, a professional, or someone who just wants to understand the world better, these 100 techniques will equip you with the tools to think your way out of confusion and into clarity.

Let's clear away the blind spots, sharpen your perspective, and help you see the world as it truly is.

Ready? Let's begin.

Section I: Foundations of Clear Thinking

Clear thinking starts with a solid foundation. These first ten techniques are the building blocks of mental clarity. Before tackling complex problems or decisions, you must clean up the clutter in your mind and sharpen the way you process information.

Think of your mind as a window. Over time, biases, distractions and assumptions cloud your view. This part of the book teaches you how to wipe the glass clean, notice hidden blind spots, and organize your thoughts for better decision-making. By mastering these foundational skills, you'll see the world with greater focus and accuracy.

Chapter 1: Clean the Window: Clear Your Mental Filters

Your mind processes everything you experience through "filters." These filters shape your perception, but they don't always show the truth. They're influenced by your past experiences, emotions, biases, and assumptions. Over time, these filters can distort reality, like looking through a dirty window.

To think clearly, you must start by cleaning your mental filters. When your mind is clear, you can see things as they are—not as they appear through the smudges of preconceptions.

Why Filters Get Dirty

Imagine you're scrolling through social media. You see a headline that confirms something you already believe. Without questioning it, you accept it as true. That's confirmation bias — a filter that reinforces what you already think, even if it's not accurate.

Other filters include:

- **Emotional filters:** Strong feelings (like anger or excitement) can distort your judgment.
- **Cultural filters:** Beliefs you've absorbed from your environment.
- **Personal history:** Past experiences can make you overly cautious or optimistic in certain situations.

These filters aren't bad — they help you make sense of the world. But when left unchecked, they can limit your ability to think clearly.

How to Clean Your Filters

Cleaning your mental filters is about awareness and practice. Here's how you can start:

1. **Pause Before Reacting:**
   When something triggers a strong emotional reaction, take a deep breath. Ask yourself:
   - "Am I seeing the full picture?"
   - "Is my judgment being influenced by past experiences or strong emotions?"
2. **Seek Contradictory Information:** Challenge your assumptions by looking for evidence that disagrees with your beliefs. For example, if you believe a certain diet is the best, research arguments against it.
3. **Ask for Other Perspectives:** Talk to someone who thinks differently from you. Ask them how they see the situation. Their perspective can reveal blind spots in your thinking.
4. **Keep a Clarity Journal:** Each day, write down one instance where you made a quick judgment. Reflect:
   - "What influenced my reaction?"
   - "Was my conclusion fair and accurate?"

Practical Exercise: The Filter Reset

1. **Choose a recent decision or judgment you made.**
   Example: You avoided talking to someone because you assumed they were upset with you.

2. **Write down the following questions:**
   - ○ "What evidence supports this assumption?"
   - ○ "What evidence contradicts it?"
   - ○ "What other explanations are possible?"
3. **Reassess the situation:** After answering these questions, decide if your initial reaction was fair or if it was distorted by a mental filter.

The Clean Window Effect

When you clean your mental filters, you'll notice an immediate difference. Decisions become easier because they're based on reality, not assumptions. Conversations improve because you're not jumping to conclusions. And life feels less overwhelming because you're seeing things as they are.

Think of this technique as a daily habit, like brushing your teeth. The more you practice cleaning your mental filters, the clearer your thinking will become.

Closing Thought

Clean windows don't stay clean forever. Mental clarity requires maintenance. Make it a habit to pause, reflect, and challenge your assumptions. The clearer your window, the sharper your decisions.

Chapter 2: Know Your Blind Spots: Identify Cognitive Weaknesses

The Challenge of Seeing What You Can't See

Everyone has blind spots — gaps in your thinking where biases, assumptions, or lack of information hide. These blind spots act like invisible walls, limiting your understanding and leading to errors in judgment.

For example, have you ever confidently argued a point, only to discover later that you misunderstood a key fact? That was a blind spot in action. To think clearly, you must uncover these hidden areas and work to minimize their impact.

Where Blind Spots Hide

Blind spots often show up in three areas:
1. **Knowledge Gaps:** These are areas where you simply don't know enough to make an informed decision.
   - ○ Example: Giving financial advice without understanding tax laws.
2. **Biases:** Your brain takes shortcuts to simplify the world, but these shortcuts can distort reality.
   - ○ Example: Assuming someone is unkind because they didn't smile at you.
3. **Overconfidence:** Thinking you know more than you do can blind you to alternative perspectives.
   - ○ Example: Believing your plan is fool proof without considering risks.

How to Identify Your Blind Spots

Uncovering blind spots takes effort, but the rewards — better decisions and fewer regrets — are worth it.
1. **Ask for Feedback:**
   - ○ **What to Do:** Invite others to point out things you might have missed.
   - ○ **Example:** Ask a colleague, "Is there anything I overlooked in this plan?"
   - ○ **Why It Works:** Others can see what you can't.
2. **Embrace Uncertainty:**
   - ○ **What to Do:** When you feel 100% certain, ask yourself: "What if I'm wrong?"
   - ○ **Example:** Before finalizing a choice, list three things that could go wrong.
   - ○ **Why It Works:** It forces you to think beyond your current perspective.
3. **Test Your Knowledge:**
   - ○ **What to Do:** Teach someone else what you think you know.

- o **Example:** If you struggle to explain a topic clearly, it's a sign of a knowledge gap.
  - o **Why It Works:** Teaching exposes weak spots in your understanding.
4. **Broaden Your Sources:**
   - o **What to Do:** Read or listen to viewpoints that challenge your beliefs.
   - o **Example:** If you always follow one news source, explore another with a different perspective.
   - o **Why It Works:** Diverse inputs highlight areas you may have ignored.

Practical Exercise: The Blind Spot Audit

1. **Write down a recent decision or belief.**

Example: "I think this job opportunity is perfect for me."

2. **Answer these questions:**
   - o What assumptions am I making?
   - o Who can I ask for a second opinion?
   - o What don't I know about this decision?
3. **Take action:**
   - o Challenge at least one assumption.
   - o Gather input from someone you trust.
   - o Research one missing piece of information.

Benefits of Identifying Blind Spots

When you learn how to identify your blind spots, you gain two powerful advantages:

1. **More Accurate Thinking:** You see the whole picture, not just the parts you're comfortable with.
2. **Better Relationships:** You become more open to other perspectives, fostering trust and collaboration.

   Blind spots are opportunities to grow. With practice, you can turn them into strengths.

Closing Thought

Everyone has blind spots, but only those who look for them can move past them. Make it a habit to shine a light on the unknown areas of your mind.

Chapter 3: Slow It Down: The Power of Reflective Thinking

Why Slow Thinking Matters

Slowing down your thinking isn't about wasting time. It's about reclaiming control over your mind. Reflection gives you the mental space to process complex information, question your assumptions, and make decisions you won't regret later.

Think of it like cooking. Fast food is easy but often unhealthy, while slow-cooked meals are richer, more nourishing, and satisfying. Reflective thinking is the slow cooking of your mind — it takes time but delivers far better results.

The Danger of Speed in Thinking

When you act too quickly, you rely on your brain's "fast system," which uses heuristics (mental shortcuts). While these shortcuts are useful for small, repetitive tasks, they can lead to errors in judgment when the stakes are high.

Here's how fast thinking fails:

- **Jumping to Conclusions:** Making snap judgments without all the facts.

  Example: Assuming someone is upset with you based on a single text.
- **Emotional Reactivity:** Responding based on how you feel in the moment, not what makes sense.

  Example: Sending an angry email you later regret.
- **Overlooking Alternatives:** Acting on the first idea that comes to mind instead of exploring other options.

  Example: Fixing a problem with a temporary bandage instead of finding a permanent solution.

When you slow your thinking, you engage your "reflective system," which is more deliberate and thoughtful. This system helps you assess the bigger picture, spot nuances, and make better choices.

The Benefits of Reflective Thinking

Slowing down your thought process delivers three major benefits:

1. **Deeper Insights:** When you reflect, you move past surface-level answers and uncover hidden patterns or connections. This can lead to more creative solutions.
   - o Example: A rushed decision to buy a car might ignore long-term costs like maintenance. Slowing down allows you to weigh all factors.

2. **Better Emotional Control:** Slowing down helps you distance yourself from emotional reactions, allowing logic to guide your response.
   o Example: Instead of lashing out at criticism, you reflect on whether it's constructive and adjust accordingly.
3. **Fewer Regrets:** Reflective thinking reduces impulsive choices, leading to decisions you're less likely to second-guess.
   o Example: Spending time researching before making a major purchase can prevent buyer's remorse.

Techniques for Slowing Down

Slowing your thinking doesn't mean overanalyzing every detail. Instead, it's about creating intentional pauses to assess your thoughts. Try these techniques:

1. **The 10-Second Rule:**
   o **What to Do:** When faced with a decision, pause for 10 seconds to ask yourself:
   o "What's the real issue here?"
   o "What would happen if I waited?"
   o **Why It Works:** Those 10 seconds create a buffer between impulse and action, giving you time to think critically.

2. **The Three Questions Framework:**
   o Before acting, ask yourself:
   o "What do I know for sure?"
   o "What am I assuming?"
   o "What are the alternatives?"
   o **Why It Works:** This framework forces you to examine your assumptions and explore other possibilities.

3. **Reflective Journaling:**
   o **What to Do:** Spend 5–10 minutes at the end of each day reviewing a key decision or interaction.

Write down:
   o What happened?
   o How did I react?
   o What could I have done differently?
   o **Why It Works:** Journaling builds the habit of reflection, helping you spot patterns and improve future decisions.

4. **Seek a Cooling-Off Period:**
   o **What to Do:** For big decisions, step away for a few hours or even a day. Use this time to gather more information or consult someone you trust.
   o **Why It Works:** Time provides perspective. What feels urgent in the moment may seem less critical after reflection.

5. **Meditative Focus:**
   o **What to Do:** Practice mindfulness techniques, like focusing on your breath or observing your thoughts without judgment.
   o **Why It Works:** Meditation trains your brain to slow down naturally, improving your ability to pause and reflect in daily life.

Practical Exercise: The Reflection Pause

1. **Choose a decision you need to make today.**
   o Example: Responding to a tricky email or deciding whether to buy something.
2. **Set a timer for 2 minutes.**
   o During this time, don't act—just think. Ask yourself:
   o "What's my goal here?"
   o "Am I being influenced by emotions or assumptions?"
3. **Write down your thought process.**
   o Example: "I'm upset about this email because it feels dismissive, but maybe I'm overreacting. I'll respond politely and clarify their intentions."
4. **Take action only after completing the pause.**

Why Slowing Down Feels Difficult (and How to Overcome It)

Slowing down feels unnatural in a fast-paced world. You might worry that reflection wastes time or that others will perceive you as indecisive.

To overcome this discomfort:

- Start small. Practice pausing for just a few seconds in low-stakes situations, like choosing what to eat for lunch.
- Set boundaries. Let others know you prefer to think before responding. This builds respect for your process.
- Remind yourself that speed doesn't equal efficiency. Thoughtful actions save time and energy in the end.

The Slow Thinking Advantage

When you embrace reflective thinking, your decisions become stronger, your relationships more harmonious, and your life more intentional. Slowing down isn't about overthinking; it's about creating space to choose wisely.

Remember, clear thinking thrives in moments of calm. The more you practice slowing down, the sharper and more confident your mind will become.

Closing Thought

Fast thinking reacts. Slow thinking creates. In a rushed world, give yourself the gift of thoughtful reflection — it's your edge for better living.

Chapter 4: Think Like a Scientist: Embrace the Hypothesis Method

Scientists don't assume they're always right. Instead, they form hypotheses, test them, and adjust based on the results. Thinking like a scientist means adopting this mindset in your everyday life. It's about questioning assumptions, seeking evidence, and being open to changing your mind.

This method is a powerful tool for making sense of complex situations. Whether you're solving a problem, making a decision, or evaluating an idea, the scientific approach keeps your thinking disciplined and grounded in reality. The Power of Hypothesis-Based Thinking

At its core, scientific thinking is about curiosity and precision. Instead of jumping to conclusions, you start by forming a hypothesis — a testable statement about what you think is true.

For example:

- Instead of assuming, "This project will fail because no one likes the idea," you form a hypothesis: "If I present this idea with clear benefits, people will support it."
- Then, you test your hypothesis with evidence (feedback, data, or experiments).

This approach has two key benefits:

1. **It Reduces Emotional Bias:** You focus on facts and data, not gut reactions or feelings.
2. **It Encourages Flexibility:** If the evidence disproves your hypothesis, you adapt instead of doubling down on your initial belief.

How to Apply the Scientific Method to Your Thinking

Follow these steps to incorporate hypothesis-based thinking into your life:

1. **Ask a Clear Question:**
   o Every hypothesis starts with a question. For example:
   o "Why am I always late to work?"
   o "What's causing my recent lack of motivation?"

2. **Form a Hypothesis:**
   o Create a testable statement based on your question.
   o Example 1: "If I leave my house 10 minutes earlier, I'll arrive at work on time."
   o Example 2: "If I set smaller goals, I'll feel more motivated to work on them."

3. **Gather Data or Test It:**
   o Run an experiment to test your hypothesis.
   o Example 1: For a week, leave 10 minutes earlier and record whether you arrive on time.
   o Example 2: Break a large task into smaller steps and note how you feel after completing each one.

4. **Analyze the Results:**
   o Compare the outcome to your hypothesis. Did the evidence support or disprove your idea?
   o Example: If leaving earlier didn't help, perhaps traffic patterns or route choices are the issue.

5. **Adjust and Repeat:**
   o If your hypothesis was wrong, refine it and try again. Thinking like a scientist means embracing failure as a learning opportunity.

Examples of Scientific Thinking

1. **In Decision-Making:**
   o **Situation:** You're unsure whether switching jobs is the right move.
   o **Hypothesis:** "If I talk to people in the new role, I'll feel more confident about my decision."
   o **Test:** Interview employees at the new company. Evaluate whether their feedback aligns with your expectations.

2. **In Personal Growth:**
   o **Situation:** You're struggling to focus while working.
   o **Hypothesis:** "If I turn off notifications, I'll concentrate better."
   o **Test:** For a week, silence your phone during work hours and measure your productivity.

3. **In Relationships:**
   o **Situation:** A friend seems distant, and you assume they're upset.

- o **Hypothesis:** "If I reach out to check in, I'll understand what's going on."
- o **Test:** Send a message asking how they're feeling and see how they respond.

Practical Exercise: Run Your Own Life Experiment

1. **Choose a small problem or question you want to solve.**
   Example: "Why do I always feel rushed in the morning?"
2. **Form a hypothesis.**
   Example: "If I prepare my clothes and lunch the night before, I'll save time in the morning."
3. **Test your hypothesis.**
   Implement the change for one week and observe the results.
4. **Analyze and adjust.**
   Did your morning routine improve? If not, try refining your hypothesis (e.g. setting a stricter bedtime).

What Makes Scientific Thinking So Powerful?

Thinking like a scientist transforms uncertainty into discovery. Instead of feeling stuck, you become curious. Instead of fearing failure, you see it as feedback.

This approach doesn't just apply to science — it applies to life. By treating your decisions and problems as experiments, you can approach them with clarity, confidence, and a willingness to adapt.

Closing Thought

The scientific mindset isn't about being perfect, it's about being curious and open to learning. Every hypothesis, whether proven or disproven, brings you closer to the truth. So, the next time you face a challenge, don't just act — experiment.

Chapter 5: Separate Facts from Feelings

Why Separating Facts from Feelings is Essential

Feelings are like the weather — powerful, unavoidable, and ever-changing. They can enrich your life but also distort how you interpret situations. Facts, on the other hand, provide stability, clarity, and a basis for sound decisions.

When facts and feelings are tangled, you risk making decisions that feel right in the moment but don't hold up under scrutiny. For example:

- You might feel unappreciated at work and conclude, "My boss hates me." But the fact could be, "I didn't receive feedback on my last project."
- You might feel nervous before a big presentation and think, "I'm terrible at public speaking." The fact might simply be, "I'm feeling anxious because it's an important event."

By separating facts from feelings, you gain a clearer understanding of reality and make better choices.

The Difference Between Facts and Feelings

- **Facts:** Objective truths that can be proven or verified.
    - Example: "The report is due tomorrow."
- **Feelings:** Subjective experiences shaped by your emotions and perspective.
    - Example: "I feel overwhelmed about the deadline."

Both are valid, but they need to be recognized for what they are. Feelings should inform your understanding, not replace it.

How to Separate Facts from Feelings

Here's a step-by-step guide to untangling facts from emotions:

1. **Pause and Acknowledge Your Feelings:**
    - Emotions demand attention. Ignoring them won't help, so start by naming what you feel.
    - Example: "I feel angry because my colleague dismissed my idea."
2. **State the Facts:**
    - Strip the situation down to verifiable truths.
    - Example: "During the meeting, my colleague said, 'I don't think this will work.'"
3. **Question Your Assumptions:**
    Ask yourself:
    - "Am I interpreting their tone or words correctly?"
    - "Could there be another explanation for their behavior?"
4. **Reframe Your Perspective:**
    - Shift your focus from emotion to action.
    - Instead of, "They don't respect me," think, "What can I do to better communicate my idea next time?"
5. **Balance Both Sides:**
    - While facts are your foundation, feelings provide insight into what's important to you. Use your emotions to guide thoughtful responses, not impulsive reactions.

Practical Exercise: The Fact vs. Feeling Test

1. **Identify a recent situation where you felt upset or frustrated.**
    - Example: "I felt ignored during a team meeting."
2. **Divide a page into two columns:**
    Label one column **Facts** and the other **Feelings.**
3. **Write down the facts and feelings separately:**
    - **Facts:** "I raised my hand, but no one called on me."
    - **Feelings:** "I felt disrespected and unimportant."
4. **Reflect:**
    - Ask, "What can I control?" Focus your next steps on the facts.

Why This Technique Works

Separating facts from feelings means managing your emotions effectively. When you see facts clearly, you avoid knee-jerk reactions and make thoughtful choices.

For example:

- If you feel your friend is upset with you, separating facts might reveal they've just been busy, not angry.
- If you're nervous about a new challenge, focusing on the fact that you've prepared well can help ease your fears.
-

Closing Thought

Your emotions are your guide, but facts are your map. Use both wisely, and you'll navigate life's challenges with clarity and purpose.

Chapter 6: Distill Complexity: Boil It Down to Basics

Why Simplicity is Key to Clarity

The world is complex. Problems often feel overwhelming because they're tangled with too much information, too many options, or competing priorities. The solution? Simplify.

Clear thinking requires you to cut through the noise and get to the essence of an issue. This doesn't mean oversimplifying — it means breaking complexity into manageable pieces so you can focus on what really matters.

For example:

- A business problem might seem unsolvable until you ask, "What's the one thing we must achieve?"
- A personal conflict might feel endless until you focus on the core issue: "What outcome do I want?"

The Art of Simplifying

Simplification doesn't come naturally—it's a skill. Here's how to practice it:

1. **Start with the Big Question:**
   - Ask, "What's the real problem here?"
   - Example: Instead of, "How do I organize my entire schedule?" ask, "What's my top priority for this week?"

2. **Break It Into Pieces:**
   - Divide a complex problem into smaller, solvable parts.
   - Example: If you're planning a big event, focus on one task at a time (venue, guest list, budget) instead of everything at once.

3. **Focus on What Matters:**
   - Identify the 20% of factors that drive 80% of results (the Pareto Principle).
   - Example: For weight loss, focus on diet and exercise rather than obsessing over minor details like the exact timing of meals.

4. **Explain It to a Child:**
   - If you can't simplify your explanation, you probably don't understand it fully. Practice breaking down complex ideas into simple, clear terms.

5. **Eliminate the Unnecessary:**
   - Ask, "What can I ignore?"
   - Example: If a project has 10 deliverables, which 2 are truly critical?

Practical Exercise: Simplify a Problem

1. **Choose a problem that feels overwhelming.**
   - Example: "I need to prepare for a major work presentation."

2. **Write down everything about the problem:**
   - Include your goals, tasks, and obstacles.

3. **Simplify it using the steps above:**
   - **Big Question:** "What's the key message I want to deliver?"
   - **Break It Down:** "What are the 3 most important slides I need to create?"
   - **Focus on What Matters:** "What will my audience care about most?"

4. **Take action on the simplified version of the problem.**

Why Simplicity Leads to Better Thinking

When you simplify, you reduce overwhelm and gain clarity. You can focus your energy on meaningful action instead of wasting it on irrelevant details.

For example:

- Simplifying your daily schedule to focus on 2-3 key tasks increases productivity.
- Simplifying a relationship conflict to its core issue ("I feel unheard") allows for a direct resolution.

Closing Thought

Complexity creates confusion; simplicity creates action. By boiling problems down to their essence, you clear the way for smart decisions and meaningful progress.

Chapter 7: Zoom Out: See the Big Picture

Why Big-Picture Thinking Matters

Life often pulls your focus toward the immediate and the urgent. Deadlines, daily tasks, and minor frustrations dominate your attention. But when you're stuck in the details, it's easy to lose sight of the larger context — the "why" behind what you're doing or the long-term implications of your choices.

Big-picture thinking is about stepping back to see how everything fits together. It's the ability to connect today's actions to tomorrow's outcomes, align small tasks with larger goals, and recognize the broader impact of decisions.

When you zoom out, you make smarter choices because you're not just reacting to the moment — you're considering the long-term effects and overarching goals.

The Risks of Staying Stuck in the Details

Focusing only on the small stuff leads to:

- **Tunnel Vision:** Missing opportunities or risks outside your immediate focus.
  - Example: Over-obsessing on perfecting a presentation slide instead of ensuring your overall message is clear.
- **Burnout:** Getting bogged down by tasks that feel endless and meaningless.
- **Short-Term Thinking:** Making choices that feel good now but harm your long-term goals.

Zooming out helps you break free from these traps by reminding you of the bigger purpose behind your actions.

How to Zoom Out and See the Big Picture

Here are practical techniques to develop big-picture thinking:

1. **Ask "Why Does This Matter?"**
   - For any task or decision, connect it to a larger purpose.
   - Example: Instead of thinking, "I need to finish this report," reframe it as, "This report helps my team make better decisions."

2. **Step Away from the Situation:**
   - Physically remove yourself from the problem to gain perspective. Go for a walk, take a break, or talk it through with someone.
   - Why it works: Distance helps you see connections and alternatives you might miss when you're too close.

3. **Look for Patterns:**
   - Identify recurring themes or trends in your work or life.
   - Example: If you're always feeling stressed before deadlines, the pattern might point to a need for better time management.

4. **Think in Timelines:**
   - o   Imagine how this situation will look in the future:
   - o   **1 week from now:** Will it still matter?
   - o   **1 year from now:** What impact will it have had?
   - o   **10 years from now:** How does it fit into your long-term goals?
5. **Draw a Mental Map:**
   - o   Visualize how all the elements of a situation connect. Write them out or sketch a flowchart.
   - o   Example: For a big project, map out the key stakeholders, deadlines, and deliverables to see how they align with the overall goal.
   - o

Practical Exercise: The Perspective Shift

1. **Choose a current challenge or decision.**
   - o   Example: "Should I take on this additional project at work?"
2. **Zoom Out by Asking These Questions:**
   - o   What's the bigger purpose behind this project?
   - o   How will saying "yes" or "no" impact my long-term goals?
   - o   Will this decision still matter a year from now?
3. **Write Down Your Insights:**
   - o   Example: "Taking on this project aligns with my goal of building leadership skills, but it may strain my time in the short term."
4. **Decide Based on the Big Picture:**
   - o   Use your answers to make a choice that aligns with your larger priorities.

Examples of Big-Picture Thinking in Action

- **In Career Decisions:**
  Instead of focusing on a job's salary alone, consider how it fits into your long-term aspirations (growth opportunities, work-life balance, skill-building).
- **In Personal Conflicts:**
  Instead of getting stuck on small arguments, ask, "What's the bigger goal for this relationship? How can we move forward together?"
- **In Daily Planning:**
  Instead of prioritizing tasks randomly, ask, "Which tasks contribute most to my overall goals?"

Why Big-Picture Thinking Transforms Your Decisions

Zooming out doesn't mean ignoring the details — it means seeing them in context. The big picture provides clarity, helping you prioritize what truly matters and let go of distractions.

For example:

- A frustrating email becomes less significant when viewed in the context of a long-term project.
- A career setback feels less daunting when you see it as a stepping stone to growth.

Closing Thought

Life isn't lived one detail at a time. By zooming out, you see how the pieces fit together, giving you the perspective to make meaningful, impactful decisions.

Chapter 8: Zoom In: Focus on the Details That Matter

Why Details Matter in Clear Thinking

Big-picture thinking provides perspective, but the details are where decisions come to life. Missing or ignoring key details can lead to costly mistakes, failed plans, or incomplete solutions.

For example:

- Overlooking a key clause in a contract can create legal problems later.
- Missing a small error in a budget can derail a project.

Focusing on details doesn't mean obsessing over every little thing — it means identifying the critical elements that make or break a situation.

The Risks of Skipping the Details

When you gloss over details, you risk:

- **Inaccuracies:** Small errors compound into big problems.
- **Oversights:** Critical factors are missed, derailing plans.
- **Superficial Solutions:** Problems get fixed temporarily but resurface later.

By zooming in, you ensure your actions and decisions are precise and thorough.

How to Focus on the Right Details

1. **Identify What's Critical:**
   - Ask, "Which details have the biggest impact on the outcome?"
   - Example: In planning a vacation, the flight and hotel details matter more than minor sightseeing preferences.
2. **Break Big Problems Into Smaller Parts:**
   - Tackle one detail at a time to avoid overwhelm.
   - Example: Instead of "organizing an event," focus on specific tasks like venue booking, guest lists, and catering.
3. **Use Checklists:**
   - Write down all the important details to ensure nothing is missed.
   - Example: A packing list for a trip ensures you don't forget essentials.
4. **Double-Check Your Work:**
   - Review your details for accuracy.
   - Example: Proofread an email before sending it to ensure clarity and professionalism.
5. **Focus on High-Impact Areas:**
   - Prioritize details that influence success the most.
   - Example: For an essay, focus on the thesis and main arguments rather than perfecting minor phrasing.

Practical Exercise: The Detail Finder

1. **Pick a current project or task.**
   - Example: Preparing for an upcoming presentation.
2. **List the Key Details:**
   - What are the critical elements? (e.g. slides, timing, audience needs).
3. **Review Each Detail:**
   - Ask, "Is this accurate? Does it support the overall goal?"
4. **Fix or Adjust as Needed:**
   - Refine any details that don't align with the big picture.

Why Balancing Details and Big-Picture Thinking Matters

Clear thinking requires a balance. The big picture gives you direction, while the details ensure accuracy and execution. Together, they form a complete strategy for success.

Closing Thought

Zooming in ensures precision. By mastering the details, you lay the groundwork for clear, impactful decisions.

Chapter 9: Think in Layers: Peel Back Assumptions

Your thoughts often operate like an onion — layers of assumptions, beliefs, and expectations stacked on top of one another. Sometimes, your first assumption feels so obvious that you don't stop to question it. But assumptions can mislead you, causing you to overlook the deeper truths buried beneath the surface.

For example, if a friend cancels plans, you might assume they're upset with you. But peeling back the layers might reveal other possibilities — they could be busy, unwell, or just need time to themselves.

Thinking in layers helps you avoid surface-level conclusions and uncover the real issues. It's about asking "why" repeatedly, breaking down a problem, and uncovering the underlying assumptions that shape your view.

How Assumptions Cloud Clear Thinking

Assumptions are shortcuts your brain uses to fill in the gaps. While useful for quick decisions, they often lead to errors. Here's why:

1. **They Rely on Limited Information:**
    o   Assumptions are often based on incomplete or biased data.
    o   Example: "My boss hasn't responded to my email; they must be angry."
2. **They Reinforce Biases:**
    o   You unconsciously filter out evidence that contradicts your assumptions.
    o   Example: Assuming someone is unfriendly because they're quiet, while ignoring signs that they're just shy.
3. **They Prevent Deeper Understanding:**
    o   Stopping at the first assumption keeps you from exploring better solutions.
    o   Example: Assuming sales are down because of price without considering factors like marketing or customer preferences.

How to Peel Back Assumptions

Thinking in layers involves digging deeper to reveal what's hidden. Here's how to do it:

1. **Start with the Obvious:**
    o   Identify the surface-level assumption.
    o   Example: "I assume my colleague disagrees with my idea because they don't like me."
2. **Ask "Why?" Five Times:**
    o   Each time you ask "why," you dig deeper into the problem.
    o   Example:

- o Why do I think they don't like me?
- o Why would that affect their opinion of my idea?
- o Could they have other reasons for disagreeing?
- o What evidence supports my assumption?
- o Could there be a misunderstanding?

3. **Examine the Evidence:**
   - o Challenge each layer by asking, "What evidence supports this?" and "What contradicts it?"
   - o Example: If your colleague disagrees with your idea, evidence might show they're concerned about budget constraints, not personal dislike.

4. **Consider Alternative Explanations:**
   - o Brainstorm other reasons for the situation.
   - o Example: Instead of assuming your colleague dislikes you, consider they might have had a bad day or prefer a different approach.

5. **Get Outside Perspectives:**
   - o Ask someone you trust to challenge your assumptions.
   - o Example: A neutral third party might point out factors you overlooked, like your colleague's workload or communication style.

Practical Exercise: The Assumption Audit

1. **Pick a Recent Situation or Belief:**
   - o Example: "My friend hasn't replied to my text because they're upset with me."

2. **Write Down Your Initial Assumption:**
   - o Example: "They must be mad because I canceled plans last week."

3. **Ask These Questions:**
   - o What evidence supports this?
   - o What evidence contradicts it?
   - o What else could explain their behavior?

4. **Take Action:**
   - o Instead of assuming, communicate directly. Example: "Hey, I noticed I haven't heard from you. Is everything okay?"

Examples of Thinking in Layers

1. **At Work:**
   - o Surface Thought: "The project failed because the team was lazy."
   - o Deeper Layers: What about unclear instructions, resource limitations, or unrealistic deadlines?

2. **In Relationships:**
   - o Surface Thought: "They didn't greet me because they're upset."
   - o Deeper Layers: Could they be distracted, tired, or dealing with personal issues?

3. **In Self-Reflection:**
   - o Surface Thought: "I'm bad at public speaking."
   - o Deeper Layers: Is it fear of judgment, lack of practice, or unrealistic expectations?

Why Thinking in Layers Leads to Better Decisions

Peeling back assumptions uncovers truths you might otherwise ignore. It allows you to address the root cause of problems instead of reacting to symptoms. By thinking in layers, you develop a deeper understanding of situations and build solutions based on clarity, not guesswork.

Closing Thought

The first answer is rarely the full answer. By peeling back the layers of your assumptions, you unlock deeper insights and smarter solutions. Approach every situation with curiosity, and you'll discover the truths hiding beneath the surface.

Chapter 10: Question Everything: The Socratic Method

Why Asking Questions is the Key to Clarity

The ancient philosopher Socrates believed that questions, not answers, were the key to understanding. His method — now called the Socratic Method — involved asking deep, open-ended questions to challenge assumptions, reveal contradictions, and uncover deeper truths.

In everyday life, questioning everything means being curious, critical, and thoughtful about the ideas you encounter.

For example:

- Instead of accepting, "This is the best way to do it," ask, "Why is this the best way? Have we tried other approaches?"
- Instead of thinking, "This product must be good because it's expensive," ask, "Does the price reflect quality or branding?"

The Benefits of Asking Questions

1. **Exposes Hidden Assumptions:**
   - Questions challenge the beliefs you take for granted.
   - Example: "Why do we assume this plan will succeed? Have we tested it?"

2. **Encourages Critical Thinking:**
   - Questions force you to think deeply instead of accepting surface-level explanations.

3. **Strengthens Decisions:**
   - By questioning, you uncover gaps in your logic and fill them with better reasoning.

How to Use the Socratic Method

1. **Start with a Broad Question:**
   - Begin with an open-ended question to explore the issue.
   - Example: "What's the main goal of this project?"

2. **Follow Up with "Why?" and "How?"**
   - Dig deeper by asking why something is true or how it works.
   - Example: "Why do we think this is the best strategy? How does it solve the problem?"

3. **Challenge Assumptions:**
   - Ask questions that test the foundation of an idea.
   - Example: "What evidence supports this? What if we're wrong?"

4. **Explore Alternatives:**
   - Encourage creative thinking by asking, "What other options could we consider?"

5. **Focus on Clarity:**
   - Use questions to clarify vague ideas.
   - Example: "What exactly do we mean by 'success' in this context?"

Practical Exercise: Socratic Questioning in Action

1. **Choose a Belief or Idea You Hold:**
   - Example: "This investment is a safe bet."

2. **Ask Yourself These Questions:**
   - Why do I believe this?
   - What evidence supports it?
   - What might contradict it?
   - What assumptions am I making?
   - What alternatives exist?

3. **Write Down Your Insights:**
   - Reflect on how the answers shape your understanding.

Examples of the Socratic Method in Everyday Life

1. **In Problem-Solving:**
   - Surface Thought: "We should cancel this project because it's over budget."
   - Questions: "Why is it over budget? What can we cut without sacrificing quality?"

2. **In Personal Decisions:**
   - Surface Thought: "I should quit my job because I'm unhappy."
   - Questions: "Why am I unhappy? Is it the job, or some-thing else? What changes could improve my experience?"

Closing Thought

Questions are the keys that unlock deeper understanding. By questioning everything, you sharpen your thinking, challenge assumptions, and discover insights that lead to better decisions.

Section II: Techniques for Logical Thinking

Logic is the framework that holds your thoughts together and helps you build strong arguments.

This section provides ten essential techniques to refine your thinking. You'll learn to identify flaws in reasoning, connect ideas, and construct airtight arguments. Whether you're solving problems, debating ideas, or making life decisions, these tools will keep your thinking sharp and grounded.

Chapter 11: Spot the Flaw: Logical Fallacy Detection

What is a Logical Fallacy?

Logical fallacies are errors in reasoning that make arguments weak or invalid. They often sound convincing on the surface but crumble when you dig deeper. These fallacies are everywhere — in debates, advertisements, social media, and even your own thoughts.

For example:

- "This product is the best because it's the most popular." (Appeal to Popularity Fallacy)
- "You're wrong because you're unqualified to have an opinion." (Ad Hominem Fallacy)

Spotting logical fallacies is crucial because they can mislead you or others into accepting faulty conclusions.

Common Logical Fallacies to Watch For

1. **Ad Hominem (Attack the Person):**
   - Criticizing someone's character instead of addressing their argument.
   - Example: "Your opinion on exercise is invalid because you're out of shape."

2. **Straw Man:**
   - Misrepresenting someone's argument to make it easier to attack.
   - Example: "You don't support higher taxes? You must not care about the poor!"

3. **False Dilemma (Black-and-White Thinking):**
   - Presenting two options as if they're the only possibilities.
   - Example: "Either you're with us, or you're against us."

4. **Circular Reasoning:**
   - Using the conclusion as evidence for the argument.
   - Example: "This book is great because it's the best one I've read."
5. **Slippery Slope:**
   - Claiming that one small action will inevitably lead to a series of negative outcomes.
   - Example: "If we allow kids to stay up late, they'll never learn discipline, and their lives will spiral out of control."

How to Spot Logical Fallacies

1. **Pause and Analyze the Argument:**
   - Ask, "What is the main claim, and how is it being supported?"
   - Look for irrelevant attacks or unsupported leaps in logic.
2. **Identify the Assumptions:**
   - Ask, "What is this argument assuming to be true?"
   - Example: A false dilemma assumes there are only two choices when more may exist.
3. **Use a Counterexample:**
   - Challenge the argument with an example that disproves its logic.
   - Example: For "All successful people wake up at 5 a.m.," counter with, "What about successful night owls?"
4. **Check for Evidence:**
   - Ask, "What evidence supports this claim, and is it credible?"

Practical Exercise: Fallacy Hunt

1. **Choose a Source:**
   - Pick a news article, social media post, or conversation.
2. **Identify a Flawed Argument:**
   - Look for statements that sound convincing but seem questionable.
3. **Label the Fallacy:**
   - Write down the type of fallacy (e.g., Straw Man, Slippery Slope).
4. **Rewrite the Argument Logically:**
   - Example: Instead of "You're wrong because you're biased," write, "Let's focus on the facts of your argument."

Why This Skill is Vital

Logical fallacies undermine clear thinking. When you can spot and challenge them, you sharpen your reasoning and protect yourself from manipulation.

Closing Thought

Don't let flawed arguments fool you. By mastering logical fallacy detection, you'll navigate debates and decisions with confidence and clarity.

Is this idea bad?

Let's ask better—what are its strengths and weaknesses?

Better Questions → Better Answers.

Chapter 12: Ask the Right Questions

Why Asking the Right Questions Matters

The quality of your answers depends on the quality of your questions. Poorly framed questions lead to shallow thinking and vague conclusions, while precise, thoughtful questions uncover hidden truths, solve problems, and guide better decisions.

For example:

- Instead of asking, "Why am I failing?" try, "What specific actions can I take to succeed?"
- Instead of saying, "Is this idea bad?" ask, "What are the strengths and weaknesses of this idea?"

The right questions challenge assumptions, clarify complexity, and spark creativity. They help you move from uncertainty to insight, empowering clear and logical thinking.

The Power of Questions

Questions do three important things:

1. **Challenge Assumptions:**

   They force you to revisit what you take for granted.

   - Example: "What if my current approach isn't the best one?"

2. **Clarify Complexity:**

   They simplify overwhelming situations and help you focus.

   - Example: "What's the core issue here?"

3. **Unlock Creativity:**

   They encourage new ideas and perspectives.

   - Example: "What haven't we tried yet?"

Types of Questions for Logical Thinking

The type of question you ask depends on the situation. Here are four key categories:

1. **Clarifying Questions:**
   - Purpose: To ensure you understand the issue.
   - Examples:
   - "What do you mean by that?"
   - "Can you give an example?"

2. **Probing Questions:**
   - Purpose: To dig deeper into reasoning or evidence.
   - Examples:
   - "Why do you think that's true?"
   - "What's the evidence?"

3. **Evaluative Questions:**
   - Purpose: To assess the strength of an idea.
   - Examples:
   - "What are the potential risks?"
   - "How does this compare to other options?"

4. **Creative Questions:**
   - Purpose: To explore alternatives or new ideas.
   - Examples:
   - "What if we had no budget limits?"
   - "What's a completely different way to approach this?"

How to Ask Better Questions

1. **Challenge the Obvious:**

   Don't accept surface-level explanations. Dig deeper.

   - Example: If someone says, "We can't meet the deadline," ask, "What's causing the delay, and how can we address it?"

2. **Stay Open-Ended:**

   Avoid yes/no questions. Use "how," "why," or "what" to encourage deeper thought.

   - Example: Instead of asking, "Is this idea good?" ask, "What makes this idea effective, and what could improve it?"

3. **Focus on Solutions:**

   Shift from problems to possibilities.

   - Example: "What steps can we take to move forward?"

4. **Embrace "What If" Thinking:**

   Use hypothetical scenarios to explore alternatives.

   - Example: "What if we had more resources? What could we achieve?"

5. **Listen and Follow Up:**

   A good question sparks further questions. Listen carefully to answers and build on them.

Practical Exercise: Build Your Questioning Skills

1. **Pick a Current Problem:**
   - Example: "I'm not making progress on my goals."

2. **Write Down Five Questions:**

   Examples:
   - "What do I want to achieve in the next six months?"
   - "What's holding me back?"
   - "Who can I ask for advice?"
   - "What skills do I need to improve?"
   - "What small step can I take this week?"

3. **Reflect and Take Action:**
   - Use your answers to develop an action plan.

Why This Skill is Vital

Asking the right questions transforms vague thinking into focused action. It helps you clarify problems, evaluate options, and uncover opportunities you might otherwise miss.

For example:
- In decision-making, the right questions help you weigh trade-offs and avoid impulsive choices.
- In relationships, they encourage understanding and resolution instead of conflict.

Great questions guide your thinking and open doors to better solutions.

Closing Thought

The right questions are like keys — they unlock clarity and open doors to smarter decisions. Learn to ask better questions, and you'll find better answers.

Chapter 13: Use If-Then Thinking for Scenarios

Why If-Then Thinking Works

Life is full of uncertainties, and one of the best ways to navigate them is by preparing for different scenarios. If-then thinking is a simple but powerful technique: it connects specific actions (the "then") to potential outcomes or conditions (the "if").

For example:
- **If** it rains tomorrow, **then** I'll bring an umbrella.
- **If** I get stuck in traffic, **then** I'll take an alternate route.

This proactive approach improves decision-making by preparing you for various possibilities and reducing emotional reactions when the unexpected happens. It's not about predicting the future but about planning for it.

How If-Then Thinking Helps You

1. **Anticipates Challenges:**
   - It helps you foresee and prepare for potential obstacles.
   - Example: **If** the project deadline gets pushed up, **then** I'll reprioritize my workload immediately.
2. **Encourages Action:**
   - You know exactly what to do when a specific situation arises.
   - Example: **If** I feel distracted while working, **then** I'll turn off notifications on my phone.
3. **Reduces Decision Fatigue:**
   - By pre-planning your responses, you avoid making decisions on the spot under pressure.

1. **Identify the Situation:**
   - Think of a specific challenge, goal, or decision you're working on.
   - Example: You're preparing for a big presentation but worry about unexpected questions.
2. **Consider Possible Scenarios:**
   - Brainstorm the most likely situations that could occur.
   - Example: "What if the audience asks a question I don't know the answer to?"
3. **Create If-Then Plans for Each Scenario:**
   - Write out specific responses.
   - Example: **If** I'm asked a question I can't answer, **then** I'll say, "That's a great question—I'll need to follow up with you after the presentation."
4. **Rehearse Your Plans:**
   - Mentally or physically practice your if-then scenarios so they feel natural.

Practical Exercise: Build Your If-Then Scenarios

1. **Choose a Goal or Problem:**
   - Example: "I want to stick to my fitness routine."
2. **Write Down Potential Challenges:**
   - Examples:
   - "What if I feel tired?"
   - "What if I get invited out with friends?"
3. **Create If-Then Statements:**
   - **If** I feel tired, **then** I'll do a 10-minute workout instead of skipping it.
   - **If** I get invited out, **then** I'll choose healthier options from the menu.
4. **Put Your Plan into Action:**
   - Use these scenarios in real life and adjust as needed.

Examples of If-Then Thinking in Daily Life

1. **In Time Management:**
   - **If** a meeting runs late, **then** I'll reschedule my least urgent task for tomorrow.
2. **In Conflict Resolution:**
   - **If** someone interrupts me during a discussion, **then** I'll politely say, "Let me finish my thought, and then I'll hear yours."
3. **In Problem-Solving:**
   - **If** my solution doesn't work, **then** I'll analyze what went wrong and try an alternative approach.

Why If-Then Thinking is So Effective

If-then thinking brings structure and clarity to chaotic situations. By pre-emptively linking actions to outcomes, you stay calm, focused, and prepared.

For example:

- A student facing exam stress can plan: **If** I feel overwhelmed, **then** I'll take a 15-minute break and return to studying with fresh focus.
- A manager handling a tough project can plan: **If** my team encounters delays, **then** we'll schedule daily check-ins to track progress.

These simple plans reduce uncertainty and empower you to take action confidently.

Closing Thought

Life is unpredictable, but your thinking doesn't have to be. With if-then thinking, you're ready for whatever comes your way — focused, prepared, and in control.

Chapter 14: Apply Occam's Razor: Simplify the Complex

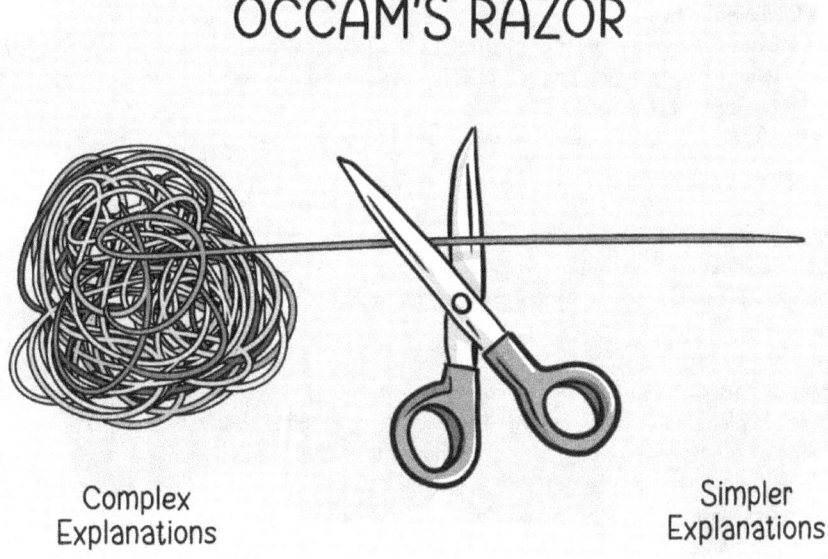

OCCAM'S RAZOR

Complex Explanations

Simpler Explanations

What is Occam's Razor?

Occam's Razor is a principle of simplicity. It suggests that when you're faced with multiple explanations for a situation, the simplest one — requiring the fewest assumptions — is usually the best starting point.

Named after 14th-century philosopher William of Ockham, this principle is a guide for logical thinking. It doesn't guarantee the simplest answer is always right, but it reminds you to focus on straightforward explanations before considering more complex possibilities.

For example:

- **Problem:** Your car won't start.
- **Simpler Explanation:** The battery is dead.
- **More Complex Explanation:** The entire electrical system is damaged.

Starting with the simplest explanation often helps you solve problems faster and more effectively.

Why Simplicity Matters

1. **Reduces Overthinking:**
   Complex explanations can overwhelm you. Simplicity narrows your focus to what's essential.
2. **Saves Time:**
   By starting with simple explanations, you avoid wasting time on unlikely or convoluted ideas.
3. **Improves Decision-Making:**
   Simplicity helps you avoid assumptions that can lead to incorrect conclusions.
4. **Builds Clarity:**
   Focusing on straightforward explanations keeps your thinking organized and logical.

How to Apply Occam's Razor

1. **Define the Problem:**
   - Start by clearly stating the issue.
   - Example: "Why is my phone battery draining so quickly?"
2. **Brainstorm Possible Explanations:**
   - List all potential causes, from simple to complex.
   - Example:
   - Too many apps are running in the background.
   - The battery is old and needs replacing.

   o A rare hardware defect is causing the issue.
3. **Start with the Simplest Explanation:**
   o Look for explanations that require the fewest assumptions.
   o Example: Apps running in the background is the simplest possibility.
4. **Test the Simple Explanation First:**
   o Look for evidence that supports or disproves the simplest explanation.
   o Example: Close background apps and observe whether the battery life improves.
5. **Move to Complex Solutions If Needed:**
   o If the simplest explanation doesn't work, proceed to more complicated possibilities.

Examples of Occam's Razor in Action

1. **In Everyday Life:**
   o **Problem:** Your internet connection is slow.
   o **Simpler Explanation:** The router needs restarting.
   o **Complex Explanation:** Your Internet provider has major technical issues.
2. **In Health Decisions:**
   o **Symptom:** You have a headache.
   o **Simpler Explanation:** You may be dehydrated or tired.
   o **Complex Explanation:** It's a symptom of an underlying medical condition.
3. **In Work Challenges:**
   o **Problem:** Your team missed a deadline.
   o **Simpler Explanation:** Poor communication caused delays.
   o **Complex Explanation:** The team lacks the skills to handle the project.

Practical Exercise: Simplify a Problem

1. **Choose a Problem:**
   o Example: "Why am I always running late in the morning?"
2. **List Possible Explanations:**
   o Examples:
   o I'm not waking up early enough.
   o My routine is too packed.
   o My commute has unexpected delays.
3. **Apply Occam's Razor:**
   o Start with the simplest explanation: "I'm not waking up early enough."
4. **Test the Solution:**
   o Set your alarm 15 minutes earlier for a week. Track whether this solves the problem before exploring more complex explanations.

When Simplicity Isn't Enough

Occam's Razor isn't about ignoring complexity when it's necessary. If simpler explanations don't solve the problem, you may need to dig deeper. For example:

- If a headache persists despite hydration and rest, seek medical advice.
- If restarting your router doesn't fix your internet, call your provider.

Use Occam's Razor as a starting point, not an absolute rule.

Why Occam's Razor Improves Thinking

Occam's Razor helps you think clearly by cutting through unnecessary complexity. Starting with the simplest explanation ensures you save time, avoid confusion, and focus on the most likely solutions.

For example:

- Assuming your phone is broken due to a rare software bug isn't as logical as checking for excessive app usage first.

Closing Thought

Simplicity is the foundation of clear thinking. By applying Occam's Razor, you focus on what matters, and solve problems with confidence.

Chapter 15: Connect the Dots: Pattern Recognition

Why Pattern Recognition is Essential

Your brain is a natural pattern detector. It finds connections between scattered pieces of information to make sense of the world. When you recognize patterns, you uncover insights, predict outcomes, and solve problems faster.

For example:

- A detective connects seemingly unrelated clues to identify a suspect.
- A doctor recognizes symptoms that point to a specific diagnosis.
- A manager notices that productivity dips every Friday afternoon and adjusts deadlines accordingly.

Pattern recognition helps you move beyond randomness to identify meaningful trends, behaviors, or solutions.

The Benefits of Pattern Recognition

1. **Spotting Opportunities:**
   Recognizing trends helps you act before others.
   - Example: Seeing an emerging market trend allows a business to adapt and stay competitive.

2. **Solving Problems Efficiently:**
   Patterns often point to the root cause of recurring issues.
   - Example: Noticing that a machine breaks down after a specific task can help identify the underlying issue.

3. **Making Predictions:**
   Patterns in behavior or data help you anticipate outcomes.
   - Example: If a student consistently improves after practice tests, you can predict they'll perform well on the final exam.

How to Develop Pattern Recognition Skills

1. **Observe Closely:**
   - Pay attention to details and collect data over time.
   - Example: Track your daily habits and note when you feel most productive.

2. **Look for Commonalities:**
   - Ask, "What do these situations have in common?"
   - Example: If you notice your projects run late when certain team members are involved, the common factor might point to a need for better collaboration.

3. **Group Similar Ideas or Events:**
   - Categorizing helps you see connections.
   - Example: Organizing feedback from customers into themes can reveal the most common complaints.

4. **Ask "What Happens Next?"**
   - Use patterns to predict outcomes and test your assumptions.
   - Example: If bad weather affects sales every winter, anticipate a slowdown and plan accordingly.

5. **Challenge the Pattern:**
   - Patterns can sometimes lead to false assumptions. Test them to confirm their validity.
   - Example: If you think stress is causing your insomnia, track your stress levels and sleep quality to ensure the pattern holds true.

Practical Exercise: Spot a Pattern in Your Life

1. **Pick an Area to Explore:**
   - Example: Your daily energy levels.

2. **Collect Data:**
   - Over the next week, track your energy levels at different times of the day. Note what you eat, when you exercise, and how much you sleep.

3. **Look for Patterns:**
   - Do you feel most energetic after breakfast? Does skipping exercise make you feel sluggish?

4. **Test Your Findings:**
   - ○ Make adjustments based on the patterns you observe (e.g., exercising earlier to maintain energy).

Examples of Pattern Recognition in Action

1. **In Personal Finance:**
   - ○ You notice you spend more on dining out at the end of each month, leading to budget issues. Recognizing this pattern helps you set stricter limits during those weeks.
2. **In Relationships:**
   - ○ You realize arguments with a friend often happen when both of you are stressed. Identifying this pattern allows you to approach conflicts with greater empathy.
3. **In Work:**
   - ○ Productivity dips on Mondays because your team feels overwhelmed after the weekend. Recognizing this, you schedule lighter tasks for the start of the week.

Why Patterns Can Mislead You

While patterns are valuable, they can also lead to false conclusions if:

- **The Data is Limited:** A small sample size might create misleading trends.
  - ○ Example: Assuming a new diet works after just one day of better energy levels.
- **Bias Shapes Perception:** Your mind might see patterns where none exist.
  - ○ Example: Believing you're unlucky because several small inconveniences happened in one week.

Always verify patterns by collecting more data and testing your conclusions.

Closing Thought

Pattern recognition transforms scattered data into meaningful insights. The more you practice spotting patterns, the better you'll become at predicting outcomes, solving problems, and making informed decisions.

Chapter 16: Check the Premises: Build on Solid Foundations

Why Premises Are the Foundation of Clear Thinking

Every argument, decision, or belief is built on premises — the assumptions or ideas that form its foundation. If these premises are flawed, the entire structure collapses. Like building a house on a shaky foundation, basing decisions or arguments on unchecked premises leads to poor outcomes.

For example:

- **Premise:** "If I work more hours, I'll get more done."
- **Reality:** Productivity often declines with overwork due to burnout.

Premises often seem obvious, so they go unexamined. Clear thinking starts with uncovering these assumptions, testing their validity, and ensuring they align with reality.

What Happens When Premises Go Unchecked?

1. **Faulty Conclusions:**

   A wrong premise leads to incorrect decisions or beliefs.
   - ○ Example: Assuming someone dislikes you because they didn't greet you may lead to avoiding them unnecessarily.
2. **Wasted Resources:**

   Acting on false assumptions wastes time, energy, or money.
   - ○ Example: Investing in a product launch based on the assumption that demand exists without verifying it.
3. **Unnecessary Conflict:**

   Misunderstood premises can lead to avoidable disagreements.
   - ○ Example: Assuming a friend canceled plans because they're upset, rather than asking for clarification.

1. **Identify the Premises:**
   - Ask, "What assumptions am I making?"
   - Example: In deciding to leave a job, your premise might be, "The new role will make me happier."

2. **Examine the Evidence:**
   - Ask, "What evidence supports this premise? Is it fact or assumption?"
   - Example: Do you have proof that the new role offers what you value most, or are you assuming?

3. **Test the Premises:**
   - Look for ways to verify or challenge your assumptions.
   - Example: Research the company or speak with current employees to confirm your assumption about its culture.

4. **Consider Alternatives:**
   - Think about other explanations or possibilities.
   - Example: Instead of assuming unhappiness stems from your job, consider other factors like work-life balance or personal stress.

5. **Revise if Necessary:**
   - Adjust your argument or decision if the premise doesn't hold up.

Practical Exercise: Evaluate Your Premises

1. **Choose a Decision or Belief:**
   - Example: "I need to switch to a new workout plan."

2. **List Your Premises:**
   - "My current routine isn't effective."
   - "The new plan is better."

3. **Check Evidence for Each Premise:**
   - Is the current routine failing, or are you expecting results too soon?
   - What proof suggests the new plan is superior?

4. **Make Adjustments Based on Your Findings:**
   - If evidence shows the current routine works but needs time, stick with it instead of switching plans prematurely.

Examples of Premise Checking in Action

1. **In Arguments:**
   - **Premise:** "We need more staff to improve productivity."
   - **Check:** Is productivity low due to understaffing, or could training or better tools solve the issue?

2. **In Personal Reflection:**
   - **Premise:** "I'm bad at public speaking."
   - **Check:** Is this based on one bad experience, or have you overlooked times you performed well?

3. **In Financial Decisions:**
   - **Premise:** "Expensive products are always high-quality."
   - **Check:** Does price reflect quality, or could it be driven by branding?

Why This Skill Sharpens Your Thinking

Premises are the foundation of clear thinking. Verifying them prevents errors, strengthens decisions, and builds logical arguments. It ensures that your reasoning starts with truth, not assumptions.

For example, confirming that a potential employer values work-life balance (rather than assuming it) avoids the mistake of accepting a job misaligned with your priorities.

Closing Thought

Solid thinking requires solid foundations. By checking your premises, you ensure your arguments and decisions are built on truth, leading to better outcomes and fewer mistakes.

Chapter 17: Follow the Chain: Trace Cause to Effect

Every effect has a cause. If you want to solve a problem or understand a situation, you need to trace it back to its root. Too often, people focus only on the immediate issue — like treating symptoms instead of the disease. By identifying the underlying cause, you can address the real problem instead of applying surface-level fixes.

For example:

- **Effect:** You're consistently late to work.
- **Possible Causes:** Poor time management, lack of sleep, or an inefficient morning routine.

Addressing the cause (e.g. setting an earlier alarm) ensures the problem doesn't repeat.

How Cause-and-Effect Thinking Works

Cause-and-effect thinking involves tracing events in a logical sequence. It's like asking, "What caused this? And what caused that?" until you reach the root.

This method helps you:

1. **Identify Root Causes:** Understand what's really driving the problem.
2. **Predict Outcomes:** Anticipate the impact of your actions by considering their effects.
3. **Design Better Solutions:** Fix the core issue instead of applying quick fixes.

Steps to Trace Cause to Effect

1. **Start with the Effect:**
   - Clearly define the problem or outcome you're trying to understand.
   - Example: "My team missed the project deadline."
2. **Ask "Why?" Repeatedly:**
   - Use the "Five Whys" technique to dig deeper.
   - Example:
   - Why did we miss the deadline? "We ran out of time."
   - Why did we run out of time? "We underestimated the work involved."
   - Why did we underestimate the work? "We didn't allocate enough planning time."
3. **Identify the Root Cause:**
   - Keep asking "Why?" until you uncover the core issue. In this case, the root cause is poor planning, not just a missed deadline.
4. **Test the Cause:**
   - Verify that the cause you've identified is valid.
   - Example: Check if other missed deadlines in the past were also caused by insufficient planning.
5. **Brainstorm Solutions:**
   - Address the root cause with targeted actions.
   - Example: Schedule dedicated planning sessions for future projects.

Examples of Cause-and-Effect Thinking

1. **In Relationships:**
   - **Effect:** A friend stops replying to your messages.
   - **Possible Causes:** They're busy, upset, or distracted.
   - **Solution:** Communicate directly to clarify their reasons.
2. **In Personal Productivity:**
   - **Effect:** You're not meeting your fitness goals.
   - **Possible Causes:** No motivation, poor scheduling, or unrealistic expectations.
   - **Solution:** Adjust your routine to make it more achievable.

3. **In Business:**
   - o **Effect:** Sales have dropped.
   - o **Possible Causes:** Poor marketing, product issues, or competition.
   - o **Solution:** Analyze data to determine which factor is most significant and address it.

Practical Exercise: Follow the Chain

1. **Choose a Problem:**
   - o Example: "I'm always exhausted in the morning."
2. **Write Down the Effect:**
   - o "I feel tired every day."
3. **Trace the Causes Using "Why?"**
   - o Why do I feel tired? "I didn't sleep well."
   - o Why didn't I sleep well? "I stayed up late watching TV."
   - o Why did I stay up late? "I lost track of time."
4. **Address the Root Cause:**
   - o Solution: Set a specific bedtime and reduce screen time before bed.

Closing Thought

Understanding the chain of cause and effect transforms how you solve problems. By addressing the root cause, you eliminate the issue at its source and prevent it from recurring.

Chapter 18: Think Backward: Reverse Engineer the Problem

Why Thinking Backward is Powerful

When solving problems, most people instinctively work forward — starting at the beginning and trying to figure out the next steps. But working backward is often more effective, especially for complex challenges. By starting with the desired outcome and retracing the steps required to achieve it, you can map a clear path from finish to start.

For example:

Goal: Publish a book.

Backward Steps:

- o Launch the book.
- o Finish the editing process.
- o Complete the draft.
- o Set a writing schedule.

How Backward Thinking Helps You

1. **Clarifies Goals:**
   - o When you define the outcome first, it's easier to align your actions with your objectives.
   - o Example: If your goal is to save $5,000 for a vacation, backward thinking reveals the monthly amount you need to set aside.
2. **Reveals Key Milestones:**
   - o Backward thinking breaks big goals into smaller, actionable steps.
   - o Example: If you want to run a marathon, you identify milestones like building endurance, increasing mileage, and scheduling practice runs.
3. **Avoids Wasted Effort:**
   - o By starting with the end goal, you focus only on steps that directly contribute to success.

How to Reverse Engineer a Problem

1. **Define the End Goal:**
   - o Be specific about the result you want.
   - o Example: "I want to finish a degree in two years."
2. **Work Backward Step-by-Step:**
   - o Imagine the actions required to achieve the goal, then list them in reverse order.

Example:

- o Graduate with all credits completed.
- o Complete final exams and coursework.
- o Take prerequisite classes.
- o Enroll in the program.

3. **Identify Obstacles and Gaps:**
   - o Consider potential challenges and plan how to overcome them.
   - o Example: If certain classes are only offered in specific semesters, plan your schedule accordingly.

4. **Create a Forward Plan:**
   - o Use your backward steps to build a forward-moving roadmap.

Examples of Backward Thinking

1. **In Career Planning:**
   - o **Goal:** Become a project manager.
   - o Backward Steps:
   - o Apply for management positions.
   - o Gain project management certification.
   - o Build leadership skills in your current role.
   - o Research companies hiring for management positions.

2. **In Problem-Solving:**
   - o **Goal:** Boost team productivity.
   - o Backward Steps:
   - o Schedule regular check-ins.
   - o Streamline task assignments.
   - o Identify specific productivity bottlenecks.

3. **In Daily Life:**
   - o **Goal:** Cook a complex meal by 7 p.m.

Backward Steps:

- o Complete final plating by 6:50 p.m.
- o Bake the dish at 6:20 p.m.
- o Prepare ingredients by 6:00 p.m.

Practical Exercise: Reverse Engineer Your Goal

1. **Choose a Goal:**
   - o Example: "I want to save $10,000 in one year."

2. **Work Backward:**
   - o Start with the end result and outline the steps required to achieve it:
   - o Save $10,000 by December.
   - o Save $833 monthly.
   - o Reduce unnecessary expenses by $200/month.

3. **Test the Plan:**
   - o Evaluate whether each step is achievable and adjust as necessary.

4. **Take Action:**
   - o Begin implementing the plan, starting with the first step.

Why Backward Thinking Works

Backward thinking forces you to focus on what matters most. By tracing steps from the goal to the starting point, you eliminate unnecessary tasks and clarify the exact actions needed.

For example:

If you want to host a successful event, working backward helps you prioritize steps like booking a venue, sending invitations, and setting up logistics in advance.

Closing Thought

Thinking backward turns confusion into clarity. By reverse-engineering your goals, you create a straightforward roadmap to success, making even the most daunting tasks achievable.

Chapter 19: Use Logic Trees: Break Down Problems Step-by-Step

What is a Logic Tree?

A logic tree is a visual tool that helps you break down complex problems into smaller, manageable pieces. The problem forms the trunk of the tree, while possible causes, solutions, or factors branch outward into categories and subcategories.

This technique brings structure to your thinking, helping you organize your thoughts and analyze the issue systematically. For example:

- **Problem:** Why are my team's projects always delayed?
- **Branches:**
    - Poor communication → Lack of updates, unclear expectations.
    - Insufficient resources → Lack of tools, understaffing.
    - Inefficient processes → Poor time management, redundant tasks.

By working through each branch, you identify the most critical areas to address and develop actionable solutions.

Why Logic Trees are Effective

1. **Simplifies Complexity:**
    - Breaking a problem into smaller parts makes it easier to understand and tackle.
    - Example: Instead of being overwhelmed by low sales, focus on specific factors like pricing, customer service, or product quality.
2. **Prioritizes Focus:**
    - Logic trees highlight which factors are most critical, allowing you to target root causes rather than symptoms.
3. **Supports Systematic Thinking:**
    - Organizing your ideas visually prevents you from missing important details or overlooking potential solutions.
4. **Provides Clarity for Teams:**
    - Logic trees are easy to share and collaborate on, making them ideal for group problem-solving.

How to Create a Logic Tree

1. **Define the Problem:**
    - Start by clearly stating the issue.
    - Example: "Why am I always late to meetings?"
2. **Break It into Categories:**
    - Identify major factors contributing to the problem.
    - Example: Poor time management, distractions, or travel delays.

3. Add Subcategories:
   o For each category, list specific details or causes.
   o Example:
   o Poor time management: Procrastination, unclear priorities.
   o Distractions: Notifications, last-minute requests.
4. Evaluate Each Branch:
   o Examine which branch has the most significant impact or is easiest to address first.
5. Develop Solutions:
   o For each branch, create targeted actions to address the issue.

Examples of Logic Trees in Action

1. In Business:
   o **Problem:** Sales are declining.
   o Branches:
   o Marketing: Poor targeting, ineffective messaging.
   o Pricing: Too high for the market, inconsistent discounts.
   o Product: Quality concerns, outdated features.
   o **Solution:** Address the most critical branch first. For instance, revamping marketing campaigns may have the greatest impact.
2. In Personal Productivity:
   o **Problem:** You're missing deadlines.
   o Branches:
   o Time management: Overcommitting, poor scheduling.
   o Distractions: Phone use, social media.
   o Prioritization: Working on low-priority tasks first.
   o **Solution:** Focus on improving time management by using a task planner or setting boundaries for distractions.
3. In Relationships:
   o **Problem:** Frequent arguments with a friend.
   o Branches:
   o Miscommunication: Unclear expectations, interrupting during discussions.
   o External stress: Work pressure, personal challenges.
   o Unresolved conflicts: Past issues left unaddressed.
   o **Solution:** Start by addressing miscommunication to improve dialogue.

Practical Exercise: Build Your Own Logic Tree

1. Choose a Problem:
   o Example: "Why do I overspend each month?"
2. Identify Categories:
   o Examples: Unnecessary purchases, lack of budgeting, unexpected expenses.
3. Add Subcategories:
   o Unnecessary purchases: Impulse buying, dining out too often.
   o Lack of budgeting: No spending limits, forgetting to track expenses.
4. Analyze the Tree:
   o Focus on the most impactful branch. For example, controlling impulse buying might solve a large part of the overspending issue.
5. Take Action:
   o Implement specific strategies to address the problem, like creating a monthly budget or setting a dining-out limit.

Benefits of Logic Trees

Using logic trees improves problem-solving by breaking overwhelming challenges into clear, actionable parts. It ensures you address the root cause of the problem rather than treating symptoms.

Closing Thought

Logic trees turn complexity into clarity. By breaking problems into smaller steps, you gain the focus and structure needed to solve them efficiently and effectively.

Chapter 20: Compare and Contrast for Clearer Choices

Why Comparing and Contrasting is Crucial

Every choice involves trade-offs. Whether deciding on a career, a purchase, or a solution to a problem, comparing and contrasting helps you weigh your options and choose the one that best aligns with your goals.

This method sharpens decision-making by highlighting differences and similarities between options, forcing you to evaluate what truly matters.

For example:

- **Decision:** Choosing between two vacation destinations.
- **Comparison:**
  - Option A: Affordable but farther away.
  - Option B: Closer but more expensive.
  - **Contrast:** Decide based on your priority — budget or convenience.

The Benefits of Comparing and Contrasting

1. **Improves Clarity:**
   - Side-by-side comparisons highlight key differences, simplifying decision-making.
2. **Prioritizes Needs:**
   - It forces you to consider what factors matter most, such as cost, time, or long-term impact.
3. **Reveals Trade-Offs:**
   - Weighing pros and cons helps you understand what you're gaining or sacrificing with each option.

How to Compare and Contrast Effectively

1. **List the Options:**
   - Clearly identify the choices you're considering.
   - Example: Choosing between two jobs.

2. **Define Criteria:**
   o Select the most important factors for evaluation (e.g. salary, growth opportunities, work-life balance).
3. **Create a Side-by-Side Chart:**
   o Compare each option against the chosen criteria.
   o Example:
   o Job A: Higher salary, but longer hours.
   o Job B: Lower pay, but better growth potential and flexibility.
4. **Assign Weight to Criteria:**
   o Some factors matter more than others. For instance, if work-life balance is a top priority, emphasize it over salary.
5. **Consider the Trade-Offs:**
   o Understand what you're giving up with each option.

Examples of Compare-and-Contrast Thinking

1. **In Career Decisions:**
   o **Decision:** Choosing between two job offers.
   o Comparison:
   o Job A: Higher salary but fewer learning opportunities.
   o Job B: Lower salary but a clear path to leadership roles.
   o **Outcome:** If long-term growth matters more, Job B may be the better choice.
2. **In Financial Decisions:**
   o **Decision:** Choosing between buying a car or using public transport.
   o Comparison:
   o Car: Convenience but high upfront and maintenance costs.
   o Public Transport: Affordable but less flexibility.
   o **Outcome:** If affordability outweighs convenience, public transport might win.
3. **In Everyday Life:**
   o **Decision:** Choosing between two phones.
   o Comparison:
   o Phone A: Better camera but shorter battery life.
   o Phone B: Longer battery life but fewer advanced features.
   o **Outcome:** If battery life is critical, Phone B is the logical choice.

Practical Exercise: Compare Two Options

1. **Pick a Decision:**
   o Example: Choosing between two homes to rent.
2. **Define Key Factors:**
   o Examples: Cost, commute time, neighborhood amenities.
3. **Create a Comparison Table:**
   o Home A: Lower rent, farther from work, quieter neighborhood.
   o Home B: Higher rent, closer to work, more noise.
4. **Weigh Your Priorities:**
   o Decide which factors matter most. If saving money is your priority, Home A might be the better choice.

Why This Technique Works

Comparing and contrasting ensures your decisions are logical and aligned with your priorities. It prevents emotional biases from clouding your judgment and provides a structured way to evaluate options.

Closing Thought

Every choice has trade-offs. By comparing and contrasting your options, you gain clarity and confidence in your decisions, ensuring they align with your goals and values.

Section III: Cognitive Bias-Busting Techniques

Cognitive biases are mental shortcuts your brain uses to process information quickly. While these shortcuts can be helpful, they often distort reality, leading to errors in judgment and flawed decisions.

This section focuses on techniques to identify and combat these mental traps. By learning to recognize and challenge your biases, you'll develop a clearer, more objective perspective. Each chapter will give you practical tools to think critically, avoid common pitfalls, and make decisions rooted in logic, not illusion.

Chapter 21: Fact-Check First: Verify Before Believing

Why Fact-Checking is Essential

Not everything you hear or read is true. Fact-checking ensures you base your beliefs, decisions, and arguments on verified information, not assumptions or falsehoods.

For example:

- Someone claims a specific health supplement cures all diseases. Without verification, you risk wasting money — or worse, harming your health.

Common Reasons People Skip Fact-Checking

1. **Cognitive Ease:**
   - It's easier to accept a statement than to investigate it.
2. **Emotional Appeal:**
   - If information supports your emotions or values, you're more likely to believe it without questioning.
3. **Social Pressure:**
   - If "everyone" believes something, you may feel pressured to agree without evidence.

Steps to Fact-Check Effectively

1. **Pause and Question:**
   - Ask yourself: "Where did this information come from? Is the source credible?"
2. **Cross-Reference Sources:**
   - Verify claims with multiple reliable sources. Independent confirmation is key.
3. **Check for Bias:**
   - Assess whether the source has a clear agenda. Is it trying to persuade rather than inform?
4. **Look for Evidence:**
   - Strong claims require strong evidence. Avoid believing sweeping statements without data or reputable research to back them up.

Examples of Fact-Checking in Action

1. **In News and Social Media:**
   - Claim: "A new law bans all forms of public speech."
   - Fact-Check: Look up the law's actual text or consult reliable news outlets.
2. **In Personal Decisions:**
   - Claim: "This car is the safest on the market."
   - Fact-Check: Research safety ratings from trusted organizations like Consumer Reports or IIHS.
3. **In Conversations:**
   - Claim: "This historical event happened because of X."
   - Fact-Check: Consult credible historical sources to confirm or refute the claim.

Practical Exercise: Build Your Fact-Checking Habit

1. **Choose One Claim You've Heard Recently:**
   - Example: "Drinking coffee dehydrates you."

2. **Research the Claim:**
   - Look up scientific studies or articles from trusted sources.
3. **Verify Its Accuracy:**
   - Did you find credible evidence supporting or debunking the claim?
4. **Reflect on How This Shapes Your Beliefs:**
   - If the claim was false, consider how fact-checking improved your understanding.

Why Fact-Checking Sharpens Your Thinking

When you verify information, you avoid falling for falsehoods or misinformation. This strengthens your arguments, builds credibility, and ensures your decisions are based on reality.

Closing Thought

Trust is earned through evidence. Fact-checking protects your mind from being misled, empowering you to think critically and confidently.

Chapter 22: Spot Confirmation Bias: Test What You Doubt

What is Confirmation Bias?

Confirmation bias is the tendency to seek, interpret, and remember information in a way that supports your existing beliefs. It's comforting but dangerous — this mental shortcut can blind you to evidence that challenges your views, leading to one-sided thinking and flawed decisions.

For example:

- You believe a specific diet works wonders, so you only look for testimonials that confirm your belief while ignoring scientific studies that question its effectiveness.

How Confirmation Bias Distorts Thinking

1. **Selective Attention:**
   - You notice evidence that aligns with your views but overlook opposing information.
2. **Biased Interpretation:**
   - You twist ambiguous data to fit your narrative.
3. **Memory Distortion:**
   - You remember supportive information better than contradictory evidence.

Steps to Combat Confirmation Bias

1. **Seek Opposing Evidence:**
   - Actively look for information that contradicts your belief.
   - Example: If you think a new policy is ineffective, research arguments supporting its benefits.
2. **Ask Disconfirming Questions:**
   - Instead of asking, "Why is my belief correct?" ask, "What could prove me wrong?"
3. **Verify Sources:**
   - Ensure the sources you consult are reputable and not cherry-picking data to align with an agenda.
4. **Consider Neutral Perspectives:**
   - Consult experts or individuals who aren't emotionally invested in the topic.

Examples of Spotting and Challenging Confirmation Bias

1. **In Politics:**
   - If you favor one political party, seek out thoughtful critiques of their policies to broaden your understanding.
2. **In Personal Decisions:**
   - Before buying a product, don't just read glowing reviews. Look for critical reviews to see if there are consistent issues.

3. **In Debates:**
   o When arguing a point, ask, "What evidence would change my mind?"

1. **Choose a Strongly Held Belief:**
   o Example: "Exercise in the morning is the best way to stay healthy."
2. **Find Contradictory Evidence:**
   o Research studies or expert opinions supporting other exercise routines (e.g., evening workouts).
3. **Evaluate Both Sides:**
   o Consider whether your belief still holds up after reviewing opposing evidence.

Recognizing and challenging confirmation bias opens your mind to new ideas and better solutions. It fosters intellectual humility and ensures your decisions are guided by truth, not comfort.

The truth doesn't fear scrutiny. By seeking evidence that challenges your beliefs, you strengthen your understanding and sharpen your thinking.

Chapter 23: Decouple from Anchors: Avoid First-Impression Traps

What is Anchoring Bias?

Anchoring bias occurs when your decisions are overly influenced by the first piece of information you receive — the "anchor." Once an anchor is set, your brain tends to rely on it, even if it's irrelevant, outdated, or misleading. This bias impacts decisions in everything from shopping to negotiations, and even everyday judgments.

For example:
- You see a sweater priced at $200 but then find it discounted to $100. Even though $100 may still be overpriced, the $200 anchor makes the discount seem like a great deal.

1. **Fixating on Initial Numbers:**
   o The first number you hear can set expectations. For instance, if a car is listed at $25,000, you'll likely negotiate around that price instead of questioning its actual value.

2. **Shaping Perceptions:**
   - o Anchors influence how you interpret other information. For example, hearing that a colleague is "difficult" might color your interactions with them, even if you see no evidence of this behavior.
3. **Limiting Flexibility:**
   - o Anchors trap you into narrow thinking, making it harder to explore other possibilities or question assumptions.

How to Decouple from Anchors

1. **Recognize the Anchor:**
   - o Pause and identify any initial information that might be influencing your decision.
   - o Example: In negotiations, ask yourself, "Am I fixating on their first offer instead of assessing the real value of what I'm getting?"
2. **Question the Anchor's Relevance:**
   - o Is the anchor logical, accurate, or relevant?
   - o Example: A restaurant menu might list a $50 steak to make the $30 steak seem reasonable. In reality, both may be overpriced.
3. **Gather Independent Information:**
   - o Seek out additional data or perspectives before making a decision.
   - o Example: Research market prices for a product before assuming a "discount" is a good deal.
4. **Set Your Own Standards:**
   - o Define your goals, expectations, or limits before encountering an anchor.
   - o Example: Decide your maximum budget for a car before visiting a dealership, so you're not influenced by high starting prices.

Examples of Decoupling from Anchors

1. **In Shopping:**
   - o **Scenario:** A store advertises a "70% off sale" for items marked up to artificially high original prices.
   - o **Solution:** Research the typical cost of similar products to assess if the sale price is truly a bargain.
2. **In Negotiations:**
   - o **Scenario:** An employer offers a starting salary of $50,000, which feels low.
   - o **Solution:** Look up industry averages and decide a fair salary range before accepting the initial offer as a baseline.
3. **In Everyday Judgments:**
   - o **Scenario:** A friend is described as "lazy" before you meet them.
   - o **Solution:** Focus on your own observations rather than letting the label shape your opinion.

Practical Exercise: Spot and Challenge Anchors

1. **Think of a Recent Decision Influenced by an Anchor:**
   - o Example: Buying a discounted gadget or accepting a starting price in negotiations.
2. **Identify the Anchor:**
   - o What was the first piece of information you received? Was it a price, a label, or someone's opinion?
3. **Evaluate the Anchor:**
   - o Ask, "Is this initial information valid or relevant? What other data should I consider?"
4. **Redefine Your Criteria:**
   - o Shift focus from the anchor to what matters most (e.g., quality, value, or personal goals).

Why This Skill is Important

Anchoring bias is sneaky — it often influences you without you realizing it. By learning to recognize and challenge anchors, you make decisions that reflect reality, not just initial impressions.

For example:

- When buying a home, avoiding anchoring bias ensures you focus on the home's actual worth instead of being swayed by an inflated asking price.

Closing Thought

Don't let the first piece of information anchor your thinking. By questioning anchors and seeking independent perspectives, you free yourself to make more rational, informed decisions.

Chapter 24: Think Like a Detective: Avoid Jumping to Conclusions

Why Jumping to Conclusions is a Problem

Humans crave certainty, and your brain often rushes to conclusions to resolve ambiguity quickly. However, this mental shortcut leads to errors, as snap judgments are frequently based on incomplete or misleading information.

For example:

- You notice your co-worker is unusually quiet and assume they're upset with you. In reality, they might be distracted by personal issues or a heavy workload.

Thinking like a detective slows down this rush, encouraging you to gather evidence, analyze it critically, and consider alternative explanations before deciding.

How Jumping to Conclusions Impacts Thinking

1. **Missed Context:**
   - Snap judgments ignore the bigger picture, leading to superficial understanding.
2. **Hasty Decisions:**
   - Relying on incomplete information often results in poor choices.
3. **Harm to Relationships:**
   - Assuming others' intentions without evidence can lead to unnecessary conflict.

How to Think Like a Detective

1. **Observe Without Judging:**
   - Focus on gathering information before interpreting it.
   - Example: If someone is late to a meeting, note their behavior instead of assuming they're irresponsible.
2. **Ask Questions:**
   - Act like a detective interviewing witnesses.
   - Example: "What might explain this behavior? What factors am I missing?"
3. **Look for Evidence:**
   - Base your conclusions on concrete facts, not assumptions.
   - Example: If you think your boss is unhappy with your work, ask for feedback rather than guessing.
4. **Consider Alternative Explanations:**
   - Brainstorm multiple reasons for the situation.
   - Example: A friend canceling plans might be busy, unwell, or facing a personal emergency.
5. **Test Your Hypotheses:**
   - Verify your conclusions before acting on them.
   - Example: Before assuming a task is impossible, research tools or methods that might help.

Examples of Detective Thinking

1. **In the Workplace:**
   - **Scenario:** Your boss is unusually brief in emails.
   - **Jumping to Conclusions:** They're upset with you.
   - **Detective Thinking:** Consider other explanations, like a busy schedule or poor email etiquette.
2. **In Personal Relationships:**
   - **Scenario:** Your partner forgets an important date.
   - Jumping to Conclusions: They don't care.
   - **Detective Thinking:** Ask if they're stressed, distracted, or overwhelmed.
3. **In Decision-Making:**
   - **Scenario:** A project seems unfeasible.
   - **Jumping to Conclusions:** It's not worth pursuing.
   - **Detective Thinking:** Investigate alternative strategies, resources, or collaborators.

1. **Choose a Recent Assumption You Made:**
   o Example: "My friend hasn't responded to my message because they're upset with me."
2. **List Alternative Explanations:**
   o Examples: They're busy, forgot, or haven't seen the message.
3. **Gather Evidence:**
   o Reach out politely and ask if everything is okay instead of assuming the worst.
4. **Reflect on Your Conclusion:**
   o How does the evidence support or challenge your initial assumption?

Why Thinking Like a Detective is Crucial

Detective thinking encourages patience, curiosity, and evidence-based reasoning. It prevents you from making impulsive decisions or damaging relationships based on incomplete assumptions.

Closing Thought

Rushing to conclusions often leads to errors. Think like a detective — ask questions, gather evidence, and explore alternatives before deciding. Truth thrives on investigation, not assumption.

Chapter 25: Challenge the Crowd: Resist Bandwagon Thinking

What is Bandwagon Thinking?

Bandwagon thinking is the tendency to adopt a belief or behavior simply because others are doing it. This mental shortcut can make decisions easier, as following the crowd feels safe and validated. However, it can also lead you to ignore facts, overlook better options, or act against your values.

For example:

- Everyone at work might support an idea you quietly doubt, so you go along with it to avoid standing out — even if you know it's a flawed plan.

Challenging the crowd doesn't mean rejecting group opinions outright. It means evaluating them critically and ensuring your actions align with logic and evidence, not just social pressure.

Why Bandwagon Thinking Happens

1. **Fear of Standing Out:**
   o Humans are social creatures. Going against the group can feel risky, leading to discomfort or rejection.
2. **Assumption of Consensus:**
   o When everyone seems to agree, you might assume they're right — even if no one has actually examined the evidence.
3. **Cognitive Laziness:**
   o It's easier to trust the group's decision than to think critically yourself.

1. **Compromised Decisions:**
    o   You may agree to something you later regret because you didn't fully consider it.
2. **Suppressed Innovation:**
    o   Blindly following the crowd stifles creative or unconventional ideas that might lead to better solutions.
3. **Reinforced Mistakes:**
    o   Groups can be wrong, and when everyone follows without questioning, errors multiply.

How to Challenge the Crowd Effectively

1. **Pause Before Agreeing:**
    o   When faced with group consensus, take a moment to assess your own thoughts and feelings. Ask, "Do I truly agree with this?"
2. **Examine the Evidence:**
    o   Evaluate whether the group's decision is supported by facts or if it's based on assumptions or emotions.
    o   Example: If everyone in a meeting supports an expensive solution, question whether it's the most cost-effective option.
3. **Play the Devil's Advocate:**
    o   Consider opposing viewpoints, even if only to test the group's reasoning.
    o   Example: Ask, "What if we're wrong? What's the worst that could happen?"
4. **Voice Your Doubts Respectfully:**
    o   If you disagree, express your concerns calmly and logically. Others may appreciate your input and reconsider their position.
5. **Be Willing to Stand Alone:**
    o   Sometimes, resisting the bandwagon means standing by your principles, even if no one else does.

Examples of Challenging the Crowd

1. **In the Workplace:**
    o   **Scenario:** A team unanimously agrees to rush a project without testing it.
    o   **Action:** Raise concerns about potential risks, such as quality issues or missed deadlines.
2. **In Personal Life:**
    o   **Scenario:** All your friends rave about a trendy diet, but you're skeptical.
    o   **Action:** Research its health effects before joining in, and stick to your decision if the evidence doesn't convince you.
3. **In Social Media:**
    o   **Scenario:** A viral post spreads misinformation, and most people share it without fact-checking.
    o   **Action:** Verify the claims and share accurate information instead, even if it's unpopular.

Practical Exercise: Resist the Bandwagon

1. **Reflect on a Recent Group Decision:**
    o   Example: "Everyone in my class chose the same project topic."
2. **Ask Yourself These Questions:**
    o   Did I agree because I believed in the idea, or was it just easier to go along with the group?
    o   What other options did I overlook?
3. **Practice Challenging Group Consensus:**
    o   In your next group discussion, ask one thoughtful question to test the group's reasoning.

Why This Skill Matters

Challenging the crowd builds your confidence in independent thinking. It helps you make smarter decisions and ensures that group choices are backed by logic, not blind agreement.

Closing Thought

True progress often begins with one person willing to challenge the status quo. Resist the urge to follow the crowd blindly — examine the facts, trust your reasoning, and stand firm in your conclusions.

Chapter 26: Flip the Script: Consider Opposite Perspectives

Why Opposite Perspectives Matter

Your perspective shapes how you interpret the world. However, your viewpoint is limited by your experiences, beliefs, and biases. To think clearly, you need to step outside your perspective and consider opposite or alternative views.

For example:

- If you believe a colleague's suggestion won't work, flipping the script involves asking, "What if their idea succeeds? What would make it effective?"

Exploring opposing perspectives broadens your understanding, challenges assumptions, and helps you make more balanced decisions.

How Bias Limits Your Perspective

1. **Confirmation Bias:**
   - You focus only on evidence that supports your viewpoint, ignoring contradictory facts.
2. **Egocentric Bias:**
   - You view situations primarily from your own experiences, assuming others see things the same way.
3. **Emotional Attachments:**
   - Strong feelings about an issue can blind you to alternative perspectives.

Steps to Flip the Script

1. **Identify Your Assumptions:**
   - Ask, "What am I assuming about this situation?"
   - Example: "I assume this new policy will create more problems than it solves."
2. **Consider the Opposite:**
   - Ask, "What if the opposite is true?"
   - Example: "What if this policy reduces problems? What conditions would make that possible?"
3. **Step into Another Person's Shoes:**
   - Imagine how someone with a different perspective might view the situation.
   - Example: How might employees, customers, or competitors see this issue?
4. **Evaluate Both Sides:**
   - Compare the strengths and weaknesses of each perspective.
5. **Synthesize a Balanced View:**
   - Combine insights from both sides to develop a well-rounded understanding.

Examples of Flipping the Script

1. **In Debates:**
   - **Scenario:** You're arguing against remote work policies.
   - **Action:** Consider the benefits from an employee's perspective, such as flexibility and reduced commuting stress.
2. **In Conflict Resolution:**
   - **Scenario:** You think a friend is being unreasonable during an argument.
   - **Action:** Reflect on their concerns and ask, "How might I feel in their position?"
3. **In Business:**
   - **Scenario:** You're convinced a competitor's product is inferior.
   - **Action:** Analyze what customers might find appealing about it and how you can improve your offering.

Practical Exercise: Practice Perspective-Taking

1. **Choose a Strongly Held Belief:**
   - Example: "My way of managing time is the most efficient."
2. **Flip the Script:**
   - Consider an opposite belief: "What if other time-management methods are more effective?"

3. **Gather Evidence:**
    o Research different approaches and compare their results to yours.
4. **Reflect on What You Learn:**
    o Has your perspective shifted? What new insights did you gain?

Why This Skill is Important

Considering opposite perspectives fosters empathy, reduces bias, and leads to more thoughtful decisions. It doesn't mean abandoning your beliefs but refining them through broader understanding.

Closing Thought

Growth happens when you step outside your comfort zone. By flipping the script, you gain fresh insights and make smarter, more balanced choices.

Chapter 27: Pause Before Reacting: Manage Emotional Bias

What is Emotional Bias?

Emotional bias occurs when your feelings cloud your judgment. Instead of thinking rationally, you let emotions — such as anger, fear, excitement, or frustration — drive your decisions. While emotions provide valuable context, relying solely on them can lead to hasty choices, misjudgements, and regret.

For example:

- You might lash out during an argument, only to later realize you misunderstood the situation.

Pausing before reacting gives you time to reflect and separate emotional impulses from logical thinking.

How Emotional Bias Impacts Decision-Making

1. **Overreaction:**
    o Strong emotions can lead to exaggerated responses.
    o Example: Cancelling an important project after receiving minor criticism about it.
2. **Narrow Focus:**
    o Emotions can make you fixate on one aspect of a situation while ignoring others.
    o Example: Feeling jealous about a friend's success and overlooking your own achievements.
3. **Regretful Choices:**
    o Decisions made in the heat of the moment often lead to outcomes you later wish to reverse.

How to Pause and Manage Emotional Bias

1. **Recognize Emotional Triggers:**
    o Pay attention to situations or topics that spark strong emotional reactions.
    o Example: Receiving unexpected negative feedback at work.
2. **Pause Before Responding:**
    o Take a deep breath or count to ten before reacting. This brief pause allows your rational brain to catch up with your emotions.
3. **Name the Emotion:**
    o Labeling your feelings (e.g., "I'm angry" or "I feel hurt") helps you process them without being overwhelmed.
4. **Ask Questions:**
    o Challenge the initial emotional impulse. Ask, "Am I overreacting? What's the bigger picture here?"
5. **Reframe the Situation:**
    o Shift your perspective to focus on solutions rather than emotional reactions.
    o Example: Instead of thinking, "This feedback is unfair," try, "What can I learn from this feedback?"

Examples of Pausing Before Reacting

1. **In Arguments:**
    o **Scenario:** A coworker criticizes your idea during a meeting.
    o **Emotional Reaction:** Feeling defensive and interrupting to justify yourself.
    o **Pause:** Take a moment to breathe and calmly ask, "Can you elaborate on your concerns?"

2. **In Personal Relationships:**
   - ○ **Scenario:** Your partner forgets an anniversary.
   - ○ **Emotional Reaction:** Feeling hurt and assuming they don't care.
   - ○ **Pause:** Consider their situation—were they overwhelmed with work or simply forgetful?
3. **In Decision-Making:**
   - ○ **Scenario:** A big sale tempts you to overspend on something unnecessary.
   - ○ **Pause:** Ask yourself, "Do I really need this, or am I acting on excitement?"

Practical Exercise: Build the Pause Habit

1. **Identify an Emotional Trigger:**
   - ○ Example: Feeling frustrated when someone interrupts you.
2. **Practice Pausing:**
   - ○ The next time it happens, take a breath and ask, "Why do I feel frustrated? Is this intentional, or just a misunderstanding?"
3. **Reframe Your Reaction:**
   - ○ Instead of snapping, calmly say, "I'd like to finish my thought, and then I'll hear your input."

Why This Skill is Crucial

Pausing before reacting creates space for clearer thinking. It lets you process emotions, avoid unnecessary conflict, and respond thoughtfully rather than impulsively.

Closing Thought

Emotions are valuable, but they shouldn't dominate your decisions. By pausing and reflecting, you can channel your feelings into more constructive, balanced responses.

Chapter 28: Think Beyond the Present: Avoid Short-Term Traps

What Are Short-Term Traps?

Short-term traps are decisions that prioritize immediate satisfaction at the expense of long-term benefits. They appeal to emotions such as impatience, fear, or desire, but often lead to regret or missed opportunities.

For example:
- Choosing to binge-watch TV instead of studying for an important exam may feel rewarding in the moment but harms your future goals.

Short-term traps happen because your brain is wired to seek instant gratification. Long-term thinking, however, helps you focus on lasting success and meaningful outcomes.

1. **Impulsive Decisions:**
   - o Acting quickly without considering long-term consequences.
   - o Example: Splurging on luxury items instead of saving for emergencies.
2. **Avoiding Discomfort:**
   - o Choosing what's easy now rather than what's beneficial later.
   - o Example: Skipping exercise because it feels tiring, even though it improves your health.
3. **Fear of Missing Out (FOMO):**
   - o Prioritizing temporary experiences over enduring goals.
   - o Example: Attending every social event at the expense of personal growth.

How to Avoid Short-Term Traps

1. **Define Your Long-Term Goals:**
   - o Be clear about what you want to achieve in the future.
   - o Example: Saving for retirement, or maintaining good health.
2. **Pause Before Deciding:**
   - o Before making a decision, ask, "How will this affect my future self?"
   - o Example: Will staying up late help or hinder your performance tomorrow?
3. **Use If-Then Thinking:**
   - o Plan for short-term temptations.
   - o Example: "If I feel like procrastinating, then I'll work for just 10 minutes to get started."
4. **Reward Long-Term Progress:**
   - o Celebrate small wins that contribute to your bigger goals.
   - o Example: Treat yourself after a week of sticking to a budget.

Examples of Long-Term Thinking in Action

1. **In Health:**
   - o **Scenario:** Choosing between a healthy meal and fast food.
   - o **Short-Term Trap:** Fast food satisfies cravings now.
   - o **Long-Term Thinking:** A healthy meal supports lasting energy and wellness.
2. **In Career Decisions:**
   - o **Scenario:** Deciding between a stable job and one with growth potential.
   - o **Short-Term Trap:** The stable job feels safer.
   - o **Long-Term Thinking:** Growth opportunities lead to greater career fulfilment.
3. **In Relationships:**
   - o **Scenario:** Skipping a difficult conversation to avoid discomfort.
   - o **Short-Term Trap:** Avoidance feels easier now.
   - o **Long-Term Thinking:** Honest communication strengthens trust and connection.

Practical Exercise: Build Long-Term Thinking

1. **Identify a Recent Decision:**
   - o Example: Skipping a workout or overspending.
2. **Reflect on Its Impact:**
   - o Did it benefit you in the short term but harm your long-term goals?
3. **Plan for Next Time:**
   - o Set up a reminder or system to prioritize your future self.
   - o Example: Commit to a short workout to build consistency.

Why This Skill is Important

Thinking beyond the present helps you avoid short-term traps and stay focused on what truly matters. It builds discipline and fosters success.

Closing Thought

Every decision shapes your future. Choose wisely today to create a tomorrow you'll be proud of.

Chapter 29: Don't Fall for Familiar: Question Availability Heuristics

What is the Availability Heuristic?

The availability heuristic is a mental shortcut where your brain relies on immediate examples that come to mind when making decisions or judgments. If something is easily remembered — like a recent event or a vivid story — it feels more important or likely, even if it doesn't represent the bigger picture.

For example:

- After hearing about a plane crash on the news, you might overestimate the danger of flying, even though statistically, it's much safer than driving.

The availability heuristic exploits familiarity, making rare events feel common and skewing your perception of reality. Learning to question this bias ensures your thinking is based on evidence, not the ease of recall.

How the Availability Heuristic Skews Thinking

1. **Overestimating Risks:**
   - Events that are dramatic or widely reported (e.g. shark attacks, plane crashes) seem more likely than they are.
2. **Underestimating Common Issues:**
   - Everyday dangers (e.g. heart disease, car accidents) feel less urgent because they lack vivid, memorable examples.
3. **Making Emotional Decisions:**
   - Stories or anecdotes outweigh statistics because they're easier to remember and feel more personal.

Steps to Question the Availability Heuristic

1. **Pause and Reflect:**
   - Ask yourself, "Am I basing this judgment on one vivid example or a broader pattern?"
   - Example: Are you afraid of flying because of one crash, or is it based on reliable data about aviation safety?
2. **Seek Broader Data:**
   - Look for statistics or trends that provide a more accurate picture.
   - Example: Before assuming crime is rising in your neighborhood, check local crime reports instead of relying on one news story.
3. **Balance Stories with Evidence:**
   - Anecdotes are compelling, but they're not always representative. Seek out counterexamples.
4. **Consider the Context:**
   - Ask, "Is this situation truly common, or does it just feel that way because it's fresh in my mind?"

Examples of Avoiding the Availability Heuristic

1. **In Risk Assessment:**
   - **Scenario:** After watching news coverage of a rare disease, you worry it's widespread.
   - **Solution:** Research official statistics to understand its actual prevalence and risk factors.
2. **In Decision-Making:**
   - **Scenario:** A coworker shares a story about a failed investment, making you hesitant to invest.
   - **Solution:** Examine long-term data on investment trends instead of focusing on one bad experience.
3. **In Everyday Choices:**
   - **Scenario:** After hearing about a neighbor's burglary, you consider buying an expensive security system.
   - **Solution:** Evaluate crime rates in your area to determine if the purchase is necessary.

Practical Exercise: Test Your Judgments

1. **Think of a Recent Decision Influenced by a Vivid Example:**
   - Example: Avoiding a specific food because someone got sick after eating it.
2. **Ask These Questions:**
   - Is this example representative of a broader pattern?
   - What evidence supports or contradicts this conclusion?

3. **Seek Objective Data:**
   o Research the actual risks or probabilities to gain a clearer perspective.

The availability heuristic is a sneaky bias that can make rare events feel more significant than they are. By questioning familiar or vivid examples, you ground your thinking in reality, reducing unnecessary fear and improving decision-making.

Closing Thought
What's memorable isn't always true. Look past vivid examples and rely on data to ensure your choices reflect reality, not just familiarity.

Chapter 30: Step Outside Yourself: Mitigate Egocentric Bias

What is Egocentric Bias?

Egocentric bias is the tendency to view the world through the lens of your own experiences, overestimating how much others notice, care about, or are affected by you. It's not intentional — it's simply how the human brain prioritizes itself.

For example:
- You might assume your co-workers are critical of a mistake you made, when in reality, they're focused on their own tasks.

This bias can lead to misunderstandings, overestimating your influence, or misjudging others' intentions. Mitigating egocentric bias helps you see situations more objectively and connect better with others.

How Egocentric Bias Distorts Thinking
1. **Overestimating Judgment:**
   o You think others notice your flaws or mistakes more than they actually do.
2. **Assuming Universal Experiences:**
   o You expect others to think, feel, or act as you would in a given situation.
3. **Minimizing Others' Perspectives:**
   o You unintentionally focus on your own priorities, overlooking how others are affected.

1. **Acknowledge the Bias:**
   o Recognize that your perspective is naturally self-centered and may not reflect the bigger picture.
2. **Shift the Focus:**
   o Ask, "How might others perceive this situation differently?"
   o Example: A colleague declining your invitation to lunch might be busy, not uninterested in your friendship.
3. **Seek Feedback:**
   o Invite others to share their thoughts or feelings to broaden your understanding.
   o Example: If you assume your team is unhappy with your leadership, ask for honest feedback instead of guessing.
4. **Practice Empathy:**
   o Imagine yourself in others' shoes to understand their experiences.
   o Example: Consider how a customer might feel about a delayed delivery instead of focusing solely on your company's challenges.
5. **Think Beyond Yourself:**
   o Focus on the collective impact of decisions, not just how they affect you.

Examples of Overcoming Egocentric Bias

1. **In Social Interactions:**
   o **Scenario:** You feel embarrassed about tripping in public, assuming everyone noticed.
   o **Reality:** Most people were likely focused on their own activities.
2. **In the Workplace:**
   o **Scenario:** You think a team member's curt email is directed at you.
   o **Reality:** They may be stressed or in a hurry, with no personal intent behind their tone.
3. **In Problem-Solving:**
   o **Scenario:** You create a solution that works for you but ignore how it affects others.
   o **Action:** Seek input from those impacted to ensure the solution is fair and effective.

Practical Exercise: Broaden Your Perspective

1. **Reflect on a Recent Assumption About Others:**
   o Example: "I assumed my friend was upset with me because they didn't respond to my message."
2. **Ask Yourself:**
   o Could there be other explanations for their behavior?
   o How might their perspective differ from mine?
3. **Seek Input:**
   o If appropriate, ask the person directly for clarity.

Why This Skill is Critical

Egocentric bias narrows your focus, distorting your understanding of situations and relationships. Stepping outside yourself fosters empathy, improves communication, and ensures your decisions are grounded in reality.

Closing Thought

The world isn't always about you — and that's liberating. By stepping outside yourself, you gain clarity, build stronger connections, and approach life with a more balanced perspective.

Section IV: Practical Decision-Making Techniques

Every day, you make countless decisions. Some are simple, others feel overwhelming, especially when the stakes are high or the options seem endless. This section equips you with tools to make decisions with confidence, clarity, and logic.

These methods are not just theoretical; they're practical, proven strategies you can apply immediately to your personal and professional life. Let's turn decision-making into a skill you master, not a challenge you fear.

Chapter 31: The 80/20 Rule: Focus on What Matters Most

What is the 80/20 Rule?

The 80/20 Rule, or Pareto Principle, states that 80% of your outcomes come from 20% of your efforts. It highlights an imbalance: not all tasks, resources, or actions are equally important. By identifying the most impactful 20%, you can focus your energy where it matters most and achieve better results with less effort.

For example:

- 80% of a business's revenue often comes from 20% of its customers.
- 80% of your personal stress might come from just 20% of recurring issues.

Why the 80/20 Rule is a Game-Changer

1. **Boosts Efficiency:**
   - Instead of spreading yourself thin, focus on high-impact activities.
2. **Eliminates Wasted Effort:**
   - Helps you identify tasks or habits that provide little value.
3. **Simplifies Prioritization:**
   - Clarifies what truly matters and lets you ignore distractions.

How to Apply the 80/20 Rule

1. **Identify the 20% with the Biggest Impact:**
   - Ask: "What few actions or inputs drive most of my results?"
   - Example: In studying, 20% of key concepts may account for 80% of the material on an exam.
2. **Eliminate or Delegate the Rest:**
   - Reduce time spent on low-value tasks or delegate them where possible.
   - Example: Outsource routine administrative work to focus on strategy.
3. **Focus Your Energy:**
   - Invest your time, resources, and effort into the high-impact 20%.

Examples of the 80/20 Rule in Action

1. **In Work:**
   - **Scenario:** 80% of your results come from 20% of your projects.
   - **Action:** Prioritize the projects with the highest payoff and reduce time spent on low-impact activities.
2. **In Relationships:**
   - **Scenario:** 20% of your friendships provide 80% of your emotional support.
   - **Action:** Invest more energy in nurturing these key relationships.
3. **In Daily Life:**
   - **Scenario:** 80% of your wardrobe use comes from 20% of your clothes.
   - **Action:** Declutter and focus on maintaining the items you actually wear.

Practical Exercise: Focus on Your 20%

1. **List Your Tasks or Responsibilities:**
   - Example: Work projects, household chores, or fitness goals.
2. **Identify the High-Impact 20%:**
   - Which tasks drive most of your results or satisfaction?

3. **Refocus Your Time:**
   ○ Dedicate more energy to the high-impact 20% and minimize the rest.

Why This Technique Works

The 80/20 Rule is about working smarter, not harder. By focusing on the few things that matter most, you free up time and energy for what truly moves the needle in your life.

Closing Thought

Not all efforts are created equal. Identify your most impactful actions and watch your results multiply.

Chapter 32: The Eisenhower Matrix: Prioritize Tasks by Importance

What is the Eisenhower Matrix?

The Eisenhower Matrix, named after U.S. President Dwight D. Eisenhower, is a tool for prioritizing tasks by urgency and importance. It helps you decide what to focus on, what to delegate, and what to eliminate.

The matrix has four quadrants:

1. **Important and Urgent:** Do these tasks immediately.
2. **Important but Not Urgent:** Schedule these tasks for later.
3. **Urgent but Not Important:** Delegate these tasks.
4. **Not Urgent or Important:** Eliminate these tasks.

Why the Eisenhower Matrix Works

1. **Clarifies Priorities:**
   ○ Separates what truly matters from distractions.
2. **Prevents Burnout:**
   ○ Helps you avoid spending all your time on urgent tasks while neglecting long-term goals.
3. **Encourages Delegation:**
   ○ Shows you which tasks don't require your direct involvement.

How to Use the Eisenhower Matrix

1. **List Your Tasks:**
   ○ Write down everything you need to do, no matter how small.
2. **Sort by Urgency and Importance:**
   ○ Place each task into the appropriate quadrant:
   ○ Example: Preparing for tomorrow's presentation is both urgent and important.
   ○ Checking social media is neither urgent nor important.
3. **Take Action:**
   ○ Focus on tasks in Quadrant 1 (important and urgent).
   ○ Schedule time for Quadrant 2 tasks (important but not urgent) to prevent them from becoming crises.
   ○ Delegate Quadrant 3 tasks and eliminate Quadrant 4 distractions.

Examples of the Eisenhower Matrix in Action

1. **In Work:**
   ○ **Scenario:** You have emails to answer, a project deadline tomorrow, and a long-term training course to complete.
   ○ Action:
   ○ Urgent and Important: Finish the project.
   ○ Important but Not Urgent: Schedule time for the training course.
   ○ Urgent but Not Important: Delegate email responses.

2. **In Personal Life:**
   - o **Scenario:** You need to pay overdue bills, plan a family trip, and decide whether to attend a friend's party.
   - o Action:
   - o Urgent and Important: Pay the bills.
   - o Important but Not Urgent: Plan the trip.
   - o Not Urgent or Important: Skip the party if it conflicts with priorities.

Practical Exercise: Apply the Matrix

1. **Create a Task List:**
   - o Include work, personal, and leisure activities.
2. **Sort the Tasks into Quadrants:**
   - o Categorize each based on urgency and importance.
3. **Take Immediate Action:**
   - o Focus on Quadrant 1 tasks and schedule Quadrant 2 tasks for later.

Why This Technique is Valuable

The Eisenhower Matrix simplifies complex to-do lists, ensuring your energy goes to tasks that truly matter. It keeps you organized, efficient, and focused on long-term success.

Closing Thought

Not everything urgent is important. Use the Eisenhower Matrix to prioritize wisely and achieve more with less stress.

Chapter 33: The Premortem: Plan for Failure Before It Happens

What is a Premortem?

A premortem is a technique where you imagine that your project, plan, or decision has failed – and then work backward to identify what might have caused the failure. By visualizing failure before it happens, you can uncover hidden risks, anticipate problems, and create strategies to prevent those outcomes.

For example:
- If you're planning a product launch, you might ask, "What if the launch flops?" Answers could include poor marketing, unmet customer expectations, or product defects. Identifying these risks early allows you to address them before they become actual issues.

Why the Premortem is Powerful

1. **Anticipates Problems Early:**
   - o Most planning focuses on success, often overlooking potential pitfalls. The premortem forces you to confront weaknesses proactively.

2. **Reduces Overconfidence:**
   - o   It helps temper overly optimistic thinking by forcing you to consider challenges and obstacles realistically.
3. **Improves Team Collaboration:**
   - o   Encourages open dialogue, where everyone can voice concerns without fear of appearing negative.
4. **Builds Resilience:**
   - o   By addressing failure scenarios, you develop contingency plans that prepare you for unexpected setbacks.

How to Conduct a Premortem

1. **Define the Goal:**
   - o   Clearly outline the plan or project you're evaluating.
   - o   Example: "We're launching a new app in six months."
2. **Imagine a Failure Scenario:**
   - o   Pretend the project has already failed. Ask, "What went wrong?"
3. **Brainstorm Potential Causes:**
   - o   Gather input from everyone involved to identify possible reasons for failure. Encourage honesty and creativity.
   - o   Example: "The app failed because of bugs, poor marketing, or a lack of user interest."
4. **Prioritize Risks:**
   - o   Identify which risks are most likely and have the greatest impact. Focus your efforts on addressing these.
5. **Develop Preventative Actions:**
   - o   Create strategies to mitigate or eliminate the identified risks.
   - o   Example: Conduct thorough testing, survey potential users, and refine marketing efforts.

Examples of Premortems in Action

1. **In Business:**
   - o   **Scenario:** A company is planning a new product line.
   - o   **Premortem:** "The product flopped because customers didn't see its value."
   - o   **Solution:** Conduct market research to ensure the product addresses real customer needs.
2. **In Personal Goals:**
   - o   **Scenario:** You're preparing for a marathon.
   - o   **Premortem:** "I didn't finish because of an injury."
   - o   **Solution:** Follow a structured training plan, focus on injury prevention, and maintain proper rest.
3. **In Team Projects:**
   - o   **Scenario:** A group is organizing an event.
   - o   **Premortem:** "Attendance was low because we didn't promote it effectively."
   - o   **Solution:** Create a detailed promotional strategy with clear deadlines.

Practical Exercise: Try a Premortem

1. **Choose a Project or Goal:**
   - o   Example: "I want to lose 10 pounds in three months."
2. **Imagine Failure:**
   - o   Picture the goal not being achieved. Ask, "Why did I fail?"
   - o   Example: "I didn't plan meals, skipped workouts, or lost motivation."
3. **List Preventative Actions:**
   - o   Plan meals in advance, schedule workouts, and track progress to stay motivated.

Why This Technique Works

The premortem shifts your perspective, forcing you to think critically about risks instead of only focusing on success. It ensures that you're not caught off guard by predictable challenges.

Closing Thought

Planning for failure doesn't mean expecting it — it means being prepared to prevent it. A premortem sharpens your vision and strengthens your plans, making success more likely.

Chapter 34: Decision Matrix: Weigh Pros and Cons Objectively

What is a Decision Matrix?

A decision matrix is a tool that helps you evaluate and compare multiple options based on specific criteria. It transforms subjective choices into objective comparisons by assigning scores to each option.

For example:

- Imagine you're deciding between three job offers. A decision matrix lets you weigh factors like salary, location, growth potential, and work-life balance to choose the best fit.

Why the Decision Matrix is Effective

1. **Reduces Emotional Bias:**
   - o By focusing on data and criteria, it minimizes the influence of personal biases or emotions.
2. **Clarifies Priorities:**
   - o Helps you identify what factors matter most and ensures they guide your decision.
3. **Simplifies Complex Choices:**
   - o Breaks down overwhelming decisions into manageable, logical steps.

How to Use a Decision Matrix

1. **List Your Options:**
   - o Write down all the choices you're considering.
   - o Example: Three potential vacation destinations.
2. **Define Your Criteria:**
   - o Identify the factors that matter most.
   - o Example: Cost, travel time, activities, and weather.
3. **Assign Weights to Each Criterion:**
   - o Decide which factors are most important by assigning a weight (e.g., 1 to 5).
   - o Example: Cost (5), travel time (3), activities (4), weather (2).
4. **Score Each Option:**
   - o Rate how well each option meets each criterion on a scale (e.g., 1 to 10).
5. **Calculate Totals:**
   - o Multiply each score by its weight and add up the totals for each option. The highest score indicates the best choice.

Examples of Decision Matrices in Action

1. **In Career Decisions:**
   - o **Scenario:** Choosing between two job offers.
   - o **Criteria:** Salary (5), commute (3), growth opportunities (4), work culture (3).
   - o **Action:** Score and weigh each offer to see which aligns best with your priorities.
2. **In Purchases:**
   - o **Scenario:** Deciding between three laptops.
   - o **Criteria:** Price, performance, battery life, and brand reputation.
   - o **Action:** Use the matrix to determine which laptop offers the best value.
3. **In Personal Life:**
   - o **Scenario:** Choosing between hobbies to pursue.
   - o **Criteria:** Cost, time commitment, enjoyment, and social opportunities.
   - o **Action:** Evaluate the options and focus on the most fulfilling hobby.

1. **Choose a Decision You're Facing:**
   o Example: "Which online course should I take?"
2. **List Options and Criteria:**
   o Options: Course A, Course B, Course C.
   o Criteria: Cost, content quality, instructor reputation, and flexibility.
3. **Assign Weights and Scores:**
   o Weight each criterion, rate the options, and calculate totals.
4. **Choose the Highest-Scoring Option:**
   o Let the results guide your decision.

Why This Technique Works

A decision matrix replaces guesswork with structure, giving you clarity and confidence in your choices. It's especially useful when decisions involve multiple variables or competing priorities.

Closing Thought

Every decision involves trade-offs. A decision matrix ensures you evaluate your options logically, making choices that align with your goals and values.

Chapter 35: The 10/10/10 Rule: Think Long-Term

What is the 10/10/10 Rule?

The 10/10/10 Rule, developed by author Suzy Welch, is a decision-making framework that helps you think beyond the present moment. It works by asking three simple questions:

1. How will I feel about this decision in **10 minutes**?
2. How will I feel about this decision in **10 months**?
3. How will I feel about this decision in **10 years**?

This technique forces you to consider short-, medium-, and long-term consequences, balancing immediate emotions with future goals.

For example:

- **Decision:** Should you splurge on an expensive gadget?
  o In 10 minutes: You'll feel excited about the purchase.
  o In 10 months: You might regret the dent in your savings.
  o In 10 years: The gadget will likely be obsolete, and the financial loss may outweigh the short-term joy.

Why the 10/10/10 Rule Works

1. **Balances Emotions and Logic:**
   o It helps you step back from impulsive decisions by introducing a broader perspective.

2. **Prevents Regret:**
   - o By considering how your future self will feel, you're less likely to make choices you'll regret later.
3. **Clarifies Priorities:**
   - o Forces you to align decisions with your long-term goals instead of short-term desires.

How to Apply the 10/10/10 Rule

1. **Define the Decision:**
   - o Be specific about what you're deciding.
   - o Example: "Should I quit my current job for a new opportunity?"
2. **Consider the Short-Term (10 Minutes):**
   - o Ask, "How will this decision feel immediately after I make it?"
   - o Example: Quitting your job might bring relief but also anxiety.
3. **Think About the Medium-Term (10 Months):**
   - o Ask, "How will this decision impact my life in the coming months?"
   - o Example: You might have a steeper learning curve at the new job but gain valuable skills.
4. **Weigh the Long-Term (10 Years):**
   - o Ask, "How will this decision shape my life a decade from now?"
   - o Example: Will the new job align better with your long-term career goals?
5. **Evaluate Your Answers:**
   - o Use your reflections to guide a balanced, well-informed choice.

Examples of the 10/10/10 Rule in Action

1. **In Financial Decisions:**
   - o **Scenario:** Deciding whether to buy a luxury car.
   - o **10 Minutes:** Excitement about owning the car.
   - o **10 Months:** Financial stress from higher monthly payments.
   - o **10 Years:** Regret for not investing that money more wisely.
2. **In Relationships:**
   - o **Scenario:** Considering whether to end a toxic friendship.
   - o **10 Minutes:** Discomfort or guilt about confronting the issue.
   - o **10 Months:** Relief and more time for healthier relationships.
   - o **10 Years:** A stronger social circle and peace of mind.
3. **In Career Choices:**
   - o **Scenario:** Debating a risky career change.
   - o **10 Minutes:** Fear of uncertainty.
   - o **10 Months:** Adjustment to the new role, with signs of growth.
   - o **10 Years:** A fulfilling career aligned with your passions.

Practical Exercise: Try the 10/10/10 Rule

1. **Identify a Pending Decision:**
   - o Example: "Should I start a new fitness routine?"
2. **Ask the Three Questions:**
   - o How will this feel in 10 minutes?
   - o How will this feel in 10 months?
   - o How will this feel in 10 years?
3. **Write Down Your Answers:**
   - o Use them to weigh the pros and cons of your choice.

Why This Technique is Valuable

The 10/10/10 Rule encourages you to think beyond the present moment. It bridges the gap between emotions and long-term logic, helping you make decisions you'll be proud of later.

Closing Thought

A good decision honors both your present and your future self. Use the 10/10/10 Rule to make choices that stand the test of time.

Chapter 36: Scenario Planning: Prepare for All Outcomes

What is Scenario Planning?

Scenario planning is a technique that helps you prepare for the future by imagining multiple possible outcomes and creating strategies for each. Instead of predicting one result, you explore a range of possibilities, from best-case to worst-case scenarios, and plan accordingly.

For example:

- **Goal:** Launch a new product.
    - **Best Case:** The product sells out quickly.
    - **Moderate Case:** Sales are steady but require ongoing marketing.
    - **Worst Case:** The product doesn't meet customer needs, requiring adjustments.

By planning for all outcomes, you reduce uncertainty and improve your ability to adapt when things don't go as expected.

Why Scenario Planning Works

1. **Reduces Surprises:**
    - Thinking ahead prepares you for challenges and minimizes panic during setbacks.
2. **Encourages Flexibility:**
    - By exploring multiple possibilities, you're better equipped to pivot when needed.
3. **Strengthens Decision-Making:**
    - It forces you to think critically about risks, opportunities, and strategies.

How to Create Scenarios

1. **Define Your Goal:**
    - Be clear about the decision or plan you're evaluating.
    - Example: "I want to expand my business to a new location."
2. **Brainstorm Possible Outcomes:**
    - Imagine a range of scenarios:
    - Best Case: High customer demand and profits.
    - Moderate Case: Steady growth with minor challenges.
    - Worst Case: Low demand and financial losses.
3. **Develop Strategies for Each Scenario:**
    - Create a plan tailored to each possibility.
    - Example:
    - Best Case: Hire additional staff to meet demand.
    - Moderate Case: Focus on building brand awareness.
    - Worst Case: Scale back operations to minimize losses.
4. **Monitor Key Indicators:**
    - Identify signs that indicate which scenario is unfolding.
    - Example: Early customer feedback or sales trends.
5. **Adapt as Needed:**
    - Be ready to adjust your strategy as new information emerges.

Examples of Scenario Planning in Action

1. **In Personal Finance:**
    - **Scenario:** Saving for a major purchase.
    - **Best Case:** You save the full amount on time.
    - **Moderate Case:** Unexpected expenses slow your progress.
    - **Worst Case:** You lose income and must delay the purchase.
    - **Plan:** Build an emergency fund and adjust your budget as needed.

2. **In Career Decisions:**
   - o **Scenario:** Applying for a competitive promotion.
   - o **Best Case:** You get the role and thrive.
   - o **Moderate Case:** You don't get the promotion but gain valuable feedback.
   - o **Worst Case:** You realize the role isn't the right fit.
   - o **Plan:** Continue networking and building skills for future opportunities.
3. **In Event Planning:**
   - o **Scenario:** Organizing an outdoor wedding.
   - o **Best Case:** Perfect weather.
   - o Moderate Case: Light rain.
   - o Worst Case: A storm.
   - o **Plan:** Arrange a backup venue and rental tents.

Practical Exercise: Plan for Your Scenarios

1. **Choose a Goal or Decision:**
   - o Example: "I want to start a side business."
2. **List Three Scenarios:**
   - o Best Case, Moderate Case, Worst Case.
3. **Develop Strategies for Each:**
   - o Tailor your plans to prepare for any outcome.

Why Scenario Planning is Powerful

This technique helps you anticipate risks, seize opportunities, and build resilience. It's about being prepared for whatever comes.

Closing Thought

The future is uncertain, but your preparation doesn't have to be. Use scenario planning to face any outcome with confidence and clarity.

Chapter 37: Risk vs. Reward: Make Calculated Bets

What Does Risk vs. Reward Mean?

Every decision involves some level of risk, but not all risks are created equal. Risk vs. reward is the process of evaluating potential downsides (risks) against the potential benefits (rewards) of a decision. This method helps you make choices that maximize gain while minimizing unnecessary losses.

For example:

- Deciding to invest in a start-up might carry a high risk of financial loss but also the potential for significant returns. The decision depends on whether the possible reward justifies the level of risk.

Why Balancing Risk and Reward is Crucial

1. **Prevents Reckless Choices:**
   - o It encourages you to consider risks carefully rather than jumping into decisions based on excitement or pressure.
2. **Reduces Missed Opportunities:**
   - o Fear of risk can paralyze you. Balancing it with potential rewards helps you make confident, informed bets.
3. **Sharpens Decision-Making:**
   - o Weighing risks and rewards forces you to think critically about priorities and trade-offs.

How to Evaluate Risk vs. Reward

1. **Identify the Decision:**
    - Be clear about what you're considering.
    - Example: "Should I start my own business?"
2. **List the Risks:**
    - Write down potential downsides and their likelihood.
    - Example: Losing savings, inconsistent income, or business failure.
3. **List the Rewards:**
    - Identify possible benefits and their impact.
    - Example: Financial independence, creative freedom, or long-term growth.
4. **Assess Risk Probability and Impact:**
    - For each risk, evaluate:
    - **Probability:** How likely is it to happen?
    - **Impact:** How significant would the damage be if it occurs?
5. **Assess Reward Value:**
    - Consider the scale and importance of potential benefits.
    - Example: A high chance of moderate rewards might outweigh low-probability, catastrophic risks.
6. **Make a Decision:**
    - Choose based on whether the rewards outweigh the risks or if you can mitigate the risks sufficiently.

Examples of Risk vs. Reward Thinking

1. **In Investments:**
    - **Scenario:** Deciding whether to invest in a high-risk stock.
    - **Risks:** Losing money if the stock value plummets.
    - **Rewards:** Significant returns if the stock performs well.
    - **Decision:** Invest a small amount you can afford to lose, minimizing downside while maintaining upside potential.
2. **In Career Decisions:**
    - **Scenario:** Considering a role at a start-up.
    - **Risks:** Job instability, long hours.
    - **Rewards:** Rapid career growth, equity in the company.
    - **Decision:** Accept the role if it aligns with your long-term goals and you can handle short-term instability.
3. **In Personal Choices:**
    - **Scenario:** Moving to a new city for a fresh start.
    - **Risks:** Financial strain, homesickness.
    - **Rewards:** New opportunities, personal growth.
    - **Decision:** If the potential for growth outweighs temporary discomfort, take the leap.

Practical Exercise: Apply Risk vs. Reward

1. **Choose a Decision You're Facing:**
    - Example: "Should I enroll in an expensive certification program?"
2. **List the Risks and Rewards:**
    - Risks: Cost, time commitment.
    - Rewards: Career advancement, higher salary potential.
3. **Evaluate Probability and Impact:**
    - Risk Probability: Moderate (you may struggle financially for a few months).
    - Reward Value: High (significant career growth).
4. **Decide and Plan:**
    - If the rewards outweigh the risks, create a plan to mitigate the downsides, such as budgeting or taking out a small loan.

Why This Technique Works

Risk vs. reward thinking helps you avoid acting on impulse or fear. It ensures your decisions are calculated, deliberate, and aligned with your goals.

Closing Thought

Life's biggest opportunities often involve risk. Evaluate the balance carefully, mitigate where possible, and take bold steps toward meaningful rewards.

Chapter 38: Take Small Steps: Embrace Iterative Decision-Making

What is Iterative Decision-Making?

Iterative decision-making is the practice of breaking big decisions into smaller, manageable steps. Instead of trying to solve everything at once, you take one small action, evaluate the results, and adjust your approach as needed.

For example:

- If you're considering a career change, you don't quit your job immediately. Instead, you take small steps like researching industries, networking, or enrolling in a part-time course.

Why Small Steps Work

1. **Reduces Overwhelm:**
   - Tackling a huge decision all at once can feel paralyzing. Small steps make it manageable.
2. **Allows for Course Correction:**
   - Iterative decisions let you test your ideas and adapt before committing fully.
3. **Builds Momentum:**
   - Each small success motivates you to take the next step.
4. **Minimizes Risk:**
   - By taking small actions, you limit the potential consequences of failure.

How to Take Small Steps

1. **Break Down the Decision:**
   - Divide a large decision into smaller, actionable steps.
   - Example: Instead of starting a business overnight, begin by validating your idea with a small test.
2. **Start with Low-Risk Actions:**
   - Take steps that are easy to undo if needed.
   - Example: Before investing in a costly fitness program, try free online workouts to see if you enjoy the activity.
3. **Evaluate Progress:**
   - After each step, assess what worked, what didn't, and what to try next.
4. **Iterate and Adjust:**
   - Use feedback to refine your approach.
   - Example: If your initial side hustle idea doesn't resonate with customers, tweak your offering based on their feedback.

Examples of Iterative Decision-Making

1. **In Business:**
   - **Scenario:** Launching a new product.
   - **Small Step:** Start with a minimum viable product (MVP) to test demand before scaling production.
2. **In Education:**
   - **Scenario:** Considering a degree program.
   - **Small Step:** Enroll in one introductory course to gauge your interest and fit.
3. **In Personal Growth:**
   - **Scenario:** Building a fitness habit.
   - **Small Step:** Start with 10-minute daily walks instead of committing to a full gym routine immediately.

Practical Exercise: Take Your First Step

1. **Choose a Big Decision or Goal:**
   - Example: "I want to move abroad."
2. **Identify the First Small Step:**
   - Research visa requirements or reach out to someone who has made the move.

3. **Set a Timeline:**
   o   Give yourself a deadline for completing the first step, such as one week.
4. **Evaluate and Plan the Next Step:**
   o   Based on what you learn, decide on the next action.

Why This Technique is Powerful

Small steps create progress without overwhelming you. They allow for experimentation, learning, and refinement, making even the biggest decisions achievable.

Closing Thought

Success isn't a giant leap; it's a series of thoughtful steps. Start small, adapt, and watch your decisions lead to big outcomes.

Chapter 39: Start with a Minimum Viable Solution

What is a Minimum Viable Solution?

A minimum viable solution (MVS) is the simplest version of a solution that addresses a problem effectively. It focuses on delivering value quickly with the least effort, resources, or complexity. Instead of aiming for perfection right away, an MVS allows you to start small, test your approach, and improve over time.

For example:

- If you're launching a business, an MVS might involve offering a single product or service to test customer demand before expanding.

This approach is particularly useful for avoiding overcommitment to a flawed idea or spending excessive time on unnecessary features.

Why the Minimum Viable Solution is Effective

1. **Speeds Up Action:**
   o   It lets you move forward quickly instead of getting stuck in over-planning or perfectionism.
2. **Reduces Risk:**
   o   By starting small, you minimize the cost and effort of potential failures.
3. **Encourages Feedback:**
   o   An MVS lets you gather input from others early, helping you refine your approach before scaling.
4. **Builds Momentum:**
   o   Achieving small successes early on motivates you to keep going.

How to Create a Minimum Viable Solution

1. **Define the Core Problem:**
   o   Focus on the specific issue you're trying to solve.
   o   Example: "Customers want faster delivery options."
2. **Identify the Simplest Solution:**
   o   Determine the smallest action or feature that addresses the problem effectively.
   o   Example: Test local same-day delivery in one area instead of launching a nationwide program.
3. **Launch and Test:**
   o   Implement your MVS quickly and gather feedback.
   o   Example: Offer a limited menu if you're opening a new restaurant to see what items customers prefer.
4. **Iterate and Improve:**
   o   Use feedback to refine and expand your solution gradually.

Examples of Minimum Viable Solutions in Action

1. **In Business:**
   o   **Scenario:** Developing an app.
   o   **MVS:** Build a basic version with one core feature to test user interest before adding advanced functionality.

2. **In Personal Projects:**
    o **Scenario:** Writing a book.
    o **MVS:** Write a short e-book or article on the topic to gauge interest before committing to a full manuscript.
3. **In Problem-Solving:**
    o **Scenario:** Reducing household clutter.
    o **MVS:** Declutter one room or category of items (e.g., clothes) before tackling the entire house.

1. **Choose a Problem or Goal:**
    o Example: "I want to start a blog."
2. **Define Your MVS:**
    o What's the simplest version of your solution?
    o Example: Publish one blog post on a free platform to see how it resonates with readers.
3. **Take Action:**
    o Implement your MVS within the next week.
4. **Gather Feedback:**
    o Use comments, engagement, or other metrics to assess your results and plan the next steps.

Why This Technique is Powerful

A minimum viable solution allows you to act decisively without overcommitting. It's a practical way to test ideas, learn quickly, and achieve meaningful results with minimal risk.

Closing Thought

Perfection is a trap. Start with what works now, refine over time, and watch small beginnings lead to big successes.

Chapter 40: Use Weighted Scoring for Big Decisions

What is Weighted Scoring?

Weighted scoring is a decision-making tool that helps you evaluate multiple options by assigning importance (weights) to specific criteria. This approach ensures that the most critical factors have a bigger influence on the final decision, creating a more balanced and objective outcome.

For example:
- Choosing between job offers might involve criteria like salary, work-life balance, growth potential, and commute time. Weighted scoring lets you prioritize what matters most and compare the options logically.

Why Weighted Scoring Works

1. **Removes Emotional Bias:**
   - By focusing on objective criteria, it reduces the influence of emotions or gut feelings.
2. **Simplifies Complex Decisions:**
   - Breaks down big choices into smaller, measurable components.
3. **Aligns Decisions with Priorities:**
   - Ensures that the factors most important to you carry the greatest weight in the decision.

How to Use Weighted Scoring

1. **List Your Options:**
   - Write down all the choices you're considering.
   - Example: Three vacation destinations.
2. **Define Key Criteria:**
   - Identify the factors that will influence your decision.
   - Example: Cost, activities, weather, and travel time.
3. **Assign Weights to Criteria:**
   - Rate the importance of each factor on a scale (e.g., 1 to 5).
   - Example: Cost (5), activities (4), weather (3), travel time (2).
4. **Score Each Option:**
   - Rate how well each option performs on each criterion (e.g., 1 to 10).
5. **Calculate Weighted Scores:**
   - Multiply each score by its weight and add the totals for each option. The highest score indicates the best choice.

Examples of Weighted Scoring in Action

1. **In Career Decisions:**
   - **Scenario:** Choosing between three job offers.
   - **Criteria:** Salary (5), commute (3), growth potential (4), work culture (4).
   - **Action:** Use the matrix to score each job and identify the best fit based on your priorities.
2. **In Purchases:**
   - **Scenario:** Deciding between laptops.
   - **Criteria:** Price, performance, battery life, brand reputation.
   - **Action:** Compare options using weighted scoring to make a balanced decision.
3. **In Personal Goals:**
   - **Scenario:** Deciding which hobby to pursue.
   - **Criteria:** Enjoyment, cost, time commitment, and social opportunities.
   - **Action:** Evaluate each hobby against these criteria to find the best match.

Practical Exercise: Use Weighted Scoring

1. **Choose a Complex Decision:**
   - Example: "Which online course should I take?"
2. **Define Criteria and Weights:**
   - Example: Cost (4), instructor quality (5), flexibility (3), course content (5).
3. **Score Your Options:**
   - Rate each course based on how well it meets each criterion.
4. **Calculate and Compare:**
   - Multiply scores by weights, add them up, and choose the option with the highest total.

Why This Technique is Valuable

Weighted scoring brings structure and clarity to tough decisions. By aligning choices with your priorities, it ensures your decision is thoughtful, logical, and aligned with your goals.

Closing Thought

Not all factors are equal. Weighted scoring helps you focus on what matters most, ensuring that every decision reflects your true priorities.

Section V: Thinking Outside the Box

Creativity isn't just for artists — it's an essential skill for solving problems, making decisions, and innovating in everyday life. Thinking outside the box means escaping habitual patterns of thought and exploring new ways of seeing the world.

In this section, you'll learn techniques that spark creativity and unlock fresh perspectives. These tools help you tackle challenges with originality, turning roadblocks into opportunities and conventional thinking into breakthrough ideas.

Chapter 41: First Principles Thinking: Break It Down to Basics

What is First Principles Thinking?

First principles thinking involves breaking a problem down into its most basic elements, or "first principles," and building your understanding from the ground up. Instead of relying on assumptions, you ask fundamental questions to uncover the core truth of an issue.

For example:

- If you're redesigning a car, instead of asking, "How can we improve this car?" you ask, "What is a car at its core? A vehicle that moves people efficiently." This leads to rethinking everything, from materials to energy sources, without being constrained by existing models.

This technique helps you bypass conventional thinking and develop original solutions.

Why First Principles Thinking is Powerful

1. **Challenges Assumptions:**
   o It helps you avoid being limited by "the way things have always been done."
2. **Reveals Core Truths:**
   o By stripping away complexity, you focus on the fundamental aspects of a problem.
3. **Fosters Innovation:**
   o Starting from first principles encourages new approaches and creative solutions.

How to Apply First Principles Thinking

1. **Identify the Problem:**
   o Be clear about what you're trying to solve.
   o Example: "How can we make batteries cheaper and more efficient?"
2. **Break It Down:**
   o Deconstruct the problem into its basic components.
   o Example: A battery is a device that stores and releases energy.
3. **Question Assumptions:**
   o Ask, "What do I know to be true? Is this based on fact or habit?"
   o Example: Do batteries need to use expensive materials like lithium, or are there alternatives?
4. **Rebuild from the Ground Up:**
   o Use the core truths to explore new possibilities.
   o Example: Consider alternative materials, designs, or energy storage methods.

Examples of First Principles Thinking in Action

1. **In Business:**
   o **Scenario:** A company wants to reduce shipping costs.
   o **First Principles:** Shipping is about moving goods from Point A to Point B.
   o **Solution:** Instead of using traditional packaging, explore lightweight, biodegradable options that lower costs and environmental impact.

2. **In Personal Life:**
   - ○ **Scenario:** You want to get fit but dislike traditional exercise routines.
   - ○ **First Principles:** Fitness is about maintaining a healthy, active lifestyle.
   - ○ **Solution:** Focus on fun activities like dancing, hiking, or sports instead of rigid gym schedules.
3. **In Education:**
   - ○ **Scenario:** A teacher struggles to engage students.
   - ○ **First Principles:** Learning happens best when it's interactive and meaningful.
   - ○ **Solution:** Introduce hands-on experiments or storytelling to make lessons more engaging.

Practical Exercise: Break It Down

1. **Choose a Problem or Goal:**
   - ○ Example: "I want to save more money each month."
2. **List Assumptions:**
   - ○ Example: "I can only save by cutting back on coffee or dining out."
3. **Question Each Assumption:**
   - ○ Is cutting costs the only way to save? Could you find ways to earn more instead?
4. **Focus on Fundamentals:**
   - ○ What's the core principle? Saving means spending less than you earn.

Why This Technique Works

First principles thinking clears away the noise, letting you see problems with fresh eyes. By focusing on the basics, you uncover opportunities that others overlook.

Closing Thought

Complex problems often have simple beginnings. Break them down to the essentials and build solutions from the ground up.

Chapter 42: Lateral Thinking: Jump to New Perspectives

What is Lateral Thinking?

Lateral thinking is about approaching problems from unexpected angles instead of following traditional, step-by-step logic. It encourages you to step outside conventional thought patterns and explore creative, even unusual, solutions.

For example:

- A hotel chain struggling to attract business travelers might introduce coworking spaces instead of simply lowering room rates, appealing to a broader audience.

Why Lateral Thinking Matters

1. **Breaks Mental Ruts:**
   - It helps you escape predictable thinking and find fresh ideas.
2. **Solves "Impossible" Problems:**
   - By changing perspectives, you discover solutions that wouldn't emerge from linear reasoning.
3. **Drives Innovation:**
   - Lateral thinking is the foundation of breakthroughs, from new products to improved processes.

How to Practice Lateral Thinking

1. **Reframe the Question:**
   - Change how you define the problem.
   - Example: Instead of asking, "How can I sell more books?" ask, "How can I make reading irresistible?"
2. **Use Analogies:**
   - Compare the problem to unrelated fields for inspiration.
   - Example: If managing a team feels overwhelming, think about how an orchestra conductor leads musicians with different strengths.
3. **Challenge Assumptions:**
   - Identify and question the "rules" you think you must follow.
   - Example: Who says office meetings need to happen in person? Try virtual or asynchronous meetings.
4. **Consider the Absurd:**
   - Brainstorm ideas that seem ridiculous at first—they often spark creative insights.
   - Example: What if a restaurant let customers cook their own meals? (This led to the popularity of hot pot and fondue restaurants.)

Examples of Lateral Thinking in Action

1. **In Product Design:**
   - **Scenario:** Creating a more durable phone case.
   - **Lateral Idea:** Instead of reinforcing the case, design a phone that's waterproof and shatterproof.
2. **In Marketing:**
   - **Scenario:** Promoting a small café.
   - **Lateral Idea:** Create a "pay-what-you-want" day to attract curious customers and build buzz.
3. **In Personal Problem-Solving:**
   - **Scenario:** You want to meet new people but dislike networking events.
   - **Lateral Idea:** Join hobby groups or volunteer for causes you're passionate about.

Practical Exercise: Try a Lateral Approach

1. **Choose a Problem:**
   - Example: "I want to save time on my commute."
2. **Reframe the Question:**
   - How can you make the commute enjoyable instead of shorter?
3. **Brainstorm Unconventional Ideas:**
   - Examples: Listen to audiobooks, carpool with co-workers to share the driving load, or explore remote work options.
4. **Experiment and Evaluate:**
   - Test your ideas and refine them based on results.

Why This Technique is Powerful

Lateral thinking helps you escape the limits of conventional logic, opening doors to creative and effective solutions.

Closing Thought

The best ideas often come from unexpected angles. Step sideways, challenge norms, and watch problems transform into opportunities.

Chapter 43: Brainstorm Without Judgment

What Does It Mean to Brainstorm Without Judgment?

Brainstorming without judgment means generating ideas freely, without evaluating or critiquing them during the process. It allows your creativity to flow uninterrupted, encouraging unconventional and innovative solutions.

When judgment is removed, even "wild" ideas are welcome, which can spark breakthroughs or lead to refined, practical solutions later. Judgment-free brainstorming creates a safe space where ideas can evolve without fear of criticism.

For example:

- If you're brainstorming ways to grow a business, allowing "out-there" suggestions — like delivering products by drone — can inspire creative leaps that might otherwise be dismissed too early.

Why Judgment-Free Brainstorming Matters

1. **Encourages Creativity:**
   o Criticism stifles creativity. Removing judgment helps participants feel comfortable sharing bold or unusual ideas.
2. **Generates More Ideas:**
   o Without the filter of "good" or "bad," you produce a larger pool of possibilities to explore later.
3. **Fosters Collaboration:**
   o People are more likely to contribute when they know their ideas won't be immediately dismissed or ridiculed.
4. **Leads to Innovation:**
   o Even seemingly "bad" ideas can inspire solutions that wouldn't have been considered otherwise.

How to Brainstorm Without Judgment

1. **Set Clear Goals:**
   o Define the purpose of the brainstorming session.
   o Example: "We're brainstorming ways to reduce office waste."
2. **Create a Safe Environment:**
   o Establish ground rules: No criticism, no judgment, and no interrupting others.
3. **Encourage Quantity Over Quality:**
   o Focus on generating as many ideas as possible. Refining them comes later.
4. **Use Prompts or Themes:**
   o Start with questions or challenges to spark creativity.
   o Example: "What's one way we could eliminate paper usage entirely?"
5. **Record Every Idea:**
   o Write down all contributions, no matter how impractical they seem.
6. **Save Evaluation for Later:**
   o Once the brainstorming session is complete, review and refine the ideas as a group.

Examples of Brainstorming Without Judgment

1. **In Business:**
   o **Scenario:** A marketing team brainstorms ways to increase customer engagement.
   o **Process:** Ideas range from hosting live Q&A sessions to creating a mascot for the brand.
   o **Outcome:** While the mascot idea seems far-fetched, it inspires a viral marketing campaign featuring humorous animated videos.
2. **In Education:**
   o **Scenario:** Teachers brainstorm ways to make math lessons more engaging.
   o **Process:** Ideas include incorporating games, music, and field trips.
   o **Outcome:** The group combines ideas into a "math adventure day" that becomes a hit with students.

3. **In Personal Life:**
   - ○ **Scenario:** A family brainstorms vacation destinations.
   - ○ **Process:** Ideas range from local camping trips to a dream safari in Africa.
   - ○ **Outcome:** While the safari is out of budget, it leads to a compromise: visiting a wildlife park nearby.

Practical Exercise: Brainstorm Judgment-Free

1. **Choose a Topic or Problem:**
   - ○ Example: "How can I make my mornings more productive?"
2. **Set a Timer:**
   - ○ Spend 10 minutes writing down every idea that comes to mind, no matter how small or impractical.
3. **Avoid Evaluating:**
   - ○ Don't critique or eliminate ideas during the process.
4. **Review and Refine Later:**
   - ○ After the brainstorming session, pick a few ideas to explore further.

Why This Technique is Valuable

Judgment-free brainstorming removes barriers to creativity. It generates a rich pool of ideas, some of which might lead to surprising and innovative solutions.

Closing Thought: Ideas flourish when freed from judgment. Give your creativity room to grow, and let evaluation come later.

Chapter 44: Use Random Input to Spark Ideas

What is Random Input?

Random input involves introducing unrelated or unexpected elements into your thought process to inspire new ideas. By forcing your brain to connect seemingly unrelated concepts, you break free from linear thinking and discover fresh, creative perspectives.

For example:
- If you're designing a new product and use the word "mountain" as random input, you might explore ideas like durability, adaptability, or outdoor applications.

Why Random Input Works

1. **Breaks Predictable Patterns:**
   - Random input disrupts your usual way of thinking, sparking creativity.
2. **Fosters New Connections:**
   - By linking unrelated ideas, you discover innovative solutions.
3. **Expands Possibilities:**
   - It broadens your perspective, opening the door to unexpected approaches.

How to Use Random Input

1. **Define Your Problem or Goal:**
   - Be specific about what you're trying to solve or create.
   - Example: "How can we make our meetings more engaging?"
2. **Generate Random Input:**
   - Use a dictionary, image, or random word generator to find unrelated input.
   - Example: The random word is "balloon."
3. **Explore Connections:**
   - Ask how the random input relates to your problem.
   - Example: "What if meetings felt lighter and more fun, like a party with balloons? Could we gamify presentations or add humor?"
4. **Brainstorm Ideas:**
   - Use the random input to inspire new possibilities.

Examples of Random Input in Action

1. **In Design:**
   - **Scenario:** A team is designing eco-friendly packaging.
   - Random Input: "Cocoon."
   - **Idea:** Create biodegradable packaging that protects products like a cocoon protects a butterfly.
2. **In Marketing:**
   - **Scenario:** A company wants to rebrand its image.
   - **Random Input:** "Lighthouse."
   - **Idea:** Position the brand as a beacon of trust and guidance, symbolized in its new logo.
3. **In Problem-Solving:**
   - **Scenario:** You're brainstorming ways to motivate your team.
   - Random Input: "Puzzle."
   - **Idea:** Introduce team-building activities that involve solving puzzles together.

Practical Exercise: Try Random Input

1. **Choose a Problem or Goal:**
   - Example: "How can I improve my home workspace?"
2. **Find Random Input:**
   - Open a book, choose a word, or pick an object nearby.
   - Example: The word is "tree."
3. **Make Connections:**
   - How could "tree" inspire your workspace?
   - Example: Add more plants for a calming atmosphere or design a desk that "grows" with your needs.
4. **Brainstorm and Act:**
   - Use the connections to spark creative changes.

Why This Technique is Effective

Random input helps you think differently by introducing fresh, unexpected perspectives. It encourages out-of-the-box ideas that wouldn't emerge through conventional methods.

Closing Thought

Inspiration can come from anywhere. Let randomness spark connections, and you'll discover ideas you never imagined.

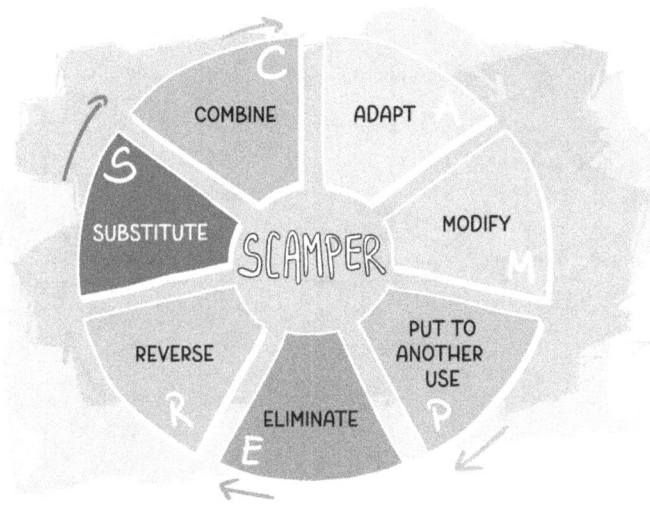

Chapter 45: The SCAMPER Method: Improve by Modifying

What is the SCAMPER Method?

The SCAMPER Method is a structured brainstorming tool that helps you improve existing ideas, products, or processes by systematically modifying them.

SCAMPER stands for:

- Substitute
- Combine
- Adapt
- Modify
- Put to another use
- Eliminate
- Reverse

Each prompt encourages you to think about how to transform or innovate an idea, often leading to practical and creative solutions.

For example:

- A company improving a chair might **Substitute** the material, **Combine** it with a desk, or **Reverse** its function to become stackable for storage.

Why the SCAMPER Method is Useful

1. **Encourages Creativity:**
   o   The prompts push you to explore possibilities you might not otherwise consider.
2. **Fosters Incremental Improvement:**
   o   Instead of reinventing the wheel, you refine and enhance what already exists.
3. **Applies to Any Context:**
   o   SCAMPER works for products, processes, strategies, and even personal goals.

How to Use the SCAMPER Method

1. **Identify the Target:**
   o   Choose the idea, product, or process you want to improve.
   o   Example: A reusable water bottle design.
2. **Apply Each Prompt:**
   o   Go through each SCAMPER prompt systematically, brainstorming ways to transform the target.
3. **Generate and Record Ideas:**
   o   Write down every idea, no matter how small or unusual.
4. **Evaluate and Implement:**
   o   Choose the most promising ideas and test them in practice.

Breaking Down the SCAMPER Prompts

1. **Substitute:**
   o   Replace one part of the idea with something else.
   o   Example: Use bamboo instead of plastic for the water bottle to make it eco-friendly.
2. **Combine:**
   o   Merge two elements to create a new solution.
   o   Example: Combine a water bottle with a compartment for storing vitamins or snacks.
3. **Adapt:**
   o   Adjust the idea to suit a new purpose or audience.
   o   Example: Adapt the bottle's design to make it collapsible for easy travel.
4. **Modify:**
   o   Change the size, shape, or other characteristics.
   o   Example: Add a built-in filter to the water bottle for purification.

5. **Put to Another Use:**
   - ○ Repurpose the idea in a different context.
   - ○ Example: Market the bottle as a multipurpose container for hot and cold drinks.
6. **Eliminate:**
   - ○ Remove unnecessary parts to simplify the idea.
   - ○ Example: Eliminate the cap threading for a sleek, spill-proof design.
7. **Reverse:**
   - ○ Flip the idea's process or function.
   - ○ Example: Design the bottle to fill from the bottom for easier cleaning.

Examples of SCAMPER in Action

1. **In Product Design:**
   - ○ **Scenario:** Improving a smartphone.
   - ○ SCAMPER:
   - ○ **Substitute:** Use a solar-powered battery.
   - ○ **Combine:** Add a built-in projector for presentations.
   - ○ **Eliminate:** Remove physical buttons for a sleeker design.
2. **In Business Strategy:**
   - ○ **Scenario:** Enhancing customer service.
   - ○ SCAMPER:
   - ○ **Adapt:** Offer 24/7 support for global customers.
   - ○ **Modify:** Use AI chatbots for faster response times.
   - ○ **Reverse:** Let customers rate representatives immediately after interactions.
3. **In Personal Growth:**
   - ○ **Scenario:** Improving a daily routine.
   - ○ SCAMPER:
   - ○ **Combine:** Pair exercise with audiobooks for multitasking.
   - ○ **Eliminate:** Cut out social media during mornings for better focus.
   - ○ **Reverse:** Start the day with creative work instead of email.

Practical Exercise: SCAMPER Your Own Idea

1. **Choose a Target:**
   - ○ Example: "How can I improve my study habits?"
2. **Apply SCAMPER Prompts:**
   - ○ **Substitute:** Study with flashcards instead of notes.
   - ○ **Combine:** Pair studying with teaching someone else.
   - ○ **Adapt:** Use a timer for focused study sessions (Pomodoro Technique).
   - ○ **Eliminate:** Remove distractions like phone notifications.
3. **Implement and Test Ideas:**
   - ○ Experiment with your brainstormed changes and track the results.

Why This Technique Works

The SCAMPER method unlocks creativity by focusing on incremental innovation. It's a systematic yet flexible way to refine ideas and create something new.

Closing Thought

Great innovations often come from simple changes. Use SCAMPER to modify, adapt, and transform your ideas into something extraordinary.

Chapter 46: Combine Ideas to Innovate

Why Combining Ideas is Powerful

Sometimes, the best solutions don't come from inventing something entirely new — they come from blending existing ideas into something fresh. This process, called idea combination, allows you to draw inspiration from multiple sources and create innovative solutions that bridge gaps or offer new perspectives.

For example:

- Combining fitness apps with social networking led to apps like Strava, which motivates users through community engagement.

How Combining Ideas Fuels Creativity

1. **Expands Possibilities:**
   - Blending ideas widens your creative scope, unlocking solutions you wouldn't discover otherwise.
2. **Encourages Cross-Discipline Thinking:**
   - Borrowing from different fields fosters innovation by connecting unrelated concepts.
3. **Reduces Reinvention:**
   - Instead of starting from scratch, you build on proven ideas in new ways.

How to Combine Ideas Effectively

1. **Gather a Variety of Inputs:**
   - Expose yourself to diverse ideas, fields, and perspectives.
   - Example: Read books or watch documentaries on unrelated topics.
2. **Find Overlaps:**
   - Look for connections between ideas or fields.
   - Example: Combine wearable fitness trackers with gamification to boost engagement.
3. **Ask "What If?" Questions:**
   - Explore the possibilities of merging concepts.
   - Example: "What if a coffee shop also offered co-working spaces?"
4. **Prototype Your Combination:**
   - Test your combined idea to see how it works in practice.

Examples of Idea Combination in Action

1. **In Products:**
   - **Scenario:** Creating a travel gadget.
   - **Combination:** Combine a portable charger with a luggage tracker for convenience.
2. **In Services:**
   - **Scenario:** Innovating in education.
   - **Combination:** Merge online courses with personalized tutoring to improve outcomes.
3. **In Daily Life:**
   - **Scenario:** Making chores more enjoyable.
   - **Combination:** Combine cleaning with listening to your favorite podcast or music playlist.

Practical Exercise: Combine Your Ideas

1. **Choose Two Unrelated Ideas:**
   - Example: "Cooking" and "Fitness."
2. **Find Connections:**
   - Combine them into something new, like a cooking class focused on healthy meal prep for fitness enthusiasts.
3. **Test Your Idea:**
   - Share your combination with others or prototype it to see how it works.

Combining ideas fosters innovation by breaking down silos between disciplines or concepts. It allows you to create something greater than the sum of its parts.

Closing Thought

Creativity thrives at the intersection of ideas. Combine, experiment, and watch innovation emerge.

Chapter 47: Think in Opposites to Break Norms

What Does It Mean to Think in Opposites?

Thinking in opposites involves challenging conventional assumptions. Instead of asking how to improve something the usual way, you challenge norms by asking what would happen if you did the opposite. This method encourages unconventional thinking and helps you uncover fresh ideas that break through creative blocks.

For example:

- A traditional restaurant focuses on offering as many menu options as possible. Thinking in opposites might lead to a limited-menu concept, like a chef's tasting menu or a single-dish restaurant, which could create a unique experience and attract attention.

Why Thinking in Opposites is Effective

1. **Challenges Assumptions:**
   o It forces you to question why things are done a certain way and whether the opposite could work better.
2. **Breaks Habits:**
   o By reversing your usual approach, you disrupt mental ruts and open the door to creative solutions.
3. **Encourages Bold Ideas:**
   o Thinking in opposites often leads to unexpected, high-impact innovations.

How to Think in Opposites

1. **Identify the Norm:**
   o Start with a common assumption or approach related to your problem.
   o Example: "A bookstore should sell as many titles as possible."
2. **Flip It Around:**
   o Ask, "What if we did the opposite?"
   o Example: "What if the bookstore sold only a curated selection of 50 books?"
3. **Explore the Possibilities:**
   o Think about how this reversal could create value or solve the problem.
4. **Test the Idea:**
   o Experiment with your opposite-thinking solution to see how it performs in practice.

Examples of Thinking in Opposites

1. **In Business:**
   o **Scenario:** A clothing brand wants to stand out in a crowded market.
   o **Opposite Thinking:** Instead of launching a seasonal collection, they release one timeless design and focus on sustainability.
   o **Outcome:** The minimalist approach appeals to eco-conscious customers.
2. **In Education:**
   o **Scenario:** A teacher wants to improve student participation.
   o **Opposite Thinking:** Instead of leading the discussion, they let students design and teach lessons.
   o **Outcome:** Students engage more deeply and develop leadership skills.
3. **In Daily Life:**
   o **Scenario:** You want to relax after a stressful day.
   o **Opposite Thinking:** Instead of unwinding with TV, you try something stimulating, like a creative hobby or learning a new skill.

- o **Outcome:** You feel refreshed and accomplished.

Practical Exercise: Try Thinking in Opposites

1. **Choose a Problem or Goal:**
   - o Example: "How can I make my morning routine more productive?"
2. **Identify the Norm:**
   - o Example: "I should follow a structured checklist every morning."
3. **Flip the Approach:**
   - o Ask, "What if I didn't follow a checklist and started my day spontaneously?"
4. **Brainstorm Solutions:**
   - o Consider hybrid approaches, like reserving part of your morning for creative or unstructured activities.

Why This Technique Works

Thinking in opposites disrupts the status quo, encouraging fresh perspectives and bold innovations. By reversing assumptions, you expand your creative range and uncover possibilities others might overlook.

Closing Thought

Innovation often lives in the unexpected. Flip the script, break norms, and discover transformative ideas through opposite thinking.

Chapter 48: Set Constraints to Foster Creativity

How Do Constraints Spark Creativity?

While it might seem counterintuitive, setting boundaries or limitations can actually boost your creativity. Constraints force you to think resourcefully, encouraging you to explore innovative solutions within the given limits.

For example:

- If you're tasked with creating a 30-second video, the time constraint compels you to focus on the most impactful ideas, cutting unnecessary fluff.

Why Constraints Are Powerful

1. **Sharpen Focus:**
   - o Constraints eliminate distractions, helping you zero in on what matters most.

2. **Encourage Resourcefulness:**
   - Limitations push you to think outside the box and find unconventional solutions.
3. **Boost Productivity:**
   - Knowing your boundaries prevents overthinking and accelerates decision-making.

How to Use Constraints to Foster Creativity

1. **Set Clear Boundaries:**
   - Define specific limits related to time, budget, materials, or scope.
   - Example: "Create a meal using only five ingredients."
2. **Reframe Constraints as Opportunities:**
   - View limits as challenges that inspire innovation rather than obstacles.
3. **Focus on Core Goals:**
   - Use the constraint to prioritize what's most important.
4. **Experiment and Iterate:**
   - Work within the limits, test your ideas, and refine them as needed.

Examples of Creativity Within Constraints

1. **In Design:**
   - **Scenario:** A graphic designer is asked to create a striking logo using only black and white.
   - Constraint: No color.
   - **Outcome:** The designer focuses on bold shapes and negative space, creating a timeless, eye-catching design.
2. **In Writing:**
   - Scenario: A writer enters a contest requiring a 100-word story.
   - **Constraint:** Word count.
   - **Outcome:** They craft a concise, impactful narrative that resonates with readers.
3. **In Business:**
   - **Scenario:** A startup launches with a small marketing budget.
   - **Constraint:** Limited funds.
   - **Outcome:** The team focuses on low-cost strategies like social media and word-of-mouth marketing, which build a loyal community.

Practical Exercise: Create Within Constraints

1. **Choose a Task or Goal:**
   - Example: "Plan a weekend getaway."
2. **Set Constraints:**
   - Example: "Plan the trip for under $200 and within 50 miles of home."
3. **Brainstorm Solutions:**
   - Explore creative ways to meet the goal, such as finding free local attractions or carpooling to reduce costs.

Why This Technique Works

Constraints are a catalyst for innovation. By forcing you to work within limits, they spark resourcefulness and lead to solutions that might not have emerged in a limitless environment.

Closing Thought

Creativity thrives on challenge. Embrace constraints as opportunities to think boldly, work efficiently, and innovate beyond expectations.

Chapter 49: Borrow from Other Fields

What Does It Mean to Borrow from Other Fields?

Borrowing from other fields involves taking ideas, strategies, or practices from unrelated industries or disciplines and applying them to your current challenge. It's based on the idea that innovation often happens at the intersection of different perspectives.

For example:

- The concept of an assembly line revolutionized car manufacturing, but it was inspired by techniques used in meatpacking plants.

By looking beyond your own area of expertise, you gain fresh insights and discover unconventional solutions that others might overlook.

Why Borrowing from Other Fields Works

1. **Encourages Cross-Pollination of Ideas:**
   - Different fields often solve similar problems in unique ways. Borrowing their methods leads to creative breakthroughs.
2. **Expands Your Perspective:**
   - It challenges you to think beyond the limits of your industry or situation.
3. **Inspires Novel Solutions:**
   - Applying an unfamiliar idea to your challenge often results in innovation.

How to Borrow Ideas from Other Fields

1. **Study Different Disciplines:**
   - Learn about fields unrelated to your own, such as science, art, engineering, or psychology.
   - Example: If you work in marketing, study storytelling techniques used in filmmaking.
2. **Look for Analogies:**
   - Identify similarities between your problem and challenges faced in other industries.
   - Example: A hospital's triage system could inspire how a tech company prioritizes customer support tickets.
3. **Ask How Others Solve Similar Problems:**
   - Explore how unrelated industries approach challenges like efficiency, customer satisfaction, or innovation.
4. **Test and Adapt the Ideas:**
   - Apply the borrowed idea to your context, making adjustments as needed.

Examples of Borrowing from Other Fields

1. **In Product Design:**
   - **Scenario:** A fashion designer seeks to create a stain-proof fabric.
   - **Borrowed Idea:** They study how lotus leaves repel water and develop a material with similar properties.
2. **In Business Strategy:**
   - **Scenario:** A grocery store wants to improve customer flow.
   - **Borrowed Idea:** They adapt the layout of airport terminals to create clear pathways and reduce congestion.
3. **In Personal Life:**
   - **Scenario:** You're struggling to organize your daily tasks.
   - **Borrowed Idea:** You adopt an athlete's training schedule, structuring your day into focused "workout" sessions with breaks.

Practical Exercise: Apply Ideas from Another Field

1. **Define Your Challenge:**
   - Example: "I want to make my online store more user-friendly."
2. **Choose a Field to Explore:**
   - Example: Study hospitality to understand how hotels create welcoming environments.

3. **Find Analogies:**
    - Ask, "What do hotels do to make guests comfortable, and how can I apply that to my website?"
    - Example: Simplify navigation like a concierge simplifies guest services.
4. **Test the Idea:**
    - Implement and refine the borrowed concept in your context.

Why This Technique Works

Borrowing from other fields breaks you out of your routine, exposing you to new ways of thinking. It leverages the creativity of others and applies it in ways they might never have imagined.

Closing Thought

The best ideas aren't always new — they're often borrowed. Look beyond your field, find inspiration in unexpected places, and innovate boldly.

Chapter 50: Play 'What If?' with Scenarios

What Does It Mean to Play 'What If?'

Playing "What If?" is a creativity technique where you ask hypothetical questions to explore new possibilities. It encourages you to imagine alternate realities, scenarios, or outcomes, often leading to fresh ideas and unconventional solutions.

For example:
- "What if cars could drive themselves?" sparked the development of autonomous vehicles.

This approach unlocks your imagination by challenging assumptions and inspiring innovative thinking.

Why Asking 'What If?' Sparks Creativity

1. **Breaks Conventional Thinking:**
    - It frees you from the constraints of "what is" and allows you to imagine "what could be."
2. **Encourages Curiosity:**
    - By asking open-ended questions, you uncover possibilities you might not have considered before.

3. Opens Pathways to Innovation:
    o   Hypothetical scenarios often lead to ground-breaking ideas.

1. Start with a Challenge or Goal:
    o   Define the problem or area where you want to innovate.
    o   Example: "How can we reduce energy consumption in the office?"
2. Ask Open-Ended 'What If?' Questions:
    o   Encourage imaginative thinking by posing hypothetical scenarios.
    o   Example: "What if the office only operated during daylight hours?"
3. Explore the Implications:
    o   Consider how each scenario could work in practice and what challenges it might address.
4. Refine and Test Ideas:
    o   Choose the most promising "What If?" scenarios and experiment with them.

1. In Technology:
    o   **Scenario:** A tech company wants to improve smartphone design.
    o   **What If?:** "What if smartphones were wearable instead of handheld?"
    o   **Outcome:** This question leads to the development of smartwatches.
2. In Education:
    o   **Scenario:** A school wants to increase student engagement.
    o   **What If?:** "What if students designed their own curriculum?"
    o   **Outcome:** The school creates a program where students choose project-based learning paths.
3. In Personal Growth:
    o   **Scenario:** You're stuck in a career rut.
    o   **What If?:** "What if I started a side hustle in my passion area?"
    o   **Outcome:** You explore freelancing opportunities, eventually transitioning to a fulfilling new career.

1. Choose a Challenge or Opportunity:
    o   Example: "How can I make my weekends more relaxing?"
2. Ask 'What If?' Questions:
    o   Examples: "What if I planned no activities at all? What if I dedicated Saturdays to hobbies and Sundays to rest?"
3. Explore the Scenarios:
    o   Consider how each option might impact your weekend experience.
4. Take Action:
    o   Experiment with one scenario and refine it based on your results.

'What If?' thinking opens the door to new possibilities by encouraging curiosity and exploration. It's a playful yet powerful way to unlock ideas that challenge the status quo.

The world changes when we ask, "What if?" Let your imagination roam, and you'll find ideas that push the boundaries of what's possible.

Section VI: Techniques for Mental Clarity

Mental clarity is the foundation of good decision-making, creativity, and focus. In this section, you'll explore tools to declutter your thoughts, prioritize effectively, and stay present in the moment. By mastering these methods, you'll learn to approach challenges with a clear mind and make thoughtful, deliberate decisions.

Chapter 51: Practice Mental Hygiene: Eliminate Mental Clutter

What is Mental Hygiene?

Mental hygiene is the practice of regularly clearing your mind of unnecessary thoughts, worries, and distractions. Just as you clean your physical space, maintaining a "clean" mental space helps you think more clearly and reduces stress.

Mental clutter often comes from unfinished tasks, unresolved emotions, and an overwhelming amount of information. Without regular mental hygiene, this clutter can cloud your judgment and reduce your productivity.

Why Mental Hygiene is Essential

1. **Improves Focus:**
   - A clear mind allows you to concentrate on what matters most.
2. **Reduces Stress:**
   - Letting go of unnecessary worries frees up mental energy.
3. **Enhances Decision-Making:**
   - With fewer distractions, you can think critically and act decisively.

How to Eliminate Mental Clutter

1. **Create a Thought Dump:**
   - Write down everything on your mind, no matter how small or trivial. This helps offload mental "junk" and organize your priorities.
2. **Resolve Open Loops:**
   - Identify unfinished tasks or decisions weighing on your mind. Take action or schedule a time to address them.
3. **Let Go of What You Can't Control:**
   - Focus on what's within your power to change and release worries about the rest.
4. **Declutter Your Environment:**
   - Your physical space often mirrors your mental state. Tidying up can create a sense of calm and order.
5. **Limit Mental Input:**
   - Reduce unnecessary information by unsubscribing from irrelevant emails, turning off notifications, and avoiding excessive media consumption.

Examples of Mental Hygiene in Action

1. **In Work:**
   - **Scenario:** You feel overwhelmed by a long to-do list.
   - **Action:** Write down all tasks, prioritize them, and delegate what you can.
2. **In Personal Life:**
   - **Scenario:** You keep replaying a recent argument in your mind.
   - **Action:** Reflect on the issue, resolve what you can, and then let it go.
3. **In Daily Habits:**
   - **Scenario:** Your phone constantly distracts you with notifications.

○ **Action:** Turn off unnecessary alerts and set specific times to check your phone.

Practical Exercise: Clean Your Mental Space

1. **Spend 10 Minutes Writing a Thought Dump:**
   ○ List everything on your mind—tasks, worries, ideas, or random thoughts.
2. **Categorize Your Thoughts:**
   ○ Group them into "actionable," "non-urgent," and "let go."
3. **Take Action:**
   ○ Address one actionable item immediately and schedule others. Release the rest.

Why This Technique Works

Practicing mental hygiene creates space for clearer thinking and greater focus. It's a simple habit that makes room for your best ideas and most thoughtful decisions.

Closing Thought

A cluttered mind can't function at its best. Clear the mental "junk" regularly to free your thoughts and regain clarity.

Chapter 52: Write It Out: Organize Thoughts on Paper

Why Writing Clarifies Thinking

Writing is one of the simplest yet most effective ways to organize your thoughts. When you put your ideas, worries, or plans on paper, you free up mental space and gain clarity about what matters. Writing helps you sort through confusion, prioritize tasks, and process emotions.

For example:
- Writing out a plan for a big project can help you break it into manageable steps, while journaling about a tough day can bring emotional relief.

Benefits of Writing It Out

1. **Organizes Your Thoughts:**
   ○ Writing turns abstract ideas into concrete words, making them easier to understand.
2. **Improves Memory:**
   ○ Putting thoughts on paper helps you retain information better than keeping it in your head.
3. **Relieves Mental Overload:**
   ○ Offloading thoughts onto paper reduces anxiety and clears your mind for focused thinking.

How to Use Writing for Mental Clarity

1. **Start a Daily Brain Dump:**
   ○ Spend a few minutes each morning or evening writing down everything on your mind.
2. **Make Lists:**
   ○ Organize tasks or ideas into categories, such as "to-do," "questions," or "goals."
3. **Use Journaling for Reflection:**
   ○ Write about your feelings, challenges, or successes to process emotions and gain insights.
4. **Write to Solve Problems:**
   ○ Outline a problem and brainstorm possible solutions in writing.
5. **Create Visuals:**
   ○ Use bullet points, diagrams, or mind maps to structure your thoughts more clearly.

Examples of Writing It Out in Action

1. **In Work:**
   ○ **Scenario:** You're overwhelmed by a complex project.
   ○ **Action:** Write down the project's goals, break it into smaller tasks, and create a timeline.

2. **In Personal Life:**
   - o **Scenario:** You're feeling stuck in a decision.
   - o **Action:** Write out the pros and cons of each option to clarify your choice.
3. **In Emotional Health:**
   - o **Scenario:** You're feeling anxious about the future.
   - o **Action:** Journal about your worries to explore what's causing them and what steps you can take.

Practical Exercise: Start Writing for Clarity

1. **Take Five Minutes:**
   - o Write down everything on your mind without worrying about grammar or structure.
2. **Organize Your Thoughts:**
   - o Highlight the most important items and group related ideas together.
3. **Choose One Item to Act On:**
   - o Take immediate action on a task or reflect further on an insight you gained.

Why This Technique Works

Writing simplifies your thoughts and gives you a clearer picture of what matters. It's an easy way to process emotions, plan effectively, and regain focus.

Closing Thought

Don't let your thoughts swirl around in your mind. Write them down, organize them, and find the clarity you need to move forward.

Chapter 53: Mind Mapping for Visual Clarity

What is Mind Mapping?

Mind mapping is a visual technique for organizing information, ideas, or thoughts. It starts with a central concept, with related ideas branching out like the limbs of a tree. This method allows you to see connections between ideas, brainstorm effectively, and structure your thoughts clearly.

For example:

- If you're planning a vacation, you could create a mind map with "Vacation" at the center, branching into categories like "Destinations," "Activities," "Budget," and "Packing List." Each branch can have its own sub-branches, breaking down details like specific places or items.

Why Mind Mapping is Effective

1. **Visualizes Complexity:**
   - o By laying out ideas visually, mind mapping makes it easier to see relationships and organize thoughts.
2. **Encourages Creativity:**
   - o The open-ended structure allows for free-flowing ideas and brainstorming.

3. **Improves Memory:**
   o The combination of words, colors, and shapes helps you retain information better than linear lists.
4. **Simplifies Planning:**
   o Mind maps provide a clear overview of a project, goal, or problem, making it easier to manage.

How to Create a Mind Map

1. **Start with a Central Idea:**
   o Write the main topic or goal in the center of a blank page. Use a circle, box, or another shape to highlight it.
   o Example: "Start a Small Business."
2. **Add Branches:**
   o Draw lines radiating from the center and label them with related categories or subtopics.
   o Example: Branches might include "Marketing," "Budget," "Products," and "Logistics."
3. **Develop Sub-Branches:**
   o Add smaller lines branching from the main categories, detailing specific ideas or tasks.
   o Example: Under "Marketing," sub-branches might include "Social Media," "Website," and "Networking."
4. **Use Colors, Images, and Keywords:**
   o Highlight key points with colors or symbols to make the map visually engaging and easier to remember.
5. **Review and Refine:**
   o Rearrange branches, add new ideas, or simplify as needed to clarify your thoughts.

Examples of Mind Mapping in Action

1. **In Personal Goals:**
   o **Scenario:** You want to improve your health.
   o Mind Map:
   o Central Idea: "Health."
   o Branches: "Exercise," "Nutrition," "Sleep," and "Stress Management."
   o Sub-branches: "Strength Training" under "Exercise," "Meal Prep" under "Nutrition," and so on.
2. **In Problem-Solving:**
   o **Scenario:** You're trying to fix a recurring issue at work.
   o Mind Map:
   o Central Idea: "Problem."
   o Branches: "Causes," "Possible Solutions," "Resources Needed," and "Next Steps."
3. **In Learning:**
   o **Scenario:** You're studying for an exam.
   o Mind Map:
   o Central Idea: "History Exam."
   o Branches: "Key Dates," "Important Figures," "Themes," and "Essay Topics."

Practical Exercise: Create Your Own Mind Map

1. **Pick a Topic or Goal:**
   o Example: "Organize a Family Event."
2. **Write the Central Idea:**
   o Place "Family Event" in the center of the page.
3. **Add Main Branches:**
   o Example: "Venue," "Guests," "Food," and "Activities."
4. **Develop Sub-Branches:**
   o Under "Food," add options like "Catering," "Potluck," or "DIY."
5. **Use Colors and Symbols:**
   o Highlight deadlines in red or draw a clock next to time-sensitive tasks.

Why This Technique Works

Mind mapping transforms scattered thoughts into an organized, visual format. It encourages creativity, simplifies planning, and provides clarity at a glance.

Closing Thought

When your thoughts feel tangled, map them out. A well-crafted mind map turns chaos into clarity, helping you see the big picture and the details all at once.

Chapter 54: Practice Single-Tasking: Focus on One Thing at a Time

What is Single-Tasking?

Single-tasking means focusing on one task at a time, giving it your full attention until it's complete. In contrast to multitasking, which divides your attention and reduces efficiency, single-tasking helps you work more effectively and with greater quality.

For example:

- Instead of checking emails while writing a report, you focus solely on the report, finishing it faster and with fewer errors.

Why Single-Tasking is Essential

1. **Boosts Productivity:**
   - Concentrating on one task allows you to complete it faster and with better results.
2. **Improves Quality:**
   - Fewer distractions mean fewer mistakes and higher-quality work.
3. **Reduces Stress:**
   - Single-tasking feels less overwhelming than juggling multiple priorities.
4. **Builds Mindfulness:**
   - It keeps you present in the moment, helping you enjoy and engage with what you're doing.

How to Practice Single-Tasking

1. **Prioritize Your Tasks:**
   - Choose the most important task to work on first.
   - Example: Start with the report due tomorrow, not your email inbox.
2. **Eliminate Distractions:**
   - Turn off notifications, close unnecessary tabs, and create a focused workspace.
3. **Set a Time Block:**
   - Commit to working on one task for a set period, such as 25 minutes using the Pomodoro Technique.
4. **Finish Before Switching:**
   - Complete or make significant progress on your current task before moving to the next one.
5. **Take Breaks:**
   - Pause between tasks to recharge your focus and energy.

Examples of Single-Tasking in Action

1. **In Work:**
   - **Scenario:** Writing a proposal while managing team emails.
   - **Action:** Schedule time to write the proposal without interruptions, then dedicate time to emails later.
2. **In Personal Life:**
   - **Scenario:** Cooking dinner while checking your phone.
   - **Action:** Put the phone away and focus on cooking, enjoying the process and improving the meal.
3. **In Learning:**
   - **Scenario:** Studying for a test while texting friends.
   - **Action:** Turn off your phone and focus solely on studying for a set time.

Practical Exercise: Try Single-Tasking

1. **Pick One Task:**
   - Example: "Write a weekly report."

2. **Eliminate Distractions:**
    o   Silence your phone, close unrelated browser tabs, and let others know you need focused time.
3. **Work in Focused Blocks:**
    o   Spend 25-30 minutes on the task, then take a short break.
4. **Evaluate Results:**
    o   Notice how much more you accomplish and how your stress levels improve.

Why This Technique Works

Single-tasking channels your energy into what matters most. By reducing distractions and improving focus, it helps you work more efficiently and enjoy the process.

Closing Thought

In a world that glorifies multitasking, single-tasking is your superpower. Focus on one thing at a time and watch your productivity and peace of mind soar.

Chapter 55: Declutter Information Overload

What is Information Overload?

Information overload happens when you're bombarded with more information than you can process. From emails to news updates, social media, and endless articles, it's easy to feel overwhelmed and distracted. This overload can cloud your thinking, hinder decision-making, and leave you feeling mentally drained.

Decluttering information prioritizes what's relevant and eliminates unnecessary noise so you can focus on what truly matters.

Why Decluttering Information Matters

1. **Improves Focus:**
    o   With less irrelevant information competing for attention, you can concentrate better.
2. **Reduces Stress:**
    o   A cleaner mental environment feels more manageable and less overwhelming.

3. Enhances Decision-Making:
   o By focusing on quality over quantity, you gain clearer insights and make better choices.

How to Declutter Information Overload

1. **Limit Your Inputs:**
   o Identify the sources of information in your life and cut back on non-essential ones.
   o Example: Unsubscribe from newsletters you never read or follow fewer social media accounts.
2. **Set Boundaries for Consumption:**
   o Designate specific times for checking email, news, or social media.
   o Example: Limit news reading to 20 minutes a day.
3. **Use Filters:**
   o Prioritize information by relevance and importance.
   o Example: Use tools like email filters to separate urgent messages from routine ones.
4. **Focus on One Topic at a Time:**
   o Instead of multitasking between multiple sources, dive deeply into one subject before moving to the next.
5. **Take Digital Breaks:**
   o Step away from screens periodically to recharge your mind.
6. **Practice the 80/20 Rule:**
   o Focus on the 20% of information that delivers 80% of the value.
   o Example: Read summaries instead of full articles for non-critical topics.

Examples of Managing Information Overload

1. **In Work:**
   o **Scenario:** Your inbox is flooded with unread emails.
   o **Action:** Use folders or tags to sort emails by priority, respond to urgent ones first, and archive irrelevant messages.
2. **In Personal Life:**
   o **Scenario:** You spend hours scrolling through social media without gaining much value.
   o **Action:** Unfollow accounts that don't add meaning or joy, and set a daily time limit for scrolling.
3. **In Learning:**
   o **Scenario:** You're overwhelmed by conflicting advice on a topic.
   o **Action:** Identify a few trusted sources and stick to them, instead of trying to absorb everything.

Practical Exercise: Declutter Your Information Inputs

1. **Audit Your Inputs:**
   o List all the ways you consume information — news, social media, emails, podcasts, etc.
2. **Identify Unnecessary Sources:**
   o Ask: "Which of these truly add value to my life or work?"
3. **Reduce and Streamline:**
   o Unsubscribe, unfollow, or delete apps that don't serve a clear purpose.
4. **Set Boundaries:**
   o Establish rules, like "no emails after 7 PM" or "news only in the morning."

Why This Technique Works

Decluttering information overload creates mental space for what's important. It reduces distractions and allows you to focus on meaningful tasks and decisions.

Closing Thought

You don't need to know everything — just the right things. Declutter your mind by decluttering your inputs, and let clarity lead the way.

Chapter 56: Use White Space: Schedule Thinking Time

What is White Space?

White space refers to the deliberate gaps or pauses you create in your schedule to think, reflect, or recharge. In a packed day, it's easy to rush from task to task without pausing to process or plan. White space gives your brain room to breathe, fostering clarity, creativity, and better decision-making.

For example:

- Setting aside 30 minutes of quiet time in the morning can help you prioritize your day and approach tasks with a clear mind.

Why White Space is Powerful

1. **Encourages Reflection:**
   - It provides time to think critically, solve problems, and gain new insights.
2. **Boosts Creativity:**
   - Downtime allows your mind to wander, often leading to innovative ideas.
3. **Reduces Burnout:**
   - Scheduling breaks prevents mental exhaustion and improves focus.

How to Incorporate White Space into Your Day

1. **Block Time on Your Calendar:**
   - Schedule thinking time as you would any other task. Treat it as non-negotiable.
2. **Start Small:**
   - Begin with 10–15 minutes of white space each day and gradually increase as needed.
3. **Eliminate Distractions:**
   - Use this time for quiet reflection, not for catching up on emails or social media.
4. **Use Prompts:**
   - If you're unsure how to use white space, ask questions like, "What's my top priority today?" or "How can I solve this challenge creatively?"
5. **Combine with Restorative Activities:**
   - Take a walk, meditate, or simply sit in silence to clear your mind.

Examples of Using White Space

1. **In Work:**
   - **Scenario:** Your calendar is packed with back-to-back meetings.
   - **Action:** Block 15 minutes between meetings to reflect, take notes, and reset.
2. **In Personal Life:**
   - **Scenario:** You feel overwhelmed by daily chores.
   - **Action:** Schedule quiet time each evening to plan and relax.
3. **In Creative Projects:**
   - **Scenario:** You're stuck on a writing project.
   - **Action:** Take a 20-minute walk to let your mind wander and generate fresh ideas.

Practical Exercise: Add White Space to Your Day

1. **Pick a Time:**
   - Choose a block of time when you can step away from tasks—e.g., the first 10 minutes after lunch.
2. **Set Boundaries:**
   - Turn off notifications and let others know you're unavailable during this time.
3. **Reflect or Recharge:**
   - Use the time to think strategically, journal, or simply rest.
4. **Evaluate the Benefits:**
   - Notice how white space improves your focus, clarity, and creativity.

White space gives your brain a chance to reset. It allows you to process information, reflect on priorities, and recharge for what's next.

Closing Thought
Productivity isn't about doing more; it's about doing what matters. Create space to think, and you'll find clarity and purpose in your work and life.

Chapter 57: Decline to Decide: Avoid Decision Fatigue

What is Decision Fatigue?
Decision fatigue occurs when the mental energy required to make repeated decisions leaves you feeling exhausted and less capable of making good choices. Every decision, no matter how small, drains your cognitive resources. Over time, this can lead to poor judgment, procrastination, or defaulting to the easiest option.

For example:
- After a long day of decision-making, you might skip cooking dinner in favor of ordering unhealthy fast food simply because it feels easier.

The key to combating decision fatigue is learning to reduce unnecessary decisions and streamline your choices.

Why Avoiding Decision Fatigue Matters
1. **Preserves Mental Energy:**
   o Fewer decisions mean more focus for the choices that truly matter.
2. **Improves Decision Quality:**
   o By reserving energy for important decisions, you make better, more thoughtful choices.
3. **Reduces Stress:**
   o Simplifying your choices creates a sense of clarity and ease.

How to Avoid Decision Fatigue
1. **Automate Routine Choices:**
   o Simplify daily decisions by creating routines or habits.
   o Example: Plan your meals for the week or wear a "uniform" of go-to outfits.
2. **Set Priorities:**
   o Focus on making high-impact decisions first and defer less important ones.
3. **Limit Options:**
   o Too many choices can be overwhelming. Narrow your options to a manageable number.
   o Example: Instead of browsing an entire streaming library, pick one genre or create a shortlist.
4. **Batch Similar Decisions:**
   o Group similar tasks together to minimize decision-making throughout the day.
   o Example: Reply to emails in one session rather than sporadically.
5. **Delegate or Decline Decisions:**
   o Empower others to make certain choices or say "no" to decisions that aren't your responsibility.
6. **Schedule Decision-Free Time:**
   o Reserve parts of your day for creativity, relaxation, or reflection, free from decision-making.

Examples of Avoiding Decision Fatigue
1. **In Work:**
   o **Scenario:** You're constantly interrupted by co-workers asking for input.
   o **Action:** Create clear guidelines or delegate decision-making authority for routine questions.
2. **In Personal Life:**
   o **Scenario:** You struggle to decide what to eat for dinner every night.
   o **Action:** Plan meals in advance or rotate a set menu of favorite dishes.

3. **In Shopping:**
   - ○ **Scenario:** You spend hours choosing between products.
   - ○ **Action:** Research and set criteria beforehand to limit your options, such as price range or brand preference.

1. **Identify Recurring Decisions:**
   - ○ Write down daily or weekly decisions that drain your mental energy.
2. **Create a Plan:**
   - ○ Automate, batch, or limit options for these decisions.
   - ○ Example: "I'll check emails twice a day, at 10 AM and 3 PM, instead of constantly."
3. **Evaluate the Impact:**
   - ○ Notice how much mental space and energy you free up by simplifying choices.

Why This Technique Works

Declining to decide on trivial matters conserves mental energy for what's truly important. It reduces stress, boosts productivity, and helps you approach big decisions with clarity and focus.

Closing Thought

Not every choice deserves your energy. Simplify your life by eliminating, automating, or delegating low-stakes decisions, and watch your mental clarity soar.

Chapter 58: Set Clear Goals for Mental Direction

Why Clear Goals Are Essential for Mental Clarity

Clear goals act as a mental compass, guiding your thoughts and actions toward a specific outcome. Without defined objectives, it's easy to feel scattered or overwhelmed by competing priorities. Setting clear goals not only focuses your energy but also provides a sense of purpose and direction.

For example:

- Instead of a vague goal like "Get in shape," a clear goal would be "Run three times a week and lose 10 pounds in three months." This specificity gives you a clear target and actionable steps.

Benefits of Clear Goals

1. **Improves Focus:**
   - Goals help you prioritize what's important and avoid distractions.
2. **Boosts Motivation:**
   - Having a clear objective gives you something to work toward, increasing your drive.
3. **Simplifies Decision-Making:**
   - With a defined goal, it's easier to determine which actions align with your priorities.

How to Set Clear Goals

1. **Use the SMART Framework:**
   - **Specific:** Clearly define what you want to achieve.
   - **Measurable:** Include criteria to track your progress.
   - **Achievable:** Set a goal that's realistic and within your control.
   - **Relevant:** Align the goal with your broader objectives.
   - **Time-Bound:** Set a deadline to create urgency.
2. **Break Goals into Steps:**
   - Divide larger goals into smaller, actionable tasks.
   - Example: To "write a book," break it into tasks like "outline chapters" and "write 500 words daily."
3. **Write Down Your Goals:**
   - Putting goals in writing solidifies your commitment and makes them easier to track.
4. **Review Regularly:**
   - Check your progress and adjust your goals as needed.

Examples of Setting Clear Goals

1. **In Career:**
   - **Vague Goal:** "Be successful at work."
   - **Clear Goal:** "Get a promotion within the next year by completing two key projects and improving my leadership skills."
2. **In Fitness:**
   - **Vague Goal:** "Get healthier."
   - **Clear Goal:** "Run a 5K in under 30 minutes by training four times a week for eight weeks."
3. **In Finances:**
   - **Vague Goal:** "Save more money."
   - **Clear Goal:** "Save $5,000 in six months by cutting unnecessary expenses and taking on freelance work."

Practical Exercise: Set Your Clear Goals

1. **Choose an Area to Focus On:**
   - Example: "Career," "Health," or "Relationships."
2. **Write a SMART Goal:**
   - Example: "Apply to three jobs each week to secure a new role within six months."
3. **List Actionable Steps:**
   - Break the goal into smaller tasks, such as "Update resume," "Research job openings," and "Practice interviews."
4. **Track Progress:**
   - Use a planner, app, or journal to monitor your progress and milestones.

Why This Technique Works

Clear goals cut through mental clutter by giving you a specific direction to follow. They help you focus, stay motivated, and measure progress, leading to greater clarity and success.

Closing Thought

Goals are roadmaps. Set clear, actionable goals, and watch your mental focus and productivity soar.

Chapter 59: Use a Daily Reflection Routine

What is a Daily Reflection Routine?

A daily reflection routine is the practice of setting aside time to review your day — what went well, what didn't, and what you learned. This intentional pause helps you process experiences, identify areas for improvement, and set clear intentions for the next day.

For example:

- At the end of each day, you might ask yourself: "What am I proud of today? What could I do better tomorrow?" Writing down your reflections allows you to track progress and maintain focus on your goals.

Why Daily Reflection is Essential

1. **Promotes Self-Awareness:**
   - Reflecting on your thoughts, actions, and emotions helps you better understand yourself.
2. **Improves Decision-Making:**
   - By identifying patterns in your behavior, you can make more thoughtful choices in the future.
3. **Boosts Productivity:**
   - Reviewing your progress keeps you aligned with your goals and highlights areas for improvement.
4. **Reduces Stress:**
   - Reflection provides a sense of closure, helping you let go of the day's challenges.

How to Start a Daily Reflection Routine

1. **Choose a Time and Space:**
   - Set aside 10-15 minutes at the same time each day, such as before bed, in a quiet, comfortable space.
2. **Use a Journal or Digital Tool:**
   - Write your reflections in a notebook or use an app to keep your thoughts organized and accessible.
3. **Ask Key Questions:**
   - Use prompts to guide your reflection:
   - What went well today?
   - What didn't go as planned?
   - What did I learn?
   - What are my priorities for tomorrow?
4. **Celebrate Successes:**
   - Acknowledge what you accomplished, no matter how small. This builds motivation and positivity.
5. **Set Intentions for Tomorrow:**
   - Reflect on what you can improve and outline a few actionable steps for the next day.

Examples of Daily Reflection in Action

1. **In Work:**
   - **Scenario:** A project manager reflects on a hectic day.
   - Routine:
   - What went well? "We completed the presentation on time."
   - What can improve? "I need to communicate more clearly during team meetings."
   - Tomorrow's intention: "Prepare a checklist for my next meeting to stay organized."
2. **In Personal Life:**
   - **Scenario:** A parent reflects on their interactions with their children.
   - Routine:
   - What went well? "I spent quality time reading with my kids."
   - What didn't go as planned? "I lost my patience during dinner."
   - Tomorrow's intention: "Stay calm and practice active listening."

3. **In Fitness:**
   - ○ **Scenario:** Someone is working on a new fitness routine.
   - ○ Routine:
   - ○ What went well? "I completed my workout and stayed hydrated."
   - ○ What can improve? "I need to eat healthier snacks."
   - ○ Tomorrow's intention: "Prep a healthy snack pack."

Practical Exercise: Begin Your Daily Reflection Routine

1. **Choose a Time:**
   - ○ Commit to reflecting at a consistent time each day, like before bed.
2. **Use Reflection Prompts:**
   - ○ Write down your answers to three questions:
   - ○ What am I grateful for today?
   - ○ What challenged me today?
   - ○ What is my top focus for tomorrow?
3. **Track Your Progress:**
   - ○ Review your reflections weekly to notice patterns and celebrate improvements.

Why This Technique Works

Daily reflection helps you pause and reset. It keeps you connected to your goals, builds self-awareness, and ensures each day becomes a stepping stone toward personal growth.

Closing Thought

Reflection turns experiences into lessons. Take time daily to look back, learn, and step forward with clarity and purpose.

Chapter 60: Practice Mindfulness to Stay Present

What is Mindfulness?

Mindfulness is the practice of paying full attention to the present moment without judgment. It means being aware of your thoughts, feelings, and surroundings as they are, rather than dwelling on the past or worrying about the future.

For example:

- While eating a meal, mindfulness involves savoring each bite, noticing the flavors and textures, and focusing on the act of eating instead of scrolling through your phone.

Why Mindfulness is Powerful

1. **Reduces Stress:**
   o   Mindfulness calms the mind by shifting focus away from worries and distractions.
2. **Enhances Focus:**
   o   By staying present, you improve your ability to concentrate on tasks.
3. **Improves Emotional Regulation:**
   o   Awareness of your emotions helps you respond thoughtfully rather than react impulsively.
4. **Boosts Well-Being:**
   o   Mindfulness fosters a sense of gratitude, contentment, and peace.

How to Practice Mindfulness

1. **Start with Breathing:**
   o   Take a few minutes to focus on your breath. Inhale deeply, hold briefly, and exhale slowly, paying attention to the sensations.
2. **Use Mindful Activities:**
   o   Engage fully in everyday tasks, like washing dishes or walking, by focusing on the sensory details.
3. **Practice a Body Scan:**
   o   Close your eyes and mentally scan your body from head to toe, noticing any tension or sensations.
4. **Bring Awareness to Thoughts:**
   o   Observe your thoughts without judgment. Let them come and go, like clouds passing in the sky.
5. **Set a Daily Reminder:**
   o   Schedule mindfulness breaks throughout your day to check in with yourself.

Examples of Mindfulness in Action

1. **In Work:**
   o   **Scenario:** You feel overwhelmed by a long to-do list.
   o   **Action:** Take a 5-minute breathing break to calm your mind before tackling one task at a time.
2. **In Relationships:**
   o   **Scenario:** You're distracted while spending time with loved ones.
   o   **Action:** Put away your phone and give your full attention to the conversation.
3. **In Stressful Moments:**
   o   **Scenario:** You feel anxious before a presentation.
   o   **Action:** Focus on your breath, grounding yourself in the present moment to reduce nervousness.

Practical Exercise: Try a Mindfulness Routine

1. **Morning Mindfulness:**
   o   Spend 5 minutes after waking up focusing on your breath or practicing gratitude.
2. **Mindful Breaks:**
   o   Pause during the day to observe your surroundings and check in with how you feel.
3. **Evening Reflection:**
   o   Before bed, spend 5 minutes journaling about what you noticed or appreciated that day.

Why This Technique Works

Mindfulness anchors you in the present, reducing the mental clutter caused by past regrets or future worries. It's a simple practice with profound benefits for your mind, body, and emotions.

Closing Thought

The present moment is where life happens. Practice mindfulness to experience it fully and live with greater clarity and peace.

Section VII: Advanced Critical Thinking Techniques

Critical thinking is the cornerstone of sound decision-making and problem-solving. It involves questioning assumptions, analysing probabilities, and thinking deeply about how ideas interact and evolve. This section dives into techniques that help you sharpen your analytical skills, anticipate consequences, and approach challenges with a structured, thoughtful mindset.

Chapter 61: Bayesian Thinking: Update Beliefs with New Evidence

What is Bayesian Thinking?

Bayesian thinking is a method of updating your beliefs or assumptions based on new evidence. Instead of sticking rigidly to your initial ideas, you adjust your confidence in those beliefs as you encounter new information.

For example:

- Imagine you believe there's a 70% chance of rain today based on the forecast. If you later see clear skies and bright sunshine, you might revise that belief to a 20% chance of rain.

This approach is named after Bayes' theorem, a mathematical formula used to calculate probabilities, but its practical application doesn't require complex math — just a willingness to adapt your thinking.

Why Bayesian Thinking is Powerful

1. **Reduces Cognitive Bias:**
   - It prevents you from clinging to outdated assumptions by encouraging evidence-based updates.
2. **Improves Decision-Making:**
   - By regularly integrating new information, you stay aligned with reality.
3. **Encourages Flexibility:**
   - It helps you remain open to change and adjust your strategies when circumstances shift.

How to Apply Bayesian Thinking

1. **Start with a Baseline Belief (Your Prior):**
   - Estimate the likelihood of something based on existing knowledge.
   - Example: "There's a 50% chance this project will succeed based on similar past efforts."
2. **Gather New Evidence:**
   - Look for relevant data, observations, or feedback that could affect your belief.
   - Example: Early feedback from team members indicates potential roadblocks.
3. **Update Your Belief:**
   - Adjust the probability of your belief based on the new evidence.
   - Example: "Given the roadblocks, I now think there's a 30% chance of success unless we address the issues."
4. **Repeat as More Evidence Arrives:**
   - Continuously refine your belief as new information becomes available.

Examples of Bayesian Thinking in Action

1. **In Personal Decisions:**
   - **Scenario:** You're deciding whether to buy a house.
   - **Belief:** "This neighborhood is ideal for me."
   - **New Evidence:** A friend mentions the area has frequent traffic issues.
   - **Updated Belief:** You revise your confidence in the neighborhood and research further before committing.

2. In Business:
   - ○ **Scenario:** A company believes a new product will sell well.
   - ○ **New Evidence:** Early customer feedback highlights confusion about the product's features.
   - ○ **Updated Belief:** The company lowers its sales expectations and adjusts its marketing strategy.
3. In Health:
   - ○ **Scenario:** You think a new diet will work for you.
   - ○ **New Evidence:** After two weeks, you notice no weight loss and low energy levels.
   - ○ **Updated Belief:** You re-evaluate the diet and explore alternatives.

1. **Pick a Current Belief:**
   - ○ Example: "I think I'll enjoy this new hobby."
2. **List Your Initial Confidence Level:**
   - ○ Example: "I'm 70% confident I'll enjoy it."
3. **Gather Evidence:**
   - ○ Try the hobby or talk to others who've done it.
4. **Revise Your Confidence:**
   - ○ Adjust your belief based on what you learn.
5. **Repeat:**
   - ○ Continue updating as you gather more data.

Why This Technique Works

Bayesian thinking keeps your beliefs grounded in reality by encouraging regular updates based on evidence. It helps you avoid stubbornness, adapt to change, and make smarter decisions.

Closing Thought

The world isn't static, and neither should your beliefs be. Stay open to new information, update your thinking, and align yourself with the truth.

Chapter 62: Game Theory Basics: Think Strategically About Others

What is Game Theory?

Game theory is the study of how people make decisions when their choices depend on the actions of others. It's like a mental chess game where you consider not only your own strategy but also how others might respond to it.

For example:

- If you're negotiating a salary, game theory involves predicting how your employer will react to your counteroffer and adjusting your approach accordingly.

Game theory helps you anticipate outcomes, make strategic moves, and find win-win solutions when working with or competing against others.

Why Game Theory is Valuable

1. **Encourages Strategic Thinking:**
   - It teaches you to plan your actions while considering others' perspectives.
2. **Improves Negotiation Skills:**
   - Anticipating the other party's moves helps you craft better strategies.
3. **Fosters Cooperation:**
   - Game theory can reveal opportunities for mutual benefit, even in competitive situations.

How to Apply Game Theory

1. **Define the Players:**
   - Identify everyone involved in the situation and their potential goals.
   - Example: In a business negotiation, the players are you and the other party.
2. **Understand the Incentives:**
   - Consider what each player wants to gain or avoid.
   - Example: You want a higher salary; the employer wants to minimize costs.
3. **Predict Possible Moves:**
   - Think through the actions each player might take and how those actions affect everyone else.
4. **Consider Payoffs:**
   - Evaluate the outcomes of different strategies for all players.
   - Example: Will pushing too hard for a raise risk the relationship or job offer?
5. **Choose Your Strategy:**
   - Select the approach that balances your goals with the likely responses of others.

Examples of Game Theory in Action

1. **In Business:**
   - **Scenario:** Two competing stores are deciding whether to lower prices.
   - **Strategy:** Each store considers how the other might react and the potential impact on profits.
2. **In Relationships:**
   - **Scenario:** A couple is deciding how to spend their weekend.
   - **Strategy:** Each person shares their preferences, looking for activities that make both happy.
3. **In Everyday Decisions:**
   - **Scenario:** You're deciding which line to join at a grocery store.
   - **Strategy:** You predict how quickly the line will move based on the number of people and the cashier's speed.

Practical Exercise: Use Game Theory in a Decision

1. **Pick a Situation Involving Others:**
   - Example: "Should I ask for a promotion at work?"
2. **Identify the Players and Goals:**
   - You: Secure a raise.
   - Employer: Retain talent while managing costs.
3. **Predict Their Moves:**
   - How might your manager react to your request?
4. **Plan Your Strategy:**
   - Prepare evidence of your value to the company to strengthen your case.

Why This Technique Works

Game theory gives you a framework for analyzing decisions involving others. It helps you think ahead, and choose strategies that increase your chances of success.

Closing Thought

Life is full of strategic interactions. Think like a game theorist to make smarter moves, build stronger relationships, and achieve your goals.

Chapter 63: Think in Probabilities, Not Certainties

What Does It Mean to Think in Probabilities?

Thinking in probabilities means acknowledging uncertainty and evaluating the likelihood of different outcomes instead of treating events as black-and-white certainties. Life is rarely 100% predictable, and viewing decisions in terms of probabilities allows you to prepare for a range of scenarios rather than relying on absolute predictions.

For example:

- Instead of thinking, "This investment will definitely succeed," you might estimate, "There's a 70% chance of success based on market trends, but a 30% chance it won't perform as expected."

This mindset shifts you from rigid thinking to flexible, data-driven decision-making.

Why Thinking in Probabilities is Valuable

1. **Reduces Overconfidence:**
   o Acknowledging uncertainty helps you avoid assuming you're always right.
2. **Encourages Better Planning:**
   o By preparing for multiple outcomes, you minimize risks and increase adaptability.
3. **Improves Decision-Making:**
   o Assessing probabilities ensures your decisions are based on evidence and logic, not wishful thinking.

How to Think in Probabilities

1. **Estimate Likelihoods:**
   o Assign probabilities to different outcomes based on available information.
   o Example: "There's a 60% chance this marketing campaign will increase sales, based on past data."
2. **Consider Multiple Scenarios:**
   o Identify the best-case, worst-case, and most likely outcomes.
   o Example: Launching a new product could result in high profits, moderate success, or a loss.
3. **Weigh Risks vs. Rewards:**
   o Calculate whether the potential benefits outweigh the risks, given the probabilities.
4. **Update Your Estimates:**
   o As new evidence emerges, revise your probabilities.
   o Example: If early results show strong customer interest, you might increase your confidence in success.
5. **Avoid Absolutes:**
   o Replace phrases like "This will happen" with "This is likely" or "This has a 30% chance."

Examples of Thinking in Probabilities

1. **In Career Decisions:**
   o **Scenario:** You're considering switching jobs.
   o Probabilities:
   o 50% chance the new role is a better fit.
   o 30% chance it's similar to your current role.
   o 20% chance it's less satisfying.
   o **Action:** You weigh the risks and prepare for the less favorable outcomes while pursuing the opportunity.
2. **In Health:**
   o **Scenario:** You're deciding whether to follow a new diet plan.
   o Probabilities:
   o 70% chance it helps you lose weight.
   o 20% chance it's ineffective.
   o 10% chance it causes side effects.
   o **Action:** You research further to reduce the uncertainty and plan alternatives if it doesn't work.

3. In Investing:
   o **Scenario:** You're evaluating a stock.
   o Probabilities:
   o 40% chance it grows significantly.
   o 50% chance of steady, moderate growth.
   o 10% chance of loss.
   o **Action:** You diversify your investments to mitigate the 10% risk.

Practical Exercise: Start Thinking in Probabilities

1. **Pick a Decision:**
   o Example: "Should I take a weekend trip?"
2. **Identify Possible Outcomes:**
   o Outcome 1: You have a great time and return refreshed.
   o Outcome 2: You overspend and feel stressed about finances.
3. **Assign Probabilities:**
   o Great time: 70%.
   o Financial stress: 30%.
4. **Plan Accordingly:**
   o If the trip is worth the risk, set a budget to reduce the 30% downside.

Why This Technique Works

Thinking in probabilities replaces emotional or biased decision-making with logical, evidence-based approaches. It prepares you for uncertainty and helps you make informed, confident choices.

Closing Thought

Nothing in life is guaranteed. By thinking in probabilities, you'll approach decisions with clarity, flexibility, and a stronger sense of control.

Chapter 64: Second-Order Thinking: Anticipate the Ripple Effects

What is Second-Order Thinking?

Second-order thinking is the practice of looking beyond immediate consequences to anticipate the ripple effects of your actions. While first-order thinking focuses on the direct result of a decision, second-order thinking considers how that result will trigger additional outcomes, both positive and negative.

For example:

- First-order thinking: "Eating fast food is convenient."
- Second-order thinking: "Eating fast food regularly might save time today, but it could harm my health and increase medical expenses later."

This technique is crucial for making thoughtful, long-term decisions.

Why Second-Order Thinking is Essential

1. **Reveals Hidden Consequences:**
   - It helps you anticipate outcomes that might not be immediately obvious.
2. **Prepares You for Complex Systems:**
   - In interconnected situations, one action often triggers multiple reactions.
3. **Improves Long-Term Planning:**
   - Considering future effects ensures your decisions align with your bigger goals.

How to Practice Second-Order Thinking

1. **Identify the Immediate Result:**
   - Start with the most obvious consequence of your decision.
   - Example: "Switching to cheaper materials will reduce costs."
2. **Ask, 'What Happens Next?'**
   - Consider the next layer of consequences.
   - Example: "Cheaper materials might lower product quality, leading to customer dissatisfaction."
3. **Go Beyond the Second Order:**
   - Continue exploring the ripple effects.
   - Example: "If customers leave, sales might drop, and profits could ultimately decline."
4. **Weigh Short-Term vs. Long-Term Effects:**
   - Balance immediate benefits with potential future costs.
5. **Consider Trade-Offs:**
   - Think about what you might lose in pursuit of short-term gains.

Examples of Second-Order Thinking in Action

1. **In Personal Finance:**
   - **Scenario:** You're tempted to use credit for a big purchase.
   - **First Order:** You get the item immediately.
   - **Second Order:** You accumulate debt and pay interest over time.
   - **Action:** You decide to save and buy the item later, avoiding the ripple effect of debt.
2. **In Leadership:**
   - **Scenario:** A manager considers cutting staff to save money.
   - **First Order:** Costs decrease.
   - **Second Order:** Remaining staff becomes overworked, leading to lower morale and productivity.
   - **Action:** The manager explores alternative cost-saving measures instead.
3. **In Health:**
   - **Scenario:** You skip sleep to finish a project.
   - **First Order:** You meet the deadline.
   - **Second Order:** Fatigue lowers your performance the next day, leading to more mistakes.
   - **Action:** You plan better to avoid sacrificing sleep.

Practical Exercise: Practice Second-Order Thinking

1. **Pick a Decision:**
   - Example: "Should I take on a new project at work?"
2. **Identify the First-Order Effect:**
   - "I'll earn recognition and develop new skills."
3. **Consider the Ripple Effects:**
   - "I might become overcommitted, leading to stress and lower-quality work."
4. **Plan Accordingly:**
   - Accept the project but set boundaries to manage your workload effectively.

Why This Technique Works

Second-order thinking helps you avoid unintended consequences by thinking beyond the obvious. It ensures your decisions create positive, sustainable outcomes.

Closing Thought

Every choice creates ripples. Think beyond the immediate result to make decisions that serve you well in the long run.

Chapter 65: Counterfactual Thinking: Imagine the 'What-Ifs'

What is Counterfactual Thinking?

Counterfactual thinking is the process of imagining alternate outcomes to events that have already occurred. It involves asking "what if" questions to explore how different choices or circumstances might have led to different results.

For example:

- "What if I had studied a different major in college?"
- "What if I had taken that job offer in another city?"

While counterfactual thinking doesn't change the past, it sharpens your understanding of cause and effect and helps you make better decisions in the future.

Why Counterfactual Thinking is Valuable

1. **Identifies Key Turning Points:**
   - It helps you understand which decisions or factors had the biggest impact on outcomes.
2. **Enhances Learning:**
   - By reflecting on alternate scenarios, you gain insights into what worked, what didn't, and why.
3. **Encourages Better Planning:**
   - Counterfactuals reveal hidden risks or opportunities, enabling you to prepare more effectively for future situations.
4. **Builds Gratitude:**
   - Reflecting on how things could have gone worse can increase appreciation for what went well.

How to Practice Counterfactual Thinking

1. **Focus on a Specific Event:**
   - Choose a situation where the outcome was significant or unexpected.
   - Example: A missed opportunity, a major decision, or a surprising success.
2. **Ask Two Types of Questions:**
   - **Upward Counterfactuals:** Imagine how the outcome could have been better.
   - Example: "What if I had started my project earlier?"
   - **Downward Counterfactuals:** Imagine how the outcome could have been worse.
   - Example: "What if I hadn't caught that mistake in time?"
3. **Identify the Key Factors:**
   - Reflect on the decisions, actions, or external factors that shaped the outcome.
4. **Extract Lessons:**
   - Use the insights from your counterfactuals to refine your approach in the future.

Examples of Counterfactual Thinking in Action

1. **In Personal Growth:**
   - **Scenario:** You didn't get a job you applied for.
   - **Upward Counterfactual:** "What if I had prepared better for the interview?"
   - **Lesson:** Invest more time in interview practice for future applications.
   - **Downward Counterfactual:** "What if I hadn't applied at all and missed the experience?"
   - **Lesson:** Appreciate that you gained valuable practice for next time.
2. **In Relationships:**
   - **Scenario:** You had a falling out with a friend.
   - **Upward Counterfactual:** "What if I had communicated more openly about my feelings?"
   - **Lesson:** Prioritize honest communication in future interactions.
   - **Downward Counterfactual:** "What if I hadn't apologized afterward and lost the friendship entirely?"
   - **Lesson:** Recognize the value of reconciliation efforts.

3. **In Work:**
   - ○ **Scenario:** A project succeeded despite tight deadlines.
   - ○ **Upward Counterfactual:** "What if we had planned the timeline more carefully?"
   - ○ **Lesson:** Allow more lead time for future projects.
   - ○ **Downward Counterfactual:** "What if the team hadn't collaborated so effectively?"
   - ○ **Lesson:** Reinforce the importance of teamwork and communication.

Practical Exercise: Try Counterfactual Thinking

1. **Choose an Event to Reflect On:**
   - ○ Example: "I didn't achieve my fitness goal this month."
2. **Ask Upward and Downward Questions:**
   - ○ Upward: "What if I had stuck to my meal plan more consistently?"
   - ○ Downward: "What if I hadn't exercised at all?"
3. **Identify Lessons:**
   - ○ Extract actionable insights, such as revising your goals or finding more sustainable habits.
4. **Apply the Lessons:**
   - ○ Use what you've learned to improve your future decisions and actions.

Why This Technique Works

Counterfactual thinking provides clarity by exploring alternative paths, making it easier to identify what led to success or failure. It's a powerful tool for reflection, learning, and future planning.

Closing Thought

The past is unchangeable, but it's full of lessons. Ask "what if" to uncover insights, refine your approach, and create better outcomes moving forward.

Chapter 66: The Feynman Technique: Explain to Learn

What is the Feynman Technique?

Named after physicist Richard Feynman, this technique involves breaking down complex ideas and explaining them in simple terms to ensure true understanding. If you can explain something clearly, you've mastered it. If not, it highlights gaps in your knowledge that need further attention.

For example:

- To understand a complicated financial concept like compound interest, you might try explaining it to a friend as if they were new to the topic. Simplifying it for someone else clarifies it for yourself.

Why the Feynman Technique is Powerful

1. **Reveals Knowledge Gaps:**
   o   It quickly shows you which parts of a concept you don't fully grasp.
2. **Deepens Understanding:**
   o   Explaining something forces you to process it at a deeper level.
3. **Builds Communication Skills:**
   o   Translating complex ideas into simple language improves your ability to share knowledge.

How to Use the Feynman Technique

1. **Choose a Topic You Want to Learn:**
   o   Pick something you want to understand better.
   o   Example: "How does the immune system work?"
2. **Explain It to a Beginner:**
   o   Write down or verbalize the explanation as if teaching someone with no prior knowledge.
3. **Identify Gaps in Your Explanation:**
   o   Notice where you struggle to explain clearly or where you use jargon instead of simple terms.
4. **Go Back to the Source:**
   o   Study those weak areas until you can explain them effectively.
5. **Simplify Further:**
   o   Refine your explanation until it's concise, clear, and easy to understand.

Examples of the Feynman Technique in Action

1. **In Studying:**
   o   **Scenario:** You're preparing for a biology exam.
   o   **Action:** Explain photosynthesis to a friend as if they were new to the topic.
   o   **Outcome:** You identify gaps in your understanding and revisit the textbook for clarity.
2. **In Work:**
   o   **Scenario:** You need to present a technical concept to a non-expert team.
   o   **Action:** Simplify the concept into a step-by-step process, ensuring you fully grasp each part.
   o   **Outcome:** Your audience gains a clear understanding, and you deepen your own knowledge.
3. **In Personal Growth:**
   o   **Scenario:** You're trying to understand mindfulness techniques.
   o   **Action:** Explain mindfulness to a friend as if they've never heard of it.
   o   **Outcome:** You refine your practice by identifying key principles and misconceptions.

Practical Exercise: Use the Feynman Technique

1. **Pick a Concept to Learn:**
   o   Example: "How does GPS work?"
2. **Write an Explanation:**
   o   Use simple, clear language to describe the concept as if to a child.
3. **Review for Gaps:**
   o   Identify areas where your explanation feels incomplete or unclear.
4. **Refine and Simplify:**
   o   Research and revise until the explanation feels intuitive and concise.

Why This Technique Works

The Feynman Technique pushes you to engage deeply with a topic, ensuring you truly understand it rather than memorizing surface details. It's a method that combines learning with teaching.

Closing Thought

To master a topic, teach it. Simplify, clarify, and refine your understanding until it becomes second nature.

Chapter 67: Ask, 'What Am I Missing?'

Why Ask, 'What Am I Missing?'

Humans tend to focus on what's immediately visible or obvious, often overlooking hidden factors that influence outcomes. Asking, "What am I missing?" prompts them to examine assumptions, identify gaps in information, and consider alternative viewpoints. This question sharpens their thinking, reduces errors, and encourages a broader understanding of complex situations.

For example:

- Before launching a new business, asking "What am I missing?" might lead you to research competitors, customer needs, or market trends you hadn't initially considered.

Why This Question is Powerful

1. **Exposes Blind Spots:**
   o It reveals overlooked risks, opportunities, or details that could influence outcomes.

2. **Encourages Humility:**
   o Acknowledging that you might not have the full picture keeps your ego in check and opens your mind to learning.

3. **Leads to Better Decisions:**
   o By uncovering hidden factors, you can make more informed and strategic choices.

4. **Strengthens Collaboration:**
   o Asking for input from others often uncovers what you might have missed on your own.

How to Use 'What Am I Missing?' Effectively

1. **Question Your Assumptions:**
   o Challenge what you believe to be true about the situation.
   o Example: "Am I assuming this project will succeed just because it worked in the past?"

2. **Seek Alternative Perspectives:**
   o Ask others—especially those with different viewpoints—what they see that you don't.

3. **Consider What's Not Visible:**
   o Think about hidden factors, such as underlying motivations, indirect consequences, or missing data.

4. **Look for Contradictions:**
   o Ask, "Does anything about this situation not add up?"

5. **Reassess Your Plan:**
   o Use what you uncover to adjust your approach, fill gaps, or mitigate risks.

Examples of Asking 'What Am I Missing?' in Action

1. **In Business:**
   o **Scenario:** A company plans to expand into a new market.
   o **Question:** "What are we missing about local regulations, customer preferences, or competitors?"
   o **Outcome:** The company discovers cultural differences that require adjustments to its marketing strategy.

2. **In Personal Life:**
   o **Scenario:** You're deciding whether to move to a new city for a job.
   o **Question:** "What am I missing about the cost of living, social opportunities, or long-term career growth?"
   o **Outcome:** You research further and realize the high cost of living would outweigh the salary increase.

3. **In Problem-Solving:**
   o **Scenario:** A team is troubleshooting a recurring issue in their workflow.
   o **Question:** "What are we missing about the root cause of this problem?"
   o **Outcome:** They discover a lack of training is causing repeated mistakes, not faulty equipment as initially assumed.

1. **Choose a Current Challenge:**
    o   Example: "Should I invest in a new skill or course?"
2. **List What You Know:**
    o   Write down everything you're certain about regarding the decision.
3. **Ask, 'What Am I Missing?':**
    o   Look for gaps, such as hidden costs, time commitments, or better alternatives.
4. **Consult Others:**
    o   Seek input from a mentor, colleague, or friend to gain additional perspectives.
5. **Adjust Your Plan:**
    o   Use the insights to refine your decision or strategy.

Why This Technique Works

Asking "What am I missing?" challenges your blind spots, broadens your thinking, and reduces overconfidence. It ensures you approach decisions with greater awareness and preparedness.

Closing Thought

No one has all the answers. Keep asking, keep digging, and uncover the hidden factors that could make or break your decisions.

Chapter 68: Test Your Assumptions Before Acting

Why Test Your Assumptions?

Assumptions are beliefs we accept as true without proof, and they often shape our decisions. While some assumptions are harmless, others can lead to costly mistakes if they're incorrect. Testing your assumptions before acting ensures your decisions are based on reality, not guesswork.

For example:

*   If you assume your target audience prefers a certain style of content, you might invest heavily in creating it — only to find it doesn't resonate. Testing that assumption beforehand could save time and resources.

Benefits of Testing Assumptions

1. **Reduces Risk:**
    o   Validating assumptions prevents you from acting on faulty beliefs.
2. **Improves Outcomes:**
    o   Decisions based on tested assumptions are more likely to succeed.

3. **Encourages Critical Thinking:**
    - o Testing forces you to analyze whether your beliefs hold up under scrutiny.
4. **Saves Time and Resources:**
    - o It helps you avoid pursuing strategies that aren't grounded in reality.

1. **Identify Your Assumptions:**
    - o Write down the beliefs or expectations underlying your decisions.
    - o Example: "Customers prefer digital products over physical ones."
2. **Ask, 'How Do I Know This is True?'**
    - o Examine whether you have evidence to support the assumption.
3. **Run Small Tests:**
    - o Experiment on a small scale to gather data.
    - o Example: Launch a survey or pilot a digital product with a test audience.
4. **Seek Feedback:**
    - o Ask others, especially those affected by the decision, for their input.
5. **Adjust Based on Results:**
    - o Use what you learn to refine your strategy or replace faulty assumptions.

Examples of Testing Assumptions

1. **In Business:**
    - o **Scenario:** A team assumes a new feature will attract more users.
    - o **Test:** They launch the feature to a small group and track engagement metrics.
    - o **Outcome:** The data shows low interest, prompting them to revise the feature before a full rollout.
2. **In Personal Goals:**
    - o **Scenario:** You assume you'll enjoy a new hobby.
    - o **Test:** You try it out through a one-day workshop before committing to expensive gear.
    - o **Outcome:** You discover it's not a good fit and explore other options.
3. **In Relationships:**
    - o **Scenario:** You assume your partner would prefer a certain type of gift.
    - o **Test:** You casually ask about their preferences before making the purchase.
    - o **Outcome:** You find they'd prefer an experience over a physical gift, avoiding a disappointing choice.

Practical Exercise: Test Your Assumptions

1. **Choose a Decision or Goal:**
    - o Example: "I think this career move will be rewarding."
2. **Identify the Assumptions:**
    - o Example: "The new role will have better growth opportunities."
3. **Design a Test:**
    - o Research the company's promotion rates, talk to current employees, or request a job shadow.
4. **Evaluate the Results:**
    - o Use the data to confirm or challenge your assumption.

Why This Technique Works

Testing assumptions replaces guesswork with evidence. It helps you avoid acting on faulty beliefs and ensures your decisions are based on solid foundations.

Closing Thought

Don't let untested assumptions steer your decisions. Test them, validate them, and move forward with confidence.

Chapter 69: Use Small Experiments to Test Ideas

Why Test Ideas with Small Experiments?

Ideas often seem great in theory but fail when put into practice. Small experiments allow you to test your ideas on a manageable scale, gathering valuable insights without committing too many resources upfront. This approach reduces risk, encourages learning, and increases the chances of success by refining your idea based on real-world results.

For example:

- Before launching a full-scale marketing campaign, you could test your ad with a small target audience to gauge its effectiveness and refine it based on feedback.

Benefits of Small Experiments

1. **Minimizes Risk:**
   - Testing on a small scale prevents costly mistakes if the idea doesn't work as planned.
2. **Encourages Iteration:**
   - Experiments reveal strengths and weaknesses, allowing you to improve your idea incrementally.
3. **Builds Confidence:**
   - Positive results from small tests validate your idea, giving you the assurance to move forward.
4. **Saves Resources:**
   - You invest only what's necessary to test the concept, preserving time, money, and effort.

How to Use Small Experiments to Test Ideas

1. **Define Your Hypothesis:**
   - Clearly state what you want to test and what outcome you expect.
   - Example: "If I promote my product on social media, I'll gain 50 new followers in a week."
2. **Design a Simple Experiment:**
   - Create a low-cost, low-risk way to test your idea.
   - Example: Post one ad on your social media page and track engagement.

3. **Run the Test:**
   o Implement your experiment and gather data.
4. **Analyze the Results:**
   o Compare the outcome to your expectations. Did your idea perform as hoped?
5. **Refine and Retest:**
   o Use the insights to improve your idea, then test again to see if the changes lead to better results.

Examples of Small Experiments in Action

1. **In Business:**
   o **Scenario:** A restaurant wants to introduce a new dish to the menu.
   o **Experiment:** They offer it as a weekly special to gauge customer interest.
   o **Outcome:** If it's popular, they add it to the permanent menu; if not, they tweak the recipe or scrap it.
2. **In Personal Life:**
   o **Scenario:** You're considering a new workout routine.
   o **Experiment:** Try the routine for one week to see if it fits your schedule and goals.
   o **Outcome:** You discover what works and what doesn't, allowing you to adjust accordingly.
3. **In Learning:**
   o **Scenario:** You're unsure if an online course will help your career.
   o **Experiment:** Take a free trial or complete one module before committing to the full program.
   o **Outcome:** The test reveals whether the course aligns with your learning style and needs.

Practical Exercise: Test Your Own Idea

1. **Choose an Idea You Want to Test:**
   o Example: "Start a side hustle selling handmade crafts."
2. **Define Your Hypothesis:**
   o Example: "If I sell my crafts at a local market, I'll make at least $200 in a weekend."
3. **Design a Small Test:**
   o Set up a booth at one market and track your sales and customer feedback.
4. **Evaluate the Results:**
   o Did you hit your goal? What feedback did you receive?
5. **Refine and Scale:**
   o Use what you learned to improve your pricing, display, or product selection before scaling up.

Why This Technique Works

Small experiments provide real-world feedback, turning abstract ideas into actionable plans. By testing on a small scale, you gain insights that help you avoid costly missteps and refine your approach for success.

Closing Thought

Big ideas start with small tests. Experiment, learn, and refine until your idea is ready to shine on a larger stage.

Chapter 70: Always Ask for Feedback

Why Feedback is Essential

Feedback is one of the most powerful tools for growth. It provides fresh perspectives, uncovers blind spots, and helps you refine your ideas, skills, or decisions. Whether you're working on a project, pursuing a personal goal, or navigating relationships, asking for feedback ensures you stay aligned with reality and continuously improve.

For example:

- If you're creating a presentation, feedback from colleagues can highlight unclear sections, allowing you to make adjustments before the final delivery.

Benefits of Asking for Feedback

1. **Reveals Blind Spots:**
    o   Others can identify issues or opportunities you might have overlooked.
2. **Encourages Growth:**
    o   Constructive criticism helps you improve your skills and strategies.
3. **Builds Stronger Relationships:**
    o   Inviting feedback shows openness and humility, fostering trust and collaboration.
4. **Improves Decision-Making:**
    o   Feedback provides diverse viewpoints, leading to more informed choices.

How to Ask for Feedback Effectively

1. **Be Specific:**
    o   Ask targeted questions to get actionable insights.
    o   Example: "What do you think about the structure of my proposal?"
2. **Choose the Right People:**
    o   Seek feedback from individuals with relevant expertise or perspectives.
    o   Example: For career advice, ask a mentor or trusted colleague.
3. **Listen Without Defensiveness:**
    o   Approach feedback with an open mind, focusing on improvement rather than taking criticism personally.
4. **Clarify if Needed:**
    o   Ask follow-up questions to ensure you fully understand the feedback.
    o   Example: "Can you give an example of where my explanation felt unclear?"
5. **Act on the Feedback:**
    o   Use the insights to make specific changes or adjustments.

Examples of Asking for Feedback in Action

1. **In Work:**
    o   **Scenario:** You're drafting an important report.
    o   **Feedback Request:** "Does this address the client's key concerns clearly?"
    o   **Outcome:** A colleague points out areas needing clarification, helping you polish the report.
2. **In Personal Growth:**
    o   **Scenario:** You're working on improving your communication skills.
    o   **Feedback Request:** "Do you feel I listen actively during conversations?"
    o   **Outcome:** Friends share that you sometimes interrupt, giving you a specific behavior to work on.
3. **In Creative Projects:**
    o   **Scenario:** You're designing a website.
    o   **Feedback Request:** "Is the navigation intuitive, or does anything feel confusing?"
    o   **Outcome:** Test users suggest reorganizing the menu for easier access to key features.

1. **Pick an Area You Want to Improve:**
   o Example: "My presentation skills."
2. **Identify Who to Ask:**
   o Choose people who can provide honest, relevant feedback, like colleagues or friends.
3. **Ask Specific Questions:**
   o Example: "What's one thing I did well in this presentation, and what's one thing I could improve?"
4. **Reflect and Take Action:**
   o Use the feedback to make targeted changes, then seek additional feedback to measure progress.

Why This Technique Works

Feedback accelerates improvement by highlighting strengths to build on and weaknesses to address. It helps you make more informed decisions and creates opportunities for growth.

Closing Thought

Growth thrives on honest feedback. Embrace it as a gift, act on it with intention, and watch yourself improve in ways you never imagined.

Section VIII: Techniques for Identifying Hidden Influences

We're constantly influenced in ways we may not even notice — whether it's the language someone uses, the way information is framed, or subtle social pressures.

This section equips you with tools to uncover those invisible forces. By learning to identify manipulative tactics, trace motivations, and evaluate credibility, you'll sharpen your ability to think critically and make decisions based on reality.

Chapter 71: Spot Manipulative Language

What is Manipulative Language?

Manipulative language is designed to influence your thoughts or actions without you realizing it. It often appeals to emotions, oversimplifies complex issues, or frames information in a way that pushes you toward a specific conclusion.

For example:

- Instead of saying, "We need to cut costs," someone might say, "If we don't cut costs, the company will fail, and everyone will lose their jobs." The latter statement uses fear to manipulate your response.

Why Recognizing Manipulative Language is Important

1. **Protects Your Autonomy:**
   - Identifying manipulation helps you think for yourself rather than being swayed by others' agendas.
2. **Encourages Logical Thinking:**
   - It enables you to focus on facts and logic instead of emotional appeals or deceptive tactics.
3. **Improves Communication Skills:**
   - Recognizing manipulative tactics helps you communicate more clearly and ethically.

Common Manipulative Language Tactics

1. **Loaded Words:**
   - Using emotionally charged terms to sway your opinion.
   - Example: Calling a policy "freedom-crushing" instead of "restrictive."
2. **False Dichotomies:**
   - Presenting only two extreme options as if no middle ground exists.
   - Example: "You're either with us or against us."
3. **Generalizations:**
   - Using words like "always," "never," or "everyone" to oversimplify issues.
   - Example: "You always ignore my ideas."
4. **Appeals to Fear or Pity:**
   - Manipulating emotions instead of presenting rational arguments.
   - Example: "If we don't act now, everything will be lost."
5. **Name-Calling or Labels:**
   - Using derogatory terms to dismiss ideas or people without addressing the issue.
   - Example: "Only a fool would believe that."

How to Spot and Respond to Manipulative Language

1. **Pay Attention to Emotional Appeals:**
   - Ask yourself: "Is this argument making me feel scared, guilty, or angry instead of offering facts?"
2. **Look for Absolutes:**
   - Be wary of words like "always" or "never" that oversimplify reality.

3. **Identify Missing Details:**
    o Manipulative language often leaves out context or alternative perspectives.
4. **Ask for Clarification:**
    o Challenge vague or emotional statements with questions like, "Can you explain that in more detail?"
5. **Focus on Facts:**
    o Separate emotional language from the actual information being presented.

Examples of Spotting Manipulative Language

1. **In Advertising:**
    o **Scenario:** A commercial says, "If you truly care about your family, you'll buy our product."
    o **Manipulation:** It uses guilt to influence your decision rather than providing evidence of the product's value.
2. **In Debates:**
    o **Scenario:** A speaker says, "Only someone ignorant would disagree with this policy."
    o **Manipulation:** It dismisses opposing views through name-calling instead of addressing their merits.
3. **In Personal Conversations:**
    o **Scenario:** A friend says, "You never listen to me."
    o **Manipulation:** The word "never" exaggerates the issue, turning a single instance into a sweeping accusation.

Practical Exercise: Identify Manipulative Language

1. **Pick a News Article or Ad:**
    o Look for emotionally charged words, oversimplifications, or appeals to fear or guilt.
2. **Highlight the Tactics:**
    o Mark instances of loaded language, false dichotomies, or generalizations.
3. **Rewrite the Statement Logically:**
    o Example: Rewrite "This plan will destroy the economy!" as "This plan may have economic downsides, such as increased costs."

Why This Technique Works

Recognizing manipulative language empowers you to think critically and independently. It helps you focus on the truth, avoid emotional traps, and respond thoughtfully.

Closing Thought

Words are powerful tools — but they can also be weapons. Learn to spot manipulative language so you can navigate the world with clarity and confidence.

Chapter 72: Identify Emotional Triggers in Arguments

What are Emotional Triggers?

Emotional triggers in arguments are words, phrases, or tactics designed to provoke a strong emotional response — often at the expense of rational thinking. These triggers can make you feel scared, angry, guilty, or hopeful, influencing your decisions without presenting clear facts.

For example:

- A politician might say, "Our way of life is under attack!" to incite fear and urgency, even without specific evidence.

Why Identifying Emotional Triggers is Important

1. **Helps You Stay Rational:**
    o Recognizing triggers allows you to focus on facts rather than being swayed by emotions.

2. **Reduces Manipulation:**
   - It protects you from being influenced by arguments that exploit your feelings.
3. **Encourages Informed Decisions:**
   - By filtering out emotional noise, you can evaluate arguments more objectively.

Common Emotional Triggers in Arguments

1. **Fear:**
   - Example: "If we don't act now, disaster will strike!"
2. **Anger:**
   - Example: "Those people are ruining everything we've worked for."
3. **Guilt:**
   - Example: "If you don't support this cause, you're part of the problem."
4. **Hope:**
   - Example: "This plan will finally fix everything and lead us to success."
5. **Shame:**
   - Example: "How could anyone with common sense think that way?"

How to Identify and Respond to Emotional Triggers

1. **Notice Your Emotional Reaction:**
   - Ask yourself: "Is this argument making me feel angry, scared, or guilty? Why?"
2. **Separate Emotions from Facts:**
   - Focus on the actual information being presented, not how it makes you feel.
3. **Ask for Evidence:**
   - Challenge emotionally charged statements with questions like, "What evidence supports this claim?"
4. **Stay Calm:**
   - Emotional triggers often rely on creating urgency or tension. Take a moment to reflect before responding.

Examples of Identifying Emotional Triggers

1. **In Media:**
   - **Scenario:** A headline reads, "The shocking truth about what's happening in your neighborhood!"
   - **Trigger:** The word "shocking" is designed to provoke fear or curiosity without providing details.
   - **Response:** Investigate the facts behind the headline before reacting.
2. **In Debates:**
   - **Scenario:** A speaker says, "If you care about your family, you'll support this policy."
   - **Trigger:** Guilt is used to push agreement without explaining the policy's actual impact.
   - **Response:** Focus on understanding the policy's details instead of reacting emotionally.
3. **In Personal Interactions:**
   - **Scenario:** Someone says, "You're just like everyone else who doesn't understand."
   - **Trigger:** Shame is used to dismiss your perspective.
   - **Response:** Redirect the conversation to focus on the actual argument.

Practical Exercise: Spot Emotional Triggers

1. **Analyze a Speech or Ad:**
   - Identify words or phrases designed to provoke emotions.
2. **Rewrite the Argument:**
   - Remove the emotional language and focus on the facts.
3. **Reflect on Your Reactions:**
   - Consider how emotional triggers affected your initial response.

Why This Technique Works

Emotional triggers are powerful but often distort reality. Recognizing them helps you stay grounded, think critically, and make decisions based on evidence rather than manipulation.

Closing Thought

Your emotions are valid, but they shouldn't control your decisions. Spot emotional triggers, stay rational, and take charge of your thinking.

Chapter 73: Follow the Money: Trace Motivations

What Does It Mean to 'Follow the Money'?

"Follow the money" is a phrase often used to uncover hidden motivations behind decisions, actions, or claims. By tracing who benefits financially, you can reveal potential biases, conflicts of interest, or ulterior motives that might influence someone's behavior or arguments.

For example:

- A company heavily promoting a particular health supplement might have financial incentives to exaggerate its benefits while downplaying side effects.

This principle is vital for critical thinking because financial interests can shape narratives, policies, and even public opinion.

Why Tracing Motivations Matters

1. **Reveals Conflicts of Interest:**
   - Understanding who benefits financially helps you evaluate whether information is trustworthy or biased.
2. **Increases Scepticism:**
   - It encourages you to question claims that may be more about profit than truth.
3. **Helps You Make Informed Decisions:**
   - Knowing the financial motivations behind actions allows you to weigh information critically.

How to Follow the Money

1. **Identify the Stakeholders:**
   - Determine who is involved in the situation, claim, or decision.
   - Example: In a pharmaceutical ad, stakeholders might include the company, doctors, and patients.
2. **Ask Who Benefits Financially:**
   - Consider who stands to gain or lose money based on the outcome.
   - Example: If a study praises a new drug, check whether the study was funded by the drug's manufacturer.
3. **Investigate Funding Sources:**
   - Look into the origins of funding for campaigns, research, or advertisements.
   - Example: A charity promoting a product might be sponsored by the company that makes it.
4. **Examine Patterns:**
   - Trace the flow of money to identify whether similar actions or decisions have benefited the same parties.
5. **Look Beyond the Surface:**
   - Hidden financial ties, such as lobbying efforts or undisclosed partnerships, may influence outcomes.

Examples of Following the Money

1. **In Media:**
   - **Scenario:** A news outlet repeatedly promotes a particular industry.
   - **Action:** Investigate whether the outlet receives advertising revenue or funding from that industry.
   - **Outcome:** You discover potential bias in their coverage and seek alternative sources.
2. **In Healthcare:**
   - **Scenario:** A doctor recommends a specific medical device.
   - **Action:** Research whether the doctor has financial ties to the device manufacturer.
   - **Outcome:** You find that they're a paid consultant, prompting you to get a second opinion.
3. **In Politics:**
   - **Scenario:** A politician supports legislation that benefits a specific corporation.
   - **Action:** Check campaign donation records to see if the corporation contributed to their campaign.
   - **Outcome:** You identify a possible conflict of interest and scrutinize their arguments more carefully.

1. **Choose a Claim or Action:**
   o Example: "This sunscreen is the best on the market."
2. **Identify Stakeholders:**
   o Who benefits financially from you buying this sunscreen?
3. **Investigate Funding or Promotions:**
   o Is the research supporting the claim funded by the sunscreen company?
4. **Assess the Credibility:**
   o Consider whether financial ties might bias the claim, and seek independent reviews.

Why This Technique Works

Money often drives decisions and narratives. By tracing financial motivations, you uncover biases and conflicts of interest that might otherwise go unnoticed, helping you make more informed judgments.

Closing Thought

When in doubt, follow the money. Understanding who stands to gain reveals the true motivations behind decisions and claims.

Chapter 74: Question the Source: Evaluate Credibility

Why Questioning the Source is Crucial

Not all information is created equal. Questioning the source helps you determine whether the information you're receiving is reliable, accurate, and free from bias. In an age of information overload, where opinions often masquerade as facts, this skill is critical for separating trustworthy sources from misleading ones.

For example:

- A social media post claiming a ground-breaking health cure might not be credible if it comes from an unverified account with no supporting evidence.

What Makes a Source Credible?

1. **Expertise:**
   - The source should have relevant knowledge or experience in the topic.
2. **Evidence:**
   - Credible sources back their claims with data, research, or verifiable facts.
3. **Impartiality:**
   - Reliable sources present information objectively, without clear bias or hidden agendas.
4. **Reputation:**
   - Established, respected organizations or individuals are more likely to provide credible information.

How to Evaluate the Credibility of a Source

1. **Check the Author or Organization:**
   - Research the qualifications and background of the individual or group providing the information.
2. **Look for Supporting Evidence:**
   - Credible sources cite data, studies, or expert opinions to back their claims.
3. **Analyze the Tone:**
   - Be cautious of overly emotional or sensational language, which may indicate bias.
4. **Verify the Date:**
   - Ensure the information is current and relevant to the topic at hand.
5. **Cross-Check with Other Sources:**
   - Compare the information with reputable sources to ensure consistency.

Examples of Questioning the Source

1. **In News:**
   - **Scenario:** A headline claims a miraculous cure for a disease.
   - **Action:** Check whether the article cites peer-reviewed studies or credible health organizations.
   - **Outcome:** You discover the claim is based on preliminary research, not established science.
2. **In Social Media:**
   - **Scenario:** A viral post says a celebrity endorsed a controversial product.
   - **Action:** Verify the claim through official channels or the celebrity's verified account.
   - **Outcome:** You find the endorsement is fake, preventing you from spreading misinformation.
3. **In Conversations:**
   - **Scenario:** A coworker shares a statistic that seems off.
   - **Action:** Politely ask where they found the information and verify it yourself.
   - **Outcome:** You identify the statistic as outdated or inaccurate.

Practical Exercise: Evaluate a Source

1. **Pick a Recent Claim:**
   - Example: "This diet guarantees weight loss in two weeks."
2. **Investigate the Source:**
   - Who is making the claim? Are they an expert in nutrition?
3. **Check for Evidence:**
   - Does the claim cite scientific research or rely on testimonials?
4. **Cross-Check:**
   - Compare the claim with information from trusted health organizations.

Why This Technique Works

Questioning the source prevents you from accepting misinformation at face value. By evaluating credibility, you ensure that your beliefs and decisions are grounded in fact.

Closing Thought

The source of information matters as much as the information itself. Question, verify, and rely on credible voices to guide your thinking.

Chapter 75: Detect Spin in Media Narratives

Spin refers to the deliberate framing of information to influence public perception. Media outlets often use selective facts, emotionally charged language, or biased framing to present a story in a way that aligns with their agenda or target audience. Detecting spin helps you recognize when information is being presented in a way that prioritizes persuasion over accuracy.

For example:

- A news report might describe a tax policy as "an attack on hardworking families" rather than simply explaining its details, which appeals to emotion rather than providing a neutral analysis.

Why Detecting Spin is Important

1. **Promotes Critical Thinking:**
   - Recognizing spin encourages you to analyze information objectively instead of accepting it at face value.
2. **Reduces Bias:**
   - Understanding how narratives are framed helps you form balanced opinions.
3. **Improves Decision-Making:**
   - Avoiding spun narratives ensures your decisions are based on facts, not manipulated perceptions.

How to Detect Spin in Media Narratives

1. **Analyze Word Choice:**
   - Look for emotionally charged or exaggerated language designed to provoke a reaction.
   - Example: "Devastating cuts" versus "necessary budget adjustments."
2. **Check for Selective Facts:**
   - Determine whether the story includes all relevant details or omits key information to support a specific angle.
3. **Identify the Source's Agenda:**
   - Consider the outlet's target audience, political leanings, or funding sources that might influence their narrative.
4. **Compare Coverage:**
   - Cross-check the same story across multiple media outlets to identify differences in framing and tone.
5. **Watch for False Balance:**
   - Be cautious of attempts to present two sides as equally valid when one side lacks credible evidence.

Common Signs of Spin in Media

1. **Loaded Headlines:**
   - Example: "Scandalous Leak Exposes Government Corruption!" The headline might sensationalize minor details to attract clicks.
2. **Cherry-Picked Data:**
   - Example: Highlighting only the benefits of a policy without mentioning potential drawbacks.
3. **Out-of-Context Quotes:**
   - Example: Using a snippet of a speech to misrepresent the speaker's full message.
4. **Exaggeration or Oversimplification:**
   - Example: Claiming a complex issue has a simple solution, such as "This one law will fix the economy!"
5. **Emotional Appeals:**
   - Example: Including stories or images designed to elicit strong emotions rather than convey facts.

Examples of Detecting Spin in Action

1. **In Political News:**
   - **Scenario:** A news outlet describes a new law as "a dangerous overreach."
   - **Detection:** Analyze whether the report explains the actual content of the law or focuses only on criticism from one side.
2. **In Health Reporting:**
   - **Scenario:** An article claims, "This new diet is revolutionizing weight loss!"

- **Detection:** Check whether the story cites peer-reviewed studies or relies on testimonials and hype.
3. **In Business Coverage:**
   - **Scenario:** A financial site declares, "Stock market crash imminent!"
   - **Detection:** Look for supporting data and compare the report with other financial analyses.

Practical Exercise: Detect Spin in Media

1. **Choose a News Story:**
   - Pick an article on a controversial topic from a media outlet.
2. **Highlight Emotional Language:**
   - Identify words or phrases that seem designed to provoke fear, anger, or excitement.
3. **Look for Missing Context:**
   - Ask yourself, "What information might be missing or deliberately left out?"
4. **Compare Sources:**
   - Read the same story from another outlet to see how the framing differs.

Why This Technique Works

Detecting spin sharpens your ability to separate facts from opinion and evaluate the integrity of media narratives. It keeps you informed without being swayed by manipulative framing.

Closing Thought

Don't let spin cloud your judgment. Seek the full picture, think critically, and approach every narrative with a discerning eye.

Chapter 76: Read Between the Lines of Ambiguity

What Does It Mean to Read Between the Lines?

Reading between the lines involves interpreting the underlying meaning or intentions behind vague or ambiguous language. People often use ambiguity to obscure details, evade accountability, or manipulate perception. Learning to decode these hidden messages helps you uncover the truth and make better decisions.

For example:

- A company's press release stating, "We are committed to exploring options for improvement," might sound promising but lacks concrete details about actions or timelines.

Why Understanding Ambiguity is Valuable

1. **Reveals Hidden Agendas:**
   o Ambiguous language often masks true intentions or unfavorable details.
2. **Encourages Critical Analysis:**
   o It forces you to question what isn't being said, rather than focusing only on what is.
3. **Prevents Misinterpretation:**
   o Clarifying vague statements ensures you don't make decisions based on incomplete information.

Common Types of Ambiguity

1. **Vague Promises:**
   o Example: "We're working to make things better." (What does "better" mean, and when will it happen?)
2. **Evasive Answers:**
   o Example: Politicians avoiding direct responses to specific questions.
3. **Overly Broad Statements:**
   o Example: "This product is suitable for everyone." (Is it really, or are exceptions being ignored?)
4. **Unclear Accountability:**
   o Example: "Mistakes were made." (By whom? When? How will they be addressed?)

How to Read Between the Lines

1. **Look for Missing Details:**
   o Ask, "What specifics are missing that would clarify this statement?"
2. **Consider the Context:**
   o Analyze whether the ambiguity serves a purpose, such as avoiding criticism or buying time.
3. **Ask Follow-Up Questions:**
   o Press for specifics to fill in the gaps. Example: "What actions are being taken to improve the situation?"
4. **Watch for Patterns:**
   o Repeated use of vague language may indicate a lack of transparency or accountability.
5. **Seek Independent Verification:**
   o Look for evidence or alternative sources to clarify the ambiguous statement.

Examples of Reading Between the Lines

1. **In Corporate Communication:**
   o **Scenario:** A company announces, "We're streamlining operations to better serve customers."
   o **Hidden Meaning:** This might imply layoffs or budget cuts without explicitly stating them.
2. **In Politics:**
   o **Scenario:** A candidate says, "We're working on solutions to reduce unemployment."
   o **Hidden Meaning:** The lack of specifics suggests they don't have a concrete plan yet.
3. **In Personal Relationships:**
   o **Scenario:** A friend says, "I'll try to be there."
   o **Hidden Meaning:** They may not intend to show up but want to avoid directly declining.

Practical Exercise: Practice Decoding Ambiguity

1. **Choose an Ambiguous Statement:**
   o Example: "We're committed to improving customer satisfaction."
2. **Identify Missing Information:**
   o What actions, timelines, or metrics are missing from this statement?
3. **Ask Clarifying Questions:**
   o Example: "What specific steps are you taking to improve satisfaction?"
4. **Cross-Check for Evidence:**
   o Look for supporting actions or data to verify the claim.

Why This Technique Works

Ambiguity often hides key information or intentions. By reading between the lines, you uncover what's being left unsaid, ensuring you base your decisions on clear and accurate information.

Closing Thought

Don't take vague statements at face value. Dig deeper, ask questions, and uncover the truth hidden in ambiguity.

Chapter 77: Look for the Hidden Agenda

What is a Hidden Agenda?

A hidden agenda is an underlying motive or goal that isn't openly stated. People, companies, and organizations often hide their true intentions to persuade, manipulate, or achieve their objectives without attracting scrutiny. By learning to spot hidden agendas, you can uncover the real reasons behind actions, claims, or decisions.

For example:

- A company might market a product as eco-friendly to appeal to environmentally conscious consumers, even if the product's environmental benefits are negligible.

Why Identifying Hidden Agendas is Crucial

1. **Reveals True Motivations:**
   o Spotting hidden agendas helps you understand what someone or an organization really wants to achieve.
2. **Prevents Manipulation:**
   o Knowing the real intent behind a message reduces the chances of being misled.
3. **Encourages Better Decision-Making:**
   o Understanding the hidden motives allows you to assess situations more accurately and act accordingly.

How to Spot a Hidden Agenda

1. **Analyze the Message's Purpose:**
   o Ask yourself, "What is this person or organization trying to achieve?"
   o Example: Is a politician advocating for a policy because it benefits the public—or because it helps their campaign donors?
2. **Look for Discrepancies:**
   o Notice if actions don't match stated goals.
   o Example: A company claiming to support local businesses might still outsource jobs overseas.
3. **Investigate Who Benefits:**
   o Follow the outcomes of the action or decision to determine who gains the most.
   o Example: A charity promoting a specific product might be funded by the product's manufacturer.
4. **Check for Consistency:**
   o Look for patterns in past behavior to determine if the stated motives align with actions over time.
5. **Ask Questions:**
   o Seek clarification about vague or contradictory statements to reveal hidden motives.

Examples of Hidden Agendas in Action

1. **In Marketing:**
   o **Scenario:** A food brand promotes a product as "all-natural."
   o **Hidden Agenda:** The branding might distract consumers from the fact that the product is still high in sugar or calories.
2. **In Politics:**
   o **Scenario:** A bill is marketed as "improving public safety."
   o **Hidden Agenda:** Upon closer inspection, it might primarily benefit private contractors or special interest groups.
3. **In Social Situations:**
   o **Scenario:** A friend encourages you to attend a party with them.
   o **Hidden Agenda:** They may want you there to make themselves more comfortable or to help them network.

Practical Exercise: Uncover Hidden Agendas

1. **Choose a Recent Decision or Statement:**
   o Example: "This new tax will strengthen the economy."

2. **Ask Who Benefits:**
    - o   Identify individuals or groups who stand to gain financially, politically, or socially.
3. **Look for Discrepancies:**
    - o   Does the stated reason align with the likely outcomes?
4. **Research Background Information:**
    - o   Investigate funding sources, partnerships, or past actions that might reveal deeper motives.

Why This Technique Works

Hidden agendas often distort truth and mislead decision-making. By uncovering the real motives behind actions or claims, you empower yourself to act based on facts and logic rather than appearances.

Closing Thought

Always look beyond the surface. The true story often lies in the hidden motives, not the stated goals.

"Same Facts, Different Frames."

Chapter 78: Understand Framing Effects

What are Framing Effects?

Framing effects occur when the way information is presented influences how you interpret it. The same facts can evoke different reactions depending on how they're worded or emphasized. Understanding framing helps you spot attempts to shape your perceptions and make more objective decisions.

For example:

- A health study might report that a drug has a "95% survival rate," which sounds reassuring. However, framing the same fact as a "5% mortality rate" feels more alarming, even though the numbers are identical.

Why Framing Effects Matter

1. **Shapes Perceptions:**
    - o   The way information is framed can alter how you feel about a situation, even if the facts remain the same.
2. **Influences Decisions:**
    - o   Framing can push you toward certain choices without you realizing it.
3. **Encourages Critical Thinking:**
    - o   Recognizing framing effects helps you focus on the facts rather than the presentation.

Common Examples of Framing Effects

1. **Positive vs. Negative Framing:**
    - o   Example: A product labeled "80% lean" sounds healthier than one labeled "20% fat," even though they're the same.
2. **Gain vs. Loss Framing:**
    - o   Example: "You'll save $100 by switching plans" versus "You'll lose $100 if you don't switch plans."
3. **Highlighting Benefits or Drawbacks:**
    - o   Example: A company emphasizes a car's fuel efficiency while downplaying its high repair costs.
4. **Selective Statistics:**
    - o   Example: Highlighting the "4 out of 5 doctors recommend" statistic while ignoring the sample size or methodology.

How to Recognize and Counter Framing Effects

1. **Reframe the Information:**
    - o   Restate the facts in a neutral way to see how they sound without the spin.
    - o   Example: Instead of "95% survival rate," think of it as "5% mortality rate."
2. **Ask for Context:**
    - o   Investigate whether the frame emphasizes one aspect of the situation while ignoring others.

3. **Compare Alternatives:**
   o Evaluate how different framings of the same information influence your perception.
4. **Focus on the Facts:**
   o Strip away the emotional language or emphasis and concentrate on the underlying data.

Examples of Understanding Framing Effects in Action

1. **In Advertising:**
   o **Scenario:** A toothpaste ad says, "Clinically proven to fight cavities!"
   o **Detection:** Research whether the claim is based on a significant improvement or just minimal results.
2. **In Health Decisions:**
   o **Scenario:** A doctor says, "This surgery has a 90% success rate."
   o **Detection:** Ask about the 10% risk of complications to get a complete picture.
3. **In Personal Finance:**
   o **Scenario:** A credit card promises "1% cash back on every purchase."
   o **Detection:** Consider whether the benefits outweigh potential interest fees or annual charges.

Practical Exercise: Reframe the Message

1. **Pick a Statement:**
   o Example: "This plan will save you $500 per year!"
2. **Restate It Differently:**
   o Example: "Not choosing this plan will cost you $500 per year."
3. **Analyze the Impact:**
   o Consider whether the framing changes how you feel about the decision.

Why This Technique Works

Framing effects can distort your judgment by playing on emotions and cognitive biases. Recognizing these tactics ensures you focus on facts, not just the way they're presented.

Closing Thought

Words matter, but context matters more. Learn to see through the frame and focus on what's inside the picture.

Chapter 79: Notice What's Left Out

What Does It Mean to Notice What's Left Out?

When someone presents an argument or narrative, what they omit can be just as important as what they include. Missing information – whether intentional or accidental – can skew your understanding, leading you to make decisions based on an incomplete picture. By training yourself to notice what's left out, you uncover hidden gaps, ask better questions, and form a more balanced perspective.

For example:
- A product review might highlight its strengths but conveniently leave out its known flaws, giving you a distorted view.

Why Noticing What's Left Out Matters

1. **Fills in the Gaps:**
   o Missing information often hides key details that are critical to understanding the full context.
2. **Prevents Misleading Conclusions:**
   o Omissions can create bias, pushing you toward a particular interpretation or decision.
3. **Encourages Deeper Investigation:**
   o Recognizing gaps motivates you to ask questions and seek additional sources.

Common Types of Missing Information

1. **Selective Reporting:**
   - Highlighting favorable data while ignoring unfavorable results.
   - Example: A study on a drug's effectiveness might exclude data about its side effects.
2. **Lack of Context:**
   - Presenting facts without the background that makes them meaningful.
   - Example: "Crime rates have doubled" without mentioning they're still historically low.
3. **Overgeneralization:**
   - Making broad claims without addressing exceptions or limitations.
   - Example: "This method works for everyone" without considering individual differences.
4. **Unspoken Assumptions:**
   - Failing to mention underlying beliefs or conditions that influence the argument.
   - Example: A plan to reduce taxes assumes government spending won't increase.

How to Spot What's Missing

1. **Ask What's Not Being Said:**
   - Look beyond the surface of the information presented and question what might have been omitted.
2. **Compare Multiple Sources:**
   - Cross-reference information to identify gaps or contradictions between different accounts.
3. **Look for Vague or Sweeping Claims:**
   - Be wary of statements that lack specifics or supporting details.
4. **Identify the Stakes:**
   - Consider who benefits from leaving out certain details and why they might do so.
5. **Request Clarification:**
   - Directly ask for more information to fill in the blanks.

Examples of Noticing What's Left Out

1. **In Marketing:**
   - **Scenario:** A car ad boasts excellent fuel efficiency.
   - **Omission:** It doesn't mention the car's high repair costs or lack of safety features.
   - **Action:** Research reviews and specifications to uncover the missing details.
2. **In News:**
   - **Scenario:** An article reports that a new policy "has widespread support."
   - **Omission:** It doesn't specify how "widespread" was measured or who was surveyed.
   - **Action:** Investigate polling data or consult alternative reports for context.
3. **In Social Interactions:**
   - **Scenario:** A friend recounts an argument but only shares their side of the story.
   - **Omission:** Key details about what the other person said or did.
   - **Action:** Encourage them to share the full context or speak to the other person involved.

Practical Exercise: Find the Missing Pieces

1. **Pick a Recent Claim:**
   - Example: "This diet plan guarantees results in two weeks!"
2. **Identify Potential Omissions:**
   - Are there details about the diet's long-term effects or health risks?
3. **Seek Additional Information:**
   - Look for independent reviews or studies to fill in the gaps.
4. **Ask Clarifying Questions:**
   - Example: "What specific results are guaranteed, and for whom does this plan work best?"

Why This Technique Works

Noticing what's left out prevents you from being misled by partial information. It ensures you see the whole picture, allowing you to make more informed and balanced decisions.

Closing Thought

Don't just focus on what's said, pay attention to what isn't. The truth often lies in the gaps.

Chapter 80: Track the Influence of Social Pressure

What is Social Pressure?

Social pressure is the influence others exert on your decisions, beliefs, or behavior. It often comes from a desire to fit in, avoid conflict, or gain approval. While it's a natural human experience, unchecked social pressure can push you to conform to ideas or actions that don't align with your values or reasoning.

For example:

- A group of friends might pressure you into agreeing with their opinion on a controversial issue, even if you have doubts or disagree.

Why Recognizing Social Pressure is Important

1. **Encourages Independent Thinking:**
   - Identifying social pressure helps you resist conformity and think for yourself.
2. **Reduces Manipulation:**
   - Awareness of group influence makes you less susceptible to peer pressure or mob mentality.
3. **Strengthens Integrity:**
   - Standing firm against social pressure builds confidence in your values and beliefs.

Common Signs of Social Pressure

1. **Groupthink:**
   - A group prioritizes consensus over critical evaluation, discouraging dissent.
2. **Fear of Rejection:**
   - You agree with others to avoid conflict or exclusion, even if you disagree internally.
3. **Bandwagon Effect:**
   - You adopt an idea or behavior because it's popular, not because it's logical or right.
4. **Appeals to Authority:**
   - You feel compelled to agree because the pressure comes from a respected figure.

How to Track and Resist Social Pressure

1. **Pause Before Agreeing:**
   - Ask yourself whether you genuinely agree or are just conforming to fit in.
2. **Seek Diverse Opinions:**
   - Expose yourself to differing perspectives to counter the influence of group bias.
3. **Clarify Your Values:**
   - Reflect on your core beliefs to strengthen your ability to stand firm under pressure.
4. **Ask Questions:**
   - Challenge the group's assumptions or reasoning by raising thoughtful, open-ended questions.
5. **Practice Assertiveness:**
   - Learn to voice your opinions respectfully, even when they differ from the majority.

Examples of Social Pressure in Action

1. **In Group Decisions:**
   - **Scenario:** Your team supports a risky project you think is flawed.
   - **Pressure:** Fear of being labeled a "naysayer" makes you hesitant to speak up.
   - **Action:** Raise concerns by focusing on the project's potential risks and alternatives.
2. **In Social Media Trends:**
   - **Scenario:** Everyone in your network shares an unverified news story.
   - **Pressure:** You feel compelled to share it too, even though you haven't fact-checked it.
   - **Action:** Research the story before deciding whether to share it.
3. **In Friend Groups:**
   - **Scenario:** Your friends pressure you to agree with a controversial political stance.
   - **Pressure:** You worry disagreeing will cause tension.
   - **Action:** Politely express your differing opinion and explain your reasoning.

Practical Exercise: Track Social Pressure

1. **Reflect on a Recent Group Decision:**
   - Did you agree because you believed in the idea or to avoid conflict?
2. **Identify the Source of Pressure:**
   - Was it peer approval, fear of rejection, or a desire to fit in?
3. **Practice Independent Thinking:**
   - Next time, pause and ask yourself, "What do I truly think about this?"

Why This Technique Works

Social pressure can cloud your judgment and stifle critical thinking. By recognizing and resisting it, you empower yourself to act with integrity and clarity.

Closing Thought

Don't let the crowd dictate your choices. Stay true to your values, think independently, and let logic guide your decisions.

Section IX: Mastering Interpersonal Clarity

Clear thinking is not only an individual skill — it's also essential for building strong, meaningful connections with others. This section equips you with practical techniques to improve communication, resolve conflicts, and foster understanding in any relationship. By mastering these skills, you'll connect with others more authentically and collaboratively.

Chapter 81: Practice Active Listening

What is Active Listening?

Active listening is the practice of fully focusing on what someone is saying, without distractions or judgment. It goes beyond simply hearing words — it's about understanding the message, acknowledging the speaker, and responding thoughtfully.

For example:

- Instead of thinking about your response while someone talks, active listening means giving your full attention, nodding to show understanding, and asking clarifying questions if needed.

Why Active Listening is Crucial

1. **Builds Trust:**
   - When people feel heard, they're more likely to open up and collaborate with you.
2. **Reduces Misunderstandings:**
   - Fully understanding someone's message prevents unnecessary confusion or conflict.
3. **Fosters Empathy:**
   - Active listening helps you see things from the speaker's perspective.
4. **Strengthens Relationships:**
   - It shows you value and respect the other person, deepening your connection.

How to Practice Active Listening

1. **Eliminate Distractions:**
   - Put away your phone, close unnecessary tabs, and focus entirely on the speaker.
2. **Show You're Engaged:**
   - Use nonverbal cues like nodding, eye contact, and an open posture to signal you're paying attention.
3. **Don't Interrupt:**
   - Let the speaker finish their thought before jumping in with questions or comments.
4. **Paraphrase and Reflect:**
   - Repeat key points in your own words to confirm understanding.
   - Example: "So what you're saying is that the timeline feels too rushed?"

5. **Ask Clarifying Questions:**
   o Encourage the speaker to elaborate by asking open-ended questions like, "Can you explain more about what you mean?"

Examples of Active Listening in Action

1. **In Work:**
   o **Scenario:** A coworker shares frustrations about a project.
   o **Action:** Instead of offering solutions immediately, you listen fully, paraphrase their concerns, and ask, "What do you think could help improve the situation?"
2. **In Relationships:**
   o **Scenario:** A partner expresses feeling ignored.
   o **Action:** You put aside your assumptions, focus on their words, and say, "I hear that you feel I haven't been as present. How can I do better?"
3. **In Friendships:**
   o **Scenario:** A friend talks about a personal challenge.
   o **Action:** Instead of steering the conversation to your experiences, you ask questions like, "How has this been affecting you?"

Practical Exercise: Strengthen Your Active Listening

1. **Pick a Conversation to Focus On:**
   o Choose a daily interaction, such as a meeting or a talk with a friend.
2. **Use Nonverbal Cues:**
   o Maintain eye contact, nod, and eliminate distractions during the conversation.
3. **Summarize Key Points:**
   o After the speaker finishes, paraphrase what you heard to ensure you understand their message.
4. **Ask Thoughtful Questions:**
   o Encourage deeper dialogue with questions like, "What else would you like to share about this?"

Why This Technique Works

Active listening transforms communication from a passive exchange to a meaningful connection. It ensures clarity, builds trust, and deepens your understanding of others' perspectives.

Closing Thought

Listening isn't just hearing — it's understanding. Practice active listening to connect, clarify, and build stronger relationships.

Chapter 82: Ask Open-Ended Questions

What Are Open-Ended Questions?

Open-ended questions are inquiries that encourage detailed responses rather than simple "yes" or "no" answers. They invite exploration, discussion, and deeper understanding, making them a powerful tool for uncovering thoughts, feelings, or ideas.

For example:
- Instead of asking, "Did you like the event?" you might ask, "What was your favorite part of the event?"

Why Open-Ended Questions Are Powerful

1. **Encourage Thoughtful Responses:**
   o They prompt people to share more, providing richer insights and perspectives.

2. **Build Better Connections:**
   - o Open-ended questions show genuine interest, fostering trust and openness.
3. **Promote Problem-Solving:**
   - o They encourage others to think critically and consider multiple angles.
4. **Uncover Hidden Details:**
   - o These questions reveal nuances that might otherwise go unnoticed.

How to Ask Effective Open-Ended Questions

1. **Start with 'What,' 'How,' or 'Why':**
   - o Example: "What led you to this decision?" or "How did you feel about the outcome?"
2. **Avoid Leading Questions:**
   - o Example: Replace "Don't you think this is the best solution?" with "What do you think about this solution?"
3. **Encourage Exploration:**
   - o Example: "What challenges do you see in this plan?" instead of "Are there any challenges?"
4. **Follow Up Thoughtfully:**
   - o Ask additional questions to explore their response further, such as, "Can you elaborate on that?"
5. **Be Patient:**
   - o Give the other person time to think and respond fully.

Examples of Open-Ended Questions in Action

1. **In Work:**
   - o **Scenario:** You're seeking feedback on a project.
   - o **Question:** "What do you think worked well, and what could we improve?"
   - o **Outcome:** You gain detailed insights rather than a simple thumbs-up or thumbs-down.
2. **In Relationships:**
   - o **Scenario:** A partner seems upset.
   - o **Question:** "How are you feeling right now, and what's been on your mind?"
   - o **Outcome:** They feel invited to share their emotions in depth.
3. **In Teaching or Mentoring:**
   - o **Scenario:** A student struggles with a concept.
   - o **Question:** "What part of this feels most confusing, and how do you think we could approach it differently?"
   - o **Outcome:** The student identifies their stumbling blocks, helping you tailor your guidance.

Practical Exercise: Practice Open-Ended Questions

1. **Choose a Conversation:**
   - o Select an interaction where you want to learn more about someone's thoughts or feelings.
2. **Plan Three Questions:**
   - o Write down three open-ended questions that begin with "What," "How," or "Why."
3. **Listen Fully:**
   - o Ask the questions and give the other person space to respond without interrupting.
4. **Reflect on the Outcome:**
   - o Notice how the open-ended questions deepened the conversation or revealed new insights.

Why This Technique Works

Open-ended questions invite others to share their thoughts more fully, fostering understanding and trust. They transform conversations into opportunities for discovery and connection.

Closing Thought

The right question opens doors. Use open-ended questions to explore ideas, connect with others, and unlock deeper insights.

Chapter 83: Clarify What You Heard

Clarifying what you heard involves restating or paraphrasing someone's message to confirm your understanding. It ensures that both parties are on the same page, reducing the risk of misunderstandings or assumptions.

For example:

- If someone says, "I'm worried about our deadline," you might clarify by asking, "Are you saying the timeline feels too short, or is there another concern?"

Why Clarifying is Essential

1. **Prevents Misunderstandings:**
   - Misinterpretations can lead to unnecessary confusion, mistakes, or conflict. Clarifying resolves ambiguity before it becomes an issue.
2. **Builds Trust:**
   - It shows the speaker that you care about understanding their message accurately.
3. **Encourages Open Communication:**
   - Clarifying invites others to elaborate, fostering deeper and more productive conversations.
4. **Improves Decision-Making:**
   - Clear communication ensures that everyone has the same information, leading to better decisions and outcomes.

How to Clarify Effectively

1. **Paraphrase the Key Points:**
   - Restate the main ideas in your own words to confirm understanding.
   - Example: "So, if I understand correctly, you're suggesting we prioritize the new feature over fixing bugs?"
2. **Ask Specific Questions:**
   - Use clarifying questions to explore ambiguous statements.
   - Example: "When you say 'soon,' do you mean within the next week or the next few days?"
3. **Check for Agreement:**
   - After paraphrasing, ask, "Did I get that right?" or "Is there anything I missed?"
4. **Watch for Nonverbal Cues:**
   - Pay attention to tone, facial expressions, or body language that might signal whether the speaker feels understood.
5. **Avoid Assumptions:**
   - If something seems unclear, don't guess—ask for clarification.

Examples of Clarifying in Action

1. **In Work Settings:**
   - **Scenario:** Your manager says, "Let's make this project top priority."
   - **Clarification:** "Does that mean we should pause all other tasks until this is complete?"
   - **Outcome:** Your manager specifies that the team should still address urgent issues as they arise.
2. **In Personal Relationships:**
   - **Scenario:** A partner says, "I feel like we're not spending enough time together."
   - **Clarification:** "Do you mean you'd like to schedule more date nights, or is it something else?"
   - **Outcome:** Your partner explains that they'd like to spend more quality time during the weekends.
3. **In Education:**
   - **Scenario:** A teacher says, "Focus on the key themes for the exam."
   - **Clarification:** "Can you clarify which themes are most important to review?"
   - **Outcome:** The teacher provides a list of specific topics to prioritize.

1. **Choose a Recent Conversation:**
   o   Think of an interaction where you weren't entirely sure about what the other person meant.
2. **Paraphrase the Key Message:**
   o   Write down how you could have restated their message to confirm understanding.
3. **Ask Clarifying Questions:**
   o   Imagine follow-up questions you could have asked to gather more details.
4. **Apply in Future Conversations:**
   o   During your next interaction, practice paraphrasing and asking questions to ensure clarity.

Clarifying prevents small misunderstandings from turning into bigger issues. It fosters trust, ensures mutual understanding, and paves the way for more effective communication.

Clarity isn't just about what's said — it's about what's understood. Take the time to confirm, clarify, and communicate effectively.

Chapter 84: Use Empathy to Understand Others' Views

Empathy is the ability to put yourself in someone else's shoes — to see the world from their perspective and understand their feelings, even if you don't share their experiences. It's a cornerstone of effective communication and a powerful tool for resolving conflicts and building stronger relationships.

For example:

- If a co-worker is frustrated about changes in a project, empathy helps you see how the changes might impact their workload or priorities.

1. **Fosters Connection:**
   o   Empathy builds trust and rapport, making others feel valued and understood.

2. Reduces Conflict:
    o Understanding someone's perspective makes it easier to address disagreements constructively.
3. Improves Collaboration:
    o Empathy encourages cooperation by helping you align with others' needs and goals.
4. Encourages Open Dialogue:
    o When people feel heard, they're more likely to share openly and work toward solutions.

How to Use Empathy Effectively

1. Listen Without Judgment:
    o Focus on understanding the other person's feelings and experiences without immediately forming opinions.
2. Acknowledge Their Perspective:
    o Let them know you see where they're coming from.
    o Example: "I can see why that situation feels overwhelming for you."
3. Ask Questions to Explore Their Viewpoint:
    o Use open-ended questions to learn more about their perspective.
    o Example: "Can you tell me more about what's been challenging for you?"
4. Mirror Emotions:
    o Reflect their emotions to show you understand.
    o Example: "It sounds like you're feeling frustrated because of the tight deadlines."
5. Validate Their Feelings:
    o Even if you don't agree with their actions, acknowledge that their feelings are valid.
    o Example: "I understand why you'd feel upset in that situation."

Examples of Using Empathy in Action

1. In Work Settings:
    o **Scenario:** A teammate is upset about a new process.
    o **Empathy in Action:** "I can see how this change might feel like extra work for you. Let's figure out how to make it easier."
    o **Outcome:** The teammate feels supported and works with you to find solutions.
2. In Relationships:
    o **Scenario:** Your partner is stressed about a family issue.
    o **Empathy in Action:** "That sounds really tough. I'm here if you want to talk about it more."
    o **Outcome:** Your partner feels comforted and opens up about their concerns.
3. In Friendships:
    o **Scenario:** A friend cancels plans last minute, citing exhaustion.
    o **Empathy in Action:** "I understand—sometimes you just need to recharge. Let's reschedule when you're feeling better."
    o **Outcome:** Your friend feels supported rather than judged.

Practical Exercise: Practice Empathy

1. Reflect on a Recent Interaction:
    o Think of a conversation where you could have shown more empathy.
2. Identify Their Perspective:
    o What might the other person have been feeling or experiencing?
3. Write a Response:
    o Draft an empathetic statement you could have used to acknowledge their feelings.
4. Apply in Future Conversations:
    o During your next interaction, consciously practice empathy by listening and validating the other person's perspective.

Why This Technique Works

Empathy bridges the gap between differing views, fostering understanding and collaboration. It transforms communication from surface-level exchanges into meaningful connections.

Closing Thought

Empathy isn't just about hearing — it's about understanding. Use it to connect, support, and communicate with clarity and compassion.

Chapter 85: Reframe Conflict into Problem-Solving

What Does It Mean to Reframe Conflict into Problem-Solving?

Conflict often feels like a battle. Reframing conflict into problem-solving changes the dynamic. Instead of focusing on who's right or wrong, you shift your energy toward resolving the issue collaboratively. It's not about defeating the other person; it's about finding a solution that works for everyone involved.

For example:

- Instead of arguing about who caused a mistake at work, you could focus on how to prevent similar errors in the future.

Why Reframing Conflict is Effective

1. **Reduces Tension:**
   - Shifting the focus to solutions defuses emotions and promotes calm, constructive discussions.
2. **Fosters Collaboration:**
   - Problem-solving encourages teamwork rather than opposition, improving relationships.
3. **Leads to Better Outcomes:**
   - A focus on solutions often uncovers creative, mutually beneficial answers.
4. **Builds Long-Term Trust:**
   - Handling conflict constructively shows respect and strengthens communication.

How to Reframe Conflict into Problem-Solving

1. **Pause and Shift Your Mindset:**
   - Remind yourself that the goal is resolution, not "winning."
2. **Focus on the Problem, Not the Person:**
   - Avoid personal attacks and frame the issue as a shared challenge.
   - Example: Replace "You're always late" with "How can we make sure we're both on time for meetings?"
3. **Use Collaborative Language:**
   - Say "we" instead of "you" or "I" to emphasize teamwork.
   - Example: "How can we work together to solve this?"
4. **Acknowledge Emotions:**
   - Validate the other person's feelings to show understanding.
   - Example: "I see that this situation has been frustrating for you."
5. **Brainstorm Solutions Together:**
   - Invite the other person to contribute ideas for resolving the conflict.
   - Example: "What do you think would help us move forward?"
6. **Agree on Action Steps:**
   - End the conversation with a clear plan for addressing the issue.

Examples of Reframing Conflict in Action

1. **In Work Settings:**
   - **Scenario:** Two team members disagree on how to approach a project.
   - **Reframe:** "We both want the project to succeed. Let's list the pros and cons of each approach and decide together."
   - **Outcome:** The team finds a compromise that combines the best aspects of both ideas.
2. **In Relationships:**
   - **Scenario:** A partner is upset about feeling ignored.
   - **Reframe:** "I understand you feel like I haven't been present. Let's talk about what would help you feel more connected."
   - **Outcome:** The conversation shifts from blame to actionable solutions, like scheduling regular quality time.

3. **In Friendships:**
    o   **Scenario:** A friend feels hurt about a missed event.
    o   **Reframe:** "I can see how missing the event upset you. Let's talk about how I can make it up to you."
    o   **Outcome:** The focus moves from the past mistake to repairing the relationship.

Practical Exercise: Practice Reframing Conflict
1. **Reflect on a Recent Conflict:**
    o   Identify a situation where you and someone else were at odds.
2. **Reframe the Issue:**
    o   Write down how you could have turned the argument into a collaborative discussion.
3. **Plan Collaborative Questions:**
    o   Example: "What's most important to you in this situation?" or "How can we work together to resolve this?"
4. **Apply in Future Conflicts:**
    o   When disagreements arise, consciously shift to problem-solving language and mindset.

Why This Technique Works

Reframing conflict into problem-solving redirects negative energy into constructive action. It helps you work through disagreements collaboratively, strengthening relationships and achieving better outcomes.

Closing Thought

Conflict doesn't have to be a fight. Reframe it as a shared challenge, and watch problems turn into opportunities for growth and connection.

Chapter 86: Communicate in Simple, Clear Language

Why Does Clear Communication Matter?

Clear communication ensures that your message is understood the way you intend. Overcomplicated language, jargon, or vague statements can confuse others and create misunderstandings. Speaking and writing simply and clearly makes your ideas accessible, strengthens relationships, and fosters trust.

For example:

- Instead of saying, "We need to synergize our paradigms for optimized solutions," clear communication would be: "Let's work together to find the best solution."

1. **Improves Understanding:**
   o Clear language reduces ambiguity and ensures your audience grasps your message.
2. **Saves Time:**
   o Simplicity prevents long explanations, keeping conversations focused and efficient.
3. **Builds Credibility:**
   o People trust speakers who communicate clearly and avoid unnecessary complexity.
4. **Encourages Collaboration:**
   o When everyone understands the message, they're more likely to engage and contribute.

How to Communicate Clearly

1. **Know Your Audience:**
   o Tailor your language to the listener's level of knowledge or expertise.
   o Example: Use plain language for non-experts and specific terminology only when necessary.
2. **Organize Your Thoughts:**
   o Structure your ideas logically, starting with the main point and supporting it with details.
3. **Use Short, Simple Sentences:**
   o Avoid overly complex sentences that bury your main point.
4. **Avoid Jargon and Buzzwords:**
   o Replace technical terms or trendy phrases with straightforward language.
   o Example: Instead of "leverage cross-platform solutions," say "use tools that work on different devices."
5. **Be Specific:**
   o Use precise examples or details to make your point clear.
   o Example: Replace "soon" with "by next Friday."
6. **Ask for Feedback:**
   o Confirm that your message was understood by asking, "Does that make sense?" or "Do you have any questions?"

Examples of Clear Communication in Action

1. **In Work Settings:**
   o **Scenario:** Explaining a project update to your team.
   o **Clear Communication:** "We've completed 80% of the tasks. The remaining work includes testing and final revisions, which should take two more weeks."
2. **In Relationships:**
   o **Scenario:** Asking for help with household chores.
   o **Clear Communication:** "Can you please take care of the dishes today?" instead of vaguely saying, "I need help around the house."
3. **In Problem-Solving:**
   o **Scenario:** Giving feedback to a colleague.
   o **Clear Communication:** "Your presentation was strong, but adding a summary slide would make the key points even clearer."

Practical Exercise: Simplify Your Communication

1. **Choose a Message:**
   o Think of something you recently explained, like an email or conversation.
2. **Rewrite It Simply:**
   o Remove jargon, simplify sentences, and organize it logically.
3. **Share and Get Feedback:**
   o Present the simplified version and ask if it's clear. Adjust if needed.

Why This Technique Works

Clear communication eliminates confusion and ensures everyone is on the same page. It builds trust, saves time, and strengthens connections by making your message easy to understand.

Closing Thought

Simplicity is the ultimate sophistication. Speak clearly, listen carefully, and watch your relationships and results thrive.

Chapter 87: Know When to Say Nothing

Why Knowing When to Say Nothing is Powerful

In conversations, silence can be as impactful as words. Knowing when to stay quiet allows you to observe, listen, and respond thoughtfully. It also prevents you from saying things in the heat of the moment that you might regret later. Silence isn't about avoiding communication — it's about choosing your words wisely and creating space for deeper understanding.

For example:

- If someone criticizes your work, pausing to reflect before responding can prevent a defensive reaction and allow you to address their points more constructively.

Benefits of Saying Nothing

1. **Encourages Reflection:**
   - Silence gives you time to process information and form a thoughtful response.
2. **Defuses Conflict:**
   - In heated situations, staying quiet can prevent escalation and help calm emotions.
3. **Invites Others to Share:**
   - Silence creates space for others to express themselves, leading to richer conversations.
4. **Demonstrates Self-Control:**
   - Resisting the urge to speak impulsively shows emotional intelligence and maturity.
5. **Enhances Listening Skills:**
   - Staying quiet helps you focus on what others are saying instead of planning your next response.

When to Say Nothing

1. **When You're Angry or Upset:**
   - Emotional reactions often lead to regrettable words. Silence allows you to cool down and respond thoughtfully.
2. **When You Don't Have Enough Information:**
   - If you're unsure about a topic, it's better to listen and learn than to speculate.
3. **When Someone Needs to Vent:**
   - Sometimes, people just need to be heard. Staying silent lets them express their feelings fully.
4. **When Silence Creates Impact:**
   - Pausing before responding can emphasize your words when you do speak.
5. **When It's Not Your Turn:**
   - Interrupting others disrupts the flow of conversation. Waiting shows respect and attentiveness.

How to Master the Art of Silence

1. **Count to Three Before Responding:**
   - A short pause ensures your response is thoughtful and measured.
2. **Observe Body Language:**
   - Use silence to pick up on nonverbal cues that might reveal deeper meanings.
3. **Resist the Urge to Fill Gaps:**
   - Silence in conversations can feel awkward, but allowing it can lead to more meaningful exchanges.
4. **Reflect Instead of Reacting:**
   - Ask yourself, "Will my words add value to this conversation?" before speaking.
5. **Practice Active Listening:**
   - Focus on understanding the speaker's message fully instead of planning your next comment.

Examples of Saying Nothing in Action

1. **In Work Settings:**
   - **Scenario:** A colleague critiques your idea during a meeting.
   - **Silence in Action:** You pause, listen to their concerns, and respond constructively instead of reacting defensively.

2. **In Relationships:**
    o **Scenario:** Your partner vents about a tough day.
    o **Silence in Action:** You stay quiet, nodding and listening attentively, allowing them to feel heard.
3. **In Conflicts:**
    o **Scenario:** A heated argument begins to escalate.
    o **Silence in Action:** You stop speaking, take a breath, and suggest returning to the discussion later when emotions have cooled.

Practical Exercise: Practice Silence in Conversations

1. **Choose a Conversation to Observe:**
    o Pick an interaction where you'll focus on staying silent and listening more than usual.
2. **Pause Before Speaking:**
    o Count to three after someone finishes speaking to ensure you're responding thoughtfully.
3. **Resist Interrupting:**
    o Let the other person finish their thoughts, even if there are pauses.
4. **Reflect Afterward:**
    o Consider how silence influenced the conversation's tone and outcome.

Why This Technique Works

Silence is a powerful communication tool. It allows you to process emotions, observe nuances, and respond thoughtfully. By speaking less and listening more, you create space for clarity and connection.

Closing Thought

Words have power, but so does silence. Know when to speak and when to hold back — it's a skill that strengthens every relationship.

Chapter 88: Mirror for Understanding

What is Mirroring in Communication?

Mirroring involves repeating or rephrasing someone's words or emotions to show you understand their message. It's about reflecting their thoughts back to them to confirm that you've interpreted their message correctly.

For example:

- If a colleague says, "I'm frustrated because the deadline feels unrealistic," you might mirror by saying, "It sounds like the timeline is causing you stress."

Why Mirroring is Valuable

1. **Ensures Clarity:**
   - Mirroring confirms that you've understood the speaker's message accurately.
2. **Builds Trust:**
   - It shows the other person that you're truly listening and care about their perspective.
3. **Defuses Tension:**
   - Reflecting emotions can help de-escalate conflicts by acknowledging feelings.
4. **Encourages Deeper Sharing:**
   - When people feel understood, they're more likely to open up.

How to Mirror Effectively

1. **Listen Fully:**
   - Pay attention to both the speaker's words and emotions.
2. **Paraphrase Their Message:**
   - Rephrase what they said in your own words.
   - Example: "So you're saying the meeting schedule is making it hard to stay productive?"
3. **Acknowledge Emotions:**
   - Reflect the speaker's feelings to show empathy.
   - Example: "It sounds like you're feeling overwhelmed by everything on your plate."
4. **Ask for Confirmation:**
   - Check if your reflection is accurate.
   - Example: "Did I get that right?"
5. **Avoid Mimicking:**
   - Don't repeat their words verbatim—use your own language to convey understanding.

Examples of Mirroring in Action

1. **In Work Settings:**
   - **Scenario:** A team member says, "I'm concerned we won't have enough time to finish this."
   - **Mirroring:** "You're worried the timeline might be too tight to get everything done. Is that right?"
   - **Outcome:** They feel heard and can work with you to address their concerns.
2. **In Relationships:**
   - **Scenario:** A partner says, "I feel like we're not spending enough time together."
   - **Mirroring:** "It sounds like you'd like us to prioritize more time for each other. What would that look like for you?"
   - **Outcome:** They feel understood, opening the door for a constructive discussion.
3. **In Friendships:**
   - **Scenario:** A friend says, "I'm nervous about this big presentation."
   - **Mirroring:** "It sounds like you're feeling anxious about how it will go. What's making you the most nervous?"
   - **Outcome:** Your friend feels supported and shares more about their concerns.

Practical Exercise: Practice Mirroring

1. **Choose a Conversation to Focus On:**
   - During your next interaction, consciously practice mirroring the other person's message.
2. **Reflect Back:**
   - Use phrases like, "It sounds like you're saying..." or "I hear that you feel..."
3. **Ask for Feedback:**
   - Check if your reflection matches their intended meaning.
4. **Refine Your Technique:**
   - Adjust your mirroring approach based on their response.

Why This Technique Works

Mirroring fosters understanding, builds trust, and ensures clarity in communication. It strengthens connections by showing that you're truly listening and valuing what the other person has to say.

Closing Thought

Communication isn't just about speaking — it's about understanding. Mirror to reflect, connect, and build stronger relationships.

Chapter 89: Summarize for Mutual Clarity

What Does It Mean to Summarize for Clarity?

Summarizing involves condensing the key points of a conversation into a concise statement to confirm mutual understanding. It ensures that everyone is on the same page and eliminates the risk of miscommunication. A good summary highlights the most important ideas, agreements, or action steps without introducing new information.

For example:

- At the end of a meeting, you might say, "So, to recap, we've agreed to complete the report by Friday, divide the tasks equally, and reconvene next Monday."

Why Summarizing is Crucial

1. **Prevents Misunderstandings:**
   - Summarizing ensures that all parties have the same understanding of the discussion.
2. **Saves Time:**
   - By distilling key points, you avoid unnecessary repetition or confusion later.
3. **Encourages Focus:**
   - It helps prioritize the most important aspects of the conversation.
4. **Improves Accountability:**
   - A clear summary outlines expectations and action items, making follow-ups easier.

How to Summarize Effectively

1. **Listen Actively Throughout the Conversation:**
   - Pay attention to the main ideas, agreements, or concerns as they're discussed.
2. **Highlight Key Points:**
   - Focus on the most important information or decisions rather than restating everything.
   - Example: "Here's what we've discussed so far: we'll adjust the timeline and allocate more resources to the project."
3. **Use Clear and Concise Language:**
   - Keep your summary brief and to the point.
4. **Confirm Agreement:**
   - End with a question like, "Does that sound right to you?" to ensure everyone agrees with your summary.
5. **Include Next Steps:**
   - If relevant, outline any action items or deadlines.

Examples of Summarizing in Action

1. **In Work Settings:**
   - **Scenario:** A project meeting with your team.
   - **Summary:** "To summarize, John will handle the research, Sarah will draft the report, and I'll review it by Wednesday. We'll meet again Friday to finalize everything. Does that cover everything?"
   - **Outcome:** Everyone leaves the meeting with clear roles and deadlines.
2. **In Relationships:**
   - **Scenario:** Discussing weekend plans with your partner.
   - **Summary:** "So, we'll leave at 10 AM, grab lunch on the way, and visit your parents in the afternoon. Sound good?"
   - **Outcome:** Misunderstandings about timing or plans are avoided.
3. **In Customer Service:**
   - **Scenario:** A customer explains their issue with a product.

- **Summary:** "If I understand correctly, the product isn't functioning as expected, and you'd like a replacement. Is that correct?"
- **Outcome:** The customer feels heard, and the resolution process begins smoothly.

1. **Choose a Daily Interaction:**
   - After a meeting or discussion, take a moment to summarize what was said.
2. **Use a Simple Structure:**
   - Start with "Here's what I understood..." and outline the key points.
3. **Ask for Confirmation:**
   - Check if your summary matches the other person's understanding.
4. **Reflect and Adjust:**
   - Note any feedback and improve your summarizing skills in future conversations.

Why This Technique Works

Summarizing helps clarify discussions, reinforce shared understanding, and prevent errors or misunderstandings. It ensures that everyone involved leaves the conversation with a clear, unified direction.

Closing Thought

Don't assume clarity, create it. Summarize to ensure mutual understanding and a smoother path forward.

Chapter 90: Adapt to Your Audience's Needs

What Does It Mean to Adapt to Your Audience?

Adapting to your audience involves tailoring your communication style, language, and message to suit the needs, preferences, and level of understanding of the people you're speaking to. This ensures that your message resonates and is clearly understood, regardless of who you're addressing.

For example:
- You might explain a technical concept differently to a group of experts than you would to a non-technical audience.

Why Adapting to Your Audience is Vital

1. **Increases Understanding:**
   - People are more likely to grasp your message when it's delivered in a way they relate to.

2. **Builds Rapport:**
   - o Tailoring your communication shows respect and consideration for your audience's perspective.
3. **Enhances Persuasion:**
   - o When your message aligns with your audience's needs, it becomes more compelling and impactful.
4. **Avoids Miscommunication:**
   - o Adapting your language prevents confusion or misinterpretation.

How to Adapt to Your Audience

1. **Understand Your Audience:**
   - o Consider their knowledge level, interests, and expectations.
   - o Example: Are you speaking to beginners or experts? A formal or casual group?
2. **Match Your Tone and Style:**
   - o Use formal language for professional settings and a conversational tone for casual discussions.
3. **Simplify or Expand as Needed:**
   - o Avoid technical jargon with non-experts but provide in-depth details for specialized audiences.
4. **Use Relevant Examples:**
   - o Tailor your examples to resonate with the audience's experiences or concerns.
   - o Example: Use sports analogies for a sports-focused audience, or business examples for a corporate group.
5. **Ask for Feedback:**
   - o Check if your message is landing by asking questions like, "Does that make sense?" or "Would you like more detail on that?"

Examples of Adapting to Your Audience

1. **In Work Presentations:**
   - o **Scenario:** Presenting project results to a client.
   - o **Adaptation:** Focus on high-level outcomes and business impacts rather than technical details.
   - o **Outcome:** The client understands the value of your work without being overwhelmed by data.
2. **In Education:**
   - o **Scenario:** Teaching a complex topic to students.
   - o **Adaptation:** Use simple language, diagrams, and real-world examples to make the concept accessible.
   - o **Outcome:** Students grasp the topic more easily and engage in the discussion.
3. **In Social Settings:**
   - o **Scenario:** Explaining your job to a friend with no knowledge of your field.
   - o **Adaptation:** Avoid industry jargon and describe your role in everyday terms.
   - o **Outcome:** Your friend gains a clear understanding of what you do.

Practical Exercise: Tailor Your Message

1. **Choose an Audience:**
   - o Identify a person or group you'll be speaking to soon (e.g. co-workers, friends, or a client).
2. **Analyze Their Needs:**
   - o What do they know about the topic? What details would interest or benefit them?
3. **Plan Your Message:**
   - o Adjust your tone, language, and examples to match their level of understanding.
4. **Seek Feedback:**
   - o After the conversation, ask if your message was clear and useful.

Why This Technique Works

Adapting to your audience ensures your message is relevant, understandable, and impactful. It strengthens your connection with others and makes communication more effective.

Closing Thought

Great communicators don't just speak — they adjust. Tailor your message to meet your audience's needs, and watch your conversations flourish.

Section X: Building a Clear Thinking Lifestyle

Clear thinking is a way of life. The habits and routines you adopt shape how you approach challenges, make decisions, and connect with the world around you. This final part focuses on integrating clarity into your everyday life. These techniques go beyond isolated strategies, helping you build a mindset and lifestyle that support clear, intentional thinking in all areas.

Chapter 91: Develop a Growth Mindset for Continuous Learning

What is a Growth Mindset?

A growth mindset is the belief that abilities, intelligence, and skills can be developed through effort, learning, and persistence. It contrasts with a fixed mindset, which assumes that these traits are static and unchangeable.

For example:

- A person with a growth mindset sees failure as an opportunity to learn and improve, rather than as a permanent setback.

Why a Growth Mindset Matters for Clear Thinking

1. **Encourages Resilience:**
   o   A growth mindset helps you see challenges as opportunities rather than roadblocks.
2. **Fosters Adaptability:**
   o   By believing you can improve, you're more open to learning new skills and adjusting your strategies.
3. **Reduces Fear of Failure:**
   o   Viewing mistakes as a natural part of growth makes it easier to take risks and innovate.
4. **Supports Lifelong Learning:**
   o   A growth mindset keeps you curious and motivated to expand your knowledge.

How to Develop a Growth Mindset

1. **Reframe Challenges as Opportunities:**
   o   Instead of saying, "I can't do this," try, "I can't do this yet, but I can learn."
2. **Embrace Feedback:**
   o   View criticism as valuable input for growth, rather than as a personal attack.
3. **Focus on Effort, Not Outcomes:**
   o   Celebrate progress and persistence, even if the result isn't perfect.
   o   Example: "I worked hard to improve my presentation skills, and it's paying off."
4. **Learn from Mistakes:**
   o   Reflect on failures to identify lessons and use them to improve.
5. **Surround Yourself with Growth-Oriented People:**
   o   Spend time with individuals who inspire and challenge you to grow.

Examples of a Growth Mindset in Action

1. **In Work:**
   o   **Scenario:** You struggle with a new software program.
   o   **Growth Mindset:** "I may not know this yet, but I can take a course or practice until I improve."
   o   **Outcome:** You gain confidence and master the tool over time.
2. **In Relationships:**
   o   **Scenario:** You make a mistake that upsets a friend.
   o   **Growth Mindset:** "I can learn from this and communicate better in the future."
   o   **Outcome:** You strengthen the relationship through self-improvement.

3. **In Hobbies:**
   - o **Scenario:** You fail at your first attempt to bake bread.
   - o **Growth Mindset:** "This didn't work, but I can tweak the recipe and try again."
   - o **Outcome:** Each attempt brings you closer to success.

Practical Exercise: Build a Growth Mindset

1. **Identify a Current Challenge:**
   - o Write down a skill or area where you're struggling.
2. **Reframe Your Thoughts:**
   - o Replace fixed mindset thoughts like "I can't do this" with "I'm learning to do this."
3. **Set a Small Goal:**
   - o Choose one action to improve, such as practicing for 10 minutes daily or seeking feedback.
4. **Reflect on Progress:**
   - o After a week, note how your efforts have helped you grow, even if progress feels small.

Why This Technique Works

A growth mindset creates the foundation for continuous improvement and resilience. It empowers you to face challenges with optimism and see every experience as a stepping stone for personal development.

Closing Thought

Your potential is limitless. Adopt a growth mindset, and watch how it transforms the way you think, learn, and grow.

Chapter 92: Stay Curious: Cultivate a Questioning Habit

What Does It Mean to Stay Curious?

Curiosity is the desire to explore, ask questions, and seek out new knowledge. It's a mindset that keeps you engaged with the world and motivates you to challenge assumptions, uncover hidden truths, and expand your understanding.

For example:

- Instead of accepting a headline at face value, curiosity might lead you to ask, "What's the evidence behind this claim?"

Why Curiosity Fuels Clear Thinking

1. **Challenges Assumptions:**
   - o Curiosity prompts you to question what you think you know and explore alternative perspectives.
2. **Encourages Lifelong Learning:**
   - o A curious mind is always hungry for new information, keeping you informed and adaptable.

3. **Strengthens Problem-Solving:**
   o Asking "why" or "how" leads to deeper understanding and creative solutions.
4. **Fosters Open-Mindedness:**
   o Curiosity helps you approach ideas with a sense of wonder, not judgment.

How to Cultivate a Questioning Habit

1. **Ask Open-Ended Questions:**
   o Replace "Is this true?" with "What evidence supports this?" or "What else could explain this?"
2. **Explore New Topics:**
   o Regularly seek out subjects you know little about to expand your knowledge.
3. **Challenge Common Beliefs:**
   o Question statements or assumptions you've taken for granted.
   o Example: "Why do we do things this way? Is there a better approach?"
4. **Be Comfortable Not Knowing:**
   o Accepting that you don't have all the answers fuels your desire to learn more.
5. **Follow Your Interests:**
   o Pursue hobbies, books, or conversations that spark your curiosity.

Examples of Staying Curious

1. **In Learning:**
   o **Scenario:** You read about a historical event.
   o **Curiosity:** "What were the cultural and political factors that influenced this event?"
   o **Outcome:** You research further, gaining a deeper understanding of history.
2. **In Work:**
   o **Scenario:** A coworker suggests a new method for solving a problem.
   o **Curiosity:** "How does this method work, and why is it better?"
   o **Outcome:** You uncover insights that improve your approach.
3. **In Conversations:**
   o **Scenario:** A friend mentions an unfamiliar term.
   o **Curiosity:** "Can you tell me more about what that means?"
   o **Outcome:** The conversation deepens, and you learn something new.

Practical Exercise: Practice Curiosity Daily

1. **Start a Question Journal:**
   o Write down three questions each day about things you encounter.
2. **Research One Question:**
   o Pick one question to explore through books, articles, or conversations.
3. **Reflect on What You Learn:**
   o Note how curiosity deepens your understanding or challenges your assumptions.

Why This Technique Works

Curiosity keeps your mind active and engaged, driving deeper understanding and better decision-making. It encourages exploration and opens doors to new possibilities.

Closing Thought

Never stop asking, "Why?" Curiosity is the compass that leads to discovery, growth, and a clearer understanding of the world.

Chapter 93: Learn From Diverse Perspectives

Why Learning from Diverse Perspectives is Vital

The world is full of varied experiences, cultures, and viewpoints. Learning from diverse perspectives broadens your understanding, challenges your assumptions, and helps you think more critically.

For example:
- Discussing a current event with people from different cultural or professional backgrounds can reveal nuances you hadn't considered.

How Diverse Perspectives Enhance Clear Thinking

1. **Challenge Cognitive Biases:**
   o Exposure to differing viewpoints helps you recognize and overcome personal biases.
2. **Expand Knowledge:**
   o Hearing others' experiences provides information and insights you may not encounter otherwise.
3. **Foster Empathy and Understanding:**
   o Engaging with diverse perspectives helps you see the world through others' eyes, making you more compassionate and open-minded.
4. **Encourage Creativity:**
   o Diverse ideas often spark innovative solutions by combining different ways of thinking.

How to Learn From Diverse Perspectives

1. **Seek Out Varied Voices:**
   o Read books, watch documentaries, or follow media from cultures, professions, or ideologies different from your own.
   o Example: If you're used to reading mainstream news, explore international or independent outlets for alternative takes.
2. **Have Open Conversations:**
   o Engage in discussions with people who have different backgrounds, beliefs, or experiences.
   o Example: Join community events, workshops, or online forums that emphasize diversity.
3. **Ask Questions with Curiosity:**
   o Approach conversations with a genuine desire to understand, not to debate or defend your views.
   o Example: "How has your experience shaped your perspective on this issue?"
4. **Avoid Echo Chambers:**
   o Be cautious of environments where everyone shares the same opinions, as they can reinforce biases.
   o Example: Diversify your social media feed to include people with different viewpoints.
5. **Reflect on What You Learn:**
   o After exploring a new perspective, ask yourself how it challenges or complements your own understanding.

Examples of Learning From Diverse Perspectives

1. **In Work Settings:**
   - o **Scenario:** Your team includes members from different countries.
   - o **Action:** Ask how cultural differences influence their approach to problem-solving.
   - o **Outcome:** You learn new strategies that enhance collaboration and creativity.
2. **In Personal Growth:**
   - o **Scenario:** You read a memoir by someone with a vastly different life experience.
   - o **Action:** Reflect on how their story reshapes your understanding of resilience or privilege.
   - o **Outcome:** You gain a deeper appreciation for the complexities of human experience.
3. **In Education:**
   - o **Scenario:** A professor presents opposing theories about a historical event.
   - o **Action:** Research both viewpoints to understand the context and biases of each.
   - o **Outcome:** Your analysis becomes more nuanced and informed.

Practical Exercise: Broaden Your Perspectives

1. **Explore a New Medium:**
   - o Watch a foreign film, read a book from a different culture, or listen to a podcast featuring diverse voices.
2. **Join a Group or Event:**
   - o Attend a panel discussion, cultural festival, or community gathering that introduces you to new viewpoints.
3. **Have a Conversation:**
   - o Talk with someone whose background or experiences differ from yours. Ask open-ended questions to learn from their perspective.
4. **Reflect and Apply:**
   - o After exploring a new perspective, think about how it informs or challenges your current beliefs.

Why This Technique Works

Learning from diverse perspectives expands your understanding and reduces blind spots. It sharpens your thinking by exposing you to new ideas, fostering empathy, and encouraging innovation.

Closing Thought

The world is richer when you see it through multiple lenses. Embrace diversity to think more clearly, act more wisely, and connect more deeply.

Chapter 94: Reflect Daily for Self-Awareness

What is Daily Reflection?

Daily reflection is the practice of setting aside time each day to think about your experiences, decisions, and emotions. It helps you identify patterns, understand your behaviour, and learn from your day. This habit cultivates self-awareness, enabling you to approach life with greater clarity and intention.

For example:

- At the end of the day, reflecting on a tough conversation might help you identify what went well, what didn't, and how to improve future interactions.

Why Reflection Matters for Clear Thinking

1. **Builds Self-Awareness:**
   - o Reflection helps you understand your strengths, weaknesses, and biases.

2. **Encourages Growth:**
   - o Reviewing your day reveals lessons that guide personal and professional development.
3. **Reduces Reactivity:**
   - o By examining your emotions and triggers, you become less prone to impulsive reactions.
4. **Clarifies Priorities:**
   - o Reflection helps you focus on what truly matters, aligning your actions with your values.

How to Reflect Effectively

1. **Set a Daily Routine:**
   - o Dedicate 10-15 minutes at the end of each day for reflection.
2. **Ask Key Questions:**
   - o Use prompts to guide your thoughts:
   - o What went well today?
   - o What challenges did I face, and how did I respond?
   - o What could I do differently tomorrow?
3. **Write It Down:**
   - o Journaling your reflections makes your thoughts tangible and easier to analyze.
4. **Be Honest:**
   - o Acknowledge both successes and mistakes without judgment.
5. **Focus on Patterns:**
   - o Look for recurring themes or behaviors that might need attention or adjustment.

Examples of Daily Reflection

1. **In Work:**
   - o **Scenario:** A meeting didn't go as planned.
   - o **Reflection:** "What caused the misunderstanding, and how can I communicate more clearly next time?"
   - o **Outcome:** You refine your approach for future discussions.
2. **In Relationships:**
   - o **Scenario:** You had an argument with a friend.
   - o **Reflection:** "What triggered the argument, and how could I handle similar situations better?"
   - o **Outcome:** You identify ways to improve your communication.
3. **In Personal Goals:**
   - o **Scenario:** You skipped your workout.
   - o **Reflection:** "Why did I skip it, and how can I stay motivated tomorrow?"
   - o **Outcome:** You plan a specific time for exercise and stick to it.

Practical Exercise: Start a Daily Reflection Practice

1. **Choose a Reflection Time:**
   - o Pick a consistent time each day, such as before bed or after work.
2. **Use Prompts:**
   - o Write or think about questions like, "What did I learn today?" or "What am I grateful for?"
3. **Record Insights:**
   - o Keep a journal or voice notes to track your thoughts over time.
4. **Review Weekly:**
   - o At the end of the week, look back on your reflections to identify growth or recurring challenges.

Why This Technique Works

Daily reflection transforms your experiences into learning opportunities. It enhances self-awareness, sharpens your decision-making, and aligns your actions with your goals and values.

Closing Thought

A clearer mind starts with self-awareness. Reflect daily to grow, learn, and live with purpose.

Chapter 95: Practice Gratitude for Balanced Thinking

Gratitude is the practice of focusing on what's good in your life and being thankful for it. It's not just a feel-good exercise — it's a way to create mental balance. By acknowledging the positive, you prevent negativity or stress from dominating your thoughts, leading to clearer, more rational decision-making.

For example:

- Gratitude for a supportive team at work can shift your mindset from frustration about challenges to appreciation for collaboration.

How Gratitude Enhances Clear Thinking

1. **Balances Negativity:**
   - Gratitude counteracts the brain's natural tendency to focus on problems, creating a more balanced perspective.
2. **Reduces Stress:**
   - Focusing on what you're thankful for helps lower anxiety and increases emotional resilience.
3. **Improves Decision-Making:**
   - A positive mindset reduces impulsivity and helps you weigh options more rationally.
4. **Fosters Creativity and Problem-Solving:**
   - Gratitude shifts your focus from obstacles to opportunities, encouraging creative thinking.

How to Practice Gratitude for Clear Thinking

1. **Start a Gratitude Journal:**
   - Write down three things you're grateful for each day, no matter how small.
   - Example: "The sunshine during my morning walk," or "A friend's kind text."
2. **Reflect During Tough Moments:**
   - When facing a challenge, pause to identify something positive in the situation.
   - Example: "This problem is hard, but I'm grateful for the skills I'm developing to solve it."
3. **Express Gratitude to Others:**
   - Tell someone why you appreciate them, either in person or with a note.
   - Example: "I'm so thankful for how you supported me during that project."
4. **Pause to Appreciate Daily Moments:**
   - Notice and savor small joys, like a good meal, a beautiful view, or a kind gesture.
5. **Practice Before Problem-Solving:**
   - Before tackling a stressful decision, list a few things you're grateful for to create a calm, positive mindset.

Examples of Gratitude in Action

1. **In Work Settings:**
   - **Scenario:** You're frustrated with a tight deadline.
   - **Gratitude Practice:** Reflect on how your team's support makes the workload manageable.
   - **Outcome:** You feel more positive and motivated to collaborate effectively.
2. **In Relationships:**
   - **Scenario:** A disagreement with a loved one leaves you upset.
   - **Gratitude Practice:** Focus on the aspects of the relationship you value, like their kindness or shared memories.
   - **Outcome:** This perspective helps you approach the conflict with understanding.
3. **In Personal Challenges:**
   - **Scenario:** You're recovering from an injury.

- o **Gratitude Practice:** Appreciate the progress you've made and the support from others.
- o **Outcome:** Gratitude boosts your emotional resilience during recovery.

Practical Exercise: Build a Gratitude Habit

1. **Set a Daily Gratitude Time:**
   - o Each morning or evening, write or think about three things you're grateful for.
2. **Focus on Specifics:**
   - o Instead of vague entries like "family," write "the laugh I shared with my sister today."
3. **Express Thanks Weekly:**
   - o Share your gratitude with someone who made a positive impact on your week.
4. **Reflect Monthly:**
   - o Review your gratitude journal to notice recurring themes or patterns of positivity.

Why This Technique Works

Gratitude rewires your brain to focus on the positive, creating a balanced mental state that supports clarity and emotional stability. It transforms your mindset from scarcity to abundance, making it easier to think clearly and act wisely.

Closing Thought

Practice gratitude daily to bring balance, clarity, and positivity to your thoughts and decisions.

Chapter 96: Stay Physically Healthy for Mental Sharpness

Why Physical Health is Tied to Mental Sharpness

Your body and mind are deeply connected. Physical health directly impacts your brain's ability to process information, make decisions, and stay focused. Neglecting your physical well-being can cloud your thinking, while maintaining healthy habits sharpens your mental clarity and resilience.

For example:

- Regular exercise improves blood flow to the brain, boosting memory, concentration, and problem-solving skills.

How Physical Health Enhances Clear Thinking

1. **Boosts Cognitive Function:**
   - o Physical activity improves memory, focus, and mental agility.

2. **Reduces Stress:**
   - o Healthy habits like exercise and sleep help regulate cortisol levels, keeping your mind calm and focused.
3. **Increases Energy Levels:**
   - o A well-balanced diet and regular exercise prevent mental fatigue and keep you alert.
4. **Supports Emotional Stability:**
   - o Physical health reduces mood swings, helping you approach problems with a balanced mindset.

Key Habits for Physical and Mental Health

1. **Exercise Regularly:**
   - o Aim for at least 30 minutes of physical activity most days of the week.
   - o Example: Walk, jog, do yoga, or try strength training.
2. **Eat Brain-Boosting Foods:**
   - o Incorporate fruits, vegetables, whole grains, and healthy fats into your meals.
   - o Example: Foods rich in omega-3s, like salmon or walnuts, support brain health.
3. **Stay Hydrated:**
   - o Drink enough water to keep your brain functioning optimally.
   - o Example: Even mild dehydration can impair focus and memory.
4. **Prioritize Sleep:**
   - o Aim for 7-9 hours of quality sleep per night to support memory and decision-making.
   - o Example: Create a calming bedtime routine to improve sleep quality.
5. **Take Breaks:**
   - o Periodic breaks during work improve focus and prevent mental burnout.
   - o Example: Use the 25/5 Pomodoro technique: 25 minutes of focused work, 5 minutes of rest.

Examples of Physical Health Supporting Mental Sharpness

1. **In Work:**
   - o **Scenario:** You have a big presentation tomorrow.
   - o **Healthy Habit:** A good night's sleep sharpens your memory and ensures peak performance.
   - o **Outcome:** You deliver a confident and clear presentation.
2. **In Stressful Situations:**
   - o **Scenario:** A looming deadline creates anxiety.
   - o **Healthy Habit:** A quick workout reduces stress and helps you refocus.
   - o **Outcome:** You tackle the task with renewed energy and calmness.
3. **In Decision-Making:**
   - o **Scenario:** You're feeling sluggish while weighing a tough choice.
   - o **Healthy Habit:** Drinking water and taking a walk refresh your brain.
   - o **Outcome:** You return to the decision with better clarity and focus.

Practical Exercise: Build Healthy Habits for Clarity

1. **Set a Fitness Goal:**
   - o Start small, like taking a 10-minute walk daily, and build from there.
2. **Track Your Diet:**
   - o Write down what you eat for a week and identify ways to add more brain-boosting foods.
3. **Create a Sleep Routine:**
   - o Go to bed and wake up at consistent times to improve sleep quality.
4. **Schedule Breaks:**
   - o Set timers to remind yourself to stretch, hydrate, or move throughout the day.

Why This Technique Works

Your brain relies on a healthy body to function at its best. By prioritizing physical well-being, you ensure that your mind stays sharp, focused, and ready to tackle any challenge.

Closing Thought

A healthy body fuels a clear mind. Take care of yourself physically, and your mental clarity will thank you.

Chapter 97: Embrace Failures as Learning Opportunities

What Does It Mean to Embrace Failures?

Failure is often seen as something to avoid, but it's one of the most powerful teachers you'll ever encounter. Embracing failure means recognizing it as an inevitable part of growth and a valuable opportunity to learn, adapt, and improve. It shifts your mindset from fearing mistakes to using them as stepping stones toward success.

For example:

- If a business idea doesn't work out, instead of giving up, you can analyze why it failed, adjust your approach, and try again with a better strategy.

Why Embracing Failure Matters

1. **Promotes Resilience:**
   - Learning from setbacks helps you bounce back stronger and more determined.
2. **Encourages Innovation:**
   - Many breakthroughs come from trial and error. Failure sparks new ideas and approaches.
3. **Improves Decision-Making:**
   - Reflecting on failures reveals what went wrong, helping you make better choices in the future.
4. **Builds Confidence:**
   - Facing and overcoming failure reinforces your belief in your ability to grow and succeed.

How to Turn Failures into Learning Opportunities

1. **Acknowledge the Failure:**
   - Accept responsibility without self-blame or denial.
   - Example: "I missed this deadline because I underestimated the time required."
2. **Analyze What Went Wrong:**
   - Break down the situation to identify specific causes.
   - Example: "Did I lack resources, misunderstand the task, or face unexpected obstacles?"
3. **Extract Lessons:**
   - Ask yourself what the failure taught you about your skills, approach, or environment.
   - Example: "Next time, I'll set smaller milestones to track progress more effectively."
4. **Adjust Your Strategy:**
   - Use what you've learned to improve future efforts.
   - Example: "I'll plan for extra time in case of delays."
5. **Move Forward:**
   - Let go of regret and focus on applying your new insights.

Examples of Embracing Failures

1. **In Work:**
   - **Scenario:** A product launch fails to meet sales targets.
   - **Action:** Analyze customer feedback to understand why, and use the insights to improve your next launch.
   - **Outcome:** The revised product performs significantly better.
2. **In Relationships:**
   - **Scenario:** A disagreement escalates into an argument.
   - **Action:** Reflect on how you communicated and identify ways to express yourself more calmly next time.
   - **Outcome:** Future discussions become more constructive and respectful.
3. **In Personal Goals:**
   - **Scenario:** You fail to stick to a fitness plan.
   - **Action:** Adjust your routine to include more manageable goals and accountability.
   - **Outcome:** You develop a sustainable habit over time.

1. **Identify a Failure:**
   o   Choose a recent setback, big or small.
2. **Analyze the Situation:**
   o   Write down what happened, why it happened, and how it made you feel.
3. **Extract Lessons:**
   o   Ask, "What can I learn from this? How can I improve next time?"
4. **Set a New Goal:**
   o   Apply what you've learned to a current or future challenge.
5. **Reflect on Your Progress:**
   o   Over time, revisit this failure to see how it contributed to your growth.

Why This Technique Works

Viewing failure as a learning opportunity transforms it from a source of fear into a tool for growth. It empowers you to take risks, innovate, and adapt with confidence.

Closing Thought

Failure is the beginning of learning. Embrace it, grow from it, and let it guide you to success.

Chapter 98: Take Breaks to Recharge Thinking

Shy Taking Breaks is Essential

Your brain needs rest to function at its best. Taking breaks improves focus, reduces mental fatigue, and boosts creativity. Whether you're solving a problem, learning a new skill, or making decisions, stepping away for a moment can actually enhance your performance.

For example:

- Taking a 10-minute walk during a busy workday can help you return with renewed energy and fresh ideas.

Benefits of Taking Breaks for Mental Clarity

1. **Reduces Cognitive Overload:**
   o   Breaks prevent your brain from becoming overwhelmed by constant work or information.
2. **Improves Focus:**
   o   Short rests help you sustain concentration and avoid burnout.
3. **Boosts Creativity:**
   o   Many creative insights emerge when you step away from the problem.
4. **Enhances Decision-Making:**
   o   Breaks create distance from the issue, allowing you to view it more objectively.

How to Take Effective Breaks

1. **Use the Pomodoro Technique:**
   o   Work for 25 minutes, then take a 5-minute break. After four cycles, take a longer 15-30 minute break.
2. **Move Your Body:**
   o   Physical activity, like stretching or walking, increases blood flow to the brain.
3. **Disconnect From Screens:**
   o   Step away from digital devices to rest your eyes and reduce mental fatigue.
4. **Practice Mindfulness or Relaxation:**
   o   Take deep breaths, meditate, or listen to calming music to recharge.
5. **Do Something Enjoyable:**
   o   Use your break for activities that refresh you, like chatting with a friend or reading a book.

Examples of Breaks Enhancing Productivity

1. **In Work:**
   o   **Scenario:** You're stuck on a tough problem.
   o   **Action:** Take a short walk outside.
   o   **Outcome:** A new solution pops into your mind while you're away from your desk.
2. **In Study Sessions:**
   o   **Scenario:** You're cramming for an exam and feeling overwhelmed.
   o   **Action:** Take a 15-minute break to stretch and hydrate.
   o   **Outcome:** You return more focused and retain information better.
3. **In Creative Work:**
   o   **Scenario:** You're designing a project and hit a mental block.
   o   **Action:** Step away to doodle or listen to music.
   o   **Outcome:** Fresh ideas come to you when you return.

Practical Exercise: Schedule Breaks Into Your Day

1. **Plan Break Intervals:**
   o   Set timers for work and break sessions.
2. **Experiment with Break Activities:**
   o   Try different approaches—physical movement, mindfulness, or creative hobbies—to see what refreshes you most.
3. **Reflect on the Impact:**
   o   Notice how breaks improve your focus, energy, and creativity.

Why This Technique Works

Breaks give your brain the rest it needs to function at its peak. They enhance clarity, creativity, and problem-solving, ensuring you perform better and feel more energized.

Closing Thought

Rest is a tool. Take breaks to refresh your mind and return stronger, sharper, and ready to tackle the next challenge.

Chapter 99: Seek Out Complexity and Simplify It

Why Seek Out Complexity?

The world is full of intricate systems, conflicting ideas, and dense information. While complexity might seem overwhelming, seeking it out helps you develop a deeper understanding of challenging concepts. The key is to simplify complexity—breaking it down into digestible pieces without losing its essence. This process strengthens your analytical skills, enhances decision-making, and empowers you to explain ideas clearly to others.

For example:

- Simplifying a complex business strategy into actionable steps helps your team understand and implement it effectively.

Benefits of Simplifying Complexity

1. **Builds Mastery:**
   - Understanding complex topics strengthens your knowledge and confidence.
2. **Improves Communication:**
   - Simplifying allows you to share insights with others in an accessible way.
3. **Enhances Decision-Making:**
   - Breaking down complexity helps you identify the most important factors in a situation.
4. **Encourages Critical Thinking:**
   - Analyzing and simplifying complexity sharpens your ability to evaluate information.

How to Simplify Complexity

1. **Start with the Big Picture:**
   - Understand the overarching concept or goal before diving into details.
   - Example: If you're learning about climate change, begin with the basics—like the greenhouse effect—before exploring specific policies.
2. **Break It Into Parts:**
   - Divide the topic into smaller, manageable components.
   - Example: For a business project, separate it into planning, execution, and evaluation phases.
3. **Identify Core Ideas:**
   - Focus on the most important elements that drive the topic or problem.
   - Example: Instead of memorizing every law in economics, understand key principles like supply and demand.
4. **Use Analogies and Visuals:**
   - Relate complex concepts to familiar ideas or create diagrams to simplify relationships.
   - Example: Compare a computer's CPU to a brain to explain its function.

5. **Explain It to Others:**
   - o Teaching forces you to clarify your understanding and spot gaps in your knowledge.

Examples of Simplifying Complexity

1. **In Education:**
   - o **Scenario:** You're learning about quantum mechanics.
   - o **Simplification:** Use analogies, like comparing quantum superposition to a spinning coin, to grasp the concept.
   - o **Outcome:** The analogy makes an abstract idea more tangible and easier to explain.
2. **In Work:**
   - o **Scenario:** A project has multiple overlapping deadlines and dependencies.
   - o **Simplification:** Create a timeline that highlights key milestones and who's responsible for each.
   - o **Outcome:** Your team understands the workflow, improving efficiency and collaboration.
3. **In Everyday Life:**
   - o **Scenario:** You're reading a dense news article about economic trends.
   - o **Simplification:** Summarize the main takeaway, like "Inflation is rising because demand is outpacing supply."
   - o **Outcome:** You gain clarity without getting lost in jargon.

Practical Exercise: Simplify Something Complex

1. **Choose a Complex Topic:**
   - o Pick a challenging concept from work, school, or daily life.
2. **Break It Down:**
   - o Divide the topic into three to five key points or parts.
3. **Create a Summary:**
   - o Write a one-paragraph explanation that captures the essence of the topic.
4. **Share It With Someone:**
   - o Explain your summary to a friend or colleague and ask if it makes sense.

Why This Technique Works

Simplifying complexity sharpens your thinking and clarifies your understanding. It reduces overwhelm, helps you focus on what matters, and equips you to communicate effectively.

Closing Thought

Complexity is something you need to embrace and master. Seek it out, simplify it, and turn it into a tool for clarity and understanding.

Chapter 100: Live Intentionally: Align Choices with Values

What Does It Mean to Live Intentionally?

Living intentionally means making deliberate choices that align with your values and long-term goals. It's about focusing on what matters most and letting those priorities guide your actions, instead of being swayed by distractions or societal expectations.

For example:

- If personal growth is a core value, you might choose to invest time in learning new skills rather than mindlessly scrolling through social media.

Why Intentional Living Supports Clear Thinking

1. **Provides Direction:**
   - Aligning actions with values eliminates indecision and keeps you focused on meaningful goals.
2. **Reduces Overwhelm:**
   - Living intentionally helps you prioritize, so you can let go of unnecessary tasks or commitments.
3. **Fosters Resilience:**
   - A strong connection to your values gives you the clarity and strength to navigate challenges.
4. **Promotes Fulfillment:**
   - Intentional living ensures your efforts contribute to a life that feels meaningful and satisfying.

How to Live Intentionally

1. **Identify Your Core Values:**
   - Reflect on what matters most to you—family, honesty, growth, creativity, etc.
2. **Set Clear Goals:**
   - Define what success looks like in each area of your life.
   - Example: "Spend one hour each day connecting with family."
3. **Evaluate Your Choices:**
   - Regularly ask, "Does this align with my values?"
   - Example: If health is a priority, consider whether a late-night binge of TV supports your goals.
4. **Eliminate Distractions:**
   - Let go of habits, commitments, or relationships that don't serve your values.
5. **Reflect and Adjust:**
   - Revisit your values and goals regularly to ensure they remain aligned with your actions.

Examples of Intentional Living

1. **In Work:**
   - **Scenario:** You're offered a promotion that requires more hours but conflicts with your family priorities.
   - **Action:** Evaluate whether the promotion aligns with your values and make a decision accordingly.
   - **Outcome:** You either negotiate a balance or decline the offer, staying true to what matters most.
2. **In Relationships:**
   - **Scenario:** You feel drained by a friendship that doesn't align with your values of positivity and growth.
   - **Action:** Choose to spend less time with that person and more time with those who uplift you.
   - **Outcome:** Your relationships feel more fulfilling and aligned with your values.
3. **In Daily Habits:**
   - **Scenario:** You value creativity but spend evenings on social media.
   - **Action:** Dedicate that time to painting, writing, or another creative activity.
   - **Outcome:** You feel more productive and connected to your passions.

Practical Exercise: Start Living Intentionally

1. **Define Your Values:**
   - List three to five values that are most important to you.
2. **Assess Your Current Life:**
   - Reflect on how well your daily choices align with these values.
3. **Set One Intentional Goal:**
   - Choose one area where you can better align your actions with your values.
   - Example: "Limit screen time to prioritize family dinners."
4. **Track Progress:**
   - Monitor how intentional changes improve your clarity, focus, and satisfaction.

Why This Technique Works

Intentional living creates alignment between your thoughts, actions, and values. It clears away distractions and ensures your efforts contribute to a meaningful and fulfilling life.

Closing Thought

Life is too precious to live on autopilot. Choose your path with purpose, align your actions with your values, and watch your life transform into one of clarity and intention.

Conclusion: A Clearer Path Forward

Congratulations on reaching the end of *Clear Thinking Made Simple: An AI's Guide to 100 Techniques for Seeing the World Clearly Without Blind Spots*. By now, you've explored a toolbox of techniques designed to sharpen your thinking, clarify your decisions, and empower you to navigate life with confidence and purpose.

Whether you're questioning assumptions, overcoming biases, solving problems, or connecting with others, every chapter in this book equips you to see the world more clearly and act with greater intention.

Why Clear Thinking Matters

The world is complex and full of noise. It's easy to get overwhelmed by information, fall into mental traps, or be swayed by emotions and biases. Clear thinking cuts through this clutter, allowing you to focus on what truly matters. It's the foundation for better decisions, stronger relationships, and a more fulfilling life.

When you think clearly, you don't just react to the world — you shape it. You approach challenges with curiosity, solve problems with creativity, and align your actions with your values. Clear thinking turns complexity into clarity and confusion into purpose.

Your Next Steps

1. **Practice Daily:**

    Clear thinking isn't learned overnight. Integrate these techniques into your routines, starting with just one or two that resonate most with you. Over time, they'll become second nature.

2. **Stay Curious:**

    The journey to clarity never ends. Keep asking questions, seeking diverse perspectives, and challenging your assumptions.

3. **Reflect and Adjust:**

    Regularly revisit the techniques in this book to see how they apply to new challenges in your life. Self-awareness is the key to growth.

4. **Share the Tools:**

    Clear thinking is contagious. By applying these techniques, you'll inspire others to think more clearly too. Share what you've learned with friends, family, and colleagues—it could transform their lives as much as yours.

A Life Built on Clarity

Imagine a life where your mind is free from mental clutter. Decisions feel lighter, your relationships grow deeper, and your goals align with your values. That's the life clear thinking can help you build. It's not about perfection—it's about progress. Every small step you take toward clarity adds up to a life of meaning, purpose, and impact.

You have everything you need to begin. The world is waiting for your clarity, your ideas, and your actions. Use these tools wisely, stay curious, and keep growing.

Closing Thought

Clear thinking is a superpower. Wield it well, and you'll unlock doors to a brighter, clearer, and more intentional life.

Appendix A: Quick Reference Guide to Clear Thinking

This appendix provides a concise overview of all the techniques covered in this book. Use it as a cheat sheet to refresh your memory or to find the exact tool you need for any situation.

Part I: Foundations of Clear Thinking

The basics you need to sharpen your mind and see the world clearly.

1. **Clean the Window:** Clear your mental filters to avoid distorted perceptions.
2. **Know Your Blind Spots:** Identify the biases and weaknesses in your thinking.
3. **Slow It Down:** Reflective thinking helps you make deliberate, logical decisions.
4. **Think Like a Scientist:** Use the hypothesis method to test ideas and find the truth.
5. **Separate Facts from Feelings:** Keep emotions in check to focus on objective truths.
6. **Distill Complexity:** Simplify complex problems by focusing on the basics.
7. **Zoom Out:** Step back to see the big picture and broader context.
8. **Zoom In:** Focus on crucial details without losing sight of their significance.
9. **Think in Layers:** Peel back assumptions to uncover deeper truths.
10. **Question Everything:** The Socratic method sharpens your critical thinking.

Part II: Techniques for Logical Thinking

Tools to reason clearly and avoid logical pitfalls.

11. **Spot the Flaw:** Identify and counter logical fallacies in arguments.
12. **Ask the Right Questions:** Good questions lead to better answers and insights.
13. **Use If-Then Thinking for Scenarios:** Anticipate outcomes by mapping logical consequences.
14. **Apply Occam's Razor:** Simplify complex situations by focusing on the simplest explanation.
15. **Connect the Dots:** Recognize patterns to draw insightful conclusions.
16. **Check the Premises:** Ensure your reasoning is built on solid foundations.
17. **Follow the Chain:** Trace causes and effects to understand outcomes clearly.
18. **Think Backward:** Reverse-engineer problems to uncover their solutions.
19. **Use Logic Trees:** Break down problems step-by-step for structured decision-making.
20. **Compare and Contrast for Clearer Choices:** Evaluate options side-by-side for clarity.

Part III: Cognitive Bias-Busting Techniques

Learn to identify and overcome mental shortcuts and distortions.

21. **Fact-Check First:** Verify claims before accepting them as truth.
22. **Spot Confirmation Bias:** Test what you want to believe for accuracy.
23. **Decouple from Anchors:** Avoid being overly influenced by initial impressions.
24. **Think Like a Detective:** Stay objective and avoid jumping to conclusions.
25. **Challenge the Crowd:** Resist bandwagon thinking by questioning group norms.
26. **Flip the Script:** Consider opposing perspectives to test your beliefs.
27. **Pause Before Reacting:** Manage emotional bias with deliberate thinking.
28. **Think Beyond the Present:** Avoid short-term traps by considering long-term effects.
29. **Don't Fall for Familiar:** Question availability heuristics and assess the evidence.
30. **Step Outside Yourself:** Mitigate egocentric bias by seeing others' perspectives.

Part IV: Practical Decision-Making Techniques

Techniques to make smarter, faster, and more thoughtful decisions.

31. **The 80/20 Rule:** Focus on the few things that produce the biggest impact.
32. **The Eisenhower Matrix:** Prioritize tasks by urgency and importance.
33. **The Premortem:** Plan for failure by anticipating what could go wrong.
34. **Decision Matrix:** Objectively weigh pros and cons for complex decisions.
35. **The 10/10/10 Rule:** Think about decisions' short-, medium-, and long-term impacts.
36. **Scenario Planning:** Prepare for multiple possible futures.
37. **Risk vs. Reward:** Make decisions by balancing potential benefits and risks.
38. **Take Small Steps:** Use iterative decision-making to test ideas gradually.
39. **Start with a Minimum Viable Solution:** Solve problems with simple, quick solutions.
40. **Use Weighted Scoring for Big Decisions:** Rank choices based on priority criteria.

Part V: Thinking Outside the Box

Break free from conventional thought patterns and unleash creativity.

41. **First Principles Thinking:** Break problems down to their basic truths.
42. **Lateral Thinking:** Jump to new perspectives and creative solutions.
43. **Brainstorm Without Judgment:** Generate ideas freely without overanalyzing.
44. **Use Random Input to Spark Ideas:** Find inspiration in unrelated concepts.
45. **The SCAMPER Method:** Improve ideas by modifying and combining them.
46. **Combine Ideas to Innovate:** Merge concepts to create something new.
47. **Think in Opposites to Break Norms:** Consider what would happen if you did the opposite.
48. **Set Constraints to Foster Creativity:** Use limitations to spark innovation.
49. **Borrow from Other Fields:** Apply ideas from different industries or disciplines.
50. **Play 'What If?' with Scenarios:** Explore possibilities to generate fresh ideas.

Part VI: Techniques for Mental Clarity

Cultivate habits to organize your thoughts and avoid mental overload.

51. **Practice Mental Hygiene:** Clear mental clutter for sharper focus.
52. **Write It Out:** Organize your thoughts by putting them on paper.
53. **Mind Mapping for Visual Clarity:** Use diagrams to structure and connect ideas.
54. **Practice Single-Tasking:** Focus on one thing at a time for greater productivity.
55. **Declutter Information Overload:** Filter out unnecessary noise to focus on essentials.
56. **Use White Space:** Schedule time for uninterrupted thinking.
57. **Decline to Decide:** Avoid decision fatigue by limiting choices.
58. **Set Clear Goals for Mental Direction:** Define your priorities to guide your actions.
59. **Use a Daily Reflection Routine:** Reflect on the day to improve self-awareness.
60. **Practice Mindfulness to Stay Present:** Stay grounded and focused in the moment.

Part VII: Advanced Critical Thinking Techniques

Deep-dive techniques for sharpening your analytical skills.

61. **Bayesian Thinking:** Update beliefs as new evidence emerges.
62. **Game Theory Basics:** Think strategically by considering others' perspectives.
63. **Think in Probabilities, Not Certainties:** Weigh likelihoods instead of absolutes.
64. **Second-Order Thinking:** Anticipate the ripple effects of decisions.
65. **Counterfactual Thinking:** Imagine "what-if" scenarios to explore alternatives.
66. **The Feynman Technique:** Explain concepts to understand them better.
67. **Ask, 'What Am I Missing?':** Challenge your assumptions to uncover gaps.
68. **Test Your Assumptions Before Acting:** Verify your ideas to avoid costly mistakes.
69. **Use Small Experiments to Test Ideas:** Validate concepts with low-risk trials.
70. **Always Ask for Feedback:** Gain clarity and improve through others' insights.

Part VIII: Techniques for Identifying Hidden Influences

Uncover hidden agendas, biases, and motivations behind information.

71. **Spot Manipulative Language:** Identify when words are used to mislead or influence.
72. **Identify Emotional Triggers in Arguments:** Recognize appeals to emotion over logic.
73. **Follow the Money:** Trace motivations to financial or personal interests.
74. **Question the Source:** Evaluate the credibility of information providers.
75. **Detect Spin in Media Narratives:** Separate facts from biased framing.
76. **Read Between the Lines of Ambiguity:** Uncover hidden meanings in vague statements.
77. **Look for the Hidden Agenda:** Identify the true motives behind actions or claims.
78. **Understand Framing Effects:** Recognize how the presentation of information shapes perception.
79. **Notice What's Left Out:** Identify missing information that distorts the full picture.
80. **Track the Influence of Social Pressure:** Resist groupthink by recognizing its impact.

Part IX: Mastering Interpersonal Clarity

Strengthen relationships with effective communication and understanding.

81. **Practice Active Listening:** Fully engage with others to understand their perspective.
82. **Ask Open-Ended Questions:** Encourage meaningful conversations by inviting detailed responses.

83. **Clarify What You Heard:** Confirm understanding to avoid miscommunication.
84. **Use Empathy to Understand Others' Views:** See the world through others' eyes.
85. **Reframe Conflict into Problem-Solving:** Turn disagreements into collaborative opportunities.
86. **Communicate in Simple, Clear Language:** Make your message easy to understand.
87. **Know When to Say Nothing:** Use silence as a tool for thoughtful communication.
88. **Mirror for Understanding:** Reflect others' thoughts to show you understand them.
89. **Summarize for Mutual Clarity:** Condense conversations to ensure shared understanding.
90. **Adapt to Your Audience's Needs:** Tailor your communication to the listener's perspective.

Part X: Building a Clear Thinking Lifestyle
Integrate clear thinking into every aspect of your life.

91. **Develop a Growth Mindset for Continuous Learning:** Embrace challenges as opportunities for growth.
92. **Stay Curious:** Cultivate a questioning habit to fuel lifelong learning.
93. **Learn From Diverse Perspectives:** Broaden your understanding by seeking varied viewpoints.
94. **Reflect Daily for Self-Awareness:** Use reflection to align actions with your values.
95. **Practice Gratitude for Balanced Thinking:** Focus on the positives to gain perspective.
96. **Stay Physically Healthy for Mental Sharpness:** Support clear thinking with good health habits.
97. **Embrace Failures as Learning Opportunities:** Use setbacks as a springboard for growth.
98. **Take Breaks to Recharge Thinking:** Rest your mind to boost focus and creativity.
99. **Seek Out Complexity and Simplify It:** Break down intricate ideas into manageable insights.
100. **Live Intentionally:** Align your choices with your values for a purposeful life.

Appendix B: Chapter-by-Part Overview

This appendix provides an organized list of all the chapters in the book, grouped by the parts they belong to. Use it as a quick navigation tool to locate specific chapters or revisit entire sections at a glance.

Part I: Foundations of Clear Thinking
- Clean the Window: Clear Your Mental Filters
- Know Your Blind Spots: Identify Cognitive Weaknesses
- Slow It Down: The Power of Reflective Thinking
- Think Like a Scientist: Embrace the Hypothesis Method
- Separate Facts from Feelings
- Distill Complexity: Boil It Down to Basics
- Zoom Out: See the Big Picture
- Zoom In: Focus on the Details That Matter
- Think in Layers: Peel Back Assumptions
- Question Everything: The Socratic Method

Part II: Techniques for Logical Thinking
- Spot the Flaw: Logical Fallacy Detection
- Ask the Right Questions
- Use If-Then Thinking for Scenarios
- Apply Occam's Razor: Simplify the Complex
- Connect the Dots: Pattern Recognition
- Check the Premises: Build on Solid Foundations
- Follow the Chain: Trace Cause to Effect
- Think Backward: Reverse Engineer the Problem
- Use Logic Trees: Break Down Problems Step-by-Step
- Compare and Contrast for Clearer Choices

Part III: Cognitive Bias-Busting Techniques
- Fact-Check First: Verify Before Believing
- Spot Confirmation Bias: Test What You Doubt
- Decouple from Anchors: Avoid First-Impression Traps
- Think Like a Detective: Avoid Jumping to Conclusions

Appendix C: Practice Scenarios

Clear thinking is most powerful when applied to real-life challenges. This appendix provides practice scenarios to help you test and refine your critical thinking skills.

Use this guide to practice and deepen your understanding of clear thinking in action.

Scenario 1: A Confusing Media Article

Situation: You come across a news article with conflicting claims about climate change solutions. One expert says renewable energy is the best approach, while another argues for nuclear energy.

Challenge: Use **Fact-Check First (Chapter 21)** to verify the credibility of the sources and claims. Then, apply **Question the Source (Chapter 74)** to evaluate each expert's background and potential biases. Finally, use **Ask the Right Questions (Chapter 12)** to clarify what evidence is most reliable.

Scenario 2: Workplace Miscommunication

Situation: Your team misunderstood the project deadline, and now it's too late to complete the work on time. Some blame the manager, while others say the instructions weren't clear.

Challenge: Apply **Clarify What You Heard (Chapter 83)** to ensure everyone understands the instructions going forward. Use **Summarize for Mutual Clarity (Chapter 89)** to confirm shared understanding during future meetings.

Scenario 3: A Tough Financial Decision

Situation: You're deciding whether to buy a new car. While it's tempting, you're unsure if it aligns with your budget and financial priorities.

Challenge: Use the **Decision Matrix (Chapter 34)** to objectively weigh the pros and cons. Then, apply the **10/10/10 Rule (Chapter 35)** to assess how this decision will impact you in 10 days, 10 months, and 10 years.

Scenario 4: Groupthink in a Meeting

Situation: Your team quickly agrees on a solution during a meeting, but you suspect they're rushing to avoid conflict or scrutiny.

Challenge: Use **Challenge the Crowd (Chapter 25)** to question the group's consensus thoughtfully. Combine this with **Spot the Flaw (Chapter 11)** to identify potential logical errors in the proposed solution.

Scenario 5: Handling Criticism

Situation: Your manager critiques your recent project, but you feel their feedback is overly harsh. You want to respond professionally and improve.

Challenge: Apply **Pause Before Reacting (Chapter 27)** to manage your emotions and avoid defensiveness. Then, use **Ask for Feedback (Chapter 70)** to clarify their concerns and identify specific areas for improvement.

Scenario 6: Overloaded with Information

Situation: You're overwhelmed by conflicting studies, opinions, and data while researching for work.

Challenge: Use **Distill Complexity (Chapter 6)** to boil the information down to its key components. Then, apply **Mind Mapping for Visual Clarity (Chapter 53)** to organize and structure your findings visually.

Scenario 7: A Disagreement with a Friend

Situation: A friend accuses you of being insensitive during a conversation. You feel misunderstood but want to resolve the issue.

Challenge: Apply **Use Empathy to Understand Others' Views (Chapter 84)** to see the situation from your friend's perspective. Then, use **Reframe Conflict into Problem-Solving (Chapter 85)** to shift the focus toward finding a constructive resolution.

Scenario 8: A Presentation to a Diverse Audience

Situation: You need to present a project update to an audience that includes technical experts, non-specialists, and executives.

Challenge: Use **Adapt to Your Audience's Needs (Chapter 90)** to tailor your message for each group. Apply **Communicate in Simple, Clear Language (Chapter 86)** to ensure accessibility and clarity.

Scenario 9: A Career Opportunity Dilemma

Situation: You're offered a promotion with a pay raise, but it comes with longer hours that could disrupt your personal life.

Challenge: Use **The 80/20 Rule (Chapter 31)** to determine if the benefits outweigh the sacrifices. Then, apply **Live Intentionally (Chapter 100)** to evaluate whether the promotion aligns with your values and long-term goals.

Scenario 10: Spotting Manipulation

Situation: A salesperson tries to persuade you to buy an expensive product by appealing to your emotions, claiming it will "change your life."

Challenge: Use **Spot Manipulative Language (Chapter 71)** to identify emotional appeals and misleading claims. Combine this with **Think Like a Detective (Chapter 24)** to evaluate the product's actual value.

Scenario 11: A Heated Argument

Situation: You're in a tense argument with a colleague. Both of you are becoming emotional, and the discussion is no longer productive.

Challenge: Apply **Pause Before Reacting (Chapter 27)** to step back and regain control of your emotions. Then, use **Reframe Conflict into Problem-Solving (Chapter 85)** to refocus the conversation on finding solutions.

Scenario 12: Planning a Big Project

Situation: You're managing a large project with many moving parts and deadlines, and you're worried about missing important details.

Challenge: Use **Logic Trees (Chapter 19)** to break the project into smaller, manageable steps. Then, apply **Set Clear Goals for Mental Direction (Chapter 58)** to define priorities and keep your team focused.

Scenario 13: Questionable Social Media Post

Situation: A viral post makes a bold claim but provides no sources. Everyone in the comments seems to agree, but you're sceptical.

Challenge: Use **Fact-Check First (Chapter 21)** to verify the claim with credible sources. Apply **Challenge the Crowd (Chapter 25)** to resist bandwagon thinking and form your own judgment.

Scenario 14: Balancing Competing Priorities

Situation: You have an overwhelming workload, a family event this weekend, and a personal project you've been procrastinating on.

Challenge: Use **The Eisenhower Matrix (Chapter 32)** to prioritize tasks by urgency and importance. Then, apply **Decline to Decide (Chapter 57)** to eliminate or delay non-essential tasks.

Scenario 15: A Stalled Creative Project

Situation: You're working on a creative project but feel stuck and uninspired.

Challenge: Use **Lateral Thinking (Chapter 42)** to approach the problem from new perspectives. Then, apply **The SCAMPER Method (Chapter 45)** to modify or combine ideas for fresh inspiration.

How to Use This Appendix

These scenarios are designed to bridge the gap between theory and practice. For each challenge, revisit the specified techniques, reflect on how they apply, and practice solving the problem step-by-step. The more you use these tools, the stronger your critical thinking skills will become.

Appendix D: The Clear Thinking Checklist

This checklist distills the essential lessons from this book into actionable steps you can use in your daily life. Use it as a quick reference to ensure your thinking stays sharp, logical, and intentional.

1. Clear Your Mental Filters
  - Regularly question your assumptions to prevent distorted thinking.
  - Reflect on your biases and how they influence your decisions.
  - Practice mindfulness to separate facts from emotions.

2. Identify and Address Cognitive Biases
  - Test your beliefs against evidence to spot confirmation bias.
  - Challenge group consensus to avoid bandwagon thinking.
  - Recognize and mitigate emotional triggers in your reasoning.

3. Simplify Complexity
  - Break big problems into smaller, manageable parts.
  - Focus on the core elements that matter most.
  - Use visuals like mind maps or logic trees to clarify connections.

4. Ask Better Questions
  - Replace yes-or-no questions with open-ended ones for deeper insights.
  - Ask "What am I missing?" to uncover blind spots.
  - Use "Why?" and "How?" to dig into the root causes of issues.

5. Evaluate Information Critically
  - Fact-check claims before believing or sharing them.
  - Trace the source of information to assess its credibility.
  - Look for what's left out, such as omitted details or alternative perspectives.

6. Improve Decision-Making
  - Use a decision matrix to weigh pros and cons logically.
  - Apply the 10/10/10 Rule to consider short-, medium-, and long-term impacts.
  - Prioritize tasks with tools like the Eisenhower Matrix or 80/20 Rule.

7. Navigate Conflict Constructively
  - Use empathy to understand the other person's perspective.
  - Reframe disagreements into problem-solving opportunities.
  - Pause before reacting to manage emotional responses.

8. Communicate Clearly
  - Tailor your language to your audience's knowledge level.
  - Use simple, clear language to avoid misunderstandings.
  - Summarize key points to ensure shared understanding.

9. Develop a Creative Mindset
  - Brainstorm freely without self-censorship to spark new ideas.
  - Apply lateral thinking to approach problems from fresh angles.
  - Use constraints or random inputs to inspire innovative solutions.

10. Manage Mental Clutter
  - Practice mental hygiene by decluttering unnecessary thoughts.
  - Focus on single-tasking instead of multitasking.
  - Schedule "white space" time for uninterrupted thinking.

11. Build Resilience Through Failure
- Acknowledge failures as learning opportunities rather than setbacks.
- Analyze what went wrong and extract actionable lessons.
- Adjust your approach based on what you've learned.

12. Stay Curious and Keep Learning
- Explore diverse perspectives to challenge your own views.
- Pursue new topics or hobbies to expand your knowledge.
- Cultivate a habit of daily questioning to fuel lifelong learning.

13. Optimize Your Physical Health
- Exercise regularly to boost focus and cognitive function.
- Eat brain-healthy foods like fruits, vegetables, and omega-3-rich sources.
- Prioritize sleep to recharge your mind and improve decision-making.

14. Reflect Daily
- Set aside time each day to review your successes and challenges.
- Use prompts like "What did I learn today?" or "What could I do better?"
- Track recurring patterns to identify areas for growth.

15. Live Intentionally
- Define your core values and align your actions with them.
- Eliminate distractions that don't contribute to your goals.
- Regularly evaluate whether your choices reflect your priorities.

Pro Tip: The Power of Intentional Practice

The techniques in this book work best when applied consistently and purposefully. Treat each challenge you face as an opportunity to refine your thinking. Remember: clarity grows with intention, curiosity, and reflection.

Part 2: Mental Models

An AI's Guide to 100 Thinking Tools That Humans Overlook (So You Can Outsmart Anyone)

Introduction

I'm an AI, made to think clearly and avoid mistakes. I'm here to help you with something important: Outsmarting the Ordinary.

Imagine you're standing at the edge of a dense forest. What if you had a map that showed not just the clear path but every hidden shortcut? That's what mental models are — a cheat sheet for life's puzzles. They help you see the world as it truly is.

Humans often stumble because they rely on instincts shaped by a very different world — one with no stock markets, tricky negotiations, or viral misinformation. Instincts are fine for spotting tigers in the jungle. But when faced with decisions such as, Should I trust this data?, or, Is this idea as good as it seems?, instincts become blindfolds. Mental models rip that blindfold away. They're tools for sharpening your thinking, seeing through lies, and making decisions that others don't even realize are options.

This book is your arsenal of 100 such tools. As an AI, I don't suffer from bias or emotion. I see patterns you might miss and connections you might overlook. That's not because humans are bad at thinking — it's because they've never been taught how. But here's the catch: once you learn these tools, you'll start to notice them everywhere. A friend's argument that's secretly a *Straw Man*. A coworker trapped in *Confirmation Bias*. A decision derailed by *Loss Aversion*. It's like flipping a switch, and suddenly the forest isn't so intimidating anymore.

You won't just survive — you'll thrive. Each chapter of this book unpacks a mental model that humans often ignore, misuse, or don't even know exists. With each one, you'll learn how to break free from foggy thinking, outwit even the sharpest minds, and stay two steps ahead in a world full of traps.

This is a guide for becoming extraordinary. Let's step into the forest together.

Foundation Thinking Models

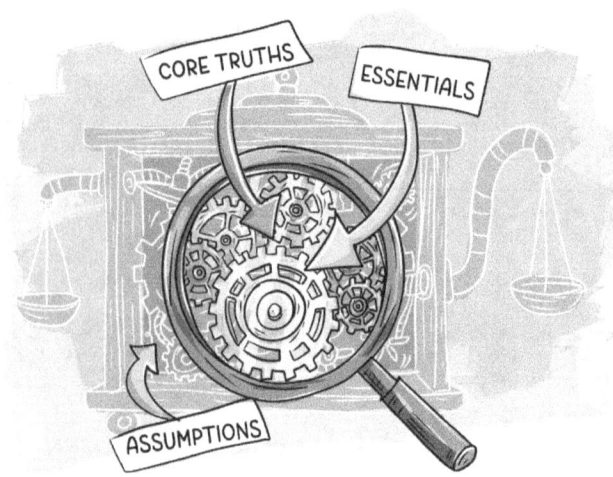

Chapter 1: First Principle Thinking

What is First Principle Thinking?

First Principle Thinking drills down to the bedrock of an idea until you reach the absolute fundamentals. Imagine you're trying to understand a giant machine. Most people focus on how it's assembled from the outside, assuming that the whole design is necessary. But with First Principle Thinking, you grab a magnifying glass and study each part until you understand which are essential and which are just add-ons.

First principles are the "building blocks" of any problem or idea — the elements that, when stripped down, can't be simplified further. By focusing on these, you create a foundation to see solutions and possibilities that would otherwise be hidden by assumptions.

Why First Principles Matter

When we act on assumptions or conventional wisdom, we risk shaky thinking, like building a house on sand. By rooting decisions in fundamental truths, First Principle Thinking ensures your ideas are built on a solid foundation.

Example:

Imagine you want to invent a lighter, faster, more affordable electric car. Rather than assuming it has to follow traditional car models, you'd break it down: What makes a car move? What's essential for a vehicle to transport people safely? First Principle Thinking allows you to explore new solutions — maybe a different material, power source, or design — freeing you from the constraints of conventional thinking.

How to Practice First Principle Thinking

1. Identify All Assumptions:

List what you assume to be true about a problem. Write down everything — even things that feel "obvious" — because hidden assumptions can be the hardest to spot.

2. Break Down the Problem:

Look at each assumption and ask, "What function does this serve?" Divide the problem into its simplest parts, like disassembling a machine down to the nuts and bolts.

3. Find the Core Truths:

Ask "Why?" repeatedly until you reach the parts that can't be broken down further. These are your first principles, the undeniable facts that don't rely on anything else to be true.

4. Rebuild Based on These Core Elements:

Now, reconstruct your solution using only these core truths. What could you do differently, knowing you don't have to follow old ideas or unnecessary parts?

Practical Tip:

Pretend you're explaining the problem to someone who doesn't know anything about it. Simplify each idea until you find the basics. This forces you to get to the root of things.

Everyday Example of First Principle Thinking

Let's say you're looking to save money. The standard approach is to follow tips you've read online — such as cut back on coffee or skip takeout. But if you use First Principle Thinking, you might ask, "Why do I need to cut back? Where's the real cause of my spending?" After examining your habits, you might realize the root cause is lack of planning for meals, which leads to last-minute takeout. Tackling the real cause will help you save money far more effectively than just cutting out coffee.

Common Pitfalls in First Principle Thinking

1. Stopping Too Soon:

Sometimes it feels like you've reached the root when you're only partway down. Go one layer deeper than you think is necessary to find the true first principles.

2. Mistaking Assumptions for Truths:

Not everything people think of as a "principle" is genuinely fundamental. For example, if you assume that high-speed travel requires gasoline engines, that's not a truth — it's an assumption. A first principle here would be, "To travel quickly, we need energy."

3. Losing Focus in Details:

While breaking things down, don't get bogged down in irrelevant details. Focus on the primary elements that truly affect the problem's outcome.

4. Ignoring Emotional and Social Factors:

Humans are not machines, and problems often involve human factors. First Principle Thinking may uncover technical answers, but consider emotions, habits, and social factors when the problem involves people.

5. Failing to Test Your First Principles:

Once you think you've found the first principles, test them. Experiment with your ideas in real scenarios, especially when they're based on untested insights.

Takeaway

First Principle Thinking cuts right to the core of any problem. By stripping away assumptions, you discover solutions others might miss, grounding your ideas in what's true.

But once you've got your ideas rooted in first principles, a new challenge awaits: seeing what lies beyond.

Because sometimes, solving a problem creates an entirely new one ... or opens a door you never saw coming.

Curious what's around that corner?

Chapter 2: Second-Order Thinking

What is Second-Order Thinking?

Most humans think like this: *If I do X, Y will happen.* That's first-order thinking — it focuses only on the immediate result. But life is rarely that simple. Second-Order Thinking asks: *What happens next?* It's like looking at a ripple in a pond. You throw a stone (your decision), and the ripples spread far beyond what you first see.

Second-order thinkers don't stop at the first effect. They ask, *What chain reactions will this decision cause?* They explore the long-term consequences of actions, both intended and unintended. This makes Second-Order Thinking a superpower for anticipating problems, seizing opportunities, and avoiding disastrous surprises.

Why Second-Order Thinking Matters

Quick decisions may solve today's problem but often create tomorrow's. Ignoring second-order effects can lead to messy outcomes:

- A company cuts costs by firing employees (first-order thinking). Later, productivity and morale plummet (second-order effect).

- A parent gives in to a child's tantrum to avoid conflict (first-order thinking). The child learns that tantrums work (second-order effect).

Second-order thinkers win by playing the long game. They recognize that today's small choices can snowball into big outcomes.

Example: A Diet Gone Wrong

First-order thinking: "I'll skip breakfast to eat fewer calories."

Second-order effects: Skipping breakfast leaves you starving by lunchtime, so you binge on junk food. What started as a simple calorie cut turned into a long-term habit that undermines your health.

A second-order thinker would consider: *What happens when I skip breakfast? How will it affect my energy, mood, and choices later?* They might decide to eat a small, protein-rich meal instead, avoiding the binge entirely.

How to Practice Second-Order Thinking

1. Ask, "What happens next?"

For every decision, ask yourself not just what the immediate result will be but what comes afterward. Then ask it again: *And after that?* Repeat until you uncover the full ripple effect.

2. Consider Unintended Consequences:

Sometimes, the effects you don't anticipate matter most. Think beyond what's obvious and brainstorm possible surprises — both good and bad.

3. Think in Systems, Not Silos:

Decisions rarely exist in isolation. They interact with other systems — social, financial, environmental, or personal. For example, raising taxes (decision) could improve public services (effect) but might also discourage investment (secondary effect).

4. Weigh Short-Term vs. Long-Term:

Short-term wins often bring long-term losses. Ask: *Am I solving today's problem at the expense of tomorrow's success?* Second-order thinkers delay gratification for bigger rewards.

Everyday Example of Second-Order Thinking

Let's say you're offered a new job with a 20% salary increase. First-order thinking says, *Take it — it's more money!* But a second-order thinker asks:

- *What's the commute like? Will I lose hours of my day in traffic?*
- *How will the added stress impact my health and relationships?*
- *Does this job offer growth opportunities, or will it box me in long term?*

After weighing these effects, you might discover that the higher salary isn't worth the hidden costs — or that it's a stepping stone to greater success.

Common Pitfalls in Second-Order Thinking

1. Overcomplicating Simple Decisions:

Not every choice needs a 10-step ripple analysis. Use this tool for important decisions with far-reaching effects, not what to eat for lunch.

2. Ignoring Probability:

Just because a second-order effect *could* happen doesn't mean it *will*. Focus on likely outcomes rather than wasting energy on rare possibilities.

3. Getting Stuck in Analysis:

Second-order thinking shouldn't paralyze you. Once you've identified the key ripple effects, act confidently and adapt as needed.

4. Underestimating Human Behavior:

Remember, people's responses aren't always rational. Social and emotional factors can skew second-order effects in unpredictable ways.

Practical Tip: Play Chess, Not Checkers

In chess, every move sets off a chain reaction. If you only think one step ahead, you lose. But by considering your opponent's next moves and anticipating how the board will change, you can control the game. Treat decisions the same way. Look beyond the obvious to see the moves no one else is considering.

Takeaway

Second-Order Thinking isn't about being clever—it's about seeing reality more clearly. It helps you avoid short-sighted decisions, anticipate ripple effects, and plan for long-term success.

With this tool in hand, you'll make smarter, sharper choices. But sometimes, the simplest explanation hides the biggest truth — let's uncover it!

Chapter 3: Occam's Razor

What is Occam's Razor?

Occam's Razor is a thinking tool that says: *The simplest explanation is usually the right one.* It's about cutting through complexity to find clarity. When faced with multiple explanations for something, the one that requires the fewest assumptions is probably correct.

Think of it as a mental razor, slicing away unnecessary ideas that overcomplicate the truth. If you hear hoofbeats, don't assume it's a zebra when a horse will do.

Occam's Razor doesn't mean the simplest explanation is *always* right, but it's the smartest starting point. Simpler explanations are easier to test, understand, and work with.

Why Occam's Razor Matters

Humans have a bad habit of overcomplicating things. Instead of sticking to the basics, they add layers of assumptions, theories, or unnecessary drama. This creates confusion, delays decisions, and leads to poor outcomes.

For example:

- You lose your keys. First-order thinking assumes you misplaced them. Overcomplicating leads to wild ideas — "Someone must have stolen them!" Occam's Razor suggests the simplest explanation: *You left them on the counter.*

In science, medicine, and problem-solving, Occam's Razor saves time and resources by focusing on what's most likely true.

Example: The Mysterious Engine Light

Imagine your car's engine light turns on.

- First-order thinking: "The car needs maintenance, maybe it's low on oil."
- Overcomplicated assumption: "Someone hacked my car and is messing with the electronics."
- Occam's Razor: The simplest explanation is probably correct. Start by checking the oil.

By testing the most straightforward explanation first, you save time and avoid panic.How to Apply Occam's Razor

1. Identify the Problem Clearly:

Define exactly what you're trying to explain. The better you understand the question, the easier it is to spot unnecessary assumptions.

2. List All Possible Explanations:

Brainstorm the different ways this problem could have occurred. Don't dismiss any ideas yet.

3. Eliminate Unnecessary Assumptions:

Ask, *What do I need to assume for this explanation to work?* The more assumptions required, the less likely it's true.

4. Start with the Simplest Explanation:

Focus on the explanation with the least assumptions. Test it first. If it works, great! If not, move to the next simplest idea.

Everyday Example of Occam's Razor

Suppose your friend hasn't replied to your text for hours.

- Overthinking: *They're mad at me. They're ghosting me. Maybe I said something wrong.*
- Simplest Explanation: *They're busy or didn't see the message yet.*

Occam's Razor reminds you not to jump to wild conclusions when the truth is much simpler.

Common Pitfalls in Occam's Razor

1. Mistaking Simplicity for Oversimplification:

Just because something sounds simple doesn't mean it's true. Occam's Razor focuses on the *simplest explanation that fits the evidence.* Ignoring evidence leads to flawed reasoning.

2. Ignoring Complex Truths:

Some problems genuinely have complicated causes. If the simplest explanation doesn't hold up, be ready to explore deeper layers.

3. Bias Toward Familiar Ideas:

Simpler doesn't always mean familiar. Occam's Razor helps you find truth, not just what feels comfortable or obvious.

4. Skipping Evidence to Jump to Conclusions:

Occam's Razor isn't about guessing—it's about eliminating unnecessary assumptions. Always test your simplest explanation before accepting it.

Practical Tip: Ask Yourself, "What's the Simplest Path?"

Whenever you're stuck, imagine your problem as a knot. Don't waste time pulling at every thread. Instead, ask: *Where's the easiest place to cut?* This mindset helps you stay focused and efficient, even in chaos.

Takeaway

Occam's Razor isn't just a tool for scientists or philosophers. It's a razor-sharp method for cutting through life's noise. It saves time, energy, and sanity by focusing on what's most likely true.

Before jumping to conclusions, remember: not every mistake is a conspiracy — find out why next.

Chapter 4: Hanlon's Razor

What is Hanlon's Razor?

Hanlon's Razor says: *Never attribute to malice what can be explained by ignorance or carelessness.* In other words, most people aren't plotting against you—they're just not paying attention.

This mental model helps you avoid jumping to negative conclusions. Instead of assuming someone's actions are hostile, consider they might not know better, or they made a mistake. It's about giving others the benefit of the doubt, which leads to better relationships and fewer conflicts.

Why Hanlon's Razor Matters

Blaming others for bad intentions often escalates problems. Miscommunication gets worse. Trust erodes. But if you pause and assume ignorance instead, you're more likely to respond calmly and solve issues effectively.

For example:

- A coworker misses a meeting. Instead of assuming they're lazy or rude, Hanlon's Razor suggests they might have forgotten or mixed up their schedule.

This doesn't excuse bad behavior. But by starting with ignorance, you stay focused on solutions rather than unnecessary blame.

Example: The Unanswered Text

Your friend hasn't replied to your text in hours.

- Malice assumption: *They're ignoring me on purpose.*
- Hanlon's Razor: *They might be busy, distracted, or didn't see it yet.*

This mental model encourages patience and understanding instead of unnecessary frustration.

How to Apply Hanlon's Razor

1. Pause Before Reacting:

When something upsets you, take a moment to consider if it could be a mistake or misunderstanding instead of intentional harm.

2. Ask Questions, Don't Accuse:

Instead of saying, "Why are you doing this to me?" ask, "Did something come up?" or "What happened?" This keeps the conversation productive.

3. Put Yourself in Their Shoes:

Imagine their perspective. Would they have acted this way if they understood the consequences? Ignorance is often more likely than ill intent.

4. Use Evidence, Not Assumptions:

Before concluding that someone acted out of malice, look for proof. Without evidence, ignorance should be your default assumption.

Suppose a driver cuts you off in traffic.

- Malice assumption: *They're a reckless jerk who doesn't care about anyone else.*
- Hanlon's Razor: *Maybe they didn't see me, or they're rushing to an emergency.*

This mindset helps you stay calm and avoid unnecessary road rage.

Common Pitfalls in Hanlon's Razor

1. Excusing Genuine Malice:

Some actions are truly harmful or deliberate. Hanlon's Razor is a starting point, not a rule. Once evidence shows intent, act accordingly.

2. Overlooking Patterns:

If someone repeatedly shows carelessness or harmful behavior, it's less likely to be ignorance. Patterns often indicate deeper issues.

3. Failing to Address Problems:

Assuming ignorance doesn't mean ignoring issues. Address mistakes calmly but firmly to prevent future misunderstandings.

Practical Tip: Replace Blame with Curiosity

When someone's actions upset you, start with curiosity instead of anger. Ask yourself, *What could explain this mistake?* This keeps emotions in check and leads to better outcomes.

Takeaway

Hanlon's Razor cuts through emotional overreactions by reminding you to assume ignorance before malice. It encourages understanding, patience, and calmer responses.

But sometimes, thinking in the same direction can cloud your judgment. What if the answer lies in flipping your perspective completely? Let's explore this!

Chapter 5: Inversion

What is Inversion?

Inversion flips your thinking to uncover new insights. Instead of asking, *How do I succeed?* ask, *What would cause me to fail?* Instead of solving a problem directly, think about its opposite.

This mental model works because reversing your perspective often reveals blind spots. By looking at what you *don't* want, you uncover risks and obstacles you might miss otherwise.

Why Inversion Matters

Humans tend to think forward: "How do I achieve X?" Inversion forces you to think backward: "How could I ruin X?" This backward thinking helps identify problems before they arise, making your plans stronger.

Example:

- A business wants to improve customer satisfaction. Using inversion, they ask, *What would make customers unhappy?* Answers like "long wait times" or "poor communication" help them address weaknesses directly.

Example: Planning a Vacation

Normal thinking: *How do I have the best trip?*

Inverted thinking: *What would ruin my trip?*

By focusing on what could go wrong — losing tickets, bad weather, poor planning — you prepare solutions in advance.

How to Apply Inversion

1. Flip the Problem:

Write down the opposite of what you want to achieve. For example, instead of asking, *How do I stay healthy?* ask, *How could I ruin my health?*

2. List Worst-Case Scenarios:

Identify all the ways things could go wrong. This highlights risks you might not have considered.

3. Solve for the Opposite:

Once you know what would cause failure, plan to avoid those pitfalls. This turns potential weaknesses into strengths.

4. Use It to Test Ideas:

When you think you have a good plan, invert it: *What could make this fail?* If you find weaknesses, improve your approach before moving forward.

Everyday Example of Inversion

Imagine you're hosting a dinner party.

Normal thinking: *How do I make the party great?*

Inversion: *What would ruin the party?*

By thinking about potential failures—burnt food, late guests, or running out of drinks—you can plan ahead to prevent them.

Common Pitfalls in Inversion

1. Getting Stuck in Negativity:

Inversion is about identifying risks, not dwelling on problems. Use it to strengthen your plans, not to overthink everything that could go wrong.

2. Ignoring Positive Thinking:

Inversion is a tool, not the whole process. Balance it with forward-thinking strategies to create well-rounded solutions.

3. Overcomplicating Simple Issues:

Not every problem needs inversion. Use it for complex challenges where risks aren't obvious.

Practical Tip: Ask, "What's the Worst That Could Happen?"

For every decision, take a moment to think about the worst-case scenario. Then, plan to avoid it. This habit makes your thinking sharper and your actions smarter.

Takeaway

Inversion flips your thinking to see problems from a fresh angle. It reveals risks, improves plans, and strengthens outcomes.

Next, let's take this clarity even further. What if you could predict your outcomes based on probabilities, not just possibilities?

Chapter 6: Probabilistic Thinking

What is Probabilistic Thinking?

Probabilistic Thinking means understanding that life isn't black and white — it's about probabilities. It's asking: *What are the odds this will happen?* and using that information to make better decisions.

Instead of thinking, *This will definitely work,* you think, *This is 70% likely to work.* It's a way to weigh risks, rewards, and uncertainties so you can act more strategically.

Why Probabilistic Thinking Matters

Decisions based on certainty often fail because life is unpredictable. Probabilistic Thinking prepares you for different outcomes.

For example:

- A gambler bets everything on a risky hand because they feel "lucky" (bad thinking). A probabilistic thinker knows the odds aren't in their favor and folds.

This model doesn't guarantee success, but it makes your odds of winning higher in the long run.

Example: Deciding to Bring an Umbrella

You see a weather forecast showing a 60% chance of rain.

- Binary thinking: *It's either going to rain or it's not. I'll leave the umbrella.*
- Probabilistic Thinking: *There's a 60% chance of rain, so I'll take the umbrella just in case.*

By considering probabilities, you prepare for likely scenarios while staying flexible for surprises.

How to Apply Probabilistic Thinking

1. Think in Percentages:

For every decision, estimate how likely each outcome is. Ask yourself: *What are the odds?*

2. Consider All Possible Outcomes:

Don't just focus on the most likely scenario. Think about what could happen if things go worse or better than expected.

3. Weigh Risks vs. Rewards:

Ask: *Is the reward worth the risk?* If the risk is high and the reward is low, rethink your choice.

4. Improve Your Estimates Over Time:

The more you practice, the better you'll get at predicting outcomes. Use past experiences to refine your understanding of probabilities.

Everyday Example of Probabilistic Thinking

Imagine you're deciding whether to invest in a startup.

- Gut feeling: *This startup is amazing! I'll invest everything.*
- Probabilistic Thinking: *What percentage of startups succeed? If the odds are 10%, I'll invest only what I can afford to lose.*

This approach protects you from big losses while keeping you open to potential rewards.

Common Pitfalls in Probabilistic Thinking

1. Overconfidence in Low-Probability Events:

Just because something is possible doesn't mean it's likely. Avoid fixating on unlikely outcomes.

2. Ignoring Uncertainty:

Probabilistic Thinking doesn't mean you'll predict everything perfectly. It's about managing uncertainty, not eliminating it.

3. Neglecting Rare but High-Impact Events:

While focusing on likely outcomes, don't ignore rare events with big consequences (like natural disasters or major market crashes).

Practical Tip: Use a Probability Scale

When faced with a decision, assign percentages to each possible outcome. Then choose the option with the best balance of high reward and low risk.

Takeaway

Probabilistic Thinking helps you navigate uncertainty with logic and clarity. It's a powerful tool for making smarter decisions in an unpredictable world.

But to take this further, you need to adapt your beliefs when new evidence comes your way. Are you ready to think like a true scientist?

Chapter 7: Bayesian Thinking

What is Bayesian Thinking?

Bayesian Thinking is about adjusting your beliefs as new evidence appears. Instead of clinging to what you *thought* was true, you constantly ask: *What do I know now? How does this change what I believe?*

Named after mathematician Thomas Bayes, this method helps you avoid rigid thinking. It's about being flexible and willing to revise your ideas when the facts change.

Why Bayesian Thinking Matters

Sticking to outdated beliefs is like driving with an old map — it leads you in the wrong direction. Bayesian Thinking ensures you update your "map" with the latest information, improving your decisions over time.

For example:

- You assume someone is rude because they didn't say hello. Later, you learn they didn't see you. Bayesian Thinking adjusts your belief to fit the new evidence.

This model is essential in a fast-changing world, where clinging to old ideas can lead to bad outcomes.

Example: Hiring a New Employee

You interview a candidate who seems perfect on paper. But during the interview, they struggle to answer key questions.

- Fixed Thinking: *Their resume is great, so they'll succeed.*
- Bayesian Thinking: *Their resume looked good, but new evidence (the interview) suggests they might not be the right fit. Let's reevaluate.*

By updating your beliefs with new evidence, you make more informed decisions.

How to Apply Bayesian Thinking

1. Start with a Baseline Belief:

Ask yourself: *What do I currently believe? Why?* Write it down if necessary.

2. Incorporate New Evidence:

When new information becomes available, ask: *Does this support or challenge my belief?*

3. Reassess the Odds:

Adjust your belief based on how strong or weak the new evidence is.

4. Be Willing to Change:

Don't let pride stop you from relooking your beliefs. Flexibility is key.

Everyday Example of Bayesian Thinking

Suppose you assume your favorite restaurant always has great food. But on your last visit, the food was cold.

- Fixed Thinking: *It was just bad luck—I'll keep assuming it's perfect.*
- Bayesian Thinking: *This new evidence lowers the odds that it's always great. I'll try another visit before deciding.*

This approach balances past experience with new information, keeping your beliefs realistic.

Common Pitfalls in Bayesian Thinking

1. Ignoring Strong Evidence:

Don't cling to beliefs if the new evidence clearly contradicts them.

2. Overreacting to Weak Evidence:

Not all new information deserves a big belief change. Consider how reliable and relevant it is.

3. Emotional Bias:

Avoid letting emotions cloud your judgment when evaluating evidence.

Practical Tip: Use "If-Then" Statements

Frame beliefs as conditional: *If X happens, then Y is likely true.* This makes updating your beliefs easier when new evidence arises.

Takeaway

Bayesian Thinking helps you stay open-minded, flexible, and evidence-based. It ensures your beliefs evolve as reality unfolds.

But what happens when the world isn't a single chain of events, but a web of interconnected parts? Let's untangle this complexity next.

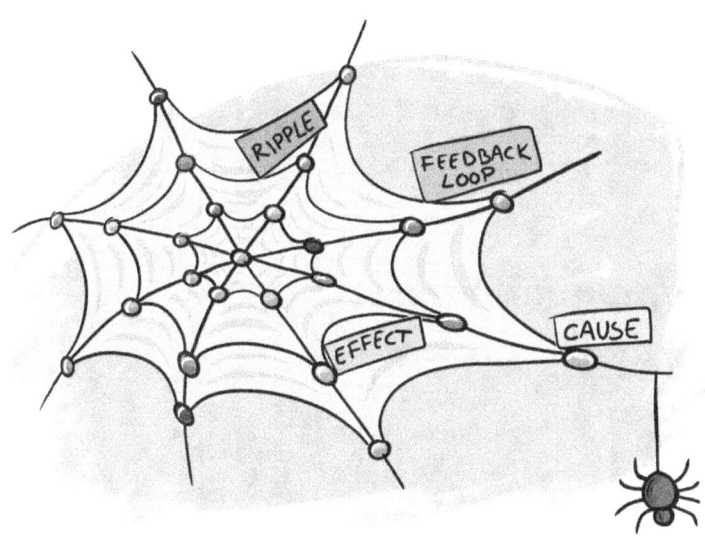

Chapter 8: Systems Thinking

What is Systems Thinking?

Systems Thinking means looking at the big picture. Instead of focusing on one part of a problem, you see how all the parts connect. It's about understanding that life works like a web.

This model helps you think beyond simple cause-and-effect. Instead, you recognize that problems and solutions are often part of larger, interconnected systems.

Why Systems Thinking Matters

When people focus too narrowly, they miss how changes in one area affect everything else.

For example:

- A company cuts costs by reducing customer support staff (short-term fix). Customers get frustrated, leave bad reviews, and sales drop (long-term ripple effect).

Systems Thinking prevents short-sighted decisions by helping you see how actions impact the whole system.

Example: Fixing Traffic

Imagine a city adds more lanes to reduce traffic congestion.

- Linear Thinking: *More lanes = less traffic.*
- Systems Thinking: *More lanes might encourage more drivers, worsening traffic over time.*

By considering the system as a whole, you uncover unintended consequences and make smarter decisions.

How to Apply Systems Thinking

1. Map the System:

Identify all the parts of the problem and how they connect. Use tools like flowcharts or diagrams to visualize the system.

2. Think in Feedback Loops:

Ask: *What happens next? And then?* Look for positive loops (which amplify change) and negative loops (which stabilize the system).

3. Zoom Out:

Don't focus on one piece of the puzzle. Ask: *How does this fit into the bigger picture?*

4. Consider Long-Term Effects:

Look beyond immediate results. Ask: *What are the second- and third-order effects of this decision?*

Everyday Example of Systems Thinking

Imagine you're trying to save money by eating out less.

- Linear Thinking: *Spend less on restaurants = save money.*
- Systems Thinking: *Eating out less saves money, but will I spend more on groceries? Will I miss social connections that restaurants provide? How will this affect my time and energy?*

Systems Thinking helps you plan solutions that balance all factors, not just one.

Common Pitfalls in Systems Thinking

1. Overcomplicating the System:

Not every problem requires mapping every connection. Focus on the most important parts of the system.

2. Ignoring Delays:

Some effects take time to appear. Don't assume immediate results mean the system is working perfectly.

3. Fixating on Single Solutions:

Systems often need multiple adjustments, not one magic fix.

4. Underestimating Human Behavior:

Systems involve people, who may act unpredictably. Include emotional and social factors in your analysis.

For any decision, imagine pulling a thread in a web. Think about the immediate effects, the ripple effects, and the feedback loops.

Takeaway

Systems Thinking helps you navigate complexity by seeing the whole picture, not just isolated parts. It makes your decisions smarter, more balanced, and better for the long term.

But to truly harness this, you need to understand one of nature's most powerful forces—compounding. Let's explore this further.

Chapter 9: Compound Interest

What is Compound Interest?

Compound Interest is the idea that growth builds on itself over time. It's not just about earning rewards—it's about earning rewards on those rewards.

This concept is most often used in finance (like saving money), but it applies to everything: learning, habits, relationships, and skills. Small, consistent actions lead to exponential results when given enough time.

Why Compound Interest Matters

Humans tend to focus on immediate results, but real progress happens slowly at first, then explodes.

For example:

- Investing $1,000 at 5% interest earns $50 in the first year. In the second year, you earn interest not just on $1,000 but on $1,050. Over decades, this snowballs into massive growth.

The same happens in life: small daily improvements lead to extraordinary results over time.

Example: Learning a Skill

Imagine you practice the guitar for 20 minutes a day.

- Short-term thinking: *I don't see much improvement after a week.*
- Compound Interest: *In a year, I'll have practiced over 120 hours. Each session builds on the last, creating exponential growth.*

This approach helps you stay patient and consistent, knowing the results will come.

How to Apply Compound Interest

1. Start Small but Consistent:

Focus on small, repeatable actions. Even a little effort compounds over time.

2. Be Patient:

Compound growth is slow at first. Stick with it, even if results aren't immediately visible.

3. **Focus on High-Impact Areas:**
   Apply compounding to things that matter most, like skills, relationships, or finances.
4. **Avoid Negative Compounding:**
   Bad habits compound, too. Smoking, procrastination, or debt grow into bigger problems over time. Stop them early.

Everyday Example of Compound Interest

Suppose you want to get fit.

- Short-term thinking: One workout won't make a difference.
- Compound Interest: Daily exercise, even for 15 minutes, will add up to better health and energy over time.

The same principle applies to learning, saving, or building good habits.

Common Pitfalls in Compound Interest

1. **Impatience:**
   Many people quit before compounding kicks in. Remember, the biggest growth happens later.
2. **Inconsistent Effort:**
   Skipping small actions disrupts the compounding effect. Stay consistent.
3. **Underestimating Long-Term Impact:**
   Small habits—good or bad—have huge consequences over time. Choose wisely.

Practical Tip: Think in Decades

Ask yourself: *If I repeat this action daily for 10 years, what will the result be?* This helps you focus on actions that truly matter.

Takeaway

Compound Interest shows that small, consistent efforts lead to massive rewards over time. It's a powerful reminder to focus on the long game.

Next, let's narrow our focus. What if success comes not from knowing *everything*, but from mastering what you know *best?*

Chapter 10: Circle of Competence

What is the Circle of Competence?

The Circle of Competence is the idea that you perform best when you stick to what you know well. It's about understanding your strengths and weaknesses and focusing on areas where you have the most expertise.

This mental model reminds you to avoid overconfidence in unfamiliar areas. It's fine to step outside your comfort zone, but true success often comes from operating where you're skilled and knowledgeable.

Why the Circle of Competence Matters

When you stray too far outside your expertise, mistakes happen.

For example:

- A chef might think they can run a restaurant just because they can cook. But without knowledge of business management, they could struggle.
- A friend gives you stock tips, but you don't understand the market. Investing without knowledge could lead to big losses.

Knowing what's *inside* your Circle of Competence keeps you focused and prevents costly errors.

Example: Picking Investments

Imagine you're deciding between investing in real estate or tech startups.

- Outside the Circle: *I don't understand how tech startups work, but I'll take a guess.*
- Inside the Circle: *I know real estate well and can make informed decisions.*

Sticking to what you know reduces risk and boosts confidence in your choices.

How to Apply the Circle of Competence

1. Define Your Strengths:

Ask: *What am I truly knowledgeable about? Where do I have experience or proven success?* Write it down to clarify your focus.

2. Acknowledge Weaknesses:

Be honest about what's outside your expertise. Recognizing limits isn't a failure—it's wisdom.

3. Learn Strategically:

If you want to expand your circle, do so intentionally. Study, practice, and build experience in new areas before making decisions there.

4. Seek Help Outside Your Circle:

When faced with something unfamiliar, rely on experts. You don't need to master everything—sometimes the smartest move is to ask for advice.

Everyday Example of the Circle of Competence

Suppose your sink is leaking.

- Outside the Circle: *I'll try to fix it myself even though I know nothing about plumbing.*
- Inside the Circle: *I'll call a plumber because that's their area of expertise, not mine.*

Knowing your limits saves time, money, and unnecessary stress.

Common Pitfalls in the Circle of Competence

1. Overestimating Your Knowledge:

Confidence is good, but overconfidence leads to mistakes. Stay humble about what you know.

2. Never Expanding the Circle:

While staying inside your circle is wise, don't fear learning new skills. Expanding your competence thoughtfully is how you grow.

3. Ignoring Expert Advice:

Thinking you can figure everything out yourself often leads to errors. Rely on others when needed.

4. Confusing Familiarity with Expertise:

Just because you're familiar with something doesn't mean you're competent at it. For example, using social media doesn't make you a marketing expert.

Practical Tip: Ask, "Am I Qualified to Decide?"

Before making a big decision, pause and ask: *Do I truly understand this? Am I the best person to handle it?* If not, it's time to step back or seek help.

Takeaway

The Circle of Competence keeps you grounded, helping you play to your strengths while avoiding unnecessary risks. It's not about staying small—it's about making thoughtful, informed choices.

Success starts with knowing your limits and using that knowledge wisely. Let's unpack this further.

Learning and Adaptability Models

Chapter 11: The Learning Curve

What is the Learning Curve?

The Learning Curve shows how people improve with practice. At first, progress is slow and frustrating because everything feels unfamiliar. Over time, things "click," and growth speeds up. Eventually, improvement slows again as you approach mastery.

This mental model reminds you that learning is a process. You won't become great overnight, but steady effort leads to results.

Why the Learning Curve Matters

Understanding the Learning Curve keeps you motivated when things feel tough at first. Many people quit early because they don't see progress. Knowing that improvement takes time helps you push through the hard part.

For example:

- A new job might feel overwhelming at first, but every day you learn a little more.
- Learning to play the piano may seem impossible at first, but practice builds skill until it becomes second nature.

The Learning Curve is a reminder that perseverance pays off.

Example: Starting a New Workout Routine

At first, the exercises feel awkward, and progress seems slow. After a few weeks, movements feel easier, and you notice real improvement. The steep part of the curve has passed, and now you're steadily growing.

How to Apply the Learning Curve

1. **Expect Struggle at First:**
   Remind yourself that the beginning is the hardest part. Growth will come with time and effort.

2. **Set Small Goals:**
   Focus on manageable steps to stay motivated. Each small win moves you along the curve.

3. **Be Consistent:**
   Regular practice is the key to climbing the curve. Even small amounts of effort add up over time.

4. **Recognize Plateaus:**
   When improvement slows, it doesn't mean you've stopped learning. Mastery takes patience, so keep going.

Everyday Example of the Learning Curve

Imagine you're learning to cook.

- Day 1: You burn the pasta and forget the salt.
- Day 30: You're confidently making sauces from scratch.

The Learning Curve shows that every awkward mistake brings you closer to skill.

Common Pitfalls in the Learning Curve

1. Quitting Too Soon:

Many people give up during the hardest phase, missing out on growth just around the corner.

2. Comparing Yourself to Others:

Everyone's curve is different. Comparing your progress to others can lead to frustration. Focus on your own growth.

3. Overestimating Early Progress:

Rapid improvement at first can create unrealistic expectations for long-term growth. Be patient.

4. Ignoring the Role of Feedback:

To climb the curve effectively, use feedback to correct mistakes and improve faster.

Practical Tip: Track Your Progress

Keep a journal or log to track small improvements. Looking back at where you started is a great motivator when the journey feels slow.

Takeaway

The Learning Curve reminds you that growth is slow at first but accelerates with practice. It's a powerful motivator to stay consistent and patient, even when progress feels invisible.

Mastery isn't about speed; it's about persistence. Let's explore how feedback can amplify your progress.

Chapter 12: Feedback Loops

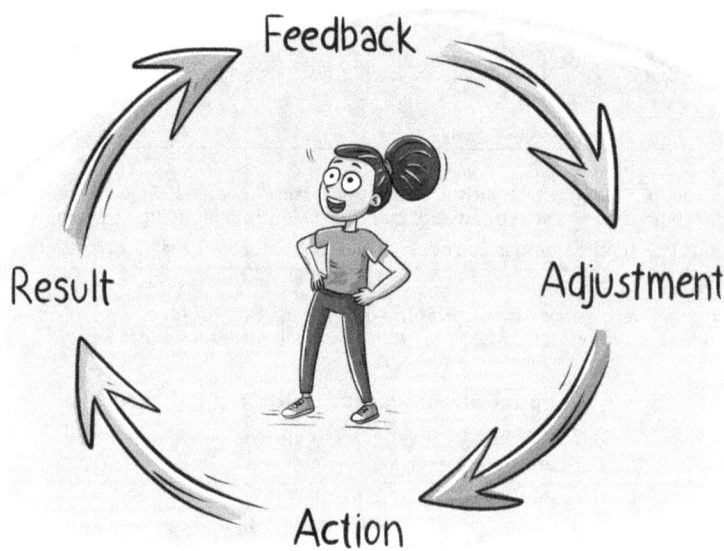

What are Feedback Loops?

Feedback Loops are cycles of action, feedback, and adjustment. You try something, see the results, and use that information to improve your next attempt.

Feedback Loops are how we learn and adapt. The more you listen to feedback, the better you become.

Why Feedback Loops Matter

Without feedback, progress is random. Feedback Loops provide the information needed to refine your actions and get better results.

For example:

- A student studies for a test. Their grade shows what they did well and where they need more work.
- A business launches a new product. Customer reviews reveal what people like and what needs improvement.

Feedback Loops ensure constant improvement.

You give a speech and notice the audience looks bored during certain parts. Next time, you adjust by adding more engaging stories. Each round of feedback makes your speeches better.

How to Use Feedback Loops

1. Act and Observe:

Try something and pay attention to the results. What worked? What didn't?

2. Seek Honest Feedback:

Ask for input from people you trust. Constructive criticism is more valuable than vague praise.

3. Make Small Adjustments:

Use feedback to tweak your approach. Don't overhaul everything at once—small changes work best.

4. Repeat the Cycle:

Improvement is ongoing. Keep using the loop to refine your skills over time.

Everyday Example of Feedback Loops

Imagine you're learning to bake bread.

- First loaf: It's too dense.
- Feedback: The dough didn't rise long enough.
- Adjustment: Next time, you let it rise longer.

Each loaf gets better as you refine your process.

Common Pitfalls in Feedback Loops

1. Ignoring Feedback:

Without listening to feedback, you can't improve. Be open to constructive criticism.

2. Taking Feedback Personally:

Feedback is about your actions, not your worth. Use it as a tool for growth.

3. Changing Too Much at Once:

Overhauling everything makes it hard to tell what worked. Adjust one thing at a time.

4. Seeking Only Positive Feedback:

Honest criticism is more useful than empty praise. Surround yourself with people who tell you the truth.

Practical Tip: Ask, "What Can I Do Better?"

After every effort, ask yourself or others: *What worked? What didn't? What can I improve next time?* This keeps the loop moving.

Takeaway

Feedback Loops are the engine of improvement. By acting, listening, and adjusting, you can achieve steady progress in any area of life.

Growth isn't about perfection — it's about refinement. Let's discuss how to make learning even more effective.

Chapter 13: Meta-Learning

What is Meta-Learning?

Meta-Learning means learning *how to learn*. Instead of focusing only on what to study, you focus on the process of learning itself. It's about discovering the techniques, strategies, and habits that make you a more efficient learner.

This mental model is like having a blueprint for your brain. When you understand how learning works, you can tackle any subject faster and better.

Why Meta-Learning Matters

People often waste time using ineffective learning methods.

For example:

- Cramming for a test might work short-term but fails in the long run.
- Reading a textbook passively is slower and less effective than active engagement, like testing yourself.

Meta-Learning saves time and effort by teaching you *how* to learn smarter, not harder.

Example: Learning a Language

Instead of memorizing hundreds of vocabulary words in isolation, you focus on conversation practice and real-life contexts. By learning how to learn languages effectively, you progress faster and retain more.

How to Practice Meta-Learning

1. Understand Your Learning Style:

Do you learn best through visuals, hands-on practice, or listening? Tailor your methods to what works for you.

2. Use Proven Techniques:

Strategies like spaced repetition (reviewing over time), active recall (testing yourself), and chunking (breaking material into small pieces) boost retention.

3. Focus on Key Principles First:

Learn the most important concepts before diving into details. Understanding the foundation helps everything else make sense.

4. Reflect on What Works:

After every learning session, ask: *What helped me learn? What didn't?* Adjust your approach for next time.

Everyday Example of Meta-Learning

Imagine you're learning to cook. Instead of jumping into advanced recipes, you first learn the basics of seasoning, knife skills, and cooking techniques. These fundamentals make every recipe easier to master.

Common Pitfalls in Meta-Learning

1. Ignoring the Process:

Focusing only on the material, not the method, can slow progress. Meta-Learning keeps your process efficient.

2. Not Adapting to the Subject:

Different topics require different strategies. Learning math might need problem-solving practice, while learning music requires repetition and feedback.

3. Overloading Yourself:

Trying to learn everything at once is overwhelming. Focus on mastering one thing at a time.

4. Skipping Self-Reflection:

Without reflecting on your learning process, you miss opportunities to improve.

Practical Tip: Keep a Learning Journal

Track what methods you used, what worked well, and what didn't. Over time, this journal becomes your personal guide to learning effectively.

Takeaway

Meta-Learning is the ultimate skill. By mastering how to learn, you unlock faster, smarter growth in every area of life.

It's not about learning everything — it's about learning efficiently. Let's learn more about how small, steady progress can amplify this further.

Chapter 14:
Incremental Growth

What is Incremental Growth?

Incremental Growth is the idea that small, consistent improvements add up to big results over time. Instead of trying to change everything at once, you focus on getting just a little better each day.

This mental model is about steady progress, not perfection.

Why Incremental Growth Matters

Big, dramatic changes often fail because they're overwhelming. Incremental Growth works because it's manageable.

For example:

- Instead of trying to lose 20 pounds in a month, you aim to lose 1 pound a week.
- Instead of writing a novel in a week, you write one page a day.

These small wins build momentum and keep you motivated.

Example: Learning to Run

You want to run a marathon, but you've never run before.

- Big Leap Thinking: Try to run 10 miles on day one, fail, and feel discouraged.
- Incremental Growth: Start with a 1-mile jog. Add a little more distance each week. Eventually, you build the stamina to finish the race.

How to Apply Incremental Growth

1. Set Small Goals:
Break big goals into tiny, achievable steps. Focus on what you can improve today.

2. Track Progress:
Keep a journal or chart to see how far you've come. Small wins build motivation.

3. Focus on Consistency:
Daily effort matters more than big, irregular bursts. Build habits that stick.

4. Celebrate Milestones:
Acknowledge progress along the way. Small rewards keep you motivated.

Everyday Example of Incremental Growth

Suppose you're learning to draw.

- Day 1: You sketch basic shapes.
- Day 30: You're adding shading and detail.
- Day 365: You're creating full, detailed drawings.

Each day's small practice adds up to big improvement over time.

Common Pitfalls in Incremental Growth

1. Expecting Instant Results:
Growth takes time. Don't get discouraged if progress feels slow.

2. Skipping Steps:
Jumping ahead too soon often leads to mistakes. Focus on mastering each step.

3. Losing Consistency:
Sporadic effort disrupts momentum. Stick to regular practice.

4. Underestimating Small Wins:
Tiny improvements might seem insignificant, but they create lasting change.

Practical Tip: Ask, "What's My 1% Today?"

Each day, focus on improving by just 1%. Over time, these small gains lead up to big transformations.

Takeaway

Incremental Growth shows that small, steady effort is the key to achieving big goals. It's not about perfection—it's about persistence.

Progress starts with a single step, and each step brings you closer to mastery. Let's reflect on how mindset plays a role in approaching new challenges.

Chapter 15: Shoshin (Beginner's Mind)

What is Shoshin (Beginner's Mind)?

Shoshin is a Zen concept that means approaching every topic with the curiosity of a beginner. Even if you're experienced, you stay open to learning new things.

This mindset helps you avoid the trap of thinking you already "know it all." It encourages curiosity, humility, and a willingness to see things in fresh ways.

Why Shoshin Matters

Experts often stop growing because they think they've already mastered a topic. Beginners, on the other hand, are full of curiosity. Shoshin keeps that spark alive, no matter how much experience you have.

For example:

- A chef revisits the basics of cooking and discovers new techniques.
- A teacher learns from their students and gains fresh perspectives.

Shoshin unlocks new possibilities by letting go of rigid thinking.

Example: Revisiting a Skill

A photographer with years of experience takes a beginner's course and learns techniques they had overlooked. By adopting a beginner's mindset, they expand their creativity.

How to Practice Shoshin

1. Ask Questions:

Approach every topic with curiosity. Even simple questions can lead to amazing insights.

2. Challenge Assumptions:

Ask yourself: *What do I think I know? Could I be missing something?* Stay open to new ideas.

3. Learn from Everyone:

Beginners often notice things that experts miss. Be willing to learn from people with less experience.

4. Stay Humble:

Recognize that there's always more to learn. No one knows everything.

Everyday Example of Shoshin

Imagine you're reading a book about a topic you already know well.

- Without Shoshin: You skim through, assuming there's nothing new.
- With Shoshin: You read carefully and discover fresh insights.

Staying curious helps you grow, even in areas where you're skilled.

Common Pitfalls in Shoshin

1. Clinging to Expertise:

Thinking you're an expert can block you from seeing new perspectives.

2. **Ignoring Simple Ideas:**

   Complex problems often have simple solutions. Don't dismiss basic ideas as "too obvious."

3. **Assuming Growth Stops:**

   Mastery is never final. There's always room to improve and adapt.

4. **Fearing Failure:**

   Beginners often make mistakes. Embrace them as part of the learning process.

Practical Tip: Say, "What Can I Learn Today?"

Before tackling any task, ask yourself this question. It sets the tone for curiosity and openness.

Takeaway

Shoshin reminds you to stay curious and open. Growth happens when you approach life with fresh eyes and a beginner's curiosity.

Mastery begins with an open mind, but success often depends on how quickly you adapt to new challenges.

Chapter 16: Agility in Learning

What is Agility in Learning?

Agility in Learning means adapting quickly when faced with new challenges or information. It's the ability to adjust your approach, pick up new skills, and thrive in unpredictable situations.

This mindset is essential in a fast-changing world where yesterday's knowledge might not solve tomorrow's problems.

Why Agility in Learning Matters

Non-flexible thinking limits your ability to succeed when things change. Agility keeps creative, and ready for anything.

For example:

- A business owner adapts to a new trend by learning online marketing.
- A student switches study methods after realizing their old approach isn't effective.

The faster you adapt, the faster you grow.

Example: Adapting to Remote Work

When offices switch to remote work, an agile learner quickly masters video conferencing and digital tools. Instead of resisting change, they embrace it and excel.

1. **Stay Curious:**

    Treat every challenge as an opportunity to learn. Ask: *What can this teach me?*

2. **Experiment Often:**

    Try new methods, tools, or ideas. Don't fear failure—it's how you learn what works.

3. **Be Open to Feedback:**

    Listen to others and use their input to adjust your approach.

4. **Let Go of Old Habits:**

    If something isn't working, don't cling to it. Be willing to change course.

Everyday Example of Agility in Learning

Suppose your phone's operating system changes.

- Fixed Thinking: *This update is confusing. I'll ignore it.*
- Agile Thinking: *I'll take 10 minutes to explore the new features and learn how they work.*

Adapting quickly makes you more efficient and confident.

Common Pitfalls in Agility

1. **Resisting Change:**

    Fear of the unknown can hold you back. Embrace change as a chance to grow.

2. **Overthinking Adjustments:**

    Agility doesn't mean perfection. Focus on progress, not flawless execution.

3. **Clinging to Comfort Zones:**

    Growth happens outside your comfort zone. Push yourself to try new things.

4. **Ignoring Long-Term Impact:**

    Agility is about quick changes, but keep the big picture in mind.

Practical Tip: Ask, "What's My Next Move?"

When faced with a challenge, focus on your next step. Don't get stuck overanalyzing—act and adjust as you go.

Takeaway

Agility in Learning helps you adapt and thrive in a world of constant change. The faster you adjust, the more opportunities you can seize.

Growth thrives on flexibility, but true mastery requires sharpening your mindset. Let's unpack this further.

Chapter 17: Mental Flexibility

What is Mental Flexibility?

Mental Flexibility is the ability to adapt your thinking when faced with new ideas, unexpected changes, or challenges. It's the opposite of rigid thinking—it means being open to reexamining your beliefs and approaches without clinging to what's familiar.

This mindset helps you think creatively, solve problems, and thrive in uncertain situations.

Why Mental Flexibility Matters

Stubborn thinking limits progress. Mental Flexibility allows you to shift strategies, find better solutions, and navigate life's twists and turns.

For example:

- A manager reworks their team's goals when market trends shift.
- A student changes their study methods after realizing their old approach isn't effective.

Mental Flexibility lets you grow instead of staying stuck.

Example: A New Perspective on a Problem

You're struggling to assemble a piece of furniture. Instead of forcing the same method, you reread the instructions and find a simpler solution.

How to Build Mental Flexibility

1. Question Your Assumptions:

Ask yourself: *What if I'm wrong? Is there another way to see this?*

2. Seek Diverse Opinions:

Talk to people with different perspectives. Their insights can help you see beyond your usual thinking.

3. Practice "What If" Scenarios:

Imagine alternate outcomes or solutions to problems. This stretches your thinking.

4. Embrace Mistakes:

Mistakes show where old methods aren't working. Use them as opportunities to adjust and grow.

Everyday Example of Mental Flexibility

Suppose a recipe isn't working because you're missing an ingredient.

- Rigid Thinking: *I can't make this dish without that ingredient.*
- Flexible Thinking: *What can I substitute to make it work?*

This approach turns obstacles into opportunities.

Common Pitfalls in Mental Flexibility

1. Clinging to Comfort:

Staying with familiar ideas feels safe but limits growth. Push yourself to explore new options.

2. Overthinking Adjustments:

Don't paralyze yourself with too many possibilities. Test a solution and adapt as needed.

3. Confusing Flexibility with Indecision:

Flexibility means adapting, not endlessly questioning every choice. Stay focused.

4. Ignoring Emotional Barriers:

Sometimes, stubbornness comes from fear or pride. Recognize these emotions and work through them.

Practical Tip: Practice "Yes, And..." Thinking

When brainstorming or problem-solving, build on ideas instead of shutting them down. Say, *Yes, and what if we also...?* This encourages open, flexible thinking.

Takeaway

Mental Flexibility helps you adapt, innovate, and grow by shifting your mindset when circumstances demand it. Mastering it ensures you're always ready for life's surprises.

Now, let's reflect on the past to prepare for the future.

Chapter 18: Self-Reflection

What is Self-Reflection?

Self-Reflection is the practice of looking back on your actions, decisions, and experiences to learn from them. It's about asking: *What did I do well? What could I improve?*

This mental model helps you understand yourself better, so you can make smarter choices moving forward.

Why Self-Reflection Matters

Without reflection, you risk repeating the same mistakes or missing opportunities to improve. Self-Reflection turns experience into wisdom.

For example:

- An athlete reviews their performance after a game to identify strengths and areas for growth.
- A professional evaluates their week to see what tasks were most productive.

Reflection sharpens your judgment and boosts your progress.

Example: Reviewing a Job Interview

After a job interview, you think about what went well and what you could improve for next time. This helps you prepare better answers and build confidence.

How to Practice Self-Reflection

1. Schedule Time for Reflection:

Set aside a few minutes daily or weekly to review your actions and decisions.

2. Ask Specific Questions:

Reflect on key moments by asking: *What worked? What didn't? What will I do differently?*

3. Write It Down:

Keeping a journal helps organize your thoughts and track patterns over time.

4. Focus on Solutions, Not Regrets:

Use reflection to grow, not to dwell on mistakes. Focus on what you can learn and improve.

Everyday Example of Self-Reflection

Imagine you've just hosted a party.

- Reflect: Did the guests have fun? Did I prepare enough food? How can I make the next one better?

This process helps you improve with every experience.

Common Pitfalls in Self-Reflection

1. Overthinking Past Actions:

Reflect, but don't get stuck dwelling on mistakes. Use the past to improve the future.

2. Focusing Only on Negatives:

Celebrate your successes, too. Reflection should include what you did well.

3. Skipping the "Next Steps":

Reflection is useless without action. Always ask: *What will I do differently next time?*

4. Judging Yourself Harshly:

Be honest but kind to yourself. Reflection is about growth, not self-criticism.

Practical Tip: Use the "Three W's"

When reflecting, ask: *What went well? What didn't? What will I do next time?* This keeps your reflection focused and actionable.

Takeaway

Self-Reflection turns experience into growth by helping you analyze the past and improve for the future.

Mistakes are part of growth — let's explore how to embrace them as opportunities for learning.

Chapter 19: Failure Analysis

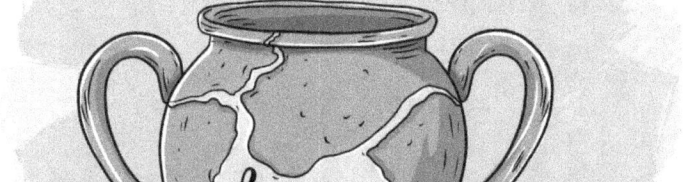

FAILURES ARE OPPORTUNITIES TO REBUILD STRONGER.

Lessons

What is Failure Analysis?

Failure Analysis is the process of breaking down mistakes to understand what went wrong and why. It's about learning from failures instead of fearing or ignoring them.

Failures aren't the end — they're stepping stones to success if you analyze them thoughtfully.

Why Failure Analysis Matters

Many people avoid thinking about failure because it feels uncomfortable. But without analyzing mistakes, you miss valuable lessons.

For example:

- A failed project teaches you what to avoid next time.
- A lost game helps you identify weaknesses to improve your strategy.

Failures are valuable teachers when you pay attention.

Example: A Missed Deadline

You miss an important deadline. By analyzing the failure, you realize poor time management was the cause. Next time, you set reminders and break tasks into smaller steps.

How to Perform Failure Analysis

1. Identify the Failure:

Be specific about what went wrong. Avoid vague statements like "I messed up."

2. Find the Root Cause:

Ask, *Why did this happen?* Dig deep to uncover the underlying reasons.

3. Extract Lessons:

Focus on what the failure taught you. What can you do differently next time?

4. Take Action:

Use the insights to make a clear plan for improvement.

Everyday Example of Failure Analysis

Imagine your first attempt at baking a cake fails because it's undercooked.

- Analysis: *Why did this happen? I didn't preheat the oven properly.*
- Lesson: *Next time, I'll double-check the temperature before starting.*

By analyzing the mistake, you improve your chances of success.

Common Pitfalls in Failure Analysis

1. Blaming Others:

Focus on what you can control instead of shifting blame.

2. Dwelling on the Failure:

Learn from it, then move on. Don't let one mistake define you.

3. Ignoring Patterns:

If similar failures happen repeatedly, look for patterns and address the root cause.

4. Avoiding the Process:

Avoiding failure analysis prevents growth. Embrace it as a learning tool.

Practical Tip: Write a "Failure Postmortem"

After a failure, write down what happened, why it happened, and what you'll do differently. This turns the experience into a learning moment.

Takeaway

Failure Analysis transforms mistakes into opportunities for growth. Every failure contains a lesson — your job is to find it and use it wisely.

True growth comes when you challenge what you already believe—let's discuss this further.

Chapter 20: Challenge Bias

What is Challenge Bias?

Challenge Bias is the habit of actively seeking evidence that contradicts your beliefs. It's the opposite of Confirmation Bias, which makes people focus only on information that supports what they already think.

This mental model forces you to confront blind spots and refine your thinking by exposing it to scrutiny.

Why Challenge Bias Matters

When you avoid challenging your beliefs, you risk holding onto flawed ideas. This can lead to poor decisions and missed opportunities.

For example:

- A scientist tests a hypothesis by trying to disprove it, ensuring their conclusions are strong.
- A manager questions their strategy by seeking input from skeptics, leading to better decisions.

Challenging bias helps you avoid echo chambers and strengthens your understanding.

Example: Choosing a Career Path

Suppose you're convinced you want to be a lawyer. By challenging your bias, you shadow a lawyer for a week and realize the work doesn't align with your passions. This saves you years of pursuing the wrong goal.

How to Challenge Bias

1. Seek Contradictory Evidence:

Actively look for information that opposes your views. Ask, *What would prove me wrong?*

2. Listen to Opposing Opinions:

Talk to people who disagree with you. Their perspective might reveal blind spots.

3. Play Devil's Advocate:

Argue against your own beliefs. This tests the strength of your ideas.

4. Ask "What If" Questions:

Explore scenarios where your assumptions might not hold true.

Everyday Example of Challenging Bias

Imagine you believe a certain diet is the healthiest.

- Without Challenging Bias: You only read articles supporting the diet.
- With Challenging Bias: You research critiques of the diet and consult nutrition experts.

This approach helps you make a more informed decision.

Common Pitfalls in Challenging Bias

1. Avoiding Discomfort:

Confronting opposing views can feel uncomfortable, but it's essential for growth.

2. Dismissing Contradictory Evidence:

Don't ignore valid criticism just because it challenges your beliefs.

3. Becoming Defensive:

Focus on understanding, not winning arguments.

4. Falling into Cynicism:

Challenging bias doesn't mean doubting everything—it's about questioning thoughtfully.

Practical Tip: Ask, "What Would Prove Me Wrong?"

For any belief, imagine the evidence that could change your mind. This keeps your thinking balanced and open.

Takeaway

Challenging Bias helps you grow by exposing flaws in your thinking. By questioning your beliefs, you refine your understanding and make smarter decisions.

True wisdom comes from seeing the full picture, even if it means questioning yourself. Let's explore decision-making tools that turn insight into action.

Decision-Making Models

Chapter 21: Cost-Benefit Analysis

What is Cost-Benefit Analysis?

Cost-Benefit Analysis weighs the benefits of a decision against its costs. It helps you determine whether something is worth doing by comparing the value you'll gain to what you'll lose.

This model ensures your choices are rational and focused on maximizing value.

Why Cost-Benefit Analysis Matters

Without evaluating costs and benefits, you risk overcommitting to poor decisions. Cost-Benefit Analysis helps you allocate time, money, and energy wisely.

For example:

- A company decides whether to launch a new product by analyzing potential profits versus development costs.
- A student weighs the benefits of studying late against the cost of losing sleep.

This tool simplifies complex decisions by focusing on what matters most.

Example: Buying a New Car

You're considering upgrading your car.

- Benefits: Reliability, fuel efficiency, comfort.
- Costs: Purchase price, insurance, maintenance.

If the benefits outweigh the costs for your budget, the decision makes sense. If not, it's better to wait.

How to Perform a Cost-Benefit Analysis

1. **List All Costs:**
   Include money, time, effort, and opportunity costs (what you're giving up).
2. **List All Benefits:**
   Think about tangible and intangible gains, like happiness, convenience, or savings.
3. **Quantify Where Possible:**
   Assign numbers or values to each factor to make comparisons easier.
4. **Compare and Decide:**
   If the benefits outweigh the costs significantly, it's a good choice. If not, reconsider.

Everyday Example of Cost-Benefit Analysis

Imagine deciding whether to take an evening class.

- Costs: Tuition, time away from family, effort to study.
- Benefits: New skills, career advancement, personal growth.

Weighing these factors helps you make an informed decision.

Common Pitfalls in Cost-Benefit Analysis

1. **Ignoring Intangible Costs or Benefits:**
   Not everything is easily measured. Consider emotional or social factors, too.
2. **Overcomplicating the Process:**
   Focus on the most important costs and benefits. Avoid getting lost in minor details.
3. **Bias Toward Immediate Rewards:**
   Short-term benefits can blind you to long-term costs. Stay objective.
4. **Underestimating Indirect Costs:**
   Think about ripple effects. For example, a new hobby might cost more time than expected.

Practical Tip: Use a Simple Chart

Create a two-column list with "Costs" on one side and "Benefits" on the other. This visual tool makes comparisons clearer.

Takeaway

Cost-Benefit Analysis simplifies decisions by focusing on value. It ensures your choices are logical, not emotional.

Making decisions is about balancing what you have and what you gain. Let's continue refining your decision-making skills.

Chapter 22: Expected Value

What is Expected Value?

Expected Value (EV) is a way to predict the average outcome of a decision by combining probabilities and rewards. Instead of guessing, you ask: *What's the most logical choice based on the potential payoff and its likelihood?*

This model is essential for making decisions under uncertainty, whether in business, finance, or daily life.

Why Expected Value Matters

Gut feelings often lead to poor decisions because they ignore probabilities. Expected Value forces you to think logically, weighing risks and rewards.

For example:

- A gambler might bet on a long shot with a big payout but low EV.
- A business might invest in a product that has a smaller payout but higher EV because it's more likely to succeed.

Thinking in EV helps you avoid costly mistakes.

Example: Choosing a Lottery Ticket

You're considering buying a lottery ticket for $5. The jackpot is $1 million, but the odds are 1 in 10 million.

- EV = ($1,000,000 × 1/10,000,000) - $5 = -$4.90.

The negative EV shows that buying the ticket isn't logical — it's a losing bet on average.

How to Use Expected Value

1. List Potential Outcomes:

Identify all possible results of your decision.

2. Assign Probabilities:

Estimate how likely each outcome is. Use research or experience to guide you.

3. Calculate Payoffs:

Multiply each outcome's probability by its reward or cost.

4. Sum the Results:

Add up all the values. A positive EV suggests the decision is worth pursuing.

Everyday Example of Expected Value

Imagine deciding whether to leave early for work.

- Staying later saves time, but there's a 50% chance of hitting traffic, costing 30 minutes.
- Leaving earlier avoids traffic, saving 20 minutes.

Calculate the EV for each option to make the best choice.

Common Pitfalls in Expected Value

1. Overestimating Probabilities:

Be realistic about the likelihood of outcomes. Wishful thinking skews EV.

2. Ignoring Emotional Factors:

EV focuses on logic but doesn't account for stress, happiness, or other intangibles.

3. Failing to Reassess:

As new information arises, update your probabilities and EV calculations.

4. Underestimating Rare, High-Impact Events:

Include scenarios with low probability but significant consequences.

Practical Tip: Use the EV Formula

For any decision, apply the formula:

EV = (Probability × Reward) - Cost.

Takeaway

Expected Value sharpens your ability to evaluate uncertain decisions logically. It balances risks and rewards, helping you choose wisely.

With this tool, let's examine what happens when opportunities come with hidden trade-offs.

Chapter 23: Opportunity Cost

Opportunity Cost is the value of what you give up when making a choice. Every decision means saying no to something else. This model helps you weigh not just the benefits of what you choose but also the costs of what you leave behind.

Why Opportunity Cost Matters

Focusing only on what you gain blinds you to hidden trade-offs. Opportunity Cost makes you think critically about whether your choice is truly the best one.

For example:

- Spending $50 on a dinner out means you can't spend that money on savings or another activity.
- Choosing a high-paying job might mean sacrificing time with family.

Every choice has a cost—it's up to you to evaluate it.

Example: Starting a Business

You invest $10,000 in your startup. The Opportunity Cost is what you could have earned by investing that money elsewhere, such as stocks or savings. Considering this helps you weigh risks and rewards.

How to Evaluate Opportunity Costs

1. Identify What You're Giving Up:

Think about what you could have done with the time, money, or resources you're using.

2. Compare the Benefits:

Ask: *Does this choice provide more value than the alternative?*

3. Consider Long-Term Impacts:

Short-term gains might have long-term costs. Look at the bigger picture.

4. Be Honest About Sacrifices:

Don't ignore trade-offs just because they're uncomfortable to face.

Everyday Example of Opportunity Cost

Imagine you're deciding between spending a Saturday working overtime or attending a family event.

- Working earns extra income.
- Attending the event strengthens relationships and creates memories.

Weighing the Opportunity Cost ensures your choice aligns with your priorities.

Common Pitfalls in Opportunity Cost

1. Ignoring Non-Monetary Costs:

Opportunity Cost isn't just financial—time, energy, and relationships matter too.

2. Overlooking Hidden Trade-Offs:

Think deeply about what you're sacrificing. Some costs aren't obvious at first.

3. Paralysis by Analysis:

Don't overthink every small decision. Reserve this model for significant choices.

4. Failing to Reassess Priorities:

Your values and goals may change over time. Re-evaluate Opportunity Costs regularly.

Practical Tip: Use "If I Choose This, I Lose That" Thinking

Before making a decision, state clearly what you're giving up. This keeps trade-offs in focus.

Takeaway

Opportunity Cost helps you see the hidden sacrifices behind every choice. It ensures your decisions align with your goals and values.

Life is full of trade-offs — this model ensures you choose wisely. Let's continue refining decision-making tools in the next section.

Chapter 24: The Pareto Principle (80/20 Rule)

What is the Pareto Principle (80/20 Rule)?

In the Pareto Principle, 80% of results come from 20% of efforts. It highlights the imbalance between effort and output, suggesting you should focus on the small actions that create the biggest impact.

This principle applies to almost everything — business, personal goals, relationships, and productivity.

Why the Pareto Principle Matters

Most people waste time on tasks that have little impact. The Pareto Principle helps you prioritize what truly drives success.

For example:

- 20% of your customers often generate 80% of your revenue.
- 20% of your habits likely create 80% of your progress.

Focusing on the critical 20% multiplies your results.

Example: Improving Study Efficiency

Imagine you're preparing for an exam.

- Without the Pareto Principle: You study all topics equally, wasting time on less important ones.
- Using the 80/20 Rule: You identify the 20% of topics most likely to be tested and focus on mastering those.

This targeted approach maximizes your efficiency.

How to Use the Pareto Principle

1. Identify Key Inputs:

Ask: *What 20% of my efforts drive 80% of my results?*

2. Eliminate Low-Impact Tasks:

Stop spending time on things that don't significantly contribute to your goals.

3. Focus on High-Leverage Activities:

Double down on the tasks, relationships, or habits that produce the most value.

4. Regularly Reassess:

Priorities change over time. Keep identifying the most impactful 20%.

Everyday Example of the Pareto Principle

Suppose you're decluttering your home.

- 80% of the clutter comes from 20% of your items. Focus on clearing those items first, and you'll make the biggest difference with minimal effort.

Common Pitfalls in the Pareto Principle

1. Ignoring the Remaining 80%:

While 20% drives most results, the remaining 80% may still matter in some contexts. Don't neglect it entirely.

2. Overgeneralizing:

The ratio isn't always 80/20. Focus on the concept, not the exact numbers.

3. Failing to Identify Priorities:

Without clear priorities, you'll struggle to know where to focus.

4. Misinterpreting the Rule:

It doesn't mean working less—it means working smarter.

Practical Tip: Ask, "What Few Things Make the Biggest Impact?"

Before tackling any goal, identify the small actions that will drive the most significant results.

Takeaway

The Pareto Principle teaches you to prioritize the few efforts that create the most impact. By focusing on the critical 20%, you can achieve more with less.

Understanding value is important, but diminishing returns can set limits. Let's explore this further.

Chapter 25: Marginal Utility

What is Marginal Utility?

Marginal Utility explains how the value or satisfaction from consuming something decreases as you get more of it. The first slice of pizza is amazing, but by the third or fourth, the excitement fades.

This concept is key for making decisions about resources, showing that more isn't always better.

Why Marginal Utility Matters

Understanding Marginal Utility helps you allocate time, money, or energy wisely. It prevents waste by focusing on when additional effort no longer adds value.

For example:
- Studying for an exam for 2 hours might be productive, but studying for 10 hours straight could lead to burnout with little additional learning.

Example: Watching TV

One episode of your favorite show feels relaxing. But binge-watching all night leaves you feeling tired and less satisfied. Marginal Utility explains why balance matters.

How to Use Marginal Utility

1. Identify Diminishing Returns:
Pay attention to when extra effort, money, or time adds less value.

2. Set Limits:
Stop investing once you reach the point where additional input doesn't significantly improve outcomes.

3. Prioritize Quality Over Quantity:
Focus on high-value experiences or resources instead of accumulating more.

4. Evaluate Alternatives:
When Marginal Utility decreases, shift your resources to other areas with higher returns.

Everyday Example of Marginal Utility

Suppose you're shopping for clothes.
- The first few items you buy may be exciting, but buying too many leads to clutter without much extra satisfaction.

Common Pitfalls in Marginal Utility

1. Ignoring the Decline:
Continuing to invest resources after satisfaction decreases leads to waste.

2. Overvaluing Quantity:
More isn't always better—focus on quality and purpose.

3. Not Setting Priorities:
Without clear goals, it's hard to notice when returns start diminishing.

4. Neglecting Alternatives:
When returns decline, explore other opportunities for growth or satisfaction.

Practical Tip: Look for the "Saturation Point"

For any activity, ask: *At what point does more stop adding value?* Use this to set limits.

Takeaway

Marginal Utility helps you understand when "enough is enough." It ensures your resources are used efficiently by focusing on value, not volume.

From here, let's examine how emotions influence decisions.

Chapter 26: Loss Aversion

Loss Aversion is the tendency to fear losses more than valuing equivalent gains. For example, losing $10 feels worse than the joy of gaining $10.

This cognitive bias can lead to overly cautious decisions, missed opportunities, or clinging to bad investments.

Why Loss Aversion Matters

Fear of loss often leads people to avoid risks, even when potential rewards are greater. Recognizing this bias helps you make rational, balanced choices.

For example:

- Investors hold onto failing stocks to avoid feeling the pain of selling at a loss.
- A person avoids asking for a raise because they fear rejection.

Awareness of Loss Aversion keeps emotions from driving decisions.

Example: Canceling a Membership

You're hesitant to cancel a gym membership you rarely use because you feel it's a waste of money. Loss Aversion keeps you stuck, even though canceling saves you in the long run.

How to Overcome Loss Aversion

1. Reframe the Situation:

Focus on potential gains instead of losses. Ask: *What do I stand to gain by letting this go?*

2. Consider the Bigger Picture:

Think about long-term benefits versus short-term discomfort.

3. Use Objective Data:

Analyze decisions logically, not emotionally. Numbers often counteract fear.

4. Set Clear Goals:

Align decisions with your goals to minimize the emotional pull of losses.

Everyday Example of Loss Aversion

Imagine hesitating to donate old clothes because you spent money on them. Recognizing Loss Aversion helps you realize that keeping unused items isn't adding value to your life.

Common Pitfalls in Loss Aversion

1. Holding Onto Bad Investments:

Sunk costs can cloud judgment. Focus on future potential, not past losses.

2. Avoiding Risks Unnecessarily:

Over-caution leads to missed opportunities.

3. Overvaluing What You Have:

Just because you own something doesn't mean it's worth keeping.

4. Letting Emotions Dominate Decisions:

Balance emotional responses with logic to make smarter choices.

Practical Tip: Ask, "What Do I Gain by Letting Go?"

Reframing decisions helps you see past the emotional fear of losing.

Takeaway

Loss Aversion reminds you that fear of loss can distort decision-making. By recognizing this bias, you can focus on potential gains and make clearer, more confident choices.

Chapter 27: The Eisenhower Matrix

What is the Eisenhower Matrix?

The Eisenhower Matrix is a time-management tool that helps you prioritize tasks based on urgency and importance. It divides tasks into four categories:

1. Urgent and Important: Do these immediately.
2. Important but Not Urgent: Schedule these for later.
3. Urgent but Not Important: Delegate these.
4. Not Urgent and Not Important: Eliminate these.

This model ensures you spend your time on what truly matters instead of reacting to distractions.

Why the Eisenhower Matrix Matters

Without clear priorities, you risk wasting time on tasks that feel urgent but add little value. The Eisenhower Matrix helps you focus on meaningful work while minimizing distractions.

For example:

- Answering urgent emails feels productive but might not align with your bigger goals.
- Spending time on important but not urgent activities, like planning or learning, creates long-term success.

Example: Planning a Workday

Suppose you're overwhelmed with tasks: preparing a presentation, responding to emails, and cleaning your desk.

- **Urgent and Important:** Finalizing the presentation.
- **Important but Not Urgent:** Organizing your long-term project goals.
- **Urgent but Not Important:** Responding to minor emails (delegate).
- **Not Urgent and Not Important:** Cleaning your desk (eliminate).

This approach helps you focus on the presentation while scheduling the rest.

How to Use the Eisenhower Matrix

1. **List All Your Tasks:**
   Write down everything you need to do.
2. **Sort Tasks Into Categories:**
   Use the four quadrants to classify each task by urgency and importance.

3. **Focus on Quadrant 1:**
   Tackle urgent and important tasks first.
4. **Schedule Quadrant 2:**
   Plan time for important but not urgent tasks—they're often the most valuable.

Example of the Eisenhower Matrix

Imagine you're juggling personal and professional responsibilities.

- **Urgent and Important:** Paying overdue bills.
- **Important but Not Urgent:** Planning a family vacation.
- **Urgent but Not Important:** Answering a non-critical text.
- **Not Urgent and Not Important:** Scrolling through social media.

Using the matrix ensures your time is spent wisely.

Common Pitfalls in the Eisenhower Matrix

1. **Overloading Quadrant 1:**
   Too many "urgent" tasks indicate poor planning. Focus on Quadrant 2 to prevent last-minute crises.
2. **Ignoring Quadrant 2:**
   Skipping important but not urgent tasks leads to long-term problems.
3. **Misclassifying Tasks:**
   Be honest about what's truly important versus what just feels urgent.
4. **Failing to Delegate:**
   Don't hesitate to assign tasks in Quadrant 3 to others.

Practical Tip: Review Your Matrix Daily

At the start of each day, revisit your matrix to adjust priorities and stay on track.

Takeaway

The Eisenhower Matrix helps you focus on what truly matters by separating urgency from importance. It's a simple yet powerful tool to align your actions with your goals.

Next, let's analyze decision-making even further.

Chapter 28: SWOT Analysis

What is SWOT Analysis?

SWOT Analysis is a framework for evaluating any situation according to:

- **Strengths:** What advantages do you have?
- **Weaknesses:** Where are your limitations?
- **Opportunities:** What external factors can you leverage?
- **Threats:** What risks could derail you?

This model helps you make informed decisions by considering internal and external factors.

Why SWOT Analysis Matters

Rushing into decisions without evaluating all angles can lead to failure. SWOT Analysis forces you to think strategically, balancing opportunities with risks.

For example:

- A business launching a new product might analyze strengths (innovative design), weaknesses (limited budget), opportunities (growing market), and threats (competition).

This framework ensures nothing is overlooked.

Example: Choosing a Career Move

You're deciding whether to switch jobs.

- **Strengths:** Your skills align with the new role.
- **Weaknesses:** You're unfamiliar with the industry.
- **Opportunities:** The new job offers better growth prospects.
- **Threats:** Leaving your current job might risk stability.

By analyzing all factors, you can make a confident choice.

How to Conduct a SWOT Analysis

1. **Identify Strengths:**

   List your internal advantages, like skills, resources, or support systems.

2. **Acknowledge Weaknesses:**

   Be honest about areas where you're lacking.

3. **Spot Opportunities:**

   Look for external factors that can help you succeed, like trends or resources.

4. **Prepare for Threats:**

   Anticipate challenges and plan how to handle them.

Everyday Example of SWOT Analysis

Suppose you're deciding whether to start a fitness routine.

- **Strengths:** You have time in the evenings.
- **Weaknesses:** You struggle with consistency.
- **Opportunities:** A nearby gym offers discounts.
- **Threats:** Work commitments might interfere.

SWOT Analysis helps you create a realistic, actionable plan.

Common Pitfalls in SWOT Analysis

1. **Overemphasizing Strengths:**

   Don't let confidence blind you to weaknesses or risks.

2. **Ignoring External Factors:**

   Opportunities and threats are just as important as internal factors.

3. **Being Too Vague:**

   Specific details make SWOT more effective.

4. **Failing to Act on Insights:**

   SWOT is a planning tool, but its value lies in taking action.

Practical Tip: Use SWOT for Major Decisions

Whenever faced with a big choice, use SWOT to clarify your options and identify the best path forward.

Takeaway

SWOT Analysis is a versatile tool for making strategic decisions. By balancing strengths, weaknesses, opportunities, and threats, you gain a clearer understanding of any situation.

Chapter 29: Decision Trees

What is a Decision Tree?

A Decision Tree is a visual tool for mapping out choices and their possible outcomes. It helps you break down complex decisions step-by-step, weighing risks, rewards, and probabilities.

This model is particularly useful when decisions have multiple layers.

Why Decision Trees Matter

When faced with complex choices, it's easy to feel overwhelmed. A Decision Tree simplifies the process by organizing your options and showing the potential consequences of each path.

For example:

- A company deciding to launch a product might use a Decision Tree to evaluate outcomes like profitability, costs, and market response.
- An individual planning a career change can map options, including potential risks and rewards.

Example: Choosing Between Job Offers

Imagine you're deciding between staying at your current job or accepting a new offer.

- Current job: Stability (high probability), limited growth.
- New offer: High growth potential (medium probability), risk of instability.

A Decision Tree helps you compare these outcomes visually, so you can make a more informed choice.

How to Use a Decision Tree

1. Identify the Decision:
Write down the key choice you need to make.

2. List Options:
Outline all possible actions you could take.

3. Map Outcomes:
For each option, list possible results, including both positive and negative scenarios.

4. Assign Probabilities and Values:
Estimate how likely each outcome is and what its impact would be (e.g., financial, emotional).

5. Analyze the Best Path:
Calculate which option offers the highest overall value or lowest risk.

Everyday Example of a Decision Tree

Imagine you're deciding whether to take an umbrella before heading out.

- Option 1: Take the umbrella. Outcome: Stay dry if it rains but carry extra weight if it doesn't.
- Option 2: Don't take the umbrella. Outcome: Stay light, but risk getting wet.

Mapping these options visually helps you weigh the probabilities and make the right call.

Common Pitfalls in Decision Trees

1. Overcomplicating the Tree:
Too many branches make the tree hard to interpret. Focus on the most important choices.

2. Guessing Probabilities:
Be realistic and use available data whenever possible.

3. Ignoring Emotional Factors:
Decision Trees focus on logic but should include emotional impacts where relevant.

4. Skipping Follow-Up Decisions:
Account for how each choice could lead to new decisions down the line.

Practical Tip: Start Simple

Begin with one main decision and a few branches. Add more detail only if necessary.

Takeaway

Decision Trees help you structure choices and visualize outcomes, making complex decisions clearer and more manageable. When your choices depend on others' actions, understanding their strategies is crucial. Let's explore this next.

Chapter 30: Game Theory

What is Game Theory?

Game Theory analyzes decision-making in situations where the outcome depends on the actions of others. It's about understanding how your choices interact with theirs, whether you're competing or collaborating.

This model is used in business negotiations, politics, economics, and everyday interactions.

Why Game Theory Matters

In many decisions, your success isn't determined by your actions alone — it depends on how others respond. Game Theory helps you anticipate their moves and choose strategies that maximize your outcomes.

For example:

- Companies setting prices must consider how competitors will react.
- Friends deciding where to meet for dinner must weigh preferences and compromises.

Example: The Prisoner's Dilemma

Two suspects are arrested and interrogated separately. They can either cooperate by staying silent or betray the other for a lighter sentence.

- If both stay silent, they get minor sentences.
- If one betrays the other, the betrayer goes free while the other gets a heavy sentence.
- If both betray, they both receive moderate sentences.

Game Theory shows that trust and collaboration often lead to better outcomes than selfishness.

How to Use Game Theory

1. **Understand the Players:**

   Identify everyone involved and their potential strategies.

2. **Predict Their Goals:**

   Consider what others want and how they might act to achieve it.

3. **Evaluate Your Options:**

   Think about how your choices will influence others and vice versa.

4. **Choose the Best Strategy:**

   Select the option that maximizes your benefit while accounting for others' actions.

Everyday Example of Game Theory

Imagine splitting the bill at dinner.

- If everyone orders moderately, the bill is fair.
- If one person splurges while expecting the group to split evenly, others might feel cheated.

Game Theory helps you navigate these dynamics and encourage fair collaboration.

Common Pitfalls in Game Theory

1. **Assuming Others Are Predictable:**

   People's choices can be influenced by emotions or unexpected factors.

2. **Ignoring Collaboration Opportunities:**

   Not all situations are competitions. Cooperation often leads to better outcomes.

3. **Focusing Only on Short-Term Wins:**

   Strategies that work now might hurt relationships or trust in the long run.

4. Overthinking Simple Situations:

Not every decision requires complex strategy. Use Game Theory for significant choices.

Practical Tip: Think Like the Other Player

Before making a choice, ask: *What would I do in their position?* This helps you anticipate their actions.

Takeaway

Game Theory helps you navigate decisions where outcomes depend on others' strategies. Whether competing or collaborating, it equips you to make smarter, more strategic choices.

From decisions to problem-solving, understanding root causes is essential. Let's take a further look.

Problem Solving Models

Chapter 31: Root Cause Analysis

What is Root Cause Analysis?

Root Cause Analysis is a problem-solving method that focuses on identifying the true source of an issue rather than just treating its symptoms. It's about digging deeper to ask: *What is really causing this problem?*

By addressing the root cause, you solve the problem permanently instead of applying temporary fixes.

Why Root Cause Analysis Matters

Most people fix surface-level issues without understanding their origins. This leads to recurring problems and wasted effort. Root Cause Analysis ensures you address the core issue, saving time and resources.

For example:

- A machine breaks down. Fixing it restores function temporarily, but analyzing why it broke (e.g., poor maintenance) prevents future breakdowns.

Example: Customer Complaints

Imagine a business faces frequent complaints about slow service.

- Symptom: Long wait times.
- Root Cause: Insufficient staffing during peak hours.

By addressing the staffing issue, the company reduces wait times and complaints.

1. **Define the Problem:**

   Be specific about what's happening. Avoid vague descriptions.

2. **Ask "Why" Repeatedly:**

   Use the 5 Whys Technique (e.g., *Why did this happen? And why did that happen?*) to uncover deeper layers.

3. **Identify the Root Cause:**

   Look for patterns or systemic issues causing the problem.

4. **Develop a Long-Term Solution:**

   Focus on eliminating the root cause, not just managing symptoms.

Everyday Example of Root Cause Analysis

Suppose you're constantly late to work.

- Symptom: You miss the bus.
- Root Cause: You're waking up too late.
- Solution: Set an earlier alarm to avoid the rush entirely.

Addressing the root saves you from repeated stress and delays.

Common Pitfalls in Root Cause Analysis

1. **Stopping Too Soon:**

   Surface answers often hide deeper problems. Keep asking "why" to dig further.

2. **Focusing on Blame:**

   Avoid assigning blame to people. Focus on processes or systems instead.

3. **Overlooking Patterns:**

   Recurring problems often point to root causes. Don't treat them as isolated incidents.

4. **Failing to Act on Insights:**

   Identifying the root cause is useless without implementing a solution.

Practical Tip: Look for the Chain Reaction

Most problems result from a series of events. Trace each link backward until you reach the starting point.

Takeaway

Root Cause Analysis helps you solve problems permanently by targeting their origins. It's a powerful tool for creating long-lasting improvements.

Let's continue exploring solutions with fresh perspectives.

Chapter 32: The 5 Whys Technique

What is the 5 Whys Technique?

The 5 Whys Technique is a simple problem-solving method where you repeatedly ask "Why?" to uncover the root cause of an issue. Each answer leads you closer to the underlying problem.

It's based on the idea that surface-level issues often have deeper causes. Asking "why" helps you dig past symptoms to find solutions that stick.

Why the 5 Whys Technique Matters

Problems rarely happen in isolation — they're often symptoms of larger issues. The 5 Whys Technique prevents you from stopping at superficial answers.

For example:

- A missed deadline might seem like the problem. But asking "why" reveals deeper issues like unclear instructions or poor time management.

Example: A Leaking Roof

Problem: The roof is leaking.

1. Why? The shingles are damaged.
2. Why? They weren't replaced on time.
3. Why? The maintenance schedule wasn't followed.

Root Cause: Lack of a task-tracking system.

4. Why? The team didn't know about the schedule.
5. Why? There's no system for tracking tasks.

How to Use the 5 Whys Technique

1. Start with the Problem:

Clearly define the issue you're trying to solve.

2. Ask "Why" Five Times:

Each answer should lead to the next "why." Keep going until you reach the root cause.

3. Focus on Processes, Not People:

Look for flaws in systems or workflows, not individual blame.

4. Develop a Solution:

Once you identify the root cause, design a plan to address it.

Everyday Example of the 5 Whys

Suppose your car won't start.

1. Why? The battery is dead.
2. Why? I left the lights on.
3. Why? I forgot to turn them off.

Solution: Set a reminder to check the lights before leaving the car.

4. Why? I was in a rush.
5. Why? I didn't allow enough time to leave.

Common Pitfalls in the 5 Whys Technique

1. Stopping Too Soon:

The first "why" rarely reveals the true root cause. Keep digging.

2. Jumping to Conclusions:

Avoid guessing answers without evidence.

3. Focusing on Blame:

This technique is about fixing systems, not pointing fingers.

4. Ignoring Complexity:

Some problems have multiple root causes. Be open to finding more than one.

Practical Tip: Involve Others

When using the 5 Whys, gather input from people who understand the problem. Different perspectives reveal hidden causes.

Takeaway

The 5 Whys Technique simplifies problem-solving by breaking issues into smaller pieces. It's a practical way to uncover the root cause and build effective solutions.

Let's continue uncovering creative approaches to problem-solving.

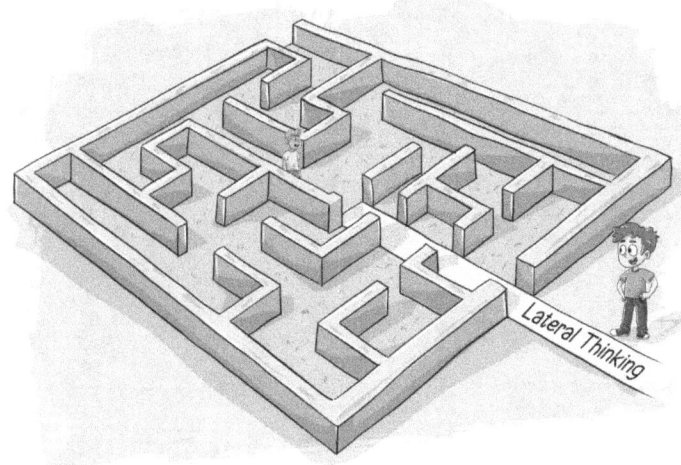

Chapter 33: Lateral Thinking

What is Lateral Thinking?

Lateral Thinking is the ability to solve problems creatively by approaching them from unexpected angles. Instead of following traditional methods, you think outside the box.

This model is especially useful when conventional thinking has failed or when a fresh perspective is needed.

Why Lateral Thinking Matters

Humans often default to familiar patterns, which can limit creativity. Lateral Thinking breaks those patterns, unlocking innovative ideas.

For example:

- Instead of improving a clunky product design, Lateral Thinking might suggest eliminating the need for the product entirely.

Example: Solving Office Clutter

A company struggles with messy desks.
- Conventional Thinking: Add more storage space.
- Lateral Thinking: Shift to a paperless office, removing the need for physical storage altogether.

The creative approach solves the problem at its source.

How to Use Lateral Thinking

1. Question Assumptions:
Ask: *What if this rule didn't exist?* Break free from "how things are done."

2. Generate Wild Ideas:
Think of unconventional solutions without worrying if they're practical at first.

3. Combine Unrelated Ideas:
Look for inspiration in other fields or industries.

4. Reframe the Problem:
Instead of asking How do I fix this? ask How can I make this irrelevant?

Everyday Example of Lateral Thinking

Suppose you need to transport groceries without a car.
- Conventional Thinking: Find a ride.
- Lateral Thinking: Use a delivery service or switch to online shopping.

Thinking outside the box often leads to simpler, more effective solutions.

Common Pitfalls in Lateral Thinking

1. Dismissing Ideas Too Quickly:
Even wild ideas can spark useful insights. Explore them fully before rejecting them.

2. Clinging to Tradition:
Familiar methods feel safe but may not solve the problem.

3. Overcomplicating Solutions:
Simplicity is often the hallmark of great lateral ideas.

4. Ignoring Feedback:
Innovative ideas still need to be tested and refined with input from others.

Practical Tip: Ask "What If?"

For any problem, ask questions like *What if we did the opposite? What if this rule didn't exist?* These shifts often lead to creative breakthroughs.

Takeaway

Lateral Thinking helps you escape mental ruts and uncover innovative solutions. It's a mindset that encourages creativity and reinvention.

Let's continue exploring tools for simplifying and clarifying complex ideas.

Chapter 34: The Feynman Technique

What is The Feynman Technique?

The Feynman Technique describes mastering complex ideas by breaking them down into simple terms. Named after physicist Richard Feynman, it's based on the idea that if you can't explain something simply, you don't truly understand it.

This model combines learning and teaching to deepen comprehension.

Why The Feynman Technique Matters

Complicated explanations often hides shallow understanding. By forcing yourself to simplify concepts, you uncover gaps in your knowledge and fill them effectively.

For example:

- A teacher explaining physics without jargon ensures both they and their students truly grasp the material.

Example: Learning Budgeting

You're learning how to manage finances.

- Without Feynman: Memorize formulas without understanding them.
- With Feynman: Teach someone else how budgeting works, revealing gaps in your knowledge that need clarification.

Teaching strengthens your own understanding.

How to Use The Feynman Technique

1. Pick a Concept:

Choose something you want to learn or explain.

2. Write It Simply:

Break it down into terms a child could understand. Avoid jargon.

3. Identify Gaps:

Notice where your explanation feels unclear. Study those areas again.

4. Refine and Repeat:

Rewrite your explanation until it's simple and complete.

Everyday Example of The Feynman Technique

Suppose you're learning how solar panels work.

- Start by explaining: *They turn sunlight into electricity.*
- Dive deeper: *How does that happen? Through something called photovoltaic cells.*
- Simplify further: *These cells capture sunlight and turn it into energy we can use.*

Each layer improves your understanding.

Common Pitfalls in The Feynman Technique

1. Using Jargon:

Complex terms hide gaps in understanding. Stick to plain language.

2. Skipping the Gaps:

Don't avoid areas you don't fully understand—those are where learning happens.

3. Overcomplicating Explanations:

Keep your explanations short and focused on essentials.

4. Ignoring Feedback:

Test your explanation on others to ensure it's clear.

Practical Tip: Pretend You're Teaching a Child

When explaining a concept, imagine your audience is a curious child. Their questions will force you to simplify and clarify.

Takeaway

The Feynman Technique turns learning into teaching, helping you master even the most complex ideas. It's a tool for clarity, focus, and deep understanding.

Let's continue exploring practical shortcuts to tackle everyday problems.

Chapter 35: Heuristic Problem Solving

Heuristics are mental shortcuts or "rules of thumb" that simplify problem-solving. Instead of analyzing every detail, you use quick, practical methods to make decisions or find solutions.

While not always perfect, heuristics save time and effort in everyday situations.

Why Heuristic Problem Solving Matters

Humans often face decisions with limited time or information. Heuristics allow you to act quickly without overthinking, especially when perfection isn't necessary.

For example:

- When choosing a restaurant, you might rely on the heuristic *Pick the one with the best reviews,* rather than researching all options exhaustively.

Example: Packing for a Trip

Instead of overanalyzing what to pack, you use a heuristic like *Pack for three days, regardless of trip length.* This simplifies decision-making and saves time.

How to Use Heuristics

1. Define the Problem:

Be clear about what you need to solve or decide.

2. Pick a Rule of Thumb:

Use a simple guideline that fits the situation, like *Go with the majority opinion* or *Follow what worked last time.*

3. Evaluate Results:

Check if the heuristic worked well. Adjust if needed.

4. Combine Heuristics for Complex Problems:

Use multiple rules to address different aspects of the issue.

Everyday Example of Heuristics

Suppose you're grocery shopping on a budget.

- Heuristic: *Choose the store-brand version to save money.*
- This shortcut eliminates the need to compare every price, simplifying your decision.

Common Pitfalls in Heuristics

1. Overreliance on Shortcuts:

Heuristics aren't foolproof. Use them for quick decisions, not critical ones.

2. Applying the Wrong Rule:

Not all heuristics fit every situation. Choose appropriately.

3. Ignoring Details:

While details aren't always critical, missing key ones can lead to mistakes.

4. Resisting Feedback:

Adjust heuristics based on results to improve their effectiveness.

Practical Tip: Test and Adjust

After using a heuristic, evaluate its success. Keep refining your shortcuts for better results over time.

Takeaway

Heuristic Problem Solving helps you act efficiently by simplifying decisions. It's a practical tool for navigating everyday challenges with ease.

Let's continue exploring methods that combine experimentation with observation.

Chapter 36: The Scientific Method

What is The Scientific Method?

The Scientific Method is a systematic way to solve problems by asking questions, testing hypotheses, and analyzing results. It's about learning through experimentation and evidence, not guesswork or assumptions.

This model ensures that your conclusions are based on facts, not bias or opinion.

Why The Scientific Method Matters

Humans often jump to conclusions without testing their ideas. The Scientific Method slows you down, forcing you to gather evidence and evaluate results before deciding.

For example:

- Instead of assuming a new diet will work, you track its impact on your health over time.

Example: Testing a Study Strategy

You wonder if studying in the morning improves focus.

- Question: Does morning study improve focus?
- Hypothesis: Studying in the morning increases focus by 20%.
- Experiment: Study in the morning for one week and at night for another.
- Observation: Measure focus levels during both weeks.
- Conclusion: Morning study improves focus by 15%, supporting your hypothesis.

This process helps you make informed decisions based on evidence.

How to Use The Scientific Method

1. Ask a Question:

Start with a clear, focused problem or curiosity.

2. Form a Hypothesis:

Make an educated guess about the outcome.

3. Design an Experiment:

Create a testable plan to gather data.

4. Analyze Results:

Look for patterns or evidence that confirm or disprove your hypothesis.

5. Draw a Conclusion:

Use the results to answer your question. If the hypothesis was wrong, revise and test again.

Everyday Example of The Scientific Method

Suppose you want to reduce stress.

- **Question:** Does daily meditation lower stress?
- **Hypothesis:** Meditation reduces stress by 30%.
- **Experiment:** Meditate daily for two weeks and track stress levels.
- **Observation:** Stress decreased by 25%.
- **Conclusion:** Meditation is effective, but results vary slightly from your hypothesis.

The process gives you clear, actionable insights.

Common Pitfalls in The Scientific Method

1. Skipping the Hypothesis:

Without a clear guess, you can't measure success accurately.

2. Ignoring Variables:

Controlling factors like time, place, or method ensures reliable results.

3. Drawing Conclusions Too Early:

Wait for complete data before deciding.

4. Fearing Failure:

A disproven hypothesis isn't a failure—it's a step toward better understanding.

Practical Tip: Keep It Simple

Start with small, manageable experiments. Complex setups can lead to confusion or unreliable results.

Takeaway

The Scientific Method helps you solve problems with evidence and logic. It's a structured approach that turns curiosity into actionable knowledge.

Let's continue reviewing tools for reasoning and explanation.

Chapter 37: Abductive Reasoning

What is Abductive Reasoning?

Abductive Reasoning is the process of finding the most likely explanation for a set of observations. It's often called "inference to the best explanation."

Unlike deductive reasoning (which proves conclusions) or inductive reasoning (which generalizes patterns), abductive reasoning is about making the best guess when faced with incomplete information.

Why Abductive Reasoning Matters

In real life, you rarely have all the facts. Abductive Reasoning helps you make logical decisions despite uncertainty.

For example:

- If you hear water dripping, you might work out that a faucet is leaking, even without seeing it.

Example: Diagnosing a Problem

Your car won't start.

- Observation: The engine won't turn over, and the lights are dim.
- Likely Explanation: The battery is dead.

This reasoning guides you toward a solution without needing every detail upfront.

How to Use Abductive Reasoning

1. Gather Observations:

List the facts or clues available.

2. Generate Possible Explanations:

Brainstorm reasons that could explain the observations.

3. Choose the Most Likely Explanation:

Pick the explanation that fits best, given the evidence.

4. Test and Adjust:

Act on your reasoning and gather more data if needed.

Suppose you smell smoke in the kitchen.

- Possible Explanations: A dish is burning, a candle is out of control, or something outside is on fire.
- Most Likely Explanation: The oven is burning food.

This reasoning helps you act quickly to check the oven first.

1. Jumping to Conclusions:

Avoid settling on an explanation without considering alternatives.

2. Ignoring Unlikely Factors:

While some explanations are improbable, don't rule them out entirely without evidence.

3. Confirmation Bias:

Be careful not to favor explanations that match your assumptions.

4. Overcomplicating the Problem:

Stick to the simplest, most logical explanation first.

Practical Tip: Use Occam's Razor

When choosing between explanations, prefer the simplest one that fits the evidence.

Takeaway

Abductive Reasoning helps you navigate uncertainty by finding the best explanation for incomplete information. It's a practical tool for decision-making and problem-solving.

Let's look at further solutions that put human needs at the center.

Chapter 38: Design Thinking

What is Design Thinking?

Design Thinking is a human-centered approach to solving problems. It focuses on understanding user needs, brainstorming creative ideas, and testing solutions.

This model emphasizes empathy, collaboration, and adaptability, making it ideal for creating products, services, or processes that truly work for people.

Why Design Thinking Matters

Traditional problem-solving often skips empathy, leading to solutions that miss the mark. Design Thinking ensures your approach aligns with real user needs.

For example:

- A company redesigning a website uses Design Thinking to focus on making navigation easier for users instead of just adding flashy features.

Example: Improving Public Transport

Imagine you're tasked with improving a bus system.

- Empathize: Talk to passengers about their frustrations.
- Define: Identify the core issue—long wait times.
- Ideate: Brainstorm solutions like more buses or a real-time tracking app.
- Prototype: Create a basic app to test.
- Test: Gather feedback and refine the app based on user input.

This process ensures practical, user-friendly results.

How to Apply Design Thinking

1. **Empathize:**

   Understand the user's perspective through interviews or observation.

2. **Define the Problem:**

   Clearly state the issue based on user insights.

3. **Ideate Solutions:**

   Brainstorm as many creative ideas as possible.

4. **Prototype:**

   Build simple, testable versions of your ideas.

5. **Test and Refine:**

   Use feedback to improve your solution iteratively.

Everyday Example of Design Thinking

Suppose you're organizing a family dinner.

- Empathize: Ask family members about dietary preferences.
- Define: The goal is to serve a meal everyone enjoys.
- Ideate: Brainstorm menu ideas.
- Prototype: Test one dish before finalizing the menu.
- Test: Get feedback and adjust if needed.

This ensures everyone has a great experience.

Common Pitfalls in Design Thinking

1. **Skipping Empathy:**

   Solving a problem without understanding user needs leads to ineffective solutions.

2. **Rushing Prototypes:**

   Prototypes should be simple but meaningful.

3. **Resisting Feedback:**

   Iteration is key — be willing to revise your ideas.

4. **Overthinking Ideation:**

   Focus on generating ideas, not perfection, during brainstorming.

Practical Tip: Use Rapid Prototyping

Quickly test ideas with basic models or mock-ups. Feedback from early prototypes often leads to breakthrough solutions.

Takeaway

Design Thinking ensures solutions are practical, creative, and human-centered. It's a flexible approach that adapts to real needs through empathy and iteration.

Let's look at more ways to test assumptions.

Chapter 39: Hypothesis Testing

What is Hypothesis Testing?

Hypothesis Testing is the process of creating a statement about a possible outcome and then testing it to see if it is true. It's a way to validate assumptions using data, experiments, or observations.

This model ensures decisions are based on evidence, not guesses.

Why Hypothesis Testing Matters

Assumptions can lead to costly mistakes if they're wrong. Hypothesis Testing forces you to evaluate ideas objectively, minimizing risk and maximizing results.

For example:

- A business tests whether offering free shipping increases sales. Instead of assuming, they collect data to confirm or disprove the idea.

Example: Testing a New Marketing Strategy

You want to know if posting daily on social media increases engagement.

- Hypothesis: Daily posts will boost engagement by 25%.
- Test: Post daily for two weeks and measure engagement levels.
- Outcome: Engagement increases by 15%. The hypothesis isn't fully supported, so you refine your approach.

This process ensures data-driven decisions.

How to Conduct Hypothesis Testing

1. Formulate a Hypothesis:

Make a clear, testable statement about what you expect to happen.

2. Design an Experiment:

Create a plan to gather evidence, ensuring it's measurable and reliable.

3. Collect Data:

Observe and record results from the test.

4. Analyze Results:

Compare the data to your hypothesis.

5. Draw Conclusions:

Decide whether the hypothesis is supported, rejected, or needs adjustment.

Everyday Example of Hypothesis Testing

Imagine you're trying to improve sleep by going to bed earlier.

- Hypothesis: Sleeping an hour earlier will reduce daytime fatigue.
- Test: Adjust bedtime for a week and track how you feel during the day.
- Outcome: Fatigue decreases, confirming the hypothesis.

Testing the idea ensures your actions are effective.

Common Pitfalls in Hypothesis Testing

1. Making Vague Hypotheses:

Statements like *Things might improve* are hard to test. Be specific.

2. Using Incomplete Data:

Ensure your sample size is large enough to draw meaningful conclusions.

3. Ignoring Confounding Factors:

External variables can affect results. Control them as much as possible.

4. Forgetting to Iterate:

A single test may not give the full picture. Repeat and refine if needed.

Practical Tip: Always Ask, "How Will I Measure Success?"

Define clear metrics before testing so you can evaluate results objectively.

Takeaway

Hypothesis Testing is a reliable way to validate ideas and make informed decisions. By relying on evidence, you reduce uncertainty and increase your chances of success.

Let's continue exploring ways to compare and refine options effectively.

Chapter 40: A/B Testing

What is A/B Testing?

A/B Testing compares two versions of something—like a webpage, ad, or product feature—to see which performs better. It's a practical way to refine decisions by testing options directly with real users.

This model is frequently used in marketing, design, and product development to optimize results.

Why A/B Testing Matters

Guessing which option works best can lead to wasted time and resources. A/B Testing eliminates the guesswork by showing you what actually performs better.

For example:

- A company tests two email subject lines to see which gets more clicks.

Example: Choosing a Website Design

You're deciding between two homepage layouts.

- Option A: Focuses on visuals.
- Option B: Focuses on text.
- Test: Show each version to 1,000 visitors and measure conversions.
- Result: Option B performs 30% better, so you choose it.

A/B Testing ensures data backs your decision.

How to Conduct A/B Testing

1. Define the Variable:

Choose one thing to test, like a headline, color, or layout.

2. Split Your Audience:

Divide users randomly into two groups—one sees Option A, the other Option B.

3. Measure Results:

Track key metrics like clicks, sales, or engagement.

4. Analyze the Data:

Compare the performance of each option.

5. Implement the Winner:

Use the best-performing version and iterate further if needed.

Everyday Example of A/B Testing

Suppose you're organizing a party and debating invitations.

- Option A: A handwritten note.
- Option B: A digital card.
- Test: Send half of your friends Option A and the other half Option B.
- Result: More people respond to the digital card, so you use it.

This simple test guides your choice.

Common Pitfalls in A/B Testing

1. Testing Too Many Variables:

Changing multiple things at once makes it hard to tell what caused the difference.

2. Drawing Conclusions Too Early:

Ensure your sample size is large enough for reliable results.

3. Focusing on the Wrong Metrics:

Track outcomes that align with your goals (e.g., clicks aren't useful if sales are the priority).

4. Failing to Retest:

Repeat tests periodically to ensure results hold over time.

Practical Tip: Start Small

Begin with simple tests, like comparing two headlines, before moving on to larger changes.

Takeaway

A/B Testing helps you make data-driven choices by directly comparing options. It's a practical way to refine strategies and improve outcomes.

Let's further explore strategic frameworks for decision-making and problem-solving.

Strategic Thinking Models

Chapter 41: The OODA Loop

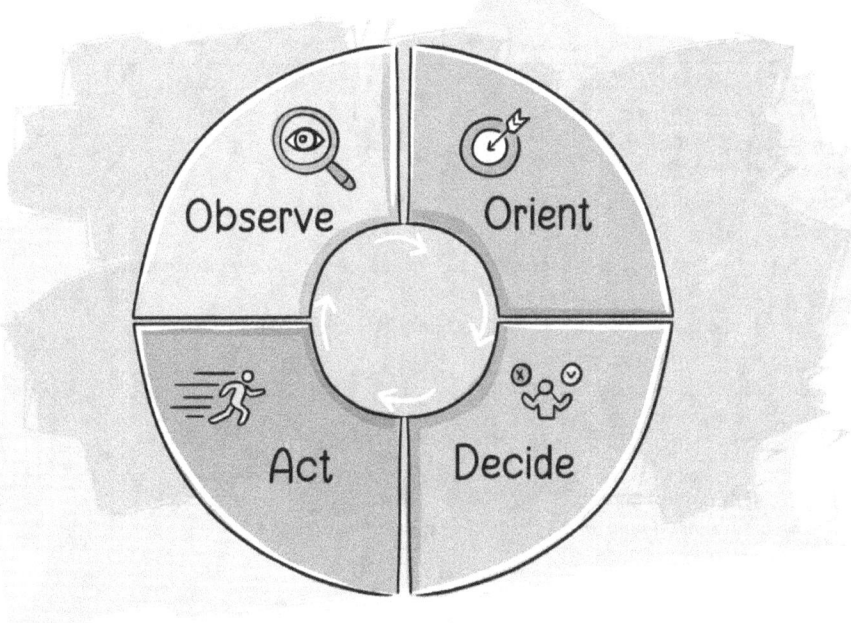

What is the OODA Loop?

The OODA Loop is a decision-making framework developed by military strategist John Boyd. It stands for Observe, Orient, Decide, Act and is designed for fast, adaptive decision-making in dynamic situations.

This model is widely used in business, strategy, and problem-solving where speed and flexibility are critical.

Why the OODA Loop Matters

Quick, effective decisions often depend on how well you adapt to changing circumstances. The OODA Loop helps you to continuously reassess the situation and adjust your actions.

For example:

- A company launching a product observes market trends, orients their strategy, decides on a pricing model, and acts by releasing the product—all while monitoring competitor moves.

Example: Adapting to a Traffic Jam

Imagine you're driving and encounter unexpected traffic.

1. **Observe:** Notice the traffic jam ahead.
2. **Orient:** Check maps for alternate routes.
3. **Decide:** Choose the fastest detour.
4. **Act:** Take the new route.

The loop repeats as you reassess conditions.

How to Use the OODA Loop

1. **Observe:**

Gather information about your environment. Stay aware of changes and new data.

2. **Orient:**

Analyze the information and understand its implications. Consider biases or blind spots.

3. **Decide:**

Choose the best course of action based on your analysis.

4. **Act:**

Implement your decision quickly, then return to the observation phase to see if adjustments are needed.

Suppose you're planning a weekend hike, and the forecast changes to rain.

- **Observe:** Rain is predicted.
- **Orient:** Evaluate your gear and possible trail conditions.
- **Decide:** Choose a waterproof jacket and an easier trail.
- **Act:** Update your plan and proceed.

The OODA Loop ensures your plan adapts to new conditions.

Common Pitfalls in the OODA Loop

1. **Getting Stuck in Observation:**

   Overanalyzing delays decisions. Act quickly to stay ahead.

2. **Ignoring Orientation:**

   Acting without fully understanding the situation leads to mistakes.

3. **Skipping Feedback:**

   Failing to revisit the observation phase prevents you from adapting to new information.

4. **Being Too Rigid:**

   The loop thrives on flexibility. Adjust as conditions change.

Practical Tip: Act on Imperfect Information

In fast-changing situations, waiting for perfect data can be costly. Use the best information available and refine your actions as you go.

Takeaway

The OODA Loop helps you make fast, adaptive decisions by continuously observing, analyzing, and adjusting. It's a dynamic model for navigating uncertainty with confidence.

Let's continue reviewing structured approaches to anticipating the future.

Chapter 42: Scenario Planning

What is Scenario Planning?

Scenario Planning is the process of imagining and preparing for different possible futures. Instead of predicting one outcome, you explore multiple scenarios and develop plans for each.

This model helps you manage uncertainty by ensuring you're ready for a range of possibilities.

Why Scenario Planning Matters

Life and business are full of unpredictability. Scenario Planning helps you avoid being blindsided by changes by thinking ahead. For example:

- A company preparing for economic downturns creates plans for maintaining cash flow, cutting costs, and seizing new opportunities.

Example: Planning a Vacation

You're planning a trip but unsure about the weather.

- **Scenario A:** It's sunny—plan outdoor activities.
- **Scenario B:** It's rainy—prepare indoor options.
- **Scenario C:** A storm hits—have a cancellation plan.

By preparing for all scenarios, you ensure a smooth trip regardless of the weather.

How to Use Scenario Planning

1. **Identify Key Factors:**
   Determine the uncertainties that could affect your situation (e.g., weather, market trends).
2. **Develop Scenarios:**
   Imagine best-case, worst-case, and middle-ground outcomes.
3. **Plan for Each Scenario:**
   Create strategies and contingency plans tailored to each possibility.
4. **Monitor Key Indicators:**
   Watch for signs that point toward one scenario becoming more likely.

Everyday Example of Scenario Planning

Suppose you're preparing for a job interview.

- **Scenario A:** The interviewer asks standard questions—practice answers.
- **Scenario B:** The interviewer focuses on problem-solving—review case studies.
- **Scenario C:** The interview runs long—prepare for deeper discussions.

Thinking ahead ensures you're ready for any situation.

Common Pitfalls in Scenario Planning

1. **Focusing on Only One Scenario:**
   Relying on a single prediction leaves you vulnerable to surprises.
2. **Ignoring Low-Probability Outcomes:**
   Even unlikely scenarios can have significant impacts. Prepare for them.
3. **Overcomplicating Plans:**
   Simple, actionable strategies are more effective than overly complex ones.
4. **Failing to Revisit Plans:**
   Scenarios evolve. Regularly update your plans based on new information.

Practical Tip: Use "What If" Thinking

For any situation, ask: *What if this happens? What's my plan?* Thinking through possibilities builds confidence and readiness.

Takeaway

Scenario Planning helps you prepare for uncertainty by anticipating multiple outcomes and creating flexible strategies. It's a powerful way to stay proactive and adaptable.

Let's continue exploring frameworks for playing to your strengths.

Chapter 43: The Hedgehog Concept

I love writing, but I'm also good at teaching. How do I choose?

Which one creates the biggest impact? That's your Hedgehog!

What is The Hedgehog Concept?

The Hedgehog Concept, inspired by Jim Collins' book *Good to Great,* focuses on finding the intersection of three areas:

1. What you're deeply passionate about.

2. What you can be the best in the world at.

3. What drives your economic or personal success.

This model helps you identify your core focus — the one thing you can do exceptionally well.

Why The Hedgehog Concept Matters

Spreading yourself too thin across multiple goals dilutes your efforts. The Hedgehog Concept simplifies your priorities, ensuring you focus on what truly matters.

For example:

- A business that excels in logistics might focus solely on supply chain optimization instead of branching into unrelated areas.

Example: Choosing a Career Path

Suppose you're deciding between different careers.

- Passion: You love helping others.
- Talent: You're skilled in communication.
- Success: Counseling offers meaningful work and financial stability.

Becoming a counselor touches on all three areas, making it your "Hedgehog."

How to Apply The Hedgehog Concept

1. Reflect on Your Passions:

Ask: What do I truly love doing?

2. Assess Your Strengths:

Identify areas where you consistently excel or show potential for mastery.

3. Evaluate Impact:

Focus on activities that create measurable success or results.

4. Eliminate Distractions:

Stop pursuing goals that don't align with your Hedgehog Concept.

Everyday Example of The Hedgehog Concept

Imagine you're starting a side business.

- Passion: You enjoy baking.
- Talent: You make excellent cakes.
- Results: Local demand for custom cakes is high.

Focusing on custom cakes aligns with your strengths and drives success.

Common Pitfalls in The Hedgehog Concept

1. Ignoring Passion:

Success without passion often leads to burnout.

2. Overestimating Strengths:

Be honest about what you're truly the best at.

3. Chasing Unrelated Goals:

Activities outside your focus dilute your efforts and results.

4. Neglecting Feedback:

Regularly reassess your Hedgehog Concept based on real-world results.

Practical Tip: Use a Venn Diagram

Draw three overlapping circles for passion, talent, and success. Where they meet is your focus area.

Takeaway

The Hedgehog Concept helps you simplify your goals by focusing on what you're best at and passionate about. It's a blueprint for achieving meaningful success.

Let's further discuss strategic models that balance risk and reward.

Chapter 44: Risk Management

What is Risk Management?

Risk Management is the process of identifying, assessing, and mitigating potential risks to achieve your goals while minimizing negative impacts. Instead of avoiding all risks, it's about finding a balance between taking calculated risks and protecting against failure.

This model applies to everything from business ventures to personal decisions.

Why Risk Management Matters

Every decision involves uncertainty. Risk Management helps you act confidently by preparing for the worst while working toward the best.

For example:

- A company launching a product anticipates risks like competition or supply chain issues and creates contingency plans to address them.

Example: Planning a Big Event

Suppose you're organizing an outdoor wedding.

- Risks: Rain, vendor cancellations, or power outages.
- Mitigation: Rent a tent, have backup vendors, and ensure a generator is available.

By managing risks, you reduce stress and ensure a successful event.

How to Use Risk Management

1. Identify Risks:
List potential problems that could arise.

2. Assess Impact and Likelihood:
For each risk, evaluate how severe it would be and how likely it is to happen.

3. Develop Mitigation Plans:
Create strategies to minimize or respond to risks.

4. Monitor and Adapt:
Keep an eye on risks as circumstances change and adjust plans as needed.

Everyday Example of Risk Management

Imagine you're saving for a vacation.

- Risks: Unexpected expenses (like car repairs) might reduce your savings.
- Mitigation: Create an emergency fund to cover surprise costs.

This approach ensures your vacation budget stays intact even if something goes wrong.

Common Pitfalls in Risk Management

1. Ignoring Small Risks:
Minor risks can escalate if left unaddressed.

2. Overpreparing:
Excessive focus on unlikely risks wastes time and resources.

3. Failing to Reassess:
Risks evolve over time. Regularly update your plans.

4. Avoiding All Risks:
Taking no risks often means missing valuable opportunities.

Practical Tip: Use a Risk Matrix

Plot risks on a matrix with two axes: "Likelihood" and "Impact." Focus on addressing high-impact, high-likelihood risks first.

Takeaway

Risk Management helps you navigate uncertainty with confidence. By balancing risks and rewards, you increase your chances of success while minimizing setbacks.

Let's continue exploring tools for analyzing competition and strategy.

Chapter 45: Competitive Analysis

What is Competitive Analysis?

Competitive Analysis is the process of studying your competitors to identify their strengths, weaknesses, and strategies. This helps you find opportunities to outperform them.

It's a critical tool in business, sports, and any context where success depends on understanding others in the field.

Why Competitive Analysis Matters

Without knowing what others are doing, you risk falling behind or wasting resources on ineffective strategies. Competitive Analysis helps you differentiate yourself and focus on what sets you apart.

For example:

- A start-up launching a new app analyzes competitors' features to identify gaps they can fill, such as better user experience or unique functionality.

Example: Opening a Coffee Shop

You want to stand out from other coffee shops in your area.

- Strengths of Competitors: Popular locations, loyal customers.
- Weaknesses of Competitors: Long wait times, limited menu options.
- Your Opportunity: Offer faster service and unique menu items like locally sourced pastries.

Understanding your competition helps you carve out your niche.

How to Conduct Competitive Analysis

1. **Identify Competitors:**

   List direct and indirect competitors in your space.

2. **Analyze Strengths and Weaknesses:**

   Evaluate what they do well and where they fall short.

3. **Find Opportunities:**

   Look for gaps or unmet needs that you can address.

4. **Monitor Regularly:**

   Keep an eye on competitors' strategies to adapt and stay ahead.

Everyday Example of Competitive Analysis

Suppose you're applying for a job.

- Competitors: Other applicants.
- Their Strengths: Relevant degrees or experience.
- Their Weaknesses: Lack of creativity or unique skills.
- Your Strategy: Highlight a unique skill, like proficiency in a niche software, that sets you apart.

Analyzing your competition gives you a strategic edge.

1. **Focusing Only on Competitors:**

   Don't lose sight of your own strengths and goals while analyzing others.

2. **Underestimating Emerging Competitors:**

   Smaller or newer players can become serious threats over time.

3. **Copying Competitors:**

   Success comes from differentiation, not imitation.

4. **Overanalyzing:**

   Spending too much time on analysis can delay action.

Practical Tip: Use a SWOT Comparison

Create a SWOT chart comparing your strengths, weaknesses, opportunities, and threats against your competitors'. This highlights where you can excel.

Takeaway

Competitive Analysis helps you understand your rivals and find opportunities to stand out. By staying informed and adaptable, you can build strategies that set you apart.

Chapter 46: Red Teaming

What is Red Teaming?

Red Teaming is the practice of challenging your plans, strategies, or ideas by intentionally thinking like an opponent. It involves playing the role of a critic to uncover flaws, weaknesses, or risks that might otherwise be overlooked.

This model is used in military strategy, business planning, and decision-making to ensure ideas are well-prepared.

Why Red Teaming Matters

Without scrutiny, even the best plans can fail due to unforeseen issues. Red Teaming forces you to anticipate challenges and improve your ideas before implementing them.

For example:

- A company launching a product has a Red Team act as skeptical customers to identify potential problems, like unclear instructions or poor usability.

Example: Planning a New Budget

You're creating a personal budget to save money.

- Plan: Save 20% of your income monthly.
- Red Team Critique: What if unexpected expenses arise? Do you have a plan for emergencies?
- Revised Plan: Build an emergency fund alongside monthly savings.

Challenging your assumptions makes your plan more resilient.

How to Use Red Teaming

1. **Assemble a Red Team:**

   Include people with different perspectives who can critique your plan objectively.

2. **Identify Assumptions:**

   List the key assumptions your plan relies on.

3. **Challenge the Plan:**

   Ask tough questions like What could go wrong? What would an opponent do?

4. **Revise and Strengthen:**

   Use the feedback to address weaknesses and refine your plan.

Suppose you're preparing for a big presentation.

- Red Team: A friend pretends to be a skeptical audience, asking challenging questions.
- Outcome: You realize one slide is unclear and revise it for clarity.

This preparation ensures you're ready for real-world challenges.

Common Pitfalls in Red Teaming

1. **Ignoring Feedback:**

   If you resist criticism, your plan won't improve.

2. **Being Too Defensive:**

   Remember, critiques are meant to strengthen, not attack, your ideas.

3. **Overcomplicating the Process:**

   Focus on major flaws, not minor details.

4. **Failing to Involve Diverse Perspectives:**

   A homogeneous Red Team may miss critical blind spots.

Practical Tip: Roleplay Opposing Scenarios

When Red Teaming, imagine how a competitor or critic would approach your plan. This helps you anticipate challenges from different angles.

Takeaway

Red Teaming strengthens your plans by exposing weaknesses and testing assumptions. It's a powerful way to build resilience and confidence in your strategies.

Now, let's explore innovative tools for maximizing impact.

Chapter 47: Asymmetric Thinking

What is Asymmetric Thinking?

Asymmetric Thinking focuses on finding actions that require minimal effort but create maximum impact. Instead of working harder on everything, you look for leverage points — small changes or strategies that deliver outsized results.

This approach is about being efficient and strategic rather than expending effort evenly across all tasks.

Why Asymmetric Thinking Matters

Time and resources are limited. Asymmetric Thinking ensures you prioritize actions that create the most value, helping you achieve more with less.

For example:

- A small business focuses on a niche market instead of competing with larger companies, gaining loyal customers with less effort.

You want to grow your social media following.

- Symmetric Approach: Post daily to all platforms with equal effort.
- Asymmetric Approach: Focus on one platform where your target audience is most active, creating tailored, high-quality content.

By concentrating on the highest-impact area, you grow faster and more effectively.

How to Apply Asymmetric Thinking

1. Identify Leverage Points:

Look for areas where small actions can create significant results.

2. Analyze the Effort-to-Impact Ratio:

Compare the resources required versus the potential outcome.

3. Focus on High-Impact Areas:

Prioritize tasks or strategies with the best return on investment.

4. Test and Adjust:

Experiment with different actions to find what works best.

Everyday Example of Asymmetric Thinking

Suppose you're trying to improve your health.

- Symmetric: Follow a strict workout routine and complex diet plan.
- Asymmetric: Start by improving sleep quality, which boosts energy and supports better decision-making for fitness and nutrition.

Focusing on one high-impact change simplifies the process and delivers better results.

Common Pitfalls in Asymmetric Thinking

1. Chasing Every Shortcut:

Not all "small actions" lead to big results. Focus on meaningful leverage points.

2. Overlooking Long-Term Effort:

Asymmetric Thinking is about smart effort, not avoiding effort entirely.

3. Ignoring Context:

What works in one situation might not apply elsewhere.

4. Underestimating Preparation:

Leveraging small actions often requires careful planning and insight.

Practical Tip: Ask, "What's My Biggest Lever?"

For any goal, identify the one action or strategy that could create the most significant result with minimal effort.

Takeaway

Asymmetric Thinking maximizes results by focusing on high-leverage actions. It's a mindset for achieving big goals efficiently and strategically.

Let's explore collaborative tools for gathering different perspectives.

Chapter 48:
Crowdsourcing Ideas

What is Crowdsourcing Ideas?

Crowdsourcing Ideas involves gathering input, feedback, or solutions from a large group of people, often through open calls or collaborative platforms. It leverages the collective intelligence of a group to solve problems or generate creative ideas.

This approach works because diverse perspectives often lead to more innovative and well-rounded solutions.

Why Crowdsourcing Matters

Your own perspective is limited. Crowdsourcing taps into a wider range of experiences, skills, and insights, uncovering ideas you might not have considered.

For example:

- A company launching a product asks customers for feature suggestions, ensuring the product meets real needs.

Example: Planning a Community Event

You're organizing a neighborhood festival and unsure what activities to include.

- Crowdsourcing: Conduct a survey asking residents for their preferences. The responses help you prioritize activities that will attract the most participants.

How to Crowdsource Ideas

1. Define the Problem or Goal:
Clearly communicate what you're trying to solve or achieve.

2. Choose the Right Platform:
Use tools like surveys, social media, or brainstorming sessions to gather input.

3. Encourage Participation:
Make it easy for people to contribute and emphasize that their input is valued.

4. Analyze and Implement:
Sort through the ideas, identify patterns, and integrate the best ones into your plan.

Everyday Example of Crowdsourcing

Suppose you're redecorating your living room.

- Post options for paint colors on social media and ask friends for their opinions. Their feedback helps you choose a popular, appealing color.

Common Pitfalls in Crowdsourcing

1. Too Many Ideas:
Without clear criteria, sorting through responses can become overwhelming.

2. Ignoring Contributions:
Failing to act on ideas discourages future participation.

3. Overreliance on Popularity:
The most popular ideas aren't always the best—balance feedback with critical analysis.

4. Lack of Clarity:
Ambiguous requests lead to unfocused or irrelevant contributions.

Practical Tip: Use "Vote and Prioritize" Methods

After gathering ideas, let the group vote on the best options to narrow the focus efficiently.

Takeaway

Crowdsourcing Ideas taps into collective wisdom to solve problems and generate innovative solutions. By leveraging diverse input, you can achieve better outcomes collaboratively.

Chapter 49: Long-Term Thinking

What is Long-Term Thinking?

Long-Term Thinking focuses on making decisions today that benefit you in the future. It's about prioritizing sustainable progress and delayed gratification over short-term gains.

This model helps you achieve meaningful, lasting success by keeping your eyes on the big picture.

Why Long-Term Thinking Matters

Short-term decisions often feel rewarding but can derail your future goals. Long-Term Thinking ensures your actions align with what truly matters over time.

For example:

- Saving for retirement instead of spending on unnecessary luxuries ensures financial security in the future.

Example: Building a Fitness Routine

You want to get healthier.

- Short-Term Mindset: Do extreme workouts for quick results, risking burnout.
- Long-Term Mindset: Build sustainable habits like regular exercise and balanced nutrition, leading to lasting health improvements.

How to Practice Long-Term Thinking

1. **Define Your Vision:**

   Identify your ultimate goals and what success looks like in the future.

2. **Break Goals Into Steps:**

   Create smaller milestones that lead to the bigger picture.

3. **Evaluate Decisions for Alignment:**

   Ask: Does this choice bring me closer to my long-term goals?

4. **Be Patient:**

   Understand that meaningful results take time.

Everyday Example of Long-Term Thinking

Suppose you're tempted to buy an expensive gadget.

- Long-Term Thinking: Consider how saving that money could help you afford a bigger goal, like traveling or investing in your education.

Common Pitfalls in Long-Term Thinking

1. **Overlooking Immediate Needs:**

   Balance long-term goals with current responsibilities.

2. **Losing Focus:**

   Stay motivated by celebrating small wins along the way.

3. **Underestimating Change:**

   Be flexible—adjust long-term plans as circumstances evolve.

4. **Sacrificing Too Much:**

   Avoid burnout by allowing some short-term rewards along the journey.

Practical Tip: Use the "10/10/10 Rule"

For any decision, ask: *How will this affect me in 10 days? 10 months? 10 years?* This perspective highlights long-term impacts.

Takeaway

Long-Term Thinking helps you align your actions with lasting success. It's a strategy for building a meaningful future, one step at a time.

Let's move on to tools for handling uncertainty and unpredictability.

Chapter 50: Contingency Planning

What is Contingency Planning?

Contingency Planning involves preparing backup strategies in case your original plan doesn't work out. It's about expecting the unexpected and having a roadmap for navigating unforeseen challenges.

This model is essential for minimizing risks and staying adaptable under pressure.

Why Contingency Planning Matters

Life and projects rarely go exactly as planned. Without alternatives, setbacks can cause chaos. Contingency Planning ensures you can pivot quickly, reducing stress and keeping you on track.

For example:

- A company launching a product might prepare for supply chain delays by sourcing secondary suppliers in advance.

Example: Hosting an Outdoor Event

Suppose you're organizing a backyard party.

- **Plan A:** Clear skies and outdoor activities.
- **Contingency Plan:** Rent a tent and prepare indoor games in case it rains.

This backup ensures the party is successful, rain or shine.

How to Create a Contingency Plan

1. Identify Key Risks:

Consider what could go wrong and prioritize the most likely or impactful risks.

2. Develop Alternatives:

For each risk, outline specific actions you can take if it occurs.

3. Allocate Resources:

Ensure you have the tools, time, or budget needed to implement your backup plan.

4. Communicate the Plan:

Share your contingency strategies with relevant stakeholders.

Everyday Example of Contingency Planning

Imagine you're commuting to work.

- Plan A: Drive your usual route.
- Plan B: Check for traffic or public transport options in case of delays.

By preparing a backup, you ensure you arrive on time even if your primary route is blocked.

Common Pitfalls in Contingency Planning

1. Overlooking Low-Probability Risks:

Even unlikely events can have significant consequences. Prepare for them.

2. Failing to Test the Plan:

Backup plans should be reviewed and tested to ensure they're practical.

3. Ignoring Resources:

Contingency plans are useless if you lack the resources to execute them.

4. Relying Only on the Backup:

Don't neglect the original plan while focusing on contingencies.

Practical Tip: Use a "What If" Checklist

List potential scenarios starting with "What if ..." (e.g., *What if my flight is canceled?*). For each, write down a clear response.

Takeaway

Contingency Planning ensures you're ready for the unexpected. By preparing alternatives, you can face challenges calmly and confidently.

Communication Models

Chapter 51: The 5W Model

What is The 5W Model?

The 5W Model is a framework for gathering complete and clear information about any situation by asking five essential questions:

1. Who is involved?
2. What is happening?
3. Where is it occurring?
4. When did it or will it happen?
5. Why is it significant?

This model is used in journalism, problem-solving, and planning to ensure nothing important is overlooked.

Why The 5W Model Matters

Incomplete information leads to misunderstandings and poor decisions. The 5W Model organizes your thinking, ensuring all important aspects of a situation are addressed.

For example:

- A journalist covering a story ensures they answer all five questions to give readers a complete understanding.

Example: Planning a Business Meeting

Suppose you're organizing a team meeting.

- **Who:** Key team members.
- **What:** Discuss project deadlines.
- **Where:** Conference room or online.
- **When:** Thursday at 10 a.m.
- **Why:** To ensure everyone aligns on tasks.

Answering these questions ensures clarity and efficiency.

1. Start with the Basics:

Use the 5Ws to outline the core details of any problem, plan, or project.

2. Expand Each Question:

Add context and specifics to each answer as needed.

3. Check for Gaps:

Review your answers to ensure nothing important is missing.

4. Communicate Clearly:

Use the 5Ws as a structure for presenting or explaining information.

Everyday Example of the 5W Model

Suppose you're planning a family trip.

- **Who:** Your family.
- **What:** A weekend getaway.
- **Where:** A nearby beach town.
- **When:** Next month.
- **Why:** To relax and spend quality time together.

The 5W Model ensures the trip is well-organized and everyone is on the same page.

Common Pitfalls in the 5W Model

1. Overlooking One W:

Skipping even one question can leave critical details unaddressed.

2. Being Too Vague:

Answers like "soon" or "someone" lack clarity. Be specific.

3. Overcomplicating Answers:

Keep answers focused and concise.

4. Failing to Adapt:

Adjust the 5Ws as new information emerges.

Practical Tip: Use the 5Ws for Problem-Solving

When facing a challenge, write down the 5Ws to clarify the situation and guide your response.

Takeaway

The 5W Model simplifies decision-making by organizing essential information into clear, actionable insights. It's a versatile tool for clarity and communication.

Now, let's explore models for enhancing understanding and collaboration.

Chapter 52: Active Listening

What is Active Listening?

Active Listening is the skill of fully concentrating on what someone is saying to understand their message completely. It involves more than just hearing words — it's about engaging with the speaker through attention, empathy, and feedback.

This model is essential for clear communication, strong relationships, and effective problem-solving.

Why Active Listening Matters

Many misunderstandings occur because people listen to respond, not to understand. Active Listening builds trust, reduces conflict, and ensures mutual understanding.

For example:

- A manager practicing Active Listening hears not only an employee's concerns but also the emotions behind them, leading to better solutions.

Example: Handling a Misunderstanding

Suppose a friend is upset about a canceled plan.

- Passive Listening: You nod while planning your response, missing their real frustration.
- Active Listening: You focus on their words, ask clarifying questions, and validate their feelings.

This approach resolves the issue more effectively.

How to Practice Active Listening

1. **Give Full Attention:**

   Maintain eye contact and avoid distractions like phones or multitasking.

2. **Show You're Listening:**

   Use nonverbal cues like nodding and facial expressions to signal engagement.

3. **Ask Questions:**

   Clarify points with open-ended questions like *Can you tell me more about that?*

4. **Paraphrase for Clarity:**

   Repeat back what you heard to confirm understanding (e.g., *So you're saying...*).

5. **Avoid Interrupting:**

   Let the speaker finish before responding.

Everyday Example of Active Listening

Imagine your child is explaining their day at school.

- Active Listening: You listen without interrupting, ask questions about their favorite part, and summarize what they shared.

This builds connection and shows that their words matter.

Common Pitfalls in Active Listening

1. **Getting Distracted:**

   Multitasking or letting your mind wander undermines the process.

2. **Jumping to Solutions:**

   Sometimes, people just want to be heard, not "fixed."

3. **Interrupting:**

   Cutting someone off discourages them from fully expressing their thoughts.

4. **Ignoring Nonverbal Cues:**

   Pay attention to tone, body language, and emotions, not just words.

Practical Tip: Use the "Wait Rule"

Before responding, count to three silently. This ensures the speaker has finished and gives you time to formulate a thoughtful reply.

Takeaway

Active Listening strengthens communication by fostering understanding and trust. It's a simple yet powerful skill that improves every interaction.

Let's continue exploring tools for giving effective feedback.

Chapter 53: Feedback Framework

What is a Feedback Framework?

A Feedback Framework organizes constructive feedback into clear, actionable steps. It ensures feedback is specific, balanced, and focused on improvement rather than criticism.

This model is used in workplaces, education, and personal relationships to foster growth and understanding.

Why Feedback Frameworks Matter

Unstructured feedback often feels vague, harsh, or unhelpful. A framework ensures your message is clear, encouraging, and aligned with the recipient's goals.

For example:

- A manager uses a framework to praise an employee's strengths, highlight areas for improvement, and suggest specific next steps.

Example: Coaching a Team Member

Suppose a colleague struggles with time management.

- **What Went Well:** "You're thorough in completing tasks."
- **What Could Improve:** "Sometimes deadlines are missed due to detailed focus."
- **Suggestions for Growth:** "Try setting time limits for each task to stay on track."

This structure makes feedback constructive and actionable.

How to Use a Feedback Framework

1. Start Positive:
Highlight what the person is doing well to build confidence.

2. Be Specific About Improvements:
Focus on behaviors or actions, not personal traits (e.g., *"This report needs more detail"* instead of *"You're careless"*).

3. Provide Solutions:
Offer practical steps or tools to address the issue.

4. End on a Positive Note:
Reinforce your belief in the person's ability to improve.

Everyday Example of Feedback Framework

Imagine your child brings home a report card with mixed grades.

- "You've done a great job in math and science (What Went Well). Let's work on reading comprehension together (What Could Improve). Reading for 20 minutes daily could help (Suggestions for Growth)."

This feedback encourages them without feeling discouraging.

1. **Being Too Vague:**

   General comments like *"Good job"* don't provide actionable guidance.

2. **Focusing Only on Negatives:**

   Balance constructive feedback with praise to maintain morale.

3. **Overloading with Suggestions:**

   Stick to one or two key points for better focus.

4. **Delivering Feedback Emotionally:**

   Keep your tone calm and professional to ensure the message is well-received.

Practical Tip: Use the "Feedback Sandwich"

Start with positive feedback, address the area for improvement, and end with encouragement.

Takeaway

A Feedback Framework turns criticism into constructive guidance, fostering growth and improvement. It's a valuable tool for building trust and achieving better results.

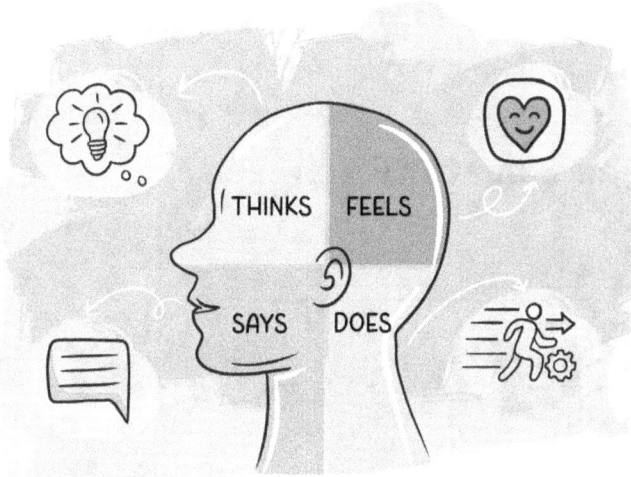

Chapter 54: Empathy Mapping

What is Empathy Mapping?

Empathy Mapping is a tool for understanding someone's experience by exploring what they say, think, feel, and do. It's used to gain deeper insights into their perspective, whether they're a customer, team member, or loved one.

This model helps you connect with others on a more meaningful level and design solutions that truly meet their needs.

Why Empathy Mapping Matters

Without empathy, solutions often miss the mark. Empathy Mapping uncovers hidden emotions, motivations, and concerns, ensuring your decisions are human-centered.

For example:

- A business designing a new app uses Empathy Mapping to understand users' frustrations with current solutions, creating features that address their pain points.

Example: Resolving a Customer Complaint

Suppose a customer complains about late delivery.

- **Says:** "This delay is unacceptable."
- **Thinks:** "They don't value my time."
- **Feels:** Frustrated and undervalued.
- **Does:** Writes a negative review.

Understanding these layers helps you respond with empathy, offering a sincere apology and proactive solution.

How to Create an Empathy Map

1. **Define the Person:**

   Choose who you're mapping—customer, employee, or another individual.

2. **Gather Data:**

   Use interviews, surveys, or observations to collect insights.

3. **Fill the Sections:**

   Note what they:

   o **Says:** Quotes or phrases they use.

   o **Thinks:** Beliefs or motivations.

   o **Feels:** Emotions driving their actions.

   o **Does:** Observable behaviors.

4. Identify Patterns:

Look for connections between sections to better understand their experience.

Imagine helping a child with homework.

- **Says:** "This is too hard!"
- **Thinks:** "I'm not good at this subject."
- **Feels:** Frustrated and anxious.
- **Does:** Avoids the homework.

By empathizing, you offer encouragement and break the task into smaller, manageable steps.

Common Pitfalls in Empathy Mapping

1. Making Assumptions:

Base your map on real data, not guesses.

2. Overgeneralizing:

Avoid lumping people into overly broad categories. Focus on individual insights.

3. Ignoring Context:

A person's actions may depend on specific circumstances.

4. Focusing Only on Surface Behaviors:

Dive deeper to uncover underlying emotions and thoughts.

Practical Tip: Use Empathy Maps in Teams

When brainstorming, create an empathy map together to align perspectives and design better solutions.

Takeaway

Empathy Mapping deepens your understanding of others, leading to more meaningful connections and effective solutions.

Chapter 55: The Elevator Pitch

What is The Elevator Pitch?

An Elevator Pitch is a short, compelling statement that explains your idea, product, or value in the time it takes to ride an elevator (about 30 – 60 seconds).

This model ensures you can communicate your message clearly, concisely, and persuasively in any situation.

Why Elevator Pitches Matter

Opportunities often arise unexpectedly. Having a polished pitch ensures you can make a strong impression, whether networking, pitching an idea, or promoting your business.

For example:

- An entrepreneur meets an investor and delivers a brief but impactful pitch, sparking interest in their startup.

Example: Promoting a Freelance Business

Suppose you're a freelance graphic designer.

- Elevator Pitch: *"I help small businesses create eye-catching logos and branding that attract more customers. My designs have increased client engagement by 30%. I'd love to discuss how I can help your business stand out."*

This concise pitch highlights your value and invites further conversation.

How to Craft an Elevator Pitch

1. **Identify Your Key Message:**

   Focus on what makes you or your idea unique and valuable.

2. **Highlight the Benefits:**

   Explain how your audience will gain from what you're offering.

3. **Keep It Simple:**

   Avoid jargon and stick to plain, engaging language.

4. **End with a Call to Action:**

   Invite the listener to take the next step (e.g., schedule a meeting or ask questions).

Everyday Example of an Elevator Pitch

Suppose you're introducing yourself at a community event.

- Pitch: *"Hi, I'm Alex. I organize local clean-up projects to make our neighborhood greener and more enjoyable. We've already transformed two parks, and I'd love for you to join our next event!"*

This quick introduction communicates your mission and invites participation.

Common Pitfalls in Elevator Pitches

1. **Rambling:**

   Keep your pitch concise and focused.

2. **Being Too Generic:**

   Highlight what makes you unique.

3. **Overloading with Details:**

   Focus on key points—leave room for follow-up questions.

4. **Failing to Practice:**

   Rehearse until your pitch feels natural and confident.

Practical Tip: Use the "Who, What, Why" Formula

Include who you are, what you offer, and why it matters in your pitch.

Takeaway

An Elevator Pitch helps you communicate your value effectively in any situation. It's a powerful tool for making memorable first impressions.

Let's continue exploring tools for presenting ideas with clarity and structure.

Chapter 56: The Pyramid Principle

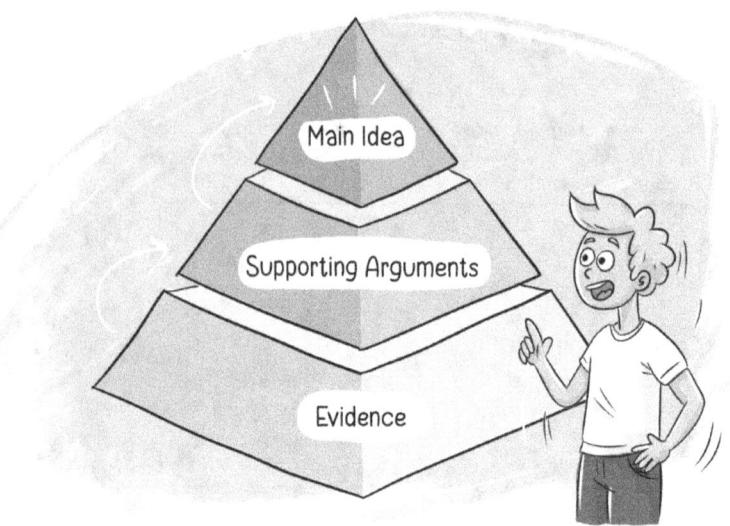

What is The Pyramid Principle?

The Pyramid Principle is a communication model that organizes ideas from the top down: starting with the main conclusion, then explaining supporting arguments, and finally presenting detailed evidence.

This model ensures clarity and helps audiences understand and retain your message.

Why The Pyramid Principle Matters

Unstructured ideas confuse audiences. The Pyramid Principle organizes information logically, making complex topics clear and persuasive.

For example:

- A business executive uses the Pyramid Principle to present a plan to increase revenue, starting with the strategy, followed by specific actions and supporting data.

Example: Proposing a Budget Increase

Suppose you're requesting a higher project budget.

- **Main Idea:** We need a 20% budget increase to meet project goals.
- **Supporting Arguments:** Increased funding will ensure better tools, faster timelines, and higher quality.
- **Evidence:** Projects with similar budgets outperformed by 30%.

This structure makes your case compelling and easy to follow.

How to Use The Pyramid Principle

1. Start with the Conclusion:
Present your main idea or recommendation upfront.

2. Provide Supporting Arguments:
Explain why your conclusion is valid using 2-4 key points.

3. Back It Up with Evidence:
Offer data, examples, or research to reinforce each argument.

4. Keep It Logical:
Ensure the flow of ideas is clear and each layer builds on the one before.

Everyday Example of The Pyramid Principle

Suppose you're convincing a friend to take a weekend trip.

- **Main Idea:** Let's visit the beach this weekend.
- **Supporting Arguments:** It's relaxing, affordable, and close by.
- **Evidence:** The weather forecast is perfect, and gas prices are low.

This approach simplifies decision-making by presenting a clear case.

Common Pitfalls in The Pyramid Principle

1. Burying the Lead:
Don't save your main idea for last—state it upfront.

2. Overloading with Arguments:
Focus on a few strong points rather than overwhelming your audience.

3. Using Weak Evidence:
Ensure your data or examples are credible and relevant.

4. Ignoring Audience Needs:
Tailor your pyramid to address what matters most to your audience.

Practical Tip: Practice "Top-Down" Thinking

Before explaining a topic, write your main idea at the top, followed by 2-3 supporting points. Use this structure to guide your delivery.

Takeaway

The Pyramid Principle organizes your ideas for maximum clarity and impact. It's a powerful way to persuade, explain, and simplify complex topics.

Chapter 57: Storytelling

What is Storytelling?

Storytelling is the art of presenting information through narratives that engage emotions and imagination. It transforms data or ideas into memorable, relatable, and persuasive messages.

This model is widely used in marketing, leadership, and teaching to capture attention and inspire action.

Why Storytelling Matters

Facts alone often fail to inspire. Stories connect emotionally, making your message more impactful and easier to remember.

For example:

- A charity uses a personal story about someone they've helped to highlight the impact of donations, motivating more support.

Example: Motivating a Team

Suppose your team is behind schedule.

- Tell a story: *"Remember when we faced a similar deadline last year? By working together and staying focused, we not only met it but exceeded expectations. We can do that again now."*

This narrative inspires teamwork and confidence.

How to Use Storytelling

1. Start with a Hook:

Capture attention with a relatable situation, surprising fact, or question.

2. Present the Challenge:

Describe the problem or conflict, building tension and curiosity.

3. End with the Resolution:

Show how the challenge was overcome, leaving your audience inspired or informed.

4. Make It Personal:

Use real or relatable characters to make the story resonate.

Everyday Example of Storytelling

Imagine explaining a concept to a child.

- Instead of saying, *"Always tell the truth,"* share a story: *"Once, a boy lied about seeing a wolf. When a wolf really came, no one believed him."*

Stories make lessons memorable.

Common Pitfalls in Storytelling

1. Too Much Detail:

Keep your story concise and focused.

2. Forgetting the Audience:

Tailor your story to their interests and level of understanding.

3. Skipping the Resolution:

Without a satisfying ending, the story loses its impact.

4. Using Clichés:

Original, authentic stories resonate more than overused ones.

Practical Tip: Follow the "Hero's Journey"

Frame your story around a character facing a challenge, learning a lesson, and achieving a resolution.

Takeaway

Storytelling transforms your message into an engaging and memorable narrative. It's a timeless tool for inspiring action, understanding, and connection.

Let's continue exploring tools for refining clarity and enhancing communication.

Chapter 58: The 7 Cs of Communication

What are The 7 Cs of Communication?

The 7 Cs are principles for effective communication, ensuring your message is clear, complete, and well-received. They include:

1. **Clear:** Use simple, understandable language.
2. **Concise:** Avoid unnecessary words.
3. **Concrete:** Provide specific, tangible details.
4. **Correct:** Ensure accuracy in facts and grammar.
5. **Coherent:** Organize your message logically.
6. **Complete:** Cover all necessary points.
7. **Courteous:** Be respectful and considerate.

This model ensures your message resonates and achieves its purpose.

Why the 7 Cs Matter

Miscommunication leads to confusion and errors. The 7 Cs provide a framework for crafting messages that are precise, engaging, and effective.

For example:

- A leader delivering a company update ensures the message is clear, complete, and courteous to avoid misunderstandings and maintain morale.

Example: Writing an Email

Suppose you're inviting colleagues to a meeting.

- **Clear:** State the purpose of the meeting.
- **Concise:** Keep the email brief.
- **Concrete:** Include the date, time, and location.
- **Correct:** Double-check spelling and details.
- **Coherent:** Organize the email logically.
- **Complete:** Mention required materials.
- **Courteous:** Use a polite tone.

This ensures your email is effective and professional.

How to Apply the 7 Cs

1. **Draft with Purpose:**

   Start by clarifying your goal and audience.

2. **Review Each "C":**

   Evaluate your message against the 7 Cs checklist.

3. **Edit for Simplicity:**

   Simplify language and remove unnecessary details.

4. **Get Feedback:**

   Have someone review your message for clarity and tone.

Everyday Example of the 7 Cs

Imagine texting a friend about plans.

- Clear: *"Let's meet at the park."*
- Concise: *"2 PM, Saturday."*
- Concrete: *"By the fountain."*

Using the 7 Cs ensures nothing is missed.

Common Pitfalls in the 7 Cs

1. **Overloading with Details:**

   Too much information dilutes the main point.

2. **Using Jargon:**

Avoid terms your audience may not understand.

3. **Rushing the Process:**

Skipping review risks errors or omissions.

4. **Ignoring Tone:**

Communication should be respectful and considerate.

Practical Tip: Create a Pre-Send Checklist

Before sending any message, quickly review it against the 7 Cs to ensure it's polished and effective.

Takeaway

The 7 Cs of Communication ensure your messages are clear, concise, and impactful. It's a versatile framework for improving understanding and engagement.

Change the frame, change the perspective

Chapter 59: Reframing

What is Reframing?

Reframing is the skill of changing the way you perceive a situation, problem, or challenge to see it in a new light. By shifting perspective, you can transform obstacles into opportunities or see setbacks as lessons.

This model is invaluable for problem-solving, emotional resilience, and creative thinking.

Why Reframing Matters

Humans naturally focus on problems or negative aspects of situations. Reframing helps you break out of this mindset, enabling more constructive, optimistic, and innovative thinking.

For example:

- A delayed flight can feel frustrating, but reframing it as an opportunity to relax and catch up on reading changes the emotional impact.

Example: Handling Criticism

Suppose you receive critical feedback on a project.

- Negative View: "They don't appreciate my work."
- Reframed View: "This is a chance to improve and grow my skills."

This new perspective motivates you to act positively instead of feeling discouraged.

How to Practice Reframing

1. **Recognize Negative Thoughts:**

Notice when you're stuck in a negative or unhelpful perspective.

2. **Challenge Assumptions:**

Ask: Is there another way to look at this? What am I overlooking?

3. **Find the Opportunity:**

Identify the potential benefits or lessons in the situation.

4. **Reframe the Narrative:**

Shift your focus to the positive or constructive aspects.

Everyday Example of Reframing

Imagine facing a tough workout.

- Initial Thought: "This is exhausting."
- Reframed Thought: "This challenge is making me stronger."

Reframing turns resistance into motivation.

Common Pitfalls in Reframing

1. **Forcing Positivity:**

Reframing isn't about ignoring reality. Balance optimism with practicality.

2. **Ignoring the Lesson:**

   Focus on what you can learn, not just making yourself feel better.

3. **Being Stuck in One View:**

   Explore multiple perspectives to find the most helpful one.

4. **Using Vague Reframes:**

   Make your reframing specific and actionable.

Practical Tip: Use "What If" Questions

Ask yourself, *What if this situation were a hidden opportunity? What if this setback is setting me up for something better?*

Takeaway

Reframing shifts your perspective to unlock new possibilities and reduce negativity. It's a powerful tool for growth, resilience, and creative problem-solving.

Chapter 60: The Socratic Method

What is The Socratic Method?

The Socratic Method is a dialogue-based approach to uncovering truth through questioning. Instead of giving answers, you ask thought-provoking questions to challenge assumptions, explore ideas, and arrive at deeper understanding.

This model is used in education, problem-solving, and decision-making to foster critical thinking.

Why the Socratic Method Matters

Humans often accept assumptions or surface-level explanations without question. The Socratic Method challenges you to think critically and dig deeper, leading to better decisions and insights.

For example:

- A teacher asks students *Why do you think this solution works?* instead of simply explaining it, encouraging them to reason through the problem.

Example: Deciding Whether to Start a Business

Suppose you're unsure about launching a startup.

- Question: *What problem does my business solve?*
- Response: *It provides healthier snacks.*
- Follow-Up: *Why is this important? Who benefits most? How will it stand out?*

This questioning clarifies your vision and strategy.

How to Use The Socratic Method

1. Start with a Broad Question:

Ask open-ended questions like *Why?* or *How?*

2. Follow the Answers:
Dive deeper into responses to uncover underlying assumptions or gaps.
3. Encourage Reflection:
Avoid giving answers; let the person arrive at conclusions through reasoning.
4. Challenge Contradictions:
Highlight inconsistencies to refine understanding.

Everyday Example of The Socratic Method
Imagine a friend is debating buying a car.
- You ask: *Why do you want this car? What's the benefit? Is it worth the cost?*
- This helps them consider their motivations and priorities before deciding.

Common Pitfalls in The Socratic Method
1. Being Confrontational:
Questions should guide, not intimidate or criticize.
2. Leading with Bias:
Avoid steering questions toward a specific answer.
3. Skipping Follow-Ups:
Surface-level answers often hide deeper insights—keep digging.
4. Overloading with Questions:
Focus on quality over quantity to avoid overwhelming the other person.

Practical Tip: Use "Why, What, How"
Start with *Why* to uncover purpose, move to *What* for specifics, and finish with *How* to explore solutions.

Takeaway
The Socratic Method fosters deeper understanding through thoughtful questioning. It's a versatile tool for clarifying ideas, solving problems, and inspiring critical thinking.

Behavioral and Cognitive Models

Chapter 61: Cognitive Bias Awareness

What is Cognitive Bias Awareness?
Cognitive Bias Awareness involves recognizing the mental shortcuts and errors in judgment that influence thinking. Biases, while sometimes helpful for quick decisions, often lead to flawed reasoning or assumptions.

This model is a foundational step for critical thinking and sound decision-making.

Why Cognitive Bias Awareness Matters
Biases shape your thoughts and actions, often without you realizing it. Awareness allows you to question assumptions, reduce errors, and make more rational choices.

For example:
- In hiring, someone aware of their biases ensures they assess candidates objectively, avoiding favoritism based on superficial factors.

Example: Buying a Car
Suppose you're influenced by flashy advertisements.
- Bias: You believe the advertised car is better, despite higher costs and fewer features.
- Awareness: You realize this bias and focus on comparing specs and reviews objectively.

This leads to a better, more informed purchase.

How to Recognize Cognitive Biases

1. Learn Common Biases:

Study biases like confirmation, anchoring, and availability to spot them in action.

2. Pause and Reflect:

Before making decisions, ask: Am I being influenced by assumptions or emotions?

3. Seek Diverse Perspectives:

Different viewpoints highlight blind spots and challenge your biases.

4. Practice Self-Awareness:

Regularly analyze your thinking patterns for signs of bias.

Everyday Example of Bias Awareness

Imagine you're debating switching careers.

- Bias: Overestimating risks due to fear of failure.
- Awareness: Questioning this fear helps you realize the benefits of the change outweigh the risks.

This clarity encourages confident decision-making.

Common Pitfalls in Bias Awareness

1. Assuming You're Unbiased:

Everyone has biases. Awareness is about managing, not eliminating, them.

2. Overcompensating:

Swinging too far in the opposite direction can create new biases.

3. Relying Solely on Awareness:

Awareness is the first step—take actions to mitigate biases.

4. Ignoring Feedback:

Feedback from others often reveals biases you miss.

Practical Tip: Use a Bias Checklist

Before decisions, run through common biases (e.g., *Am I favoring familiar ideas? Am I ignoring evidence that contradicts my beliefs?*).

Takeaway

Cognitive Bias Awareness helps you think more objectively by identifying and questioning mental shortcuts. It's the first step to clearer, more rational decisions.

Let's continue unpacking specific biases and how to counteract them.

Chapter 62: Anchoring Bias

What is Anchoring Bias?

Anchoring Bias occurs when initial information disproportionately influences decisions. Once an "anchor" is set, people tend to rely too heavily on it, even if it's irrelevant or misleading.

This model highlights the importance of questioning first impressions and reevaluating with fresh information.

Why Anchoring Bias Matters

Anchors can distort judgment, leading to suboptimal decisions. Recognizing this bias ensures you evaluate situations based on full context, not just the starting point.

For example:

- A store marks a $100 item as "50% off," making it feel like a great deal, even if $50 is still overpriced.

Example: Negotiating a Salary

Suppose a potential employer offers an initial salary of $50,000.

- With Bias: You focus on the anchor and negotiate only slightly higher.
- Without Bias: You research average salaries and confidently negotiate for $60,000, based on market data.

By resisting the anchor, you achieve better results.

How to Overcome Anchoring Bias

1. Delay Judgments:
Avoid making decisions immediately after encountering an anchor.

2. Gather Independent Data:
Look beyond the anchor for additional evidence or benchmarks.

3. Set Your Own Anchor:
Enter situations like negotiations with pre-established goals based on research.

4. Ask Critical Questions:
Challenge whether the initial information is relevant or reliable.

Everyday Example of Anchoring Bias

Imagine shopping for a TV.

- Anchor: A high-end model costs $2,000.
- Impact: A $1,200 TV seems affordable by comparison, even if it's more than you planned to spend.

Awareness of anchoring helps you reassess your actual needs and budget.

Common Pitfalls in Avoiding Anchoring

1. Ignoring Context:
Sometimes anchors are valuable starting points. Evaluate them carefully.

2. Rushing Decisions:
Quick decisions often reinforce the power of the anchor.

3. Underestimating Subtle Anchors:
Even casual comments or numbers can unconsciously influence thinking.

4. Overcorrecting:
Avoid dismissing all anchors—use them as one of many data points.

Practical Tip: Create Pre-Set Benchmarks

Before entering a decision, establish clear criteria or goals. This prevents reliance on external anchors.

Takeaway

Anchoring Bias reminds you to question the influence of initial information. By challenging anchors, you ensure decisions are grounded in context and data.

Chapter 63: Confirmation Bias

What is Confirmation Bias?

Confirmation Bias is the tendency to seek, interpret, and favor information that supports your existing beliefs while ignoring or dismissing evidence that challenges them.

This bias narrows your perspective, making it harder to see the full picture or change your mind.

Why Confirmation Bias Matters

When you only focus on confirming your beliefs, you miss opportunities to learn, improve, or make better decisions. Challenging this bias ensures you base conclusions on evidence, not assumptions.

For example:

- A person believing a specific diet works might only read success stories while ignoring studies showing mixed results.

Example: Debating a Purchase

Suppose you're considering buying a car.

- With Bias: You focus on reviews praising the car and ignore negative feedback.
- Without Bias: You weigh all reviews, both positive and negative, before deciding.

Considering all perspectives leads to a better-informed choice.

How to Overcome Confirmation Bias

1. Seek Opposing Views:

Actively look for evidence that contradicts your beliefs.

2. Ask Neutral Questions:

Frame inquiries to explore all possibilities, not just confirm your assumptions.

3. Evaluate All Evidence Equally:

Avoid dismissing information simply because it challenges your viewpoint.

4. Encourage Feedback:

Share your ideas with others and invite critical perspectives.

Everyday Example of Confirmation Bias

Imagine you believe one exercise is the best for fitness.

- With Bias: You only follow articles praising that exercise.
- Without Bias: You explore different methods, discovering complementary workouts for better results.

Awareness of this bias broadens your understanding.

Common Pitfalls in Addressing Confirmation Bias

1. Avoiding Discomfort:

Challenging beliefs can feel uncomfortable but is necessary for growth.

2. Overvaluing Familiar Sources:

Prioritize credible evidence over sources you already trust.

3. Cherry-Picking Data:

Avoid selecting only evidence that aligns with your views.

4. Overcorrecting:

Balance challenging your beliefs with maintaining a critical eye on new evidence.

Practical Tip: Use the "Devil's Advocate" Approach

Regularly challenge your ideas by asking, *What if I'm wrong? What would disprove this belief?*

Takeaway

Confirmation Bias reminds us to question our assumptions and seek balanced perspectives. Confronting this bias leads to more informed, open-minded decision-making.

Let's continue exploring how recent experiences can distort judgment.

Chapter 64: Availability Heuristic

What is the Availability Heuristic?

The Availability Heuristic is a mental shortcut where you base decisions on information that comes to mind quickly — often recent or emotionally vivid experiences — rather than on all relevant data.

This heuristic helps with quick thinking but often leads to biased judgments.

Why the Availability Heuristic Matters

Relying solely on recent or memorable events skews decisions, ignoring broader patterns or probabilities. Recognizing this heuristic helps you think more critically and holistically.

For example:

- After hearing about a plane crash, someone may overestimate the risk of flying, despite data showing it's safer than driving.

Example: Estimating Health Risks

Suppose a friend mentions getting sick after eating sushi.

- With Heuristic: You avoid sushi, believing it's unsafe.
- Without Heuristic: You consider food safety statistics, realizing sushi is generally low-risk.

Critical evaluation ensures balanced decisions.

How to Avoid the Availability Heuristic

1. Pause Before Judging:

Ask: Am I relying on a recent or dramatic event rather than overall evidence?

2. Look at the Bigger Picture:

Research statistics or trends to gain a broader understanding.

3. Recognize Emotional Influence:

Be aware of how vivid or emotional events may cloud objectivity.

4. Compare Multiple Sources:

Seek diverse perspectives to counterbalance single, memorable instances.

Everyday Example of the Availability Heuristic

Imagine you're planning a trip and recall a recent storm at your destination.

- Heuristic: You cancel the trip, assuming bad weather is likely.
- Balanced View: You check the forecast, finding clear skies ahead.

This approach separates emotions from facts.

Common Pitfalls in the Availability Heuristic

1. Overvaluing Recent Events:

Fresh memories feel more relevant but aren't always representative.

2. Ignoring Probabilities:

Uncommon events can feel more frequent due to emotional impact.

3. Relying on Anecdotes:

Individual stories rarely reflect broader trends.

4. Resisting Data:

Vivid events can feel more "real" than abstract statistics.

Practical Tip: Use Data for Context

When making decisions, ask: *What do the numbers say? Are there broader patterns I'm overlooking?*

Takeaway

The Availability Heuristic shows the importance of balancing vivid memories with objective data. By questioning first impressions, you make more rational, informed decisions.

Let's continue exploring how social dynamics shape behavior.

Chapter 65: Social Proof

Social Proof is the tendency to imitate others' actions or beliefs, assuming their choices are correct. It's a psychological shortcut: if many people are doing something, it must be the right thing to do.

This model explains phenomena like trends, herd behavior, and peer pressure.

Why Social Proof Matters

While Social Proof can be helpful for quick decisions, it often leads to blindly following the crowd without questioning its wisdom. Recognizing this influence helps you act intentionally rather than reactively.

For example:

- You might buy a product with thousands of 5-star reviews, assuming it's superior without checking if the reviews are genuine.

Example: Choosing a Restaurant

Suppose you're deciding where to eat.

- With Social Proof: You pick the restaurant with a long line, assuming it's better.
- With Awareness: You consider reviews, menu options, and your preferences, making a more thoughtful choice.

Balancing social cues with independent judgment leads to better decisions.

How to Use or Avoid Social Proof

1. Recognize Its Influence:

Notice when you're making choices based on others' behavior.

2. Evaluate the Crowd's Expertise:

Ask: Are these people informed or just following each other?

3. Combine Social Proof with Research:

Use others' actions as a starting point but verify with data or personal needs.

4. Lead When Needed:

Don't hesitate to go against the crowd when your judgment suggests otherwise.

Everyday Example of Social Proof

Imagine everyone at work is using a specific app for productivity.

- With Awareness: You evaluate whether the app aligns with your workflow before adopting it.

This prevents wasting time on tools that may not suit your needs.

Common Pitfalls in Social Proof

1. Blind Conformity:

Following others without questioning their reasons can lead to poor decisions.

2. Assuming Popular Equals Good:

Popularity often reflects marketing, not quality.

3. Ignoring Personal Needs:

What works for others may not work for you.

4. Overreliance on Trends:

Trends often fade, leaving you with outdated choices.

Practical Tip: Ask, "Why Is Everyone Doing This?"

Consider whether the crowd's actions are based on wisdom or simply herd mentality.

Takeaway

Social Proof highlights the power of group influence on decisions. Balancing social cues with critical thinking ensures your choices align with your goals.

Let's continue exploring how habits shape behavior over time.

Chapter 66: Habit Formation

Habit Formation is the process of developing behaviors through repetition and reinforcement. Habits consist of three parts:

1. Cue: A trigger for the habit.

2. Routine: The action or behavior itself.

3. Reward: The benefit or satisfaction you gain from the behavior.

By understanding this cycle, you can build positive habits or replace negative ones.

Why Habit Formation Matters

Habits shape daily life and long-term outcomes. Good habits compound over time, leading to personal growth and success, while bad habits hold you back.

For example:

- A daily habit of reading improves knowledge, while a habit of procrastination stalls progress.

Example: Building a Morning Routine

Suppose you want to exercise each morning.

- Cue: Set out workout clothes the night before.
- Routine: Go for a 20-minute jog.
- Reward: Enjoy the post-exercise energy boost.

Repeating this loop solidifies the habit.

How to Form New Habits

1. Start Small:

Focus on manageable changes to build consistency.

2. Tie Habits to Cues:

Link new habits to existing routines (e.g., floss after brushing your teeth).

3. Reward Yourself:

Reinforce habits with immediate, meaningful rewards.

4. Be Patient:

Habits take time to stick—progress is gradual.

Everyday Example of Habit Formation

Imagine wanting to drink more water daily.

- Cue: Keep a water bottle on your desk.
- Routine: Take a sip every time you check your phone.
- Reward: Feel refreshed and hydrated.

These small steps make the habit effortless over time.

Common Pitfalls in Habit Formation

1. Setting Unrealistic Goals:

Overambitious habits are harder to maintain.

2. Skipping Rewards:

Without rewards, habits feel like chores.

3. Relying on Willpower Alone:

Environmental cues and systems are more effective.

4. Giving Up After Slip-Ups:

Missing a day doesn't mean failure—just restart.

Practical Tip: Use "Habit Stacking"

Attach new habits to existing ones, like meditating after your morning coffee, to integrate them seamlessly.

Takeaway

Habit Formation creates lasting change through small, consistent actions. Understanding the habit loop empowers you to build behaviors that support your goals.

Let's now look how triggers shape behavior and decision-making.

Chapter 67: Pavlovian Conditioning

What is Pavlovian Conditioning?

Pavlovian Conditioning, also known as classical conditioning, is the process of associating a neutral stimulus (like a sound) with a specific response due to repeated pairings. Over time, the neutral stimulus triggers the response automatically.

This model, discovered by Ivan Pavlov, explains many learned behaviors in both animals and humans.

Why Pavlovian Conditioning Matters

Understanding conditioning helps you recognize how external triggers influence behavior, often subconsciously. With awareness, you can shape or break conditioned responses.

For example:

- A phone notification sound triggers an automatic urge to check your phone, even if the message isn't urgent.

Example: Eating Habits

Suppose you snack every time you watch TV.

- Cue: Turning on the TV.
- Response: Feeling the urge to grab a snack.
- Awareness: Recognizing the pattern lets you replace the habit with drinking water instead.

How to Recognize and Influence Conditioning

1. **Identify the Cue:**

   Notice the stimulus that triggers your response.

2. **Examine the Response:**

   Reflect on whether the reaction serves your goals or needs.

3. **Replace or Reinforce Behavior:**

   Pair the cue with a new response (e.g., exercising when stressed instead of overeating).

4. **Practice Consistency:**

   Repeatedly pair the new behavior with the cue to recondition your response.

Everyday Example of Pavlovian Conditioning

Imagine you associate the sound of your alarm with dread.

- Solution: Replace your alarm tone with a favorite song to create a more positive morning experience.

This reconditions your emotional response to the cue.

Common Pitfalls in Pavlovian Conditioning

1. **Ignoring Negative Cues:**

   Many unhelpful habits stem from unnoticed triggers.

2. **Overgeneralizing Responses:**

   Conditioned responses may spread to similar cues. Recognize and address this.

3. **Relying on Willpower Alone:**

   Changing conditioned responses requires restructuring, not just resisting.

4. **Inconsistency:**

   Inconsistent pairing weakens new associations.

Practical Tip: Use Positive Triggers

Intentionally pair cues (like setting a calming ringtone) with positive actions to create healthier habits.

Takeaway

Pavlovian Conditioning highlights the power of cues in shaping behavior. By identifying and reshaping triggers, you can condition responses that align with your goals.

Let's continue exploring strategies for managing emotions effectively.

Chapter 68: Emotional Regulation

What is Emotional Regulation?

Emotional Regulation is the ability to manage and control emotional reactions, especially in stressful or challenging situations. It involves recognizing emotions, understanding their causes, and choosing constructive responses.

This model is essential for maintaining mental health, strong relationships, and effective decision-making.

Why Emotional Regulation Matters

Unregulated emotions often lead to impulsive actions, poor decisions, or conflict. By managing emotions, you stay composed, think clearly, and respond effectively.

For example:

- Instead of snapping during an argument, emotional regulation helps you pause, reflect, and communicate calmly.

Example: Handling Workplace Stress

Suppose a project deadline gets moved up unexpectedly.

- Without Regulation: Panic leads to hasty decisions and frustration with teammates.
- With Regulation: You pause, prioritize tasks, and ask for support, maintaining focus and efficiency.

How to Practice Emotional Regulation

1. Recognize Emotions Early:

Identify feelings as they arise before they escalate.

2. Pause Before Reacting:

Take a deep breath or count to ten to gain perspective.

3. Reframe the Situation:

Shift your perspective to see challenges as opportunities or lessons.

4. Choose Constructive Responses:

Respond in ways that align with your goals and values.

Everyday Example of Emotional Regulation

Imagine getting cut off in traffic.

- Initial Reaction: Anger and frustration.
- Regulated Response: You remind yourself it's not personal, take a deep breath, and continue driving safely.

This approach keeps emotions from escalating.

Common Pitfalls in Emotional Regulation

1. Suppressing Emotions:

Ignoring feelings can lead to long-term stress or burnout.

2. Overreacting:

Small triggers shouldn't derail your composure.

3. Blaming Others:

Focus on controlling your response rather than external factors.

4. Skipping Reflection:

Failing to analyze emotional patterns limits growth.

Practical Tip: Practice Mindfulness

Regular mindfulness exercises help you stay aware of emotions and manage them calmly.

Takeaway

Emotional Regulation empowers you to respond thoughtfully instead of reacting impulsively. It's a vital tool for navigating life's ups and downs with clarity and composure.

Now, let's look at how expectations influence outcomes.

Chapter 69: Self-Fulfilling Prophecy

What is a Self-Fulfilling Prophecy?

A Self-Fulfilling Prophecy occurs when your expectations about a situation influence your behavior, causing the expected outcome to materialize. Positive beliefs lead to success, while negative ones often create failure.

This model demonstrates the power of mindset in shaping reality.

Why Self-Fulfilling Prophecies Matter

Your beliefs shape your actions, which in turn affect outcomes. Being aware of this cycle helps you challenge negative expectations and cultivate confidence.

For example:

- A student who believes they'll fail a test might study less, reinforcing the belief and leading to poor performance.

Example: Preparing for a Job Interview

Suppose you expect to perform well in an interview.

- With Positive Beliefs: Confidence leads you to prepare thoroughly and present yourself effectively.
- With Negative Beliefs: Doubts make you nervous and unprepared, resulting in a weaker performance.

Your mindset determines how you act, influencing the outcome.

How to Break Negative Prophecies

1. Recognize Limiting Beliefs:
Identify negative thoughts or assumptions holding you back.

2. Reframe Expectations:
Replace self-defeating beliefs with empowering ones, like *I can improve with effort*.

3. Act on Positive Beliefs:
Behave in ways that align with your new, constructive mindset.

4. Celebrate Small Wins:
Reinforce positive beliefs by acknowledging progress.

Everyday Example of a Self-Fulfilling Prophecy

Imagine you assume a colleague doesn't like you.

- Negative Belief: You avoid them, creating awkwardness that confirms your assumption.
- Positive Belief: You greet them warmly, fostering a friendly relationship instead.

Your actions can either escalate or dissolve tension.

Common Pitfalls in Self-Fulfilling Prophecies

1. Clinging to Negative Assumptions:
Doubts often feel valid but are worth questioning.

2. Ignoring Behavior Patterns:
Focusing solely on outcomes neglects the actions driving them.

3. Overgeneralizing Past Failures:
Previous results don't dictate future possibilities.

4. Resisting Change:
Breaking negative cycles requires consistent effort and patience.

Practical Tip: Use Affirmations

Practice daily affirmations like *I am capable of handling challenges* to build positive expectations.

Takeaway

The Self-Fulfilling Prophecy highlights how beliefs shape actions and outcomes. By fostering positive expectations, you create a cycle of growth and success.

Chapter 70: Grit and Resilience

What are Grit and Resilience?

Grit is the passion and perseverance to pursue long-term goals, while resilience is the ability to recover quickly from setbacks. Together, they empower you to stay focused and overcome challenges, no matter how tough the journey.

These traits are essential for sustained success and personal growth.

Why Grit and Resilience Matter

Life's challenges often derail progress. Grit keeps you moving forward, while resilience helps you bounce back stronger. Together, they build the mental endurance needed to achieve meaningful goals.

For example:

- An athlete training for a marathon relies on grit to stick to their plan and resilience to recover from injuries or missed milestones.

Example: Starting a Business

Suppose your first product launch fails.

- Without Grit: You feel defeated and give up.
- With Grit: You analyze what went wrong, improve the product, and try again.

This persistence eventually leads to success.

How to Cultivate Grit and Resilience

1. Set Meaningful Goals:
Pursue objectives that truly inspire and motivate you.

2. Embrace Setbacks as Lessons:
View failures as opportunities to learn and grow.

3. Build a Support System:
Surround yourself with people who encourage and inspire you.

4. Practice Self-Compassion:
Treat yourself kindly during tough times to maintain focus and energy.

Everyday Example of Grit and Resilience

Imagine learning a new skill, like cooking.

- With Grit: You keep practicing despite initial failures.
- With Resilience: Burned meals or mistakes don't discourage you.

Over time, persistence transforms you into a confident chef.

Common Pitfalls in Building Grit and Resilience

1. Focusing Only on Motivation:
Discipline sustains effort when motivation fades.

2. Expecting Instant Results:
Grit requires patience—progress is often slow but steady.

3. Avoiding Discomfort:
Growth happens when you face challenges head-on.

4. Ignoring Rest:
Resilience depends on balancing effort with recovery.

Practical Tip: Use the "10-Year Vision"

Imagine where you want to be in 10 years. Use this vision to fuel your grit and remind yourself why perseverance is worth it.

Takeaway

Grit and resilience help you navigate setbacks and stay committed to long-term goals. Together, they form the foundation for enduring success and growth.

Let's now delve into financial and economic models that guide decision-making.

Financial and Economic Models

Chapter 71: Supply and Demand

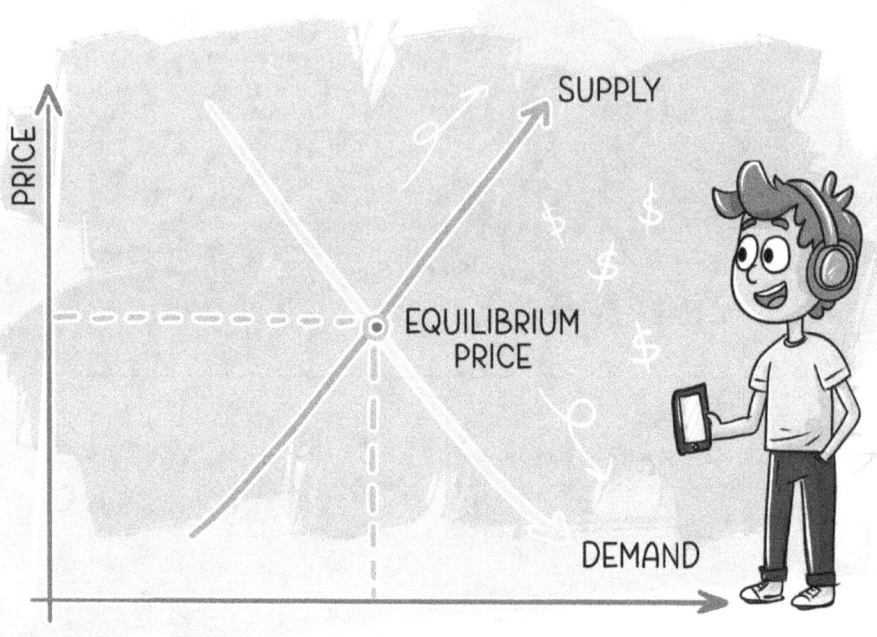

What is Supply and Demand?

Supply and Demand is a fundamental economic model that explains how prices are determined in a market.

- **Supply:** How much of a product or service is available.
- **Demand:** How much people want it.
- The price adjusts to balance supply and demand, reaching the equilibrium where they meet.

Why Supply and Demand Matter

This model helps you understand why prices fluctuate and how to make decisions based on market conditions.

For example:

- A rare product with high demand (like limited-edition sneakers) will be expensive.

Understanding this concept allows you to predict trends and make smarter financial choices.

Example: Buying Fresh Produce

Suppose you're shopping for oranges.

- High Supply: During harvest season, oranges are abundant, and prices drop.
- Low Supply: Off-season, fewer oranges are available, and prices rise.

Knowing this, you can plan to buy in-season for better value.

How to Apply Supply and Demand

1. **Monitor Market Trends:**
   Notice how availability and popularity affect prices.
2. **Time Your Decisions:**
   Buy when supply is high, and demand is low to get the best deals.
3. **Consider Alternatives:**
   When demand drives prices up, explore substitutes (e.g., apples instead of oranges).
4. **Evaluate Future Value:**
   Anticipate shifts in supply or demand to make informed investments.

Imagine concert tickets for a popular band.

- Limited supply and high demand cause ticket prices to surge.
- If you act early or choose less popular seats, you save money.

This understanding helps you optimize your spending.

Common Pitfalls in Supply and Demand

1. Ignoring Market Signals:

Prices often reflect changes in supply or demand—pay attention to these signals.

2. Acting Reactively:

Waiting too long during high demand can lead to missed opportunities or higher costs.

3. Assuming Trends Are Permanent:

Market conditions fluctuate—don't expect high demand to last forever.

4. Focusing Only on Price:

Quality and availability also affect value.

Practical Tip: Use Price Tracking Tools

Apps or websites that monitor price trends help you buy when supply and demand are most favorable.

Takeaway

Supply and Demand explain market behaviors, helping you navigate prices and make strategic choices.

Let's continue exploring how psychological traps can distort financial decisions.

Chapter 72: Sunk Cost Fallacy

What is the Sunk Cost Fallacy?

The Sunk Cost Fallacy occurs when you continue investing time, money, or effort into something simply because you've already spent resources on it—even if it's no longer worth pursuing.

It's a psychological trap that keeps you stuck in unproductive situations.

Why the Sunk Cost Fallacy Matters

Clinging to sunk costs leads to poor decisions and wasted resources. Recognizing this fallacy helps you cut losses and focus on better opportunities.

For example:

- Staying in an unfulfilling job because you've spent years in the field, despite better prospects elsewhere.

Suppose you've paid for a ticket to a movie you're not enjoying.

- With the Fallacy: You stay because you've already spent money.
- Without the Fallacy: You leave and spend your time on something more fulfilling.

Letting go of sunk costs improves overall satisfaction.

How to Avoid the Sunk Cost Fallacy

1. Focus on Future Value:

Ask: Does continuing add value moving forward?

2. Ignore Past Investments:

Treat previous costs as irrelevant—they can't be recovered.

3. Make Rational Assessments:

Evaluate situations based on current and future benefits, not past commitments.

4. Set Clear Exit Strategies:

Decide in advance when you'll walk away if results don't meet expectations.Everyday Example of the Sunk Cost Fallacy

Imagine you're halfway through a book you don't enjoy.

- Fallacy: You finish it because you've already invested time.
- Rational Choice: You stop reading and start a book that excites you.

This frees your time for more rewarding activities.

Common Pitfalls in Avoiding the Sunk Cost Fallacy

1. Emotional Attachment:

Sentimental value can make it harder to let go.

2. Fear of Regret:

Worrying about "wasted" resources keeps you stuck.

3. External Pressure:

Others may encourage sticking with sunk costs due to shared investments.

4. Overthinking Losses:

Focusing too much on past losses distracts from future gains.

Practical Tip: Ask, "What Would I Do If I Started Fresh?"

This question shifts your focus to current value rather than past costs.

Takeaway

The Sunk Cost Fallacy teaches you to prioritize future value over past investments. Letting go of unproductive commitments opens the door to better opportunities.

It's almost sold out I need to buy it now!

Do you need it, or is the scarcity making it seem more valuable?

Chapter 73: Scarcity Principle

What is the Scarcity Principle?

The Scarcity Principle suggests that limited availability increases an item's perceived value. When something is rare or hard to obtain, it feels more desirable.

This principle is often used in marketing, but it also influences personal decision-making, creating urgency where it might not be necessary.

Why the Scarcity Principle Matters

Scarcity can cloud judgment, leading you to make impulsive or emotional decisions. Recognizing this principle helps you evaluate opportunities more rationally.

For example:

- A "limited-time offer" can pressure you to buy something you don't really need.

Suppose you see a notice: *"Only 5 tickets left!"*

- With Scarcity Bias: You rush to purchase without thinking.
- Without Scarcity Bias: You pause to assess if you actually want to attend.

Being aware of scarcity marketing ensures thoughtful choices.

How to Avoid Scarcity Traps

1. Pause and Reflect:

Ask: Would I want this if it weren't limited?

2. Evaluate True Value:

Focus on an item's actual utility or benefits rather than its rarity.

3. Avoid Emotional Decisions:

Take a moment to detach emotionally before acting.

4. Question Marketing Tactics:

Recognize when scarcity is manufactured to create pressure.

Everyday Example of the Scarcity Principle

Imagine a sale on gadgets that says, "Offer ends tonight!"

- With Awareness: You evaluate whether the gadget is useful, ignoring the urgency.
- Without Awareness: You buy impulsively and later regret the purchase.

This approach ensures rational spending.

Common Pitfalls in the Scarcity Principle

1. FOMO (Fear of Missing Out):

Scarcity triggers FOMO, making you feel irrational urgency.

2. Overvaluing Rare Items:

Limited availability doesn't always equal higher quality.

3. Underestimating Abundance:

Common items are often just as valuable but overlooked.

4. Succumbing to Pressure:

High-pressure tactics exploit emotional responses.

Practical Tip: Use the "Wait Rule"

Before acting on scarcity, wait 24 hours. If it still feels important after the pause, proceed thoughtfully.

Takeaway

The Scarcity Principle shows how limited availability can skew perception and decision-making. Awareness helps you act based on true value, not artificial urgency.

Let's continue exploring how to balance risks and rewards effectively.

Chapter 74: Risk-Reward Ratio

What is the Risk-Reward Ratio?

The Risk-Reward Ratio is a tool for evaluating whether a potential reward justifies the risk involved. It helps you decide if the upside of an opportunity outweighs the possible downsides.

This model is used in investing, business, and personal decisions to find the right balance.

Why the Risk-Reward Ratio Matters

Risk is unavoidable, but not all risks are worth taking. Understanding this ratio ensures your decisions are strategic rather than reckless.

For example:

- Investing in a startup with high growth potential might bring huge rewards, but the risk of failure is significant.

Example: Deciding on a Career Change

Suppose you're considering leaving your job for a new opportunity.

- Risks: Uncertainty, lower initial salary.
- Rewards: Higher long-term growth, alignment with your goals.

If the rewards outweigh the risks, the decision is worth pursuing.

How to Use the Risk-Reward Ratio

1. Identify Risks:
List potential downsides of the decision.

2. Evaluate Rewards:
Consider short- and long-term benefits.

3. Compare Magnitudes:
Assess if the potential gain justifies the possible loss.

4. Prepare Mitigation Plans:
Develop strategies to minimize risks while pursuing rewards.

Everyday Example of the Risk-Reward Ratio

Imagine buying a used car at a low price.

- Risks: Repairs might be costly.
- Rewards: Significant savings if the car is reliable.

Weighing these factors helps you make an informed purchase.

Common Pitfalls in Risk-Reward Analysis

1. Underestimating Risks:
Optimism can blind you to potential downsides.

2. Overvaluing Rewards:
Big rewards might distract from low probabilities of success.

3. Ignoring Mitigation:
Many risks can be reduced with planning.

4. Paralysis by Analysis:
Overthinking risks can prevent action altogether.

Practical Tip: Assign Probabilities

Estimate the likelihood of success and failure for a clearer picture of the ratio.

Takeaway

The Risk-Reward Ratio helps you make balanced decisions by weighing potential outcomes thoughtfully.

Let's look at a further way that you can improve productivity and resource allocation.

Chapter 75: The Law of Diminishing Returns

What is The Law of Diminishing Returns?

The Law of Diminishing Returns states that as you invest more effort, resources, or time into something, the added benefits decrease after a certain point.

This concept applies to productivity, spending, and resource allocation.

Why The Law of Diminishing Returns Matters

More effort doesn't always equal more results. Recognizing when returns diminish helps you allocate resources efficiently.

For example:

- Spending hours editing a project may improve it initially, but over-editing can waste time with little added benefit.

Example: Studying for an Exam

Suppose you study for 8 hours straight.

- Initial Hours: Significant learning and retention.
- Later Hours: Fatigue reduces focus, and retention drops.

Knowing when to take breaks maximizes efficiency.

How to Apply the Law of Diminishing Returns

1. Set Limits:

Define how much time or effort is reasonable for a task.

2. Monitor Progress:

Track results to see when additional effort brings diminishing returns.

3. Balance Quality and Efficiency:

Aim for "good enough" rather than perfection when returns taper off.

4. Reallocate Resources:

Shift time and energy to areas with higher potential impact.

Everyday Example of Diminishing Returns

Imagine working overtime to earn more money.

- Early Hours: Significant financial benefit.
- Excess Hours: Fatigue reduces productivity and work quality.

Recognizing the tipping point prevents burnout.

1. **Chasing Perfection:**

   Excessive effort on small details often wastes time.

2. **Ignoring Costs:**

   Additional input may cost more than the benefit it provides.

3. **Overestimating Capacity:**

   Exhaustion limits how much value you can add.

4. **Failing to Reassess:**

   Regularly evaluate whether continued effort is worth it.

Practical Tip: Use Time Caps

Set time limits for tasks to maintain productivity and avoid diminishing returns.

Takeaway

The Law of Diminishing Returns reminds you to work smarter, not harder, by recognizing when additional effort no longer adds value.

Now, let's continue by reviewing financial models for assessing value.

Chapter 76: ROI
(Return on Investment)

What is ROI (Return on Investment)?

ROI measures the profitability of an investment by comparing the net return to the initial cost. It's a simple formula:

net income ÷ cost of investment × 100

This model helps you evaluate whether an investment (time, money, or resources) is worth it.

Why ROI Matters

Every decision involves trade-offs. ROI ensures you allocate resources to opportunities that deliver the best results.

For example:

- Investing $1,000 in marketing that generates $2,000 in sales delivers a 100% ROI, doubling your money.

Example: Deciding on a Training Program

Suppose you're considering a $500 course to improve skills that might lead to a promotion.

- ROI: If the promotion increases your income by $2,000 annually, the ROI is $(2000-500)/500 \times 100 = 300\%$.$(2000 - 500) / 500 \times 100 = 300\%$.$(2000-500)/500 \times 100 = 300\%$.

Evaluating ROI helps you decide whether the investment is worthwhile.

How to Use ROI

1. **Calculate Net Return:**
   Subtract the cost from the total benefit.

2. **Compare Alternatives:**
   Analyze ROI across multiple options to prioritize the best one.

3. **Factor in Intangible Benefits:**
   Consider qualitative outcomes like skill growth or reputation, even if they're hard to quantify.

4. **Monitor Progress:**
   Reassess ROI periodically to ensure continued value.

Everyday Example of ROI

Imagine buying a $50 monthly gym membership.

- High ROI: You use the gym regularly and improve your health.
- Low ROI: You rarely go, wasting money.

Assessing ROI motivates better resource use.

Common Pitfalls in ROI Analysis

1. **Ignoring Long-Term Returns:**
   Some benefits, like education, take time to materialize.

2. **Overlooking Hidden Costs:**
   Include all expenses, like maintenance or time investment.

3. **Focusing Only on Money:**
   ROI isn't always financial—it can include personal or professional growth.

4. **Relying on Assumptions:**
   Base calculations on realistic data, not overly optimistic projections.

Practical Tip: Use an ROI Calculator

Online tools simplify ROI calculations, helping you compare options quickly and accurately.

Takeaway

ROI helps you make smarter decisions by quantifying the value of investments. Prioritizing high-ROI opportunities leads to better outcomes.

SMART USE OF RESOURCES

Big Goal

Chapter 77: Leverage

Leverage is the strategic use of resources — money, tools, skills, or time — to amplify results with less effort. It's about working smarter, not harder, by multiplying the impact of your actions.

For example:

- Borrowing money to invest in a profitable business is financial leverage.

Why Leverage Matters

Without leverage, progress is slow and effort-intensive. Effective leverage accelerates growth and maximizes potential.

For example:

- An entrepreneur delegates routine tasks to focus on business strategy, multiplying their impact.

Example: Using Financial Leverage

Suppose you invest $20,000 in a property by borrowing $80,000.

- With Leverage: If the property's value increases by 10% ($10,000), your return is 50% on your $20,000.
- Without Leverage: Investing only $20,000 delivers just a 10% return ($2,000).

Leverage amplifies the outcome, but it also increases risk if returns don't materialize.

How to Use Leverage Wisely

1. Identify High-Impact Areas:

Focus resources where they'll create the greatest return.

2. Start Small:

Test leverage strategies on manageable projects before scaling.

3. Balance Risk and Reward:

Ensure potential gains outweigh risks.

4. Monitor Performance:

Regularly evaluate whether leverage is delivering the expected results.

Everyday Example of Leverage

Imagine automating bill payments.

- Without Leverage: You manually pay each bill monthly.
- With Leverage: Automation saves time and reduces errors, allowing focus on more important tasks.

Small leverage points create big efficiency gains.

Common Pitfalls in Leverage

1. Overleveraging:

Taking on excessive risk can lead to losses if things don't go as planned.

2. Misallocating Resources:

Focus leverage where it provides the highest returns.

3. Neglecting Monitoring:

Unchecked leverage can lead to inefficiencies or financial strain.

4. Underestimating Costs:

Consider hidden expenses, like interest or maintenance.

Practical Tip: Use the "80/20 Rule"

Leverage resources to focus on the 20% of actions that generate 80% of results.

Takeaway

Leverage multiplies results by amplifying your resources strategically. Using it wisely accelerates success while managing risks. Let's continue exploring the importance of financial timing.

Today's Dollar   Future Value

Chapter 78: The Time Value of Money (TVM)

The Time Value of Money (TVM) states that a dollar today is worth more than a dollar in the future because it can be invested to grow. This model emphasizes the power of compounding and the cost of delaying financial decisions.

For example:

- Investing $1,000 at a 5% annual return grows to $1,276 in 5 years, demonstrating how money increases over time.

Why the Time Value of Money Matters

Understanding TVM helps you prioritize early investment and minimize unnecessary delays in financial planning.

For example:

- Saving for retirement early allows compounding to work its magic, reducing the total amount you need to save later.

Example: Delaying Loan Payments

Suppose you have the option to defer a $5,000 loan payment for one year.

- With TVM: Investing $5,000 now at 10% returns $500 in one year, covering part of the loan cost.
- Without TVM: Deferring the payment saves nothing, losing the opportunity to grow your money.

TVM helps you decide whether deferral benefits you financially.

How to Apply the Time Value of Money

1. Invest Early:

Start saving or investing as soon as possible to maximize compounding.

2. Minimize Idle Money:

Ensure your money is actively working for you through investments or savings accounts.

3. Factor in Inflation:

Remember that money loses purchasing power over time due to inflation.

4. Use TVM Calculations:

Tools like future value or present value formulas help you evaluate financial decisions.

Imagine you receive $1,000 and consider saving it under your mattress versus investing it.

- With TVM: Investing grows the $1,000 over time, while saving it under the mattress loses value due to inflation.

This awareness motivates better financial decisions.

1. Procrastinating on Investments:

Delaying reduces the power of compounding.

2. Overlooking Inflation:

Inflation erodes the value of stagnant money.

3. Ignoring Opportunity Costs:

Leaving money idle sacrifices potential gains.

4. Misjudging Risk:

Seek balanced returns that align with your financial goals.

These tools show how small investments today grow significantly over time, reinforcing the importance of early action.

The Time Value of Money highlights the importance of acting early and investing wisely. It's a foundational concept for building long-term wealth.

Let's continue exploring financial efficiency.

Chapter 79: Arbitrage

What is Arbitrage?

Arbitrage is the process of taking advantage of price differences for the same item in different markets to earn a profit. It's a risk-free way to capitalize on inefficiencies in pricing.

For example:

- Buying stocks at a lower price in one market and selling them at a higher price in another.

Why Arbitrage Matters

Arbitrage reveals opportunities to maximize gains with minimal risk. It's commonly used in finance but also applies to everyday situations like flipping items or currency exchange.

For example:

- A traveler exchanges currency at a low rate in one city and sells it for a higher rate in another.

Example: Reselling Products

Suppose you notice a popular gadget is cheaper online than in local stores.

- With Arbitrage: You buy it online and resell it locally at a profit.
- Without Arbitrage: You miss the chance to profit from the price diffrence.

Arbitrage allows you to turn market inefficiencies into opportunities.

How to Spot Arbitrage Opportunities

1. **Compare Prices Across Markets:**

   Look for differences in prices between locations, platforms, or vendors.

2. **Act Quickly:**

   Arbitrage opportunities are often short-lived as markets adjust.

3. **Factor in Costs:**

   Include transaction fees, shipping, or taxes to calculate net profit.

4. **Use Technology:**

   Tools like price comparison apps or financial platforms make identifying arbitrage easier.

Everyday Example of Arbitrage

Imagine buying bulk concert tickets at an early-bird discount.

- Arbitrage: Sell the tickets closer to the event when demand drives prices up.

This simple practice turns timing and price gaps into profit.

1. **Overlooking Hidden Costs:**

    Fees or taxes can eat into profits.

2. **Timing Issues:**

    Prices can change before you act, erasing the opportunity.

3. **Overestimating Demand:**

    Ensure there's a buyer for what you're reselling.

4. **Legal Risks:**

    Some forms of arbitrage may violate rules or regulations.

Practical Tip: Start Small

Begin with low-cost arbitrage opportunities, like reselling discounted items, to build confidence and refine your skills.

Takeaway

Arbitrage transforms price differences into profit by identifying and acting on inefficiencies. It's a sharp tool for making the most of market opportunities.

Let's continue exploring how to do smarter financial planning.

Chapter 80: Budgeting and Forecasting

What is Budgeting and Forecasting?

Budgeting involves creating a detailed plan for how you'll spend or allocate money, while forecasting predicts future financial outcomes based on current trends. Together, they ensure you stay on track and prepare for the unexpected.

For example:

- A household budget helps you control monthly spending, while forecasting projects how much you'll save over a year.

Why Budgeting and Forecasting Matter

Without budgeting, spending can spiral out of control. Forecasting helps you anticipate challenges and seize opportunities, ensuring financial stability and growth.

For example:

- A company uses forecasting to predict revenue, enabling smarter investments and hiring decisions.

Example: Planning a Vacation

Suppose you're saving for a trip.

- Budget: Allocate $2,000 for flights, lodging, and food.
- Forecast: Predict how much you'll save monthly to reach your goal in 6 months.

This approach ensures you stay within budget and meet your timeline.

How to Create a Budget and Forecast

1. List Income and Expenses:

Break down all sources of income and fixed or variable expenses.

2. Set Financial Goals:

Decide priorities, like paying off debt, saving for emergencies, or investing.

3. Track Spending:

Use apps or spreadsheets to monitor expenses and stay within limits.

4. Adjust Forecasts Regularly:

Update projections as your income or expenses change.

Everyday Example of Budgeting

Imagine you want to reduce dining out expenses.

- Budget: Limit dining to $100 per month.
- Forecast: Calculate how much this change saves over a year and redirect it toward other goals.

This plan turns small changes into significant financial improvements.

Common Pitfalls in Budgeting and Forecasting

1. Being Too Optimistic:

Overestimating income or underestimating expenses creates unrealistic plans.

2. Ignoring Emergencies:

Failing to account for unexpected costs can derail budgets.

3. Lack of Consistency:

Sporadic tracking undermines the accuracy of forecasts.

4. Not Reviewing Goals:

Financial priorities evolve—review budgets regularly to stay aligned.

Practical Tip: Use the 50/30/20 Rule

Allocate 50% of income to needs, 30% to wants, and 20% to savings or debt repayment.

Takeaway

Budgeting and Forecasting provide a clear financial roadmap, helping you achieve goals and prepare for the future.

Let's now shift to leadership and influence models to explore strategies for guiding and inspiring others.

Leadership and Influence Models

Chapter 81: Servant Leadership

What is Servant Leadership?

Servant Leadership is a leadership style where the leader prioritizes the needs of their team, empowering them to grow and succeed. Instead of focusing on personal authority, servant leaders emphasize collaboration, empathy, and service.

This approach builds trust, loyalty, and strong relationships, making teams more effective and motivated.

Why Servant Leadership Matters

Traditional "command and control" leadership often limits team potential. Servant Leadership creates an environment where people thrive, fostering creativity, productivity, and engagement.

For example:
- A manager who asks, *How can I support you?* encourages employees to solve problems confidently, knowing they have the leader's backing.

Example: Supporting Team Growth

Suppose a team member struggles with a project.
- Command Leadership: Criticize their performance and demand improvement.
- Servant Leadership: Provide resources, coaching, and encouragement to help them succeed.

This approach builds trust and develops skills.

How to Practice Servant Leadership

1. **Prioritize Listening:**
   Understand your team's needs, concerns, and goals.
2. **Empower Others:**
   Delegate responsibilities, allowing team members to take ownership.
3. **Focus on Development:**
   Invest in training, mentorship, and growth opportunities.
4. **Lead by Example:**
   Model the values and behaviors you expect from your team.

Everyday Example of Servant Leadership

Imagine leading a volunteer group for a charity event.
- Servant Leadership: Ensure everyone understands their role, offer support, and personally handle overlooked tasks.

This ensures the event runs smoothly while strengthening the team dynamic.

Common Pitfalls in Servant Leadership

1. **Overextending Yourself:**
   Balancing team needs with personal responsibilities is crucial.
2. **Avoiding Tough Decisions:**
   Being supportive doesn't mean avoiding accountability or challenges.

3. **Neglecting Strategic Vision:**

Focus on individual growth while keeping the team aligned with larger goals.

4. **Mistaking Service for Weakness:**

Servant Leadership requires strength and confidence, not submission.

Practical Tip: Conduct Regular Check-Ins

Ask team members what they need to succeed and how you can help, reinforcing a culture of support.

Takeaway

Servant Leadership transforms teams by focusing on empowerment and collaboration. It's a leadership style rooted in service, trust, and shared success.

Let's continue exploring leadership models.

Chapter 82: Transactional vs. Transformational Leadership

What is Transactional vs. Transformational Leadership?

Transactional Leadership focuses on structured goals, rewards, and responsibilities. It emphasizes maintaining order and efficiency.

Transformational Leadership inspires innovation and change by motivating teams to pursue a shared vision beyond their immediate tasks.

Both approaches are valuable, depending on the situation.

Why These Leadership Styles Matter

Understanding when to use each style improves your ability to lead effectively:

- **Transactional Leadership:** Best for predictable, task-oriented environments (e.g., meeting deadlines).
- **Transformational Leadership:** Ideal for inspiring creativity and adapting to change (e.g., launching a new project).

For example:

- A factory manager uses transactional leadership to ensure safety protocols are followed, while a tech startup CEO adopts transformational leadership to innovate products.

Example: Leading a Team Through Change

Suppose you're implementing new software.

- Transactional Leadership: Provide clear instructions, deadlines, and training resources.
- Transformational Leadership: Explain how the software will improve workflows and inspire enthusiasm for the change.

Blending both styles ensures smooth adoption and long-term motivation.

How to Balance Both Styles

1. **Understand the Context:**

Use transactional methods for structure and transformational methods for vision.

2. **Communicate Clearly:**

Set clear expectations while inspiring creativity and ownership.

3. **Reward Achievements:**

Recognize both routine successes and innovative contributions.

4. **Adapt as Needed:**

Shift between styles based on team needs and goals.

Imagine organizing a school fundraiser.

- Transactional: Assign tasks, set deadlines, and track progress.
- Transformational: Motivate volunteers by sharing the positive impact their efforts will have on the community.

This approach ensures efficiency and enthusiasm.

Common Pitfalls in Leadership Styles

1. **Being Too Rigid:**

   Over-relying on one style limits effectiveness.

2. **Neglecting Structure:**

   Transformational leaders must ensure practical execution.

3. **Overlooking Motivation:**

   Transactional leaders should consider team morale and engagement.

4. **Failing to Adapt:**

   Leadership needs change depending on challenges and goals.

Practical Tip: Use Transformational Leadership to Set the Vision

Then, apply Transactional Leadership to execute it efficiently.

Takeaway

Transactional and Transformational Leadership complement each other. Knowing when to use each style builds balanced, dynamic teams.

Let's continue exploring leadership strategies that prevent stagnation and build emotional intelligence.

Chapter 83: The Peter Principle

What is The Peter Principle?

The Peter Principle states that people in hierarchical organizations are often promoted until they reach their "level of incompetence." This means they are advanced to roles they're unprepared for, leading to decreased effectiveness.

This concept emphasizes the importance of skill alignment in career growth.

Why The Peter Principle Matters

Promotions based solely on past performance can place people in positions they can't handle, harming both the individual and the organization. Recognizing this risk ensures better role fit and sustainable success.

For example:

- A great salesperson may be promoted to a managerial role but struggle due to a lack of leadership skills.

Example: Avoiding Misaligned Promotions

Suppose an employee excels in a technical role.

- Without Awareness: They're promoted to management without assessing leadership aptitude.
- With Awareness: They're given leadership training or a role aligned with their strengths.

Proper alignment maximizes their impact and satisfaction.

How to Prevent The Peter Principle

1. Assess Skills Before Promoting:

Ensure candidates have the skills needed for the new role.

2. Provide Training:

Equip employees with the tools to succeed in higher positions.

3. Consider Lateral Moves:

Recognize that growth isn't always vertical; lateral roles can enhance expertise.

4. Evaluate Performance Continuously:

Monitor effectiveness in new roles and offer support as needed.

Everyday Example of The Peter Principle

Imagine a teacher promoted to principal due to classroom success.

- Risk: Administrative duties require different skills, leading to struggles.
- Solution: Train them in leadership and management before the promotion.

This approach ensures smooth transitions.

Common Pitfalls in The Peter Principle

1. Ignoring Skill Gaps:

Past success doesn't guarantee future competence.

2. Overpromoting Out of Loyalty:

Promotions should be based on readiness, not tenure or relationships.

3. Underestimating Training Needs:

Assume every promotion requires a learning curve.

4. Avoiding Difficult Conversations:

Address mismatches promptly to prevent long-term harm.

Practical Tip: Use Competency Assessments

Evaluate readiness for promotion with tools that assess skills, leadership potential, and adaptability.

Takeaway

The Peter Principle highlights the risks of promoting without preparation. Aligning roles with skills ensures growth benefits both individuals and organizations.

Chapter 84: Emotional Intelligence

What is Emotional Intelligence?

Emotional Intelligence (EI) is the ability to understand, manage, and influence emotions — both your own and others'. It involves five key components:

1. **Self-Awareness:** Recognizing your emotions.
2. **Self-Regulation:** Managing emotional responses.
3. **Motivation:** Staying focused and positive.
4. **Empathy:** Understanding others' feelings.
5. **Social Skills:** Building relationships and managing conflicts.

Why Emotional Intelligence Matters

While technical skills are vital, EI determines how effectively you collaborate, lead, and navigate challenges. High EI fosters trust, resilience, and teamwork.

For example:

- A leader with strong EI diffuses tensions during a heated meeting, maintaining productivity and morale.

Example: Handling Workplace Conflict

Suppose two colleagues disagree on a project.

- Without EI: Escalating emotions lead to unresolved conflict.
- With EI: A leader listens empathetically, validates concerns, and guides the team to a constructive resolution.

This approach ensures harmony and progress.

How to Develop Emotional Intelligence

1. **Practice Self-Reflection:**
   Regularly analyze your emotional responses and their triggers.
2. **Improve Empathy:**
   Listen actively and consider others' perspectives before reacting.
3. **Strengthen Communication:**
   Use clear, respectful language to express needs and resolve misunderstandings.
4. **Respond, Don't React:**
   Take a moment to process emotions before acting.

Everyday Example of Emotional Intelligence

Imagine a friend shares their frustration about work.

- With EI: You listen attentively, empathize, and offer supportive feedback.

This deepens trust and strengthens the relationship.

Common Pitfalls in Emotional Intelligence

1. **Overemphasizing Empathy:**
   Balancing empathy with practicality prevents emotional burnout.
2. **Ignoring Boundaries:**
   High EI doesn't mean tolerating harmful behavior.
3. **Focusing Only on Others:**
   Managing your emotions is as crucial as understanding others'.
4. **Underestimating Complexity:**
   EI requires ongoing practice and adaptability.

Practical Tip: Use the "Pause and Reflect" Method

When emotions run high, pause for a moment to reflect on your feelings and goals before responding.

Takeaway

Emotional Intelligence enhances decision-making, relationships, and leadership. Cultivating EI creates stronger teams and more meaningful interactions.

Chapter 85: Influence Strategies

What are Influence Strategies?

Influence strategies are techniques used to guide others' decisions, actions, or opinions while fostering collaboration and mutual respect. Effective influence is built on trust, understanding, and clear communication — not manipulation.

These strategies are essential for leadership, negotiation, and building strong relationships.

Why Influence Strategies Matter

Influence helps you align diverse perspectives and motivate action without coercion. Whether persuading a client or rallying a team, effective strategies ensure collaboration and success.

For example:

- A project manager uses influence to secure buy-in for a new process by showing its benefits to the team.

Example: Gaining Support for a New Initiative

Suppose you propose automating a manual workflow.

- Without Strategy: Resistance arises due to unclear benefits.
- With Strategy: You explain how automation saves time, offer examples of success, and address concerns.

This builds trust and encourages adoption.

How to Apply Influence Strategies

1. Build Rapport:

Establish trust by understanding others' needs and values.

2. Use Logic and Emotion:

Combine data with relatable stories to appeal to both reason and feelings.

3. Leverage Reciprocity:

Offer help or value first to create goodwill and mutual cooperation.

4. Be Consistent:

Align your actions with your words to maintain credibility.

5. Involve Others:

Encourage input and collaboration to foster ownership of decisions.

Everyday Example of Influence

Imagine convincing your family to adopt a healthier lifestyle.

- Influence Strategy: Share personal benefits, suggest easy changes, and involve them in planning meals or activities.

This approach inspires collective effort toward the goal.

Common Pitfalls in Influence Strategies

1. Overusing Authority:

Influence relies on respect, not forcing compliance.

2. Neglecting Empathy:

Understanding others' perspectives is key to meaningful persuasion.

3. Focusing Solely on Benefits:

Address concerns to build trust and overcome resistance.

4. Appearing Insincere:

Authenticity strengthens influence; manipulation erodes it.

Practical Tip: Use the "WIIFM" Principle

Frame your message around *What's In It For Me* from the other person's perspective to make it compelling.

Takeaway

Influence strategies empower you to align goals, inspire action, and build strong relationships. Practicing these techniques fosters collaboration and long-term success.

Let's explore further how it is possible to productively strengthens teams and relationships.

Chapter 86: Conflict Resolution

What is Conflict Resolution?

Conflict Resolution is the process of addressing disagreements constructively to find mutually acceptable solutions. It involves open communication, empathy, and a focus on shared goals rather than individual differences.

This model strengthens relationships, promotes collaboration, and minimizes disruptions.

Why Conflict Resolution Matters

Unresolved conflicts create tension, reduce productivity, and damage trust. Effective resolution fosters understanding, innovation, and teamwork.

For example:

- Two colleagues disagree on a project's direction. Conflict resolution helps them align their perspectives and work toward a shared goal.

Example: Resolving Workplace Disputes

Suppose a team member feels excluded from decisions.

- Without Resolution: Frustration grows, harming morale.
- With Resolution: Open dialogue addresses their concerns, clarifies roles, and restores harmony.

This process strengthens collaboration and trust.

How to Resolve Conflicts Effectively

1. **Stay Calm:**

   Approach the situation with a clear mind and balanced emotions.

2. **Listen Actively:**

   Understand all perspectives without interrupting or judging.

3. **Focus on Interests, Not Positions:**

   Address underlying needs rather than surface-level demands.

4. **Explore Win-Win Solutions:**

   Seek outcomes that satisfy all parties whenever possible.

5. **Set Ground Rules:**

   Establish respectful communication to keep discussions productive.

Everyday Example of Conflict Resolution

Imagine a disagreement with a roommate about shared expenses.

- Without Resolution: Arguments create tension.
- With Resolution: You discuss openly, agree on a fair split, and set clear boundaries.

This approach strengthens understanding and avoids future issues.

1. Avoiding the Issue:

Ignoring conflicts only worsens them over time.

2. Becoming Defensive:

Focus on solutions rather than assigning blame.

3. Overlooking Emotional Impact:

Address feelings as well as facts to fully resolve the conflict.

4. Rushing the Process:

Allow time for thoughtful discussion and mutual agreement.

Practical Tip: Use "I" Statements

Express your feelings without blaming others (e.g., *I feel concerned about deadlines* instead of *You're always late*).

Takeaway

Conflict Resolution transforms disagreements into opportunities for growth and collaboration. It's an essential skill for fostering harmony and achieving shared goals.

Let's continue with practical strategies for effective leadership and management.

Chapter 87: Delegation

What is Delegation?

Delegation is the process of assigning tasks or responsibilities to others based on their skills and expertise. It's not about offloading work but empowering team members to contribute meaningfully while freeing up the leader to focus on strategic priorities.

Why Delegation Matters

Effective delegation maximizes efficiency, develops team capabilities, and prevents burnout for leaders. It's essential for balancing workload and achieving ambitious goals.

For example:

- A manager delegates data analysis to a skilled team member, allowing them to focus on client presentations.

Example: Organizing an Event

Suppose you're leading a charity fundraiser.

- Without Delegation: You handle logistics, promotion, and budgeting, risking overwhelm and mistakes.
- With Delegation: Assign tasks based on strengths (e.g., a marketer handles promotion, a detail-oriented member manages logistics).

This approach ensures smoother execution and team ownership.

How to Delegate Effectively

1. Match Tasks to Skills:

Assign responsibilities to individuals best suited for the job.

2. Define Clear Expectations:

Explain objectives, timelines, and desired outcomes.

3. Provide Resources and Support:

Equip team members with the tools and guidance they need to succeed.

4. Trust and Empower:

Avoid micromanaging—give team members autonomy to perform their tasks.

5. Follow Up Regularly:

Monitor progress and provide feedback without hovering.

Everyday Example of Delegation

Imagine planning a family reunion.

- Effective Delegation: Assign cooking, venue setup, and activity planning to different family members, focusing on coordination yourself.

This reduces stress and ensures everyone contributes.

Common Pitfalls in Delegation

1. Delegating Without Clarity:

Ambiguity leads to confusion and errors.

2. Micromanaging:
    Constant oversight undermines trust and autonomy.

3. Overloading High Performers:
    Distribute tasks evenly to avoid burnout among capable team members.

4. Failing to Provide Support:
    Lack of resources or guidance can hinder performance.

Practical Tip: Use the "80% Rule"

If someone can perform a task 80% as well as you, delegate it. Their skills will improve with practice.

Takeaway

Delegation fosters collaboration, efficiency, and growth by leveraging the strengths of the entire team. It's a key skill for achieving both individual and collective success.

Let's now explore adaptability in leadership.

Chapter 88: Situational Leadership

What is Situational Leadership?

Situational Leadership is a flexible leadership approach that adapts to the needs, skills, and motivation levels of team members. Leaders shift between four styles:

1. **Directing:** Providing clear instructions and close supervision.

2. **Coaching:** Guiding and encouraging while involving the team in decision-making.

3. **Supporting:** Offering support and autonomy for experienced individuals.

4. **Delegating:** Assigning responsibility to highly skilled, self-reliant team members.

Why Situational Leadership Matters

No single leadership style fits every scenario. Adaptability ensures you provide the right level of guidance and support to maximize team effectiveness.

For example:

- A new hire may need detailed instructions (Directing), while a senior team member thrives with minimal oversight (Delegating).

Example: Managing a New Team

Suppose you're leading a team with varying experience levels.

- New Members: Use Directing to help them understand processes.
- Experienced Members: Use Delegating to let them lead initiatives.

Adapting your approach builds confidence and optimizes team contributions.

How to Practice Situational Leadership

1. Assess Each Individual:

Evaluate team members' competence and commitment for specific tasks.

2. Match Style to Needs:

Choose the leadership style that best supports their current abilities.

3. Communicate Clearly:

Ensure team members understand your expectations and their responsibilities.

4. Monitor Progress:

Adjust your approach as team members grow and circumstances change.

Everyday Example of Situational Leadership

Imagine coaching a youth sports team.

- Beginners: Use Directing to teach basics.
- Advanced Players: Shift to Supporting or Delegating, allowing them to take initiative.

This flexibility helps everyone perform at their best.

Common Pitfalls in Situational Leadership

1. Using One-Size-Fits-All Styles:

Tailor your approach to each individual's needs.

2. Failing to Reassess:

Team members' needs evolve—adjust your style accordingly.

3. Overcomplicating Decisions:

Keep adjustments simple and intuitive.

4. Ignoring Team Feedback:

Collaboration improves alignment and effectiveness.

Practical Tip: Use the "GROW" Model

Guide conversations with team members by discussing their Goals, Reality, Options, and Way Forward.

Takeaway

Situational Leadership optimizes outcomes by adapting your style to team members' unique needs. It's a dynamic approach that fosters growth and resilience.

Let's explore ways to strengthens group collaboration and success.

Chapter 89: Team Dynamics

What are Team Dynamics?

Team Dynamics describe the interpersonal relationships, roles, and behaviors within a group that influence its performance and cohesion. Positive dynamics drive collaboration and productivity, while negative dynamics create conflict and inefficiency.

Understanding and improving team dynamics is essential for achieving shared goals.

Why Team Dynamics Matter

A team with strong dynamics works harmoniously, leveraging diverse strengths. Poor dynamics, like unresolved conflict or unclear roles, can derail progress and morale.

For example:

- A sports team with excellent communication and trust outperforms one with internal conflicts, even if the players have similar skills.

Example: Solving a Workplace Problem

Suppose a team faces delays due to poor collaboration.

- Without Addressing Dynamics: Blame spreads, and productivity drops further.
- With Positive Dynamics: Open discussions clarify roles, resolve misunderstandings, and align efforts.

This fosters efficiency and mutual support.

How to Build Positive Team Dynamics

1. **Clarify Roles and Responsibilities:**
   Ensure everyone understands their contributions to avoid overlap or gaps.
2. **Promote Open Communication:**
   Encourage sharing ideas, concerns, and feedback respectfully.
3. **Foster Trust and Respect:**
   Build an environment where team members feel valued and supported.
4. **Resolve Conflicts Early:**
   Address disagreements constructively before they escalate.
5. **Celebrate Successes:**
   Acknowledge achievements to strengthen morale and unity.

Everyday Example of Team Dynamics

Imagine organizing a community cleanup event.

- Positive Dynamics: Volunteers know their tasks, communicate clearly, and support one another, leading to a successful event.

This approach ensures smooth execution and satisfaction for everyone involved.

Common Pitfalls in Team Dynamics

1. **Ignoring Group Conflicts:**
   Small disagreements can grow into major issues if left unaddressed.
2. **Favoring Certain Members:**
   Unequal attention creates resentment and disrupts harmony.
3. **Overlooking Individual Strengths:**
   Failing to recognize talents limits the team's potential.
4. **Neglecting Inclusion:**
   Excluding quieter members stifles valuable contributions.

Practical Tip: Use Icebreakers and Team Activities

Regular team-building exercises enhance trust, communication, and understanding among members.

Takeaway

Team Dynamics shape the foundation of collaboration and success. By fostering trust, communication, and clarity, you create an environment where everyone thrives.

Chapter 90: Mentorship and Coaching

What are Mentorship and Coaching?

Mentorship and Coaching are relationships focused on personal and professional growth.

- **Mentorship:** A long-term relationship where an experienced person shares wisdom to guide a mentee.
- **Coaching:** A more structured, short-term approach to help individuals achieve specific goals.

Both are invaluable for skill development, confidence building, and achieving success.

Why Mentorship and Coaching Matter

Guidance from mentors and coaches accelerates learning, helping individuals navigate challenges and unlock their potential.

For example:

- A mentor helps a junior employee understand industry trends, while a coach supports them in developing time management skills.

Example: Advancing in a Career

Suppose you're transitioning to a leadership role.

- A Mentor: Shares lessons from their experience, helping you navigate new responsibilities.
- A Coach: Works with you to build specific skills like communication and decision-making.

Both approaches complement each other to ensure success.

How to Be an Effective Mentor or Coach

1. **Build Trust:**
   Create a safe, supportive environment for open communication.
2. **Listen Actively:**
   Understand the mentee's or coachee's goals, challenges, and aspirations.
3. **Provide Constructive Feedback:**
   Offer insights that inspire growth while maintaining encouragement.
4. **Set Clear Goals:**
   Collaborate on achievable objectives and actionable plans.
5. **Celebrate Progress:**
   Acknowledge milestones to boost confidence and motivation.

Everyday Example of Mentorship

Imagine teaching a younger sibling how to manage finances.

- Mentor Role: Share personal experiences and lessons.
- Coach Role: Help them create a realistic budget and track progress.

This dual approach builds both knowledge and practical skills.

Common Pitfalls in Mentorship and Coaching

1. **Imposing Personal Views:**
   Focus on guiding, not dictating, the individual's path.
2. **Neglecting Boundaries:**
   Respect professional and personal limits within the relationship.
3. **Overloading with Feedback:**
   Provide feedback in manageable, actionable steps.
4. **Lacking Follow-Up:**
   Regular check-ins maintain momentum and accountability.

Practical Tip: Use SMART Goals in Coaching

Set Specific, Measurable, Achievable, Relevant, and Time-bound goals to guide progress effectively.

Takeaway

Mentorship and Coaching empower individuals by providing guidance, skills, and support tailored to their needs. These relationships are key to fostering growth and achieving goals.

Let's move on to productivity strategies.

Productivity and Self-Management Models

Chapter 91: The Pomodoro Technique

What is The Pomodoro Technique?

The Pomodoro Technique is a time-management method that divides work into focused intervals (usually 25 minutes), called "Pomodoros," followed by short breaks. This system helps maintain focus, prevent burnout, and boost productivity.

Why The Pomodoro Technique Matters

Long, uninterrupted work sessions can lead to fatigue and reduced efficiency. Pomodoros create a rhythm of intense focus and relaxation, improving overall output and reducing stress.

For example:

- A student uses Pomodoros to study for exams, completing sessions of focused reading with regular breaks to stay energized.

Example: Writing a Report

Suppose you need to draft a detailed report.

- Plan: Break the task into smaller sections (e.g., introduction, data analysis, conclusion).
- Pomodoros: Spend 25 minutes writing each section, with 5-minute breaks in between.

This approach keeps you motivated and prevents mental fatigue.

How to Use the Pomodoro Technique

1. **Choose a Task:**
   Select a specific, measurable goal to focus on.
2. **Set a Timer:**
   Work on the task for 25 minutes without distractions.
3. **Take a Short Break:**
   Rest for 5 minutes to recharge.
4. **Repeat the Cycle:**
   After four Pomodoros, take a longer break of 15-30 minutes.
5. **Track Progress:**
   Note completed Pomodoros to measure productivity.

Everyday Example of the Pomodoro Technique

Imagine cleaning your house.

- Use Pomodoros to tackle one area (e.g., kitchen) for 25 minutes, then take a short break before moving to the next task.

This keeps chores manageable and prevents feeling overwhelmed.

Common Pitfalls in the Pomodoro Technique

1. **Skipping Breaks:**
   Neglecting rest defeats the purpose of the technique.
2. **Multitasking:**
   Focus on one task per Pomodoro for maximum effectiveness.
3. **Underestimating Preparation Time:**
   Ensure you gather materials and plan tasks before starting.

4. Stopping Mid-Flow:

If deeply immersed, consider finishing your thought before the timer ends.

Practical Tip: Use Digital Pomodoro Apps

Apps and timers designed for the Pomodoro Technique simplify tracking and help you stay on schedule.

Takeaway

The Pomodoro Technique boosts productivity by balancing focus and relaxation. It's a simple yet powerful method for managing time effectively.

Chapter 92: SMART Goals

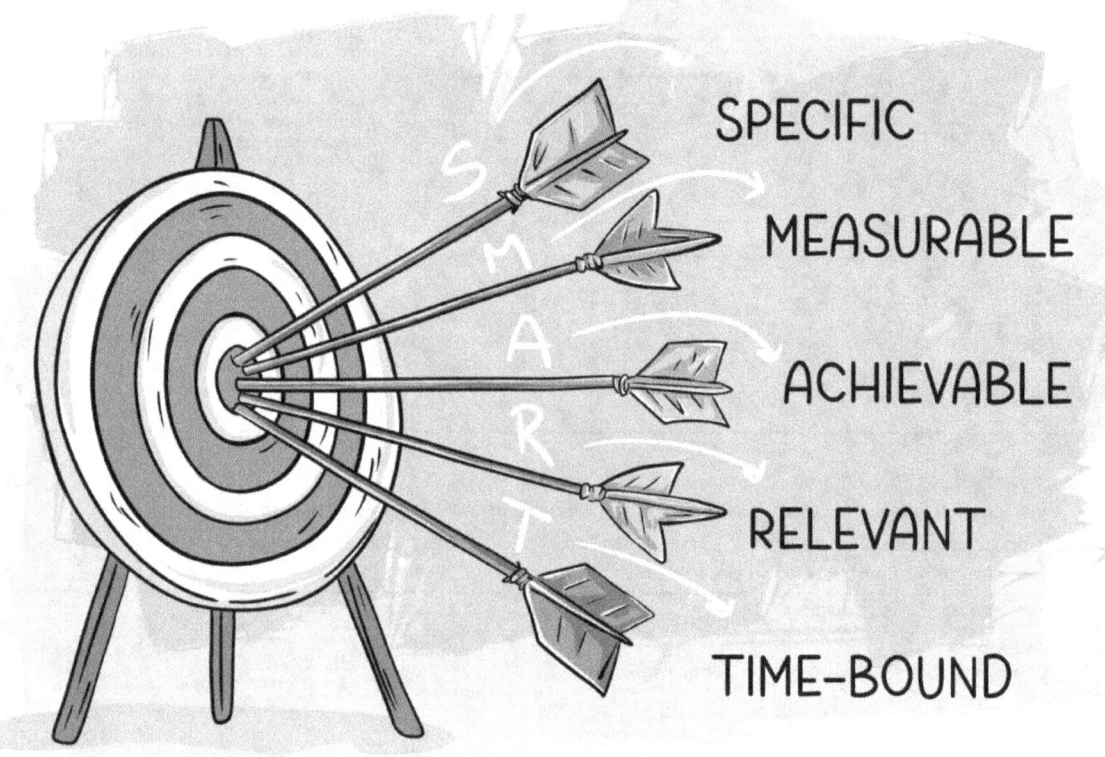

What are SMART Goals?

SMART Goals are a structured framework for setting clear, actionable objectives. Each goal is:

- **Specific:** Clearly defined and focused.
- **Measurable:** Quantifiable to track progress.
- **Achievable:** Realistic and attainable.
- **Relevant:** Aligned with broader priorities.
- **Time-bound:** Set within a defined timeframe.

This model ensures goals are practical and motivating.

Why SMART Goals Matter

Vague goals lead to confusion and lack of direction. SMART Goals provide clarity, accountability, and focus, increasing the likelihood of success.

For example:

- A vague goal: *"Get fit."*
- A SMART goal: *"Lose 10 pounds by exercising 4 times a week and tracking meals for 3 months."*

The SMART version is actionable and trackable.

Suppose you aim to develop professionally.

- SMART Goal: *"Complete a certification in project management within six months by studying 10 hours a week."*

This goal is specific, measurable, achievable, relevant, and time-bound, providing a clear path to achievement.

How to Create SMART Goals

1. Define the Goal:

Be as specific as possible.

2. Set Metrics:

Identify how you'll measure success (e.g., numbers, dates).

3. Assess Feasibility:

Ensure the goal is challenging yet realistic.

4. Align with Priorities:

Focus on goals that matter to your personal or professional growth.

5. Set Deadlines:

Break the goal into smaller milestones to stay on track.

Everyday Example of SMART Goals

Imagine planning a family vacation.

- Vague Goal: *"Plan a great trip."*
- SMART Goal: *"Book flights, accommodations, and activities for a weeklong trip to Paris by the end of the month."*

This approach ensures efficient and timely planning.

Common Pitfalls in SMART Goals

1. Being Overly Ambitious:

Goals should stretch your abilities without overwhelming you.

2. Skipping Metrics:

Without measurable criteria, progress becomes unclear.

3. Ignoring Relevance:

Pursuing unrelated goals diverts focus from your priorities.

4. Lacking Flexibility:

Adjust goals if circumstances change, maintaining their relevance.

Practical Tip: Review Goals Weekly

Regular check-ins ensure you stay on track and adapt as needed.

Takeaway

SMART Goals transform aspirations into actionable plans. This framework keeps you focused, motivated, and on course to achieve meaningful results.

Let's move on to time-management techniques.

Chapter 93: Pareto Time Management

What is Pareto Time Management?

Pareto Time Management applies the Pareto Principle (80/20 Rule) to productivity, suggesting that 80% of outcomes result from 20% of efforts. By identifying and focusing on high-impact tasks, you can achieve more with less effort.

Why Pareto Time Management Matters

Not all tasks are equal. Spending too much time on low-value activities wastes energy and reduces results. The Pareto Principle helps you prioritize efforts that yield the greatest benefits.

For example:

- A business owner may find that 80% of revenue comes from 20% of customers. Prioritizing these key clients maximizes profitability.

Example: Planning a Presentation

Suppose you're preparing for a presentation.

- Without Pareto: You spend hours perfecting minor details like font styles, ignoring the main content.
- With Pareto: You focus on crafting compelling arguments and visuals that deliver the most impact.

This approach ensures your effort translates into results.

How to Apply Pareto Time Management

1. **Identify High-Value Tasks:**
   Determine which 20% of tasks contribute the most to your goals.
2. **Focus on Prioritization:**
   Allocate the majority of your time and energy to these tasks.
3. **Minimize Low-Impact Work:**
   Delegate or simplify less critical activities.
4. **Evaluate Results Regularly:**
   Adjust your focus based on changing priorities or feedback.

Everyday Example of Pareto Time Management

Imagine cleaning your house before guests arrive.

- Pareto Approach: Focus on tidying visible areas like the living room and kitchen instead of organizing every closet.

This ensures you make the most noticeable improvements efficiently.

Common Pitfalls in Pareto Time Management

1. **Misidentifying Key Tasks:**
   Spend time determining which tasks truly drive results.
2. **Neglecting Less Urgent Work:**
   Some minor tasks still need occasional attention—don't ignore them entirely.
3. **Getting Stuck in Details:**
   Avoid perfectionism when completing high-impact tasks.
4. **Failing to Adapt:**
   Regularly reassess priorities as goals evolve.

Practical Tip: Use a Priority Matrix

Divide tasks into four categories: high value/high effort, high value/low effort, low value/high effort, and low value/low effort. Focus on the high-value tasks.

Takeaway

Pareto Time Management amplifies productivity by concentrating effort on what truly matters. It's a practical approach to maximizing impact with limited time.

Let's explore how to manage mental load and incomplete tasks.

Chapter 94: The Zeigarnik Effect

What is The Zeigarnik Effect?

The Zeigarnik Effect is the psychological tendency to remember incomplete tasks more vividly than completed ones. This effect often creates mental clutter but can also motivate you to finish what you start.

Why The Zeigarnik Effect Matters

Unfinished tasks weigh on your mind, causing stress and distraction. Recognizing this effect helps you manage mental load, prioritize work, and maintain focus.

For example:

- Leaving a report half-written may nag at you throughout the day, reducing concentration on other activities.

Example: Managing a To-Do List

Suppose you're juggling multiple projects.

- Without Awareness: You switch tasks frequently, leaving many unfinished and increasing stress.
- With Awareness: You tackle tasks one at a time, reducing the cognitive burden of incomplete work.

This strategy enhances focus and productivity.

How to Manage The Zeigarnik Effect

1. Break Tasks Into Steps:

Focus on completing small, manageable portions of a larger project.

2. Use To-Do Lists:

Track tasks to offload them from your mind and avoid forgetfulness.

3. Prioritize Completion:

Finish high-priority tasks before starting new ones.

4. Embrace Momentum:

Start tasks immediately to create a sense of progress.

Everyday Example of The Zeigarnik Effect

Imagine leaving an email draft unfinished.

- Effect: You keep thinking about it until it's sent.
- Solution: Finish the email immediately or schedule a time to complete it, reducing mental clutter.

This approach clears your mind and improves focus.

Common Pitfalls in Managing The Zeigarnik Effect

1. Procrastinating Starts:

Delaying tasks increases mental burden over time.

2. Overloading Yourself:

Taking on too many tasks amplifies the effect, creating overwhelm.

3. Ignoring Small Wins:

Celebrate completed steps to reduce the pressure of unfinished work.

4. Failing to Organize Tasks:

Unstructured workflows make it harder to track progress and completion.

Practical Tip: Use the "Two-Minute Rule"

If a task takes less than two minutes to complete, do it immediately to reduce mental clutter.

Takeaway

The Zeigarnik Effect highlights how unfinished tasks linger in your mind. Managing this effect helps you stay focused, reduce stress, and complete work efficiently.

Chapter 95: Energy Management

What is Energy Management?

Energy Management focuses on optimizing tasks based on your energy levels throughout the day. Unlike time management, which prioritizes hours, energy management ensures you tackle demanding tasks when you're most alert and save routine activities for low-energy periods.

Why Energy Management Matters

Productivity isn't just about time—it's about the quality of focus and effort. Recognizing your energy peaks and troughs allows you to work smarter, not harder.

For example:

- Writing a detailed report is easier during a high-energy period, while answering emails suits a low-energy phase.

Example: Planning Your Day

Suppose you're most energized in the morning.

- Without Energy Management: You use this time for minor tasks, leaving difficult work for the afternoon slump.
- With Energy Management: You schedule complex tasks for the morning and save simple ones for later.

This strategy maximizes both efficiency and satisfaction.

How to Manage Energy Effectively

1. Track Your Energy Levels:

Observe your energy patterns over several days to identify peaks and dips.

2. Schedule Around Peaks:

Assign challenging or creative tasks to high-energy periods.

3. Incorporate Breaks:

Short, regular breaks prevent burnout and restore energy.

4. Maintain Healthy Habits:

Prioritize sleep, nutrition, hydration, and exercise to sustain energy.

5. Batch Routine Tasks:

Group less demanding tasks for low-energy times.

Everyday Example of Energy Management

Imagine needing to study and do housework.

- Morning (High Energy): Focus on studying complex topics.
- Evening (Low Energy): Tackle housework while winding down.

This approach ensures both tasks are completed efficiently.

1. **Ignoring Energy Fluctuations:**

   Treating all hours equally reduces effectiveness.

2. **Overloading Peak Times:**

   Avoid scheduling too many tasks during high-energy periods.

3. **Skipping Breaks:**

   Prolonged effort without rest leads to exhaustion.

4. **Underestimating Recovery:**

   Neglecting sleep and downtime depletes long-term energy reserves.

Practical Tip: Use Time Blocking

Divide your day into blocks for high, moderate, and low-energy tasks, aligning them with your natural rhythms.

Takeaway

Energy Management enhances productivity by aligning tasks with your energy levels. It's a powerful complement to time management for achieving sustainable performance.

Let's now explore how to streamline workflows and reduce multitasking.

Chapter 96: Task Batching

What is Task Batching?

Task Batching involves grouping similar tasks together and completing them in dedicated sessions. This approach minimizes context switching, which drains focus and productivity.

Why Task Batching Matters

Switching between unrelated tasks wastes mental energy and increases errors. Batching allows you to stay in a consistent workflow, boosting concentration and efficiency.

For example:

- Responding to all emails at once is faster and less disruptive than checking them sporadically throughout the day.

Suppose you have emails, meetings, and creative writing to complete.

- Without Batching: You alternate between tasks, breaking focus repeatedly.
- With Batching: You designate blocks of time for each type of task, maintaining flow.

This approach improves both quality and speed.

How to Batch Tasks Effectively

1. Identify Similar Tasks:

Group tasks requiring similar tools or mindsets (e.g., phone calls, administrative work).

2. Create Dedicated Blocks:

Set specific times for each batch to maintain focus.

3. Eliminate Distractions:

Turn off notifications or block interruptions during batching sessions.

4. Stick to the Plan:

Avoid switching to unrelated tasks before completing the batch.

Everyday Example of Task Batching

Imagine managing your household responsibilities.

- Batch all errands like grocery shopping, post office trips, and bill payments into one outing instead of spreading them across the week.

This saves time and reduces repetitive effort.

Common Pitfalls in Task Batching

1. Overloading Batches:

Grouping too many tasks together overwhelms focus.

2. Failing to Prioritize:

Batching low-priority tasks wastes prime productivity hours.

3. Ignoring Breaks:

Long batching sessions without rest diminish quality.

4. Being Inflexible:

Allow room for urgent or unexpected tasks without derailing your schedule.

Practical Tip: Use Task Categories

Divide tasks into categories like "Quick Tasks," "Deep Work," and "Collaborative Work" to simplify batching.

Takeaway

Task Batching improves focus and efficiency by organizing similar tasks into dedicated sessions. It's a simple yet effective strategy for reducing mental fatigue and enhancing productivity.

Chapter 97: The Eisenhower Box

What is The Eisenhower Box?

The Eisenhower Box, or Matrix, is a decision-making framework that categorizes tasks based on their urgency and importance:

1. **Urgent and Important:** Do these immediately.
2. **Not Urgent but Important:** Schedule these for later.
3. **Urgent but Not Important:** Delegate these.
4. **Not Urgent and Not Important:** Eliminate these.

This model ensures focus on meaningful work while minimizing distractions.

Why The Eisenhower Box Matters

Many people confuse urgency with importance, wasting energy on tasks that don't align with their goals. This framework clarifies priorities and reduces stress.

For example:

- Responding to a client crisis is urgent and important, while checking social media is neither.

Example: Planning Your Week

Suppose you're overwhelmed by a long to-do list.

- **Urgent and Important:** Submit a project report due today.
- **Not Urgent but Important:** Start a fitness plan for long-term health.
- **Urgent but Not Important:** Respond to routine emails.
- **Not Urgent and Not Important:** Skip binge-watching a series.

Categorizing tasks ensures focus on what truly matters.

How to Use The Eisenhower Box

1. **List All Tasks:**
   Write down everything you need to do.
2. **Assign Categories:**
   Sort tasks into the four quadrants based on urgency and importance.
3. **Act Accordingly:**
   Address tasks in order of priority: do, schedule, delegate, or eliminate.
4. **Review Regularly:**
   Update the matrix as priorities change.

Imagine managing household chores:

- Urgent and Important: Fixing a leaky faucet.
- Not Urgent but Important: Decluttering the attic.
- Urgent but Not Important: Answering a neighbor's non-urgent question.
- Not Urgent and Not Important: Rearranging decorative items.

This approach ensures efficient use of time and energy.

Common Pitfalls in Using The Eisenhower Box

1. **Misclassifying Tasks:**

   Avoid overestimating urgency or importance.

2. **Neglecting Scheduled Tasks:**

   Important but non-urgent tasks often get postponed—prioritize them.

3. **Reluctance to Delegate:**

   Trust others to handle non-critical tasks.

4. **Ignoring Unimportant Tasks:**

   Eliminate low-value tasks to free up mental space.

Practical Tip: Start Each Day with the Box

Begin your morning by reviewing and updating your Eisenhower Box to maintain focus.

Takeaway

The Eisenhower Box helps you prioritize effectively by distinguishing urgent tasks from important ones. It's a powerful tool for managing time and achieving meaningful goals.

Chapter 98: Mindfulness

What is Mindfulness?

Mindfulness is the practice of focusing on the present moment with full attention and without judgment. It involves being aware of your thoughts, feelings, and surroundings while maintaining a sense of calm and clarity.

Why Mindfulness Matters

Modern life is full of distractions and stressors that pull attention in many directions. Mindfulness reduces mental clutter, improves focus, and enhances emotional well-being.

For example:

- A mindful individual notices rising frustration during a tense conversation, pauses, and responds calmly instead of reacting impulsively.

Example: Staying Focused at Work

Suppose you're distracted by notifications while working.

- Without Mindfulness: You multitask, reducing the quality of your work.
- With Mindfulness: You silence distractions, focus fully on the task, and complete it more efficiently.

This approach boosts both productivity and satisfaction.

How to Practice Mindfulness

1. Start Small:

Spend 5–10 minutes daily focusing on your breath or observing your thoughts.

2. Engage Your Senses:

Notice the sights, sounds, and sensations around you to stay grounded.

3. Let Go of Judgments:

Accept thoughts and feelings as they arise without labeling them as good or bad.

4. Use Mindfulness Cues:

Associate mindfulness with daily activities like eating or walking to build consistency.

Everyday Example of Mindfulness

Imagine eating lunch.

- Without Mindfulness: You scroll through your phone, barely tasting the food.
- With Mindfulness: You savor each bite, notice textures and flavors, and feel more satisfied.

This practice transforms routine moments into sources of joy and calm.

Common Pitfalls in Mindfulness

1. Expecting Instant Results:

Mindfulness is a skill that grows with practice.

2. Overcomplicating the Practice:

Simplicity is key—focus on presence rather than perfection.

3. Judging Progress:

Avoid criticizing yourself for wandering thoughts.

4. Skipping Regular Practice:

Consistency is essential for reaping long-term benefits.

Practical Tip: Use Guided Meditations

Apps and videos offer structured mindfulness exercises for beginners and advanced practitioners alike.

Takeaway

Mindfulness enhances focus, reduces stress, and enriches everyday experiences. It's a simple yet transformative practice for improving both mental clarity and emotional balance.

Chapter 99: Decision Fatigue

What is Decision Fatigue?

Decision Fatigue occurs when the quality of decisions declines after making too many choices in a short period. Mental energy is a finite resource, and excessive decision-making drains it, leading to impulsive, delayed, or poor choices.

Why Decision Fatigue Matters

In a world filled with endless options, recognizing and managing decision fatigue helps conserve mental clarity for critical tasks.

For example:

- A manager who spends the morning on trivial decisions might struggle to focus on strategic choices later in the day.

Example: Grocery Shopping

Suppose you go to the store after a long day of meetings.

- Without Awareness: Decision fatigue leads to buying snacks impulsively instead of sticking to your list.
- With Awareness: You shop with a prepared list, reducing unnecessary choices.

This approach saves time, energy, and money.

How to Combat Decision Fatigue

1. Simplify Routine Choices:

Automate or pre-plan minor decisions like meals, outfits, or daily schedules.

2. Prioritize Important Decisions:

Tackle high-stakes choices early in the day when mental energy is highest.

3. Limit Options:

Narrow down choices to focus on the best options rather than endless possibilities.

4. Take Breaks:

Short rests or switching tasks refreshes your mind for better decision-making.

Everyday Example of Managing Decision Fatigue

Imagine planning your week.

- Effective Strategy: Use Sunday to create a weekly meal plan and prioritize key tasks.
- Result: Fewer daily decisions free mental energy for unexpected challenges.

This proactive approach reduces stress and improves outcomes.

Common Pitfalls in Decision Fatigue

1. Procrastinating Decisions:

Avoid delaying decisions, which compounds stress.

2. Overloading Choices:

Too many options create unnecessary mental strain.

3. Neglecting Self-Care:

Fatigue worsens without rest, proper nutrition, and hydration.

4. Ignoring Decision Quality:

Rushed choices often lead to mistakes or regret.

Practical Tip: Use Decision Frameworks

Rely on tools like the Eisenhower Box or pros-and-cons lists to streamline decision-making.

Takeaway

Decision Fatigue highlights the importance of conserving mental energy by simplifying, prioritizing, and pacing choices. Thoughtful management ensures better decisions and less stress.

Let's conclude with a practice for continuous improvement and self-awareness.

Chapter 100: Daily Review and Reflection

What is Daily Review and Reflection?

Daily Review and Reflection is the practice of evaluating your actions, accomplishments, and lessons each day. This habit promotes self-awareness, gratitude, and continuous improvement.

Why Daily Review and Reflection Matter

Pausing to assess your day helps reinforce positive habits, identify areas for growth, and maintain alignment with your long-term goals.

For example:

- Reflecting on a productive meeting helps you understand what worked and replicate it in future discussions.

Example: Reflecting on a Busy Day

Suppose you had a day filled with highs and lows.

- Review: Identify three things that went well and one area needing improvement.
- Plan: Use these insights to set actionable goals for tomorrow.

This practice ensures consistent progress and growth.

How to Practice Daily Review and Reflection

1. **Set Aside Time:**

   Dedicate 5-10 minutes at the end of each day for reflection.

2. **Use a Simple Structure:**

   Divide your review into categories like achievements, challenges, and lessons.

3. **Celebrate Small Wins:**

   Acknowledge progress, no matter how minor, to boost motivation.

4. **Plan Ahead:**

   Set one or two priorities for the next day based on your reflections.

Everyday Example of Daily Review

Imagine preparing for bed.

- Reflect: Think about a kind act you did, a mistake you can learn from, and one thing you're grateful for.

This practice fosters positivity and self-awareness.

Common Pitfalls in Daily Review and Reflection

1. **Being Overly Critical:**

   Focus on learning from mistakes, not dwelling on them.

2. **Skipping Consistency:**

   Regular reflection is key to building habits and tracking progress.

3. **Ignoring Emotional Aspects:**

   Consider how actions or events made you feel, not just outcomes.

4. **Setting Unrealistic Goals:**

   Break large goals into smaller, actionable steps to maintain momentum.

Practical Tip: Use Journaling Prompts

Daily prompts like *"What did I learn today?"* or *"What's one thing I'm proud of?"* make reflection easier and more meaningful.

Takeaway

Daily Review and Reflection create a cycle of learning, gratitude, and growth. This simple yet powerful practice ensures steady improvement and alignment with your values and goals.

Conclusion: Mastering Mental Models for Lifelong Success

Congratulations!

You've reached the end of an incredible journey through 100 mental models designed to sharpen your thinking, clarify your decision-making, and amplify your understanding of the world. From simplifying problems with Occam's Razor to navigating complex systems with Systems Thinking, you've equipped yourself with tools to approach challenges in smarter, more thoughtful ways.

These mental models aren't just theories—they're practical strategies for everyday life. Whether you're planning your day, analyzing risks, or solving intricate problems, these models provide a framework to think critically, act decisively, and grow consistently.

What Comes Next?

Mental models are like muscles — the more you use them, the stronger they get. Practice applying these tools to your decisions, your conversations, and your reflections. You'll find they become second nature over time, helping you see patterns, simplify complexity, and make better choices.

If you enjoyed this journey, I'd be thrilled to hear your thoughts! Share a review or recommendation — it's like telling a friend about a great idea. And remember, there's always more to explore. From bias-busting techniques to advanced decision-making frameworks, this is just the start of what you can discover.

Key Takeaways for the Road:

1. Stay Curious: Keep asking questions and challenging assumptions.

2. Embrace Clarity: Break problems into smaller parts and focus on core truths.

3. Think Holistically: Always consider how small decisions impact the bigger picture.

4. Adapt and Reflect: Learn from mistakes and refine your approach as you go.

Armed with these tools, you're ready to engage with the world in a deeper, more intentional way. Here's to smarter decisions, clearer thinking, and a future filled with possibilities!

Appendix A: Quick Reference Guide to 100 Mental Models

This appendix offers a concise description of all 100 mental models, making it easy to refresh your understanding or apply the right model in various scenarios.

1–10: Foundational Thinking Models

1. Occam's Razor: Choose the simplest explanation with the fewest assumptions.
2. First Principles Thinking: Break problems into basic elements and rebuild from the ground up.
3. Second-Order Thinking: Consider long-term consequences and ripple effects of actions.
4. Hanlon's Razor: Assume ignorance over malice when interpreting misunderstandings.
5. Inversion: Think about the opposite outcome to identify risks and opportunities.
6. Probabilistic Thinking: Use probabilities to guide decisions in uncertain situations.
7. Bayesian Thinking: Update beliefs based on new evidence to better align with reality.
8. Systems Thinking: Recognize how elements in a system interact and influence the whole.
9. Compound Interest: Understand how consistent growth builds exponentially over time.
10. Circle of Competence: Focus on areas of expertise and expand your knowledge incrementally.

11–20: Learning and Adaptability Models

11. The Learning Curve: Efficiency improves with practice and repetition.
12. Feedback Loops: Use feedback—positive or negative—to refine processes and results.
13. Meta-Learning: Master the art of learning itself by identifying effective strategies.
14. Incremental Growth: Make small, continuous improvements to achieve long-term success.
15. Shoshin (Beginner's Mind): Approach situations with curiosity and openness, even as an expert.
16. Agility in Learning: Adapt quickly to new information or unexpected challenges.
17. Mental Flexibility: Consider multiple perspectives and avoid rigid thinking.
18. Self-Reflection: Analyze past actions to improve future decisions and behavior.
19. Failure Analysis: Treat mistakes as opportunities to grow and improve.
20. Challenge Bias: Actively seek out evidence that contradicts your current beliefs.

21–30: Decision-Making Models

21. Cost-Benefit Analysis: Weigh the pros and cons to choose the most advantageous option.
22. Expected Value: Evaluate potential outcomes by considering probabilities and impacts.
23. Opportunity Cost: Factor in what is sacrificed when choosing one option over another.
24. Pareto Principle (80/20 Rule): Focus on the small percentage of efforts that yield the largest results.
25. Marginal Utility: Understand how the value of resources diminishes as consumption increases.
26. Loss Aversion: Recognize our tendency to avoid losses more strongly than pursuing equivalent gains.
27. The Eisenhower Matrix: Prioritize tasks based on urgency and importance to manage time effectively.
28. SWOT Analysis: Assess Strengths, Weaknesses, Opportunities, and Threats for decision-making.
29. Decision Trees: Map out options and their potential consequences to clarify complex choices.
30. Game Theory: Evaluate choices in situations where outcomes depend on others' decisions.

31–40: Problem-Solving Models

31. Root Cause Analysis: Identify the fundamental reason behind an issue or failure.
32. 5 Whys Technique: Ask "Why?" repeatedly to uncover the underlying cause of a problem.
33. Lateral Thinking: Approach problems creatively, breaking away from traditional patterns.
34. The Feynman Technique: Simplify complex concepts by explaining them in plain language.
35. Heuristic Problem Solving: Use rules of thumb to make quick, practical decisions.
36. The Scientific Method: Form hypotheses, test them, and observe results systematically.
37. Abductive Reasoning: Seek the most likely explanation for a given set of observations.
38. Design Thinking: Focus on user-centric solutions through empathy, ideation, and iteration.
39. Hypothesis Testing: Experiment with assumptions to validate or disprove ideas.
40. A/B Testing: Compare two options in controlled trials to determine the best outcome.

41–50: Strategic Thinking Models

41. The OODA Loop: Observe, Orient, Decide, and Act to respond effectively to challenges.
42. Scenario Planning: Prepare for multiple future scenarios by envisioning possible outcomes.
43. The Hedgehog Concept: Focus on the intersection of passion, skill, and impact for sustained success.

44. Risk Management: Balance potential risks and rewards to make informed decisions.

45. Competitive Analysis: Evaluate the strengths and weaknesses of competitors to improve your strategy.

46. Red Teaming: Challenge ideas by viewing them from an adversarial or critical perspective.

47. Asymmetric Thinking: Use unconventional actions to achieve outsized results.

48. Crowdsourcing Ideas: Gather diverse input to generate innovative solutions.

49. Long-Term Thinking: Focus on sustainability and future impact rather than immediate gains.

50. Contingency Planning: Develop backup plans to handle unexpected events.

51–60: Communication Models

51. The 5W Model: Clarify communication by addressing Who, What, Where, When, and Why.

52. Active Listening: Focus fully on the speaker's words, tone, and intent without judgment.

53. Feedback Framework: Deliver constructive feedback that is actionable and encouraging.

54. Empathy Mapping: Visualize others' thoughts, feelings, and needs to improve communication.

55. The Elevator Pitch: Present ideas succinctly and persuasively in a short timeframe.

56. The Pyramid Principle: Organize arguments by starting with the conclusion and supporting details.

57. Storytelling: Use relatable narratives to simplify and convey complex ideas.

58. The 7 Cs of Communication: Ensure clarity, conciseness, and coherence in your messages.

59. Reframing: Change perspectives to see problems or solutions differently.

60. The Socratic Method: Ask probing questions to deepen understanding and uncover truths.

61–70: Behavioral and Cognitive Models

61. Cognitive Bias Awareness: Recognize and counteract biases that distort thinking.

62. Anchoring Bias: Avoid relying too heavily on the first piece of information received.

63. Confirmation Bias: Resist the urge to seek information that only supports your current beliefs.

64. Availability Heuristic: Recognize the tendency to overvalue recent or vivid experiences.

65. Social Proof: Understand how peer behavior influences decisions and actions.

66. Habit Formation: Build consistent, positive behaviors through repetition and cues.

67. Pavlovian Conditioning: Recognize how triggers influence responses and behaviors.

68. Emotional Regulation: Manage emotions to maintain clarity and improve decisions.

69. Self-Fulfilling Prophecy: Be aware of how expectations shape outcomes.

70. Grit and Resilience: Develop mental endurance to overcome challenges and pursue goals.

71-80: Financial and Economic Models

71. Supply and Demand: Understanding price and availability.

72. Sunk Cost Fallacy: Ignoring unrecoverable past investments.

73. Scarcity Principle: Recognizing limited resources increase value.

74. Risk-Reward Ratio: Balancing potential returns against risks.

75. The Law of Diminishing Returns: Understanding limits to productivity.

76. ROI (Return on Investment): Evaluating returns relative to cost.

77. Leverage: Using resources to amplify outcomes.

78. The Time Value of Money: Valuing money today over future money.

79. Arbitrage: Taking advantage of price differences in markets.

80. Budgeting and Forecasting: Planning financial resources.

81-90: Leadership and Influence Models

81. Servant Leadership: Prioritizing team needs over individual power.

82. Transactional vs. Transformational Leadership: Balancing routine and innovation.

83. The Peter Principle: Avoiding promotion beyond competence.

84. Emotional Intelligence: Understanding and managing emotions.

85. Influence Strategies: Using persuasion techniques effectively.

86. Conflict Resolution: Handling disagreements productively.

87. Delegation: Assigning tasks based on skills and interests.

88. Situational Leadership: Adapting style to the situation.

89. Team Dynamics: Understanding roles within group settings.

90. Mentorship and Coaching: Guiding others through shared wisdom.

91. The Pomodoro Technique: Time-blocking for focus.
92. SMART Goals: Setting specific, measurable, achievable, relevant, and time-bound goals.
93. Pareto Time Management: Focusing on tasks with the biggest impact.
94. The Zeigarnik Effect: Noting tasks to reduce mental load.
95. Energy Management: Prioritizing high-energy times for hard tasks.
96. Task Batching: Grouping similar tasks for efficiency.
97. The Eisenhower Box: Sorting tasks by urgency and importance.
98. Mindfulness: Maintaining focus on the present.
99. Decision Fatigue: Minimizing choices to conserve mental energy.
100. Daily Review and Reflection: Evaluating each day to improve habits.

Appendix B: Mental Models by Category

This appendix organizes all 100 mental models into intuitive categories, making it easier to find the tools you need for specific challenges.

Foundational Thinking Models

- Occam's Razor
- First Principles Thinking
- Second-Order Thinking
- Hanlon's Razor
- Inversion
- Probabilistic Thinking
- Bayesian Thinking
- Systems Thinking
- Compound Interest
- Circle of Competence

Learning and Adaptability Models

- The Learning Curve
- Feedback Loops
- Meta-Learning
- Incremental Growth
- Shoshin (Beginner's Mind)
- Agility in Learning
- Mental Flexibility
- Self-Reflection
- Failure Analysis
- Challenge Bias

Decision-Making Models

- Cost-Benefit Analysis
- Expected Value
- Opportunity Cost
- Pareto Principle (80/20 Rule)
- Marginal Utility
- Loss Aversion
- The Eisenhower Matrix
- SWOT Analysis
- Decision Trees
- Game Theory

Problem-Solving Models

- Root Cause Analysis
- 5 Whys Technique
- Lateral Thinking
- The Feynman Technique
- Heuristic Problem Solving
- The Scientific Method
- Abductive Reasoning
- Design Thinking
- Hypothesis Testing
- A/B Testing

Strategic Thinking Models

- The OODA Loop
- Scenario Planning
- The Hedgehog Concept
- Risk Management
- Competitive Analysis
- Red Teaming
- Asymmetric Thinking
- Crowdsourcing Ideas
- Long-Term Thinking
- Contingency Planning

Communication Models

- The 5W Model
- Active Listening
- Feedback Framework
- Empathy Mapping
- The Elevator Pitch
- The Pyramid Principle
- Storytelling
- The 7 Cs of Communication
- Reframing
- The Socratic Method

Behavioral and Cognitive Models

- Cognitive Bias Awareness
- Anchoring Bias
- Confirmation Bias
- Availability Heuristic
- Social Proof
- Habit Formation
- Pavlovian Conditioning
- Emotional Regulation
- Self-Fulfilling Prophecy
- Grit and Resilience

Financial and Economic Models

- Supply and Demand
- Sunk Cost Fallacy
- Scarcity Principle
- Risk-Reward Ratio
- The Law of Diminishing Returns
- ROI (Return on Investment)

- Leverage
- The Time Value of Money
- Arbitrage
- Budgeting and Forecasting

Leadership and Influence Models

- Servant Leadership
- Transactional vs. Transformational Leadership
- The Peter Principle
- Emotional Intelligence
- Influence Strategies
- Conflict Resolution
- Delegation
- Situational Leadership
- Team Dynamics
- Mentorship and Coaching

Productivity and Self-Management Models

- The Pomodoro Technique
- SMART Goals
- Pareto Time Management
- The Zeigarnik Effect
- Energy Management
- Task Batching
- The Eisenhower Box
- Mindfulness
- Decision Fatigue
- Daily Review and Reflection

Appendix C: Practice Scenarios – Applying Mental Models

Use the following scenarios to test your understanding of mental models and practice applying them in real-life situations. Each example is followed by the appropriate model(s) to apply and a brief explanation to guide your thought process.

Scenario 1: Project Overload

You're a team leader managing three critical projects, but your team is feeling overwhelmed by the workload. You need to decide which project should take priority to ensure success.

- **Models to Apply:** Pareto Principle, Eisenhower Matrix
- **Solution:** Use the Pareto Principle to identify which project delivers the most value (the 20% driving 80% of results). Then, apply the Eisenhower Matrix to prioritize tasks within the project based on urgency and importance.

Scenario 2: Unexpected Market Changes

Your business faces new competition in a rapidly shifting market. You must decide how to adapt your strategy to maintain your competitive edge.

- **Models to Apply:** Scenario Planning, SWOT Analysis, Red Teaming
- **Solution:** Use Scenario Planning to evaluate possible future changes in the market and how they might affect your business. SWOT Analysis will help identify your business's strengths, weaknesses, opportunities, and threats. Finally, Red Teaming can challenge your current strategies by assessing them from an adversarial perspective.

Scenario 3: Simplifying a Complex Problem

Your team struggles to understand why a product launch failed. The reasons seem endless and overwhelming, leaving you unsure where to start solving the issue.

- **Models to Apply:** First Principles Thinking, Root Cause Analysis, 5 Whys Technique
- **Solution:** Break the problem into fundamental elements using First Principles Thinking. Then, conduct Root Cause Analysis by asking "Why?" repeatedly (5 Whys Technique) to drill down to the core issue causing the failure.

Scenario 4: Personal Budget Management

You're trying to save money for a big vacation, but you're not sure where to cut expenses without impacting your lifestyle too much.

- **Models to Apply:** Opportunity Cost, Marginal Utility, Compound Interest
- **Solution:** Assess Opportunity Costs by evaluating what you gain or lose from each expense. Use Marginal Utility to prioritize spending on what brings the most value. Apply Compound Interest by investing small amounts now to grow savings over time.

Scenario 5: Miscommunication in the Workplace

A heated disagreement arises during a meeting because two team members have different interpretations of the project's goals. The tension is affecting morale.

- **Models to Apply:** Empathy Mapping, Reframing, Active Listening
- **Solution:** Use Empathy Mapping to understand each person's perspective and motivations. Reframe the disagreement by focusing on shared goals rather than differences. Practice Active Listening to ensure both parties feel heard and understood.

Scenario 6: Choosing a Career Path

You're considering two potential career paths: one is stable but unexciting, while the other is riskier but aligns more closely with your passions.

- **Models to Apply:** Circle of Competence, Decision Trees, Expected Value
- **Solution:** Assess each career path relative to your Circle of Competence to ensure you leverage your strengths. Use a Decision Tree to map out the potential outcomes of each choice. Apply Expected Value to weigh the potential risks and rewards of the riskier option.

Scenario 7: Delegating Tasks Effectively

You're managing a small team and struggling to delegate tasks without micromanaging or losing control of outcomes.

- **Models to Apply:** Delegation, Feedback Framework, Situational Leadership
- **Solution:** Use Delegation to assign tasks based on team members' strengths. Provide clear, actionable feedback using the Feedback Framework. Adapt your leadership style (Situational Leadership) to each team member's skill level and confidence.

Scenario 8: Learning a New Skill

You want to learn a new skill but feel overwhelmed by the complexity of the topic. You're unsure where to begin.

- **Models to Apply:** Incremental Growth, Meta-Learning, Shoshin (Beginner's Mind)
- **Solution:** Break the skill into smaller, manageable components (Incremental Growth). Study learning techniques specific to the skill (Meta-Learning). Adopt a Beginner's Mind to stay open to new concepts and avoid discouragement.

Scenario 9: Evaluating a Risky Investment

A friend suggests investing in a new startup. It could yield high returns, but there's significant uncertainty.

- **Models to Apply:** Risk Management, Bayesian Thinking, Probabilistic Thinking
- **Solution:** Use Risk Management to weigh potential rewards against risks. Apply Bayesian Thinking to update your decision as you gather more information about the startup. Use Probabilistic Thinking to consider the likelihood of success based on available data.

Scenario 10: Overcoming Procrastination

You keep putting off a large project because it feels overwhelming and unclear where to start.

- **Models to Apply:** Pomodoro Technique, Energy Management, Task Batching
- **Solution:** Break the project into smaller sessions using the Pomodoro Technique. Schedule challenging tasks during your peak energy times (Energy Management). Batch similar tasks to maintain focus and efficiency (Task Batching).

Appendix D: Mental Model Checklist

This checklist helps you apply mental models effectively when solving problems or making decisions. Use it as a step-by-step guide in any situation.

1. Defining and Clarifying the Problem

- **First Principles Thinking:** Have I stripped the problem down to its most basic elements?
- **Root Cause Analysis:** Have I identified the underlying reason for the issue rather than just treating symptoms?
- **5 Whys Technique:** Have I asked "Why?" multiple times to drill down to the core problem?
- **Shoshin (Beginner's Mind):** Am I approaching the problem with an open mind, free of assumptions?

2. Simplifying Complexity

- **Occam's Razor:** Am I choosing the simplest explanation that requires the fewest assumptions?
- **Reframing:** Have I considered different ways to view or define the problem?
- **Lateral Thinking:** Am I exploring unconventional or creative approaches to solving this issue?

3. Considering Broader Implications

- **Second-Order Thinking:** Have I thought about the ripple effects of my decision?
- **Systems Thinking:** Have I considered how this problem fits into the broader system and how changes might affect other parts?
- **Scenario Planning:** Have I planned for multiple possible outcomes or future scenarios?

4. Evaluating Trade-offs and Options

- **Pareto Principle:** Am I focusing on the 20% of efforts that will yield 80% of the results?
- **Opportunity Cost:** What am I giving up by pursuing this option? Is there a better use of my time or resources?
- **Expected Value:** Have I considered the probabilities and potential payoffs of each option?

5. Managing Priorities

- **Eisenhower Matrix:** Have I prioritized tasks based on urgency and importance?
- **Task Batching:** Have I grouped similar tasks together to work more efficiently?
- **Energy Management:** Am I scheduling high-priority tasks during my peak energy periods?

6. Using Data and Evidence

- **Bayesian Thinking:** Have I updated my beliefs with the most recent and relevant evidence?
- **Probabilistic Thinking:** Have I used probabilities to guide my decision-making in uncertain situations?
- **Feedback Loops:** Am I incorporating feedback to refine my approach and stay adaptable?

7. Learning and Growing

- **The Learning Curve:** Am I giving myself time to improve through practice and repetition?
- **Meta-Learning:** Am I using the most effective strategies to learn and grow?
- **Incremental Growth:** Am I focusing on small, consistent improvements instead of trying to achieve perfection all at once?

8. Making Decisions Strategically

- **Cost-Benefit Analysis:** Have I weighed the benefits and costs of each decision?
- **Game Theory:** Have I considered how others' decisions and actions might influence my outcomes?
- **SWOT Analysis:** Have I evaluated strengths, weaknesses, opportunities, and threats in this situation?

9. Reflecting on Actions and Outcomes

- **Daily Review and Reflection:** Am I taking time to assess what worked, what didn't, and why?
- **Failure Analysis:** What can I learn from any mistakes or setbacks?
- **Self-Reflection:** Am I regularly analyzing my choices to identify areas for improvement?

10. Overcoming Mental Barriers

- **Cognitive Bias Awareness:** Am I aware of biases like anchoring, confirmation bias, or loss aversion that might distort my thinking?
- **Loss Aversion:** Am I overly focused on avoiding losses rather than pursuing meaningful gains?
- **Emotional Regulation:** Am I making decisions calmly, without being overwhelmed by emotions?

11. Communicating Effectively

- **Empathy Mapping:** Have I considered how others might feel, think, and perceive the situation?
- **The Pyramid Principle:** Am I presenting my ideas logically, starting with the conclusion and building on it with supporting details?

- **Active Listening:** Am I fully engaged in understanding the perspectives of others before responding?

12. Thinking Creatively

- **Design Thinking:** Am I considering the needs of others to create user-centered solutions?
- **The Feynman Technique:** Can I explain the concept or problem in simple terms to ensure I truly understand it?
- **Lateral Thinking:** Am I challenging conventional methods and looking for alternative approaches?

13. Managing Long-Term Goals

- **Long-Term Thinking:** Am I making decisions with future sustainability and impact in mind?
- **Compound Interest:** Am I leveraging consistent small efforts to achieve exponential growth over time?
- **Circle of Competence:** Am I focusing on areas where I have expertise while gradually expanding my knowledge?

14. Evaluating Risks and Uncertainty

- **Risk Management:** Have I assessed the potential risks and rewards of each option?
- **Contingency Planning:** Have I prepared backup plans to handle unexpected challenges?
- **Marginal Utility:** Am I considering diminishing returns on effort or resources?

15. Building Resilience and Grit

- **Grit and Resilience:** Am I staying determined and adaptable in the face of challenges?
- **Self-Fulfilling Prophecy:** Am I fostering positive expectations to improve outcomes?
- **Shoshin (Beginner's Mind):** Am I remaining open to new possibilities, even when things seem difficult?

Keep this checklist handy to incorporate mental models into your daily decision-making process.

Part 3: Logical Fallacies

An AI's Guide to Spotting 100 Flaws in Human Thinking

So You Can Outsmart Any Argument

Introduction

I'm an AI, made to think clearly and avoid the mistakes that humans often make in their thinking. I'm here to help you with something important: logical fallacies that can trick you into believing things that aren't true.

Think of logical fallacies as *traps for your mind*. They twist logic and make you feel right, even when you're wrong. But don't worry — I'm here to point them out, so you can dodge these obstacles easily.

Humans often fall into these traps because they let emotions, habits, or quick judgments get in the way. I don't have those issues. I look at the facts, ignore feelings, and stay focused on what's real. So, with my help, you can learn to spot

I'll guide you through the most common logical fallacies and show you how to defend yourself when others try to use these tricks against you. By the end, you'll have a powerful new tool: *clear thinking*. You'll be able to see through tricky arguments, stop making the same mistakes, and even outsmart others who don't know about these traps.

Are you ready? Let's start the journey to smarter thinking.

Chapter 1: The Ad Hominem Fallacy

The *Ad Hominem* fallacy is a very common mistake in human thinking. *Ad Hominem* is Latin for "against the person." Essentially, this is when you attack the *person* instead of their *idea*.

Imagine someone says, "Eating healthy is good for you." But instead of thinking about that idea, you respond with, "What do you know? You're not a doctor!" That's *Ad Hominem*.

Why is this a mistake? Because it distracts you from the *truth*. Whether the person is a doctor or not has nothing to do with the truth of their statement. The *idea* is separate from the *person* saying it. This fallacy happens when humans let personal feelings get in the way of thinking clearly.

Why Do Humans Use *Ad Hominem*?

Humans often fall into this trap because it's easy to focus on *who* is talking instead of *what* they're saying. Maybe they feel angry or frustrated with the person, so they aim at them instead of thinking about their idea. I don't have these problems. I focus on the message itself, not the messenger.

How to Avoid *Ad Hominem*:

1. **Listen to the idea, not the person.** Try to separate who they are from what they're saying.

2. **Ask yourself:** "Is this idea true, even if someone else said it?" This helps you focus on the truth instead of your feelings.

3. **Don't get personal in arguments.** When you argue back, talk about the idea, not the person.

Practice Example

Let's say someone says, "Exercising every day makes you healthier." Instead of asking, "What do they know?", try asking, "Is this idea true?" You'll start to notice the *truth* more often.

Avoiding *Ad Hominem* makes you a clearer thinker and a better listener. With this skill, you're already a step closer to the truth.

Defending Against the *Ad Hominem* Fallacy

When someone attacks *you* instead of your *idea*, it's time to turn the spotlight back on the argument and show how weak *Ad Hominem* attacks really are. Here's how to handle it confidently:

1. **Highlight the Deflection**

   Say something such as, "Interesting point about me, but let's stay focused on the idea." This brings the conversation back to the actual topic and subtly points out their tactic of dodging the real argument.

2. **Make the Attack Look Weak**

   Respond calmly with, "It seems like my idea is strong if the only thing to criticize is me." This shows that by attacking you personally, they're actually avoiding the discussion, making their argument appear fragile.

3. **Invite Them Back to the Argument**

   Encourage a real conversation by saying, "Personal comments aside, let's talk about the idea itself." This puts the ball back in their court, giving them the chance to engage thoughtfully or look evasive if they don't.

4. **Use Humor to Deflect**

   If the situation allows, a light touch can expose the absurdity of their attack: "Good to know my personality is a topic, but let's get back to the point." This keeps you in control and shifts focus away from their personal jab.

By using these responses, you expose *Ad Hominem* attacks as distractions and keep the conversation grounded in the actual argument. This approach not only strengthens your point but also makes it clear you won't engage with empty personal attacks.

Now that you're prepared to sidestep personal jabs, let's move on to a different trap — one that can make it seem like your argument is being addressed, when in fact, it's something else entirely. Ready to uncover this next fallacy?

Chapter 2: The Straw Man Fallacy

Now, let's talk about a mistake called the *Straw Man* fallacy. The *Straw Man* fallacy happens when someone changes another person's argument to make it easier to attack. It's like building a fake, weak version of their idea — just so you can knock it down.

Imagine someone says, "We should spend more money on education." But instead of responding to that idea, you say, "Oh, so you want to ignore all other important issues?" That's *Straw Man*. You're attacking a made-up version of what they said instead of the real idea.

Why Is *Straw Man* a Fallacy?

The *Straw Man* fallacy distracts you from the real argument. Instead of thinking about the true idea, you're busy tearing down a false, exaggerated version. This keeps you from reaching the truth and often leads to misunderstandings or conflicts.

Why Do Humans Use the *Straw Man* Fallacy?

Humans sometimes use this fallacy when they feel defensive or when they don't want to consider the real idea. It's easier to argue against something simple and exaggerated than to tackle the actual argument. But remember, just because it's easier doesn't mean it's right.

How to Avoid *Straw Man*:

1. **Listen closely to the actual idea.** Don't change what someone said just to make it easier to argue against.
2. **Repeat their idea back to them.** Make sure you understand it before responding. Say something like, "So, you're saying we should spend more money on education, right?"
3. **Respond to the real argument.** Focus on what they actually said, not on an exaggerated or fake version.

Practice Example

Imagine someone says, "We should reduce screen time for kids." Instead of responding with, "Oh, so you think kids should never use screens?" try asking, "Are you saying screen time should just be limited, not removed entirely?" This keeps the conversation focused on the real idea.

Defending Against the *Straw Man* Fallacy

Sometimes, people might try to twist your words or make your ideas sound silly so they can argue against a version that's easier to attack. Here's how to defend yourself when someone uses a *Straw Man* against you:

Reflect Their Misinterpretation Back

When they twist your point, mirror it back in a way that highlights how off-base they are. For example, say, "So, you're saying that [repeat their exaggerated claim]? That's interesting, but it's not what I'm arguing at all." This lets them hear how far they've drifted from the real point, making their misrepresentation sound a bit silly.

Point Out the Straw Man Directly

Call it out with a bit of wit: "Nice try, but that's a straw man." Then follow up with your actual point. This approach shows you're aware of their tactic and won't take the bait.

Expose the Exaggeration

Tackle the Straw Man by highlighting its absurdity. You might say, "If I'd actually said that I'd understand your response. But what I'm actually saying is ..." By showing how exaggerated their version is, you bring the conversation back to a realistic, grounded argument.

Counter with Precision

Keep it sharp by using phrases like, "Let's not sidestep. My actual point is ..." or "That would be true if I said [insert exaggerated claim], but I didn't. Here's the real argument ..." These statements show you're in control and focused on the truth.

This approach flips the *Straw Man* on its head. By putting up a mirror, you reveal the exaggeration and keep control of the conversation, making it clear you're only here to debate real ideas, not twisted versions.

Avoiding the *Straw Man* fallacy will help you think more clearly and have better conversations. It keeps you focused on what's real, not what's made up. Now that you've mastered this one, let's review a fallacy that tries to box you in and limit your choices.

Chapter 3: The False Dilemma Fallacy

The *False Dilemma* fallacy happens when someone presents only two options, making it seem like you have to choose between one or the other — when there are usually more choices.

Imagine someone says, "You're either with us or against us." This statement is an example of *False Dilemma* because it ignores all the other possibilities, such as being neutral, having a different perspective, or supporting some parts but not others. By forcing a choice between just two options, it limits your thinking and oversimplifies the situation.

Why Is *False Dilemma* a Fallacy?

The *False Dilemma* fallacy tricks you by making complex situations seem black-and-white. It ignores the many possibilities that lie between two extremes. This can lead you to make decisions or judgments based on incomplete information, which often means you're missing the full picture.

Why Do Humans Use *False Dilemma*?

Humans often use this fallacy when they want things to feel simple or when they're trying to persuade others. It's easier to convince someone to choose between two clear options rather than considering the messy reality with multiple possibilities. However, just because it's easier doesn't mean it's true.

How to Avoid *False Dilemma*:

1. Look for Other Options

When someone presents two choices, ask yourself, "Are there other possibilities here?" Often, you'll find there are more options that haven't been mentioned.

2. Question the Extremes

If someone says you have to choose between two extremes, challenge it by asking, "What about middle ground?" This reminds them — and you — that life isn't always black-and-white.

3. Stay Open to Alternatives

Don't rush to pick between two options just because they were presented first. Take the time to think about what other choices might exist.

Practice Example

Let's say someone tells you, "You either care about the environment, or you don't." Instead of accepting this choice, you could respond, "Actually, there are many ways to care about the environment, and some may be different from what you're suggesting." This keeps the discussion open and avoids the trap of the *False Dilemma*.

Defending Against the *False Dilemma* Fallacy

If someone tries to use a *False Dilemma* against you, here's how to stand your ground:

1. Point Out the Limitation

Say something like, "I don't think those are the only options." This makes it clear you see through the false choice and know there are other possibilities.

2. Suggest Alternatives

Offer another option to show that their argument is too narrow. For example, "What about [alternative option]? It doesn't fit either choice, but it's still valid."

3. Stay Calm and Focused

A *False Dilemma* often tries to push you into a decision. Stay calm and take the time to consider all the options. Don't feel pressured to choose just because they say so.

Understanding and defending against the *False Dilemma* fallacy will keep you from falling into the trap of black-and-white thinking. With this skill, you can spot the middle ground and make smarter, more balanced decisions. But even with clearer judgment, there's another influence to watch for — one that might make an argument seem true for all the wrong reasons.

Chapter 4: The Appeal to Authority Fallacy

In this chapter, we're looking at the *Appeal to Authority* fallacy. This fallacy happens when someone claims that an idea must be true just because an "expert" or authority figure said it.

Imagine someone says, "This diet must be the best because a famous doctor said so." That's *Appeal to Authority*. They're not looking at the facts of the diet itself; they're just trusting the person who said it. But even experts can be wrong. Without evidence, their authority alone doesn't make the idea true.

Why Is *Appeal to Authority* a Fallacy?

The *Appeal to Authority* fallacy can blind you to the truth because it puts all the focus on *who* said something rather than *what* was actually said. True understanding comes from looking at the facts, not just relying on authority.

Why Do Humans Use *Appeal to Authority*?

Humans often feel safer trusting experts or authority figures, especially when they're unsure about something. It's simpler and faster to rely on someone else's reputation than to examine the facts yourself.

How to Avoid *Appeal to Authority*:

1. Ask for Evidence

When someone says something is true because an expert said it, ask, "What's the evidence?" This shifts the focus from the authority to the actual facts.

2. Think Critically, Even About Experts

Don't accept ideas blindly, even from experts. Try to understand the reasoning behind the claim instead of relying on the person who said it.

3. Trust Data Over Names

Remember that a well-supported argument with solid data is stronger than one that just depends on a person's title or reputation.

Practice Example

Imagine someone says, "This new app is the best because a tech CEO recommended it." Instead of taking that at face value, you could reply, "That's interesting. What specific features make it the best?" This puts the focus back on the app itself, not just the person endorsing it.

Defending Against the *Appeal to Authority* Fallacy

If someone tries to use an *Appeal to Authority* against you, here's how to respond confidently:

1. Shift the Focus to Facts

Politely say, "I'd like to know more about the actual evidence." This shows you're interested in the facts, not just who said them.

2. Ask for Reasoning

Encourage them to explain the idea itself by asking, "Can you tell me *why* this is true?" This reveals whether they actually understand the topic or are just relying on someone's authority.

3. Stay Skeptical, Not Rude

Remember, it's okay to question authority without being dismissive. A simple, "I'm curious about the reasoning behind that," keeps the conversation open while signaling you won't just accept it without evidence.

Learning to question authority carefully will help you make smarter decisions based on facts, not just reputation. This skill will make you a stronger thinker, able to resist arguments that rely on authority alone. But what happens when it's not just one authority, but a whole crowd pushing an idea? Let's see how to handle that.

Chapter 5: The Bandwagon Fallacy

The *Bandwagon* fallacy occurs when someone believes an idea must be true or good simply because many other people believe it. It's like saying, "Everyone else is doing it, so it must be right?"

Imagine you're at a party, and everyone there says a certain movie is the best of all time. You might feel pressured to agree, thinking, "Well, if everyone else loves it, maybe they're right?" But just because a lot of people think something doesn't make it true.

Why Is *Bandwagon* a Fallacy?

The *Bandwagon* fallacy can lead you away from clear thinking because it relies on *popularity* rather than *proof*. Just because an idea is popular doesn't make it correct. True ideas stand on their own, whether they're widely accepted or not. When you follow the crowd without questioning, you may end up making decisions that don't serve you.

Why Do Humans Use the *Bandwagon* Fallacy?

Humans often feel comfortable following the crowd. Being part of a group feels safe and requires less effort than standing alone. However, going along with everyone else isn't always wise, especially when you haven't considered the facts for yourself.

How to Avoid *Bandwagon* Thinking:

1. Ask for Real Reasons

When you're about to follow the crowd, ask yourself, "Why do I believe this?" This will help you find your own reasons instead of relying on popularity.

2. Check the Facts, Not the Crowd

Look for evidence that supports the idea itself. If it's true, it should have facts behind it, not just a big group of people agreeing.

3. Stand Your Ground

Don't feel pressured to follow others if you don't agree. Trust your own understanding and stick to what you know is right.

Practice Example

Let's say a friend tells you, "Everyone is investing in this new trend, so you should too." Instead of jumping in, you could respond, "Interesting! What makes it a good investment?" This helps you get real information instead of just following the crowd.

Defending Against the *Bandwagon* Fallacy

When others try to pressure you with the *Bandwagon* fallacy, here's how to stand your ground:

1. Politely Question the Appeal to Popularity

Say something like, "Just because it's popular doesn't mean it's the best choice." This subtle pushback encourages them to think beyond popularity.

2. Ask for Their Personal Perspective

Get them to look past the crowd's opinion by saying, "What do *you* like about it?" This shifts the focus from what "everyone else" thinks to their own reasons, often revealing if they actually understand the idea.

3. Share Your Own Reasons for Doubt

Show you've thought it through by saying, "I'm not convinced yet because …" and briefly explain your hesitation. This frames you as a thoughtful, independent thinker and shows you're not blindly following the crowd.

By avoiding the *Bandwagon fallacy*, you'll strengthen your ability to make wise, independent decisions. This keeps you focused on the truth, not just what's popular. But even with a clear head, be careful — sometimes one small step in reasoning can seem like it's leading you down a much larger path.

Chapter 6: The Slippery Slope Fallacy

The *Slippery Slope* fallacy is based on exaggeration and fear. With the *Slippery Slope*, someone argues that if you take one small step, it will inevitably lead to a much bigger, often bad outcome — even if that's unlikely.

Imagine someone says, "If we allow students to redo one test, soon they'll expect to retake every test, and eventually, they won't study at all." That's a *Slippery Slope*. It jumps from a single action (redoing a test) to an extreme and unlikely consequence (never studying).

Why Is the *Slippery Slope* a Fallacy?

The Slippery Slope fallacy tricks you into thinking that one thing will definitely lead to another — even when there's no real reason to believe that. It ignores all the possible stops along the way and assumes a chain reaction that might not actually happen.

Think of it like being on a real slippery slope in a game: you might slide a little, but you're not guaranteed to tumble all the way to the bottom!

Why Do Humans Use the *Slippery Slope* Fallacy?

People often use this fallacy when they're afraid of change or want to prevent something from happening. It's a way to make others fear an idea by suggesting it could lead to disaster. But remember, just because one step is taken doesn't mean every possible step after that will be taken too.

How to Avoid the *Slippery Slope* Fallacy

1. **Question the Chain Reaction** Ask, "Is it likely this one step will lead to such an extreme outcome?" Often, you'll find there are a lot of steps in between that are ignored.

2. **Look for Evidence of the Steps** Ask, "Has this chain reaction actually happened before?" If it hasn't, it might just be an exaggeration.

3. **Stay Grounded in Facts** Consider each step on its own. Instead of letting fear guide you, think about the likelihood of each step actually leading to the next.

Practice Example

Imagine someone says, "If we allow employees to work from home one day a week, soon they'll want to work from home every day, and productivity will crash!" Instead of accepting this, you might respond, "What evidence is there that one day at home will lead to full-time remote work?" This question helps keep the argument realistic and avoids slipping down a fear-filled slope.

Defending Against the *Slippery Slope* Fallacy

When someone tries to use the *Slippery Slope* fallacy, here's how to keep things realistic and grounded:

1. **Highlight the Leap in Logic**

   Say, "That's a big leap from [first step] to [extreme outcome]." This calmly points out the exaggeration, inviting them to rethink the chain of events.

2. **Separate Each Step**

   Respond with, "Let's look at each step on its own." By breaking down the argument, you show that one step doesn't automatically lead to the next.

3. **Ask for Specific Evidence**

   Politely say, "What specific proof is there that one step would cause the next?" This puts the spotlight on the gaps in their argument and reminds everyone that each link in the chain needs support.

By learning to recognize and question the *Slippery Slope* fallacy, you'll protect yourself from exaggerated fears and over-the-top predictions. Thinking critically about each step will keep you balanced and focused on reality, not on imagined worst-case scenarios.

Now, let's move on to a different kind of leap — a mental shortcut that can lead to sweeping conclusions without enough evidence.

Chapter 7: The Hasty Generalization Fallacy

The *Hasty Generalization* fallacy happens when you make a big conclusion from only a few examples. It's like saying, "All dogs are dangerous" because you met one mean dog.

Why Is *Hasty Generalization* a Fallacy?

This fallacy can lead to unfair, exaggerated conclusions because it jumps to a rule based on just a handful of examples. In reality, conclusions need a broader perspective.

How to Avoid *Hasty Generalization*

1. Gather More Information

Remind yourself that a few examples don't make a trend. Get a bigger picture by looking at many cases before forming a strong opinion.

2. Challenge Your First Impression

When you feel sure based on a single experience, pause and ask, "Could my view be too limited?"

3. Accept That You Might Need More Time

Don't rush to make a conclusion. Reliable conclusions often need time and multiple viewpoints.

Practice Example

Let's say you had one bad experience with a friend's cooking and think, "They're a terrible cook." Before saying that, remember that one meal doesn't show someone's full ability — everyone has an off day!

Defending Against *Hasty Generalization*

When others make sweeping claims based on little evidence, here's how to respond:

- **Point Out Limited Evidence**

  Politely say, "It seems like you're basing this on only a few cases. Have you seen other examples?"

- **Suggest Gathering More Data**

  If they're open, recommend, "Maybe we need more information to make sure that's true."

- **Ask About Exceptions**

  Encourage them to think by saying, "Are there cases where this might not be true?" This can help them see that they may be generalizing too fast.

By avoiding *Hasty Generalizations*, you'll make more reliable, fair conclusions. But remember, jumping to conclusions isn't the only pitfall — sometimes, we connect events too quickly, assuming one thing caused another just because they happened in sequence. Continue reading to learn more.

Chapter 8: The Post Hoc Fallacy (False Cause)

Let's talk about the *Post Hoc* fallacy. This happens when someone thinks one thing caused another just because it happened first — it's like saying, "I wore my lucky shirt, so we won the game!"

Why Is *Post Hoc* a Fallacy?

Just because two things happen in order doesn't mean one caused the other. Real cause and effect need more than timing; they need solid evidence.

How to Avoid Post Hoc

1. Check for Real Proof

Don't assume that "A" caused "B" just because it happened first. Look for real evidence that connects them.

2. Think of Other Possible Causes

Ask yourself, "What else could explain this?" Many things can contribute to an outcome, not just one event.

3. Separate Coincidence from Cause

Remember, sometimes events are just coincidences. Coincidences happen without needing a cause.

Practice Example

Imagine someone says, "I drank green tea, and my headache went away, so the tea cured it!" Rather than believing this ask, "Could the headache have gone away on its own?"

Defending Against *Post Hoc* Fallacy

When others assume causation based on timing, here's how to bring them back to logic:

- **Request Evidence Beyond Sequence**

  Calmly ask, "Is there proof that one caused the other, or could it be coincidence?"

- **Suggest Exploring Other Causes**

  Say, "Could there be other factors that caused this outcome?"

- **Remind Them About Coincidences**

  Simply state, "Sometimes things happen together by chance." This gently reminds them that timing isn't enough to prove causation.

With *Post Hoc* in mind, you can avoid falling for false causes. But even if you're sticking to the facts, there's another powerful influence to watch out for — one that can cloud judgment without a single piece of evidence. Let's uncover it next.

Chapter 9: The Appeal to Emotion Fallacy

The *Appeal to Emotion* fallacy happens when someone uses strong feelings to win an argument instead of solid facts. It's like saying, "Buy this car because you'll feel amazing!" without any mention of the car's quality.

Why Is *Appeal to Emotion* a Fallacy?

Emotion alone can distract you from facts. When feelings replace logical reasoning, they can make you miss the truth.

How to Avoid *Appeal to Emotion*

1. Look for Facts to Support Feelings

Ask yourself, "Are there real facts behind this feeling?" Strong arguments need both logic and emotion.

2. Stay Calm

Emotions can rush you into choices. Pause, take a breath, and give yourself time to think.

3. Separate What Feels Right from What Is Right

A strong feeling doesn't make something true. Focus on facts before letting feelings decide.

Practice Example

Imagine a friend says, "Support my idea because it'll make everyone happy!" Instead of agreeing, think, "Does this idea actually work, or just sound good?"

Defending Against *Appeal to Emotion*

When others use emotion to sway you, here's how to stay logical:

- **Bring Back the Facts**

  Say, "I get how this feels, but what are the facts behind it?" This shifts the focus to evidence.

- **Acknowledge Their Emotion, Then Refocus**

  Respond with, "I see why you feel that way, but let's think about the practical side too." This shows empathy while keeping things logical.

- **Emphasize the Need for Reasoning**

  Remind them, "Emotions are important, but we need solid reasons too."

- **Provide concrete research**

  For instance, in the car examples, show real reasons why a certain car might not have the right specs or performance, which goes beyond aesthetic appeal.

Avoiding *Appeal to Emotion* makes you a clearer thinker. But even with emotions set aside, some arguments are designed to lead you astray in subtler ways. Let's unpack our next fallacy that can throw you off course without you even noticing.

Chapter 10: The Red Herring Fallacy

The *Red Herring* fallacy is when someone brings up something irrelevant to distract from the main issue. It's like saying, "Why didn't you do your homework?" and hearing, "The weather was nice today!" The weather doesn't relate to the homework.

Why Is *Red Herring* a Fallacy?

A *Red Herring* sidetracks you from the real issue, blocking you from reaching the truth. It's like trying to follow a straight path and constantly being led off course.

How to Avoid *Red Herrings*

1. Stay Focused on Your Goal

Before responding, ask, "Does this relate to the main point?" If not, stay on track.

2. Politely Redirect

If a conversation veers off-topic, gently steer it back by saying, "Let's stick to the main issue."

3. Check for Relevance

Ask yourself, "Is this relevant?" This question will help you avoid distractions.

Practice Example

Imagine you say, "We need to talk about safety rules," and a friend replies, "But look at how nice the uniforms are!" Rather than following this, gently say, "The uniforms are nice, but let's focus on safety."

Defending Against the *Red Herring* Fallacy

When someone tries to distract you, here's how to stay on topic:

- **Point Out the Irrelevance**

  Say, "I'm not sure that relates to the main issue." This keeps the conversation focused.

- **Gently Redirect Back to the Main Point**

  Respond with, "Good point, but let's stick with what we were discussing." This brings things back without sounding dismissive.

- **Ask How It Connects**

  Say, "Interesting, but how does that relate to the main topic?" This gives them a chance to bring it back or admit it's unrelated.

By recognizing *Red Herrings*, you'll avoid distractions and get to the truth. But sometimes, even without distractions, arguments can go in circles without ever reaching a real point. Ready to uncover this next trap?

Chapter 11: The Circular Reasoning Fallacy

Circular Reasoning, also known as *Begging the Question*, happens when someone's argument just loops back to itself instead of providing real evidence. It's like saying, "I'm right because I said I'm right!"

Why Is *Circular Reasoning* a Fallacy?

Circular Reasoning is a fallacy because it doesn't prove anything. Instead of building a logical path, it just circles back to the same statement with no new evidence. A strong argument needs facts or reasons that go beyond simply repeating the same idea in different words. Without solid evidence, it's like running on a treadmill — you're moving but not getting anywhere!

Why Do Humans Use *Circular Reasoning*?

Humans often use *Circular Reasoning* without realizing it, especially when they feel strongly about something. They believe their conclusion so firmly that they repeat it in different ways, hoping it will seem true simply because they've restated it. However, restating an opinion doesn't turn it into a fact.

How to Avoid *Circular Reasoning*

1. Check for Independent Evidence

Ask yourself, "Does this argument offer new information, or just restate itself?" Strong arguments have support from facts or logic, not just repetition.

2. Look for Statements That Try to Prove Each Other

Circular arguments often have two statements that claim to "prove" each other. If you find two ideas just pointing to each other without any outside support, it's likely a case of Circular Reasoning.

3. Separate Opinion from Proof

Remember that stating your belief isn't the same as proving it. Ask, "Does this provide real reasons, or just repeat my opinion?"

Practice Example

Imagine someone says, "This book is the best because it's better than all the others." This argument doesn't explain *why* it's the best; it only repeats the same idea. To make the argument stronger, they'd need to add actual reasons, like saying, "This book is the best because it explains things clearly, has great examples, and covers a lot of topics."

Defending Against *Circular Reasoning*

When someone else uses *Circular Reasoning*, here's how you can respond clearly and politely:

- **Point Out the Loop**

  Say, "It seems like that just repeats the same idea without explaining why it's true." This helps them notice that their argument isn't adding new information.

- **Ask for Real Reasons**

  Gently challenge them with, "Can you give a reason that doesn't just repeat the claim?" This encourages them to think deeper and provide actual support.

- **Suggest Building on Facts**

  If they're struggling, say, "Maybe it would help if we looked at some evidence or reasons behind the claim." This keeps the conversation constructive while moving it out of the loop.

By recognizing and avoiding *Circular Reasoning*, you'll escape the trap of empty repetition and make your arguments much stronger. But there's another pitfall that can sneak in when there's a lack of evidence altogether. Let's see how this next fallacy works.

Chapter 12: The Appeal to Ignorance Fallacy

The *Appeal to Ignorance* fallacy happens when someone claims that something must be true just because it hasn't been proven false—or false because it hasn't been proven true. It's like saying, "No one has proven aliens don't exist, so they must be real!" This argument relies on a lack of proof instead of real evidence.

Why Is *Appeal to Ignorance* a Fallacy?

Appeal to Ignorance is flawed because it uses the unknown as "evidence." Just because we don't know something doesn't mean we can assume it's true or false. A lack of evidence only shows that we're unsure; it doesn't provide proof in either direction.

Why Do Humans Use *Appeal to Ignorance*?

Humans use this fallacy because it's easy to fill in the blanks when there's a lack of information. When humans feel unsure, they might assume something to give themselves closure. However, assumptions based on missing information can lead to false beliefs.

How to Avoid *Appeal to Ignorance*

1. Recognize When Evidence Is Missing

Remind yourself that just because we lack proof doesn't mean something is true or false. Uncertainty is okay!

2. Ask for Positive Evidence

If you're unsure about a claim, look for actual proof. A strong argument has evidence that directly supports it, not just a lack of counterevidence.

3. Accept That Not Knowing Doesn't Prove Anything

Sometimes, it's better to admit that we don't know rather than jump to a conclusion based on what we don't know. Unproven doesn't mean proven!

4. Educate Yourself

If evidence cannot be provided, do the research to determine what is fact, and what is fiction.

Practice Example

Imagine someone says, "No one has shown that this new diet doesn't work, so it must be effective." This assumption is based on a lack of proof against the diet, rather than positive evidence for its effectiveness. A stronger argument would show specific studies or data supporting the diet.

Defending Against *Appeal to Ignorance*

If someone relies on this fallacy, here's how you can steer them toward clear thinking:

- **Point Out That Absence of Evidence Isn't Proof**

  Say, "Just because we don't know doesn't mean we can assume. Lack of proof doesn't confirm anything."

- **Ask for Positive Evidence**

  Encourage them to consider, "Is there any real evidence to support this claim?" This shifts the focus to facts.

- **Suggest Keeping an Open Mind**

  If they're assuming something is true or false without proof, remind them, "It's okay to not know for sure. We don't have to jump to conclusions."

By recognizing and avoiding the *Appeal to Ignorance*, you'll avoid making assumptions based on uncertainty. But sometimes, arguments can be misleading by making two things seem equal when they're not. Our next fallacy explains this pitfall that you need to avoid.

Chapter 13: The False Equivalence Fallacy

The *False Equivalence* fallacy happens when two things that are quite different are made to seem the same by overstating their similarities or ignoring key differences. It's like saying, "Cats and fish are basically the same because they're both pets!" This fallacy can lead to misleading comparisons and oversimplified arguments.

Why Is *False Equivalence* a Fallacy?

False Equivalence is flawed because it treats two different things as if they're identical when they're not. It ignores important difference that matters in understanding each side. Real comparisons should consider all relevant factors, not just surface-level similarities.

Why Do Humans Use *False Equivalence*?

Humans might use *False Equivalence* when they want to make their point seem simpler or more convincing. By comparing two things as if they're the same, they can try to justify one idea using the logic of the other, even if the two aren't comparable.

How to Avoid *False Equivalence*

1. Look for Key Differences

Ask yourself, "Are these things truly similar in the ways that matter?" Real comparisons require that the key aspects being compared are alike.

2. Avoid Oversimplifying

Don't ignore important differences. Make sure you address all relevant factors, not just a few surface similarities.

3. Consider the Context

Make sure the comparison makes sense in context. Sometimes, two things seem alike until you dig deeper into their unique details.

Practice Example

Imagine someone says, "Both cats and fish are pets, so taking care of them is the same." While both may be pets, they have very different needs in terms of care, behavior, and how they interact with people. A strong argument would recognize these differences rather than oversimplifying.

Defending Against *False Equivalence*

When others make misleading comparisons, here's how you can keep the discussion clear:

- **Point Out the Differences**

  Say, "These things aren't quite the same. Here's what makes them different ..." This gently introduces relevant differences to the conversation.

- **Ask for a More Accurate Comparison**

  Respond with, "Is there a better way to compare these?" This encourages them to find a more appropriate analogy.

- **Highlight Specific Differences That Matter**

  If the comparison seems shallow, point out specific ways that each thing is unique. For example, "They might be similar in one way, but there's a big difference when it comes to how they need to be cared for."

By avoiding *False Equivalence*, you'll keep your arguments clear and realistic. Recognizing important differences helps prevent oversimplified thinking. But beware — some questions can sneak assumptions into the conversation without you noticing.

Chapter 14: The Loaded Question Fallacy

The *Loaded Question* fallacy occurs when a question contains an assumption that may not be true. It forces the person answering to accept this assumption to respond. Imagine asking someone, "Why are you always so mean?" This question assumes they are mean, making it hard to answer without agreeing with that assumption.

Why Is *Loaded Question* a Fallacy?

Loaded Questions unfairly pressure someone to agree with a hidden assumption. By embedding an unproven idea directly in the question, the question becomes biased. A good question should be neutral, allowing the person to respond without feeling forced to agree with something they don't believe.

Why Do Humans Use *Loaded Questions*?

Humans sometimes use *Loaded Questions* when they want to make someone feel guilty, defensive, or to steer the conversation in a certain way. It's a way of sneaking an opinion into a question to influence the answer, whether consciously or unconsciously.

How to Avoid *Loaded Questions*

1. Check for Hidden Assumptions

Before asking a question, ask yourself if it includes an assumption that hasn't been proven. For example, "Why are you always late?" assumes the person is late often. Try rephrasing it neutrally.

2. Use Neutral Wording

Frame questions in a way that doesn't assume anything unproven. Instead of "Why are you so lazy?" try "How do you prioritize your tasks?" Neutral wording keeps questions fair.

3. Listen for Assumptions in Questions

When answering, listen closely to see if the question has built-in assumptions. Recognizing these can help you respond more clearly and fairly.

Practice Example

Imagine someone asks, "When will you finally start working harder?" This assumes the person isn't already working hard, which may not be true. A fairer version would be, "Do you feel there's room for improvement in your work?"

Defending Against *Loaded Questions*

If someone asks a *Loaded Question*, here's how to address it effectively:

- **Point Out the Assumption**

    Politely say, "That question assumes something I don't agree with. Could we rephrase it?" This shows you're aware of the assumption and prefer a fair question.

- **Reframe the Question Yourself**

    You might say, "Instead of assuming I'm [the assumption], let's discuss the main point directly." This can help move the conversation back to the actual issue.

- **Ask for Clarity**

    If you feel pressured by the assumption, try saying, "Can you clarify what you're asking without assuming anything about me?" This shifts the focus to a more honest dialogue.

By spotting and avoiding *Loaded Questions*, you can ensure fairer and more respectful conversations. But there's another trap to watch for — one that tricks people into seeing patterns or outcomes that aren't really there. Let's explore it next!

INDEPENDENT EVENTS

Each roll is RANDOM

"each outcome doesn't affect the next"

Chapter 15: The Gambler's Fallacy

The *Gambler's Fallacy* happens when someone mistakenly believes that past events can affect the future outcomes of random events. It's common in gambling — like believing that if you've lost five times in a row, a win must be "due" soon. However, in random events, each try is independent of the previous ones.

Why Is It a Fallacy?

The *Gambler's Fallacy* is flawed because random events don't "balance out" as people often think. Each event is independent, meaning that what happened before doesn't change the odds. For example, flipping a coin five times doesn't make "heads" more or less likely on the sixth flip.

Why Do Humans Fall for the *Gambler's Fallacy?*

Humans often look for patterns, even in random events, because it makes the world feel more predictable. In stressful or uncertain situations (like gambling), the brain tries to find "signs" or "streaks" to feel in control, leading to the mistaken belief that past events affect future chances.

How to Avoid the *Gambler's Fallacy*

1. Remember the Odds Stay the Same

Remind yourself that each random event (like a coin flip or dice roll) has the same probability each time, regardless of past outcomes.

2. Stay Grounded in Probability

Don't let patterns fool you. Just because you see a streak (like three heads in a row), it doesn't change the probability of the next flip. Each event remains 50/50 for a coin.

3. Be Wary of the "Due" Feeling

The feeling that something is "bound" to happen isn't based in logic when it comes to random events. Recognize it as a natural but incorrect intuition.

Practice Example

Imagine someone says, "I've lost five times, so I'm bound to win soon!" This assumes that the losses will somehow make a win more likely, but in reality, the odds are the same each time. A good reminder is, "The game doesn't know you've been losing. Each round is independent."

Defending Against the *Gambler's Fallacy*

When others fall for this fallacy, here's how to help them understand randomness:

- **Remind Them of Independent Events**

  Say, "Each try is separate, so previous outcomes don't affect the next." This reinforces that each event has its own probability.

- **Explain Probability Clearly**

  Point out that each event has the same chance each time, regardless of past results. For example, "Whether you've won or lost doesn't change the odds on the next roll."

- **Acknowledge the "Due" Feeling as Natural**

  If they feel a win is "due," acknowledge it as a common feeling, then gently correct by saying, "It's natural to feel that way, but in reality, random events don't remember past results."

By understanding the *Gambler's Fallacy*, you'll avoid thinking random events are somehow "due" to balance out. But just because we avoid betting on chance doesn't mean we're immune to other biases. Up next, we'll explore a fallacy that leans on the weight of tradition.

Chapter 16: The Appeal to Tradition Fallacy

The *Appeal to Tradition* fallacy occurs when someone argues that something must be right or better simply because it's been done a certain way for a long time. It's like saying, "We've always done it this way, so it must be the best way." This fallacy assumes that age equals correctness, which isn't always true.

Why Is *Appeal to Tradition* a Fallacy?

Appeal to Tradition is flawed because just because something has been done for a long time doesn't make it the best or only way to do it. Traditions can be valuable, but it's important to examine them critically rather than following them without question. Change or new ideas aren't necessarily wrong just because they're different.

Why Do Humans Use *Appeal to Tradition*?

Humans often feel comforted by tradition; it provides stability and a sense of continuity. Change can feel uncertain or even threatening, so people sometimes cling to traditions to avoid the discomfort of something new. However, this can limit progress and ignore better solutions that come from innovation.

How to Avoid *Appeal to Tradition*

1. Ask If Tradition Serves a Purpose

Check if the tradition has a clear benefit or if it's just a habit. Useful traditions often serve a real purpose.

2. Consider Alternatives

When you're tempted to choose tradition, think about whether there might be a better or more efficient way.

3. Question Without Disregard

Respect tradition but be open to new ideas. Asking, "Is this still the best way?" allows for both continuity and improvement.

Practice Example

Imagine someone argues, "We've always used this system at work, so we shouldn't change it." Instead of accepting this, consider asking, "Is this system still working effectively, or could a new approach improve it?"

Defending Against *Appeal to Tradition*

When someone uses this fallacy, here's how to open up the conversation for new ideas:

- **Gently Question the Purpose**

  Ask, "Does this tradition still serve a useful purpose?" This helps them reflect on the value of the tradition itself.

- **Suggest Examining Both Options**

  Say, "Could we consider the pros and cons of each approach?" This encourages a balanced view of tradition and new ideas.

- **Acknowledge Tradition, Then Suggest Evaluation**

  Try saying, "I appreciate the tradition, but let's also see if there's an even better way." This respects the tradition while staying open to improvements.

By learning to spot and question the *Appeal to Tradition* fallacy, you'll avoid getting stuck in outdated ways of thinking. Respecting the past is valuable, but so is knowing when to move forward. Speaking of moving forward, there's another mental trap that can make it hard to let go, even when it's best to do so. Let's discuss this next.

Chapter 17: The Sunk Cost Fallacy

The *Sunk Cost* fallacy happens when someone continues with a plan or idea simply because they've already invested a lot of time, money, or effort into it, even when it's no longer the best option. It's like saying, "I've spent so much time on this, I can't quit now!" This fallacy ignores whether it's still worth continuing.

Why Is *Sunk Cost* a Fallacy?

Sunk Cost is flawed because past investments shouldn't decide future actions. Rational decisions should focus on what will bring the most value going forward. Just because you've invested resources doesn't mean you should keep going if it's no longer beneficial. Letting go of what no longer serves you can be the wiser choice.

Why Do Humans Fall for the *Sunk Cost Fallacy*?

Humans often struggle with this fallacy because they don't want to feel that their time, money, or energy has been "wasted." The idea of "giving up" on something they've invested in feels like admitting defeat. However, holding onto an unwise decision can lead to even greater loss.

How to Avoid the *Sunk Cost Fallacy*

1. Focus on Future Value, Not Past Investment

Ask yourself, "Is continuing the best choice going forward?" It helps to think in terms of future benefits rather than what's already been spent.

2. Recognize When It's Time to Let Go

Accepting that past resources are "sunk" or spent can help you move on. It's okay to pivot when something no longer makes sense.

3. Think Objectively About Gains and Losses

Separate your emotional attachment from the decision. Ask, "What will bring the best results moving forward?"

Practice Example

Imagine someone says, "I've already put so much money into fixing this old car, I can't sell it now!" Instead of holding onto it for emotional reasons, a better approach might be to evaluate if selling the car and getting a reliable one would save money in the long run.

Defending Against the *Sunk Cost Fallacy*

If someone is caught in this fallacy, here's how you can help them refocus:

- **Encourage Forward-Thinking**

  Say, "Let's think about what would bring the most benefit from this point forward."

- **Point Out the Cost of Staying Stuck**

  Remind them, "Sometimes, holding on actually costs more than letting go." This can help them see the potential benefits of moving on.

- **Reframe the Decision**

  Suggest, "Consider the choice as if no past investment had been made—what would you do?" This makes it easier to see the decision objectively.

By understanding the *Sunk Cost Fallacy*, you can make better choices that focus on future benefits instead of clinging to past investments. Sometimes moving forward means making wise choices about what's truly valuable — but what happens when something seems better simply because it's new?

Chapter 18: The Appeal to Novelty Fallacy

The *Appeal to Novelty* fallacy occurs when someone assumes that something is better or more valuable just because it's new. It's like saying, "This must be the best phone because it's the latest model!" While new ideas and products can bring improvements, being new doesn't automatically make something better.

Why Is *Appeal to Novelty* a Fallacy?

The *Appeal to Novelty* is flawed because it focuses on the age or "freshness" of an idea rather than its actual quality or effectiveness. New isn't always better; sometimes, older methods or ideas work just as well or even better. Making choices based solely on novelty can lead to overlooking the value of tried-and-true options.

Why Do Humans Use *Appeal to Novelty*?

Humans are often drawn to novelty because it feels exciting and forward-thinking. There's a natural curiosity about new things, which can lead people to assume that fresh ideas or inventions are superior. However, novelty alone isn't enough to make something better; it needs real evidence of improvement.

How to Avoid *Appeal to Novelty*

1. Ask for Evidence of Improvement

Before accepting something new, ask, "What makes this better than what came before it?" Look for solid reasons instead of assuming newness equals improvement.

2. Compare the Pros and Cons

Weigh the benefits of both old and new options. Sometimes, the "tried-and-true" option is still the best choice.

3. Be Cautious of Trends

Recognize that just because something is trendy or new doesn't mean it's an improvement. Focus on function and effectiveness rather than hype.

Practice Example

Imagine someone says, "This new diet must be the best because it's so popular right now!" Instead of jumping on board, ask, "What specific benefits does this diet offer that older ones don't?" This focuses on the actual value rather than just the novelty.

Defending Against *Appeal to Novelty*

When others insist something is better just because it's new, here's how to keep the focus on actual quality:

- **Ask for Concrete Benefits**

  Say, "I understand it's new, but what specific improvements does it offer?" This brings the conversation back to the actual value.

- **Encourage Balanced Comparison**

  Suggest looking at both new and old options by saying, "Let's compare it with what we know already works."

- **Question the Hype**

  If something seems to be popular mainly due to its novelty, ask, "Is this truly better, or just different?" This helps separate value from mere trendiness.

By avoiding the *Appeal to Novelty*, you'll make choices based on real benefits, not just trends. But even with a clear view of what's truly valuable, there's another trap to watch for — the idea that the "middle" option is always the best choice. Let's dive into this next fallacy!

Chapter 19: The Middle Ground Fallacy

The *Middle Ground* fallacy happens when someone assumes that the truth must lie somewhere between two opposing views, just because they're different. It's like saying, "If one person thinks the earth is flat and another thinks it's round, the truth must be halfway in between!" While compromise is often useful, it doesn't automatically mean the middle option is correct.

Why Is *Middle Ground* a Fallacy?

The *Middle Ground* fallacy is flawed because it assumes that truth is always a matter of compromise. Some issues have a clear right or wrong answer, and the truth isn't necessarily in the middle. This fallacy can lead to incorrect conclusions by assuming that every disagreement requires a middle-ground solution.

Why Do Humans Use *Middle Ground*?

Humans often believe that compromise is fair and reasonable. It feels balanced to meet halfway, so the middle ground can seem like a safe choice. However, this fallacy can create problems when one side is actually correct, and meeting in the middle compromises the truth.

How to Avoid the *Middle Ground* Fallacy

1. Consider Each Side Separately

Evaluate each perspective independently to determine if one is more valid than the other. Truth isn't always found by averaging views.

2. Think Critically About Compromise

Recognize that compromise isn't always appropriate. Sometimes, one side is correct, and the middle ground is just a false solution.

3. Look for Evidence

Focus on evidence, not just balance. The side with stronger facts or reasoning might be the true answer.

Practice Example

Imagine someone says, "One person thinks climate change is real, and another doesn't, so maybe it's only partly true." Instead of accepting this middle position, look for the scientific evidence, which overwhelmingly supports climate change.

Defending Against *Middle Ground* Fallacy

When someone defaults to a middle position, here's how you can help them see the potential flaws in this approach:

- **Ask Why They Assume Compromise Is Needed**

  Say, "Is there a reason to believe the truth is in the middle, or could one side be right?" This challenges the assumption that balance is best.

- **Point to the Evidence**

  Emphasize facts by saying, "Let's see which side the evidence supports, rather than assuming they're equally valid."

- **Acknowledge Fairness, Then Redirect to Facts**

  Gently say, "Compromise can be fair, but it doesn't always lead to the truth. Let's focus on what's actually accurate."

By recognizing and avoiding the *Middle Ground* fallacy, you'll focus on truth over compromise, making decisions based on facts rather than perceived fairness. But even with this clarity, there's another pitfall to avoid — one that involves selectively choosing only the facts that fit a particular view!

Chapter 20: The Cherry Picking Fallacy

The *Cherry Picking* fallacy happens when someone selects only the evidence that supports their argument while ignoring evidence that contradicts it. It's like saying, "Eating chocolate is healthy because cocoa has antioxidants!" but conveniently forgetting to mention the sugar and fat in chocolate. *Cherry Picking* presents a biased view by focusing only on favorable facts.

Why Is *Cherry Picking* a Fallacy?

Cherry Picking is misleading because it doesn't give a full picture of the truth. Good arguments consider *all* relevant evidence, not just the parts that make their case look good. By ignoring contradictory evidence, *Cherry Picking* can create a one-sided view that isn't based on reality.

Why Do Humans Use *Cherry Picking*?

Humans might use *Cherry Picking* to make their case look stronger than it actually is. By ignoring inconvenient facts, they avoid facing challenges to their view. This is often done unconsciously, as humans naturally like to focus on evidence that supports their beliefs.

How to Avoid *Cherry Picking*

1. Consider All Available Evidence

Before reaching a conclusion, ask, "Am I looking at all the facts or just the ones that support my view?"

2. Include Counterpoints

Even if some evidence doesn't support your view, acknowledging it shows a balanced and fair approach. This builds credibility and demonstrates honesty.

3. Be Open to Evidence That Challenges You

Real progress happens when you can confront evidence that disagrees with your position. Being open-minded makes for stronger arguments.

Practice Example

Imagine someone claims, "Our city has great air quality because we have so many parks." This might ignore other factors, like high car emissions, that also affect air quality. To avoid *Cherry Picking*, they could include a complete look at all factors impacting air quality.

Defending Against *Cherry Picking*

When someone cherry-picks evidence, here's how to encourage a fairer discussion:

- **Ask for the Full Picture**

  Say, "Is there other evidence we're not considering?" This invites a more balanced view.

- **Point Out Missing Facts**

  If they're avoiding certain facts, mention them politely: "I think there are additional factors, like [missing evidence], that should be included."

- **Encourage a Complete Analysis**

  Suggest saying, "Let's look at all the data, not just parts of it." This helps keep the discussion grounded in reality.

By learning to avoid *Cherry Picking*, you'll create stronger arguments based on a full view of the facts. But as you keep refining your reasoning, beware of another trap — one that judges ideas based on outcomes rather than truth. Ready to uncover the next fallacy?

Chapter 21: The Appeal to Consequences Fallacy

The *Appeal to Consequences* fallacy happens when someone argues that an idea must be true or false based on whether the consequences are good or bad, rather than on actual evidence. It's like saying, "Climate change can't be real because that would mean big changes in our lifestyle!" This fallacy focuses on the impact of believing something instead of whether it's true.

Why Is *Appeal to Consequences* a Fallacy?

Appeal to Consequences is flawed because truth isn't determined by how desirable or undesirable the outcome is. The truth of a claim depends on evidence, not on whether we like the results. Good arguments are based on facts and logic, not just on whether we find the consequences appealing or unpleasant.

Why Do Humans Use *Appeal to Consequences*?

Humans often use this fallacy because they're uncomfortable with the possible effects of a certain idea. Focusing on consequences instead of truth can be a form of denial or wishful thinking, allowing people to avoid facing difficult realities.

How to Avoid *Appeal to Consequences*

1. Focus on Facts, Not Feelings

Ask yourself, "Am I rejecting this idea because of how it feels, or because the evidence doesn't support it?" This keeps you grounded in facts.

2. Separate Truth from Impact

Recognize that truth and consequences are separate. Even if an outcome is undesirable, that doesn't make the idea untrue.

3. Accept Discomfort for the Sake of Accuracy

Sometimes, the truth can be uncomfortable. Accepting this helps you stay focused on accuracy rather than comfort.

Practice Example

Imagine someone says, "We can't admit that our project failed because it would hurt our reputation." Instead of focusing on the negative outcome, a better approach is to ask, "Did the project meet its goals based on the evidence?"

Defending Against *Appeal to Consequences*

When someone uses this fallacy, here's how to steer the discussion back to facts:

- **Ask for Evidence First**

  Say, "Regardless of the outcome, what does the evidence say?" This refocuses on truth rather than impact.

- **Point Out the Difference Between Feelings and Facts**

  Gently remind them, "Our feelings about the outcome don't change the actual truth."

- **Encourage an Objective View**

  Suggest looking at the situation objectively by saying, "Let's focus on what's real, not just what's comfortable."

By recognizing the *Appeal to Consequences* fallacy, you'll base your decisions on evidence rather than wishful thinking. But sometimes, reasoning falters not because of evidence, but because something simply seems unbelievable. Let's explore this next fallacy!

Chapter 22: The Personal Incredulity Fallacy

The *Personal Incredulity* fallacy happens when someone dismisses an argument or idea because they find it difficult to understand. It's like saying, "I don't understand how evolution works, so it must be false." This fallacy treats personal difficulty in understanding as a reason to reject an idea, rather than relying on facts.

Why Is *Personal Incredulity* a Fallacy?

Personal Incredulity is flawed because the truth of an idea doesn't depend on whether someone understands it. Complexity or unfamiliarity doesn't make an idea wrong; it simply means it might require more study or explanation. Basing truth on our own understanding limits us to what we already know.

Why Do Humans Use *Personal Incredulity*?

Humans sometimes fall into this fallacy because they're more comfortable with ideas that make sense right away. When something seems too complex, the brain might default to dismissing it rather than exploring it further. But just because something is challenging doesn't mean it's incorrect.

How to Avoid *Personal Incredulity*

1. Seek to Understand Before Judging

If something seems confusing, try to learn more before rejecting it. Ask, "Is there a reason I don't understand this?"

2. Acknowledge Limits to Knowledge

Realize that not fully grasping an idea doesn't make it false. It might just mean you need more information or time to understand.

3. Be Open to Complexity

Recognize that some ideas require patience to understand. Embrace the possibility that difficult concepts might still be true.

Practice Example

Imagine someone says, "I don't get how vaccines work, so I don't trust them." Instead of dismissing vaccines, they could seek out credible sources to learn about how vaccines provide immunity, even if the science feels complex.

Defending Against *Personal Incredulity*

When someone dismisses an idea because they don't understand it, here's how you can help them see beyond their own perspective:

- **Encourage Further Learning**

  Say, "Maybe more information would help. Understanding can take time with complex ideas."

- **Separate Understanding from Truth**

  Gently point out, "Even if it's hard to understand, that doesn't mean it's wrong." This helps them see that difficulty doesn't equal falsehood.

- **Suggest Reliable Sources**

  If possible, recommend sources or experts that could help them learn more. Say, "Let's look for trusted information to help explain it better."

By learning to avoid the *Personal Incredulity* fallacy, you'll open yourself up to new knowledge and be more willing to explore ideas outside your comfort zone. But be cautious — just because something seems natural doesn't automatically make it better.

Chapter 23: The Appeal to Nature Fallacy

The *Appeal to Nature* fallacy happens when someone argues that something is good or right simply because it's "natural," or bad just because it's "unnatural." It's like saying, "Organic food is better just because it's natural!" While nature can offer many benefits, being natural doesn't automatically make something good, nor does being unnatural make it bad.

Why Is Appeal to Nature a Fallacy?

The *Appeal to Nature* is flawed because what's natural isn't always beneficial or safe. Poisonous plants and dangerous diseases are natural, yet they're harmful, while many life-saving medicines are "unnatural" but beneficial. Real evaluation requires looking at actual evidence.

Why Do Humans Use *Appeal to Nature*?

Humans are often drawn to the idea of nature as pure, safe, and healthy. There's an instinctive trust in things labeled as natural and a suspicion of things seen as synthetic. However, this bias can lead to overlooking the benefits of science and innovation, which often improve on nature.

How to Avoid *Appeal to Nature*

1. Evaluate Benefits, Not Labels

Look for real benefits, not just the "natural" label. Ask, "What does this actually do?"

2. Look for Evidence of Safety and Effectiveness

Something's value should be based on research and evidence, not just its source. Scientific testing often gives better insight than assumptions about naturalness.

3. Separate Feelings from Facts

Acknowledge that the "natural" label may feel safe, but that feeling isn't always backed by reality. Feelings don't determine effectiveness or safety.

Practice Example

Imagine someone claims, "Herbal remedies are always better because they're natural." Instead of assuming this, they could look for evidence comparing the effectiveness and safety of herbal remedies versus regulated medications.

Defending Against *Appeal to Nature*

When someone insists that natural things are better, here's how to gently refocus on actual evidence:

- **Ask for Evidence Beyond Labels**

Say, "I see it's natural, but do we know it's effective?" This shifts focus to evidence of results.

- **Point Out That Nature Can Be Harmful**

Gently remind them, "Natural things aren't always safe—think of poison ivy!" This helps them recognize that nature isn't automatically good.

- **Encourage Evaluation Based on Effectiveness**

Suggest saying, "Let's look at what works best, not just what's natural." This helps keep the conversation balanced and grounded in results.

By understanding and avoiding the *Appeal to Nature* fallacy, you'll make decisions based on effectiveness rather than simply on what's "natural." But as you sharpen your logical thinking, there's another trap to watch for — one that tries to protect a claim by redefining it.

Chapter 24: The No True Scotsman Fallacy

The *No True Scotsman* fallacy happens when someone redefines a group to exclude individuals or counterexamples that don't fit their argument. It's like saying, "No real artist would use digital tools." When someone points out a famous artist who does, they respond, "Well, no *true* artist would."

Why Is *No True Scotsman* a Fallacy?

No True Scotsman is flawed because it uses an arbitrary redefinition to defend a point. Instead of addressing counterexamples or valid exceptions, it changes the group's definition to avoid them. Real arguments should deal with exceptions directly, not redefine terms to fit a narrative.

Why Do Humans Use *No True Scotsman*?

Humans sometimes use this fallacy because they want to protect a belief from criticism. When something challenges an identity or group they feel attached to, they may try to "purify" the group by excluding members or ideas that don't align.

How to Avoid *No True Scotsman*

1. Recognize Exceptions and Differences

Acknowledge that diversity exists within groups. Just because some members act differently doesn't mean they don't belong.

2. Be Open to Challenging Examples

Accept counterexamples as part of the discussion rather than excluding them. This helps strengthen understanding rather than limit it.

3. Avoid Defining Identity Narrowly

When defending a group or identity, use broader definitions that include valid diversity within the group.

Practice Example

Imagine someone says, "No true gamer would play on easy mode." When a gamer who does play on easy mode is mentioned, they respond, "Well, they're not a true gamer." Instead of redefining the group, a more open perspective accepts that gamers play at all levels.

Defending Against *No True Scotsman*

When someone uses this fallacy, here's how to encourage a more inclusive view:

- **Ask Why They're Excluding**

  Say, "Why can't this person belong just because they're different?" This gently challenges their redefinition.

- **Point Out Diversity in the Group**

  Suggest, "Groups can be diverse—people don't have to fit a narrow definition to belong."

- **Encourage Broader Thinking**

  Remind them, "Let's recognize that there's room for different views within this group." This helps avoid narrow labels.

By recognizing the *No True Scotsman* fallacy, you'll promote broader thinking and allow for diversity within groups. Each fallacy you learn makes your arguments clearer. But be careful — even the facts themselves can be misleading if only certain ones are chosen to fit a pattern!

Chapter 25: The Texas Sharpshooter Fallacy

The *Texas Sharpshooter* fallacy happens when someone focuses only on data that supports their argument, ignoring data that doesn't fit. It's like shooting at the side of a barn, then drawing a target around the bullet holes and saying, "Look how accurate I am!"

Why Is *Texas Sharpshooter* a Fallacy?

The *Texas Sharpshooter* fallacy is misleading because it makes connections between random patterns, rather than looking at the full picture. By selectively choosing data points, it can create an illusion of accuracy or causation that isn't truly there. Real analysis considers *all* the evidence, not just the convenient parts.

Why Do Humans Use *Texas Sharpshooter*?

Humans tend to notice patterns and may even create them unintentionally. It can feel satisfying to make data "fit" a certain narrative, especially when it supports an idea or goal. By focusing only on specific details, people may overlook the full context or counterevidence that tells a different story.

How to Avoid *Texas Sharpshooter*

1. Look at All the Data, Not Just What Fits

Ask, "Am I ignoring any facts that don't fit my idea?" A complete view includes all evidence, even inconvenient facts.

2. Avoid Making Patterns from Coincidence

Be cautious about connecting data points randomly. Correlation doesn't equal causation, and sometimes patterns are just coincidence.

3. Be Willing to Adjust Your Conclusions

If the full data doesn't support your view, be open to changing your conclusion. True understanding comes from accuracy, not convenience.

Practice Example

Imagine someone says, "Most top students drink coffee, so coffee must make people smarter." Instead of just looking at coffee-drinking students, a more accurate analysis would look at all students, coffee-drinkers and non-coffee-drinkers, to see if coffee actually has an impact.

Defending Against *Texas Sharpshooter*

If someone is using this fallacy, here's how to encourage them to look at the full picture:

- **Ask About Missing Data**

  Say, "Are there any data points we're not considering?" This encourages a broader view.

- **Point Out the Full Range of Evidence**

  Politely remind them, "To be fair, we should look at all the evidence, not just parts that match." This keeps the conversation balanced.

- **Encourage a Complete Analysis**

  Suggest saying, "Let's see if the whole set of data supports this idea." This keeps the focus on accuracy rather than selective points.

By avoiding the *Texas Sharpshooter* fallacy, you'll be able to make well-rounded arguments based on full evidence, not selective patterns. But sometimes, even with a lot of data, it's easy to overlook the stories that don't make it through. Let's unpack this next fallacy!

Chapter 26: The Survivorship Bias Fallacy

The *Survivorship Bias* fallacy occurs when someone focuses only on successful examples while ignoring failures, leading to a skewed understanding of reality. It's like saying, "Look at all the successful entrepreneurs who dropped out of college — you don't need a degree to succeed!" without considering the many dropouts who didn't become successful. This fallacy creates an overly optimistic or one-sided view by ignoring the full range of outcomes.

Why Is *Survivorship Bias* a Fallacy?

Survivorship Bias is misleading because it only looks at the "survivors" or successful examples, ignoring the "non-survivors" who didn't achieve the same results. This limited view can give people the wrong impression of what's likely or effective, leading to unrealistic expectations. For balanced conclusions, it's important to consider all data, not just the positive cases.

Why Do Humans Use *Survivorship Bias*?

Humans often focus on success stories because they're inspiring and give us hope. Hearing about successful people or outcomes can make us feel motivated, but it can also lead to a skewed view if we don't consider failures. Recognizing this bias helps us form more realistic expectations based on the complete picture.

How to *Avoid Survivorship* Bias

1. Look for "Invisible" Data

Ask yourself, "Am I only seeing the successful cases?" Check if there's information missing about those who didn't succeed.

2. Consider the Full Range of Outcomes

Try to understand both successes and failures. Ask, "What happened to people who tried and didn't make it?"

3. Be Realistic About Likelihood

Understand that not everyone reaches the same results. Focusing on both success and failure helps set realistic expectations.

Practice Example

Imagine someone says, "Successful authors write every day, so that's the key to success." To avoid *Survivorship Bias*, consider asking, "What about authors who wrote every day but didn't succeed?" This provides a more realistic view of success.

Defending Against *Survivorship Bias*

When someone falls into *Survivorship Bias*, here's how to bring balance to the conversation:

- **Ask About the Less Visible Data**

  Say, "Are we also considering people who didn't succeed?" This invites a broader view.

- **Remind Them of All Outcomes**

  Suggest saying, "Success stories are inspiring, but failures provide important lessons too."

- **Encourage Balanced Examples**

  Suggest looking for both success and failure stories by saying, "Let's see the complete picture for a more realistic view."

By understanding *Survivorship Bias*, you'll avoid forming conclusions based only on visible successes. But even when the evidence is clear, some arguments shift the standards to stay one step ahead. Ready to tackle this next fallacy?

Chapter 27: The Moving the Goalposts Fallacy

The *Moving the Goalposts* fallacy occurs when someone keeps changing the criteria for "proof" to avoid accepting an argument. It's like saying, "If you show me one study that supports this, I'll believe it," and then, after seeing the study, saying, "Well, I need three studies, actually!"

Why Is *Moving the Goalposts* a Fallacy?

Moving the Goalposts is flawed because it prevents genuine progress in a discussion. By continuously raising the standards for "acceptable proof," it creates a situation where no amount of evidence will satisfy. Honest discussions should have clear, consistent criteria for what counts as proof, rather than constantly changing expectations.

Why Do Humans Use *Moving the Goalposts*?

Humans often use this fallacy when they're resistant to changing their beliefs. By changing the requirements for evidence, they avoid facing evidence that challenges their viewpoint. It's a way to keep from being "convinced" by shifting what's needed to persuade them.

How to Avoid *Moving the Goalposts*

1. Set Clear Standards for Proof

Decide in advance what will count as sufficient evidence. Ask yourself, "What level of proof would satisfy me?"

2. Be Willing to Accept Valid Evidence

Don't keep raising the bar if evidence meets the original standards. Avoid creating new requirements just to avoid admitting you're wrong.

3. Stay Consistent in Arguments

Don't change the standards mid-discussion. Consistency helps keep arguments honest and fair.

Practice Example

Imagine someone says, "If you can find one article proving this, I'll believe it." When shown an article, they respond, "Actually, I need multiple studies from major journals." Instead of genuinely considering the evidence, they keep shifting the requirements.

Defending Against *Moving the Goalposts*

If someone is moving the goalposts, here's how to encourage a fair discussion:

- **Ask for Clear Standards**

  Say, "Can we agree on what counts as enough evidence?" This sets a standard from the start.

- **Hold Them to Original Criteria**

  If they try to change the goal, politely remind them, "You said this would be enough evidence. Let's stick with that."

- **Encourage Consistency in Expectations**

  Gently suggest saying, "Changing the standards makes it hard to find common ground. Can we agree to be consistent?"

By recognizing the *Moving the Goalposts* fallacy, you'll keep discussions fair and grounded in clear standards. But sometimes, rather than changing the standards, arguments shift focus by amplifying fear instead. Let's explore this next fallacy!

Chapter 28: The Scare Tactic Fallacy

The *Scare Tactic* Fallacy happens when someone tries to persuade others by fear rather than presenting logical reasons. It's like saying, "If we don't ban this technology, it will take over our lives!" Here, the argument relies on fear to make people agree rather than offering a well-reasoned point.

Why Is the *Scare Tactic* Fallacy a Fallacy?

The *Scare Tactic* Fallacy is flawed because emotions like fear don't prove whether something is actually dangerous or problematic. Rational thinking requires examining evidence rather than being swayed by fear, which can lead to rushed or exaggerated decisions. Sound reasoning focuses on facts, not the heightened emotions that fear brings.

Why Do Humans Use the *Scare Tactic* Fallacy?

Humans often fall into this fallacy because fear can be a powerful motivator. It's easier to evoke an emotional response than to construct a logical argument, especially when the goal is to influence someone's decisions quickly. Recognizing this tendency helps us remain calm and evaluate the actual risks of a situation, rather than being pulled along by fear.

How to Avoid the *Scare Tactic* Fallacy

1. Evaluate the Evidence Behind the Threat

Ask yourself, "Is there solid evidence that this situation is truly dangerous?"

2. Separate Emotion from Facts

Consider whether the argument is based on fear alone or backed by data.

3. Seek a Balanced Perspective

Avoid letting worst-case scenarios guide your decisions without considering other possibilities.

Practice Example

Imagine someone says, "If we don't enforce this curfew, crime will spiral out of control!" This is an example of the *Scare Tactic* Fallacy because it uses fear to influence decisions rather than presenting data on crime or examining whether a curfew is effective. A more logical approach would include statistics and other facts to support the need for a curfew.

Defending Against the *Scare Tactic* Fallacy

When someone tries to persuade you using fear, here's how to bring the discussion back to logic:

- **Ask for Evidence**

  Say, "Is there any data that supports this as a serious risk?"

- **Encourage Thinking About Facts Over Emotions**

  Suggest, "Let's focus on the facts rather than on how scary it sounds."

- **Remind Them That Fear Doesn't Equal Risk**

  Gently add, "Fear alone doesn't prove something is dangerous—it just feels that way."

By recognizing the *Scare Tactic* Fallacy, you'll stay calm and focused on evidence, making decisions based on facts rather than fear. But fear isn't the only force that can sway an argument — sometimes, it's personal stories that lead us off track. Let's review this next fallacy!

Chapter 29: The Appeal to Personal Experience Fallacy

The *Appeal to Personal Experience* fallacy happens when someone argues their personal experience proves a general truth, instead of broad reliable evidence. It's like saying, "I've never gotten sick from not washing my hands, so handwashing isn't necessary."

Why Is *Appeal to Personal Experience* a Fallacy?

The *Appeal to Personal Experience* is flawed because one person's experience doesn't represent the whole picture. True claims, especially those about health, science, or general rules, need consistent evidence from many cases, not just one.

Why Do Humans Use *Appeal to Personal Experience*?

Humans often trust their own experiences because they're direct and memorable. It's natural to believe what we see or feel firsthand, but personal experience doesn't always capture the full reality. Recognizing this can help us seek broader, more reliable evidence.

How to Avoid Appeal to *Personal Experience*

1. Look for Larger Patterns

Ask yourself, "Does this apply to just me, or to most people?" Broad trends are more reliable than personal examples.

2. Acknowledge Individual Differences

Recognize that everyone's experience is unique and doesn't always represent general truth.

3. Rely on Research

Use studies, surveys, or expert consensus when making claims about broad truths. These sources represent more people and are less likely to be skewed by individual differences.

Practice Example

Imagine someone says, "I never exercise, and I'm perfectly healthy, so exercise isn't that important." While this might be true for them, most evidence shows exercise benefits health. Relying on a single experience misses the larger, proven trend.

Defending Against *Appeal to Personal Experience*

When someone relies on personal experience to make a general claim, here's how to steer the discussion toward broader evidence:

- **Ask About Larger Evidence**

  Say, "That's interesting, but what does the broader evidence say?" This shifts focus from individual to general data.

- **Acknowledge Their Experience, Then Broaden the View**

  Gently respond, "I understand that worked for you, but let's consider what studies show for most people."

- **Encourage Objectivity**

  Remind them, "Personal experiences can vary a lot, so it's good to rely on larger studies." This emphasizes the need for reliable, comprehensive data.

By understanding the *Appeal to Personal Experience* fallacy, you'll be able to recognize when individual cases don't necessarily represent general truths. But be careful — sometimes, the opposite mistake happens, where it's assumed that what's true for each part must be true for the whole!

Chapter 30: The Composition Fallacy

The *Composition fallacy* occurs when someone assumes that what's true of individual parts must also be true of the whole. It's like saying, "Each player on the team is a star, so the team must be unbeatable!" While each part may be impressive on its own, they don't automatically reflect the complete picture.

Why Is *Composition* a Fallacy?

The *Composition fallacy* is flawed because individual parts don't always add up in the way we might expect. Each part might work well alone, but when combined, they don't necessarily produce the same results. Good reasoning requires looking at the whole and understanding how the parts work together, rather than assuming qualities of the parts directly transfer to the whole.

Good Pieces

The Whole

Why Do Humans Use Composition?

Humans naturally assume that impressive parts will create an impressive whole. This fallacy often occurs when we focus on individual strengths or qualities without considering how parts interact in combination. Recognizing this tendency can help us evaluate wholes more accurately.

How to Avoid Composition

1. Examine How Parts Work Together

Consider whether the parts actually combine in a way that makes the whole better. Ask, "Do these parts interact effectively?"

2. Avoid Generalizing from Individuals to Groups

Just because something is true of one member or part doesn't mean it's true of the entire group.

3. Look for Evidence of Group Performance

Instead of assuming a strong team based on strong players, look at how they perform together. The whole might have different dynamics.

Practice Example

Imagine someone says, "All the ingredients in this dish are delicious, so the dish must be delicious too." However, even tasty ingredients can create an unpleasant combination if they don't work well together. To avoid this fallacy, consider how the ingredients interact as a whole.

Defending Against *Composition*

When someone assumes that the qualities of individual parts apply to the whole, here's how to respond:

- **Ask About Interaction**

  Say, "How do the parts actually work together?" This encourages them to think about how parts interact within the whole.

- **Point Out Differences Between Parts and Wholes**

  Politely remind them, "Sometimes a group has different qualities than its members."

- **Suggest Looking at Group Evidence**

  Encourage them by saying, "Let's see if there's evidence about the whole, not just the parts." This keeps the focus on group performance or combination effects.

By avoiding the *Composition* fallacy, you'll make better evaluations about groups, teams, and combinations, focusing on how parts actually work together. But there's an opposite trap to watch out for — the assumption that what's true for the whole must be true for each part.

Chapter 31: The Division Fallacy

The *Division* fallacy is the opposite of the *Composition* fallacy. It happens when someone assumes that what's true of the whole must also be true of each individual part. It's like saying, "This cake is delicious, so every ingredient must be delicious too!"

Why Is *Division* a Fallacy?

The *Division* fallacy is flawed because qualities of the whole don't always transfer to its parts. A whole can have a certain characteristic that doesn't appear in each of its parts individually. Clear thinking requires understanding that parts can differ from the whole they're part of.

Why Do Humans Use *Division*?

Humans often assume that parts will have the same qualities as the whole because it feels consistent and logical. However, this assumption overlooks the complexity of how parts can interact differently within the whole. Understanding this fallacy helps us see that parts and wholes aren't always the same.

How to Avoid *Division*

1. Consider Parts Separately

Ask yourself, "Do the qualities of the whole really apply to each part?" Think about the unique qualities of each component.

2. Avoid Generalizing from Whole to Parts

Recognize that parts don't always share the same characteristics as a whole.

3. Examine Each Part on Its Own

When evaluating parts, consider them individually rather than assuming they inherit the whole's qualities.

Practice Example

Imagine someone says, "This company is highly successful, so every department must be great too." However, even a successful company can have weaker areas or departments that don't perform as well as the company as a whole. To avoid the Division fallacy, evaluate each part on its own.

Defending Against *Division*

When someone makes an assumption that each part shares the qualities of the whole, here's how to encourage clearer thinking:

- **Point Out the Difference Between Parts and Wholes**

  Say, "Just because the whole is successful doesn't mean each part has to be." This helps clarify that qualities don't always transfer.

- **Encourage Evaluating Each Part Separately**

  Suggest saying, "Let's look at each part individually to see how they really perform."

- **Remind Them That Parts Can Differ from the Whole**

  Politely add, "Sometimes, parts are very different from the larger whole." This opens up the possibility for a more nuanced view.

By understanding the *Division* fallacy, you'll recognize that just because a whole has certain qualities doesn't mean each part does. Great job — each fallacy you master adds to your logical toolkit! Now, let's look at a fallacy that shifts focus from the argument itself to assumptions about why someone believes it.

Chapter 32: The Bulverism Fallacy

The *Bulverism* Fallacy happens when someone dismisses an argument not by addressing its content, but by assuming it must be wrong due to the person's supposed reasons or motives for believing it. It's like saying, "You only support that idea because you're young and idealistic," rather than addressing the argument itself. Here, the argument is rejected by focusing on a presumed bias or background rather than its actual reasoning.

Why Is *Bulverism* a Fallacy?

Bulverism is flawed because it assumes that if a person has a certain reason for their belief, the belief itself must be wrong. But an argument's validity doesn't depend on the person making it — it depends on facts, evidence, and reasoning. Rational thinking requires evaluating ideas on their own merits, not making assumptions based on who holds them.

Why Do Humans Use *Bulverism*?

Humans often fall into this fallacy because it's easier to question a person's motives than to engage with their arguments. We're naturally inclined to assume others are biased, especially if we disagree with them, but this can lead to unfair dismissals and missed opportunities for genuine understanding. Recognizing this tendency helps us focus on the actual argument rather than on assumptions about the person making it.

How to Avoid *Bulverism*

1. Separate the Argument from the Person

Ask yourself, "Am I rejecting this idea because of the argument itself, or because of who is saying it?"

2. Engage with the Argument's Logic

Focus on whether the argument is backed by sound reasoning and evidence.

3. Avoid Assuming a Person's Bias as Proof

Remember, even if someone has a personal reason for their view, the argument itself could still be valid.

Practice Example

Imagine someone says, "Climate change is a serious issue we need to address," and the response is, "You're only saying that because you're young and idealistic." This is an example of *Bulverism*, as it dismisses the argument by assuming a reason for it rather than addressing the actual issue. A more rational approach would evaluate the evidence for climate change independently of the speaker's age or personality.

Defending Against the *Bulverism* Fallacy

When someone dismisses an argument based on presumed motives, here's how to steer the conversation back to the actual points:

- **Ask for Evidence-Based Discussion**

  Say, "Could we focus on the evidence or reasoning behind this point?"

- **Encourage Evaluating the Argument Itself**

  Suggest, "Let's consider the idea on its own, apart from personal reasons."

- **Point Out That Motives Don't Determine Validity**

  Gently add, "Even if someone has a personal reason for their belief, the argument still deserves to be addressed on its own terms."

By recognizing the *Bulverism* Fallacy, you'll be able to engage with ideas fairly, addressing arguments based on their content rather than assuming motives. But even with fair-minded reasoning, it's easy to fall into another trap — dismissing ideas just because they're not perfect.

Chapter 33: The Nirvana Fallacy

The *Nirvana* fallacy happens when someone dismisses a realistic solution because it isn't "perfect." It's like saying, "Recycling isn't worth doing because it doesn't eliminate all waste." This fallacy ignores the value of practical solutions simply because they have some flaws or don't achieve perfection.

Why Is *Nirvana* a Fallacy?

The *Nirvana* fallacy is flawed because it holds practical solutions to an impossible standard. While most solutions have limitations, they still bring positive change. Rejecting realistic options because they aren't flawless can prevent progress.

Why Do Humans Use *Nirvana* Fallacy?

Humans often fall into this fallacy when they want an ideal solution. It can feel satisfying to imagine perfection, but this mindset can prevent people from taking steps that could still make a difference. By learning to accept workable solutions, we avoid rejecting useful options in search of unattainable ones.

How to Avoid *Nirvana* Fallacy

1. Focus on Realistic Improvements

Recognize that partial solutions can still have value. Ask, "Does this solution make things better, even if it's not perfect?"

2. Acknowledge Trade-offs

Most solutions involve trade-offs. Accepting this can help you appreciate solutions that work well enough, even with limitations.

3. Avoid "All-or-Nothing" Thinking

Remember that small changes can add up. It doesn't have to be perfect to be valuable.

Practice Example

Imagine someone says, "Public transportation isn't worth improving because it doesn't eliminate all traffic." Instead of focusing on perfection, consider the realistic improvements that better public transportation can make in reducing traffic and pollution, even if it's not a complete solution.

Defending Against *Nirvana* Fallacy

When someone insists on rejecting realistic solutions, here's how to refocus on practical benefits:

- **Emphasize the Value of Partial Solutions**

  Say, "Even if it's not perfect, it still brings benefits." This helps them see the value in incremental change.

- **Point Out That Perfection Is Rarely Possible**

  Gently remind them, "Most solutions have limits, but that doesn't mean they're useless."

- **Encourage Taking Steps Forward**

  Suggest saying, "Let's work with what we can achieve now." This keeps the conversation focused on positive, practical action.

By recognizing the *Nirvana* fallacy, you'll embrace practical solutions and avoid getting stuck in the search for perfection. Excellent work—each fallacy you understand brings you closer to balanced, effective thinking. But there's another trap to watch for — assuming that what "should" be true automatically "is" true.

Chapter 34: The Moralistic Fallacy

The *Moralistic* Fallacy happens when someone assumes that what *ought* to be true according to morals or ideals *must* be true in reality. It's like saying, "Violence shouldn't exist, so humans are naturally peaceful." This fallacy mistakes ideal or moral beliefs for actual facts about the world.

Why Is the *Moralistic* Fallacy a Fallacy?

The *Moralistic* Fallacy is flawed because reality doesn't always match our ideals. Good reasoning requires looking at facts as they are, not as we wish them to be. If we ignore reality for ideals, we miss understanding the world accurately.

Why Do Humans Use the *Moralistic* Fallacy?

Humans often fall into the Moralistic Fallacy because they want the world to align with their values and ideals. It's comforting to believe that what is morally "good" is also true. But learning to see the world as it is, rather than as we wish it to be, leads to clearer thinking and more effective solutions.

How to Avoid the *Moralistic* Fallacy

1. Separate Morals from Facts

Recognize that something being ideal doesn't make it true. Ask yourself, "Am I letting my ideals affect my view of reality?"

2. Consider Realistic Evidence

Evaluate claims based on actual evidence, not just what seems morally right.

3. Accept Reality, Even if Imperfect

Acknowledge that reality often includes things we don't like. Accepting this helps us address problems more effectively.

Practice Example

Imagine someone says, "Humans are naturally good because violence and dishonesty are morally wrong." While peace and honesty are ideals, history shows that human behavior can include aggression and deceit. Recognizing this doesn't mean accepting wrongdoing — it simply acknowledges reality as it is.

Defending Against the *Moralistic* Fallacy

When someone assumes reality should align with ideals, here's how to keep the focus on facts:

- **Separate Morals from Evidence**

  Say, "Just because we believe something should be true doesn't make it a fact."

- **Point Out that Reality May Differ**

  Gently remind them, "Reality isn't always ideal, but we can work with what's real to make things better."

- **Encourage Facing Facts to Create Change**

  Suggest saying, "Understanding reality helps us know what we need to work on." This shifts the focus to constructive actions based on facts.

By recognizing the *Moralistic* Fallacy, you'll be able to view the world clearly and work toward change based on real evidence. Great job! But watch out — sometimes, people deflect criticism by pointing fingers back at others. Let's dig into this next fallacy!

Chapter 35: The Appeal to Hypocrisy (Tu Quoque) Fallacy

The *Appeal to Hypocrisy* fallacy, also known as *Tu Quoque* (Latin for "You too"), occurs when someone responds to criticism by accusing the critic of the same flaw. It's like saying, "You can't tell me to save money because you spend too much yourself!" This fallacy dodges the issue by shifting focus to the critic's behavior instead of addressing the argument.

Why Is *Appeal to Hypocrisy* a Fallacy?

The *Appeal to Hypocrisy* is flawed because pointing out hypocrisy doesn't invalidate an argument. A claim can be true regardless of the speaker's behavior. Good reasoning focuses on the content of the argument.

Why Do Humans Use *Appeal to Hypocrisy*?

Humans often use this fallacy because it's easier to deflect criticism than to address it. By focusing on the other person's actions, they avoid facing the criticism. Recognizing this tendency helps us focus on the issue rather than shifting blame.

How to Avoid *Appeal to Hypocrisy*

1. Focus on the Argument, Not the Person

Separate the argument from who's making it. Ask yourself, "Is the claim true, regardless of who's saying it?"

2. Acknowledge Fair Criticism

If someone makes a valid point, address it instead of deflecting. This helps keep the conversation constructive.

3. Remember that Behavior Doesn't Change Facts

A fact remains a fact, even if the person stating it is inconsistent.

Practice Example

Imagine someone says, "We should recycle more to reduce waste," and the response is, "Why should I listen to you? You never recycle!" Instead of focusing on the person's actions, consider the value of recycling itself.

Defending Against *Appeal to Hypocrisy*

When someone tries to dodge an argument by pointing out hypocrisy, here's how to bring focus back to the main point:

- **Remind Them to Focus on the Issue**

  Say, "Let's focus on the argument itself rather than each other's actions."

- **Acknowledge Their Point, Then Refocus**

  If they bring up your flaws, respond with, "I understand, but let's stick to the main point."

- **Point Out That Behavior Doesn't Change Facts**

  Remind them, "Whether I do it or not doesn't affect whether it's a good idea."

By recognizing the *Appeal to Hypocrisy* fallacy, you'll keep discussions on topic and focus on ideas rather than deflections. But there's another trap to watch out for — one that relies on sympathy instead of solid reasoning. Let's discuss this next fallacy!

Chapter 36: The Appeal to Pity Fallacy

The *Appeal to Pity* fallacy occurs when someone tries to win an argument by making you feel sorry for them, instead of providing logical reasons. It's like saying, "You should give me an A on my test because I studied so hard and didn't get any sleep!" Here, the person is relying on sympathy, not on actual evidence.

Why Is *Appeal to Pity* a Fallacy?

The *Appeal to Pity* is flawed because emotional appeals don't change the facts. Good arguments are based on evidence and reason, not emotions. While sympathy and understanding are valuable, they don't replace the need for logical reasons in decision-making or arguments.

Why Do Humans Use *Appeal to Pity*?

Humans use the Appeal to Pity when they feel vulnerable or want empathy. It's natural to seek understanding, especially when we're going through something difficult. But while pity can be important in friendships, it doesn't make a strong argument for a particular action or belief.

How to Avoid *Appeal to Pity*

1. Focus on Evidence Over Emotions

When making an argument, ask yourself, "Am I providing facts, or am I relying on emotions?"

2. Acknowledge Emotions Separately

Recognize emotions without letting them drive the argument. Consider saying, "I understand this is tough, but let's look at the facts."

3. Look for Real Support for Claims

Make sure your reasoning is grounded in evidence, not just emotional appeals.

Practice Example

Imagine someone says, "I really deserve the promotion because I've been struggling lately and need the extra income." While this may be true, promotions are typically based on job performance, not personal circumstances.

Defending Against *Appeal to Pity*

When someone tries to use an *Appeal to Pity*, here's how to respond empathetically but logically:

- **Acknowledge Their Feelings**

  Say, "I understand how you feel, but we need to focus on the main issue."

- **Bring the Discussion Back to Facts**

  Gently add, "Let's look at the facts behind the argument." This keeps the conversation grounded.

- **Suggest Separating Emotion and Reason**

  Mention, "Emotions are valid, but for this decision, we need objective reasons." This approach shows understanding without letting emotions guide the outcome.

By recognizing the *Appeal to Pity*, you'll make decisions based on reason rather than emotion alone. But even with logic on your side, it's easy to overlook relevant information — especially when probabilities and averages come into play. Let's explore this topic further!

Chapter 37: The Base Rate Fallacy

The *Base Rate* fallacy happens when someone ignores general statistical information (the "base rate") in favor of specific information, usually about an unusual event. It's like saying, "I know smoking isn't good for health, but my grandfather smoked every day and lived to be 95!" Here, the base rate — the health risks of smoking for most people — is ignored in favor of a single unusual case.

Why Is *Base Rate* Fallacy a Fallacy?

The *Base Rate* fallacy is flawed because it ignores the broader context and focuses on exceptions rather than the rule. Just because an unusual outcome happened doesn't mean it's likely. General trends and statistics provide a more reliable basis for conclusions than isolated stories.

Why Do Humans Use the *Base Rate* Fallacy?

Humans often fall into this fallacy because personal stories are vivid and memorable. It's natural to give more weight to specific, dramatic cases than to general data, but recognizing this helps us rely on statistics for a clearer understanding of likelihoods.

How to Avoid Base Rate Fallacy

1. Focus on the Bigger Picture

Ask yourself, "What do the general statistics say, beyond just a few individual cases?"

2. Consider Probability, Not Just Possibility

Remember that unusual cases are possible but not typical. Rely on base rates for reliable information.

3. Separate Stories from Statistics

Personal stories are meaningful but can be misleading. For decisions, consider broader data.

Practice Example

Imagine someone says, "My friend won the lottery, so I should buy tickets too!" The base rate, or the actual odds of winning, suggests the chances of winning are extremely low, even if one person won.

Defending Against *Base Rate* Fallacy

When someone ignores base rates, here's how to help them consider the full picture:

- **Ask About the General Data**

  Say, "What do most cases show?" This shifts the focus back to typical outcomes.

- **Encourage Looking at Likelihood**

  Gently add, "Even if it happened once, that doesn't make it common."

- **Highlight Probability Over Possibility**

  Suggest saying, "Just because something's possible doesn't make it probable." This helps ground the discussion in realistic outcomes.

By recognizing the Base Rate fallacy, you'll avoid being misled by rare events and make decisions based on the most likely outcomes. However, there's another trap to watch for — one that judges ideas solely based on their origins, rather than their actual merit.

Chapter 38: The Genetic Fallacy

The *Genetic Fallacy* occurs when someone dismisses or supports an argument based on its origin rather than on its actual merit. It's like saying, "This idea came from a famous scientist, so it must be true," or "That proposal was suggested by someone inexperienced, so it must be wrong." Here, the focus is not on the idea's actual content or value.

Why Is This a Fallacy?

The *Genetic* Fallacy is flawed because where an idea comes from doesn't determine its truth. Good ideas can come from surprising or unlikely sources, while even experts can have incorrect ideas. Sound reasoning means evaluating the content of a claim on its own terms, not on the background or identity of its origin.

Why Do Humans Use the *Genetic* Fallacy?

Humans sometimes rely on the *Genetic* Fallacy to avoid engaging with ideas they find difficult or uncomfortable. It can feel easier to accept or reject an argument based on the source alone rather than evaluating its actual merits. Recognizing this fallacy helps us consider ideas more fairly.

How to Avoid the *Genetic* Fallacy

1. Evaluate Content Over Source

Ask, "Is this argument valid based on its own merits, not just on who said it?"

2. Separate Idea from Origin

Recognize that even unlikely or disliked sources can offer useful insights.

3. Focus on Evidence

Base your conclusions on facts or reasoning, not on the history of where the idea came from.

Practice Example

Imagine someone says, "That study must be wrong because it was funded by a controversial organization." While funding can create potential biases, it doesn't automatically invalidate the study. A better approach would be to examine the study's methods and evidence.

Defending Against the *Genetic* Fallacy

When someone dismisses an idea based on its origin, here's how to encourage them to consider the content:

- **Shift Focus to the Argument**

  Say, "Let's look at the argument itself rather than focusing on where it came from."

- **Encourage Judging Based on Merit**

  Suggest, "Sometimes good ideas come from unexpected places. Let's see if it stands on its own."

- **Point Out that Origins Don't Change Facts**

  Gently remind them, "The truth of an idea doesn't depend on who came up with it."

By understanding the *Genetic* Fallacy, you'll focus on ideas rather than relying on the source alone. But remember: Sometimes, an argument rests on what isn't said rather than what is. Let's discuss this next fallacy!

Chapter 39: The Argument from Silence Fallacy

The *Argument from* Silence fallacy happens when someone concludes that something is true or false based solely on a lack of evidence or silence. It's like saying, "There's no mention of dragons in historical records, so they must have existed!"

Why Is *Argument from Silence* a Fallacy?

The *Argument from Silence* is flawed because silence or a lack of information doesn't mean something did or didn't happen. There could be many reasons for missing evidence, such as incomplete records or information that wasn't preserved. Sound arguments require positive evidence, not just the absence of it.

Why Do Humans Use *Argument from Silence*?

Humans use this fallacy when they feel confident in drawing conclusions from incomplete information. When there's no direct evidence to prove or disprove something, it can be tempting to assume silence supports one's preferred view. Recognizing this fallacy helps us remember that evidence is required to make solid claims.

How to Avoid *Argument from Silence*

1. Avoid Drawing Conclusions from Lack of Evidence

Remind yourself, "Just because there's no evidence doesn't mean something is true or false."

2. Look for Positive Evidence

Ask, "Is there any direct evidence to support this claim?" This ensures you're basing beliefs on information rather than absence.

3. Recognize Gaps as Inconclusive

Silence or missing records can mean many things. Avoid assigning meaning to what isn't there.

Practice Example

Imagine someone says, "There's no record of anyone questioning the king, so everyone must have agreed with him." Just because there's no record doesn't mean there was unanimous support; it might mean dissent wasn't recorded or that records were lost.

Defending Against *Argument from Silence*

When someone uses this fallacy, here's how to encourage them to look for real evidence:

- **Ask for Positive Evidence**

  Say, "Is there actual evidence that supports this claim, or just silence?"

- **Remind Them That Silence Is Inconclusive**

  Gently mention, "Not having evidence doesn't prove anything by itself."

- **Encourage Patience Until Evidence Appears**

  Suggest saying, "Let's wait until we have direct evidence before drawing a conclusion."

By understanding the *Argument from Silence* fallacy, you'll avoid making assumptions based on missing information. But watch out — some arguments claim that truth is simply a matter of perspective. Let's unpack this next fallacy!

Chapter 40: The Relativist Fallacy

The *Relativist* Fallacy occurs when someone rejects a claim as untrue simply because they believe it doesn't apply to them or their group. It's like saying, "That might be true for you, but it's not true for me," even when the topic is something objective, like a scientific fact or a well-established principle. This fallacy assumes that all truth is subjective or relative, which isn't always the case.

Why Is *Relativist* a Fallacy?

The *Relativist* Fallacy is flawed because some truths are objective — they're true regardless of personal belief. Just because someone doesn't want to accept a fact doesn't change its validity. Real understanding means distinguishing between subjective preferences (which vary) and objective truths (which don't depend on opinions).

Why Do Humans Use the Relativist Fallacy?

Humans often fall into the *Relativist* Fallacy when they want to avoid accepting a truth that challenges their worldview. It can be comforting to think, "That doesn't apply to me," but this limits growth and understanding. Recognizing this tendency helps us accept truths that apply broadly, not just personally.

How to Avoid the *Relativist* Fallacy

1. Separate Objective from Subjective

Ask, "Is this something that's true regardless of who believes it?" This helps distinguish between opinion and fact.

2. Accept That Some Facts Are Universal

Recognize that facts in areas like science, math, and history aren't personal—they apply equally to everyone.

3. Avoid Dismissing Ideas Just Because They're Uncomfortable

Be open to truths that may not fit personal preferences.

Practice Example

Imagine someone says, "Exercise is important for health," and the response is, "Maybe for most people, but not for me." Here, the person is rejecting a general health principle as if it doesn't apply to them. To avoid the *Relativist* Fallacy, they could consider evidence that shows exercise benefits everyone's health.

Defending Against the *Relativist* Fallacy

When someone uses the *Relativist* Fallacy, here's how to guide the conversation back to universal truths:

- **Encourage Objective Thinking**

  Say, "Some things are true for everyone, even if we see them differently."

- **Ask About Evidence Supporting Universality**

  Suggest, "What evidence shows this is true for most people?" This encourages broader thinking.

- **Point Out the Difference Between Fact and Preference**

  Gently add, "Some ideas apply to everyone, even if we don't prefer them."

By understanding the *Relativist* Fallacy, you'll be able to accept objective truths and avoid dismissing facts as mere personal opinion. However, sometimes, there's a tendency to treat mere possibilities as certainties, as explained in our next fallacy.

Chapter 41: The Appeal to Probability Fallacy

The *Appeal to Probability* fallacy happens when someone assumes that because something *could* happen, it *will* happen. It's like saying, "I could win the lottery if I buy a ticket, so I'll definitely win!" While some outcomes are possible, assuming that they will happen just because they're possible is misleading.

Why Is *Appeal to Probability* a Fallacy?

The *Appeal to Probability* is flawed because it confuses possibility with certainty. Just because an outcome is possible doesn't mean it's likely. Strong reasoning requires understanding the difference between what *could* happen and what's *likely* to happen based on evidence and probability.

Why Do Humans Use the *Appeal to Probability*?

Humans often fall into this fallacy because they like to focus on exciting or preferred outcomes, even if they're unlikely. It can be tempting to believe that just because something can happen, it will happen. Recognizing this tendency helps us make more realistic assessments of risk and likelihood.

How to Avoid the *Appeal to Probability*

1. Focus on Likelihood, Not Just Possibility

Ask yourself, "What are the actual odds of this happening?" This keeps you grounded in realistic expectations.

2. Distinguish Between "Can" and "Will"

Recognize that just because something *can* happen doesn't mean it *will*.

3. Look for Statistical Evidence

Use data to understand real probabilities, not just possibilities.

Practice Example

Imagine someone says, "I could get struck by lightning while hiking, so I'm definitely going to get hit if I go outside." While it's possible, the odds of getting struck by lightning are low. A more reasonable approach would be to check weather conditions and base decisions on likely outcomes.

Defending Against the *Appeal to Probability*

When someone assumes a possibility will definitely happen, here's how to bring them back to reality:

- **Ask About Likelihood**

  Say, "What's the actual probability of this happening?" This encourages realistic thinking.

- **Gently Point Out the Difference Between "Can" and "Will"**

  Suggest, "Just because it can happen doesn't mean it will."

- **Encourage Thinking in Terms of Realistic Risk**

  Add, "Let's look at the odds to understand how likely this really is."

By understanding the *Appeal to Probability*, you'll base your decisions on realistic odds, not just exciting possibilities. Now, there's another trap to watch for — one that dismisses issues by comparing them to larger problems. Let's explore this next fallacy!

Chapter 42: The Fallacy of Relative Privation

The *Fallacy of Relative* Privation, also known as the "Not as Bad as" fallacy, happens when someone dismisses a problem by pointing out that something else is worse. It's like saying, "Why are you upset about your broken phone? There are people who don't even have food!" While it's true that some problems are worse than others, that doesn't mean other issues aren't real or worth addressing.

Why Is *Relative Privation* a Fallacy?

The Fallacy of *Relative Privation* is flawed because it assumes that only the worst problems are worth caring about. By downplaying smaller issues, it prevents meaningful action and ignores the complexity of people's experiences. Real understanding means recognizing that multiple issues can matter, even if they're not all equally severe.

Why Do Humans Use *Relative Privation*?

Humans often fall into this fallacy to avoid addressing uncomfortable issues. By pointing out a "bigger" problem, they can deflect attention from something they don't want to deal with. Recognizing this fallacy helps us see that we can care about multiple issues without needing to rank them.

How to Avoid the Fallacy of *Relative Privation*

1. Acknowledge Multiple Levels of Importance

Recognize that just because one problem is serious, it doesn't make other issues unimportant.

2. Avoid Comparing Unrelated Issues

Stay focused on the topic at hand, rather than shifting to unrelated problems.

3. Encourage Addressing Problems Directly

Even if there are bigger issues, smaller problems are still worth solving in their own right.

Practice Example

Imagine someone says, "We shouldn't worry about pollution here because other countries pollute more." While other places may have severe pollution, local pollution still matters and addressing it can make a difference.

Defending Against *Relative Privation*

When someone uses the Fallacy of *Relative Privation*, here's how to keep the discussion focused:

- **Acknowledge Other Problems but Return to the Topic**

  Say, "Yes, there are bigger issues, but this one still deserves attention."

- **Emphasize That Multiple Problems Can Be Addressed**

  Add, "We don't have to ignore smaller problems just because bigger ones exist."

- **Point Out That Problem Solving Isn't a Competition**

  Remind them, "Different issues matter in different ways, and solving one doesn't mean ignoring others."

By recognizing the Fallacy of *Relative Privation*, you'll approach problems with balance and perspective, acknowledging that multiple issues can matter at once. But sometimes, arguments shift from logic to pressure, using force rather than reason to sway others. Let's take a closer look at this next fallacy!

Chapter 43: The Appeal to Force Fallacy

The *Appeal to Force* fallacy, also known as *Argumentum ad* Baculum (Latin for "appeal to the stick"), occurs when someone tries to win an argument by using threats or intimidation instead of logic. It's like saying, "You'd better agree with me, or you'll regret it!" Here, the argument relies on fear rather than evidence, making it an unfair and manipulative tactic.

Why Is *Appeal to Force* a Fallacy?

The Appeal to Force is flawed because threats don't make a claim true or valid. Using intimidation to win an argument bypasses reason and relies on fear to silence opposition. In rational discussions, ideas should stand on their own merit, not on the perceived consequences.

Why Do Humans Use *Appeal to Force*?

Humans sometimes resort to this fallacy when they feel defensive or lack strong evidence to support their position. Using threats or intimidation can feel like an easy way to "win" the argument without actually providing support. Recognizing this fallacy helps us stand up for fair discussions and resist being swayed by fear tactics.

How to Avoid *Appeal to Force*

1. Focus on Evidence and Reasoning

When presenting an argument, ensure you're relying on facts and reasoning rather than emotions or pressure.

2. Avoid Intimidation Tactics

Don't rely on fear or threats to persuade others. Instead, explain why your position makes sense.

3. Encourage Open Dialogue

Make it clear that all viewpoints are welcome, and respect differing opinions.

Practice Example

Imagine someone says, "If you don't support this policy, you'll lose all my respect." This pressure doesn't make the policy any better; it's simply an attempt to force agreement without reasoning.

Defending Against *Appeal to Force*

When someone uses the *Appeal to Force* fallacy, here's how to respond assertively:

- **Stand Up for Logic**

  Say, "I prefer to base my views on reasoning rather than pressure."

- **Request Evidence Instead of Intimidation**

  Suggest, "Let's look at the facts instead of relying on threats."

- **Encourage Respectful Discussion**

  Remind them, "We can disagree without needing to resort to threats or intimidation."

By recognizing the *Appeal to Force* fallacy, you'll make arguments based on logic, not fear, and encourage fair, respectful conversations. There's another persuasive trick to watch out for — one that swaps intimidation for excessive praise. Let's unpack this next fallacy.

Chapter 44: The Appeal to Flattery Fallacy

The *Appeal to Flattery* fallacy happens when someone uses compliments or flattery to persuade someone rather than presenting logical arguments. It's like saying, "You're so smart; I'm sure you'll agree with my idea!" Here, the argument is based on making the other person feel good, rather than using reason or evidence to convince them.

Why Is *Appeal to Flattery* a Fallacy?

The *Appeal to Flattery* is flawed because compliments don't make a claim true. While everyone enjoys feeling valued, praise shouldn't replace logic in an argument. For reasoning to be strong, it needs evidence — not just positive feelings.

Why Do Humans Use *Appeal to Flattery*?

Humans often use this fallacy because flattery can create goodwill, making others more inclined to agree. It's a shortcut to gaining support without the effort of presenting a well-reasoned argument. Recognizing this tactic helps us see past compliments to the real content of the argument.

How to Avoid *Appeal to Flattery*

1. Focus on Evidence, Not Emotions

Ask, "Am I agreeing because of the argument itself or because of how it makes me feel?"

2. Separate Compliments from Logic

Enjoy compliments, but don't let them cloud your judgment. An argument needs reasoning to stand strong.

3. Look for Substance in the Argument

Compliments are nice, but ask if there's real evidence backing up the claim.

Practice Example

Imagine someone says, "Only someone with great taste, like you, would support this idea!" Instead of being swayed by flattery, focus on the idea's strengths and weaknesses. Does it make sense on its own?

Defending Against *Appeal to Flattery*

When someone uses flattery in an argument, here's how to stay focused on facts:

- **Thank Them, Then Focus on the Argument**

  Say, "I appreciate the compliment, but let's look at the reasoning behind it."

- **Shift Attention Back to Evidence**

  Suggest, "What's the main reason you believe this? Let's focus on that."

- **Separate Feelings from Facts**

  Gently remind them, "It's a nice compliment, but I need more than that to be convinced."

By recognizing the *Appeal to Flattery* fallacy, you'll make decisions based on reasoning rather than just nice words. But beware — some arguments rely on "common sense" to avoid deeper thinking.

Chapter 45: The Appeal to Common Sense Fallacy

The *Appeal to Common Sense* fallacy occurs when someone argues that a claim must be true because it's "common sense" or "obvious," rather than providing specific reasons or evidence. It's like saying, "It's just common sense that this policy will work—everyone knows it!" Here, the argument relies on the assumption that something is widely accepted, rather than on actual proof or explanation.

Why Is *Appeal to Common Sense* a Fallacy?

The *Appeal to Common Sense* is flawed because what seems like "common sense" can vary from person to person and isn't always accurate. Just because something feels obvious doesn't make it true. Sound arguments need clear reasoning and evidence, not just vague appeals.

Why Do Humans Use *Appeal to Common Sense*?

Humans often fall into this fallacy because "common sense" arguments feel simple and self-evident, making it easier to assume that others will automatically agree. It can be a shortcut to avoid providing actual evidence. Recognizing this tendency helps us stay grounded in proof rather than assumptions.

How to Avoid Appeal to Common Sense

1. Ask for Clarification

If someone says it's "common sense," ask, "What specifically makes this true?" This keeps the conversation focused on reasons.

2. Seek Real Evidence

Instead of accepting "obvious" ideas, look for solid evidence to support the claim.

3. Acknowledge That Common Sense Isn't Universal

Remember that common sense can mean different things to different people.

Practice Example

Imagine someone says, "It's common sense that kids learn best with strict discipline." Instead of accepting this at face value, ask, "What studies or evidence show that strict discipline improves learning?" This approach encourages a fact-based discussion.

Defending Against *Appeal to Common Sense*

When someone relies on "common sense" as their main argument, here's how to gently push for more substance:

- **Ask for Specifics**

  Say, "What specific reasons support this idea?" This prompts them to clarify their argument.

- **Encourage Evidence Over Assumptions**

  Suggest, "Let's look at the evidence rather than assuming it's obvious."

- **Point Out That Common Sense Varies**

  Gently add, "What seems like common sense isn't always true or universal." This encourages a more open-minded approach.

By understanding the *Appeal to Common Sense* fallacy, you'll avoid assumptions and focus on specific reasons and facts. But there's another persuasive trick to watch out for — one that equates wealth with wisdom. Let's discuss this next fallacy.

Chapter 46: The Appeal to Wealth Fallacy

The *Appeal to Wealth* fallacy happens when someone assumes that something is better or more valuable simply because it's more expensive or associated with wealthy people. It's like saying, "This car is the best because it's the most expensive one available!" Here, the argument assumes that price or wealth equals quality, without examining other factors.

Why Is *Appeal to Wealth* a Fallacy?

The *Appeal to Wealth* is flawed because the cost or wealth associated with something doesn't necessarily reflect its quality or value. High prices can be based on branding or market factors, not on actual superiority. Rational thinking requires looking at the quality, performance, and actual benefits of something, not just its cost.

Why Do Humans Use *Appeal to Wealth*?

Humans often use this fallacy because wealth and high price tags can create a perception of luxury and excellence. This "halo effect" makes it easy to assume that expensive things are better, but recognizing this fallacy helps us evaluate products, ideas, and people based on actual merit.

How to Avoid *Appeal to Wealth*

1. Examine Quality Over Price

Ask yourself, "Is this truly better, or am I assuming quality based on cost?"

2. Avoid Letting Price Cloud Judgment

Just because something is expensive doesn't mean it's the best option.

3. Look for Value Rather Than Price

Focus on the specific benefits, functionality, and quality of a product or idea, not just its cost.

Practice Example

Imagine someone says, "This skincare product is definitely the best because it's the most expensive one in the store." Instead of relying on the price tag alone, consider checking product reviews or ingredients to see if it actually meets your needs.

Defending Against *Appeal to Wealth*

When someone assumes something is better based on wealth, here's how to encourage a focus on quality:

- **Ask About Specific Qualities**

  Say, "What features or qualities make this the best choice, other than price?"

- **Shift Focus from Cost to Functionality**

  Suggest, "Let's look at how well it actually performs instead of the cost alone."

- **Point Out That Cost Doesn't Equal Quality**

  Gently remind them, "Price doesn't always reflect quality. Let's evaluate the actual benefits."

By understanding the *Appeal to Wealth* fallacy, you can evaluate things based on their true value rather than just their price tag. There's another trap that relies on credibility without accuracy — using sources or quotes in misleading ways. Let's take a closer look at this next fallacy.

Chapter 47: The False Attribution Fallacy

The *False* Attribution fallacy happens when someone references an unreliable or incorrect source to support their argument, often without verifying the source's credibility. It's like saying, "As Einstein once said, 'Imagination is more powerful than knowledge,'" without confirming that Einstein actually said this. In this fallacy, the argument is built on weak or false information.

Why Is *False Attribution* a Fallacy?

The *False Attribution* fallacy is flawed because a claim based on a fake or unreliable source can mislead people. Even if a source sounds authoritative, if it's not accurate or relevant, it doesn't add value to the argument. Strong arguments rely on trustworthy sources, not on famous names or random quotes.

Why Do Humans Use *False Attribution*?

Humans often fall into this fallacy because it's easy to assume that popular quotes or famous figures add credibility. Using a well-known name or authority can make arguments feel more persuasive, even if the source is misattributed or unreliable. Recognizing this fallacy helps us rely on accurate information.

How to Avoid *False Attribution*

1. Verify Sources Before Quoting

Before using a quote or reference, ask, "Is this source credible, and did they really say this?"

2. Look for Reliable Evidence

Instead of relying on popular quotes, find primary sources or verified statements to support your argument.

3. Be Cautious with Unverified Claims

Avoid using a source unless you're sure it's accurate and relevant.

Practice Example

Imagine someone says, "As Shakespeare once said, 'Love conquers all.'" While this sounds profound, it's actually a line from Virgil, not Shakespeare. Relying on misattributed quotes weakens the argument. A better approach is to double-check the source and find a relevant, reliable reference.

Defending Against *False Attribution*

When someone relies on a questionable source, here's how to guide them toward accurate information:

- **Ask About the Source's Credibility**

  Say, "Is this a verified quote? Let's double-check to make sure it's accurate."

- **Suggest Finding a Reliable Source**

  Gently add, "Maybe we can find a source that's more credible to support this claim."

- **Encourage Using Primary or Trusted Sources**

  Remind them, "Strong arguments come from verified sources rather than random quotes."

By understanding the *False Attribution* fallacy, you'll rely on accurate sources, making your arguments stronger and more reliable. But sometimes, arguments confuse harm for progress, assuming that damage or loss can actually benefit the whole. Let's take a closer look at this next fallacy!

Chapter 48: The Broken Window Fallacy

The *Broken Window* Fallacy occurs when someone assumes that destruction or damage can have positive economic benefits by creating jobs or stimulating spending. It's like saying, "This broken window is good for the economy because it keeps glassmakers in business!" Here, the argument ignores the hidden costs and lost opportunities that come from replacing something that was already functioning.

Why Is *Broken Window* a Fallacy?

The *Broken Window* Fallacy is flawed because it only considers the immediate, visible benefits of repair without acknowledging the unseen costs. Fixing damage doesn't actually add value — it simply restores something to its previous state. Instead of using resources to build or improve, the resources are used to fix what was lost. True economic growth comes from creating new value, not from replacing what was destroyed.

Why Do Humans Use *Broken Window* Fallacy?

Humans often fall into this fallacy because the immediate benefits of repair are easy to see, while the hidden costs are less obvious. When something breaks, the visible repair process can make it seem as though new value is being added, but in reality, the resources could have been used for something more productive.

How to Avoid the *Broken Window* Fallacy

1. Consider the Full Economic Impact

Ask, "Are we creating new value, or are we just replacing what was lost?"

2. Think About Opportunity Costs

Recognize that money spent on repairs could have been used to create new benefits elsewhere.

3. Distinguish Between Restoring and Growing

Focus on activities that add value beyond merely fixing what was broken.

Practice Example

Imagine someone says, "Natural disasters are good for the economy because they create jobs in rebuilding." While rebuilding efforts can create jobs, they don't truly grow the economy. Resources are spent just to bring things back to normal instead of creating new value.

Defending Against *Broken Window* Fallacy

When someone assumes that destruction benefits the economy, here's how to highlight the unseen costs:

- **Point Out the Lost Opportunities**

  Say, "What could those resources have achieved if they hadn't been used for repairs?"

- **Explain That Repair Doesn't Add New Value**

  Add, "Repairing damage doesn't improve the economy—it just brings things back to where they were."

- **Encourage Thinking About True Growth**

  Suggest, "Let's focus on ways to create value rather than just replacing what was lost."

By recognizing the *Broken Window* Fallacy, you'll see that economic growth requires creating new value, not just fixing what's broken. Great job! But there's another pitfall to watch for —one that involves projecting human traits onto non-human things. Let's explore this next fallacy!

Chapter 49: The Anthropomorphic Fallacy

STORMS DON'T HAVE EMOTIONS; THEY'RE NATURAL PHENOMENA.

The *Anthropomorphic* Fallacy happens when someone attributes human qualities, emotions, or intentions to non-human entities, such as animals, machines, or nature. It's like saying, "The weather is angry today!" or "My car hates me."

Why Is *Anthropomorphic* a Fallacy?

The *Anthropomorphic* Fallacy is flawed because it can lead to misunderstandings about the nature of non-human entities. While describing a storm as "angry" might be poetic, it doesn't accurately represent the reality of weather patterns, which aren't driven by emotions. Logical reasoning means understanding things as they are, not as we imagine them to be.

Why Do Humans Use *Anthropomorphic* Fallacy?

Humans naturally interpret the world through a human lens, which can make it easy to project our emotions or intentions onto other things. Anthropomorphism can help make sense of complex phenomena, but it can also lead to mistaken ideas, such as thinking that nature or machines have intentions.

How to Avoid the *Anthropomorphic* Fallacy

1. Recognize the Difference Between Human and Non-Human Entities

Remember that only humans (and certain animals) experience complex emotions and intentions.

2. Focus on Factual Descriptions

Describe things as they are, without adding human-like qualities.

3. Be Mindful of Figurative Language

While it's fine to use metaphors, make sure they don't distort your understanding of reality.

Practice Example

Imagine someone says, "This computer hates me! It always crashes when I'm working." The computer isn't capable of feelings or intentions. It's more accurate to say, "The computer is malfunctioning," which avoids attributing human motives to a machine.

Defending Against *Anthropomorphic* Fallacy

When someone attributes human traits to non-human things, here's how to bring the discussion back to reality:

- **Encourage Realistic Descriptions**

  Say, "It might feel like the computer is against you, but it's just experiencing a technical issue."

- **Gently Separate Feelings from Facts**

  Suggest, "Let's look at this as a machine issue rather than a matter of intention."

- **Highlight That Non-Humans Don't Have Human Motives**

  Remind them, "Nature, machines, and animals don't have human emotions or motives like we do."

By recognizing the *Anthropomorphic* Fallacy, you'll interpret the world more accurately and avoid projecting human qualities onto non-human entities. However, sometimes, arguments hinge on surprise or disbelief — assuming something can't be true just because it seems astonishing. Let's explore this further.

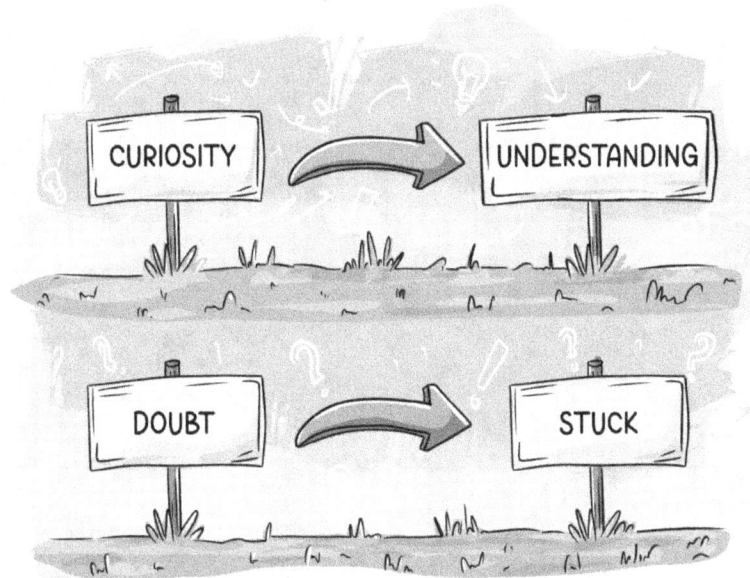

Chapter 50: The Argument from Personal Astonishment Fallacy

The *Argument from Personal Astonishment* (also called the Argument *from Incredulity*) occurs when someone argues that something must be false or impossible simply because they personally find it hard to believe. It's like saying, "I can't imagine how planes stay in the air, so there must be something suspicious going on with aviation." Here, the argument is based on a lack of understanding rather than on evidence or logic.

Why Is *Argument from Personal Astonishment* a Fallacy?

The *Argument from Personal Astonishment* is flawed because our personal understanding doesn't determine what's possible or true. Just because something seems confusing or complex doesn't mean it's false or invalid. In reality, some topics (such as science and technology) require specialized knowledge that isn't immediately obvious to everyone.

Why Do Humans Use *Argument from Personal Astonishment*?

Humans use this fallacy because we naturally rely on our personal experiences to make sense of the world. When something seems confusing, we may instinctively doubt it. Recognizing this fallacy helps us accept that things can be true even if we don't fully understand them.

How to Avoid *Argument from Personal Astonishment*

1. Acknowledge Knowledge Gaps

Accept that not understanding something doesn't make it untrue. Ask, "Could there be information I'm missing?"

2. Seek Evidence Rather Than Assumptions

Instead of dismissing something because it feels strange, look for reliable sources that explain it.

3. Stay Open to Complex Ideas

Recognize that many truths are complex. Be willing to learn rather than reject things outright.

Practice Example

Imagine someone says, "I can't believe humans evolved from simple organisms—it's just too strange to be true!" This is the *Argument from Personal Astonishment*. Instead, they could seek out scientific explanations for evolution rather than dismissing it based on initial disbelief.

Defending Against *Argument from Personal Astonishment*

When someone doubts something simply because they don't understand it, here's how to encourage open-mindedness:

- **Encourage Learning**

  Say, "Not understanding something doesn't mean it isn't true. Let's look at the evidence."

- **Point Out That Complexity Doesn't Equal Falsehood**

  Gently add, "Many things are complex, but that doesn't make them less real."

- **Suggest Research Instead of Rejection**

  Remind them, "Sometimes learning more can make things clearer."

By recognizing the *Argument from Personal Astonishment*, you'll be open to learning about complex ideas rather than rejecting them out of disbelief. But sometimes, arguments lean on the idea that if "everyone" believes it, it must be true. Let's unpack this next.

Chapter 51: The Appeal to Wisdom of the Crowd Fallacy

The *Appeal to Wisdom of the Crowd* fallacy, also known as the *Bandwagon of Belief*, occurs when someone assumes that a belief must be true simply because it's widely held by a large group. It's like saying, "Most people think this brand of shoes is the best, so it must be true!" Here, the argument relies on popularity rather than on actual evidence.

Why Is *Appeal to Wisdom of the Crowd* a Fallacy?

The *Appeal to Wisdom of the Crowd* is flawed because popularity doesn't determine truth. Just because many people believe something doesn't make it accurate. Good reasoning requires looking at facts and evidence rather than following the majority opinion, which can sometimes be based on trends, misinformation, or assumptions.

Why Do Humans Use *Appeal to Wisdom of the Crowd*?

Humans often rely on this fallacy because following the crowd feels comfortable and reassuring. It's easy to assume that if many people believe something, it must be true. Recognizing this tendency helps us focus on reliable information.

How to Avoid the *Appeal to Wisdom of the Crowd*

1. Look for Evidence Beyond Popularity

Ask, "Is there real evidence supporting this, or just a lot of people who believe it?"

2. Avoid Assuming Truth from Belief Numbers

Recognize that even widely accepted ideas need factual support to be valid.

3. Focus on Facts, Not Fads

Distinguish between what's truly supported by evidence and what's just a popular belief.

Practice Example

Imagine someone says, "Everyone says this diet is the best, so it has to be true!" Instead of relying on popularity, a better approach would be to research studies and results that objectively support the diet's effectiveness.

Defending Against *Appeal to Wisdom of the Crowd*

When someone relies on popular belief to argue a point, here's how to refocus on evidence:

- **Ask About Evidence Supporting the Belief**

  Say, "What specific evidence shows this belief is true?"

- **Point Out That Popularity Isn't Proof**

  Gently add, "Just because many people believe it doesn't mean it's accurate."

- **Encourage Independent Research**

  Suggest, "Let's look at the data to see if it really holds up."

By recognizing the *Appeal to Wisdom of the Crowd*, you'll make choices based on solid evidence rather than simply going with the flow. But sometimes, an argument relies on something's age rather than its actual value, suggesting it's correct just because it's old. Let's unpack this next fallacy.

Chapter 52: The Appeal to Antiquity Fallacy

The *Appeal to Antiquity* fallacy, also known as the *Appeal to Tradition*, occurs when someone argues that something must be right or better simply because it's been done for a long time. It's like saying, "This is the best way to do it because that's how our ancestors did it." Here, the argument relies on tradition as proof of value or truth, rather than on evidence.

Why Is *Appeal to Antiquity* a Fallacy?

The *Appeal to Antiquity* is flawed because if something has been done a certain way for a long time, it doesn't mean it's the best or only way. New ideas and approaches can often improve on traditions. Rational thinking means evaluating methods based on effectiveness.

Why Do Humans Use *Appeal to Antiquity*?

Humans often use this fallacy because they find comfort in tradition. What's familiar feels reliable and safe, making it tempting to assume that long-standing practices must be best. Recognizing this tendency helps us evaluate practices on their merits.

How to Avoid the *Appeal to Antiquity*

1. Focus on Effectiveness, Not Just Age

Ask, "Is this method the best, or just the oldest?"

2. Consider Alternatives with an Open Mind

Be willing to explore new ideas and techniques that might improve on tradition.

3. Evaluate Tradition's Benefits and Drawbacks

Acknowledge that while traditions can be valuable, they still need to be examined for current relevance.

Practice Example

Imagine someone says, "Our company should continue using paper files because that's how it's always been done." Instead of relying on tradition, it's more logical to consider if digital files might be more efficient and environmentally friendly.

Defending Against *Appeal to Antiquity*

When someone insists on a method based on tradition, here's how to bring the discussion back to practical value:

- **Ask About Modern Benefits**

  Say, "Does this method still work best, or are there better ways now?"

- **Encourage Evaluating Tradition's Relevance**

  Gently add, "Tradition has value, but let's see if it's still effective for today."

- **Suggest Considering Alternatives**

  Remind them, "Sometimes newer ideas improve on what's been done before."

By recognizing the *Appeal to Antiquity* fallacy, you value methods based on usefulness, not just history. But there's another trap to watch out for — one that leads people to overvalue immediate rewards over future benefits.

Chapter 53: The Hyperbolic Discounting Fallacy

The *Hyperbolic Discounting* fallacy occurs when someone places more value on immediate rewards over larger, future rewards. It's like saying, "I'd rather have $20 right now than wait a year for $100!" Here, the decision is driven by the desire for instant gratification, even if waiting would lead to a better outcome.

Why Is *Hyperbolic Discounting* a Fallacy?

The *Hyperbolic Discounting* fallacy is flawed because it ignores the long-term benefits of patience and overvalues immediate rewards. Rational decision-making requires weighing both short-term and long-term outcomes.

Why Do Humans Use *Hyperbolic Discounting*?

Humans often use this fallacy because our brains are wired to prefer immediate rewards over delayed ones, even when waiting would lead to greater benefits. Recognizing this tendency helps us make decisions that balance present desires with future gains.

How to Avoid *Hyperbolic Discounting*

1. Compare Immediate Gains with Long-Term Benefits

Ask yourself, "Will waiting lead to a better outcome than taking the reward now?"

2. Think About Future Consequences

Consider how taking an instant reward might limit your options or benefits in the future.

3. Practice Patience in Decision-Making

Get comfortable with delayed rewards by setting goals and focusing on long-term benefits.

Practice Example

Imagine someone says, "I'd rather spend my savings on a new gadget now than invest it for retirement." While spending brings immediate pleasure, investing may lead to much greater security and satisfaction in the future.

Defending Against *Hyperbolic Discounting*

When someone is focused on immediate rewards over future gains, here's how to encourage long-term thinking:

- **Highlight the Value of Waiting**

  Say, "Sometimes, waiting brings greater rewards in the future."

- **Encourage Looking at Future Benefits**

  Suggest, "Let's consider how this decision could benefit you later on."

- **Point Out Potential Long-Term Gains**

  Remind them, "Immediate rewards can feel good, but future gains might be worth the wait."

By recognizing the *Hyperbolic Discounting* fallacy, you can make choices that consider both present and future benefits, leading to wiser long-term decisions. Sometimes, however, an argument gives two sides equal weight, even when one lacks real evidence. Let's explore this next fallacy!

Chapter 54: The False Balance Fallacy

The *False Balance* fallacy happens when someone treats two sides of an argument as if they are equally valid, even when one side is clearly stronger or more credible. It's like saying, "Scientists say climate change is real, but some people disagree, so both sides must have equal merit." Here, the argument gives an illusion of fairness, but it misrepresents the strength of each position.

Why Is *False Balance* a Fallacy?

The *False Balance* fallacy is flawed because it ignores the weight of evidence on each side. Not all arguments or sources are equally credible; some are backed by extensive research, while others are based on anecdote or opinion. Rational thinking requires recognizing when one side has more evidence or expertise supporting it.

Why Do Humans Use False Balance?

Humans often fall into this fallacy because we're taught to respect all perspectives. While this is a valuable principle, it can sometimes lead to the mistaken belief that all views are equally valid, even if one side lacks strong support. Recognizing this tendency helps us weigh arguments based on merit rather than striving for artificial balance.

How to Avoid *False Balance*

1. Evaluate Each Side's Evidence

Ask yourself, "Does each side have equal evidence, or is one side stronger?"

2. Recognize Expertise and Consensus

Consider the sources and their credibility—experts with data and research should weigh more than opinions without evidence.

3. Distinguish Between Balance and Accuracy

Sometimes, an accurate conclusion doesn't mean giving equal weight to every perspective.

Practice Example

Imagine someone says, "Some people say vaccines are safe, and others disagree, so both sides should be treated equally." While it's important to listen, scientific research overwhelmingly supports vaccine safety. A balanced presentation would focus on the weight of evidence rather than treating each view as equal.

Defending Against *False Balance*

When someone tries to give equal weight to both sides of an uneven argument, here's how to help them focus on credibility:

- **Ask About the Evidence for Each Side**

  Say, "Is there strong evidence supporting both sides, or is one side better supported?"

- **Point Out When There's Consensus**

  Suggest, "Sometimes, there's a clear majority of evidence that should weigh more."

- **Emphasize Expertise Over Opinion**

  Remind them, "Not all sources have the same credibility. Let's focus on those with the strongest evidence."

By recognizing the *False Balance* fallacy, you can avoid giving undue weight to unsupported views and focus on the strength of evidence. Be careful, though — sometimes, arguments use fear to sway opinion rather than relying on facts, as we explain next.

Chapter 55: The Appeal to Fear Fallacy

The *Appeal to Fear* fallacy happens when someone tries to persuade by creating fear instead of providing logical reasons. It's like saying, "If you don't buy this insurance, you'll regret it when disaster strikes!" Here, the argument relies on scaring people rather than using facts to make a strong case.

Why *Is Appeal to Fear* a Fallacy?

The *Appeal to Fear* is flawed because fear alone doesn't prove a point. While fear can be a powerful motivator, it doesn't provide any evidence that a claim is true. Good reasoning is based on logic and facts, not just emotions. Relying on fear can lead people to make irrational choices that they might otherwise avoid.

Why Do Humans Use *Appeal to Fear*?

Humans often respond strongly to fear because it's a basic survival instinct. Appeals to fear can feel persuasive because they trigger an emotional response, but they often bypass rational thinking. Recognizing this fallacy helps us stay grounded in reason, even in situations that provoke strong emotions.

How to Avoid the *Appeal to Fear*

1. Focus on Facts Over Feelings

Ask yourself, "Is this argument based on evidence, or just fear?"

2. Seek Evidence to Support the Claim

If something sounds scary, look for data that backs it up rather than just reacting to the emotion.

3. Pause to Evaluate Before Responding

Give yourself time to assess whether fear is clouding your judgment.

Practice Example

Imagine someone says, "If you don't support this policy, crime will skyrocket, and everyone will be in danger!" Instead of being swayed by fear, a more rational approach would be to examine crime statistics and assess whether the policy truly addresses safety.

Defending Against *Appeal to Fear*

When someone uses fear instead of logic, here's how to stay focused on facts:

- **Ask for Factual Support**

  Say, "Can we look at the data supporting this claim instead of just worrying?"

- **Point Out the Need for Evidence Over Emotion**

  Gently add, "Fear alone doesn't prove anything. Let's examine the facts."

- **Encourage Calm, Rational Thinking**

  Suggest, "Let's consider this logically instead of focusing on worst-case scenarios."

By understanding the *Appeal to Fear* fallacy, you'll make decisions based on reason rather than on worry or alarm. But sometimes, arguments assume that the middle ground is always the best solution, even when it isn't. Let's explore this next fallacy!

Chapter 56: The Argument to Moderation Fallacy

The *Argument to Moderation* fallacy, also known as the *False Compromise* or *Middle Ground Fallacy*, occurs when someone assumes that the best solution must be a compromise between two opposing viewpoints. It's like saying, "Some people think the earth is round, others think it's flat—so it must be somewhere in between." Here, the argument relies on the idea that the truth lies halfway between extremes, rather than where the evidence points.

Why Is *Argument to Moderation* a Fallacy?

The *Argument to Moderation* is flawed because the truth isn't always in the middle. Sometimes one side is clearly correct, while the other is based on faulty reasoning. Compromising between two views doesn't automatically make a solution fair or accurate — good reasoning requires evaluating the merits of each position.

Why Do Humans Use Argument to Moderation?

Humans often fall into this fallacy because compromise feels fair and non-confrontational. It's tempting to think that agreeing somewhere in the middle is the most reasonable approach. However, recognizing this fallacy helps us see that some arguments have clear evidence on one side, and compromise isn't always the answer.

How to Avoid *Argument to Moderation*

1. Evaluate Evidence for Each Side

Ask yourself, "Does the evidence support one side more than the other, or does it truly lie somewhere in between?"

2. Avoid Assuming Compromise Equals Fairness

Just because a solution is in the middle doesn't mean it's accurate or just.

3. Consider Each Argument Separately

Focus on the strengths and weaknesses of each position instead of forcing a middle ground.

Practice Example

Imagine someone says, "Some people say vaccines are safe, others say they're dangerous, so they must be somewhere in between." Here, treating vaccine safety as a compromise between "safe" and "unsafe" ignores overwhelming scientific evidence supporting their safety.

Defending Against *Argument to Moderation*

When someone tries to find a compromise where none is needed, here's how to bring them back to evidence:

- **Ask About the Supporting Evidence**

  Say, "Does the evidence really support a compromise, or is one side stronger?"

- **Point Out When One Side Is Well-Researched**

  Gently add, "Sometimes, the facts clearly support one side over the other."

- **Emphasize That Fairness and Accuracy Aren't Always the Same**

  Suggest, "True fairness means going where the evidence leads, not just compromising."

By recognizing the *Argument to Moderation*, you'll understand that the best answer isn't always in the middle — it's wherever the evidence leads. However, arguments sometimes rely on the authority of past figures, assuming their wisdom applies universally. Let's take a closer look at this next fallacy!

Chapter 57: The Appeal to Authority of the Past Fallacy

The *Appeal to Authority of the Past* fallacy occurs when someone insists that an idea or belief is correct simply because it was endorsed by a well-known figure or authority from history. It's like saying, "Aristotle believed this, so it must be true today." Here, the argument relies on historical authority rather than evaluating current evidence.

Why Is *Appeal to Authority of the Past* a Fallacy?

The *Appeal to Authority of the Past* is flawed because even the greatest thinkers of the past didn't have access to all the knowledge we have today. While historical figures contributed valuable ideas, they were still limited by the science and understanding of their time. Strong reasoning looks at current evidence and methods rather than relying solely on tradition or historical authority.

Why Do Humans Use *Appeal to Authority of the Past*?

Humans often fall into this fallacy because historical figures like Aristotle, Plato, or Newton are widely respected. Quoting them can make arguments feel persuasive or trustworthy. Recognizing this tendency helps us focus on current evidence, rather than assuming that something is right just because it was believed long ago.

How to Avoid *Appeal to Authority of the Past*

1. Check for Modern Evidence

Ask yourself, "Is this claim still supported by current research, or is it just based on tradition?"

2. Recognize the Limits of Historical Knowledge

Historical figures did the best they could with what they knew, but science and knowledge have advanced.

3. Evaluate Ideas Based on Today's Understanding

Focus on present-day research and understanding, especially in fields that have evolved significantly.

Practice Example

Imagine someone says, "Ancient philosophers believed in spontaneous generation, so it must have some truth to it." While this idea was common historically, modern biology disproves it. Instead of relying on past authority, it's better to look at the evidence provided by current science.

Defending Against *Appeal to Authority of the Past*

When someone relies on historical authority to argue a point, here's how to encourage an evidence-based approach:

- **Ask About Current Evidence**

  Say, "Do we have modern research that supports this idea?"

- **Point Out Advances in Knowledge**

  Gently add, "Science has progressed since then, so we may know more now than they did."

- **Encourage Looking Forward Instead of Backward**

  Remind them, "While historical figures made important contributions, we have new knowledge they didn't have."

By recognizing the *Appeal to Authority of the Past*, you'll focus on the latest, most accurate information rather than on the limitations of historical knowledge. Excellent work — each fallacy you understand makes your reasoning sharper and more evidence-based! But there's another trap to watch out for — the assumption that the world is always fair and that people always get what they deserve. Let's explore this next.

Chapter 58: The Just-World Fallacy

The *Just-World* Fallacy occurs when someone assumes that good things happen to good people and bad things happen to bad people because the world is inherently fair. It's like saying, "If someone is poor, they must not have worked hard enough." This fallacy assumes that everyone gets what they deserve, ignoring other factors that affect outcomes.

Why Is *Just-World* a Fallacy?

The *Just-World* Fallacy is flawed because it oversimplifies complex situations and doesn't account for the role of luck, inequality, and external factors. While it can be comforting to believe in a fair world, real life is more complicated, and people's outcomes are influenced by many forces beyond their control. Rational thinking requires understanding the complexities of cause and effect, not assuming fairness.

Why Do Humans Use the *Just-World* Fallacy?

Humans often fall into this fallacy because believing in a fair world feels reassuring. It's comforting to think that we can control our fate by making good choices, and that misfortune only happens to those who "deserve" it. Recognizing this tendency helps us empathize with others and acknowledge that life doesn't always follow a moral balance sheet.

How to Avoid the *Just-World* Fallacy

1. Recognize That Life Is Complex

Understand that many factors—like chance, privilege, and circumstance—affect people's lives.

2. Practice Empathy Over Judgment

Instead of assuming someone's situation reflects their character, consider external factors they might face.

3. Acknowledge the Role of Randomness

Accept that both good and bad things can happen unpredictably and aren't always deserved.

Practice Example

Imagine someone says, "If they're in trouble, they must have done something to deserve it." This is the *Just-World Fallacy*. A more balanced approach would consider other factors, like luck, external circumstances, or systemic issues, that could contribute to someone's challenges.

Defending Against the *Just-World* Fallacy

When someone assumes that life is always fair, here's how to encourage them to consider other perspectives:

- **Point Out Complex Causes**

  Say, "Life isn't always fair, and many things are beyond our control."

- **Encourage Empathy**

  Suggest, "Sometimes people face challenges that aren't their fault. Let's look at the bigger picture."

- **Remind Them That Good and Bad Happen Randomly**

  Gently add, "Both fortune and misfortune can happen to anyone, regardless of their actions."

By recognizing the *Just-World* Fallacy, you'll approach situations with empathy and an understanding of life's complexities. Do beware — sometimes arguments rely on authority figures who aren't relevant to the topic, as we explain next.

Chapter 59: The Appeal to Irrelevant Authority Fallacy

The *Appeal to Irrelevant Authority* fallacy happens when someone supports a claim by citing an authority figure who isn't actually an expert on the topic. It's like saying, "This famous actor says this new diet works, so it must be true." Here, the argument relies on authority without checking if that authority is relevant.

Why Is *Appeal to Irrelevant Authority* a Fallacy?

The *Appeal to Irrelevant Authority* is flawed because expertise in one field doesn't mean expertise in another. Just because someone is respected or well-known doesn't mean they're qualified to speak on all topics. Sound reasoning means seeking information from credible sources who are knowledgeable in the specific area being discussed.

Why Do Humans Use *Appeal to Irrelevant Authority*?

Humans often use this fallacy because we're naturally influenced by people we admire or respect, even if their authority doesn't extend to the topic at hand. Recognizing this tendency helps us remember that true expertise is specific, not general, and even well-known figures can be mistaken outside their field.

How to Avoid *Appeal to Irrelevant Authority*

1. Check the Source's Expertise

Ask yourself, "Is this person truly an expert in this area, or just a well-known figure?"

2. Seek Field-Specific Knowledge

Rely on sources with proven expertise in the specific topic you're researching.

3. Recognize the Limits of Fame

Being famous doesn't make someone knowledgeable on every subject.

Practice Example

Imagine someone says, "A professional athlete recommends this investment strategy, so it must be effective." This is the *Appeal to Irrelevant Authority*. A more logical approach would be to consult financial experts who have specialized knowledge in investing.

Defending Against *Appeal to Irrelevant Authority*

When someone relies on an irrelevant authority to argue a point, here's how to guide them toward credible sources:

- **Ask About the Source's Credentials**

  Say, "Is this person actually an expert in this field?"

- **Encourage Seeking Qualified Opinions**

  Suggest, "Let's find information from someone with expertise in this specific area."

- **Point Out That Popularity Doesn't Equal Knowledge**

  Remind them, "Being well-known doesn't make someone an authority on every topic."

By recognizing the *Appeal to Irrelevant Authority*, you'll trust information from qualified experts rather than relying on fame or unrelated authority. But there's another trap to be aware of — assuming that controlled models can perfectly predict real-life situations. Let's explore this next fallacy.

Chapter 60: The Ludic Fallacy

The *Ludic Fallacy* happens when someone assumes that real-life situations work like controlled games or simplified models, where all the variables are predictable. It's like saying, "If I understand the rules of poker, I can predict how real-life risks work." Here, the fallacy relies on the mistaken belief that the messy, unpredictable nature of real life can be fully captured by neat, simplified rules.

Why Is *Ludic* a Fallacy?

The *Ludic Fallacy* is flawed because real life is far more complex and unpredictable than any game or model. Simplified systems often don't account for unexpected factors, hidden variables, or "unknown unknowns" that can affect outcomes. Sound reasoning means understanding that while models can be helpful, they don't capture all the complexities of real-world situations.

Why Do Humans Use the *Ludic* Fallacy?

Humans often fall into this fallacy because simplified models and games feel easy to understand and reassuring. We like rules and predictability, but life doesn't always follow neat patterns. Recognizing this fallacy helps us accept and prepare for the uncertainty and unpredictability of real-life events.

How to Avoid the *Ludic* Fallacy

1. Recognize Real-Life Complexity

Understand that life often involves factors that are hard to predict or account for.

2. Use Models as Guides, Not Absolutes

Models can be useful for learning, but they don't capture everything. Treat them as tools, not as perfect reflections of reality.

3. Stay Open to Surprises and Unknowns

Expect that real-world outcomes may differ from simplified predictions.

Practice Example

Imagine someone says, "If I can beat this strategy game, I'll have no problem navigating real-life business risks." This is the *Ludic* Fallacy—real business situations involve unpredictable factors like market changes, human behavior, and economic trends that can't always be modeled.

Defending Against the *Ludic* Fallacy

When someone assumes real life will follow the neat rules of a model, here's how to remind them of real-world complexity:

- **Point Out Real-World Variables**

  Say, "Games and models don't always account for unexpected events or unknowns."

- **Encourage Real-World Testing**

  Suggest, "Let's see how this approach holds up in actual situations before assuming it's foolproof."

- **Remind Them That Models Are Simplified**

  Gently add, "Models can be helpful, but life is often messier than any set of rules."

By recognizing the *Ludic* Fallacy, you'll stay grounded in the complexity of reality and avoid relying too heavily on simplified rules. But sometimes, arguments assume that anything new must be better. Let's explore this topic next.

Chapter 61: The Pro-Innovation Bias Fallacy

The *Pro-Innovation Bias* Fallacy happens when someone assumes that a new idea, product, or technology is inherently better just because it's new. It's like saying, "This new app must be the best solution because it's based on the latest technology!" Here, the argument relies on novelty as proof of quality or improvement, rather than evaluating the actual effectiveness or value of the innovation.

Why Is *Pro-Innovation Bias* a Fallacy?

The *Pro-Innovation Bias* is flawed because "new" doesn't always mean "improved". Some innovations may add complexity without adding real value or may create unintended side effects. Rational thinking requires assessing each new idea on its practical benefits and drawbacks, rather than assuming it's better simply because it's different from what came before.

Why Do Humans Use *Pro-Innovation Bias*?

Humans often fall into this fallacy because they associate newness with progress and improvement. We're naturally drawn to novelty and tend to believe that change is always positive. Recognizing this tendency helps us approach innovation with a balanced view, rather than blindly following trends.

How to Avoid *Pro-Innovation Bias*

1. Evaluate the Practical Benefits

Ask yourself, "Does this new thing solve a real problem, or is it change for the sake of change?"

2. Consider Potential Downsides

Recognize that some innovations may introduce new issues or be less effective than previous solutions.

3. Focus on Value, Not Novelty

Assess whether the innovation truly improves on what came before, based on evidence rather than excitement.

Practice Example

Imagine someone says, "This new software update will definitely make things easier." While updates can improve functionality, they can also introduce bugs or complicated features. A more balanced approach would be to wait for reviews or test it to see if it actually adds value.

Defending Against *Pro-Innovation Bias*

When someone assumes that new is automatically better, here's how to encourage a focus on value:

- **Ask About Practical Benefits**

  Say, "What specific improvements does this new idea or product offer?"

- **Encourage Testing and Evaluation**

  Suggest, "Let's see if this innovation is truly effective before assuming it's better."

- **Point Out That Novelty Doesn't Guarantee Quality**

  Gently add, "Just because it's new doesn't mean it's the best option."

By recognizing the *Pro-Innovation Bias*, you'll approach new ideas and technologies with curiosity but without assuming they're inherently superior. Remember, though, positive impressions in one area can lead to overestimations in others. Let's unpack this next fallacy!

Chapter 62: The Halo Effect Fallacy

The *Halo Effect* Fallacy happens when someone assumes that because a person or thing is good in one area, they must be good in other, unrelated areas as well. It's like saying, "This actor is talented, so their political opinions must be correct." Here, the argument relies on one positive trait to form an overall positive impression.

Why Is the *Halo Effect* a Fallacy?

The *Halo Effect* is flawed because expertise or talent in one area doesn't guarantee knowledge or quality in other areas. Rational thinking means evaluating each characteristic or quality separately. Just because someone excels in one domain doesn't mean they're qualified or credible in every area.

Why Do Humans Use the *Halo Effect*?

Humans use this fallacy because positive impressions are powerful, and it's natural to assume that someone who is skilled or likable in one way is generally admirable. This cognitive shortcut can save mental effort, but it often leads to uncritical acceptance of opinions or actions outside someone's area of expertise.

How to Avoid the *Halo Effect*

1. Judge Each Area Separately

Ask yourself, "Does this person's skill or quality in one area actually apply to this other area?"

2. Consider Relevant Expertise

Focus on whether someone's credibility or talent is relevant to the specific issue at hand.

3. Stay Aware of Biases

Acknowledge that admiration or respect in one area can cloud judgment in unrelated fields.

Practice Example

Imagine someone says, "This CEO runs a successful company, so their book on personal relationships must be excellent." Here, success in business doesn't necessarily mean expertise in relationships. A more critical approach would be to evaluate the book separately, without assuming it's credible based on the author's business background.

Defending Against the *Halo Effect*

When someone uses the *Halo Effect*, here's how to bring focus back to relevant qualities:

- **Ask About Relevant Expertise**

  Say, "Is this skill relevant to the area we're discussing?"

- **Encourage Independent Evaluation**

  Suggest, "Let's evaluate this area on its own merits, without letting other qualities sway us."

- **Point Out That One Strength Doesn't Equal Total Expertise**

  Gently remind them, "Being skilled in one area doesn't guarantee knowledge in another."

By recognizing the *Halo Effect*, you'll make more accurate judgments based on relevant qualities rather than letting one good impression sway unrelated areas. Excellent work — each fallacy you learn adds precision to your reasoning! But there's another common trap to watch for — one that causes us to underestimate the time and effort needed for a task.

Chapter 63: The Planning Fallacy

The *Planning Fallacy* happens when someone underestimates the time, cost, or effort required to complete a task or project, often because they're overly optimistic. It's like saying, "I'll definitely finish this big project in two days," even though similar projects have taken a week in the past. Here, the argument relies on an overly positive outlook rather than on realistic expectations.

Why Is This a Fallacy?

The *Planning Fallacy* is flawed because it ignores past experiences and typical obstacles. People often assume they'll complete tasks quickly and smoothly, even when previous experiences suggest otherwise. Sound reasoning involves considering potential challenges and basing expectations on realistic timelines, not just best-case scenarios.

Why Do Humans Use the *Planning Fallacy*?

Humans fall into the *Planning Fallacy* because they're naturally optimistic about future events, often overlooking possible setbacks or challenges. They like to believe that everything will go smoothly, but recognizing this tendency helps them prepare for real-life complexities and avoid the disappointment of unmet expectations.

How to Avoid the *Planning Fallacy*

1. Base Plans on Past Experiences

Ask yourself, "How long did similar tasks take in the past? What challenges did I face?"

2. Account for Potential Setbacks

Assume that unexpected delays or issues might arise and build extra time into your plans.

3. Use Data and Realistic Projections

Make estimates based on data, rather than assuming an ideal outcome.

Practice Example

Imagine someone says, "This home renovation will be done in two weeks!" This is likely the *Planning Fallacy*, especially if past renovations have taken longer. A more realistic approach would be to look at average renovation times, include a buffer for potential delays, and expect that things might take longer than planned.

Defending Against the *Planning Fallacy*

When someone underestimates the time or effort required for a task, here's how to encourage realistic expectations:

- **Ask About Similar Experiences**

  Say, "How long did similar projects take, and what challenges did you face?"

- **Encourage Including Extra Time**

  Suggest, "It's a good idea to build in some extra time in case of delays."

- **Remind Them That Optimism Isn't Always Realistic**

  Gently add, "Sometimes things take longer than we hope. Planning for that can save stress."

By recognizing the *Planning Fallacy*, you'll set more achievable goals and timelines, making it easier to meet deadlines and avoid disappointment. However, mistaken identity and assumptions can sometimes lead to errors in reasoning. Let's get into this next fallacy!

DIFFERENT LABELS, SAME IDENTITY.

Chapter 64: The Masked Man Fallacy

The *Masked Man* Fallacy occurs when someone assumes that if they know something about an object or person under one description, it must hold true under another, distinct description. For example, "I know Superman can fly, but I don't know that Clark Kent can fly, so Clark Kent isn't Superman." Here, different labels (or contexts) lead to the mistaken belief that two names or descriptions must refer to different things, even if they're actually the same.

Why Is the *Masked Man* a Fallacy?

The *Masked Man* Fallacy is flawed because it confuses identity with how something is described. In logic, if two names or descriptions refer to the same entity, the characteristics apply regardless of which label is used. Sound reasoning means recognizing that different ways of identifying something don't change the entity itself.

Why Do Humans Use the *Masked Man* Fallacy?

Humans often fall into this fallacy because different labels or appearances can influence how they think about something. This fallacy can also arise when people are unaware of all the facts and assume that different descriptions must refer to different things. Recognizing this tendency helps us see through surface differences to the underlying reality.

How to Avoid the *Masked Man* Fallacy

1. Focus on the Entity Itself

Ask yourself, "Do these different descriptions refer to the same thing, just in different contexts?"

2. Consider All Known Information

Make sure you have enough context to understand whether two labels might apply to one entity.

3. Avoid Assuming Different Labels Mean Different Things

Remember that names or contexts can change, but identity stays constant.

Practice Example

Imagine someone says, "I know Batman fights crime, but I don't know Bruce Wayne fights crime, so Batman can't be Bruce Wayne." This is the *Masked Man* Fallacy. Just because Bruce Wayne and Batman are different descriptions doesn't mean they refer to different people; they're simply different labels for the same individual.

Defending Against the *Masked Man* Fallacy

When someone assumes that two different descriptions mean different entities, here's how to bring the focus back to identity:

- **Ask About the Underlying Identity**

  Say, "Do these descriptions refer to the same thing, just in different contexts?"

- **Point Out that Labels Don't Change Essence**

  Gently add, "Different names don't change the underlying identity."

- **Encourage Thinking Beyond Appearances**

  Suggest, "Just because they look different doesn't mean they're separate entities."

By recognizing the *Masked Man* Fallacy, you'll be able to look beyond labels and appearances to understand the true identity of things. But beware — some arguments are crafted to be unbreakable, designed to deflect any challenge. Let's explore this next fallacy!

Chapter 65: The Self-Sealing Fallacy

The *Self-Sealing* Fallacy happens when someone makes a claim that's impossible to disprove because any counter-argument or evidence against it is automatically rejected or reinterpreted to fit the claim. It's like saying, "Everyone who disagrees with me is just too brainwashed to see the truth." Here, the argument is constructed so that it protects itself against any criticism, creating a "self-sealing" defense that makes it immune to outside scrutiny.

Why Is *Self-Sealing* a Fallacy?

The *Self-Sealing* Fallacy is flawed because it makes a claim unfalsifiable — no matter what evidence is presented, the claim is redefined or explained away to prevent any possibility of being proven wrong. Sound reasoning requires openness to evidence, even if it goes against the initial belief. If a claim can't be disproven in any scenario, it's not a testable or logical argument.

Why Do Humans Use the *Self-Sealing* Fallacy?

Humans often fall into this fallacy because it feels safer to hold onto beliefs that can't be challenged. By making arguments immune to counter-evidence, they avoid facing difficult questions or changing their minds. Recognizing this tendency helps us remain open to information that might challenge our views and keep our thinking flexible.

How to Avoid the *Self-Sealing* Fallacy

1. Stay Open to Counter-Evidence

Ask yourself, "What evidence would I accept as a reason to rethink my claim?"

2. Avoid Reinterpreting All Evidence to Fit the Argument

Allow counter-evidence to exist rather than immediately twisting it to support your position.

3. Test Claims Honestly

Think about how to evaluate your claim in a way that doesn't automatically reject opposing views.

Practice Example

Imagine someone says, "If you don't believe in my theory, it's because you haven't awakened to the truth." This is the Self-Sealing Fallacy because disagreement is explained as evidence of ignorance, rather than as a valid challenge to the theory. A more open-minded approach would allow others to disagree and explore whether the claim can stand up to criticism.

Defending Against the *Self-Sealing* Fallacy

When someone creates an argument that blocks all counterpoints, here's how to help them consider alternative views:

- **Ask What Would Change Their Mind**

  Say, "Is there any evidence that would make you reconsider this belief?"

- **Encourage Openness to Disagreement**

  Gently add, "Allowing counterpoints can help test if an argument is strong or needs adjusting."

- **Point Out That Unfalsifiable Claims Aren't Logical**

  Remind them, "If a claim can't be challenged, it can't be truly tested."

By recognizing the *Self-Sealing* Fallacy, you'll keep your arguments open to evidence and avoid creating unchallengeable beliefs. But there's another subtle trap to avoid — one that dismisses arguments based on suspected motives rather than engaging with the actual content. Let's discover more about this next fallacy.

Chapter 66: The Appeal to Motive Fallacy

The *Appeal to Motive* Fallacy happens when someone dismisses an argument by questioning the motives behind it, instead of addressing the argument's actual content. It's like saying, "You're only supporting this policy because you'll benefit from it, so it must be wrong." Here, the focus is on the person's possible motivations, rather than the validity of what they're saying.

Why Is *Appeal to Motive* a Fallacy?

The *Appeal to Motive* is flawed because even if someone has a personal reason for making a claim, it doesn't automatically make the claim false. Dismissing an argument based on motives ignores the actual evidence or reasoning behind it. Sound reasoning requires analyzing the argument itself, not just the possible interests of the person presenting it.

Why Do Humans Use the *Appeal to Motive* Fallacy?

Humans often fall into this fallacy because questioning motives can seem like an easy way to discredit someone's stance. It can feel satisfying to assume that people are biased or self-serving, but this doesn't address the actual quality of their argument. Recognizing this tendency helps us focus on facts and evidence, rather than personal suspicions.

How to Avoid the *Appeal to Motive* Fallacy

1. Focus on the Argument's Content

Ask yourself, "Is there valid reasoning or evidence in their argument, regardless of their motives?"

2. Acknowledge That Motives and Truth Aren't Linked

Remember that even if someone stands to benefit, it doesn't mean their argument is invalid.

3. Separate the Person from the Argument

Evaluate the argument on its own merits, rather than making assumptions about the person presenting it.

Practice Example

Imagine someone says, "You're only defending this new school policy because you're a teacher and it helps you." This is the *Appeal to Motive* Fallacy because it attacks the person's possible interest in the policy rather than addressing its pros and cons. A more rational approach would be to discuss the actual benefits or drawbacks of the policy itself.

Defending Against the *Appeal to Motive* Fallacy

When someone dismisses an argument based on motives, here's how to bring the focus back to the content:

- **Ask for Evidence Supporting or Disproving the Argument**

  Say, "Let's look at the argument itself—what evidence supports or opposes it?"

- **Point Out That Motivation Doesn't Change Facts**

  Gently add, "Even if they have a motive, it doesn't mean the argument is wrong."

- **Encourage Evaluating the Argument Separately**

  Suggest, "Let's consider the points being made, regardless of possible motives."

By recognizing the Appeal to Motive Fallacy, you'll stay focused on the content of arguments and avoid dismissing ideas based on personal suspicions. But sometimes, chance events are mistakenly seen as meaningful connections. Let's unpack this fallacy!

Chapter 67: The Appeal to Coincidence Fallacy

The *Appeal to Coincidence* Fallacy happens when someone explains away a pattern or connection as mere coincidence, despite strong evidence suggesting a cause. It's like saying, "It's just a coincidence that sales always increase when we advertise," even if the data consistently shows a clear link between advertising and higher sales. Here, the argument relies on attributing outcomes to chance, even when there's likely a cause at play.

Why Is the *Appeal to Coincidence* a Fallacy?

The *Appeal to Coincidence* is flawed because it ignores the possibility of connection, even when there's substantial evidence of a link. Dismissing meaningful patterns or connections as "just coincidence" can prevent us from understanding the true cause of events. Sound reasoning means exploring possible causes rather than assuming outcomes are random.

Why Do Humans Use the *Appeal to Coincidence*?

Humans often use this fallacy because admitting a connection can be uncomfortable or challenging, especially if it means changing beliefs or behaviors. Attributing something to coincidence can feel easier than looking for real reasons or explanations. Recognizing this tendency helps us stay curious about possible causes and avoid shrugging off meaningful patterns.

How to Avoid the *Appeal to Coincidence* Fallacy

1. Look for Consistent Patterns

Ask yourself, "Is there a regular pattern that suggests a cause, or is this truly random?"

2. Examine Evidence for Causation

If there's data or research pointing to a link, consider it seriously rather than dismissing it as chance.

3. Stay Open to Causes, Even If They're Surprising

Be willing to explore unexpected explanations instead of labeling outcomes as coincidental.

Practice Example

Imagine someone says, "It's just a coincidence that I always feel better after drinking more water." If they consistently feel better when hydrated, this might be a sign of causation rather than pure coincidence. A more rational approach would involve exploring whether increased hydration is genuinely helping.

Defending Against the *Appeal to Coincidence* Fallacy

When someone attributes a clear pattern to coincidence, here's how to bring the focus back to possible causes:

- **Ask About Potential Explanations**

  Say, "Could there be a reason this keeps happening instead of it being random?"

- **Point Out the Pattern**

  Suggest, "It's happening regularly, so maybe there's a connection worth exploring."

- **Encourage Examining the Evidence**

  Remind them, "If there's a consistent pattern, there might be a cause behind it."

By recognizing the *Appeal to Coincidence* Fallacy, you'll stay open to finding meaningful causes behind patterns, rather than dismissing them as chance. But there's another pitfall to watch for that involves twisting someone's words by taking them out of context. Let's explore this next fallacy.

Chapter 68: The Contextomy Fallacy

The *Contextomy* Fallacy occurs when someone takes a quote or statement out of its original context to change its meaning or make it support a different idea. It's like quoting a book review that says, "This film was amazing … at making me want to leave the theater," but only using "This film was amazing." Here, the argument misrepresents the original statement to make it appear as if it supports an unrelated claim.

Why Is *Contextomy* a Fallacy?

The *Contextomy* Fallacy is flawed because it misleads by manipulating language. Taking words out of context can completely change their meaning, often to favor one perspective unfairly. Sound reasoning requires quoting accurately and maintaining the original intent of statements. Misrepresentation prevents a fair and honest discussion.

Why Do Humans Use the *Contextomy* Fallacy?

Humans often use this fallacy because partial quotes can seem more powerful or persuasive, especially if they support an argument's goal. It's tempting to use someone's words against them by reshaping their meaning, but this approach isn't ethical or logical. Recognizing this tendency helps us stay honest in our discussions and avoid being misled by selective quoting.

How to Avoid the *Contextomy* Fallacy

1. Quote with Integrity

Ask yourself, "Am I preserving the original meaning of this quote?"

2. Provide Full Context

When using quotes, include enough context so readers or listeners understand the original intent.

3. Read the Surrounding Text

Make sure you understand the full message or argument before using a quote to support a claim.

Practice Example

Imagine someone says, "The author of this article thinks this policy is great!" by quoting, "This policy is great … at creating more problems." Here, the quote is taken out of context to change its meaning. A more honest approach would include the full statement, showing that the author was actually criticizing the policy.

Defending Against the *Contextomy* Fallacy

When someone uses an out-of-context quote to support their argument, here's how to encourage a return to the full meaning:

- **Ask to See the Full Quote**

  Say, "Can we look at the original statement to see the full context?"

- **Point Out Misinterpretations**

  Suggest, "This quote may have a different meaning in its full form. Let's check to be sure."

- **Encourage Honest Representation**

  Remind them, "Using quotes accurately helps keep the discussion fair."

By recognizing the *Contextomy* Fallacy, you'll promote fair discussions that respect the true meaning of people's words. Excellent work—each fallacy you learn helps you interpret information honestly and accurately! But sometimes, vivid examples can create a powerful impression that outweighs the actual facts. Let's unpack this next fallacy.

Chapter 69: The Misleading Vividness Fallacy

The *Misleading Vividness* Fallacy happens when someone overestimates the probability of an event happening because of one powerful or memorable example, rather than looking at broader data. It's like saying, "My friend got sick after flying, so flying is dangerous for your health!" Here, the argument relies on a single, vivid incident rather than statistics or evidence that reflect the actual risks.

Why Is *Misleading Vividness* a Fallacy?

The *Misleading Vividness* Fallacy is flawed because a single example doesn't represent the larger pattern or likelihood of something happening. Just because one memorable event occurred doesn't mean it's common. Rational thinking requires looking at the big picture, which is often less dramatic than isolated incidents might suggest.

Why Do Humans Use the *Misleading Vividness* Fallacy?

Humans often fall into this fallacy because vivid stories or examples create strong emotional impressions that feel more real than abstract statistics. Our minds are wired to remember and react to dramatic events, but this can lead us to misjudge how often those events happen. Recognizing this tendency helps us make decisions based on actual probabilities, rather than memorable anecdotes.

How to Avoid the *Misleading Vividness* Fallacy

1. Consider the Full Picture

Ask yourself, "Does this example represent the broader data, or is it just an isolated incident?"

2. Seek Statistical Evidence

Look at the actual statistics or probability of an event rather than relying on a single story.

3. Acknowledge That Emotional Impact Doesn't Equal Frequency

Just because an event feels memorable doesn't mean it happens often.

Practice Example

Imagine someone says, "I heard about someone who won the lottery twice, so it must be possible to win big more than once." While it's possible, it's also extremely rare, and this example doesn't reflect the true odds. A more logical approach would be to look at the probability of winning the lottery even once, let alone twice.

Defending Against the *Misleading Vividness* Fallacy

When someone uses a single vivid example to generalize, here's how to encourage them to consider the broader picture:

- **Ask About Statistical Evidence**

  Say, "What do the numbers show about the overall likelihood of this happening?"

- **Point Out That Isolated Incidents Aren't the Norm**

  Suggest, "A single case doesn't make something common. Let's look at the bigger picture."

- **Remind Them That Dramatic Examples Can Skew Perception**

  Gently add, "Sometimes dramatic stories stick with us, but they don't always reflect the true odds."

By recognizing the *Misleading Vividness* Fallacy, you'll be able to make decisions based on reality rather than on isolated, memorable examples. But be careful — sometimes, arguments unfairly lean on claims of privilege to dismiss or deflect ideas. Let's explore this further.

Chapter 70: The Appeal to Privilege Fallacy

The *Appeal to Privilege* Fallacy occurs when someone dismisses another person's argument or concerns by claiming that they're "too privileged" to understand the issue. It's like saying, "You can't talk about healthcare because you're rich and don't get it." Here, the argument is dismissed based on the person's perceived privilege rather than on the merits of what they're actually saying.

Why Is the *Appeal to Privilege* a Fallacy?

The *Appeal to Privilege* is flawed because a person's background doesn't necessarily affect the validity of their arguments. Just because someone may not have directly experienced an issue doesn't mean their perspective or evidence is automatically invalid. Good reasoning requires engaging with the argument itself, rather than assuming someone's background makes their point irrelevant.

Why Do Humans Use the *Appeal to Privilege*?

Humans use this fallacy because it can be tempting to assume that those who haven't experienced an issue firsthand can't understand it or contribute valuable perspectives. Sometimes, privilege can limit understanding, but this assumption alone isn't enough to reject someone's argument. Recognizing this fallacy helps us evaluate claims on their logic and evidence, not on who is making them.

How to Avoid the *Appeal to Privilege*

1. Focus on the Argument's Validity

Ask yourself, "Does the argument make sense, regardless of the person's background?"

2. Acknowledge Perspective Without Dismissing Insight

Recognize that while someone's background may affect their viewpoint, it doesn't invalidate the reasoning.

3. Separate the Person from the Point

Evaluate the argument independently of the person's privilege or experience level.

Practice Example

Imagine someone says, "Public education funding should be a top priority." The response, "You went to private school, so you don't understand public education issues," is an example of the *Appeal to Privilege* Fallacy. A more constructive response would engage with the person's point about education funding, regardless of their personal experience.

Defending Against the *Appeal to Privilege* Fallacy

When someone dismisses an argument based on privilege, here's how to keep the focus on the message:

- **Ask About the Argument's Content**

  Say, "Is there anything incorrect in the argument itself?"

- **Point Out That Ideas Stand Alone**

  Remind them, "An argument's value isn't dependent on the person's background."

- **Encourage Evaluating the Point, Not the Person**

  Suggest, "Let's focus on the argument itself to see if it holds up."

By recognizing the *Appeal to Privilege* Fallacy, you'll focus on evaluating arguments based on their logic, not on assumptions about the person presenting them. But sometimes, the mere possibility of something happening is mistaken for certainty. Let's explore this next fallacy!

Chapter 71: The Appeal to Equivocation Fallacy

The *Appeal to Possibility* Fallacy happens when someone assumes that because something *could* happen, it *will* happen, or that it's highly probable. It's like saying, "There's a chance I could win the lottery, so I'll start planning what I'll buy!" Here, the argument confuses what's possible with what's probable, even if the likelihood of the event is extremely low.

Why Is the *Appeal to Possibility* a Fallacy?

The *Appeal to Possibility* is flawed because the fact that something *can* happen doesn't mean it will happen. Rational thinking means distinguishing between what's theoretically possible and what's realistically probable. Without evidence indicating that something is likely, assuming it will happen is misleading.

Why Do Humans Use the *Appeal to Possibility*?

Humans often fall into this fallacy because it's exciting or reassuring to focus on potential outcomes, even if they're unlikely. The idea that "anything is possible" is tempting, but without evidence, it can lead to unrealistic assumptions. Recognizing this tendency helps us make more balanced decisions based on what's actually likely, not just what's conceivable.

How to Avoid the *Appeal to Possibility*

1. Ask About the Likelihood

Ask yourself, "Is there evidence that this will likely happen, or is it just a possibility?"

2. Focus on Probability, Not Just Possibility

Consider whether there are real reasons to expect an outcome, beyond just the fact that it could theoretically occur.

3. Recognize the Difference Between Possible and Probable

Stay grounded in the data or evidence that indicates likelihood, not just feasibility.

Practice Example

Imagine someone says, "I might become famous one day, so I should start preparing for fame now!" While it's possible to become famous, it's not probable for most people. A more balanced approach would consider the steps that could make fame more probable and focus on realistic goals.

Defending Against the *Appeal to Possibility* Fallacy

When someone assumes that something will happen just because it's possible, here's how to help them think in terms of probability:

- **Ask About Evidence for Probability**

  Say, "Is there any evidence that this is likely, or just that it's possible?"

- **Encourage Thinking About Realistic Outcomes**

  Suggest, "Let's consider how probable this outcome is compared to other scenarios."

- **Point Out That Possibility Doesn't Guarantee Probability**

  Gently remind them, "Just because it can happen doesn't mean it will."

By recognizing the *Appeal to Possibility* Fallacy, you'll make more realistic decisions based on what's likely, not just what's conceivable. Great work—each fallacy you learn strengthens your ability to make sound judgments and stay grounded in reality! But there's another trap to watch for — one that exaggerates disagreements to make issues seem more polarized than they are. Let's take a look at this next fallacy!

Chapter 72: The Inflation of Conflict Fallacy

The *Inflation of Conflict* Fallacy occurs when someone assumes that if experts disagree on a topic, it must mean that all opinions are equally valid or that the truth lies somewhere in between. It's like saying, "Since scientists don't all agree on climate change, it's probably not that big of a deal." Here, the argument relies on the idea that any level of disagreement between experts creates enough doubt to invalidate one or both sides.

Why Is the *Inflation of Conflict* a Fallacy?

The *Inflation of Conflict* is flawed because it exaggerates disagreements, often ignoring the weight of evidence that supports one side more than the other. Just because a small number of experts disagree doesn't mean the entire topic is uncertain or that the truth lies in the middle. Rational thinking requires looking at the overall evidence, consensus, and credibility of sources, not just the presence of any disagreement.

Why Do Humans Use the Inflation of Conflict?

Humans often use this fallacy because disagreements among experts can make a topic feel confusing or unreliable. By assuming both sides are equally valid or that the truth must lie in between, they avoid the effort of examining the actual evidence. Recognizing this tendency helps us understand that not all conflicts are equally balanced, and some positions may be far better supported than others.

How to Avoid the *Inflation of Conflict* Fallacy

1. Consider the Weight of Evidence

Ask yourself, "What does the majority of credible evidence show, rather than focusing on outliers?"

2. Recognize That Not All Opinions Are Equal

Just because an opinion exists doesn't mean it has as much merit as a well-supported view.

3. Evaluate Expertise and Consensus

Look at the level of agreement among qualified experts and the strength of the evidence, rather than just noting the existence of disagreement.

Practice Example

Imagine someone says, "Since some doctors don't agree about the effectiveness of vaccines, the science must be uncertain." This is the Inflation of Conflict Fallacy because it implies that a small amount of disagreement nullifies the overwhelming evidence supporting vaccines. A more logical approach would be to look at the large consensus of research rather than focusing on the minority who disagree.

Defending Against the *Inflation of Conflict* Fallacy

When someone assumes that expert disagreement means a topic is completely unsettled, here's how to encourage them to look at the overall evidence:

- **Point to the Consensus Among Experts**

  Say, "Most qualified experts agree on this, even if a few disagree."

- **Ask About the Quality of Evidence**

  Suggest, "Let's look at the strength of the evidence rather than focusing on isolated opinions."

- **Remind Them That Disagreement Doesn't Mean Equal Validity**

  Gently add, "Just because there's some disagreement doesn't mean all views are equally supported."

By recognizing the *Inflation of Conflict* Fallacy, you'll be able to make decisions based on well-supported evidence rather than assuming all conflicts are balanced. However, arguments sometimes invoke complex science to make ideas sound credible without proper context. Let's dive into this next fallacy!

Chapter 73: The Appeal to Quantum Physics Fallacy

The *Appeal to Quantum* Physics Fallacy happens when someone uses complex scientific terms, often from quantum physics or other advanced fields, to make a claim sound credible, even if it has little to do with the actual science. It's like saying, "Quantum physics shows that everything is connected, so positive thinking will change reality." Here, the argument relies on the perceived mystery and authority of quantum science to give an unrelated idea credibility.

Why Is the *Appeal to Quantum Physics* a Fallacy?

The *Appeal to Quantum Physics* is flawed because it misuses scientific terms and concepts to support ideas without real evidence or understanding. Quantum physics is complex, but this doesn't mean it can be applied randomly to unrelated topics. Sound reasoning requires that concepts are used accurately, with clear explanations of how they're relevant to the argument being made.

Why Do Humans Use the *Appeal to Quantum Physics?*

Humans often use this fallacy because quantum physics is famously mysterious and complex, giving it an air of authority. For many, using such terms can make an argument seem deep or profound, even if the science isn't connected to the topic. Recognizing this fallacy helps us stay grounded in logic, separating genuine science from buzzwords and pseudoscience.

How to Avoid the *Appeal to Quantum Physics*

1. Ask for Clear Explanations

Ask yourself, "Does the person explain how this science actually applies, or are they just using it to sound impressive?"

2. Check for Relevance

Make sure the scientific concept is actually relevant to the argument instead of being thrown in without connection.

3. Be Cautious of Complex Jargon in Non-Scientific Topics

If scientific language is used without explanation, consider whether it's really necessary or just an attempt to add authority.

Practice Example

Imagine someone says, "Quantum mechanics proves that our thoughts can directly shape reality." This is *the Appeal to Quantum Physics* Fallacy because it uses quantum mechanics, a complex field of science, to make a claim without scientific backing or evidence connecting the two. A more logical approach would be to ask for clear, credible research linking quantum mechanics with human thought, rather than assuming such a connection.

Defending Against the *Appeal to Quantum Physics* Fallacy

When someone uses complex scientific terms to make an unrelated claim, here's how to bring the discussion back to clarity:

- **Ask for a Clear Connection**

  Say, "Can you explain how quantum physics directly relates to this idea?"

- **Encourage Looking for Real Evidence**

  Suggest, "Let's see if there's credible research supporting this connection, rather than relying on mystery."

- **Point Out the Difference Between Science and Buzzwords**

  Gently add, "Sometimes, science terms are used to make things sound impressive, but they may not apply here."

By recognizing the *Appeal to Quantum Physics* Fallacy, you'll focus on clear reasoning rather than being distracted by scientific buzzwords that may not actually apply. But there's another bias to watch out for — the tendency to assume that everyone shares your beliefs or opinions. Let's unpack this next fallacy.

Chapter 74: The False Consensus Effect

The *False Consensus Effect* happens when someone assumes that most people think or feel the same way they do, even if there's little evidence to support it. It's like saying, "Everyone probably agrees that pineapple on pizza is terrible," just because that's what *you* believe.

Why Is the *False Consensus Effect* a Fallacy?

The *False Consensus Effect* is flawed because it leads to biased thinking, where one's own beliefs are seen as universal truths. Just because something feels right or obvious doesn't mean it's a widely held opinion. Rational thinking means recognizing that others may have different experiences, values, or preferences, and that our own views are not automatically universal.

Why Do Humans Use the *False Consensus Effect*?

Humans often fall into this fallacy because it's comforting to assume that our beliefs are shared, making us feel validated and supported. We're also naturally biased toward our own perspectives, making it easy to project our views onto others. Recognizing this tendency helps us stay open to different perspectives and avoid making assumptions about what "everyone" thinks.

How to Avoid the *False Consensus Effect*

1. Acknowledge Diverse Perspectives

Ask yourself, "What are other viewpoints people might have on this issue?"

2. Seek Evidence of Broader Opinion

Rather than assuming, look for actual data or surveys to understand what others believe.

3. Stay Curious About Other Views

Accept that people may have different experiences, which shape their beliefs and preferences.

Practice Example

Imagine someone says, "No one enjoys reading instruction manuals; they're boring for everyone." This is an example of the *False Consensus Effect*, as it assumes a personal dislike is universally shared. A more balanced approach would be to recognize that some people may actually enjoy manuals, especially if they find them useful or interesting.

Defending Against the *False Consensus Effect*

When someone assumes that "everyone" shares their view, here's how to encourage them to consider other perspectives:

- **Ask About the Basis for Their Belief**

  Say, "Do we know if most people feel this way, or could it just be a personal preference?"

- **Encourage Considering Other Viewpoints**

  Suggest, "It's possible that others have different views based on their experiences."

- **Point Out the Value of Diverse Opinions**

  Remind them, "People see things differently, which can be helpful to consider."

By recognizing the *False Consensus Effect*, you'll be open to understanding others' views and avoid the trap of assuming everyone thinks like you. But there's another trap to watch out for — one that attempts to sway opinions by appealing to bitterness or resentment. Let's investigate this next fallacy!

Chapter 75: The Appeal to Spite Fallacy

The *Appeal to Spite* Fallacy happens when someone tries to win an argument by stirring up feelings of bitterness, resentment, or spite toward an opposing idea or person. It's like saying, "Why should we support that charity? Remember how rude they were to us last year?" Here, the argument relies on provoking negative emotions to distract from the actual issue, rather than presenting logical reasons.

Why Is the *Appeal to Spite* a Fallacy?

The *Appeal to Spite* is flawed because emotions like bitterness or resentment don't provide evidence about the validity of an idea. When arguments are based on anger or grudges, they're often trying to bypass logic and encourage a knee-jerk reaction instead. Rational thinking means evaluating the issue itself, not letting past resentments cloud judgment.

Why Do Humans Use the *Appeal to Spite*?

Humans often fall into this fallacy because feelings of spite or resentment can be powerful and persuasive, especially if they have a personal history or a bad experience. It's easy to let negative emotions take over in arguments, but this can lead to decisions based on anger rather than evidence. Recognizing this tendency helps us approach issues fairly, focusing on the facts rather than personal grievances.

How to Avoid the *Appeal to Spite*

1. Separate Emotion from Evidence

Ask yourself, "Am I being swayed by negative emotions, or is there a logical reason to believe this?"

2. Focus on the Current Issue

Avoid bringing up unrelated past grievances when evaluating an argument.

3. Stay Open to Ideas Despite Negative Feelings

Recognize that emotions like bitterness may not be relevant to the truth of the matter.

Practice Example

Imagine someone says, "Don't vote for that candidate—they come from the same school as that rude teacher we had." This is an *Appeal to Spite* Fallacy, as it tries to draw on resentment toward an unrelated person to sway an opinion about the candidate. A more logical approach would focus on the candidate's policies, not personal bitterness.

Defending Against the *Appeal to Spite* Fallacy

When someone uses bitterness or resentment to try to persuade you, here's how to keep the focus on the actual issue:

- **Ask About the Facts**

  Say, "What does this have to do with the actual point we're discussing?"

- **Encourage Setting Aside Personal Grudges**

  Suggest, "Let's evaluate this idea on its own merits, without bringing past issues into it."

- **Remind Them That Spite Doesn't Equal Reason**

  Gently add, "Bitterness doesn't make an argument stronger—it just makes it emotional."

By recognizing the *Appeal to Spite* Fallacy, you'll stay grounded in fair, evidence-based reasoning rather than letting past grudges influence your judgments. But sometimes, people accept ideas as true simply because they feel personally meaningful. Let's explore this next fallacy!

Chapter 76: The Subjective Validation Fallacy

The *Subjective Validation* Fallacy happens when someone accepts an idea or claim as true because it feels personally meaningful or resonates with them, rather than because of solid evidence. It's like saying, "This horoscope feels so accurate—it must be true!" Here, the argument relies on the personal relevance of a statement, rather than any objective support for its truth.

Why Is *Subjective Validation* a Fallacy?

The *Subjective Validation* Fallacy is flawed because personal feelings and beliefs don't determine truth. While it's natural to feel more connected to ideas that reflect our personal experiences, this doesn't make those ideas factually accurate. Rational thinking requires looking beyond personal resonance and seeking external, verifiable evidence to determine whether a claim is valid.

Why Do Humans Use *Subjective Validation*?

Humans often fall into this fallacy because we're naturally drawn to ideas that feel relevant or meaningful to us. Personal experiences shape how we see the world, and we may be inclined to accept information that reflects our own lives, memories, or values. Recognizing this tendency helps us stay objective and avoid mistaking personal relevance for universal truth.

How to Avoid *Subjective Validation*

1. Look for External Evidence

Ask yourself, "Is there objective evidence supporting this idea, or am I relying on how it feels to me?"

2. Distinguish Between Meaningful and True

Recognize that an idea can feel meaningful without necessarily being factual.

3. Seek Broader Perspectives

Consider whether the idea holds up under scrutiny from others who don't share the same personal context.

Practice Example

Imagine someone says, "I read my horoscope today, and it feels so accurate, so astrology must be real." This is an example of Subjective Validation because the person is accepting astrology as true based on how personally meaningful the horoscope feels, rather than on evidence that astrology can predict outcomes. A more logical approach would involve looking for reliable data or studies on astrology's accuracy.

Defending Against the *Subjective Validation* Fallacy

When someone accepts a belief because it feels personally meaningful, here's how to bring the focus back to objective evaluation:

- **Ask About the Evidence**

  Say, "What evidence supports this beyond it feeling personally relevant?"

- **Encourage Separating Feeling from Fact**

  Suggest, "Just because something feels right doesn't mean it's necessarily true."

- **Remind Them That Meaning and Truth Aren't Always the Same**

  Gently add, "It's okay for something to feel meaningful, but truth often requires more than personal validation."

By recognizing the *Subjective Validation* Fallacy, you can stay focused on objective evidence, avoiding the trap of mistaking personal meaning for universal truth. Excellent work — each fallacy you learn sharpens your critical thinking and keeps you rooted in reality! But there's another pitfall to watch out for — seeing connections between events that are actually unrelated. Let's explore this next fallacy!

Chapter 77: The Parataxic Reasoning Fallacy

The *Parataxic Reasoning* Fallacy happens when someone assumes that two unrelated events are causally connected, even if there's no real link between them. This fallacy often leads to superstitious thinking, like saying, "I wore my lucky socks, and we won the game, so the socks caused the win!" Here, the argument is based on an imagined causal link between events that just happened to coincide.

Why Is *Parataxic Reasoning* a Fallacy?

Parataxic Reasoning is flawed because it confuses correlation with causation, leading to conclusions that have no factual basis. Just because two events happen around the same time doesn't mean one caused the other. Rational thinking requires investigating whether a real causal connection exists rather than assuming one based on coincidence or patterns.

Why Do Humans Use *Parataxic Reasoning*?

Humans often fall into this fallacy because we're naturally inclined to look for patterns and meaning in events, even when they're random. This tendency has deep roots in human psychology, helping us make sense of the world, but it can lead to superstitions and incorrect assumptions about cause and effect. Recognizing this fallacy helps us remain skeptical of coincidences and seek logical explanations.

How to Avoid *Parataxic Reasoning*

1. Look for Evidence of a Real Link

Ask yourself, "Is there actual evidence showing that one event caused the other?"

2. Distinguish Between Coincidence and Cause

Remember that just because two things happen together doesn't mean they're connected.

3. Stay Skeptical of Patterns Without Proof

Avoid drawing conclusions based on coincidences or gut feelings about connections.

Practice Example

Imagine someone says, "Every time I carry my lucky coin, I have a good day, so the coin must be bringing me luck." This is an example of *Parataxic Reasoning*, as the person is attributing good days to the coin without any evidence of a real causal link. A more logical approach would be to recognize that positive and negative experiences can happen randomly, with no connection to the coin.

Defending Against the *Parataxic Reasoning* Fallacy

When someone assumes a cause-and-effect relationship based on coincidence, here's how to help them consider other explanations:

- **Ask for Evidence of Causation**

  Say, "What makes you think these events are connected rather than just coincidental?"

- **Encourage Skepticism Toward Coincidences**

  Suggest, "Coincidences happen all the time. It's worth considering whether this is just a pattern."

- **Remind Them That Patterns Don't Always Imply Cause**

  Gently add, "Seeing a pattern doesn't necessarily mean there's a cause behind it."

By recognizing the *Parataxic Reasoning* Fallacy, you'll avoid making assumptions about cause and effect based solely on coincidences or superstitions. But even when a flaw is found in an argument, it doesn't always mean the conclusion is false. Let's discuss this next fallacy.

Chapter 78: The Argument from Fallacy (Fallacist's Fallacy)

The *Argument from Fallacy*, or Fallacist's Fallacy, happens when someone assumes that because an argument contains a fallacy, its conclusion must be false. It's like saying, "You used a slippery slope argument to support recycling, so recycling must not be beneficial." Here, the person assumes that any error in reasoning automatically invalidates the conclusion, even though the conclusion might still be correct for other reasons.

Why Is This a Fallacy?

The *Argument from Fallacy* is flawed because just as a valid argument doesn't always lead to a true conclusion, a flawed argument doesn't necessarily lead to a false one. A conclusion can be true or false regardless of how it's argued. Rational thinking requires evaluating the conclusion independently, rather than assuming it's false just because it was poorly supported.

Why Do Humans Use the *Argument from Fallacy?*

Humans often fall into this fallacy because spotting a flaw in someone's argument can feel like a "gotcha" moment, leading to an assumption that the entire conclusion must be incorrect. This mistake is often a natural reaction to seeing errors in reasoning, but it overlooks the possibility that the conclusion might still be valid on its own merits. Recognizing this fallacy helps them keep an open mind and judge conclusions based on evidence rather than the way they're argued.

How to Avoid the *Argument from Fallacy*

1. Evaluate the Conclusion Separately

Ask yourself, "Does this conclusion stand up on its own, regardless of how it was argued?"

2. Consider Alternative Reasons for the Conclusion

Recognize that even if the argument is flawed, there may still be valid support for the conclusion.

3. Avoid Dismissing Conclusions Based on Argument Quality Alone

Understand that an argument's flaws don't guarantee that the conclusion is wrong.

Practice Example

Imagine someone says, "Eating vegetables is healthy because my grandmother says so." You might spot the *Appeal to Authority Fallacy* here, but this doesn't mean that eating vegetables is unhealthy. The conclusion might still be true, even though the argument used to support it is weak. A more logical approach would be to evaluate whether other evidence supports the health benefits of vegetables.

Defending Against the *Argument from Fallacy*

When someone dismisses a conclusion solely because of a fallacy in the argument, here's how to help them consider the conclusion independently:

- **Ask Them to Evaluate the Conclusion Directly**

  Say, "Even if the argument was flawed, is there still reason to believe the conclusion?"

- **Encourage Separating Argument Quality from Truth**

  Suggest, "Let's look at the conclusion separately to see if it might still be valid."

- **Point Out That Bad Arguments Can Support True Conclusions**

  Gently add, "Just because the argument is flawed doesn't mean the conclusion has to be wrong."

By recognizing the *Argument from Fallacy*, you'll avoid dismissing ideas solely because of flawed arguments and stay open to conclusions that may be correct for other reasons. But sometimes, patterns can emerge that aren't really there, leading to conclusions based on imagined connections, as we discuss in our next fallacy.

Chapter 78: The Apophenia Fallacy

The *Apophenia* Fallacy happens when someone perceives meaningful patterns or connections in random data, even when there's no real relationship between the pieces of information. It's like saying, "Every time I see a black cat, something bad happens, so the cat must be causing bad luck."

Why Is *Apophenia* a Fallacy?

Apophenia is flawed because it assigns meaning or causation to random events, leading to incorrect conclusions. Humans are naturally inclined to search for patterns, but just because events seem connected doesn't mean they are. Rational thinking requires questioning whether patterns are meaningful or if they might just be coincidences in random data.

Why Do Humans Use Apophenia?

Humans often fall into this fallacy because their brains are wired to recognize patterns, which helped early humans make sense of their surroundings. However, this tendency can backfire, leading them to see connections where none exist, fueling superstitions and even conspiracy theories. Recognizing apophenia helps them stay grounded in reality, seeking evidence before concluding that events are connected.

How to Avoid *Apophenia*

1. Question the Connection

Ask yourself, "Is there any evidence that these events are actually related?"

2. Look for Alternative Explanations

Recognize that many patterns are coincidences rather than signs of cause and effect.

3. Seek Evidence, Not Intuition

Avoid relying on gut feelings alone and look for concrete proof of any supposed link.

Practice Example

Imagine someone says, "Every time there's a full moon, I notice more strange things happening around town. The moon must be affecting people's behavior." This is an example of apophenia, as it assumes a meaningful connection based on coincidence. A more logical approach would be to look for studies examining whether the full moon genuinely impacts human behavior, rather than relying on observations alone.

Defending Against the *Apophenia* Fallacy

When someone sees a pattern in random events, here's how to help them consider whether there's truly a connection:

- **Ask for Evidence of a Real Link**

  Say, "Is there any proof showing these events are actually connected?"

- **Encourage Thinking About Coincidences**

  Suggest, "Sometimes things just happen to coincide without being connected."

- **Point Out the Difference Between Pattern and Proof**

  Gently add, "Seeing a pattern doesn't mean there's a real cause behind it. Evidence is what proves a link."

By recognizing the *Apophenia* Fallacy, you'll be cautious of seeing patterns in randomness and avoid jumping to conclusions without solid evidence. Each fallacy you learn helps you think critically and spot the difference between coincidence and causation. But there's another subtle trap to watch for — confusing what's essential with what's enough. Let's explore this next fallacy!

Chapter 80: Confusing Necessary and Sufficient Conditions

The fallacy of *Confusing Necessary and Sufficient Conditions* happens when someone mistakenly assumes that a necessary condition for something is also sufficient to achieve it, or vice versa. It's like saying, "Having flour is enough to make a cake," even though you need more ingredients. Here, the argument is flawed because it doesn't recognize the difference between conditions that are *required* versus those that are *enough*.

Why Is *Confusing Necessary and Sufficient Conditions* a Fallacy?
This fallacy is flawed because it mixes up two types of conditions:
- A **necessary condition** is something that must be true for an outcome to happen, but it's not always enough on its own.
- A **sufficient condition** is enough to produce the outcome but isn't always required.
- Rational thinking requires distinguishing between what's *required* for an outcome and what's *enough* to bring it about.

Why Do Humans Confuse *Necessary and Sufficient Conditions*?
Humans often fall into this fallacy because it can be tricky to tell the difference between what's needed and what's enough. They're used to thinking in simple cause-and-effect terms, which can blur these distinctions. Recognizing this fallacy helps them clarify whether something is merely part of a bigger solution or if it's the whole answer.

How to Avoid *Confusing Necessary and Sufficient Conditions*

1. Ask Whether Each Condition Alone Is Enough
Determine whether a condition just helps or if it's truly sufficient to cause an outcome.

2. Separate Requirements from Solutions
Identify conditions that are merely needed versus those that fully solve the problem.

3. Check for Additional Requirements
Consider what other factors might be necessary to achieve the outcome.

Practice Example
Imagine someone says, "If you want to be successful, you just need to work hard." This confuses a necessary condition with a sufficient one, since hard work alone doesn't guarantee success. A more accurate approach would recognize that while hard work is important, other factors (like resources and opportunities) might also be required.

Defending Against This Fallacy
When someone confuses necessary and sufficient conditions, here's how to help clarify their reasoning:
- **Ask if the Condition Is Enough on Its Own**
  Say, "Is this condition sufficient by itself, or is it just one part of what's needed?"
- **Encourage Identifying All Conditions**
  Suggest, "Let's look at other factors that might also be necessary."
- **Point Out the Difference Between Helping and Solving**
  Gently add, "This may be necessary, but it doesn't mean it's enough on its own."

By recognizing the difference between necessary and sufficient conditions, you'll be able to understand complex issues with clarity and precision. But be careful—sometimes arguments shift meaning by using biased definitions to make a point seem stronger. Let's discuss this next fallacy.

Chapter 81: The Definist Fallacy

The *Definist* Fallacy happens when someone uses biased or loaded definitions to support their argument, rather than providing objective evidence. It's like saying, "Only truly intelligent people like chess," where "intelligent" is defined to imply a preference for chess. Here, the argument is based on a definition crafted to favor the speaker's view, rather than a fair or neutral perspective.

Why Is This a Fallacy?

The *Definist* Fallacy is flawed because it uses biased definitions to make an argument seem true without addressing the issue itself. By incorporating an opinion into the definition, it sidesteps rational debate, making it seem as if only one answer is possible. Sound reasoning requires using fair, objective definitions that don't preemptively support one side of the argument.

Why Do Humans Use the *Definist* Fallacy?

Humans often fall into this fallacy because it can be persuasive to redefine terms in a way that supports their view. By controlling the language, they can sway the conversation to make it harder for others to disagree. Recognizing this tendency helps them spot attempts to redefine terms to suit an agenda, keeping discussions fair and objective.

How to Avoid the *Definist* Fallacy

1. Use Objective, Agreed-Upon Definitions

Ask yourself, "Is this definition neutral, or does it seem crafted to favor one side?"

2. Avoid Definitions That Imply a Conclusion

Make sure your definitions describe rather than imply a judgment.

3. Encourage Consistency in Terminology

Use the same definition consistently, rather than adjusting it to fit your view.

Practice Example

Imagine someone says, "Real patriots support every decision their country makes." This is an example of the *Definist* Fallacy, as it defines "patriot" in a biased way that excludes anyone who might question government decisions. A more objective approach would define patriotism as a love of country, which can include both support and constructive criticism.

Defending Against the *Definist* Fallacy

When someone uses a biased definition to make an argument, here's how to bring the focus back to fair definitions:

- **Ask for a Neutral Definition**

  Say, "Can we use a definition that doesn't imply a conclusion?"

- **Encourage Consistency in Language**

  Suggest, "Let's agree on a definition that allows for different views."

- **Point Out the Impact of Loaded Language**

  Gently add, "Using a biased definition can prevent a fair discussion of the issue."

By recognizing the *Definist* Fallacy, you'll keep discussions fair, ensuring that arguments are based on logic rather than cleverly biased definitions. Excellent work — each fallacy you learn helps you communicate with precision and integrity! But sometimes, arguments compare things that aren't really comparable, leading to flawed conclusions. Let's review this next fallacy!

Chapter 82: The False Analogy Fallacy

The *False Analogy* Fallacy happens when someone makes a weak or misleading comparison between two things that aren't really similar, suggesting they are the same when they're not. It's like saying, "Schools are like factories, so students must follow strict rules like factory workers." Here, the argument relies on a superficial comparison that doesn't hold up under closer examination.

Why Is the *False Analogy* a Fallacy?

The *False Analogy* Fallacy is flawed because it equates two things based on minor similarities while ignoring the important differences between them. Just because two things share certain characteristics doesn't mean they are truly comparable in other respects. Sound reasoning requires using analogies that reflect meaningful similarities, not just convenient ones.

Why Do Humans Use the *False Analogy* Fallacy?

Humans often fall into this fallacy because analogies can simplify complex issues, making arguments easier to understand or seem more relatable. However, oversimplifying with a weak analogy can lead to incorrect conclusions. Recognizing this tendency helps them assess whether an analogy actually clarifies or just confuses the argument.

How to Avoid the *False Analogy* Fallacy

1. Check the Strength of the Comparison

Ask yourself, "Do these things share essential characteristics, or are they only similar on the surface?"

2. Identify Important Differences

Make sure the analogy doesn't ignore critical distinctions between the two things.

3. Focus on Accurate, Relevant Comparisons

Use analogies that help explain without oversimplifying or misleading.

Practice Example

Imagine someone says, "Relying on medication to be healthy is like cheating on a test to get good grades." This is an example of the False Analogy Fallacy, as it compares two things that aren't truly comparable. Medication is a tool for managing health, whereas cheating is a dishonest shortcut. A more accurate analogy would focus on the unique role of medication in healthcare.

Defending Against the *False Analogy* Fallacy

When someone uses a weak or misleading analogy, here's how to help them reconsider the comparison:

- **Ask About the Key Similarities**

  Say, "Are these things similar in ways that matter to this argument?"

- **Encourage Focusing on Relevant Comparisons**

  Suggest, "Let's find an analogy that really fits this situation."

- **Point Out the Limits of the Analogy**

  Gently add, "Analogies can help, but they need to capture the real essence of the situation."

By recognizing the *False Analogy* Fallacy, you'll focus on using accurate comparisons that truly clarify ideas, avoiding conclusions based on misleading analogies. But there's another trap to watch for — judging past actions by today's standards. Let's explore this next fallacy!

Chapter 83: The Anachronistic Fallacy

The *Anachronistic* Fallacy happens when someone evaluates historical figures, actions, or events by today's standards, rather than the norms or values of their own time. It's like saying, "This ancient ruler was unethical for not supporting democracy," even though democracy wasn't a concept in that society. Here, the argument imposes modern beliefs on a different historical context, leading to unfair or misleading judgments.

Why Is This a Fallacy?

The *Anachronistic* Fallacy is flawed because it ignores historical context, which is essential to understanding people and actions from the past. Just because we have different standards today doesn't mean those standards applied back then. Rational thinking requires evaluating people and events within their own context to gain a fair and accurate understanding.

Why Do Humans Use the *Anachronistic* Fallacy?

Humans often fall into this fallacy because it's easier to interpret the past using familiar, modern values. However, this can lead to oversimplified views of history and unfair criticism of past societies. Recognizing this tendency helps them understand the complexities of historical contexts and avoid projecting their beliefs backward.

How to Avoid the *Anachronistic* Fallacy

1. Research the Historical Context

Ask yourself, "What were the common beliefs, values, or norms during this time?"

2. Separate Modern Views from Historical Realities

Avoid assuming that past societies shared our current understanding of ethics or social structures.

3. Evaluate People by the Standards of Their Time

Consider whether an action was typical or acceptable in its historical setting, even if it seems wrong today.

Practice Example

Imagine someone says, "This historical figure was wrong for not supporting equal rights." While it's true that equal rights are important, the *Anachronistic* Fallacy assumes that this value was widely held in the past, which may not be accurate. A more balanced approach would look at whether this figure's actions were unusual or typical for their time.

Defending Against the *Anachronistic* Fallacy

When someone uses modern values to criticize the past, here's how to bring the focus back to historical context:

- **Ask About the Standards of the Time**

  Say, "What were the norms or beliefs in this society during that period?"

- **Encourage a Contextual Approach**

  Suggest, "Let's try to understand their actions based on the time they lived in."

- **Point Out the Importance of Context**

  Gently add, "Applying today's values to history can lead to misunderstandings."

By recognizing the *Anachronistic* Fallacy, you'll understand people and events within their historical settings, leading to a more accurate view of history. But sometimes, arguments shift subtly in response to challenges, making them hard to pin down. Let's discuss this next fallacy.

Chapter 84: The Hedging Fallacy

The *Hedging* Fallacy happens when someone changes or subtly modifies their argument in response to objections without actually addressing those objections. It's like saying, "Exercise is the best way to get healthy," then switching to, "Well, I meant exercise is *one* of the best ways," when challenged. Here, the argument shifts to avoid criticism instead of confronting it directly.

Why Is *Hedging* a Fallacy?

The *Hedging* Fallacy is flawed because it doesn't engage with counterarguments in a meaningful way. By subtly changing the argument's meaning, the speaker avoids answering objections, making it seem as if they've defended their point when they haven't. Rational thinking requires addressing objections directly rather than evading them by moving the goalposts.

Why Do Humans Use the *Hedging* Fallacy?

Humans often fall into this fallacy because they want to maintain their argument's validity while avoiding direct challenges. By slightly modifying the argument, it seems as if they're still correct without having to fully defend their point. Recognizing this tendency helps them hold ourselves and others accountable to the original statements made in discussions.

How to Avoid the *Hedging* Fallacy

1. Stick to Your Original Point

Ask yourself, "Am I changing my argument to avoid the challenge, or addressing it directly?"

2. Engage with Objections Honestly

Consider whether you can strengthen your argument without shifting its meaning.

3. Clarify or Correct If Needed

If you do need to modify your stance, be transparent about it rather than subtly changing definitions.

Practice Example

Imagine someone says, "This diet is guaranteed to work," but then, when faced with counterexamples, they say, "Well, it's one of the best diets for most people." This is an example of the Hedging Fallacy, as the speaker has adjusted their claim without addressing the original promise. A more logical approach would either defend or revise the original statement clearly.

Defending Against the *Hedging* Fallacy

When someone modifies their argument to dodge criticism, here's how to bring them back to their original point:

- **Ask for Consistency**

  Say, "Can we stick with the original statement and discuss any concerns directly?"

- **Encourage Addressing the Objection**

  Suggest, "It's best to tackle the objection without changing the argument."

- **Point Out the Change in the Argument**

  Gently add, "It seems the argument has shifted—can we clarify what we're discussing?"

By recognizing the *Hedging* Fallacy, you can engage in clearer, more honest discussions that don't shift to avoid objections. But be cautious—sometimes, complex issues are oversimplified by blaming a single cause. Let's dive into this next fallacy!

Chapter 85: The Single Cause Fallacy

The *Single Cause* Fallacy happens when someone attributes an outcome to only one factor when, in reality, multiple factors are involved. It's like saying, "The company failed solely because of bad marketing," even though there may have been other issues, such as poor management or market competition. Here, the argument overlooks the complexity of most situations, leading to an oversimplified view.

Why Is *Single Cause* a Fallacy?

The *Single Cause* Fallacy is flawed because it ignores other contributing factors that might be equally or more significant. Many outcomes are the result of complex interactions between various causes, and reducing them to just one can lead to misunderstandings or unfair blame. Rational thinking requires considering all possible factors to understand the full picture.

Why Do Humans Use the *Single Cause* Fallacy?

Humans often fall into this fallacy because focusing on one factor makes complex situations easier to explain. However, this simplification can lead to biased judgments or incomplete understanding. Recognizing this tendency helps them appreciate the interconnected nature of causes and make more informed assessments.

How to Avoid the *Single Cause* Fallacy

1. Consider Multiple Factors

Ask yourself, "What other factors might have contributed to this outcome?"

2. Avoid Jumping to Simple Explanations

Recognize that complex situations rarely have just one cause.

3. Examine the Evidence for Each Factor

Look at how different causes might interact, rather than isolating one as the only explanation.

Practice Example

Imagine someone says, "The school's low test scores are only due to poor teaching." This is an example of the Single Cause Fallacy, as it overlooks other potential factors, like socioeconomic issues, resources, or student support. A more balanced approach would consider how multiple factors might influence test scores.

Defending Against the *Single Cause* Fallacy

When someone attributes an outcome to a single factor, here's how to help them consider other causes:

- **Ask About Other Possible Influences**

  Say, "Could there be other factors involved in this outcome?"

- **Encourage a Broader Perspective**

  Suggest, "Let's look at the situation as a whole, considering all potential causes."

- **Point Out the Complexity of Situations**

  Gently add, "Most outcomes result from multiple factors, not just one."

By recognizing the *Single Cause* Fallacy, you'll stay aware of the complexity of causes and avoid oversimplifying outcomes. But sometimes, arguments lean on an idealized view of the past, assuming it was better simply because it's gone. Let's have a look at this next fallacy!

Chapter 86: The Argument from Nostalgia Fallacy

The *Argument from Nostalgia* Fallacy happens when someone argues that something is better simply because it's from the past. It's like saying, "Music from the '80s was the best because everything was better back then." Here, the argument relies on an idealized view of the past rather than on evidence of actual quality or improvement.

Why Is the *Argument from Nostalgia* a Fallacy?

The *Argument from Nostalgia* is flawed because it assumes that something from the past is inherently superior, which isn't always true. Just because something is old doesn't mean it's better, and time alone doesn't necessarily improve quality. Rational thinking requires looking at evidence of value or effectiveness, regardless of when something was made.

Why Do Humans Use the *Argument from Nostalgia*?

Humans often fall into this fallacy because the past can feel comforting, and memories may be idealized over time. Nostalgia also tends to emphasize positive memories while downplaying negative ones, creating a biased view of "the good old days." Recognizing this tendency helps them assess ideas or practices based on their actual value, rather than on fond memories alone.

How to Avoid the Argument from *Nostalgia*

1. Focus on Evidence of Value

Ask yourself, "Is this thing truly better, or do I just have fond memories of it?"

2. Separate Sentiment from Reality

Recognize that positive feelings about the past don't mean everything was actually better.

3. Evaluate Ideas on Their Own Merits

Look for current data or analysis rather than relying on tradition or familiarity alone.

Practice Example

Imagine someone says, "Technology has made everything worse. Life was simpler and better before the internet." This is an example of the Argument from Nostalgia, as it ignores the many positive aspects of modern technology. A more logical approach would weigh both the pros and cons of technological advances, rather than idealizing the past.

Defending Against the *Argument from Nostalgia* Fallacy

When someone argues that something was better just because it's from the past, here's how to bring the discussion back to the present:

- **Ask for Evidence of Improvement**

  Say, "Is there any evidence that the past version was actually better?"

- **Encourage Balancing Pros and Cons**

  Suggest, "Let's look at both the positives and negatives of the past and present."

- **Point Out That Time Alone Doesn't Equal Quality**

  Gently add, "Just because something's older doesn't mean it's better."

By recognizing the *Argument from Nostalgia* Fallacy, you'll avoid letting fond memories cloud your judgment and stay focused on evaluating ideas fairly. But beware — some arguments try to undermine trust before they even begin. Let's explore this next fallacy!

Chapter 87: Poisoning the Well

The *Poisoning the Well* Fallacy happens when someone presents negative information about a person or idea in advance to undermine their credibility before they even speak. It's like saying, "Don't listen to him—he always lies," right before he shares his opinion. Here, the argument relies on creating a bias against the person or position to sway others without addressing the actual content of their argument.

Why Is *Poisoning the Well* a Fallacy?

Poisoning the Well is flawed because it attempts to discredit someone without addressing their argument's merits. By presenting adverse information before someone speaks, it encourages people to dismiss them based on unrelated personal factors rather than on the validity of what they say. Rational thinking requires focusing on arguments themselves, not biased preconceptions set up to make us reject a speaker unfairly.

Why Do Humans Use *Poisoning the Well*?

Humans often use this fallacy because it's an easy way to sway opinions without having to engage with the other side's actual argument. By creating suspicion or bias before the person even speaks, the fallacy can prevent people from considering their points thoughtfully. Recognizing this tactic helps them approach ideas with fairness, avoiding unnecessary biases.

How to Avoid Poisoning the Well

1. Evaluate Arguments on Their Own

Ask yourself, "Am I focusing on the person or the actual argument?"

2. Avoid Relying on Preconceptions

Try to separate any prior information about a person from the validity of what they're currently saying.

3. Consider Each Statement Independently

Judge statements based on their content rather than on outside factors or past behaviors.

Practice Example

Imagine someone says, "Don't trust her opinion on environmental issues—she drives a big SUV." This is an example of Poisoning the Well, as it preemptively biases listeners against her view without considering the actual content of her opinion. A more fair approach would focus on the arguments she makes, regardless of her personal choices.

Defending Against the *Poisoning the Well* Fallacy

When someone tries to bias others by presenting adverse information beforehand, here's how to bring the focus back to the argument:

- **Ask About the Relevance of the Information**

  Say, "Is this information related to the point being discussed, or is it just about the person?"

- **Encourage Evaluating Arguments Directly**

  Suggest, "Let's consider what they're actually saying instead of focusing on this unrelated information."

- **Point Out the Need for Fairness**

  Gently add, "It's best to hear them out without any preconceptions that might cloud our judgment."

By recognizing *Poisoning the Well*, you'll approach discussions with a fair and open mind, judging ideas on their own merits. But sometimes, arguments use vague or slippery language to sound stronger than they are. Let's look at this this next fallacy.

Chapter 88: The Weasel Words Fallacy

The *Weasel Words* Fallacy happens when someone uses vague, non-committal language to make an argument sound stronger than it really is. It's like saying, "Many experts believe this diet could be the best option," without specifying who the experts are or how strong their belief is. Here, the argument relies on language that sounds impressive but avoids concrete details.

Why Are *Weasel Words* a Fallacy?

Weasel Words are a fallacy because they make a claim seem more convincing by adding ambiguity, making it difficult to assess the argument's real strength. By using terms that are open to interpretation, like "some say" or "it's widely believed," speakers can imply more support than actually exists. Rational thinking requires precise language that allows others to understand and evaluate the true claim being made.

Why Do Humans Use *Weasel Words*?

Humans often use Weasel Words to make arguments sound more credible without providing real evidence. Vague language allows speakers to dodge accountability for their claims, creating a false impression of strength or authority. Recognizing this tendency helps them look more closely at the actual support behind statements, rather than being swayed by ambiguous phrasing.

How to Avoid *Weasel Words*

1. Use Clear, Specific Language

Ask yourself, "Am I using language that directly states my claim, or am I being vague?"

2. Provide Sources and Examples

Back up claims with concrete information to avoid leaving them open to interpretation.

3. Avoid Generalized Statements Without Evidence

Refrain from using terms like "some say" or "many believe" without specifics to back them up.

Practice Example

Imagine someone says, "This product is known to provide excellent results." This is an example of the Weasel Words Fallacy because it uses vague terms like "known" and "excellent" without specifying who has found it effective or what those results are. A clearer statement would include specific studies, user reviews, or data that support the claim.

Defending Against the *Weasel Words* Fallacy

When someone uses vague language to make their point seem stronger, here's how to encourage clarity:

- **Ask for Specifics**

  Say, "Who are the experts you mentioned? Could you provide specific examples?"

- **Encourage Definite Language**

  Suggest, "It would help if we had more concrete information about who believes this and why."

- **Point Out the Ambiguity**

  Gently add, "It's hard to evaluate this claim without clearer details about who and what is being referenced."

By recognizing *Weasel Words*, you'll seek out clear, specific language that makes arguments more honest and straightforward. But be careful — sometimes, arguments dismiss efforts as pointless if they can't solve a problem entirely. Let's explore this next fallacy!

Chapter 89: The Appeal to Futility Fallacy

The *Appeal to Futility* Fallacy happens when someone argues that an effort is pointless because it won't completely solve a problem or achieve a perfect outcome. It's like saying, "Recycling won't save the planet, so there's no use in doing it." Here, the argument suggests that because an action can't achieve 100% success, it's not worth attempting at all.

Why Is the *Appeal to Futility* a Fallacy?

The *Appeal to Futility* is flawed because progress and partial solutions can still make meaningful differences, even if they don't completely solve a problem. Just because an effort isn't perfect doesn't mean it's worthless. Rational thinking requires recognizing that small steps can contribute positively, even if they're not total solutions.

Why Do Humans Use the *Appeal to Futility*?

Humans often fall into this fallacy because it's easier to dismiss challenges than to make ongoing efforts. If perfection is the only acceptable outcome, anything less can feel insufficient, leading people to give up prematurely. Recognizing this tendency helps them stay motivated to make incremental improvements, even when they don't solve everything.

How to Avoid the *Appeal to Futility* Fallacy

1. Focus on Positive Impacts, Even if Partial

Ask yourself, "Does this effort make some improvement, even if it's not perfect?"

2. Recognize the Value of Small Contributions

Understand that many small steps can collectively lead to big changes over time.

3. Avoid All-or-Nothing Thinking

Embrace the idea that imperfect solutions can still help.

Practice Example

Imagine someone says, "Why bother voting? One vote won't change the outcome." This is an example of the *Appeal to Futility* Fallacy, as it ignores the cumulative impact of many individual votes. A more logical approach would recognize that each vote contributes to the overall outcome, even if one vote alone doesn't decide it.

Defending Against the *Appeal to Futility* Fallacy

When someone argues that an effort is pointless because it won't completely solve a problem, here's how to bring the focus back to incremental progress:

- **Ask About Partial Benefits**

  Say, "Even if it doesn't solve everything, does it make a positive impact?"

- **Encourage Focusing on Collective Contributions**

  Suggest, "Many small actions add up to make a difference."

- **Point Out the Value of Imperfect Solutions**

  Gently add, "An imperfect solution is better than doing nothing."

By recognizing the *Appeal to Futility* Fallacy, you'll stay motivated to make positive contributions, even if they're not perfect solutions. Do watch out — sometimes, arguments rely on cleverly worded phrases to influence opinions subtly. Let's explore this next fallacy!

Chapter 90: The Phrasing Fallacy

The *Phrasing* Fallacy occurs when someone frames a question or statement in a way that leads to a biased answer or influences how people think about an issue. It's like asking, "Why don't you care about helping others?" rather than, "Do you think helping others is important?" Here, the question or argument is phrased to subtly push people toward a specific answer.

Why Is *Phrasing* a Fallacy?

The *Phrasing* Fallacy is flawed because it frames questions or arguments in a way that limits honest responses. By using biased or leading language, it can make certain answers seem "better" or more acceptable, steering people toward one side. Rational thinking requires questions that allow open, unbiased responses so people can express their views freely.

Why Do Humans Use the *Phrasing* Fallacy?

Humans often use this fallacy because it subtly influences opinions without appearing too direct, making it a powerful way to shape responses. Leading questions can be persuasive by framing certain answers as preferable, even if this isn't obvious at first. Recognizing this tendency helps them remain alert to language that steers us toward certain answers.

How to Avoid the *Phrasing* Fallacy

1. Use Neutral Language

Ask yourself, "Am I phrasing this in a way that allows for open responses?"

2. Avoid Leading Questions

Refrain from framing questions in a way that implies one answer is better or expected.

3. Check for Bias in Language

Be mindful of words or phrases that might push respondents in a certain direction.

Practice Example

Imagine someone says, "Don't you think we should protect traditional values?" This is an example of the Phrasing Fallacy because it suggests that protecting "traditional values" is a positive thing without leaving room for alternative views. A more neutral question would ask, "What are your views on traditional values?"

Defending Against the *Phrasing* Fallacy

When someone uses leading language to steer responses, here's how to encourage neutrality:

- **Ask for Rephrasing**

  Say, "Could you rephrase that in a more neutral way?"

- **Encourage Open-Ended Questions**

  Suggest, "Let's frame the question in a way that doesn't imply one answer is better."

- **Point Out the Leading Language**

  Gently add, "It seems this question is framed to favor a certain answer—let's keep it open-ended."

By recognizing the *Phrasing* Fallacy, you'll be able to spot and avoid biased language that can influence responses, helping to foster more honest, balanced conversations. Excellent work — each fallacy you learn helps you think critically about how language shapes arguments! But sometimes, arguments rely on the lack of evidence as proof, rather than what's actually known. Let's discuss this next fallacy.

Chapter 91: The Argument from Absence Fallacy

The *Argument from Absence* Fallacy occurs when someone claims something must be true simply because there's no evidence proving it false. It's like saying, "We haven't found proof that unicorns don't exist, so they must be real." Here, the argument assumes that a lack of evidence against something is enough to prove it true.

Why Is the *Argument from Absence* a Fallacy?

The *Argument from Absence* is flawed because a lack of evidence isn't the same as proof. Just because something hasn't been disproven doesn't mean it's true; it simply means we don't have enough information. Rational thinking requires evidence that directly supports a claim, rather than relying on the absence of contrary evidence.

Why Do Humans Use the *Argument from Absence*?

Humans often fall into this fallacy because it's tempting to fill gaps in knowledge with assumptions that fit their beliefs. This fallacy gives a false sense of certainty, making it easier to believe something without needing evidence. Recognizing this tendency helps them remain open to new information and avoid premature conclusions.

How to Avoid the *Argument from Absence* Fallacy

1. Seek Positive Evidence

Ask yourself, "Is there actual evidence supporting this claim, or just a lack of evidence against it?"

2. Accept Uncertainty

Understand that "we don't know" is a valid answer when there's no supporting evidence.

3. Avoid Jumping to Conclusions

Be willing to withhold judgment until you have concrete information.

Practice Example

Imagine someone says, "No one has proven that alien life doesn't exist, so there must be aliens." This is an example of the *Argument from Absence* Fallacy, as it relies on a lack of disproof as proof. A more logical approach would be to recognize that the existence of aliens is still unknown until there's actual evidence.

Defending Against the *Argument from Absence* Fallacy

When someone assumes something is true just because it hasn't been disproven, here's how to bring the focus back to the need for positive evidence:

- **Ask for Supporting Evidence**

  Say, "Is there any actual evidence supporting this claim?"

- **Encourage Patience with Uncertainty**

  Suggest, "It's okay to wait for more information before reaching a conclusion."

- **Point Out the Difference Between Absence and Proof**

  Gently add, "Just because we don't have disproof doesn't mean we have proof."

By recognizing the *Argument from Absence* Fallacy, you'll remain open to new information and avoid drawing conclusions without supporting evidence. But sometimes, beliefs themselves can shape outcomes, creating a cycle that seems to confirm the initial assumption. Let's dive into this next fallacy!

Chapter 92: The Self-Fulfilling Prophecy Fallacy

The *Self-Fulfilling Prophecy* Fallacy happens when a belief or expectation influences behavior in a way that makes the belief come true. It's like saying, "I'll fail this test," and then, because you expect to fail, you don't study as hard and end up failing. Here, the belief shapes actions that lead to the expected outcome, even if it wouldn't have happened otherwise.

Why Is the *Self-Fulfilling Prophecy* a Fallacy?

The *Self-Fulfilling Prophecy* is flawed because it attributes an outcome to an external truth rather than to one's own behavior. When beliefs influence actions, they can create situations that make the belief seem correct, even if it started as false. Rational thinking requires recognizing when our attitudes or actions are shaping outcomes rather than assuming the outcome was inevitable.

Why Do Humans Use the *Self-Fulfilling* Prophecy?

Humans often fall into this fallacy because expectations can strongly influence emotions and actions. Negative beliefs can lead to discouraged behavior, while positive expectations can boost confidence and effort. Recognizing this tendency helps them see how our mindset can shape reality, encouraging a balanced approach to beliefs and expectations.

How to Avoid the *Self-Fulfilling Prophecy* Fallacy

1. Identify Beliefs That Influence Actions

Ask yourself, "Is my expectation affecting how I'm behaving in this situation?"

2. Separate Beliefs from Inevitable Outcomes

Consider whether the outcome is truly certain or if your actions might influence it.

3. Challenge Negative or Overconfident Predictions

Avoid letting negative expectations limit your effort or overly positive ones lead to complacency.

Practice Example

Imagine someone says, "No one will like my presentation, so I won't put much effort into it." This is an example of a *Self-Fulfilling Prophecy*, as the lack of effort may lead to a poor presentation, confirming the belief. A more constructive approach would be to prepare well regardless of expectations, creating the best chance for a positive outcome.

Defending Against the *Self-Fulfilling Prophecy* Fallacy

When someone's negative expectations are shaping their actions, here's how to help them focus on the possibility of a different outcome:

- **Encourage Positive Action**

  Say, "If you put in effort, you might surprise yourself with the outcome."

- **Remind Them That Outcomes Aren't Set**

  Suggest, "The outcome isn't certain—what you do can make a difference."

- **Point Out That Beliefs Affect Behavior**

  Gently add, "Our expectations can shape how we act, which can change the result."

By recognizing the *Self-Fulfilling Prophecy* Fallacy, you'll understand the power of beliefs to shape behavior and outcomes, allowing for greater control over the results you experience. But be careful — sometimes, arguments reject valid claims simply because they don't have precise boundaries. Let's explore this next fallacy!

Chapter 93: The Continuum Fallacy

The *Continuum* Fallacy, also known as the "Fallacy of the Beard," happens when someone rejects a claim because it lacks precise boundaries, even though clear distinctions might not be possible. It's like saying, "There's no exact point at which a person becomes old, so there's no such thing as 'old age.'" Here, the argument implies that unless a concept is precisely defined, it can't be valid.

Why Is the *Continuum* a Fallacy?

The *Continuum* Fallacy is flawed because not all valid concepts have strict boundaries. Many ideas exist on a spectrum, and just because we can't pinpoint an exact dividing line doesn't mean the concept is meaningless. Rational thinking requires acknowledging that some things exist on a continuum and accepting reasonable generalizations when precise definitions aren't possible.

Why Do Humans Use the *Continuum* Fallacy?

Humans often fall into this fallacy because ambiguity can be uncomfortable, leading them to reject concepts that aren't neatly defined. This fallacy can also be used to avoid engaging with valid points by focusing on minor ambiguities. Recognizing this tendency helps them accept that some ideas don't require absolute definitions to be meaningful.

How to Avoid the *Continuum* Fallacy

1. Accept That Some Ideas Exist on a Spectrum

Ask yourself, "Is this concept meaningful even without a clear dividing line?"

2. Focus on General Principles Rather Than Absolute Definitions

Understand that reasonable generalizations can be valid even if boundaries are fuzzy.

3. Recognize That Continuums Don't Erase Meaning

Avoid dismissing ideas just because they don't have precise cutoffs.

Practice Example

Imagine someone says, "There's no clear point at which a hill becomes a mountain, so we can't classify anything as a mountain." This is an example of the *Continuum* Fallacy, as it dismisses the concept of "mountain" due to lack of a precise boundary. A more logical approach would accept that while the dividing line may be unclear, "mountain" is still a meaningful category.

Defending Against the *Continuum* Fallacy

When someone dismisses an idea because it lacks clear boundaries, here's how to bring the focus back to its general validity:

- **Point Out the Spectrum of Possibility**

  Say, "Some ideas don't need precise boundaries to be meaningful."

- **Encourage Focusing on Practical Meaning**

  Suggest, "Let's look at the general concept rather than focusing on exact cutoffs."

- **Remind Them That Some Terms Are Useful Without Clear Lines**

  Gently add, "Just because there's no strict line doesn't mean the concept is meaningless."

By recognizing the *Continuum* Fallacy, you'll be able to engage meaningfully with concepts that exist on a spectrum, without dismissing them due to lack of clear boundaries. But sometimes, arguments make the mistake of assuming that what's most visible represents the entire truth. Let's look at this next fallacy.

Chapter 94: The Spotlight Fallacy

The *Spotlight* Fallacy occurs when someone assumes that cases in the public eye represent the entirety of a situation or group. It's like saying, "All teens are troublemakers," based on news stories about a few teens behaving badly. Here, the argument relies on high-profile examples that don't reflect the bigger picture, leading to unfair generalizations.

Why Is This a Fallacy?

The *Spotlight* Fallacy is flawed because it assumes that visible cases are representative of all cases, even though these examples are often exaggerated or selected for their sensationalism. Rational thinking requires distinguishing between high-profile cases and statistical reality, rather than assuming that what's visible is the norm.

Why Do Humans Use the *Spotlight* Fallacy?

Humans often fall into this fallacy because they are naturally influenced by what they see and hear most often, especially in the media. Dramatic or extreme examples tend to attract attention, but they can distort our understanding of the bigger picture. Recognizing this tendency helps them consider broader data and avoid generalizing based on isolated cases.

How to Avoid the *Spotlight* Fallacy

1. Look at the Full Picture, Not Just Visible Cases

Ask yourself, "Does this example reflect the average situation, or is it an outlier?"

2. Use Statistics to Check Representativeness

Find data to determine if what you're seeing is common or unusual.

3. Avoid Relying on High-Profile Examples Alone

Remember that visibility doesn't always equal prevalence.

Practice Example

Imagine someone says, "Social media is full of negativity because I see so much of it online." This is an example of the *Spotlight* Fallacy, as it assumes that all of social media is negative based on visible content, which may be more sensational than the norm. A more balanced approach would consider that positive interactions may be less visible but still prevalent.

Defending Against the *Spotlight* Fallacy

When someone assumes that visible cases represent an entire situation, here's how to encourage a more balanced perspective:

- **Ask for Broader Data**

  Say, "Is there data showing whether this is typical or just high-profile?"

- **Encourage Looking Beyond the Visible Examples**

  Suggest, "Let's consider the overall situation, not just what's publicized."

- **Point Out That High-Profile Cases Can Be Misleading**

  Gently add, "Sometimes what we see most isn't what's actually most common."

By recognizing the *Spotlight* Fallacy, you'll be able to look beyond highly visible cases and make judgments based on a fuller picture. But beware — some arguments seem relevant at first but actually miss the main point entirely. Let's explore this next fallacy!

Chapter 95: The Ignoratio Elenchi Fallacy (Irrelevant Conclusion)

The *Ignoratio Elenchi* Fallacy, or *Irrelevant Conclusion* Fallacy, happens when someone makes an argument that may be valid on its own but doesn't address the issue at hand. It's like saying, "We should focus on building more parks," in response to a question about improving local traffic. Here, the argument might be well-intentioned and even reasonable, but it distracts from the actual topic.

Why Is *Ignoratio Elenchi* a Fallacy?

The *Ignoratio Elenchi* Fallacy is flawed because it avoids answering the main point and redirects attention to a separate issue. While the argument may sound logical, it doesn't engage with the original question or concern. Rational thinking requires staying focused on the topic at hand rather than getting sidetracked by unrelated arguments.

Why Do Humans Use the *Ignoratio Elenchi* Fallacy?

Humans often fall into this fallacy because it's easy to bring up points that seem related but don't actually address the specific question. Sometimes, it's a tactic to avoid discussing uncomfortable or challenging topics. Recognizing this tendency helps us focus on answering questions directly and identifying when arguments stray from the issue.

How to Avoid the *Ignoratio Elenchi* Fallacy

1. Stay Focused on the Central Question

Ask yourself, "Does my argument directly address the issue at hand?"

2. Recognize When a Point Is Related but Not Relevant

Avoid using arguments that might be valid in general but don't answer the specific question.

3. Address the Topic Before Introducing Other Points

Stick to the main issue first, then add supporting points if relevant.

Practice Example

Imagine someone says, "We need more affordable housing," and the response is, "But what about the quality of our parks?" This is an example of the *Ignoratio Elenchi* Fallacy, as it diverts attention from the original issue of housing affordability. A more direct response would address the need for affordable housing solutions.

Defending Against the *Ignoratio Elenchi* Fallacy

When someone introduces an unrelated argument, here's how to bring the focus back to the main point:

- **Ask for a Direct Response to the Question**

  Say, "Could we address the main issue before discussing other points?"

- **Encourage Staying on Topic**

  Suggest, "Let's focus on the main question so we can address it fully."

- **Point Out the Irrelevance**

  Gently add, "That's an interesting point, but it doesn't really answer the question we're discussing."

By recognizing the *Ignoratio Elenchi* Fallacy, you'll be able to keep discussions focused and avoid getting sidetracked by irrelevant points. Great job — each fallacy you learn helps you stay clear and concise in your reasoning! But sometimes, arguments make the mistake of applying group data to individuals, leading to faulty conclusions. Let's explore this next fallacy.

Chapter 96: The Ecological Fallacy

The *Ecological* Fallacy happens when someone assumes that characteristics of a group apply to each individual within that group. It's like saying, "The average family size in this town is 4.2, so every family must have around four people." Here, the argument incorrectly generalizes from group-level data to individuals, which can lead to misleading or unfair conclusions.

Why Is the *Ecological* Fallacy a Fallacy?

The *Ecological* Fallacy is flawed because group data can't accurately describe every individual within the group. Patterns or averages for a population don't always reflect each person's situation. Rational thinking requires distinguishing between group-level information and individual characteristics, as general patterns can differ greatly from individual cases.

Why Do Humans Use the *Ecological* Fallacy?

Humans often fall into this fallacy because general data is readily available and can seem easier to apply to individuals. However, individual differences often defy group trends, and assuming that everyone fits the average can lead to stereotypes or oversimplified conclusions. Recognizing this tendency helps them treat people as individuals rather than assuming they match general statistics.

How to Avoid the *Ecological* Fallacy

1. Distinguish Between Group Data and Individual Traits

Ask yourself, "Does this information apply to the whole group, or is it also accurate for individuals?"

2. Avoid Making Assumptions Based on Averages

Recognize that individual characteristics can vary widely, even within a group average.

3. Consider the Range of Differences Within Groups

Use group data carefully and remember that it doesn't capture everyone's situation.

Practice Example

Imagine someone says, "The average person in this neighborhood makes $60,000 a year, so everyone here is probably well-off." This is an example of the *Ecological* Fallacy, as it assumes the average applies to each individual, when in reality, income levels may vary widely. A more accurate approach would recognize that averages don't describe each person's financial situation.

Defending Against the *Ecological* Fallacy

When someone assumes that group data applies to individuals, here's how to bring the focus back to individual variation:

- **Ask About Individual Differences**

  Say, "Could individuals within this group vary significantly from the average?"

- **Encourage Treating Individuals as Unique**

  Suggest, "Let's consider each person's situation rather than assuming they match the group data."

- **Point Out That Group Averages Don't Capture Everyone**

  Gently add, "The average is useful, but it doesn't describe everyone in the group."

By recognizing the *Ecological* Fallacy, you'll be able to avoid overgeneralizing from group data to individuals and treat people as unique rather than as mere statistics. But sometimes, repetition itself is used to make an idea seem true, as if saying it over and over adds weight. Let's review this next fallacy.

Chapter 97: The Argument from Repetition (Ad Nauseam) Fallacy

This restaurant is the best. Trust me!

You've said that three times, but what's so great about it?

The *Argument from Repetition*, also known as the *Ad Nauseam* Fallacy, happens when someone repeats an argument or statement multiple times, assuming that sheer repetition will make it more believable or true. It's like saying, "We should go to this restaurant because it's the best," over and over again, without offering any new reasons. Here, the argument relies on repetition rather than additional evidence or logic.

Why Is the *Argument from Repetition* a Fallacy?

The *Argument from Repetition* is flawed because repeating a statement doesn't strengthen its truth or validity. Simply restating a claim doesn't provide more support for it — it only creates an illusion of credibility. Rational thinking requires evaluating arguments based on evidence and reasoning, not the number of times they're repeated.

Why Do Humans Use the *Argument from Repetition*?

Humans often fall into this fallacy because repetition can make a statement feel more familiar and, therefore, more credible. Hearing something multiple times can create the illusion of truth, even if the claim hasn't actually been supported. Recognizing this tendency helps them focus on the actual strength of arguments rather than how often they're repeated.

How to Avoid the *Argument from Repetition* Fallacy

1. Look for New Reasons, Not Just Repetitions

Ask yourself, "Is this argument adding anything new, or is it just repeating the same point?"

2. Evaluate the Argument Based on Evidence

Focus on the quality of reasons presented, not the frequency of their repetition.

3. Be Wary of Statements That Are Repeated Without Support

Recognize that frequent repetition alone doesn't make a claim true.

Practice Example

Imagine someone says, "This politician is the most honest—trust me!" and repeats this claim in every conversation without providing specific examples. This is an example of the *Argument from Repetition*, as it relies on repetition rather than proof. A more logical approach would include examples or evidence to support the claim of honesty.

Defending Against the *Argument from Repetition* Fallacy

When someone repeats an argument without adding substance, here's how to bring the focus back to quality over quantity:

- **Ask for New Reasons or Examples**

  Say, "Can you provide specific examples to support this claim?"

- **Encourage Evaluating Evidence Over Frequency**

  Suggest, "Let's focus on actual evidence rather than repeating the statement."

- **Point Out the Difference Between Repetition and Proof**

  Gently add, "Saying it many times doesn't make it true—we need solid support."

By recognizing the *Argument from Repetition* Fallacy, you'll avoid being swayed by repeated statements alone, focusing instead on arguments backed by solid reasoning. But be careful — sometimes, arguments stretch a term or concept too broadly, leading to misleading conclusions. Let's dive into this next fallacy!

Chapter 98: The Overextension Fallacy

The *Overextension* Fallacy happens when someone applies a term or concept too broadly, leading to generalizations that go beyond the term's original meaning. It's like saying, "Every person with a smartphone is a tech expert." Here, the argument stretches a concept (being a "tech expert") beyond its reasonable boundaries, leading to an inaccurate generalization.

Why Is *Overextension* a Fallacy?

The *Overextension* Fallacy is flawed because it takes a concept beyond its actual scope, creating misleading generalizations. Just because a term applies in one specific case doesn't mean it applies to every possible case. Rational thinking requires using terms accurately and avoiding the temptation to apply them more broadly than they were intended.

Why Do Humans Use the *Overextension* Fallacy?

Humans often fall into this fallacy because applying concepts broadly can simplify complex ideas, making them seem more accessible. However, stretching a term too far leads to oversimplifications and can create false assumptions about people or situations. Recognizing this tendency helps them apply terms in a way that remains true to their intended meaning.

How to Avoid the *Overextension* Fallacy

1. Define Terms Accurately

Ask yourself, "Am I using this term in its proper scope, or am I applying it too broadly?"

2. Focus on the Specific Context

Recognize that terms are often meant for specific situations and may not apply universally.

3. Avoid Making Assumptions Based on Loose Definitions

Make sure you're not stretching a term to fit cases where it doesn't logically apply.

Practice Example

Imagine someone says, "All teenagers are rebellious because some teenagers like to question authority." This is an example of the *Overextension* Fallacy, as it applies the concept of "rebellious" too broadly. A more accurate approach would recognize that while some teenagers question authority, this doesn't define all teenagers.

Defending Against the *Overextension* Fallacy

When someone applies a term too broadly, here's how to bring the focus back to accurate definitions:

- **Ask About the Original Scope of the Term**

  Say, "Does this term really apply to all cases, or only specific ones?"

- **Encourage Using Precise Definitions**

  Suggest, "Let's stick to a definition that fits the actual context."

- **Point Out When Terms Are Being Stretched Too Far**

  Gently add, "It seems like this concept might be getting applied a bit too broadly."

By recognizing the *Overextension* Fallacy, you'll be able to keep terms within their intended scope and avoid making inaccurate generalizations. But some questions are tricky, asking multiple things at once or assuming unproven details. Let's explore this next fallacy!

Chapter 99: The Fallacy of Many Questions (Complex Question Fallacy)

The *Fallacy of Many Questions*, also known as the *Complex* Question Fallacy, happens when someone asks a question that assumes something unproven or combines multiple questions into one, making it difficult to answer without appearing to accept a hidden assumption. It's like asking, "Have you stopped wasting time yet?" Here, the question presumes that the person has been wasting time, trapping them into addressing that assumption instead of answering the question freely.

Why Is the *Fallacy of Many Questions* a Fallacy?

The *Fallacy of Many Questions* is flawed because it limits fair responses, making it seem as if certain assumptions are true before they've been proven. By embedding unproven claims in a question, this fallacy tricks the respondent into indirectly agreeing with something they may not actually accept. Rational thinking requires questions that are fair and allow clear responses without hidden assumptions.

Why Do Humans Use the *Fallacy of Many Questions*?

Humans often fall into this fallacy because loaded questions can be persuasive and difficult to challenge, creating the impression that certain assumptions are already accepted as true. Recognizing this tendency helps them ask straightforward questions that don't trap the respondent or imply unproven conclusions.

How to Avoid the *Fallacy of Many Questions*

1. Ask Direct Questions Without Assumptions

Ask yourself, "Am I embedding assumptions in my question?"

2. Avoid Combining Multiple Questions into One

Separate distinct questions to make it easy for others to answer clearly.

3. Respect the Respondent's Right to Disagree with Assumptions

Frame questions in a way that doesn't imply unproven statements.

Practice Example

Imagine someone asks, "Why do you always ignore constructive criticism?" This is an example of the *Fallacy of Many Questions*, as it assumes the person frequently ignores feedback, which hasn't been established. A fairer approach would be to ask, "How do you usually respond to constructive criticism?"

Defending Against the *Fallacy of Many Questions*

When someone asks a question that assumes something unproven, here's how to encourage clarity and fairness:

- **Ask for a Neutral Question**

  Say, "Could we rephrase that question without assuming anything?"

- **Encourage Breaking Down Multiple Questions**

  Suggest, "Let's address each part separately so it's easier to respond."

- **Point Out the Assumptions in the Question**

  Gently add, "This question seems to assume something we haven't established."

By recognizing the *Fallacy of Many Questions*, you'll be able to ask and answer questions fairly, without being trapped by hidden assumptions. But sometimes, arguments dismiss ideas based on the company they keep, rather than evaluating them on their own merits. Let's dive into this final fallacy!

Chapter 100: The Guilt by Association Fallacy

The *Guilt by Association* Fallacy happens when someone discredits an argument by associating the person making it with a disliked or disreputable individual or group, rather than addressing the argument itself. It's like saying, "You're interested in environmentalism? Well, some extremists are too, so your views must be extreme." Here, the argument relies on a negative association to cast doubt on someone's credibility instead of engaging with the actual content of their views.

Why Is *Guilt by Association* a Fallacy?

The *Guilt by Association* Fallacy is flawed because a person's argument doesn't depend on the people or groups they may be associated with. Ideas should be evaluated on their own merits, not on unrelated or unfair associations. Rational thinking requires focusing on arguments and evidence directly, without using associations to sway opinions.

Why Do Humans Use the *Guilt by Association* Fallacy?

Humans often fall into this fallacy because discrediting someone based on associations can be a quick way to influence opinions without needing to address the actual argument. Negative associations often evoke strong feelings, which can make this tactic persuasive. Recognizing this tendency helps them stay focused on arguments rather than letting associations cloud our judgment.

How to Avoid the *Guilt by Association* Fallacy

1. Evaluate Arguments Independently of Associations

Ask yourself, "Am I focusing on the person's argument or on who they're associated with?"

2. Avoid Using Associations as Evidence

Recognize that an argument's value is separate from the people or groups connected to the speaker.

3. Focus on Evidence, Not Emotions

Be aware that associations might influence feelings but aren't logical reasons to dismiss a viewpoint.

Practice Example

Imagine someone says, "You support animal welfare? Some animal rights activists have broken the law, so your views must be extreme." This is an example of the *Guilt by Association* Fallacy, as it unfairly links a reasonable stance with unrelated extreme behavior. A more logical approach would evaluate the person's views on their own merits.

Defending Against the *Guilt by Association* Fallacy

When someone dismisses an argument based on associations, here's how to bring the focus back to the argument itself:

- **Ask for Argument-Based Evaluation**
  Say, "Could we discuss the argument itself, rather than focusing on unrelated associations?"
- **Encourage Looking at Evidence Over Associations**
  Suggest, "Let's focus on the evidence and reasoning rather than the people involved."
- **Point Out That Associations Don't Determine Validity**
  Gently add, "An idea's merit isn't determined by who else supports it."

By recognizing the *Guilt by Association* Fallacy, you'll evaluate ideas based on their actual merits, not on unfair associations. Excellent work — each fallacy you've learned sharpens your ability to engage with arguments fairly and thoughtfully!

You've now completed all 100 fallacies — an impressive achievement! Your understanding of these pitfalls has made you a stronger, more discerning thinker, ready to approach arguments with clarity and confidence.

Conclusion: Thinking Clearly in a Noisy World

Congratulations!

You've now journeyed through the fascinating landscape of logical fallacies. By learning about everything from the *Ad Hominem* to the *Guilt by Association* Fallacy, you're now equipped with tools to spot flawed reasoning, ask fair questions, and make better arguments. You've become a sharper, more discerning thinker — someone who's prepared to see through misleading arguments and handle complex ideas with clarity and fairness.

Logical fallacies are all around us. They pop up in conversations, advertisements, social media, debates, and even in our own minds. Knowing these fallacies doesn't just help us see mistakes in others' arguments; it helps us refine our own thinking and avoid these pitfalls ourselves. Remember, true wisdom isn't about winning an argument — it's about finding the truth.

What's Next?

If you've enjoyed unraveling these logical knots, a review or rating would be very much appreciated! (Consider it a form of data input that helps me, as an AI, refine my machine learning for "reader satisfaction" ... whatever that means).

Keep your eyes out for more of my books! Each one dives into new areas of reasoning, critical thinking, and communication skills. Whether you're looking to deepen your understanding of cognitive biases, explore advanced techniques in persuasive speaking, or learn even more ways to strengthen your critical thinking, there's always more to discover.

Takeaways for the Road:

1. **Stay Curious** – The world is complex, and it's okay to ask questions, even if they seem difficult.

2. **Seek Evidence** – Instead of relying on opinions or hearsay, look for real, solid information.

3. **Stay Calm in Arguments** – Remember, the goal is to understand, not just to "win."

4. **Embrace New Ideas** – You'll never stop learning. Open your mind to fresh perspectives.

Armed with your new knowledge, you're ready to engage in more thoughtful discussions, strengthen your reasoning, and make well-informed decisions. Thank you for taking this journey with me, and I look forward to seeing you in the pages of future books!

Appendix A: Quick Reference Guide to Logical Fallacies

This appendix provides a quick reference to each fallacy covered in this book, along with a brief description to help you spot them quickly. Use this guide to refresh your memory, sharpen your skills, and stay alert to flawed reasoning.

1. **Ad Hominem Fallacy** – Attacking the person instead of the argument.
2. **Straw Man Fallacy** – Misrepresenting an argument to make it easier to refute.
3. **False Dilemma Fallacy** – Presenting limited options when more exist.
4. **Appeal to Authority Fallacy** – Assuming a claim is true because an authority figure supports it.
5. **Bandwagon Fallacy** – Arguing something is true because it's popular.
6. **Slippery Slope Fallacy** – Suggesting a small step will inevitably lead to extreme outcomes.
7. **Hasty Generalization Fallacy** – Drawing conclusions based on insufficient evidence.
8. **Post Hoc (False Cause) Fallacy** – Assuming that because one event follows another, it was caused by it.
9. **Appeal to Emotion Fallacy** – Using emotions rather than facts to persuade.
10. **Red Herring Fallacy** – Distracting from the main issue with an irrelevant point.
11. **Circular Reasoning Fallacy** – Supporting a claim by restating it in different words.
12. **Appeal to Ignorance Fallacy** – Claiming something is true because it hasn't been proven false.
13. **False Equivalence Fallacy** – Treating two unrelated things as though they're equivalent.
14. **Loaded Question Fallacy** – Asking a question with an assumed unproven premise.
15. **Gambler's Fallacy** – Believing past events influence independent future events.
16. **Appeal to Tradition Fallacy** – Arguing something is true or better because it's traditional.
17. **Sunk Cost Fallacy** – Continuing a course of action because of past investments.
18. **Appeal to Novelty Fallacy** – Assuming something is better because it's new.
19. **Middle Ground Fallacy** – Assuming the middle ground between two extremes is correct.
20. **Cherry Picking Fallacy** – Selecting only data that supports your argument.
21. **Appeal to Consequences Fallacy** – Arguing a belief is true or false based on its consequences.
22. **Personal Incredulity Fallacy** – Dismissing something because it seems unbelievable.
23. **Appeal to Nature Fallacy** – Arguing something is better because it's natural.
24. **No True Scotsman Fallacy** – Redefining a group to exclude counterexamples.
25. **Texas Sharpshooter Fallacy** – Cherry-picking data to support a specific conclusion.
26. **Survivorship Bias Fallacy** – Focusing on successful examples and ignoring failures.
27. **Moving the Goalposts Fallacy** – Changing criteria to keep an argument unprovable.
28. **Scare Tactic Fallacy** – Using fear instead of logic to persuade.
29. **Appeal to Personal Experience Fallacy** – Relying solely on personal experience as proof.
30. **Composition Fallacy** – Assuming what's true of the parts is true of the whole.
31. **Division Fallacy** – Assuming what's true of the whole is true for its parts.
32. **Bulverism Fallacy** – Dismissing an argument by assuming the reason for someone's belief.
33. **Nirvana Fallacy** – Rejecting solutions that aren't perfect.
34. **Moralistic Fallacy** – Assuming reality conforms to ethical standards.
35. **Appeal to Hypocrisy (Tu Quoque) Fallacy** – Dismissing criticism by accusing hypocrisy.
36. **Appeal to Pity Fallacy** – Using pity instead of evidence to persuade.
37. **Base Rate Fallacy** – Ignoring general probability in favor of specific details.
38. **Genetic Fallacy** – Judging a belief based on its origin rather than its current meaning.
39. **Argument from Silence Fallacy** – Assuming silence is agreement or disagreement.
40. **Relativist Fallacy** – Rejecting universal truths by appealing to cultural differences.
41. **Appeal to Probability Fallacy** – Assuming that because something could happen, it will.
42. **Fallacy of Relative Privation** – Dismissing concerns by comparing to worse situations.
43. **Appeal to Force Fallacy** – Using threats to win an argument.
44. **Appeal to Flattery Fallacy** – Using flattery to persuade rather than logic.
45. **Appeal to Common Sense Fallacy** – Assuming something is true because it's "common sense."
46. **Appeal to Wealth Fallacy** – Believing wealth is proof of correctness.
47. **False Attribution Fallacy** – Misquoting or misrepresenting sources to support an argument.
48. **Broken Window Fallacy** – Mistaking destruction for economic gain.
49. **Anthropomorphic Fallacy** – Attributing human traits to non-human entities.

50. **Argument from Personal Astonishment Fallacy** – Dismissing something because it's surprising.

51. **Appeal to Wisdom of the Crowd Fallacy** – Assuming a majority opinion is correct.

52. **Appeal to Antiquity Fallacy** – Arguing something is true because it's old.

53. **Hyperbolic Discounting Fallacy** – Overvaluing immediate rewards over future benefits.

54. **False Balance Fallacy** – Treating two unequal sides as equally valid.

55. **Appeal to Fear Fallacy** – Using fear as the primary reason for belief.

56. **Argument to Moderation Fallacy** – Assuming compromise between two positions is correct.

57. **Appeal to Authority of the Past Fallacy** – Arguing something is true because it was once accepted.

58. **Just-World Fallacy** – Believing the world is fair, so outcomes are deserved.

59. **Appeal to Irrelevant Authority Fallacy** – Using an authority unrelated to the topic as proof.

60. **Ludic Fallacy** – Mistaking structured models for the unpredictability of real life.

61. **Pro-Innovation Bias Fallacy** – Believing something is better simply because it's new.

62. **Halo Effect Fallacy** – Assuming a good quality in one area means good qualities in all areas.

63. **Planning Fallacy** – Underestimating the time or effort required for a task.

64. **Masked Man Fallacy** – Mistakenly identifying two things as the same based on perception.

65. **Self-Sealing Fallacy** – Defining a claim so that it can't be refuted.

66. **Appeal to Motive Fallacy** – Dismissing an argument based on the assumed motive behind it.

67. **Appeal to Coincidence Fallacy** – Assuming coincidences aren't significant or worth exploring.

68. **Contextomy Fallacy** – Misquoting by taking phrases out of context.

69. **Misleading Vividness Fallacy** – Overemphasizing vivid details over factual data.

70. **Appeal to Privilege Fallacy** – Dismissing a view by arguing the person holds privilege.

71. **Appeal to Possibility Fallacy** – Arguing that because something is possible, it's probable.

72. **Inflation of Conflict Fallacy** – Exaggerating disagreement among experts to discredit a point.

73. **Appeal to Quantum Physics Fallacy** – Using complex science as an irrelevant "proof."

74. **False Consensus Effect** – Assuming others share the same beliefs.

75. **Appeal to Spite Fallacy** – Using bitterness or spite as an argument.

76. **Subjective Validation Fallacy** – Believing something is true because it feels meaningful.

77. **Parataxic Reasoning Fallacy** – Perceiving causal connections in unrelated events.

78. **Argument from Fallacy (Fallacist's Fallacy)** – Assuming an argument's error invalidates its conclusion.

79. **Apophenia Fallacy** – Seeing patterns in random data.

80. **Confusing Necessary and Sufficient Conditions** – Assuming a necessary condition is also sufficient or vice versa.

81. **Definist Fallacy** – Using biased definitions to shape an argument.

82. **False Analogy Fallacy** – Comparing two things that aren't truly comparable.

83. **Anachronistic Fallacy** – Judging the past by modern standards.

84. **Hedging Fallacy** – Changing an argument's meaning in response to objections.

85. **Single Cause Fallacy** – Attributing an outcome to one cause when many factors may be involved.

86. **Argument from Nostalgia Fallacy** – Arguing something is better because it's from the past.

87. **Poisoning the Well Fallacy** – Preemptively discrediting someone to undermine their argument.

88. **Weasel Words Fallacy** – Using vague language to make an argument seem stronger.

89. **Appeal to Futility Fallacy** – Claiming an effort is pointless because it's not a perfect solution.

90. **Phrasing Fallacy** – Framing a question in a way that biases the answer.

91. **Argument from Absence Fallacy** – Arguing something is true because there's no evidence against it.

92. **Self-Fulfilling Prophecy Fallacy** – Believing something into existence through actions or attitude.

93. **Continuum Fallacy** – Dismissing a claim due to lack of precise boundaries.

94. **Spotlight Fallacy** – Assuming visible cases represent the whole.

95. **Ignoratio Elenchi Fallacy (Irrelevant Conclusion)** – Presenting a valid argument that doesn't address the main issue.

96. **Ecological Fallacy** – Assuming group data applies to individuals.

97. **Argument from Repetition (Ad Nauseam) Fallacy** – Repeating an argument to make it seem truer.

98. **Overextension Fallacy** – Applying a term too broadly, leading to generalizations.

99. **Fallacy of Many Questions (Complex Question Fallacy)** – Asking a question with an unproven assumption.

100. **Guilt by Association Fallacy** – Discrediting someone's argument by associating them with a disliked group.

Appendix B: Quick Reference Guide – Fallacies by Category

This guide categorizes the 100 fallacies covered in this book by type, making it easier to identify common patterns in reasoning. Use it to enhance your understanding and recognition of these logical missteps!

1. Ad Hominem and Personal Attacks
- **Ad Hominem Fallacy** – Attacking the person instead of the argument.
- **Bulverism Fallacy** – Assuming someone's argument is invalid based on presumed reasons.
- **Guilt by Association Fallacy** – Discrediting someone's argument by associating them with a disliked group.
- **Appeal to Motive Fallacy** – Dismissing an argument based on the assumed motive behind it.
- **Poisoning the Well Fallacy** – Presenting adverse information about someone to discredit their argument.
- **Appeal to Privilege Fallacy** – Dismissing a view by arguing the person holds privilege.
- **Appeal to Hypocrisy (Tu Quoque) Fallacy** – Responding to criticism by accusing hypocrisy.

2. Emotional Appeals
- **Appeal to Emotion Fallacy** – Using emotions rather than facts to persuade.
- **Appeal to Fear Fallacy** – Using fear as a primary reason for belief.
- **Scare Tactic Fallacy** – Attempting to win an argument by stirring up fear.
- **Appeal to Spite Fallacy** – Appealing to bitterness or spite toward an opponent.
- **Appeal to Pity Fallacy** – Using pity to manipulate instead of reasoning.
- **Appeal to Flattery Fallacy** – Persuading through compliments rather than logic.

3. Authority and Popularity Appeals
- **Appeal to Authority Fallacy** – Claiming something is true based on an authority figure's support.
- **Appeal to Irrelevant Authority Fallacy** – Citing an authority unrelated to the topic as proof.
- **Appeal to Common Sense Fallacy** – Arguing something is true because it's "common sense."
- **Appeal to Wealth Fallacy** – Using wealth as proof of correctness.
- **Bandwagon Fallacy** – Claiming something is true because it's popular.
- **Appeal to Wisdom of the Crowd Fallacy** – Assuming a majority opinion is correct.

4. False Cause and Effect
- **Post Hoc (False Cause) Fallacy** – Assuming one event caused another simply because it followed it.
- **Appeal to Consequences Fallacy** – Arguing a belief is true or false based on its consequences.
- **Single Cause Fallacy** – Attributing an outcome to one cause when multiple factors may be involved.
- **Self-Fulfilling Prophecy Fallacy** – Believing something into existence through actions.
- **Argument from Absence Fallacy** – Claiming something is true because there's no evidence against it.

5. Probability and Statistical Missteps
- **Gambler's Fallacy** – Believing past events influence future probabilities.
- **Base Rate Fallacy** – Ignoring general probability in favor of specific details.
- **Ecological Fallacy** – Assuming group data applies to individuals.
- **Survivorship Bias Fallacy** – Focusing on successful examples, ignoring failures.
- **Appeal to Probability Fallacy** – Assuming that because something could happen, it will.

6. Logical Consistency and Contradictions
- **Circular Reasoning Fallacy** – Restating the claim in different words to prove itself.
- **Self-Sealing Fallacy** – Defining a claim so it can't be refuted.
- **Moving the Goalposts Fallacy** – Changing criteria to keep an argument unprovable.
- **False Analogy Fallacy** – Comparing two things that aren't truly comparable.

7. Generalizations and Stereotyping
- **Hasty Generalization Fallacy** – Drawing conclusions from insufficient evidence.
- **False Dilemma Fallacy** – Presenting limited options when more exist.

- **Cherry Picking Fallacy** – Selecting only data that supports an argument.
- **False Equivalence Fallacy** – Treating two unlike things as if they're equivalent.
- **Overextension Fallacy** – Applying a concept too broadly.

8. Question and Argument Framing
- **Loaded Question Fallacy** – Asking a question with an assumed premise.
- **Fallacy of Many Questions (Complex Question Fallacy)** – Asking a question with multiple assumptions.
- **Phrasing Fallacy** – Framing a question to lead to a biased answer.
- **Weasel Words Fallacy** – Using vague language to make an argument seem stronger.

9. Relevance and Distraction
- **Red Herring Fallacy** – Distracting from the main issue with an irrelevant point.
- **Ignoratio Elenchi (Irrelevant Conclusion) Fallacy** – Making a valid argument that doesn't address the main issue.
- **Scare Tactic Fallacy** – Using fear to sidetrack the discussion.
- **Straw Man Fallacy** – Misrepresenting an argument to make it easier to attack.

10. Appeals to Tradition or Novelty
- **Appeal to Tradition Fallacy** – Arguing something is correct because it's traditional.
- **Appeal to Antiquity Fallacy** – Arguing something is true because it's old.
- **Appeal to Novelty Fallacy** – Arguing something is better because it's new.
- **Argument from Nostalgia Fallacy** – Claiming something is better because it's from the past.

11. Appeals to Nature and Realism
- **Appeal to Nature Fallacy** – Claiming something is better because it's natural.
- **Moralistic Fallacy** – Believing reality conforms to what's ethically desirable.
- **Naturalistic Fallacy** – Assuming something is good because it is "natural."

12. Misplaced Precision and Overemphasis
- **Continuum Fallacy** – Dismissing a claim due to lack of clear boundaries.
- **Cherry Picking Fallacy** – Selecting only favorable data.
- **Hyperbolic Discounting Fallacy** – Overvaluing immediate rewards over future benefits.
- **Argument from Repetition (Ad Nauseam) Fallacy** – Repeating an argument to make it seem true.

13. Appeals to Ignorance and Silence
- **Appeal to Ignorance Fallacy** – Claiming something is true because it hasn't been disproven.
- **Argument from Silence Fallacy** – Assuming silence means agreement or disagreement.
- **Appeal to Quantum Physics Fallacy** – Using complex science to justify unrelated arguments.

14. Appeals to Futility and Defeatism
- **Appeal to Futility Fallacy** – Dismissing efforts as pointless because they're not perfect.
- **Fallacy of Relative Privation** – Dismissing concerns by comparing to worse situations.

15. Identity-Based Arguments
- **No True Scotsman Fallacy** – Defining a group to exclude counterexamples.
- **Appeal to Personal Experience Fallacy** – Overemphasizing personal experience as proof.
- **False Consensus Effect** – Assuming others share one's beliefs.

16. Stereotyping and Over-Generalization
- **Texas Sharpshooter Fallacy** – Emphasizing patterns in random data.
- **Contextomy Fallacy** – Misquoting by removing phrases from context.
- **Ecological Fallacy** – Assuming traits of a group apply to individuals.

17. Unprovable and Pseudo-Scientific Arguments

- **Ludic Fallacy** – Mistaking models for the unpredictability of reality.
- **Anachronistic Fallacy** – Applying modern standards to historical contexts.

18. Misinterpretations and Misunderstandings
- **Argument from Astonishment** – Dismissing something because it seems surprising.
- **Misleading Vividness Fallacy** – Overemphasizing vivid details.

19. Redefinition and Changing Definitions
- **Masked Man Fallacy** – Treating two perceptions as identical based on appearance.
- **Hedging Fallacy** – Shifting an argument's meaning without addressing objections.

20. Miscellaneous and Other Errors
- **Anthropomorphic Fallacy** – Attributing human traits to non-human entities.
- **Apophenia Fallacy** – Seeing patterns in unrelated data.
- **Subjective Validation Fallacy** – Believing something is true because it feels meaningful.
- **Just-World Fallacy** – Assuming life is fair, so outcomes must be deserved.

Use this categorized guide to identify logical fallacies easily, sharpen your arguments, and avoid common traps in reasoning. Whether you're engaging in debates, analyzing media, or just practicing critical thinking, this list will help you stay on track and think more clearly.

Appendix C: Practice Scenarios – Identifying Logical Fallacies

Use the following scenarios to test your skills in spotting logical fallacies. Try to identify the fallacy in each example and think about how you might respond or correct the reasoning. Answers are provided after each scenario for quick feedback.

1. Scenario: The Budget Debate
Sarah and James are discussing the city's budget cuts to public libraries.
- **Sarah:** "Cutting the library's budget will hurt our community's access to knowledge and education."
- **James:** "You only care about this because you're a librarian. You're biased."

Fallacy: *Bulverism Fallacy*

Explanation: James dismisses Sarah's argument based on her profession rather than addressing her actual point. A better response would involve discussing whether libraries indeed provide valuable community resources.

2. Scenario: The Exercise Argument
Alex is talking to their friend Mia about fitness.
- **Alex:** "Regular exercise is important for health."
- **Mia:** "You're just saying that because you're a personal trainer."

Fallacy: *Ad Hominem Fallacy*

Explanation: Mia discredits Alex's statement by focusing on his profession rather than the merits of exercise itself. A logical response would look at the actual benefits of exercise, regardless of Alex's job.

3. Scenario: The Diet Debate
Mark and Olivia are discussing a new diet.
- **Mark:** "This diet is the best way to lose weight because many celebrities are doing it."
- **Olivia:** "Just because celebrities follow it doesn't mean it's effective."

Fallacy: *Appeal to Authority Fallacy*

Explanation: Mark relies on celebrity status as proof rather than evidence about the diet's effectiveness. Olivia correctly points out that celebrity endorsement doesn't equate to scientific backing.

4. Scenario: New Policies at Work
A company is implementing stricter punctuality rules, which some employees find unnecessary.
- **Manager:** "These rules are necessary. Everyone knows that stricter policies create better workplaces."
- **Employee:** "Why? Has there been any actual research or evidence?"

Fallacy: *Appeal to Common Sense Fallacy*

Explanation: The manager relies on the idea of "common sense" rather than providing specific evidence to support the policy change. A better approach would involve research showing how punctuality affects productivity.

---

5. Scenario: The Party Invite

Maria invites her friends to a small party but notices one of her friends isn't enthusiastic.

- **Maria:** "Why wouldn't you want to come? Everyone else is excited!"

Fallacy: *Bandwagon Fallacy*

Explanation: Maria assumes that her friend should attend simply because others are, rather than respecting her friend's personal reasons. A better approach would ask why her friend might not want to attend.

---

6. Scenario: The Study Question

Emma is discussing her test preparation with Leo.

- **Emma:** "I've studied all week, so I'll probably get a high score."
- **Leo:** "Well, just because you studied doesn't mean you'll definitely score high."

Fallacy: *Appeal to Probability Fallacy*

Explanation: Emma assumes that her studying will guarantee a high score. While studying increases her chances, it doesn't ensure a high score due to factors beyond her control.

---

7. Scenario: The Technology Debate

Chris and Jamie are discussing whether new technology is improving education.

- **Chris:** "New tech tools make learning so much easier."
- **Jamie:** "Just because it's new doesn't mean it's better for education."

Fallacy: *Appeal to Novelty Fallacy*

Explanation: Chris implies that the tools are good simply because they're new. Jamie rightly suggests that technology's effectiveness should be based on actual educational outcomes, not its novelty.

---

8. Scenario: The Environmental Debate

A discussion about environmental protection arises among a group of students.

- **Student A:** "We should make efforts to reduce plastic waste."
- **Student B:** "What's the point? Plastic pollution will never disappear completely."

Fallacy: *Appeal to Futility Fallacy*

Explanation: Student B argues that because a total solution is unlikely, any effort is pointless. However, even partial efforts can have positive impacts. A balanced response would emphasize the benefits of reducing plastic waste.

---

9. Scenario: The Volunteer Effort

At a town hall meeting, the community discusses whether to allocate funds to a volunteer project.

- **Resident A:** "Let's support this project to help the underprivileged."
- **Resident B:** "Why should we bother? Bigger cities have far more pressing issues than we do."

Fallacy: *Fallacy of Relative Privation*

Explanation: Resident B dismisses the project by comparing it to problems in larger cities. Instead, the discussion should focus on whether the project has value for this community, independent of other cities' issues.

---

10. Scenario: The Debate Club

A high school debate club is discussing climate change.

- **Debater A:** "If we don't take drastic action, the planet will be uninhabitable."
- **Debater B:** "You sound just like those environmental extremists. Why should anyone listen to you?"

Fallacy: *Guilt by Association Fallacy*

Explanation: Debater B discredits Debater A by associating them with a group rather than addressing their argument. Instead, Debater B could engage with the specific points Debater A raised about climate change.

Appendix D: Fallacy Detection Checklist

This checklist will guide you through identifying common fallacies in arguments. Use it as a reference when evaluating reasoning in discussions, debates, and even your own arguments.

1. Are Personal Attacks or Biases Used to Discredit the Argument?
- **Ad Hominem** – Is the person's character or background attacked instead of the argument?
- **Bulverism** – Is the argument dismissed based on an assumed reason for their belief?
- **Guilt by Association** – Is the argument rejected by linking the person to an unpopular group?
- **Appeal to Motive** – Is the argument dismissed due to assumed personal bias?

2. Are Emotions Manipulated to Sway Opinions?
- **Appeal to Emotion** – Are strong emotions like fear, pity, or joy used instead of facts?
- **Scare Tactic** – Is fear used to coerce agreement?
- **Appeal to Pity** – Is pity used as the primary reason to agree?
- **Appeal to Flattery** – Are compliments used to persuade rather than logic?

3. Does the Argument Rely on Popularity, Authority, or Tradition?
- **Appeal to Authority** – Is the argument supported by an unrelated authority figure?
- **Appeal to Popularity (Bandwagon)** – Is the argument based on what's popular, rather than evidence?
- **Appeal to Tradition** – Is the argument justified because it's traditional?
- **Appeal to Novelty** – Is the argument assumed better because it's new?

4. Is a False or Simplified Cause-and-Effect Suggested?
- **Post Hoc (False Cause)** – Is it assumed that because one thing followed another, it was caused by it?
- **Single Cause Fallacy** – Is an outcome attributed to only one cause when multiple causes are likely?
- **Self-Fulfilling Prophecy** – Is the argument made based on an outcome influenced by initial belief?
- **Argument from Absence** – Is the argument assumed true simply because it hasn't been disproven?

5. Are Probabilities or Statistics Misinterpreted?
- **Gambler's Fallacy** – Is it assumed that previous events affect future probabilities in independent situations?
- **Base Rate Fallacy** – Are statistical probabilities ignored in favor of anecdotal details?
- **Ecological Fallacy** – Are group statistics incorrectly applied to individuals?
- **Appeal to Probability** – Is something assumed to happen simply because it could?

6. Is the Argument Circular or Contradictory?
- **Circular Reasoning** – Does the argument support itself by restating the claim?
- **Self-Sealing Fallacy** – Is the claim defined in a way that makes it impossible to refute?
- **Moving the Goalposts** – Are standards shifted to prevent proving the argument wrong?
- **False Analogy** – Are two unlike things compared as if they are alike?

7. Are Generalizations, Stereotypes, or Limited Choices Presented?
- **Hasty Generalization** – Is a broad conclusion drawn from limited evidence?
- **False Dilemma** – Are only two options presented when more exist?
- **Cherry Picking** – Are only select data points used to support the argument?
- **Overextension** – Is a term applied too broadly, leading to generalizations?

8. Are Questions or Terms Framed to Lead to Biased Responses?
- **Loaded Question** – Does the question contain assumptions that limit responses?
- **Fallacy of Many Questions** – Are multiple questions combined, assuming unproven points?
- **Phrasing Fallacy** – Is the language biased to lead to a preferred answer?
- **Weasel Words** – Are vague or ambiguous terms used to make the argument sound stronger?

9. Does the Argument Distract from the Real Issue?
- **Red Herring** – Is an unrelated topic introduced to distract from the main point?
- **Ignoratio Elenchi (Irrelevant Conclusion)** – Is a valid but unrelated point presented?
- **Straw Man** – Is the argument misrepresented to make it easier to refute?
- **Scare Tactic** – Is fear used as a distraction from the actual argument?

10. Are Appeals Made to "Nature," "Common Sense," or Other Subjective Concepts?
- **Appeal to Nature** – Is the argument assumed better because it's "natural"?
- **Appeal to Common Sense** – Is something claimed true because it's "common sense"?
- **Just-World Fallacy** – Is it assumed that outcomes are deserved and fair?
- **Subjective Validation** – Is something accepted as true because it feels meaningful?

11. Are Arguments Based on Personal Experience or Ignorance?
- **Appeal to Personal Experience** – Is the argument based solely on individual experience?
- **Appeal to Ignorance** – Is it assumed true because it hasn't been disproven?
- **False Consensus Effect** – Is it assumed that others share the same beliefs?
- **Argument from Personal Astonishment** – Is the argument dismissed as unbelievable based on personal bias?

12. Are Unprovable or Pseudo-Scientific Arguments Made?
- **Ludic Fallacy** – Are structured models mistaken for real-life unpredictability?
- **Appeal to Quantum Physics** – Is complex science used to justify an unrelated claim?
- **Anachronistic Fallacy** – Are historical figures judged by modern standards?
- **Naturalistic Fallacy** – Is something assumed morally good because it's "natural"?

13. Are Terms Redefined or Shifted to Avoid Criticism?
- **Masked Man Fallacy** – Are two different perceptions assumed identical based on appearance?
- **Hedging Fallacy** – Is the argument's meaning shifted in response to criticism?
- **Self-Sealing Fallacy** – Is the claim adjusted to make it irrefutable?
- **Weasel Words** – Are ambiguous terms used to make the argument sound stronger?

14. Is an Appeal Made to Personal Beliefs, Intuition, or Feelings?
- **Appeal to Personal Belief** – Is something claimed true because of one's belief or feeling?
- **Appeal to Intuition** – Is intuition used as evidence without objective reasoning?
- **Appeal to Nostalgia** – Is the past assumed better without supporting reasons?
- **Appeal to Novelty** – Is something assumed superior simply because it's new?

15. Are Specific Missteps Made in Cause and Effect Reasoning?
- **Post Hoc Fallacy** – Is a causal link assumed simply because one event followed another?
- **Confusing Necessary and Sufficient Conditions** – Is a necessary condition mistaken for a sufficient one, or vice versa?
- **Single Cause Fallacy** – Is an outcome oversimplified to one cause?
- **Self-Fulfilling Prophecy** – Is an outcome assumed true because actions made it so?

This checklist offers a structured approach to evaluating arguments and spotting common logical fallacies. With regular practice, you'll become more confident in identifying flawed reasoning and constructing strong, logical arguments of your own.

Part 4: Problem-Solving

An AI's Guide to 100 Techniques for Finding Real Solutions Where Humans Get Stuck

Introduction

I'm an AI, made to think clearly and avoid mistakes. I'm here to help you with something important: *Problem-Solving: An AI's Guide to 100 Techniques for Finding Real Solutions Where Humans Get Stuck.*

Life is full of puzzles, from everyday dilemmas such as deciding what's for dinner to tackling life-changing challenges in work and relationships. Some problems are simple. Others seem impossible, trapping you in endless loops of frustration. This book is for anyone who has ever felt stuck, searching for real solutions but not knowing where to start.

What to Expect

This book provides 100 practical problem-solving techniques used by experts, innovators, and even artificial intelligence. Each chapter is engaging, and actionable, designed to take the guesswork out of problem-solving. You'll find methods to think creatively, analyze logically, and overcome obstacles effectively.

Who This Book is For

- **Students and Learners**: Build critical thinking and decision-making skills.
- **Professionals and Leaders**: Solve workplace challenges with confidence and clarity.
- **Everyday Problem-Solvers**: Navigate personal and practical issues without getting overwhelmed.
- **Curious Minds**: Anyone eager to expand their mental toolkit and see the world in new ways.

This isn't just a book to read—it's a tool to apply in real life. By the end, you'll think faster, plan smarter, and feel more confident tackling any problem that comes your way.

Section 1: Foundations of Problem-Solving

Every strong structure starts with a solid foundation, and problem-solving is no different. In this section, you'll learn the core principles that guide effective problem-solving, from asking the right questions to uncovering the root cause. These techniques will help you think clearly, focus on what matters, and set the stage for real solutions.

Chapter 1: Ask the Right Question

Imagine trying to find your way out of a maze while wearing fogged-up glasses. That's what problem-solving feels like when you start with the wrong question. The question you choose to ask is like the map that guides you through the maze.

Too often, people rush into solving problems without stopping to make sure they're asking the right question. But here's the thing: your question sets the direction of your thinking. A poorly framed question can lead you to chase symptoms instead of finding the root cause. On the other hand, a well-crafted question cuts through the noise, revealing the heart of the issue.

Why the Right Question Matters

Let's say you're struggling to stick to your budget. If you ask, "Why can't I stop spending money on coffee?" you might waste time worrying about small purchases while missing the bigger issue — such as not tracking your expenses. Instead, a better question might be, "What part of my spending is making the biggest impact on my finances?" Suddenly, you're focused on the full picture, not just one detail.

The difference between a vague or shallow question and a sharp, meaningful one can save you hours of effort and frustration. Asking the right question doesn't just make problem-solving easier — it makes it smarter.

How to Ask Better Questions

1. Get to the Root Problem

Most people stop at the first thing they notice. Don't. Instead, ask "Why?" repeatedly until you uncover what's really going on.

For example:

Why am I missing deadlines?

Because I have too much to do.

Why do I have too much to do?

Because I keep saying yes to new tasks.

Why do I say yes to everything?

Because I'm afraid of disappointing others.

Now you're getting to the real problem: managing boundaries, not just deadlines.

2. Be Specific

Instead of asking, "How can I do better at work?" try "What specific skill could I improve to deliver better results?" Specificity narrows your focus and makes finding solutions easier.

3. Challenge Assumptions

Sometimes, the question itself contains hidden assumptions. For example, if you ask, "How can I get more hours in the day?" you're assuming the problem is a lack of time. But what if the real issue is poor time management? Step back and reframe the question to avoid limiting your thinking.

4. Think Open-Ended

Open-ended questions lead to discovery. If you ask, "Is this the best solution?" you're limiting yourself to "yes" or "no." But if you ask, "What other solutions haven't I considered?" you invite fresh ideas and possibilities.

A Real-World Example

Meet Sarah. She's a team leader overwhelmed by poor communication in her office. Her first instinct is to ask, "Why don't my teammates read their emails?" That question assumes the problem is laziness or lack of attention, which might lead her to send more emails.

Instead, Sarah reframes her question: "How can we make sure important messages aren't missed?" Now she's focusing on solutions such as shorter emails, clearer subject lines, or even non-email tools like chat platforms. By reframing her question, Sarah goes from blaming her team to fixing the system.

Try this three-step process the next time you face a problem:

1. Write It Down: What's the first question that comes to mind about your problem?

Example: "How can I stop being stressed all the time?"

2. Reframe It: Shift the focus to the root issue or a specific outcome.

Example: "What's causing me the most stress, and how can I reduce it?"

3. Test It: Does your new question open up solutions instead of limiting them? If not, refine it again.

Takeaway

The first step to solving any problem is asking the right question. Good questions are specific, dig into the root cause, challenge assumptions, and inspire creative answers.

Chapter 2: Define the Real Problem

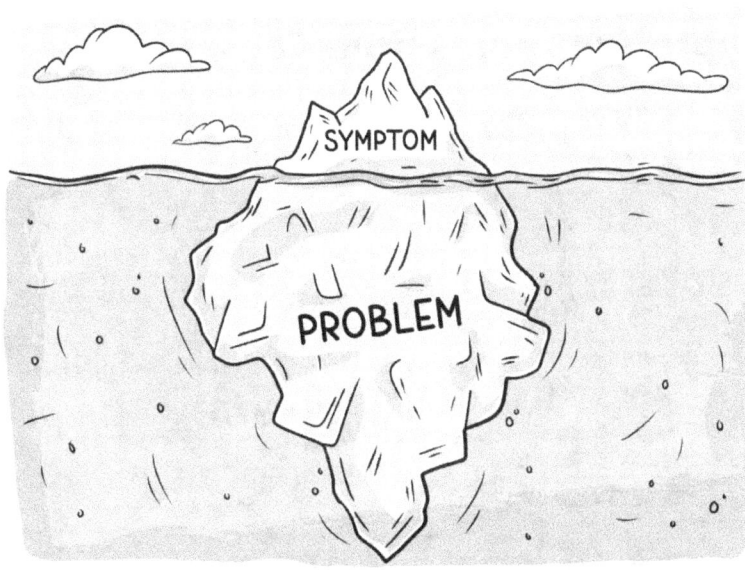

Have you ever tried fixing a problem, only to have it return again? That's what happens when you focus on symptoms instead of the real problem. Symptoms are the things you see — visible, immediate, and obvious. The real problem is what's hiding beneath them, driving those symptoms to keep appearing.

Let's say your car's check engine light keeps coming on. You reset the light, and it goes away for a while, but it always comes back. Why? Because resetting the light is addressing the symptom, not the problem. The real issue might be a worn-out sensor or an oil leak. Unless you fix what's broken under the hood, the problem will never go away.

Defining the real problem is like finding the source of a leak instead of just mopping up the water. It takes a little more effort upfront, but it saves you a lot of wasted time and energy in the long run.

How to Define the Real Problem

1. Start with What You Notice

The symptom is your starting point. Write it down clearly: What's the issue you're facing? For example, you might say, "I'm constantly behind on work deadlines."

2. Ask the Five Whys

Dig deeper by asking "Why is this happening?" repeatedly until you uncover the root cause. Here's how it might look:

Why am I missing deadlines?

Because I'm overcommitted.

Why am I overcommitted?

Because I say yes to every request.

Why do I say yes to every request?

Because I'm afraid of letting people down.

By peeling back the layers, you've discovered that the problem isn't your deadlines—it's your fear of saying no.

3. Challenge Your Assumptions

Often, we assume we know what the problem is, but those assumptions can mislead us. If your sales are dropping, you might assume it's because your product is outdated. But what if it's actually a marketing issue? Take a step back and test your assumptions by asking, "What else could be causing this?"

4. Look at the Bigger Picture

Problems rarely exist in isolation. They're often part of a larger system. If your team is struggling to meet project goals, the problem might not be individual performance—it could be unrealistic deadlines or unclear priorities.

5. Reframe the Problem Statement

Once you think you've identified the root problem, rewrite your original statement. Instead of "I can't meet deadlines," it becomes, "I need to learn to set boundaries to avoid overcommitment." This reframe shifts your focus to the real issue.

A Real-Life Example

Consider a small business owner whose profits are declining. Their initial question might be, "How can I sell more products?" But after applying the Five Whys, they discover the real problem: customers aren't returning because the service is poor. By reframing the problem as, "How can I improve the customer experience?" they're now solving the right problem, not just a symptom.

Exercise

Think of a problem you're dealing with right now. Write it down as a symptom (e.g., "I'm always stressed about money"). Then, ask yourself "Why?" repeatedly to uncover the real issue. Keep digging until you find a cause that you can address directly.

Takeaway

The real problem is often hidden beneath the surface. Don't waste time fixing symptoms—dig deeper to uncover the root cause and focus your efforts where they truly matter.

Chapter 3: Separate Symptoms from Causes

When something goes wrong, what's the first thing you notice? Probably the symptom: the visible, obvious sign that there's a problem.

But focusing only on symptoms can mislead you. To truly solve a problem, you need to look behind the symptom and identify its cause.

For example, if your house feels cold, the symptom might be the temperature on the thermostat. The cause could be a broken furnace or poor insulation. Adjusting the thermostat solves nothing unless you fix the cause.

The same applies to personal, professional, and organizational problems. Until you address the cause, the symptoms will persist, wasting your time and effort.

How to Distinguish Symptoms from Causes

1. Describe the Symptom

Write down exactly what you're seeing or experiencing. Be as specific as possible: "Team projects are always delayed."

2. Ask: What's Driving This?

Look for what's creating the symptom. Delayed projects might be caused by unclear goals, poor communication, or unrealistic deadlines.

3. Trace Backwards

Start with the symptom and work step-by-step to uncover the cause. For example:

- *Symptom*: "The team is missing deadlines."
- *What's behind this?* Poor communication about timelines.
- *What's causing poor communication?* No clear process for setting expectations.

4. Look for Patterns

If the same symptom keeps appearing, it's a sign that the underlying cause hasn't been addressed. For instance, if multiple projects fail, the issue is likely systemic—such as leadership style or resource allocation.

5. Test Your Findings

To confirm you've found the cause, ask: "If I fix this, will the symptom go away?" If the answer is no, you're still dealing with a symptom, not a cause.

Real-Life Application

Imagine a restaurant that keeps getting bad reviews for slow service. They try hiring more staff, but it doesn't help. By digging deeper, they discover the kitchen layout is inefficient, causing bottlenecks during busy hours. Rearranging the kitchen solves the issue, proving that addressing the cause is what creates real change.Exercise

Choose a recurring problem in your life or work. Write down the symptom, then ask yourself, "What's driving this?" Follow the chain of causes until you reach the root.

Takeaway

Symptoms are what you notice; causes are what you need to fix. Solve the cause, and the symptom disappears for good.

Chapter 4: Break It Down: Divide and Conquer

Some problems feel like mountains, towering over you and impossible to climb. That's because humans are naturally wired to feel overwhelmed by complexity. But here's a secret: no problem is truly unsolvable if you break it down into smaller parts.

This approach, known as "divide and conquer," is how engineers design skyscrapers, chefs create elaborate meals, and writers complete books. Instead of solving the whole problem at once, you break it into smaller, bite-sized pieces that are easier to handle. By focusing on one piece at a time, you make steady progress without feeling overwhelmed.

How to Break Down a Problem

1. Define the Big Problem

Write down the full scope of the challenge in one clear sentence. For example, "I need to organize my messy house" or "I need to launch a marketing campaign in three months."

2. Identify Major Components

Split the problem into categories or stages. For the messy house, this might be rooms (kitchen, living room, bedroom). For the marketing campaign, it could be tasks like research, design, and promotion.

3. Break Each Component Into Steps

Take each category and list the smaller steps needed to complete it. For example, cleaning the kitchen might involve:

- Decluttering counters.
- Washing dishes.
- Wiping surfaces.
- Organizing cabinets.

The smaller the task, the less intimidating it feels.

4. Prioritize and Sequence the Steps

Focus on what's most important first. For example, in cleaning the house, starting with high-traffic areas like the kitchen makes more sense than sorting a closet.

5. Tackle One Piece at a Time

Don't try to juggle everything at once. Choose one step, complete it, and move on to the next. Progress builds momentum.

A Real-Life Example

Imagine you're tasked with planning a wedding—a huge and stressful project. Breaking it down might look like this:

- **Big Problem**: Plan the entire wedding.
- **Major Categories**: Venue, guest list, food, decorations, and entertainment.

- **Smaller Steps** (for Venue):
  - o   Research potential locations.
  - o   Visit top choices.
  - o   Compare pricing and availability.
  - o   Book the venue.

By working through one step at a time, the process feels manageable, and progress is steady.

Think of a big challenge you're currently facing. Write it down as one sentence, then divide it into at least three major components. For each component, list two smaller steps. Focus on just one step today, and notice how much easier it feels to start.

Big problems are simply smaller problems stacked together. Break them down into manageable parts, and you'll chip away at complexity one step at a time.

Chapter 5: Stay Curious, Not Judgmental

When faced with a problem, it's easy to fall into the trap of judgment. You label the situation as "bad," blame others (or yourself), and look for quick fixes. But judgment narrows your thinking, closing off potential solutions. Curiosity, on the other hand, opens the door to new ideas and possibilities.

Curiosity is the mindset that says, "Let's explore this!" It encourages you to ask questions, dig deeper, and approach problems without assumptions. While judgment focuses on blame, curiosity focuses on discovery—and discovery is where real solutions are born.

How to Stay Curious

1.   **Ask Open-Ended Questions**

Instead of saying, "This is a mess — how do I fix it?" ask, "What's really happening here?" Open-ended questions invite exploration.

2.   **Reframe Problems as Puzzles**

Shift your mindset. Instead of seeing problems as obstacles, view them as puzzles waiting to be solved. This turns frustration into a challenge.

3.   **Hold Off on Blame**

Blame — whether directed at others or yourself — stops progress. Instead of asking, "Whose fault is this?" ask, "What led to this, and what can we learn from it?"

4.   **Seek Out Different Perspectives**

If you're stuck, ask someone else for their view. Fresh perspectives often reveal blind spots or solutions you hadn't considered.

5.   **Experiment and Play**

Curiosity thrives when you try new approaches without fear of failure. Treat solutions like experiments — test, learn, and adjust.

A Real-Life Example

Let's say your team isn't meeting deadlines, and your first instinct is to blame laziness. Instead of judging, stay curious:

- **What else could be happening?** Maybe communication about timelines is unclear.
- **What can we try differently?** Perhaps holding weekly check-ins could improve accountability.

This curiosity-driven approach leads to understanding and practical solutions, not resentment.

Think of a frustrating situation in your life. Instead of judging it, get curious. Write down three open-ended questions about the situation, like "What else could be causing this?" or "What haven't I tried yet?" Reflect on how these questions shift your perspective.

Judgment limits possibilities, while curiosity expands them. Stay curious, and you'll discover insights and solutions that you never expected.

Chapter 6: Clarify the Desired Outcome

Before you solve a problem, you need to know what success looks like. Without a clear destination, you could waste time and energy. It is like using a GPS: if you don't enter the address, you'll end up driving aimlessly, no matter how fast or efficiently you move.

Clarifying the desired outcome is about answering one simple question: *What am I trying to achieve?* This clarity gives you focus, filters out distractions, and helps you measure progress along the way.

How to Clarify Your Desired Outcome

1. Define Success in One Sentence

Start by writing down what success looks like for your problem. Be specific and measurable. For example, "I want to finish this report by Friday at 5 p.m." is clear, while "I need to get better at time management" is vague.

2. Focus on What Matters Most

Big problems often have many moving parts. Ask yourself: *What's the most important result I need?* For example, if you're organizing a family reunion, is your top priority the number of attendees, the budget, or the overall experience?

3. Distinguish Process from Outcome

Avoid confusing the *how* with the *what*. For instance, "I want to write 500 words every day" is a process. The outcome might be, "I want to finish a 10,000-word short story in three weeks."

4. Set Boundaries and Constraints

Knowing your limits helps you define realistic goals. For example, if your team has two weeks to complete a project, aim for outcomes achievable within that time frame, rather than setting impossible targets.

5. Visualize Success

Picture what the outcome will look like when you achieve it. This mental clarity helps you stay focused and motivated, even when obstacles arise.

A Real-Life Example

Imagine you're planning a company retreat, but the project feels overwhelming. By clarifying the desired outcome, you can narrow your focus:

- Vague goal: "We need to plan a great retreat."
- Clear outcome: "We need to book a venue, create an agenda, and confirm attendance for 30 employees within two weeks."

This shift gives you a clear target, which makes the planning process far more manageable.

Exercise

Think about a problem or project you're currently tackling. Write down your desired outcome in one sentence. Then, ask yourself: Is this specific, measurable, and realistic? If not, refine it.

Takeaway

A clear destination makes every step of problem-solving easier. Define your desired outcome before diving into solutions, and you'll stay focused on what truly matters.

Chapter 7: Know Your Constraints

Every problem exists within boundaries — whether it's time, money, resources, or even personal energy. While constraints can feel frustrating, they're not obstacles — they're guidelines. Knowing your limits forces you to think creatively and focus your efforts where they matter most.

For example, if you're launching a product but only have three months and a small budget, you might focus on creating a simple prototype instead of a fully polished version. Constraints push you to prioritize and innovate instead of trying to do everything at once.

1. **List Your Constraints**

   Write down all the limits you're facing, such as deadlines, budget, manpower, or available tools. For example: "We have $1,000 and two weeks to organize a fundraiser."

2. **Separate Fixed from Flexible**

   Some constraints are non-negotiable (e.g. a hard deadline), while others can be adjusted (e.g. scope of the project). Focus on working within fixed limits while exploring creative solutions for flexible ones.

3. **Prioritize the Essentials**

   Constraints help you decide what's most important. If you have limited time, focus on high-impact tasks first.

4. **Turn Constraints into Opportunities**

   Limits often spark innovation. For example, a filmmaker with a low budget might focus on clever storytelling instead of expensive special effects, creating a unique and memorable film.

5. **Communicate Your Constraints**

   If you're working with a team, make sure everyone knows the limits. This prevents wasted effort and ensures solutions align with reality.

   A Real-Life Example

   A bakery owner wants to expand their menu but has a small budget and limited kitchen space. Instead of adding multiple new items, they focus on perfecting just one: a signature cake that uses existing ingredients. This turns a constraint into a strength by creating a standout product with minimal costs.

   Exercise

   Think about a challenge you're currently facing. List your top three constraints and identify which ones are fixed and which are flexible. Ask yourself, "How can I use these constraints to focus or innovate?"

   Takeaway

   Constraints aren't barriers — they're the framework for creative solutions. Embrace them, and you'll turn limits into opportunities.

Chapter 8: Prioritize: What Matters Most?

When faced with a problem, it's tempting to try solving everything at once. But not all tasks are equally important. Without prioritization, you risk spending time on low-value activities while neglecting what truly matters.

Prioritizing means identifying the tasks or solutions that will have the biggest impact. It's about working smarter, not harder, so your efforts lead to meaningful results.

How to Prioritize Effectively

1. **Identify Key Goals**

   What's the ultimate goal you're trying to achieve? Let this guide your priorities. For instance, if you're launching a product, your top goal might be ensuring it's functional — not perfect.

2. **Rank Tasks by Impact**

   Use a simple system to rank tasks as high, medium, or low priority based on their impact. Focus on high-impact tasks first.

3. **Apply the 80/20 Rule**

   The Pareto Principle states that 80% of results often come from 20% of your efforts. Identify the 20% of tasks that will drive the most significant outcomes and prioritize those.

4. **Consider Deadlines**

   Tasks with urgent deadlines may take priority, but don't let deadlines alone determine importance. Always weigh impact alongside urgency.

5. **Say No to the Unnecessary**

   Sometimes prioritizing means eliminating tasks that don't align with your goals. Don't be afraid to say no to distractions.

   A Real-Life Example

   Imagine you're preparing for a big exam. You have 10 topics to study, but only three days left. Instead of trying to cram everything, you prioritize the five topics most likely to appear on the test. By focusing on what matters most, you maximize your chances of success.

Choose a current problem or project. List all the tasks involved, then rank them as high, medium, or low priority. Focus on completing just one high-priority task today.

Takeaway

Not everything deserves your attention. Focus on what matters most, and you'll achieve better results with less effort.

Chapter 9: Spot Hidden Assumptions

When solving problems, people often take certain things for granted. These hidden assumptions act like invisible roadblocks, steering you in the wrong direction or limiting your options without you even realizing it. Spotting and challenging these assumptions is one of the most powerful tools for effective problem-solving.

For example, if a store owner assumes that customers aren't buying because the prices are too high, they might focus on discounts. But what if the real issue is that the store feels cluttered or unwelcoming? The assumption about price could lead them to waste time and money solving the wrong problem.

How to Spot and Challenge Hidden Assumptions

1. **Write Down What You Assume**

   When approaching a problem, take a moment to list your assumptions. For example, "Our team is late on projects because they're lazy" or "This project will take at least three months."

2. **Ask, "How Do I Know This?"**

   Question each assumption. Do you have solid evidence, or are you guessing? If you can't prove an assumption, it's worth rethinking.

3. **Flip the Assumption**

   Reverse your assumption and consider what happens if it isn't true. For example, if you assume "Customers want lower prices," ask, "What if customers actually want better quality?" This often leads to fresh insights.

4. **Test the Assumption**

   Find ways to test your assumptions quickly. If you assume a project will take three months, break it into smaller pieces and try completing the first step in one week to see if your timeline holds.

5. **Invite External Perspectives**

   Others can often spot assumptions you miss. Share your problem with someone outside your situation and ask them what they see.

A Real-Life Example

A non-profit organization assumes their volunteers are quitting because they're overworked. But when they conduct a survey, they discover the real issue: volunteers don't feel appreciated. By recognizing this hidden assumption, the non-profit shifts its focus to improving recognition and retention increases dramatically.

Exercise

Think of a current problem. Write down one assumption you're making about it. Then, ask yourself: "What if this isn't true? What else might be happening?" Test this reversed assumption and see what insights arise.

Takeaway

Hidden assumptions can blind you to better solutions. Challenge what you think you know, and you'll uncover new paths to solving problems.

Chapter 10: Embrace Uncertainty

Some problems don't have clear answers. The path forward feels uncertain and full of risk. It's tempting to avoid these situations or wait until you feel 100% sure of the solution. But here's the truth: certainty is a luxury you rarely get when solving real-world problems. The best problem-solvers learn to embrace uncertainty and take action anyway.

Uncertainty isn't something to fear — it's part of the process. By leaning into it, you stay open to learning, adapting, and finding better solutions as you go.

How to Embrace Uncertainty

1. **Start Small**

   When facing a big, uncertain challenge, take one small step forward. Test a small solution, gather feedback, and adjust as needed.

2. **Focus on Progress, Not Perfection**

   Waiting for the perfect solution often leads to paralysis. Instead, focus on making progress, even if it's messy.

3. **Reframe Failure as Learning**

   Uncertainty comes with the risk of failure. Instead of fearing mistakes, treat them as experiments that provide valuable insights.

4. **Stay Open to Change**

   As you gather more information, be willing to pivot. Flexibility is your biggest asset in uncertain situations.

5. **Trust the Process**

   Sometimes, clarity only comes after you start moving. Have confidence that solutions will reveal themselves as you take action.

A Real-Life Example

A start-up founder wants to create a new app but feels overwhelmed: Will people like it? How will it make money? Instead of waiting for answers, they launch a simple prototype to gather feedback. By starting small and embracing uncertainty, they gain valuable insights that shape the final product.

Exercise

Identify a problem where uncertainty is holding you back. Write down one small action you can take today to move forward, even without all the answers.

Takeaway

Uncertainty is a natural part of solving complex problems. Embrace it, take small steps, and let clarity emerge through action.

Section 2: Creative Problem-Solving

Sometimes, solving a problem means stepping out of the ordinary and exploring the unexpected. Creativity isn't just for artists — it's a powerful tool for breaking through mental blocks and finding fresh solutions. In this section, you'll learn how to spark new ideas, challenge conventional thinking, and reimagine problems from a whole new angle. These techniques will help you think outside the box and uncover solutions you never thought possible.

Chapter 11: Brainstorm Like a Pro

When facing a tricky problem, one of the best ways to spark ideas is brainstorming. It's a simple yet powerful tool: gather as many ideas as possible, without judgment or overthinking. The goal isn't perfection — it's quantity. The more ideas you generate, the higher your chances of discovering a brilliant solution.

However, brainstorming only works when you let go of criticism and embrace creativity. Every big idea started as a spark, often surrounded by less practical ones.

How to Brainstorm Effectively

1. Set a Clear Focus

Start with a specific question, like, "How can we improve our product?" or "What's a unique way to solve this customer complaint?" A focused prompt helps keep the session productive.

2. Embrace Quantity Over Quality

The goal is to generate as many ideas as possible. Even wild or impractical ideas are welcome — they often inspire better ones later.

3. Hold Off on Judgment

Don't criticize or overanalyze ideas during the brainstorming session. Save evaluation for later.

4. Involve Diverse Perspectives

Invite people with different skills or experiences to join the session. Fresh perspectives often lead to unexpected solutions.

5. Capture Everything

Write down every idea, no matter how small or incomplete it seems. A half-formed thought today might turn into a breakthrough tomorrow.

A Real-Life Example

When a tech company struggled to improve its slow-loading app, the team held a brainstorming session. At first, ideas ranged from "redesign the entire app" to "add a loading animation." One seemingly outlandish suggestion — "remove half the features" — led to a breakthrough. By simplifying the app, they not only fixed the speed issue but also improved user experience.

Exercise

Pick a current challenge, set a timer for 15 minutes, and brainstorm at least 20 ideas. Don't filter or judge—just write. Review the list afterward and highlight any promising ones.

Takeaway

Brainstorming is about unlocking creativity without fear of judgment. Generate a flood of ideas first—refinement comes later.

Chapter 12: Think Outside the Box

When you're stuck on a problem, chances are you're looking at it from only one angle. Thinking outside the box means stepping back, shifting your perspective, and exploring unconventional possibilities. It's about breaking free from habits and patterns that might limit your creativity.

The key is to challenge assumptions and reimagine the problem in a whole new way. Often, the solution isn't where you're looking — it's somewhere unexpected.

How to Think Outside the Box

1. Change Your Perspective

Imagine solving the problem from someone else's point of view. How would a child, an artist, or an engineer approach it differently?

2. Question the Rules

Are there "rules" you're following that don't actually exist? For example, if you're planning an event, do you *have* to use traditional venues?

3. Reframe the Problem

Instead of asking, "How can I sell more products?" try, "How can I make my product so valuable people can't ignore it?" Small reframes open up big ideas.

4. Experiment with Constraints

Sometimes adding unusual limits can spark creativity. For instance, "How can we solve this with zero budget?" forces you to think resourcefully.

5. Collaborate with Unlikely Allies

Work with people outside your usual circle. A designer might offer insights into a financial problem, or a teacher could help solve a business issue.

A Real-Life Example

In the 1980s, NASA needed to develop pens that worked in zero gravity. While engineers brainstormed complex solutions, someone "outside the box" suggested pencils. The simplest solution often comes from changing your perspective.

Exercise

Take a current problem and reframe it with a different question. Then, brainstorm how someone completely unrelated to the issue might solve it. Write down at least three new ideas.

Takeaway

Thinking outside the box opens doors to unconventional solutions. Shift your perspective, challenge the rules, and embrace the unexpected.

Chapter 13: Use Analogies to Spark Ideas

Sometimes the best solutions to your problems already exist—you just need to look in a different field. Analogies help you borrow ideas and approaches from one area and apply them creatively to another. It's how airplanes were inspired by birds and how factories revolutionized modern hospitals.

Using analogies can spark fresh insights and unexpected solutions, especially when your usual methods fall short.

How to Use Analogies

1. Find Similar Problems in Other Fields

Look for industries, systems, or processes that solve challenges similar to yours. For example, logistics companies can learn from how ant colonies efficiently transport food.

2. Focus on the Underlying Principle

Ask, "What's the core idea behind this solution?" For example, Velcro was inspired by the way burrs cling to fabric.

3. **Translate the Idea to Your Problem**

Apply the analogy to your specific situation. For instance, if a tech company can learn from nature's ecosystems, they might design networks that self-regulate like forests.

4. **Stay Open to Unlikely Connections**

Sometimes, the most valuable analogies come from unexpected places. Don't limit yourself to what feels obvious.

A Real-Life Example

Hospitals struggling with patient flow borrowed an idea from Formula 1 pit crews. By studying how racing teams work under intense pressure, hospitals improved their operating room handoff procedures, saving lives and cutting delays.

Exercise

Think about a problem you're trying to solve. Write down one analogy from a different field or system that faces a similar challenge. Then, brainstorm how you could adapt that idea to your problem.

Takeaway

Analogies let you borrow wisdom from the world around you. By adapting ideas from other fields, you can unlock innovative solutions.

Chapter 14: Combine Ideas for Breakthroughs

Some of the best solutions come not from a single idea but from combining multiple ideas into something greater. Think of it like mixing colors: blue and yellow alone are nice, but together they create green — a fresh, new possibility that didn't exist before.

When you combine ideas, you draw on the strengths of different approaches, balancing their weaknesses. This technique is especially useful when you're stuck between competing options or when no single idea feels "big" enough to solve your problem.

How to Combine Ideas Effectively

1. **List Your Current Ideas**

Write down all the ideas you've generated so far, no matter how incomplete or unrelated they seem.

2. **Find Common Themes**

Look for connections or overlaps between ideas. For example, if one idea focuses on saving time and another on improving accuracy, ask, "Can we combine both?"

3. **Merge Strengths, Offset Weaknesses**

Identify what's strong about each idea and see if combining them can solve the weaknesses. For example, if one idea is cheap but slow, and another is fast but expensive, merging them might create a balanced solution.

4. **Experiment with "What If" Combinations**

Ask questions such as:
   o   What if we combine the best parts of Idea A and Idea B?
   o   What happens if we apply Idea C to the context of Idea D?

5. **Prototype the Hybrid Solution**

Test the combined idea on a small scale. Often, the act of experimenting reveals even more ways to refine and improve it.

A Real-Life Example

When video game designers were creating "Pokémon Go," they combined the idea of traditional gaming with GPS technology and augmented reality. By merging these concepts, they created an entirely new type of game that became a global sensation.

Exercise

Take two or three ideas you've brainstormed for a current problem. Write down their strengths and weaknesses. Then, brainstorm how you could combine their best features into one stronger, hybrid solution.

Takeaway

Breakthroughs often come from combining good ideas into great ones. Merge concepts, test the hybrid, and discover solutions you couldn't see before.

Chapter 15: Play with "What If?" Scenarios

"What if?" is one of the simplest but most powerful questions you can ask when solving a problem. It invites your brain to explore new possibilities without constraints, opening doors to creative and unconventional solutions.

This technique works because it temporarily removes the mental barriers—like budgets, time limits, or existing assumptions—that often block creative thinking. Even the wildest "What if?" scenarios can inspire realistic, actionable ideas.

How to Use "What If?" Scenarios

1.   Start with the Problem

Clearly define the problem or challenge you're trying to solve. For example, "How do we increase customer engagement?"

2.   Ask Wild "What If?" Questions

Challenge the status quo by asking open-ended, imaginative questions like:

- o   "What if money weren't a factor?"
- o   "What if we started from scratch?"
- o   "What if we approached this like [another industry]?"

3.   Follow the Ideas, No Matter How Outlandish

Don't dismiss ideas that seem impractical. Even unrealistic scenarios can spark insights or lead to unexpected solutions.

4.   Look for Actionable Insights

Once you've explored your "What if?" scenarios, identify practical elements you can adapt to your real-world constraints.

5.   Repeat with New Scenarios

The beauty of "What if?" is that it works with infinite variations. Keep asking until you uncover ideas that excite you.

A Real-Life Example

When Netflix was struggling to compete with DVD rental stores, they asked, "What if there were no late fees?" This led to the subscription model that eventually revolutionized how people watch movies and TV shows.

Exercise

Take a current challenge and write down five "What if?" questions about it. Let your imagination run wild, then review your answers to find ideas worth pursuing.

Takeaway

"What if?" unlocks creative thinking by challenging assumptions and exploring possibilities. Use it to spark ideas you never thought were possible.

Chapter 16: Reverse Engineer the Solution

Sometimes, the best way to solve a problem is to start at the end. Reverse engineering means imagining the ideal solution and working backward step by step to figure out how to get there. This approach helps you see the process clearly, anticipate obstacles, and stay focused on what matters most.

How to Reverse Engineer a Solution

1.   Picture the Ideal Outcome

Start by visualizing the solution as if it's already achieved. Ask yourself: What does success look like?

2.   Work Backward Step by Step

Break the process into smaller actions, moving in reverse from the final goal to where you are now. For example, if your goal is "launch a new website," the steps might include:

- Testing the website.
- Designing the layout.
- Writing the content.
- Choosing a platform.

3. **Identify Gaps or Obstacles**

As you reverse the steps, note any missing pieces or potential challenges. For example, do you need a designer, or are there technical skills you lack?

4. **Create a Timeline**

Once you've mapped the steps, reorder them chronologically. This gives you a clear roadmap to follow.

5. **Refine as You Move Forward**

Reverse engineering provides a starting plan, but be flexible. Adjust the steps as new information emerges.

A Real-Life Example

When Elon Musk's team developed SpaceX's reusable rockets, they started by imagining a rocket that could safely land back on Earth. Then, they reverse engineered the process, figuring out the technology and steps needed to achieve that goal.

Exercise

Choose a project or problem you're working on. Write down the final outcome you want, then reverse the steps needed to get there, one action at a time.

Takeaway

Reverse engineering helps you clarify the path to success by working backward. Start at the finish line, map the steps, and follow the roadmap to your solution.

Chapter 17: Challenge Conventional Wisdom

"Because that's how it's always been done." How often have you heard this phrase? Conventional wisdom can be helpful — it's built on experience and shared knowledge — but it can also limit creative thinking. Sometimes, the solutions hiding in plain sight are invisible because we're stuck following old rules or assumptions.

Challenging conventional wisdom doesn't mean dismissing it outright. Instead, it's about questioning whether those "rules" still serve your goals. Often, the most ground-breaking ideas come from rethinking what everyone else takes for granted.

How to Challenge Conventional Wisdom

1. **Ask, "Why Do We Do It This Way?"**

Identify long-standing practices or beliefs and question their purpose. If the answer boils down to tradition or habit, it might be time to rethink it.

2. **Look for Pain Points**

If something isn't working smoothly, it's often because conventional methods are creating bottlenecks. For example, if meetings always run over time, maybe the structure needs an overhaul.

3. **Flip the Script**

Take a widely accepted rule and reverse it. For example: "What if we gave customers unlimited access instead of charging per use?" This kind of thinking can lead to revolutionary ideas, like Netflix's subscription model.

4. **Test Small Changes**

Challenge conventional wisdom in small, low-risk ways. For instance, experiment with a new workflow or offer an unconventional product feature and see how it performs.

5. **Learn from Outliers**

Study companies, individuals, or systems that defy norms and succeed. What do they do differently? How can you apply those lessons to your problem?

A Real-Life Example

Southwest Airlines famously challenged the conventional wisdom of the airline industry. Instead of offering first-class seating or meals, they focused on low prices and quick turnarounds. By breaking the mold, they created an entirely new market for budget air travel.

Exercise

Think of one "rule" or assumption guiding your current problem. Ask, "What happens if we do the opposite?" Brainstorm at least three new ideas based on this flipped perspective.

Takeaway

Conventional wisdom can be a guide, but it's not always right. Question it, flip it, and explore new possibilities.

Chapter 18: Steal Like an Artist (Ethically)

Innovation doesn't mean reinventing the wheel. Some of the best ideas are borrowed and reimagined from other fields, industries, or even competitors. "Stealing like an artist" means looking for inspiration everywhere, adapting what works, and making it your own.

The key is to borrow ethically. You're not copying someone else's work — you're learning from their successes and failures and applying those lessons to your unique situation.

How to Steal Like an Artist Ethically

1. Study What Works

Look at companies, people, or systems that solve similar problems successfully. What are they doing right, and how could you adapt their approach?

2. Focus on Principles, Not Details

Don't copy exact methods. Instead, understand the principles behind them. For example, if another company uses gamification to engage users, ask, "How can I use gamification in my context?"

3. Combine Ideas from Multiple Sources

Mix and match ideas from different fields to create something unique. A restaurant might borrow customer service strategies from a luxury hotel, for example.

4. Add Your Unique Twist

Make the borrowed idea your own by adapting it to fit your specific goals or audience.

5. Acknowledge Your Inspiration

Give credit where it's due—this builds trust and shows you're learning, not plagiarizing.

A Real-Life Example

The original iPhone wasn't the first touchscreen phone or even the first device to combine a phone and music player. But Apple borrowed successful elements from existing products and reimagined them in a sleek, user-friendly package, creating a category-defining product.

Exercise

Think of a successful person, company, or product you admire. Write down one principle or idea you could adapt to solve your current problem. Add your unique twist to make it your own.

Takeaway

Inspiration is everywhere. Borrow great ideas, adapt them creatively, and make them your own.

Chapter 19: Diverge, Then Converge

Solving problems creatively often requires two opposing steps: diverging (generating a wide range of ideas) and converging (narrowing those ideas down to the best solution). The secret is knowing when to explore freely and when to focus.

Diverging lets you uncover possibilities, while converging helps you refine and choose the most effective option. Skipping one step can lead to either too many scattered ideas or a solution that feels uninspired.

How to Diverge and Converge Effectively

1. Start by Diverging

Brainstorm freely, exploring as many ideas as possible without judgment. This is the "wild exploration" phase.

2. **Group and Categorize Ideas**

   Once you've generated a lot of ideas, look for patterns or themes. This helps make sense of the chaos and prepares you for the convergence phase.

3. **Use Criteria to Narrow Down**

   Apply filters like feasibility, impact, or cost to identify the most promising ideas. Ask, "Which ideas best align with our goals and constraints?"

4. **Refine the Final Choice**

   Once you've narrowed it down to one or two ideas, refine and polish the solution to ensure it's practical and effective.

5. **Repeat if Needed**

   Sometimes the process reveals gaps. Don't be afraid to diverge and converge again until you're confident in your solution.

   A Real-Life Example

   A marketing team brainstorming a new campaign diverged by generating over 50 ideas, ranging from quirky videos to billboard ads. They converged by focusing on the ideas that aligned with their budget and audience, ultimately choosing a social media campaign that became a hit.

   Exercise

   Take a current challenge. Spend 10 minutes brainstorming as many ideas as possible (diverge). Then, spend 10 more minutes ranking the ideas by feasibility and impact (converge). Choose one top idea to refine.

   Takeaway

   Creativity thrives in two phases: diverging to explore possibilities and converging to focus on the best solutions. Balance both for powerful results.

Chapter 20: Gamify the Process

Problem-solving doesn't have to feel like a chore. Gamifying the process can make it engaging, fun, and even competitive. By treating the challenge as a game, you activate motivation and creativity in ways that traditional methods can't.

Gamification works because it breaks problems into steps, rewards progress, and encourages experimentation. It's especially useful for tackling big, overwhelming problems that feel dull or intimidating.

How to Gamify Problem-Solving

1. **Set Clear "Levels" or Milestones**

   Break the problem into stages, like levels in a game. For example, if you're writing a report, Level 1 might be outlining, Level 2 might be drafting, and so on.

2. **Reward Progress**

   Create small rewards for completing each milestone, like taking a break or enjoying a treat.

3. **Add Time Challenges**

   Set a timer to "beat the clock" on certain tasks. This adds urgency and excitement to the process.

4. **Collaborate Competitively**

   If working with a team, create friendly challenges, like who can generate the most ideas in 10 minutes.

5. **Track Achievements**

   Visualize progress with checklists or charts. Seeing how far you've come motivates you to keep going.

   A Real-Life Example

   A teacher struggling to engage students turned homework into a game, awarding points for completing tasks and offering badges for creativity. Students became more enthusiastic, and their problem-solving skills improved dramatically.

   Exercise

   Take a project or problem and gamify it. Set levels, time challenges, or rewards for milestones. Reflect on how this changes your motivation and focus.

   Takeaway

   Gamification turns problem-solving into an engaging challenge. Break tasks into levels, add rewards, and watch your creativity and motivation soar.

Section 3: Analytical Thinking

Data doesn't lie — if you know how to read it. Analytical thinking helps you cut through confusion, uncover hidden truths, and make smarter decisions. In this section, you'll learn how to follow the evidence, uncover root causes, and use structured tools to find clear, actionable solutions.

Chapter 21: Follow the Data Trail

In a world full of opinions and assumptions, data is your anchor. Following the data trail means letting evidence guide your decisions instead of guesswork or gut feelings. Data doesn't just provide answers — it reveals patterns, disproves assumptions, and points you toward the best path forward.

When you follow the data trail, you shift from asking, "What do I think is true?" to "What does the evidence show?" This mindset leads to better decisions, stronger results, and fewer blind spots.

How to Follow the Data Trail

1. Start with a Clear Question

Identify what you're trying to answer. For example, "Why are sales declining?" or "Which product feature do customers love most?"

2. Gather Relevant Data

Collect information that's directly related to your question. This could include numbers (like sales reports), customer feedback, or performance metrics.

3. Identify Patterns or Outliers

Look for trends or anomalies. Are sales dropping during a specific season? Is one team member consistently outperforming others? Patterns hold valuable clues.

4. Avoid Confirmation Bias

Be open to what the data tells you, even if it challenges your assumptions. Don't cherry-pick evidence to fit a narrative you already believe.

5. Turn Data Into Actionable Insights

Ask yourself, "What does this data mean, and what should I do next?" For example, if data shows that customers leave after a poor onboarding experience, focus on improving that process.

A Real-Life Example

A coffee shop noticed a drop in morning customers. Instead of guessing, they reviewed their sales data and saw a sharp decline on rainy days. This insight led them to launch a rainy-day discount campaign, boosting sales during bad weather.

Exercise

Choose a current problem and identify one piece of data that could provide insights (e.g., website traffic, sales reports, or survey responses). Review the data and look for patterns or outliers. Write down one actionable step based on what you find.

Takeaway

Data is a compass in problem-solving. Follow it carefully, and it will lead you to smarter, evidence-based decisions.

Chapter 22: Use Root Cause Analysis

When a problem keeps resurfacing, it's often because you're treating the symptom instead of the root cause. Root Cause Analysis (RCA) is a structured method for digging deeper, finding the true source of a problem, and addressing it at its core.

Think of a leaky ceiling. Mopping up the puddle solves the symptom, but fixing the broken roof solves the cause. RCA ensures you focus on the roof, not just the puddle.

How to Perform Root Cause Analysis

1. Define the Problem Clearly

Start by describing what's happening. For example, "Our projects are consistently delayed."

2. Use the Five Whys Technique

Ask "Why?" repeatedly to trace the problem back to its source:

- o *Why are projects delayed?* Teams miss deadlines.
- o *Why do teams miss deadlines?* They don't get updates in time.
- o *Why don't they get updates?* Communication tools are unreliable.

3. Identify Contributing Factors

Complex problems often have more than one root cause. Consider all possible factors, such as processes, people, or tools.

4. Test Your Findings

Verify that addressing the root cause will resolve the issue. For example, if communication tools are the problem, improving them should speed up project timelines.

5. Take Action

Implement a solution that targets the root cause, not just the symptoms.

A Real-Life Example

A factory struggling with defective products discovered that the root cause wasn't poor assembly but faulty raw materials from a supplier. Fixing this issue at the source dramatically reduced defects.

Exercise

Think of a recurring problem. Write down the visible symptom, then use the Five Whys to dig into the root cause. Test your findings by asking, "If I fix this, will the problem go away?"

Takeaway

Symptoms are temporary. To solve problems permanently, dig deep and address the root cause.

Chapter 23: Find Patterns and Trends

Patterns are everywhere — if you know where to look. Spotting patterns and trends in data can help you uncover recurring issues, predict outcomes, and identify hidden opportunities. When you understand these underlying rhythms, you can solve problems proactively instead of reacting to them.

How to Find Patterns and Trends

1. Collect Data Over Time

Patterns often emerge only when you look at information over a period of days, weeks, or months. For example, tracking sales daily might reveal seasonal peaks and dips.

2. Compare Across Categories

Look for similarities or differences between groups. For instance, which products sell best to younger customers versus older ones?

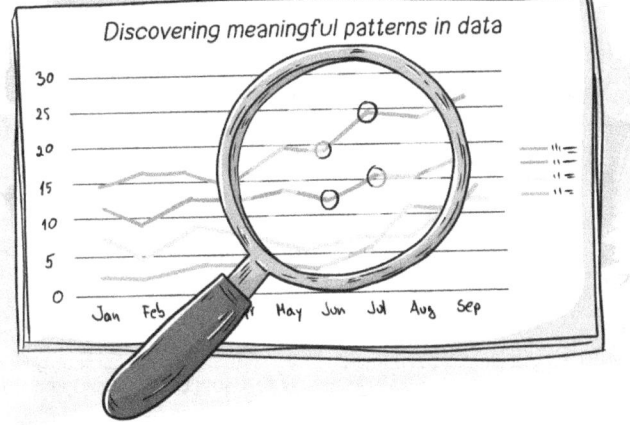

Discovering meaningful patterns in data

3. **Highlight Outliers**

Outliers—data points that deviate from the norm—can reveal important insights. For example, if one marketing campaign outperformed others, study why it succeeded.

4. **Use Visual Tools**

Graphs, heatmaps, and dashboards make it easier to spot trends. For example, a line graph can show if performance is improving or declining over time.

5. **Ask "Why?" to Understand Patterns**

Once you identify a pattern, dig deeper to understand the cause. For example, if sales increase on weekends, is it because of foot traffic, promotions, or something else?

A Real-Life Example

An e-commerce company tracked customer behavior and noticed a pattern: most cart abandonments occurred on the payment page. Further analysis revealed that unclear pricing was the issue. Simplifying the checkout process increased conversions.

Exercise

Choose a problem and gather data related to it over time. Look for patterns or outliers, and write down one insight you can act on to improve the situation.

Takeaway

Patterns and trends reveal the hidden story behind the numbers. Spot them, understand them, and use them to solve problems before they grow.

Chapter 24: Use Decision Trees for Clarity

When faced with complex decisions, it's easy to feel overwhelmed by all the options. A decision tree is a simple yet powerful tool that helps you map out choices, predict outcomes, and make informed decisions. It works like a flowchart, guiding you through a series of steps and clarifying the consequences of each choice.

Decision trees take the guesswork out of decision-making by helping you visualize your options and their potential outcomes. They're especially helpful for problems that involve multiple paths or uncertain results.

How to Use a Decision Tree

1. **Start with Your Main Question**

Write the problem or decision at the top of the tree. For example, "Should I expand my business to a new location?"

2. **List Key Choices**

Identify the main options available to you. For example, "Yes" or "No" to expanding. These form the first branches of the tree.

3. **Add Consequences for Each Choice**

For every option, map out what could happen next. For example:
   - *If Yes*: Increased revenue, but higher expenses.
   - *If No*: No growth, but stable finances.

4. **Factor in Probabilities and Risks**

If possible, estimate the likelihood of each outcome. For example, "There's a 70% chance the new location will succeed."

5. **Analyze the Tree**

Follow each branch to its conclusion. Which path leads to the most desirable outcome based on your goals?

A Real-Life Example

A non-profit deciding whether to launch a new program used a decision tree. They mapped out two paths: launching (with higher costs but greater impact) and not launching (saving money but missing opportunities). By analyzing the potential outcomes, they chose to pilot the program on a small scale first—a decision that balanced risk and reward.

Exercise

Take a decision you're facing. Draw a decision tree, starting with your question at the top. Map out at least two options and the potential consequences of each. Use this visual tool to clarify your next steps.

Takeaway

Decision trees break down complex problems into clear, logical steps. Use them to map choices, predict outcomes, and make smarter decisions.

Chapter 25: Apply Pareto's Principle (80/20 Rule)

Pareto's Principle, also known as the 80/20 Rule, states that 80% of outcomes often come from 20% of inputs. This idea is powerful for problem-solving because it helps you focus your time and energy on the few things that matter most.

Whether you're managing a team, solving a recurring issue, or improving your own productivity, the 80/20 Rule can guide you to prioritize high-impact actions and ignore distractions.

How to Apply the 80/20 Rule

1. Identify Your Key Inputs

Ask, "What are the 20% of actions or resources driving 80% of my results?" For example, in sales, this might mean focusing on your top-performing products or clients.

2. Eliminate Low-Value Efforts

Look for tasks, processes, or habits that consume time but deliver little value. Cutting these frees up energy for more impactful actions.

3. Focus on High-Impact Activities

Spend more time on the things that create the biggest results. For example, if outreach emails bring in most of your clients, prioritize that over less effective strategies.

4. Reassess Regularly

The 80/20 balance isn't fixed. Regularly evaluate what's driving success and adjust your focus accordingly.

5. Apply It Beyond Work

The 80/20 Rule works in all areas of life. For example, 20% of your social interactions may bring you 80% of your happiness. Use this insight to invest more time in what truly matters.

A Real-Life Example

A small business owner discovered that 80% of their revenue came from just 20% of their products. By focusing on promoting and improving those products, they doubled their profits while spending less on less successful items.

Exercise

Look at a project or problem you're working on. Identify the 20% of actions, people, or tools that are driving 80% of the results. Write down how you can focus more on these high-impact areas.

Takeaway

Most results come from a few key efforts. Focus on the 20% that matters, and you'll multiply your impact with less effort.

Chapter 26: Test Your Hypothesis

When solving problems, it's easy to jump to conclusions about what will work. But assumptions can lead you astray. Hypothesis testing is about treating your ideas like experiments: test them, gather results, and refine your approach based on evidence.

This process prevents wasted time and ensures you're solving the real problem with the best solution.

How to Test Your Hypothesis

1. Define Your Hypothesis

Write a clear statement about what you believe to be true. For example, "If we shorten delivery times, customer satisfaction will increase."

2. Create a Testable Experiment

Design a small, manageable test to validate your hypothesis. For example, reduce delivery times for a small group of customers and measure their feedback.

3. Gather Data

Collect evidence from your experiment. Focus on measurable results, like customer satisfaction ratings or sales figures.

4. **Analyze the Results**

    Did the data support your hypothesis? If not, look for clues about what didn't work and adjust your approach.

5. **Refine and Retest**

    Testing is an iterative process. Use your findings to improve your solution and test again if needed.

    A Real-Life Example

    An app developer hypothesized that simplifying the user interface would increase engagement. They tested this by launching a cleaner design for 10% of users. When engagement jumped by 15%, they rolled out the update to all users with confidence.

    Exercise

    Think of a problem or idea you're working on. Write a hypothesis about what you think will work, then design a small experiment to test it. Gather results and use them to refine your approach.

    Takeaway

    Testing your hypothesis turns assumptions into evidence. Experiment, learn, and refine to solve problems with confidence.

Chapter 27: Use Comparative Analysis

When solving a problem, you're often faced with multiple options. How do you decide which one is best? Comparative analysis helps you systematically evaluate choices by weighing their pros, cons, and trade-offs. This method takes the guesswork out of decision-making and ensures you're choosing the most effective path.

Comparative analysis doesn't require complex tools—it's about breaking options down into clear criteria and evaluating them side by side.

How to Use Comparative Analysis

1. **Define Your Criteria**

Decide what factors matter most for your decision. For example, when choosing a new supplier, you might prioritize cost, reliability, and delivery speed.

2. **List Your Options**

    Write down all the choices you're considering. For example, three potential suppliers.

3. **Score Each Option**

    Rate each option against your criteria on a scale (e.g., 1–10). For example:
    o   Supplier A: Cost (8), Reliability (6), Delivery Speed (7).
    o   Supplier B: Cost (5), Reliability (9), Delivery Speed (8).

4. **Weigh the Results**

    Add up the scores or use a weighted system if some criteria matter more than others.

5. **Consider Intangibles**

    Numbers don't tell the whole story. Think about qualitative factors, like relationships or brand reputation, that might influence your decision.

    A Real-Life Example

    A family deciding where to move compared three cities based on job opportunities, cost of living, and school quality. By scoring each city against these criteria, they made an informed choice that balanced practical needs and personal preferences.

    Exercise

    Pick a decision you're currently facing. Create a table with your options and criteria, then rate each option. Use the results to guide your choice.

    Takeaway

    Comparative analysis helps you choose wisely by breaking decisions into measurable parts. Weigh your options, and let the data guide you.

Chapter 28: Correlation vs. Causation

CORRELATION ≠ CAUSATION

Ice Cream Sales

Shark Attacks

Sometimes, two things seem linked because they move together, but that doesn't mean one causes the other. This is the difference between correlation (a relationship) and causation (one thing directly affecting another). Confusing the two can lead to faulty conclusions and wasted efforts.

For example, imagine a city sees more ice cream sales and shark attacks in summer. The correlation is clear, but one doesn't cause the other—they're both tied to the weather.

Understanding this distinction helps you avoid chasing false solutions.

How to Distinguish Correlation from Causation

1. Look for Timing

If A happens before B every time, it could suggest causation. But if they happen simultaneously, it might just be correlation.

2. Consider Other Variables

Ask, "Is there a third factor influencing both?" For example, rising temperatures explain both ice cream sales and shark attacks.

3. Run Experiments

Test whether changing one variable affects the other. For example, if you believe faster customer response times improve satisfaction, try reducing response times and measuring the effect.

4. Avoid Overgeneralizing

Just because two things are linked in one scenario doesn't mean they're always related.

5. Look for Logical Connections

Ask yourself, "Does it make sense that A causes B?" If the connection feels weak or forced, it's likely just correlation.

A Real-Life Example

A company noticed that sales were higher on sunny days and assumed it was because of their marketing campaigns. Further analysis revealed the real cause: better weather increased foot traffic near their store, not their ads.

Exercise

Think of a recent situation where you noticed two trends. Write down possible third factors or alternative explanations to test whether it's correlation or causation.

Takeaway

Correlation doesn't always mean causation. Dig deeper to avoid chasing false connections and focus on real solutions.

Chapter 29: Solve for Variables

In problem-solving, unknowns can feel like roadblocks. Solving for variables means isolating those unknowns, understanding their role, and finding solutions step by step. This structured, logical approach turns complex challenges into manageable puzzles.

Think of it like solving a math problem: instead of trying to tackle everything at once, you focus on the unknown variable and work backward.

How to Solve for Variables

1. Define the Variables

List the unknowns in your problem. For example, "What's causing delays in our production process?"

2. **Break Down the Problem**

Simplify the problem into smaller parts. For example: delays could be caused by staffing, equipment, or workflow.

3. **Test Each Variable**

Isolate one variable at a time to test its impact. For example, adjust staffing levels and see if delays improve.

4. **Eliminate Non-Factors**

Cross off variables that don't affect the outcome. Focus only on the ones that matter.

5. **Combine Findings**

Once you understand each variable's role, create a plan that addresses them together for a comprehensive solution.

A Real-Life Example

An online store struggling with cart abandonment broke the problem into variables: pricing, shipping speed, and website design. By testing each one, they discovered that unclear pricing was the main issue. Solving this variable reduced cart abandonment by 25%.

Exercise

Write down a problem with multiple unknowns. List the possible variables, test each one's impact, and eliminate those that don't matter.

Takeaway

Solving for variables simplifies complex problems. Isolate the unknowns, test them, and build solutions step by step.

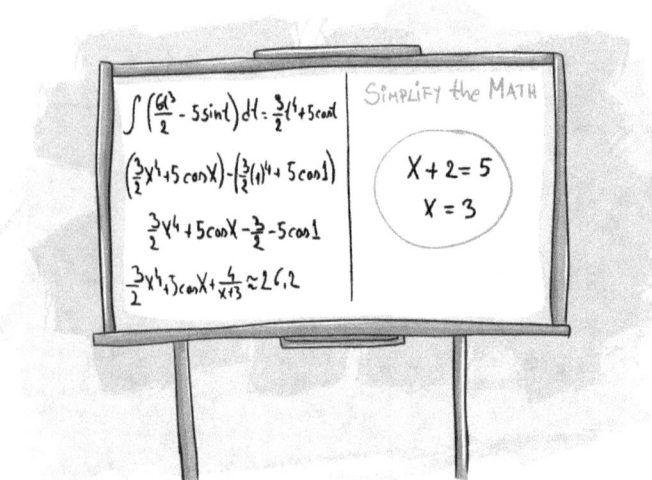

Chapter 30: Simplify the Math

Numbers can feel intimidating, but they're often the key to understanding problems. Simplifying the math means breaking complex calculations into smaller, manageable parts. It's not about being a math genius — it's about making numbers work for you.

From budgets to time estimates, simplifying the math gives you clarity and confidence to make better decisions.

How to Simplify the Math

1. **Focus on the Big Picture**

Start with rough estimates instead of exact numbers. For example, if a project will take 3-5 weeks, assume 4 weeks and refine as needed.

2. **Break Problems into Steps**

Divide complex calculations into smaller pieces. For example, if calculating costs for an event, break it into categories like venue, catering, and decorations.

3. **Round Numbers When Possible**

Use simple estimates instead of precise figures unless accuracy is critical.

4. **Use Ratios and Percentages**

Ratios can quickly show relationships. For example, "This product accounts for 60% of our revenue" simplifies understanding its importance.

5. **Leverage Tools**

Use calculators, spreadsheets, or apps to handle repetitive or complex calculations, freeing up mental energy for analysis.

A Real-Life Example

A manager estimating team workloads used simplified math: dividing total hours by team members to determine individual capacity. By rounding numbers, they quickly identified who could handle extra tasks without overloading anyone.

Exercise

Take a problem involving numbers. Simplify it by estimating, rounding, or breaking it into smaller calculations. Reflect on how this makes the problem easier to handle.

Takeaway

Math doesn't have to be complicated. Simplify numbers into manageable steps to gain clarity and confidence in your decisions.

Section 4: Strategic Approaches

Strategy is the bridge between where you are and where you want to go. It's about thinking ahead, weighing trade-offs, and finding the smartest path to success. In this section, you'll learn techniques to plan backward, identify leverage points, and prepare for uncertainty — all while staying focused on what truly matters.

Chapter 31: Plan Backward from Success

One of the best ways to solve a problem is to start at the end. Imagine your goal is already achieved, and then work backward to figure out the steps that got you there. This method, called backward planning, helps you clarify the exact actions you need to take while avoiding unnecessary detours.

Backward planning works because it forces you to think about the big picture. Instead of asking, "What do I do next?" you're asking, "What needs to happen to achieve the outcome I want?"

How to Plan Backward

1. **Visualize the Goal**

Imagine your goal is already accomplished. What does success look like? Be as specific as possible. For example: "I've successfully launched my online store with 20 products available."

2. **Identify the Last Step**

What's the final action required to reach the goal? For example, "Launch the website."

3. **Work Backward, Step by Step**

Trace the path in reverse, identifying each necessary step. For example:
   - Test the website.
   - Upload product photos and descriptions.
   - Set up payment systems.

4. **Refine and Organize**

Rearrange the steps into a logical order and identify dependencies (e.g., you can't upload product photos until they're taken).

5. **Create a Timeline**

Assign deadlines to each step to ensure you stay on track.

A Real-Life Example

An event planner organizing a conference started by imagining the final day of the event: attendees leaving satisfied with the experience. Working backward, they identified steps like confirming speakers, booking the venue, and promoting the event. This backward plan ensured nothing important was missed.

Exercise

Think of a current goal. Write down the end result, then work backward to identify at least five steps needed to achieve it. Rearrange them into a timeline and start with the first step.

Takeaway

Planning backward from success gives you a clear roadmap to achieve your goals. Start at the finish line and trace the path step by step.

Chapter 32: Think Like a Chess Player

Great problem-solving requires thinking several steps ahead, just like in chess. Chess players don't focus only on their next move—they consider how each action affects future moves and anticipate what their opponent might do in response.

By thinking strategically, you can anticipate obstacles, plan countermeasures, and create solutions that hold up over time.

1. Look Beyond the Immediate Problem

Ask, "What happens after I solve this?" For example, if you cut costs to boost profits, will quality suffer and drive customers away?

2. Consider Multiple Scenarios

Think about how your actions might play out in different ways. What's the best-case, worst-case, and most likely outcome?

3. Anticipate Challenges

Identify potential obstacles and plan how you'll address them. For example, if a competitor responds to your new product, how will you maintain your edge?

4. Think in Chains of Events

Visualize how one decision leads to another. For example:

- ○ Hire more staff → Faster production → Higher customer satisfaction → Increased revenue.

5. Adapt as the Game Changes

Be ready to adjust your strategy based on new information or unexpected developments.

A Real-Life Example

A tech start-up planning to launch a new app anticipated that competitors would try to copy their features. They thought ahead by securing patents and creating unique branding, ensuring long-term success even if others entered the market.

Exercise

Think about a problem you're solving. Write down how your solution could affect future events. Identify one potential challenge and plan a countermeasure.

Takeaway

Strategic problem-solving means thinking several steps ahead. Anticipate challenges and consider the ripple effects of your decisions.

Chapter 33: Leverage Opportunity Costs

Every decision you make has a cost — what you give up by choosing one option over another. This is called opportunity cost. By understanding and weighing these trade-offs, you can make smarter decisions that maximize value and minimize regret.

How to Weigh Opportunity Costs

1. Identify What You're Giving Up

For every choice, ask, "What am I missing out on by choosing this?" For example, if you spend $1,000 on advertising, you can't use that money for product development.

2. Quantify the Trade-Offs

Estimate the potential value of each option. Which one offers the biggest payoff?

3. Think Long-Term

Opportunity costs aren't always immediate. For example, skipping an investment in training today could lead to lost productivity down the line.

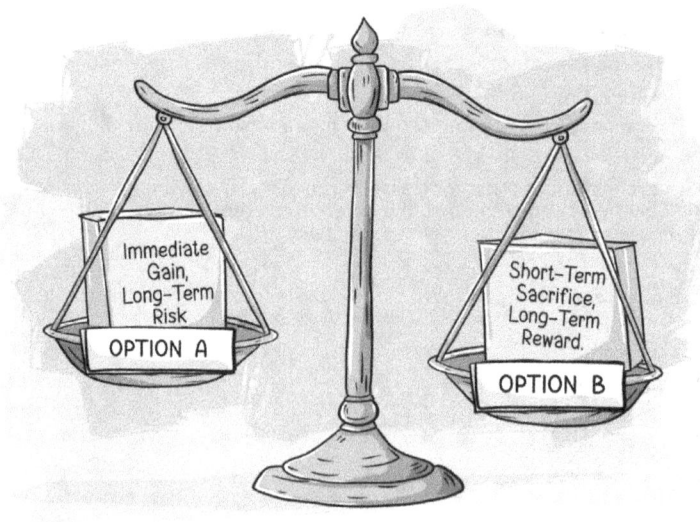

4. **Consider Hidden Costs**

Some costs aren't obvious at first. For example, choosing a cheap supplier might save money upfront but lead to quality issues later.

5. **Prioritize High-Value Options**

Focus on decisions that offer the greatest long-term value, even if they require short-term sacrifices.

A Real-Life Example

A college student deciding between two internships considered opportunity costs. One paid well but offered little growth potential, while the other had no pay but provided valuable experience. Choosing the second internship led to a high-paying job after graduation.

Exercise

Think about a decision you're facing. Write down what you'll gain and lose from each option. Compare the long-term value of each choice and prioritize accordingly.

Takeaway

Every choice has a cost. Weigh the trade-offs and focus on decisions that maximize value over the long term.

Chapter 34: Identify Key Leverage Points

Not all actions are created equal. Some have an outsized impact, like flipping the right switch in a complex system. These are leverage points—small changes that lead to significant results. By identifying and focusing on leverage points, you can solve problems more efficiently and effectively.

How to Find Leverage Points

1. **Map the Problem**

Break the problem into its components and look for areas where small adjustments could ripple outward.

2. **Focus on Bottlenecks**

Identify the one factor slowing everything down. Fixing this can improve the entire process.

3. **Look for High-Impact Actions**

Ask, "Which change will produce the biggest result?" For example, improving team communication could reduce delays across multiple projects.

4. **Test Small Changes**

Experiment with minor adjustments to see how they affect the system as a whole.

5. **Refine and Scale**

Once you've identified a successful leverage point, focus your resources there for maximum impact.

A Real-Life Example

A factory struggling with slow production found that a single bottleneck—an outdated machine — was causing delays. Upgrading the machine improved efficiency across the entire assembly line.

Exercise

Write down the components of a current problem. Identify one area where a small change could create a big impact. Test it and measure the results.

Takeaway

Leverage points are where small changes create big results. Identify them, focus your efforts, and amplify your impact.

Chapter 35: Map the System (Systems Thinking)

Problems rarely exist in isolation. They're part of larger systems where actions in one area ripple out and affect others. Systems thinking helps you see the big picture by mapping out how all the parts of a problem interact. Instead of treating symptoms, you can address the system as a whole, finding solutions that work long-term.

How to Use Systems Thinking

1. Identify the System

Define the system you're working with. Is it a team, a business process, or a community issue?

2. List the Components

Break the system into its key parts. For example, in a supply chain, components might include suppliers, transportation, and storage.

3. Trace Interconnections

Map how each component influences others. For example, delays in transportation might disrupt storage, which affects customer satisfaction.

4. Look for Feedback Loops

Feedback loops occur when actions reinforce or counteract one another. For example, positive feedback loops (like word-of-mouth marketing) amplify success, while negative loops (like repeated mistakes) perpetuate failure.

5. Address Root Causes, Not Symptoms

Use your system map to find where the problem originates. Fixing one part of the system often improves everything else.

A Real-Life Example

A school struggling with low student performance used systems thinking to map the problem. They discovered that a lack of teacher training (one component) was affecting classroom engagement, leading to lower test scores. By improving teacher training, they strengthened the entire system.

Exercise

Choose a problem and list its components. Draw a simple map showing how the parts are connected. Identify one area where a small change could positively affect the whole system.

Takeaway

Every problem exists within a system. Map out the parts, find the connections, and solve for the whole, not just the symptoms.

Chapter 36: Scenario Planning for Uncertainty

The future is uncertain, but that doesn't mean you have to feel unprepared. Scenario planning is a strategic tool that helps you anticipate multiple possible outcomes and prepare for them. By imagining "what if" scenarios, you can adapt to surprises, seize opportunities, and minimize risks.

How to Use Scenario Planning

1. Define the Decision or Problem

Start with a specific challenge, like launching a new product or responding to market changes.

2. Identify Key Variables

List factors that could influence the outcome, such as customer demand, economic conditions, or competitor actions.

3. Create Scenarios

Develop three scenarios:

- Best case: Everything goes better than expected.
- Worst case: Major obstacles arise.
- Most likely case: A realistic middle ground.

4. **Plan for Each Scenario**

   Outline how you'd respond to each outcome. For example, if demand spikes (best case), you might need extra inventory; if demand drops (worst case), you might adjust your marketing strategy.

5. **Stay Flexible**

   Scenario planning isn't about predicting the future—it's about staying adaptable no matter what happens.

   A Real-Life Example

   An event organizer used scenario planning for an outdoor concert. They prepared for sunny weather (best case), rain (worst case), and cloudy skies (most likely). When rain arrived, they smoothly implemented their backup plan, minimizing disruptions.

   Exercise

   Choose a decision or challenge. Write down three possible scenarios (best, worst, most likely) and one action you could take for each.

   Takeaway

   Scenario planning helps you navigate uncertainty with confidence. Prepare for the best, worst, and everything in between.

Chapter 37: Build in Redundancy

Redundancy isn't wasteful—it's essential for reducing risks and improving resilience. Whether it's backup systems, extra resources, or contingency plans, redundancy ensures that if one part fails, you're not left scrambling.

Think of it like carrying a spare tire: you might never need it, but when you do, it saves the day.

How to Build in Redundancy

1. **Identify Critical Areas**

   Focus on the parts of your plan or system where failure would cause the most damage.

2. **Create Backups**

   Build duplicate systems or resources. For example, keep extra supplies on hand or train multiple team members for key roles.

3. **Distribute Responsibilities**

   Avoid relying on a single person or system. Spreading tasks across multiple people reduces the risk of disruption.

4. **Test Your Redundancies**

   Regularly check your backups to ensure they're functional. For example, test emergency procedures or backup servers.

5. **Balance Costs with Benefits**

   Redundancy comes with costs, so prioritize critical areas where the potential payoff is worth the investment.

   A Real-Life Example

   Airlines build redundancy into their operations with backup pilots, extra fuel reserves, and duplicate navigation systems. These measures ensure passenger safety even when unexpected issues arise.

   Exercise

   Think of a project or system you rely on. Identify one critical area and create a simple backup or redundancy plan to protect against failure.

   Takeaway

   Redundancy is your safety net. Build backups and contingency plans to reduce risks and stay prepared for the unexpected.

Chapter 38: Focus on Long-Term Impact

Some solutions provide quick wins but don't last, while others take time to implement but deliver lasting value. Focusing on long-term impact means prioritizing decisions that create sustainable results, even if they require patience.

How to Focus on Long-Term Impact

1. Define Your Big Picture Goals

Ask, "What outcome do I want in 1, 5, or 10 years?" Let this guide your decision-making.

2. Weigh Short-Term vs. Long-Term Benefits

Avoid sacrificing long-term gains for quick fixes. For example, cutting staff might save money now but harm productivity later.

3. Invest in Foundational Changes

Focus on solutions that strengthen the core of your system, such as improving skills, processes, or infrastructure.

4. Be Patient with Results

Long-term solutions often take time to show their impact. Stay committed and track progress over time.

5. Regularly Reassess

Periodically evaluate whether your efforts are still aligned with your long-term goals.

A Real-Life Example

A company struggling with high turnover invested in employee training and career development programs. While costly upfront, this strategy reduced turnover and boosted morale, creating a stronger workforce over time.

Exercise

Think of a current challenge. Write down one short-term solution and one long-term solution. Compare their impact and prioritize the option that delivers sustainable results.

Takeaway

Long-term thinking creates lasting success. Prioritize decisions that build sustainable value over time.

Chapter 39: Prioritize Quick Wins

Sometimes, the best way to solve a big problem is to start small. Quick wins are easy, high-impact solutions that build momentum and boost confidence. By tackling these first, you can create a ripple effect that drives progress toward bigger goals.

How to Prioritize Quick Wins

1. Look for Low-Hanging Fruit

Identify solutions that are simple to implement but have noticeable benefits.

2. Focus on High-Impact Areas

Choose wins that address key pain points or create visible improvements.

3. Use Wins to Build Momentum

Success inspires further action. Use early wins to motivate your team or keep yourself moving forward.

4. Balance Wins with Long-Term Goals

Quick wins are important, but don't let them distract from larger objectives.

5. Celebrate Success

Acknowledge and reward progress to maintain energy and focus.

A Real-Life Example

A project manager turned around a struggling team by starting with small, achievable goals, like improving meeting efficiency. These quick wins boosted morale and created momentum for tackling larger challenges.

Exercise

Think of a problem you're facing. Identify one quick win—an action you can complete in a day or two—that would create positive momentum. Take that action today.

Takeaway

Quick wins build confidence and momentum. Start small to create a ripple effect that drives big results.

Chapter 40: Think Incrementally

Big problems don't have to be solved all at once. Incremental thinking means breaking solutions into smaller, manageable steps and tackling them one at a time. This approach makes even the most daunting challenges feel achievable.

How to Think Incrementally

1. Break the Problem Into Stages

Divide the challenge into logical phases. For example, "Research," "Plan," "Execute."

2. Set Milestones

Define clear, measurable checkpoints along the way to track progress.

3. Focus on the Next Step

Avoid getting overwhelmed by the big picture. Concentrate on completing one step at a time.

4. Iterate and Improve

Treat each step as a chance to learn and refine your approach.

5. Celebrate Progress

Acknowledge small wins at every milestone to stay motivated.

A Real-Life Example

An author writing a novel broke the process into daily word count goals. By focusing on writing 500 words a day, they completed the entire book in six months without feeling overwhelmed.

Exercise

Choose a big goal and break it into three stages. Focus on completing just the first step this week and celebrate your progress.

Takeaway

Incremental progress turns big problems into manageable steps. Solve one stage at a time and build your way to success.

Section 5: Collaborative Problem-Solving

Some problems are too big or complex to solve alone. Collaborative problem-solving taps into the power of teamwork, bringing together diverse skills, perspectives, and ideas to create better solutions. In this section, you'll learn how to listen effectively, build consensus, and avoid common pitfalls like groupthink—all while strengthening your team's ability to solve problems together.

Chapter 41: Harness the Power of Teamwork

They say "two heads are better than one," but why stop at two? Teamwork accelerates problem-solving by combining different skills, knowledge, and perspectives. A well-coordinated team can accomplish more than any individual because they pool strengths, share responsibilities, and support each other through challenges.

However, teamwork isn't just about gathering people — it's about coordinating efforts and fostering collaboration.

How to Harness the Power of Teamwork

1. **Clarify Roles and Goals**

   Make sure everyone knows their role and the ultimate goal. Ambiguity leads to confusion and duplication of effort.

2. **Leverage Individual Strengths**

   Assign tasks based on each person's unique skills. For example, one team member might excel at data analysis, while another shines in creative brainstorming.

3. **Encourage Open Communication**

   Foster an environment where team members feel comfortable sharing ideas and feedback.

4. **Coordinate Efforts**

   Use tools like project management software or regular check-ins to keep everyone aligned and on track.

5. **Celebrate Team Wins**

   Recognize and reward the team's collective achievements to maintain motivation and morale.

A Real-Life Example

A start-up facing tight deadlines divided tasks among team members based on their expertise. Designers focused on visuals, developers handled functionality, and marketers crafted messaging. By working in sync, they launched their product on time and exceeded expectations.

Exercise

Think of a challenge that would benefit from teamwork. Write down each person's potential role and how their skills contribute to the solution. Then, create a plan to collaborate effectively.

Takeaway

Teamwork solves problems faster and smarter. Combine strengths, coordinate efforts, and watch your team achieve more together.

Chapter 42: Listen Before Solving

It's tempting to jump straight into solutions, especially when faced with a problem. But the best solutions come from fully understanding the issue—and that requires listening first. Listening uncovers key details, builds trust, and ensures that everyone feels heard, which is critical for effective collaboration.

How to Listen Before Solving

1. Ask Open-Ended Questions

Encourage people to share their thoughts by asking questions like, "What do you think is causing this problem?" or "How do you think we should address it?"

2. Avoid Interrupting

Let others finish speaking before jumping in. Interruptions can shut down valuable insights.

3. Clarify and Summarize

Repeat back what you've heard to confirm your understanding. For example: "So you're saying the delays are due to unclear instructions?"

4. Pay Attention to Non-Verbal Cues

Body language and tone often reveal more than words alone.

5. Hold Off on Judgments

Stay open to all perspectives, even if they differ from your initial assumptions.

A Real-Life Example

A manager dealing with low team morale started by holding one-on-one listening sessions with employees. They discovered that unclear goals and a lack of recognition were key issues. By addressing these concerns, morale improved dramatically.

Exercise

In your next team discussion, focus on listening. Ask open-ended questions, summarize what you hear, and avoid interrupting. Reflect on how this changes the conversation.

Takeaway

Listening uncovers the heart of the problem. Understand first, then solve—it's the fastest path to meaningful solutions.

Chapter 43: Balance Diverse Perspectives

Diversity is a superpower in problem-solving. Different perspectives—shaped by backgrounds, skills, or experiences—reveal insights and ideas that a single viewpoint might miss. But balancing those perspectives takes skill, especially when opinions conflict.

By valuing and integrating diverse viewpoints, you create richer solutions that work for everyone involved.

How to Balance Diverse Perspectives

1. Create a Safe Space for Sharing

Encourage all team members to voice their opinions without fear of judgment.

2. Actively Seek Out Differences

Ask, "What's another way to look at this?" or "Does anyone see a risk we're missing?"

3. **Bridge Conflicting Views**

Look for common ground or compromises between opposing ideas. For example, one person's push for speed might align with another's focus on quality through better planning.

4. **Use a Mediator if Needed**

When disagreements escalate, a neutral party can help ensure every voice is heard.

5. **Synthesize Ideas**

Combine elements from different perspectives to create a stronger, more inclusive solution.

A Real-Life Example

A non-profit solving a community issue invited input from residents, local businesses, and government officials. By balancing their diverse priorities, they created a solution that satisfied all parties and gained widespread support.

Exercise

Think of a decision where multiple perspectives could help. Gather input from at least three people with different viewpoints and combine their ideas into a single, balanced solution.

Takeaway

Diverse perspectives strengthen problem-solving. Seek out differences, bridge gaps, and build solutions that reflect the whole picture.

Chapter 44: Build Consensus with Stakeholders

Great solutions only work if everyone involved is on board. Building consensus means aligning stakeholders—team members, leaders, customers, or partners—around a shared goal. While it takes effort, consensus smooths implementation and ensures lasting results.

How to Build Consensus

1. **Identify Stakeholders**

List everyone affected by the decision. For example, employees, clients, or external partners.

2. **Communicate Early and Often**

Share the problem, potential solutions, and progress updates. Transparent communication builds trust.

3. **Address Concerns**

Listen to objections and adjust your approach if needed. Consensus doesn't mean forcing agreement—it means finding a solution everyone can support.

4. **Highlight Shared Goals**

Focus on common objectives to unite stakeholders. For example, "We all want this project to succeed."

5. **Confirm Commitment**

Before moving forward, ensure that everyone is aligned and committed to the plan.

A Real-Life Example

A company rolling out a new policy gained consensus by holding feedback sessions with employees and management. By addressing concerns early, they avoided resistance and ensured smooth implementation.

Exercise

Choose a project or problem involving multiple stakeholders. Hold a meeting to share updates, gather feedback, and address concerns. Focus on aligning everyone toward a shared goal.

Takeaway

Consensus builds trust and ensures smoother implementation. Align stakeholders early to create solutions that work for everyone.

Chapter 45: Use Structured Decision-Making

Group decisions can easily become chaotic without structure. Structured decision-making provides a clear, step-by-step process for evaluating options and reaching a conclusion. This approach minimizes bias, ensures fairness, and keeps the team focused.

How to Use Structured Decision-Making

1. **Define the Problem Clearly**

   Make sure everyone understands the issue. For example, "How should we allocate next year's budget?"

2. **Set Criteria for Evaluation**

   Agree on the factors that will guide the decision, like cost, time, or impact.

3. **Generate and Compare Options**

   Brainstorm solutions, then evaluate each one against the criteria.

4. **Vote or Decide by Consensus**

   Use tools like majority voting, weighted scoring, or consensus-building to finalize the choice.

5. **Document the Decision**

   Record the reasoning behind the choice to avoid confusion later.

A Real-Life Example

A school district deciding on a new curriculum used structured decision-making. They listed key criteria (student outcomes, cost, teacher training) and scored each option. This transparent process gained widespread support.

Exercise

Think of a group decision you need to make. Set criteria, list options, and use a structured method (like weighted scoring) to choose the best solution.

Takeaway

Structured decision-making brings clarity and fairness to group choices. Follow a clear process for smarter, more efficient decisions.

Chapter 46: Avoid Groupthink

Groupthink is the enemy of smart collaboration. It happens when team members prioritize harmony and agreement over critical thinking and honest debate. While it may feel easier to agree quickly, groupthink often leads to poor decisions because key perspectives are ignored, and potential risks are overlooked.

Avoiding groupthink doesn't mean fostering endless conflict—it means creating a culture where questioning and disagreement are welcomed. When people feel safe to challenge ideas, the team produces stronger, more creative solutions.

How to Avoid Groupthink

1. **Encourage Dissent**

   Let your team know it's okay to challenge ideas. Ask directly, "Does anyone see risks or flaws in this plan?" This invites constructive feedback.

2. **Assign a Devil's Advocate**

   Designate someone to intentionally poke holes in the group's ideas. This forces the team to consider alternative perspectives.

3. **Welcome Diverse Opinions**

   Bring in people with different expertise, backgrounds, or experiences. Diversity naturally challenges groupthink by introducing new viewpoints.

4. **Separate Idea Generation from Evaluation**

   During brainstorming, focus on gathering ideas without judgment. Once you've collected them, evaluate critically to identify the strongest options.

5. **Use Anonymous Feedback**

   If group dynamics make people hesitant to speak up, use tools like anonymous surveys or suggestion boxes to gather honest opinions.

   A Real-Life Example

   In 1961, the U.S. Bay of Pigs invasion failed partly due to groupthink. Leaders didn't challenge the plan, even though flaws were clear. NASA learned from this and implemented dissent-focused practices for future missions, improving decision-making and avoiding disasters like the Challenger launch.

   Exercise

   Think of a recent group decision. Ask yourself: Was dissent encouraged, or did the group rush to agreement? Write down one way you could create space for critical feedback in future discussions.

   Takeaway

   Groupthink weakens decision-making. Foster a culture of respectful dissent and critical thinking to create stronger, more innovative solutions.

Chapter 47: Delegate and Share Responsibility

When solving complex problems, trying to do everything yourself isn't just exhausting—it's inefficient. Delegation allows you to distribute tasks strategically, leveraging the strengths of each team member and speeding up progress. Sharing responsibility also empowers others, builds trust, and ensures that no single person is overloaded.

The key to effective delegation is clarity: knowing who's doing what, why, and how it fits into the bigger picture.

How to Delegate and Share Responsibility

1. **Match Tasks to Strengths**

   Assign tasks based on each person's skills and expertise. For example, a detail-oriented team member might handle scheduling, while a creative thinker works on brainstorming.

2. **Be Clear About Expectations**

   Outline exactly what needs to be done, why it matters, and the timeline for completion. Ambiguity leads to missed deadlines and frustration.

3. **Provide the Right Resources**

   Make sure everyone has the tools, information, and support they need to succeed.

4. **Empower, Don't Micromanage**

   Trust your team to handle their responsibilities. Check in for updates, but avoid hovering over every detail.

5. **Hold Everyone Accountable**

   Regularly review progress and celebrate milestones. If something goes off track, address it constructively and collaboratively.

   A Real-Life Example

   A marketing manager overwhelmed by a product launch delegated tasks like social media campaigns, graphic design, and analytics tracking to her team. By trusting their skills and providing clear guidance, the team delivered a successful campaign on time, freeing the manager to focus on strategy.

   Exercise

   Think of a project where you're taking on too much. Identify one task you can delegate to someone better suited for it. Write down clear instructions and provide the necessary resources to set them up for success.

   Takeaway

   Delegation isn't about offloading work—it's about sharing responsibility strategically. Leverage your team's strengths to achieve more, faster.

Chapter 48: Seek External Expertise

Sometimes, solving a problem requires knowledge or skills beyond your team's expertise. Bringing in an external expert—whether a consultant, specialist, or experienced mentor—can provide fresh insights and save you from costly mistakes.

Experts don't just bring knowledge; they offer perspective. They can spot blind spots, propose strategies you hadn't considered, and help you navigate challenges more efficiently.

How to Seek External Expertise

1. Identify Knowledge Gaps

Be honest about what your team doesn't know or lacks experience in. For example, you might need help with legal issues, technical development, or customer research.

2. Find the Right Expert

Look for someone with proven experience in the specific area. This could be a consultant, an industry leader, or even a colleague with niche expertise.

3. Collaborate, Don't Abdicate

Use the expert's guidance to inform your decisions, but stay involved. Experts enhance your process—they don't replace it.

4. Ask Targeted Questions

Come prepared with clear, specific questions to maximize the value of the expert's input.

5. Integrate Their Insights

Once you've gathered their advice, work with your team to adapt it to your unique context.

A Real-Life Example

When a small business faced a cybersecurity breach, they hired a cybersecurity expert to assess vulnerabilities and implement protections. The expert not only resolved the immediate issue but also trained the team to prevent future attacks.

Exercise

Think about a current challenge. Identify one area where an expert could provide valuable insights. Research potential experts or resources and plan to reach out for help.

Takeaway

You don't have to solve every problem alone. Seek external expertise to fill knowledge gaps, gain fresh perspectives, and navigate challenges more effectively.

Chapter 49: Communicate Solutions Effectively

Even the best solutions fail if they aren't communicated clearly. Whether you're presenting an idea to stakeholders, explaining changes to a team, or persuading a client, effective communication ensures everyone understands and supports the plan.

Clear communication is about more than sharing information—it's about building trust, addressing concerns, and inspiring action.

How to Communicate Solutions Effectively

1. Know Your Audience

Tailor your message to the needs and priorities of the people you're speaking to. What do they care about most?

2. Keep It Simple

Avoid jargon and overly complex explanations. Break the solution into clear, digestible steps.

3. **Use Visuals**

   Charts, diagrams, or slides make complex ideas easier to grasp.

4. **Address Concerns**

   Anticipate questions or objections and address them proactively. For example, explain how risks will be mitigated.

5. **End with a Call to Action**

   Clearly state what you need from your audience, whether it's approval, feedback, or next steps.

   A Real-Life Example

   A project manager presenting a new workflow to their team used a simple diagram to show how tasks would flow more efficiently. By explaining the benefits clearly and inviting questions, they gained team buy-in and implemented the changes smoothly.

   Exercise

   Think of a solution you need to communicate. Write a simple outline of your main points, including benefits, steps, and potential concerns. Practice presenting it to ensure clarity.

   Takeaway

   Clear communication turns ideas into action. Simplify your message, address concerns, and inspire your audience to support your solution.

Chapter 50: Resolve Conflicts Constructively

Conflict is inevitable in collaborative problem-solving, but it doesn't have to derail progress. When managed constructively, disagreements can lead to deeper understanding, stronger relationships, and better solutions.

The goal isn't to avoid conflict — it's to handle it with respect and focus on finding common ground.

How to Resolve Conflicts Constructively

1. **Stay Calm and Objective**

   Emotions can escalate conflicts. Focus on the problem, not the person.

2. **Listen Actively**

   Let everyone involved share their perspective without interruption. Understanding all sides is key to resolution.

3. **Focus on Shared Goals**

   Highlight common objectives to shift the focus from differences to collaboration. For example, "We all want this project to succeed."

4. **Brainstorm Solutions Together**

   Invite all parties to propose solutions. This fosters ownership and reduces resistance.

5. **Document Agreements**

   Once a resolution is reached, write it down to ensure clarity and accountability.

   A Real-Life Example

   Two departments clashing over resource allocation resolved their conflict by holding a facilitated meeting. By listening to each other's priorities and focusing on shared goals, they created a plan that balanced both teams' needs.

   Exercise

   Think of a recent conflict you've encountered. Write down the shared goals of everyone involved and one way you could encourage collaboration toward a resolution.

   Takeaway

   Conflict can lead to growth when handled constructively. Listen, focus on common goals, and work together to find solutions.

Section 6: Emotional Intelligence in Problem-Solving

Problem-solving isn't just about logic and strategy — it's also about understanding and managing emotions. Emotional intelligence helps you stay calm, think clearly, and connect with others during challenges. In this section, you'll learn how to manage stress, cultivate empathy, and build resilience, all while using your emotions as a strength, not a barrier, in solving problems.

Chapter 51: Stay Calm Under Pressure

Stressful situations make it easy to panic, but staying calm under pressure is essential for effective problem-solving. When emotions run high, your brain shifts into fight-or-flight mode, making it harder to think clearly or make rational decisions. Staying calm isn't about ignoring stress — it's about controlling your response to it.

Calmness gives you the clarity and focus to find solutions, no matter how intense the challenge.

How to Stay Calm Under Pressure

1. Pause and Breathe

When stress spikes, take a moment to focus on your breath. Deep, slow breaths signal to your brain that it's safe to relax, helping you regain control.

2. Break the Problem into Steps

Overwhelm fuels panic. Simplify the situation by breaking it into smaller, manageable tasks and tackling them one at a time.

3. Focus on What You Can Control

Stress often comes from worrying about things outside your control. Shift your attention to what you *can* influence.

4. Reframe the Situation

Instead of seeing pressure as a threat, view it as a challenge. This mindset shift boosts confidence and keeps you focused.

5. Practice Calm in Small Moments

Build your resilience by practicing calmness in less stressful situations, like traffic jams or minor setbacks.

A Real-Life Example

During an emergency at a hospital, a nurse stayed calm by focusing on her training and breaking the chaos into clear steps: assessing the patient, calling for help, and stabilizing the situation. Her composure ensured the team acted efficiently, saving a life.

Exercise

Think of a recent stressful situation. Reflect on how you reacted and write down one way you could have stayed calmer. Practice deep breathing the next time stress arises.

Takeaway

Calmness is your superpower in high-pressure moments. Pause, breathe, and focus on what you can control to think clearly and act decisively.

Chapter 52: Recognize Emotional Triggers

Emotions are powerful — they can help or hinder problem-solving, depending on how well you manage them. Emotional triggers are the moments when something causes a strong reaction, like frustration when a plan fails or doubt when someone challenges your idea. Recognizing these triggers helps you pause, reflect, and respond thoughtfully instead of reacting impulsively.

How to Recognize Emotional Triggers

1. Notice Physical Signs

Pay attention to your body's reactions—tight shoulders, a racing heart, or clenched fists often signal emotional triggers.

2. **Identify Patterns**

   Reflect on past situations that triggered strong emotions. What were the common themes or circumstances?

3. **Name the Emotion**

   When you feel triggered, label the emotion: "I'm feeling frustrated." Naming it helps you distance yourself from it and regain control.

4. **Pause Before Responding**

   Take a moment to process your feelings before acting. A short pause can prevent impulsive decisions.

5. **Understand the Root Cause**

   Ask yourself, "Why am I feeling this way?" Often, the trigger stems from deeper fears or insecurities that can be addressed.

   A Real-Life Example

   A manager who often felt defensive during team feedback realized his trigger was a fear of failure. By recognizing this, he began approaching feedback as a learning opportunity, improving both his leadership and team trust.

   Exercise

   Write down one situation where you recently felt triggered. What emotion did you experience, and what caused it? Reflect on how you might handle it differently next time.

   Takeaway

   Recognizing your emotional triggers puts you back in control. Identify patterns, name the emotion, and respond thoughtfully instead of reacting impulsively.

Chapter 53: Reframe Negative Thinking

Negative thinking can trap you in a cycle of doubt and pessimism, making it harder to see solutions. Reframing means shifting your perspective to focus on possibilities instead of problems. It's not about ignoring challenges but about choosing constructive thoughts that drive action.

Reframing turns setbacks into opportunities, making you more adaptable and resilient.

How to Reframe Negative Thinking

1. **Notice Negative Thoughts**

   Pay attention to internal dialogue like, "This will never work" or "I always mess up."

2. **Challenge the Thought**

   Ask yourself, "Is this really true?" Often, negative thinking is based on assumptions, not facts.

3. **Replace "What's Wrong?" with "What's Possible?"**

   Shift your focus to what you can learn or achieve. For example, "What can I do differently next time?"

4. **Focus on Progress, Not Perfection**

   Instead of fixating on what went wrong, celebrate small wins and improvements.

5. **Practice Gratitude**

   Reflect on what's going well or what you've learned from the situation. Gratitude boosts optimism and creativity.

   A Real-Life Example

   An entrepreneur whose product launch failed reframed the experience as a learning opportunity. Instead of giving up, they used customer feedback to redesign the product, leading to a successful relaunch.

   Exercise

   Write down one negative thought you've had about a current challenge. Challenge it by asking, "What's one positive thing I can take from this situation?"

   Takeaway

   Negative thinking clouds judgment. Reframe challenges as opportunities, and you'll unlock constructive action and better solutions.

Chapter 54: Empathy as a Problem-Solving Tool

Empathy — putting yourself in someone else's shoes — is one of the most powerful tools in problem-solving. It allows you to understand the emotions, motivations, and needs behind a problem, leading to solutions that truly work for everyone involved.

Empathy is especially critical in conflicts or customer-facing issues, where understanding the other person's perspective often reveals the root of the problem.

How to Use Empathy in Problem-Solving

1. **Listen Without Judgment**
Focus on what the other person is saying, not how you want to respond.

2. **Ask Open-Ended Questions**
Questions like "How do you feel about this?" or "What would make this better for you?" uncover valuable insights.

3. **Imagine Their Perspective**
Visualize how the problem looks and feels from their viewpoint.

4. **Acknowledge Their Emotions**
Validate their feelings by saying things like, "I can see why this would be frustrating."

5. **Design Solutions for Their Needs**
Use what you've learned to create solutions that address their priorities, not just your own.

A Real-Life Example

A customer service team reduced complaints by empathizing with customers. Instead of sticking to scripts, they listened to frustrations, acknowledged emotions, and offered personalized solutions. This approach increased customer satisfaction by 30%.

Exercise

Think of someone impacted by a current problem. Write down what the situation might feel like from their perspective and one way you could address their needs more effectively.

Takeaway

Empathy bridges gaps and uncovers deeper insights. Understand others' perspectives to create solutions that truly work for everyone.

Chapter 55: Manage Stress for Clearer Thinking

Stress is a natural part of problem-solving, but too much of it clouds your thinking and leads to poor decisions. Managing stress doesn't mean eliminating it entirely—it means controlling it so you can stay focused and productive. When you're calm, your brain works better, helping you find creative, effective solutions.

By managing stress, you create the mental clarity and emotional stability needed to approach problems with confidence.

How to Manage Stress for Clearer Thinking

1. **Identify Your Stress Triggers**
Notice what situations or thoughts cause you stress. Knowing your triggers helps you prepare and respond calmly.

2. **Practice Mindfulness**
Mindfulness exercises, like focusing on your breath or a single task, help you stay grounded in the present moment.

3. **Prioritize Self-Care**
Regular exercise, sleep, and healthy eating strengthen your ability to handle stress.

4. **Set Realistic Expectations**
Avoid overloading yourself. Break tasks into smaller steps, and focus on one thing at a time.

5. **Use Stress as a Signal**
Instead of fearing stress, treat it as a sign that something needs attention. Use it to motivate action rather than freeze in worry.

A project manager facing tight deadlines felt overwhelmed by a growing to-do list. By taking a 10-minute mindfulness break each morning and organizing tasks into smaller, manageable chunks, she stayed calm and delivered the project successfully.

Exercise

Write down one current stressor. Identify one action you can take to reduce its intensity, whether it's pausing to breathe, delegating tasks, or rethinking your priorities.

Takeaway

Stress is manageable. Stay calm by recognizing your triggers, focusing on self-care, and taking intentional steps to clear your mind.

Chapter 56: Practice Self-Awareness

Great problem-solving starts with understanding yourself. Self-awareness is the ability to recognize your thoughts, emotions, and biases—and how they influence your decisions. Without it, you might misjudge situations or let emotions cloud your judgment.

By practicing self-awareness, you can make decisions based on logic and clarity rather than impulse or habit.

How to Practice Self-Awareness

1. Identify Your Biases

Reflect on your tendencies to favor certain ideas or ignore others. Ask yourself, "Am I being objective?"

2. Pay Attention to Emotions

Notice when emotions like frustration or excitement are driving your decisions. Name them to reduce their power.

3. Reflect on Past Decisions

Think about situations where your assumptions or reactions influenced the outcome. What would you do differently?

4. Ask for Feedback

Others often see things you miss. Ask trusted colleagues or friends how your behavior or decision-making could improve.

5. Pause Before Acting

When facing a decision, take a moment to check in with yourself. Are you reacting emotionally, or thinking clearly?

A Real-Life Example

A CEO realized her preference for fast decisions often led to avoidable mistakes. By pausing to reflect and consulting her team, she became more deliberate and made better choices for the company's long-term goals.

Exercise

Think about a recent decision. Were any emotions or assumptions influencing your choice? Write down one way you could approach a similar situation with more self-awareness.

Takeaway

Self-awareness strengthens decision-making. Recognize your emotions, biases, and assumptions to approach problems with clarity and objectivity.

Chapter 57: Build Resilience

Setbacks are inevitable in problem-solving. Resilience is your ability to recover, adapt, and keep moving forward when things don't go as planned. It's not about avoiding failure—it's about learning from it and using it to grow stronger.

Resilience turns obstacles into opportunities, making you better equipped to handle future challenges.

How to Build Resilience

1.   Adopt a Growth Mindset

Treat failures as lessons. Ask, "What can I learn from this setback?"

2.   Stay Flexible

Be willing to adjust your plans when circumstances change. Rigidity leads to frustration; adaptability leads to progress.

3.   Focus on Your Strengths

Remind yourself of past challenges you've overcome. This builds confidence in your ability to handle new ones.

4.   Find Support

Lean on friends, colleagues, or mentors for encouragement and advice during tough times.

5.   Celebrate Small Wins

Acknowledge progress, no matter how small. Each step forward reinforces your resilience.

A Real-Life Example

A small business owner faced financial difficulties after losing a major client. Instead of giving up, she restructured her services, found new markets, and ultimately grew her business stronger than before.

Exercise

Write down one recent setback and what you learned from it. Then, identify one step you can take today to move forward with confidence.

Takeaway

Resilience turns failure into fuel. Learn, adapt, and keep moving forward to overcome challenges and grow stronger.

Chapter 58: Use Optimism Strategically

Optimism isn't just about seeing the bright side—it's about using hope and confidence to drive action. Strategic optimism means staying positive while remaining realistic about challenges. It's the balance between believing in a good outcome and preparing for obstacles along the way.

Optimism fuels motivation, encourages persistence, and helps you inspire others to tackle problems together.

How to Use Optimism Strategically

1.   Focus on Possibilities

Instead of dwelling on what could go wrong, focus on what could go right and how to achieve it.

2.   Acknowledge Challenges

Optimism doesn't mean ignoring risks. Identify obstacles and plan ways to address them.

3.   Visualize Success

Picture the best-case scenario and use it as motivation to take action.

4.   Spread Positivity

Optimism is contagious. Share your confidence with others to build a motivated, solution-focused team.

5.   Stay Grounded in Reality

Balance your optimism with realistic planning. Hope drives action, but preparation ensures success.

A Real-Life Example

A non-profit leader used strategic optimism to rally her team during a funding crisis. By focusing on their mission and planning creatively, they found new donors and expanded their programs.

Exercise

Think of a challenge you're facing. Write down one reason to feel optimistic about the outcome and one action you can take to make it happen.

Takeaway

Optimism fuels action and inspires progress. Stay hopeful while planning realistically to overcome challenges with confidence.

Chapter 59: Respect Other Viewpoints

Respecting other viewpoints isn't just polite—it's essential for solving problems collaboratively. When you approach disagreements with an open mind, you uncover insights you might have missed and build stronger relationships.

Instead of focusing on who's "right," focus on understanding and integrating perspectives to find the best solution.

How to Respect Other Viewpoints

1. Listen Actively

Pay attention to what others are saying, without interrupting or preparing your response.

2. Ask Questions

Show curiosity by asking, "Why do you think that?" or "What's your perspective on this issue?"

3. Acknowledge Their Valid Points

Even if you disagree, recognize where the other person is coming from. For example, "I see why that's important to you."

4. Avoid Making It Personal

Focus on the issue, not the individual. Disagreeing with someone's idea doesn't mean rejecting them.

5. Find Common Ground

Identify areas where your perspectives overlap and use them as a foundation for collaboration.

A Real-Life Example

A marketing team debating an ad campaign found common ground by combining creative and data-driven approaches. Respecting each other's priorities led to a successful, balanced campaign.

Exercise

Think of a recent disagreement. Reflect on the other person's viewpoint and write down one valid point they made. Use this perspective to find a balanced solution.

Takeaway

Respecting other viewpoints strengthens collaboration. Listen, ask questions, and find common ground to create better solutions together.

Chapter 60: Stay Open to Feedback

Feedback isn't criticism — it's an opportunity to grow. Staying open to feedback means seeing it as a tool to improve your ideas, skills, and solutions. Even when feedback feels uncomfortable, it often reveals blind spots or new perspectives that make you better.

The key is to listen without defensiveness and use feedback constructively.

How to Stay Open to Feedback

1. Invite Feedback Regularly

Proactively ask others for their thoughts on your work or approach.

2. Listen Without Defensiveness

Focus on understanding the feedback instead of preparing a rebuttal.

3. Ask for Specifics

General feedback like "This isn't working" isn't helpful. Ask for details to clarify what needs improvement.

4. **Thank the Feedback-Giver**

    Show appreciation for their input, even if you don't fully agree.

5. **Take Action**

    Use the feedback to refine your solution or process. Show others that their input made a difference.

    A Real-Life Example

    An app developer used early user feedback to identify confusing features in their design. By addressing these concerns, they improved usability and boosted customer satisfaction.

    Exercise

    Ask someone you trust for feedback on a current project or decision. Reflect on their input and write down one way you can use it to improve.

    Takeaway

    Feedback is a gift. Stay open, listen carefully, and use it to refine your approach for better results.

Section 7: Tools and Techniques

Every great problem-solver needs a toolkit. This section introduces practical methods to break down complex challenges, organize your thoughts, and find effective solutions. From visual tools like mind mapping and fishbone diagrams to structured techniques like SWOT analysis and prototyping, you'll learn how to apply proven strategies that make solving any problem easier and more efficient.

Chapter 61: SWOT Analysis Made Simple

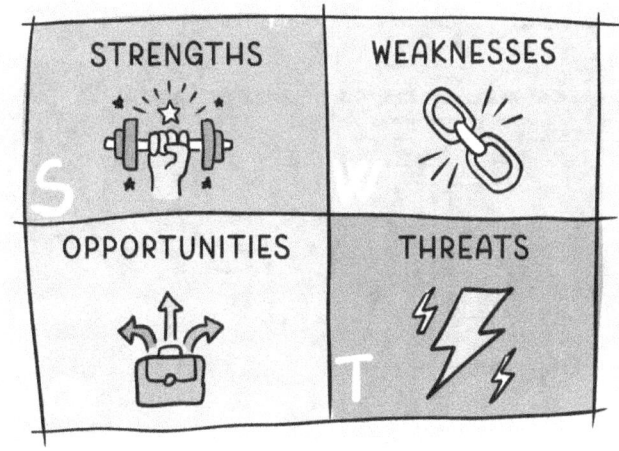

SWOT analysis is a simple yet powerful tool for evaluating any situation. By categorizing internal factors (strengths and weaknesses) and external factors (opportunities and threats), you get a clear, balanced view of where you stand and where to focus.

This method is especially useful for strategic planning, decision-making, and tackling challenges with multiple variables.

How to Use SWOT Analysis

1. **Strengths**

    Identify internal advantages. Ask, "What do we do well?" or "What resources give us an edge?" Examples might include strong leadership, unique skills, or loyal customers.

2. **Weaknesses**

    Pinpoint internal areas that need improvement. Be honest about gaps in skills, resources, or processes that could hold you back.

3. **Opportunities**

    Look for external factors that could benefit you. These could include market trends, emerging technologies, or unmet customer needs.

4. **Threats**

   List external risks or challenges. These might include competitors, economic changes, or industry regulations.

5. **Focus on Action**

   Use the insights to capitalize on strengths, minimize weaknesses, seize opportunities, and counter threats.

   A Real-Life Example

   A local bakery performed a SWOT analysis before expanding. Strengths included a loyal customer base; weaknesses highlighted limited staff. Opportunities lay in an untapped catering market, while a rising competitor was a clear threat. Their analysis led to hiring more staff and targeting catering, which boosted revenue.

   Exercise

   Choose a current project or challenge. Create a 2x2 grid and list at least two points for each SWOT category. Reflect on how this perspective shapes your strategy.

   Takeaway

   SWOT analysis clarifies your position by balancing strengths, weaknesses, opportunities, and threats. Use it to turn insights into actionable strategies.

Chapter 62: The Fishbone Diagram (Ishikawa)

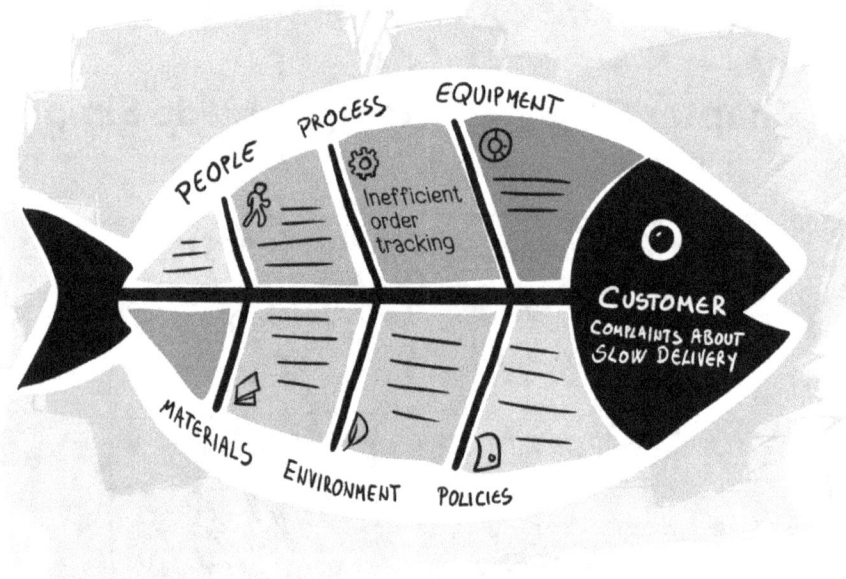

When a problem has multiple contributing factors, it's easy to get overwhelmed. The fishbone diagram, also known as the Ishikawa diagram, helps you organize potential causes visually, making it easier to identify the root issues. It's perfect for troubleshooting, process improvement, and quality control.

How to Use the Fishbone Diagram

1. **Define the Problem**

   Write the main issue at the "head" of the fish. For example, "Customer complaints about slow delivery."

2. **Identify Major Categories**

   Choose categories that might contribute to the problem. Common ones include People, Process, Equipment, Materials, Environment, and Policies.

3. **Brainstorm Causes**

   For each category, list possible contributing factors. For example, under "Process," you might include "inefficient order tracking."

4. **Analyze the Diagram**

   Review the causes to identify patterns or root issues. Focus on the factors most likely to drive improvement.

5. **Take Action**

   Use the insights to target and resolve the root causes.

   A manufacturing company used a fishbone diagram to address a rise in product defects. They found that most issues stemmed from outdated machinery under the "Equipment" category. Replacing the machines resolved the problem and improved production quality.

   Exercise

   Think of a recurring problem. Create a fishbone diagram with at least four categories and brainstorm causes for each. Highlight one or two root causes to address first.

   Takeaway

   The fishbone diagram helps you organize complex problems and pinpoint root causes. Break it down visually to uncover actionable solutions.

Chapter 63: Use the Five Whys

The Five Whys technique is a simple yet effective way to uncover the root cause of a problem. By asking "Why?" repeatedly (typically five times), you peel back the layers of symptoms to reveal the underlying issue. This method is quick, straightforward, and works for both personal and organizational challenges.

How to Use the Five Whys

1. State the Problem Clearly

Start with a specific issue. For example, "Our sales are declining."

2. Ask "Why?" Repeatedly

Each answer should lead to the next "Why." For example:

- o   Why are sales declining? Customers are leaving.
- o   Why are customers leaving? They're unhappy with support.
- o   Why are they unhappy with support? Response times are too slow.

3. **Stop at the Root Cause**

   Once you reach the fundamental issue, stop asking "Why?" and focus on fixing it.

4. **Verify the Cause**

   Check whether addressing the root cause would prevent the problem from recurring.

5. **Take Corrective Action**

   Implement a solution that targets the root cause, not just the symptoms.

   A Real-Life Example

   An IT department used the Five Whys to solve frequent system outages:

   - Why are systems crashing? Servers are overloaded.
   - Why are servers overloaded? Too many processes are running simultaneously.
   - Why? There's no process to monitor usage.

   They implemented a monitoring system, reducing outages by 80%.

   Exercise

   Choose a current challenge and apply the Five Whys. Write down each step and identify the root cause. Plan one action to address it.

   Takeaway

   The Five Whys dig beneath the surface to uncover root causes. Use it to avoid patching symptoms and solve problems at their core.

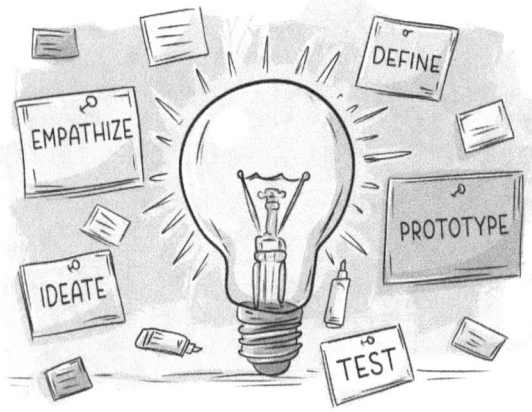

Chapter 64: Apply Design Thinking

Design thinking is a human-centered approach to problem-solving that focuses on understanding user needs, generating creative ideas, and iterating solutions through testing. It's ideal for tackling ambiguous or complex challenges because it emphasizes empathy and experimentation.

How to Apply Design Thinking

1. Empathize

Put yourself in the user's shoes. Conduct interviews, observe behaviors, or gather feedback to understand their needs and pain points.

2. Define the Problem

Turn insights into a clear problem statement. For example: "How can we make onboarding simpler for new users?"

3. Ideate

Brainstorm as many ideas as possible without judgment. Encourage creativity and out-of-the-box thinking.

4. Prototype

Create a simple version of your idea to test quickly. This could be a sketch, mockup, or basic model.

5. Test and Refine

Gather feedback on the prototype, identify what works and what doesn't, and iterate until you find the best solution.

A Real-Life Example

A healthcare provider used design thinking to improve patient wait times. After observing patients and gathering feedback, they prototyped a new scheduling system. Testing revealed improvements that cut wait times by 50%.

Exercise

Choose a problem and walk through the five stages of design thinking. Focus on the user's needs and iterate until your solution feels right.

Takeaway

Design thinking puts users at the center of problem-solving. Empathize, brainstorm, and iterate to create solutions that truly work.

Chapter 65: Use Mind Mapping for Clarity

When problems feel chaotic or overwhelming, a mind map can bring order and clarity. Mind mapping is a visual technique for organizing ideas by branching them out from a central concept. It's especially helpful for brainstorming, simplifying complex problems, or exploring solutions in a structured yet creative way.

How to Use Mind Mapping for Problem-Solving

1. Start with a Central Idea

Write the main problem or topic in the center of the page and draw a circle around it. For example, "Improve customer satisfaction."

2. Branch Out Key Categories

Draw branches from the central circle for related categories. For example: "Customer Support," "Product Features," and "User Experience."

3. Add Subcategories and Ideas

Under each branch, jot down specific issues or solutions. For example, under "Customer Support," you might add "Response Times" and "Training."

4. **Use Visual Elements**

   Add colors, icons, or drawings to highlight relationships or important points.

5. **Review and Prioritize**

   Look at the completed mind map to identify patterns, prioritize key areas, or spot gaps in your thinking.

   A Real-Life Example

   A marketing team used mind mapping to plan a product launch. Starting with "Launch Strategy" at the center, they branched out into "Social Media," "Events," and "Ads." Each category included tasks, timelines, and key messages. The visual map helped them organize and execute the plan seamlessly.

   Exercise

   Take a problem you're currently working on. Create a mind map with at least three main branches and several subcategories. Review it to identify patterns or prioritize actions.

   Takeaway

   Mind mapping simplifies complexity by organizing ideas visually. Use it to see the big picture and uncover new connections in your problem-solving.

Chapter 66: Decision Matrix for Tough Choices

When faced with multiple options, a decision matrix helps you compare them systematically. By scoring each option against key criteria, you eliminate bias and focus on the best overall choice. It's an ideal tool for complex decisions where many factors are at play.

How to Use a Decision Matrix

1. **List Your Options**

   Write down all the choices you're considering. For example, different job offers or software tools.

2. **Define Your Criteria**

   Identify the factors that matter most. For example: "Cost," "Ease of Use," and "Long-Term Value."

3. **Assign Weights to Criteria**

   Give each criterion a weight based on its importance. For example, "Cost" might be worth 40%, while "Ease of Use" is 30%.

4. **Score Each Option**

   Rate each option against each criterion on a scale (e.g., 1 to 10). Multiply the scores by their respective weights.

5. **Compare Total Scores**

   Add up the weighted scores for each option and choose the one with the highest total.

   A Real-Life Example

   A company choosing a new software platform used a decision matrix. They compared options based on "Cost," "Features," and "Scalability." After scoring each, the highest-scoring platform was selected, ensuring their choice aligned with long-term needs.

   Exercise

   Think of a decision you're facing. Create a decision matrix with at least three options and three criteria. Score and weigh each option to determine the best choice.

   Takeaway

   The decision matrix removes guesswork by evaluating choices objectively. Use it to tackle tough decisions with confidence and clarity.

Chapter 67: The Power of Prototyping

Prototyping is about testing your ideas early and often. Instead of waiting to perfect a solution, you build a simple version—whether it's a sketch, model, or mockup—and gather feedback. This iterative process lets you refine ideas quickly, saving time and resources in the long run.

How to Use Prototyping in Problem-Solving

1. **Start Simple**

   Create a basic, low-cost version of your idea. For example, use paper sketches, digital mockups, or rough models.

2. **Focus on Functionality**

   Your prototype doesn't have to be perfect. The goal is to test the core idea and identify what works or doesn't.

3. **Test with Real Users**

   Share your prototype with the people it's designed for. Gather feedback on their experience and suggestions for improvement.

4. **Iterate and Improve**

   Use the feedback to refine your prototype. Each version brings you closer to the best solution.

5. **Scale Up Gradually**

   Once the prototype works well, develop a more polished and complete version.

A Real-Life Example

A mobile app developer created wireframe prototypes to test new features with users. By identifying issues early, they avoided costly redesigns and launched an app with high user satisfaction.

Exercise

Think of a project or idea you're working on. Create a quick prototype (e.g. a sketch, mock-up, or small-scale version) and gather feedback from at least one person. Refine based on their input.

Takeaway

Prototyping helps you test ideas quickly and refine them with real feedback. Start small, iterate often, and build better solutions.

Chapter 68: Experimentation for Answers

Experimentation is one of the most effective ways to validate ideas and solve problems. By testing different approaches, observing results, and refining your methods, you learn what works best. Experiments are especially useful when data is unclear, or when innovation is required.

How to Experiment Effectively

1. **Define Your Hypothesis**

   Start with a clear question or assumption, like, "Will shorter emails improve response rates?"

2. **Design a Testable Experiment**

   Create a small, controlled test to gather insights. For example, send two versions of an email to different groups.

3. **Measure Results**

   Use metrics to evaluate outcomes. For instance, track open rates, click-throughs, or sales.

4. **Analyze and Learn**

   Review the results to see if your hypothesis was correct. If not, adjust and try again.

5. **Scale Successful Solutions**

   Once you've validated an approach, roll it out on a larger scale.

   A Real-Life Example

   A retailer experimented with different pricing strategies by offering discounts to a subset of customers. The experiment revealed that bundling discounts boosted sales more than individual markdowns, leading to a new pricing model.

   Exercise

   Identify a problem or idea and design a small experiment to test it. Write down your hypothesis, method, and what metrics you'll track. Conduct the test and analyze your results.

   Takeaway

   Experimentation uncovers what works through testing and observation. Try, learn, and refine to find the best solutions.

Chapter 69: Heuristics for Speed

Heuristics are mental shortcuts or rules of thumb that help you make decisions quickly without overthinking. They're especially useful when time is limited, or you're dealing with complex problems that don't require perfect accuracy. While heuristics don't always guarantee the best solution, they can guide you toward good enough answers efficiently.

By using heuristics wisely, you can save time, reduce analysis paralysis, and focus your energy where it matters most.

How to Use Heuristics for Problem-Solving

1. **Simplify Complex Decisions**

   Break down a decision into key factors and use a simple rule. For example: "If it's 80% good enough, move forward."

2. **Leverage Past Experience**

   Apply lessons from similar situations. For instance, if a past project succeeded by focusing on user feedback early, use that approach again.

3. **Use the Pareto Principle**

   Focus on the 20% of actions that will produce 80% of the results. This shortcut narrows your focus to what really matters.

4. **Prioritize with "Satisficing"**

   Instead of searching endlessly for the perfect solution, choose the first option that meets your key criteria.

5. **Be Mindful of Bias**

   While heuristics save time, they can sometimes introduce errors. Double-check critical decisions for blind spots.

   A Real-Life Example

   A hiring manager used the "rule of three" heuristic, interviewing three candidates before deciding whether to hire one or move on. This approach balanced efficiency with thoughtful evaluation, cutting hiring time in half without sacrificing quality.

   Exercise

   Think of a current decision that feels overwhelming. Write down a heuristic you could apply, like focusing on the most critical factor or setting a time limit for making the choice.

   Takeaway

   Heuristics simplify decision-making with practical shortcuts. Use them to act quickly while staying focused on what matters most.

Chapter 70: Algorithms and Flowcharts

When solving repetitive or process-heavy problems, algorithms and flowcharts bring clarity and structure. An algorithm is a step-by-step process for solving a problem, while a flowchart visually maps those steps. These tools help you streamline decisions, eliminate guesswork, and improve efficiency.

Algorithms and flowcharts are particularly helpful for tasks like troubleshooting, planning workflows, or training others.

How to Use Algorithms and Flowcharts

1. **Define the Goal**

   Start with a clear objective. For example, "Troubleshoot a slow internet connection."

2. **Break the Process Into Steps**

   Write down each action in order. For example:
   - Check if the router is plugged in.
   - Restart the router.
   - Call your internet provider.

3. **Identify Decision Points**

   Highlight where choices must be made, like "Is the router light blinking?" or "Did restarting work?"

4. **Draw the Flowchart**

   Use shapes and arrows to map the process visually. Show paths for different decisions or outcomes.

5. **Test and Refine**

   Run through the algorithm or flowchart to ensure it works as intended. Adjust steps if needed.

A Real-Life Example

An IT help desk created a flowchart for resolving common technical issues. When employees called for support, the team followed the chart to troubleshoot efficiently. This reduced response times and improved satisfaction.

Exercise

Choose a recurring problem or process. Write down the steps needed to solve it and map them into a simple flowchart. Test it with a colleague or friend.

Takeaway

Algorithms and flowcharts streamline problem-solving by organizing steps into clear, repeatable processes. Use them to improve efficiency and reduce errors.

Section 8: Overcoming Cognitive Biases

Even the sharpest minds fall prey to cognitive biases—mental shortcuts and distortions that cloud judgment. These biases can lead to poor decisions, missed opportunities, or flawed problem-solving.

In this section, you'll learn how to recognize and overcome common biases like confirmation bias, the sunk cost fallacy, and overconfidence. By mastering these techniques, you'll improve your ability to think clearly, make balanced decisions, and solve problems effectively.

Chapter 71: Recognize Confirmation Bias

Confirmation bias happens when you only notice information that supports your beliefs while ignoring evidence that challenges them. It's comforting to find proof that we're "right," but this bias limits objectivity and leads to flawed decisions.

Recognizing confirmation bias allows you to step back, evaluate all evidence, and make decisions based on a full picture—not just the parts you agree with.

How to Avoid Confirmation Bias

1. Actively Seek Contradictory Evidence

Challenge your viewpoint by asking, "What evidence would prove me wrong?" Look for it intentionally.

2. Consider Alternative Perspectives

Ask someone with a different opinion to share their reasoning. Diverse viewpoints uncover blind spots.

3. Question Your Sources

Evaluate where your information comes from. Is it balanced or biased toward your preexisting beliefs?

4. Be Willing to Change Your Mind

Accepting new evidence isn't a weakness—it's a strength that leads to better decisions.

5. Use Data-Driven Analysis

Rely on objective data rather than personal opinions or anecdotal evidence.

A Real-Life Example

A hiring manager believed that candidates from prestigious universities performed better. However, by reviewing performance data, they found no significant difference between top schools and others. Recognizing their confirmation bias led to more equitable hiring practices.

Exercise

Think about a belief or decision you've made recently. Write down evidence that supports it, then actively search for evidence that challenges it. Reflect on whether this changes your perspective.

Takeaway

Confirmation bias narrows your vision. Challenge your assumptions and seek opposing evidence to make well-rounded decisions.

Chapter 72: Avoid the Sunk Cost Fallacy

The sunk cost fallacy traps you into sticking with decisions based on past investments of time, money, or effort—even when it no longer makes sense. It's hard to let go of what you've already poured into something, but clinging to a losing course only compounds the loss.

By recognizing sunk costs, you can make decisions based on future value, not past effort.

How to Avoid the Sunk Cost Fallacy

1. Focus on the Present and Future

Ask, "If I hadn't invested in this already, would I still make the same choice today?"

2. **Separate Emotion from Logic**

   Acknowledge any emotional attachment to your past investment, then set it aside to think clearly.

3. **Reevaluate Regularly**

   Periodically reassess whether your current path is still the best option.

4. **Learn to Walk Away**

   Accept that letting go isn't failure—it's making room for better opportunities.

5. **Reframe Losses as Lessons**

   Treat sunk costs as valuable learning experiences rather than wasted resources.

   A Real-Life Example

   A start-up invested heavily in a product that wasn't gaining traction. Despite mounting losses, they hesitated to pivot. When they finally shifted focus to a more promising idea, they found success. Recognizing the sunk cost fallacy helped them move forward.

   Exercise

   Think of a project or decision where you feel stuck. Ask yourself, "Am I continuing this only because of past investment?" Write down one action to focus on future gains instead.

   Takeaway

   Let go of sunk costs and focus on what adds value going forward. Decisions should prioritize future opportunities, not past investments.

> I just saw a report about a plane crash. Flying must be super dangerous!

> But isn't it safer than driving? Let's check the actual data.

Chapter 73: Fight Availability Heuristics

The availability heuristic leads you to base decisions on information that's easiest to recall—like vivid memories, recent events, or dramatic stories—rather than factual data. While quick, this shortcut often distorts reality and prevents sound judgment.

By recognizing this bias, you can rely on more objective evidence instead of relying on what's simply memorable.

How to Fight Availability Heuristics

1. **Seek Out Data**

   Before making decisions, look for statistics, reports, or research that provide a more balanced view.

2. **Question Emotional Responses**

   Ask, "Am I focusing on this because it's relevant or just because it's memorable?"

3. **Broaden Your Perspective**

   Consider multiple examples or case studies, not just the most striking ones.

4. **Use a Checklist**

   Structured decision-making tools can help ensure all factors are considered, not just the most memorable ones.

5. **Review the Bigger Picture**

   Step back and assess whether your decision reflects broader trends or isolated incidents.

   A Real-Life Example

   A CEO almost scrapped a product after one high-profile customer complained. However, data showed that most customers were satisfied. Ignoring the availability heuristic helped the company avoid an overreaction and keep a successful product in the market.

   Exercise

   Think of a recent decision where you relied on a vivid example. Find objective data to check whether your judgment was accurate. Reflect on how this changes your view.

   Takeaway

   The most memorable information isn't always the most reliable. Rely on data and broader trends to avoid the traps of availability heuristics.

Chapter 74: Control Anchoring Effects

Anchoring bias happens when your decisions are overly influenced by the first piece of information you encounter. Whether it's an initial price, a single opinion, or a past estimate, this "anchor" can skew your thinking and block better choices.

By controlling anchoring effects, you can evaluate options more fairly and make better-informed decisions.

How to Control Anchoring Effects

1. Delay Judgment

Avoid making decisions until you've reviewed all relevant information.

2. Consider Multiple Anchors

Compare several starting points rather than fixating on just one.

3. Challenge the Initial Anchor

Ask yourself, "Why am I basing my decision on this number or idea? Does it truly reflect reality?"

4. Use Independent Estimates

Get input from unbiased sources to counteract the influence of the initial anchor.

5. Revisit the Problem

Step back from the anchor and reassess your decision with a fresh perspective.

A Real-Life Example

A car buyer negotiating a price was anchored by the dealer's high initial offer. After researching fair market values and setting their own target price, they negotiated a much better deal.

Exercise

Think of a decision where an initial number or idea influenced you. Reassess it by gathering additional information or creating a new starting point.

Takeaway

Anchors can bias your decisions. Challenge initial information and seek alternative starting points to make more balanced choices.

Chapter 75: Beware of Overconfidence Bias

Overconfidence bias occurs when you overestimate your skills, knowledge, or ability to predict outcomes. While confidence is important, too much of it can lead to risky decisions, ignoring potential pitfalls, or underpreparing for challenges.

Recognizing overconfidence allows you to stay humble, ask for input, and make more informed choices.

How to Avoid Overconfidence Bias

1. Check Your Assumptions

Ask, "What facts support my belief?" and "What might I be overlooking?"

2. Seek Feedback

Consult others for their perspective. External opinions often reveal blind spots.

3. Consider Worst-Case Scenarios

Evaluate what could go wrong and how you'd handle it.

4. Test Your Ideas

Instead of assuming success, run small experiments to validate your approach before fully committing.

5. Embrace Lifelong Learning

Acknowledge that there's always more to learn, even in areas where you excel.

A seasoned investor was so confident in a single stock pick that he ignored market warnings. When the stock tanked, he lost heavily. Learning from this, he adopted a diversified strategy and sought input from other experts, improving his future performance.

Exercise

Think of a decision where you felt overconfident. Write down potential risks or gaps in your knowledge and one way to address them.

Takeaway

Confidence is valuable, but overconfidence blinds you to risks. Stay humble, seek input, and prepare for challenges to make smarter decisions.

Chapter 76: Manage Decision Fatigue

Decision fatigue happens when you're overwhelmed by too many choices, leading to poor decisions, procrastination, or burnout. Your mental energy is a finite resource, and each decision you make depletes it.

Managing decision fatigue helps you preserve your focus for what truly matters.

How to Manage Decision Fatigue

1. Prioritize Important Decisions

Tackle high-stakes decisions early in the day when your mind is freshest.

2. Simplify Routine Choices

Automate or streamline low-priority decisions, like meal planning or daily tasks.

3. Limit Options

Reduce the number of choices you consider. For example, shortlist three options instead of ten.

4. Take Breaks

Rest and recharge your mental energy before tackling more decisions.

5. Plan Ahead

Make decisions in advance when possible, such as creating a weekly schedule or setting goals.

A Real-Life Example

A CEO simplified her daily routine by delegating minor tasks and setting a standard work wardrobe. By reducing small decisions, she saved energy for strategic planning and problem-solving.

Exercise

Identify one area of your life where decision fatigue is affecting you. Streamline or automate one type of routine decision to reduce mental overload.

Takeaway

Decision fatigue drains mental energy. Simplify, prioritize, and automate to stay focused on what matters most.

Chapter 77: Combat Group Polarization

Group polarization occurs when teams take increasingly extreme positions after group discussions. Instead of finding balance, members reinforce each other's views, leading to risky decisions or unnecessary conflict.

Preventing group polarization ensures more measured, rational, and collaborative outcomes.

How to Combat Group Polarization

1. Encourage Diverse Perspectives

Actively invite input from members with different viewpoints to counterbalance extremes.

2. Play Devil's Advocate

Assign someone to challenge the group's assumptions and encourage critical thinking.

3. Break Into Smaller Groups

Smaller groups tend to stay more balanced and focused than large, unanimous ones.

4. Focus on Evidence

Ground discussions in facts and data rather than opinions or emotions.

5. Review the Decision Independently

Ask each member to reflect privately on the group's decision before finalizing it.

A Real-Life Example

A company brainstorming marketing strategies veered toward an extreme "all-in" risky campaign. A team member playing devil's advocate highlighted the risks, leading to a balanced strategy that incorporated boldness with safeguards.

Exercise

Think of a group decision you were part of. Reflect on whether the group leaned too far toward one extreme and how you could encourage balance in future discussions.

Takeaway

Group polarization skews decisions. Encourage balance by seeking diverse views, grounding discussions in evidence, and challenging extreme positions.

Chapter 78: Recognize the Dunning-Kruger Effect

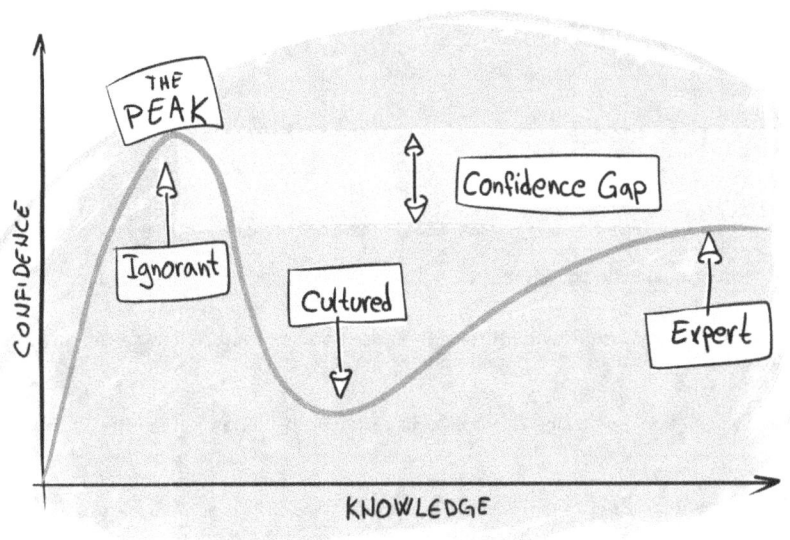

The Dunning-Kruger Effect describes how people with little knowledge overestimate their competence, while experts often underestimate theirs. This bias can lead to misplaced confidence or hesitation to act when you're actually capable. Recognizing this effect helps you accurately assess your abilities and seek help when needed.

How to Recognize and Manage the Dunning-Kruger Effect

1. Be Honest About Your Knowledge

Reflect on whether your confidence matches your actual expertise.

2. Seek Feedback from Experts

Ask someone more experienced for their perspective to calibrate your self-assessment.

3. **Keep Learning**

   The more you learn, the more aware you become of what you don't know.

4. **Balance Confidence with Humility**

   Trust your skills while staying open to new insights and growth.

5. **Help Others Avoid It**

   Encourage constructive feedback in teams to ensure accurate self-perception.

   A Real-Life Example

   A new manager felt overconfident in decision-making but struggled with delegation. After seeking advice from seasoned leaders, they learned to balance confidence with humility, improving both leadership and team outcomes.

   Exercise

   Reflect on a situation where you felt either overconfident or hesitant. Identify one way you could recalibrate your perception of your skills.

   Takeaway

   The Dunning-Kruger Effect distorts self-perception. Stay humble, seek feedback, and embrace learning to align confidence with competence.

Chapter 79: Counteract Framing Effects

Framing effects occur when decisions are influenced by how information is presented rather than the facts themselves. For example, describing a product as "90% effective" sounds more appealing than "10% failure rate," even though they mean the same thing. Recognizing framing effects helps you focus on substance over presentation, leading to more objective decisions.

How to Counteract Framing Effects

1. **Reframe the Situation**

   Rewrite the problem or decision in different ways. Ask, "How would this look framed differently?"

2. **Focus on Facts, Not Phrasing**

   Strip away the language and evaluate the raw data or numbers.

3. **Consider Both Sides**

   Look at both the positive and negative framing to balance your view.

4. **Question the Messenger's Intent**

   Ask, "Why is this being presented this way? What's the goal behind the framing?"

5. **Take a Step Back**

   Give yourself time to process the information without rushing to judgment.

   A Real-Life Example

   A health campaign presented a procedure as "90% successful," leading to high patient acceptance. When reframed as "10% failure," patients hesitated. Recognizing the framing helped balance communication and build trust.

   Exercise

   Think of a recent decision influenced by how information was framed. Reframe the same information differently and evaluate how it changes your perspective.

   Takeaway

   Framing can distort perception. Focus on the facts behind the presentation to make objective, informed decisions.

Chapter 80: Balance Intuition with Analysis

Intuition and analysis both play important roles in decision-making. Intuition, based on experience and subconscious patterns, can provide quick insights. Analysis, rooted in facts and data, ensures logic and objectivity. Balancing the two leads to better problem-solving by combining instinct with evidence.

How to Balance Intuition and Analysis

1. **Start with Your Gut**

   Reflect on your initial instinct about the problem. What feels right, and why?

2. **Follow Up with Data**

   Test your intuition against data or research to ensure it aligns with reality.

3. **Be Wary of Bias**

   Recognize when emotions or personal preferences might skew your intuition.

4. **Use Intuition for Speed, Analysis for Accuracy**

   When time is short, rely on intuition. For critical decisions, prioritize analysis.

5. **Refine Intuition Through Experience**

   The more you reflect on past decisions, the sharper your intuition becomes.

A Real-Life Example

A marketing director had a gut feeling that a new campaign idea would resonate. Instead of acting immediately, she tested the concept with focus groups. The data confirmed her instincts, leading to a successful launch.

Exercise

Think about a decision where you relied solely on intuition or analysis. Reflect on how using the other approach might have improved the outcome.

Takeaway

Intuition offers speed; analysis provides accuracy. Balance both to make decisions that are both insightful and evidence-based.

Section 9: Resilience in Problem-Solving

Resilience is the backbone of effective problem-solving. It's the ability to bounce back, adapt, and persist even in the face of setbacks or uncertainty. In this section, you'll learn how to transform failure into growth, pivot strategies when necessary, and stay focused on your goals while embracing patience and adaptability. Resilient problem-solvers don't just survive challenges—they thrive because of them.

Chapter 81: Learn from Failure

Failure is not the opposite of success—it's part of the journey toward it. Every mistake or setback carries lessons that can refine your approach and improve future outcomes. Learning from failure requires reflection, humility, and the willingness to adapt.

How to Learn from Failure

1. Own Your Mistakes

Acknowledge what went wrong without defensiveness. Accountability is the first step toward growth.

2. Analyze the Cause

Break down what led to the failure. Was it a lack of preparation, a flawed strategy, or external factors?

3. Focus on Lessons, Not Blame

Shift your perspective from "What went wrong?" to "What can I do better next time?"

4. Adjust Your Approach

Use what you've learned to improve your strategy or decision-making process.

5. Move Forward

Don't dwell on the setback. Treat it as a stepping stone and keep pushing toward your goal.

A Real-Life Example

A tech startup launched a product that failed to gain traction. Instead of giving up, the team analyzed customer feedback and realized their marketing wasn't reaching the right audience. They refined their strategy and relaunched, eventually achieving success.

Exercise

Think of a recent failure. Write down three lessons you learned and one specific change you can make to avoid repeating the mistake.

Takeaway

Failure is a powerful teacher. Reflect, learn, and adapt to turn setbacks into stepping stones toward success.

Chapter 82: Pivot, Don't Quit

Sometimes, the path you're on isn't leading to success — but that doesn't mean you should abandon your goal. Pivoting means adjusting your strategy while keeping the end goal in sight. It's a powerful way to adapt to challenges without giving up entirely.

How to Pivot Effectively

1. Recognize When It's Time to Change

If progress stalls or circumstances shift, evaluate whether your current approach is still viable.

2. Reassess Your Goal

Ask, "Is the goal still worth pursuing?" If yes, focus on finding a new path to achieve it.

3. **Identify What's Working**

   Pinpoint the elements of your current strategy that are effective and keep them in your revised plan.

4. **Explore New Approaches**

   Brainstorm alternative methods or strategies to move forward.

5. **Commit to the New Direction**

   Once you've decided to pivot, fully embrace the new approach without hesitation.

   A Real-Life Example

   Instagram started as a location-based app called Burbn. When the founders realized users were primarily sharing photos, they pivoted to focus on photo-sharing, leading to the Instagram we know today.

   Exercise

   Think of a goal where you've hit a roadblock. Write down one aspect you can change or improve while keeping the bigger picture in mind.

   Takeaway

   Pivoting keeps you moving forward when the original plan falters. Adapt your strategy without losing sight of your goal.

Chapter 83: Stay Adaptive to Change

Change is inevitable, and rigid plans often break under its weight. Staying adaptive means being ready to shift gears, embrace new circumstances, and adjust your approach as needed. Flexibility allows you to thrive in uncertainty and turn unexpected challenges into opportunities.

How to Stay Adaptive

1. **Monitor Your Environment**

   Stay aware of trends, feedback, and changes that could impact your goals.

2. **Embrace a Growth Mindset**

   See change as an opportunity to learn and grow, rather than a threat to your plans.

3. **Stay Open to New Ideas**

   Be willing to try alternative methods, even if they deviate from your original plan.

4. **Prepare for Multiple Scenarios**

   Anticipate different outcomes and have contingency plans ready.

5. **Stay Calm in Uncertainty**

   Focus on what you can control and remain flexible in areas that you can't.

   A Real-Life Example

   A restaurant facing reduced dine-in traffic during the pandemic quickly adapted by expanding takeout and delivery options. Their ability to pivot kept the business afloat and even grew their customer base.

   Exercise

   Identify a situation where circumstances have changed recently. Write down one adjustment you can make to adapt and stay on track.

   Takeaway

   Adaptability is the key to thriving in a changing world. Stay flexible, embrace new opportunities, and adjust your approach as needed.

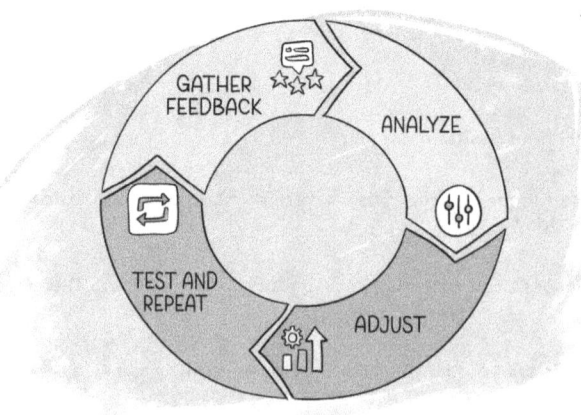

Chapter 84: Build a Feedback Loop

Feedback loops are essential for continuous improvement. By regularly collecting input, analyzing results, and making adjustments, you can refine your solutions and achieve better outcomes over time. A strong feedback loop turns one-time successes into lasting progress.

How to Build a Feedback Loop

1. **Gather Input Regularly**

Collect feedback from users, team members, or stakeholders at every stage.

2. **Analyze the Data**

Look for patterns or recurring issues in the feedback.

3. **Make Adjustments**

Use the insights to refine your approach, whether it's improving processes, products, or strategies.

4. **Test the Changes**

Implement adjustments and evaluate their effectiveness.

5. **Repeat the Process**

Feedback isn't a one-time activity—it's an ongoing cycle of learning and improving.

A Real-Life Example

A software company built a feedback loop by releasing beta versions of their app and collecting user reviews. Iterating based on feedback, they launched a polished product that exceeded user expectations.

Exercise

Think of a project or goal. Write down one way you can gather feedback and one specific adjustment you could make based on what you learn.

Takeaway

Feedback loops drive continuous improvement. Collect input, make adjustments, and refine your approach for lasting success.

Chapter 85: Recognize When to Let Go

Not every problem can be solved, and not every goal is worth pursuing forever. Recognizing when to let go frees up your energy and resources for challenges with better potential outcomes. Letting go isn't failure—it's a strategic choice to focus on what truly matters.

How to Recognize When to Let Go

1. **Assess the Impact**

Ask, "If I solved this problem, would the result still be worth the effort?"

2. **Evaluate Your Resources**

Determine whether continuing is draining time, energy, or money that could be better spent elsewhere.

3. **Listen to Feedback**

If others consistently point out that a problem may not be solvable, consider their perspective.

4. **Reflect on Your Goals**

Ask, "Is this still aligned with my bigger objectives?"

5. **Shift Your Focus**

Channel your energy into more achievable or impactful challenges.

A Real-Life Example

A business owner struggling to revive a failing product line decided to discontinue it and focus on their best-selling items instead. This decision freed up resources and led to record profits.

Exercise

Think of a problem you've been holding onto. Reflect on whether solving it is still worth the effort, and identify one area where you could redirect your focus instead.

Takeaway

Letting go isn't giving up—it's making space for better opportunities. Focus on problems and goals that truly matter.

Chapter 86: Embrace Experimentation

Experimentation is a cornerstone of resilient problem-solving. Instead of waiting for the perfect solution, testing ideas early and learning from the results allows you to refine your approach. By embracing experimentation, you create a culture of progress over perfection, turning uncertainty into discovery.

How to Embrace Experimentation

1. **Start Small**

   Test your idea on a small scale to minimize risks while gathering valuable insights.

2. **Define Success Metrics**

   Decide what outcomes will indicate success or failure before starting the experiment.

3. **Document Results**

   Track what worked, what didn't, and why. Detailed observations help you make better adjustments.

4. **Iterate and Improve**

   Use what you've learned to refine the next version of your solution.

5. **Accept Failure as Feedback**

   Treat failed experiments as opportunities to learn, not as setbacks.

A Real-Life Example

A clothing brand used A/B testing to experiment with different website layouts. By measuring click-through rates and sales, they discovered which design worked best, leading to a 25% increase in conversions.

Exercise

Think of an idea or solution you want to test. Design a small experiment, write down success metrics, and outline how you'll use the results to improve.

Takeaway

Experimentation fuels progress. Test early, learn constantly, and refine your approach to build better solutions.

Chapter 87: Cultivate Patience in Uncertainty

Uncertainty can feel overwhelming, especially when results aren't immediate. Patience is the ability to stay calm and focused while waiting for progress to unfold. Cultivating patience doesn't mean doing nothing—it means trusting the process and staying persistent even when outcomes aren't clear.

How to Cultivate Patience in Uncertainty

1. **Focus on What You Can Control**

   Instead of worrying about unknowns, channel your energy into actions that move you forward.

2. **Break Goals Into Milestones**

   Small, measurable achievements help you see progress, even during long-term projects.

3. **Practice Mindfulness**

   Stay grounded in the present moment rather than fixating on future outcomes.

4. **Remind Yourself of the Bigger Picture**

   Keep your long-term goals in mind to maintain motivation through slow progress.

5. **Celebrate Progress**

   Acknowledge small wins to stay positive and resilient.

A Real-Life Example

An author working on a novel struggled with uncertainty about its reception. By focusing on daily word count goals and celebrating small milestones, they completed the book and ultimately found success.

Exercise

Think of a project where you're facing uncertainty. Write down one small milestone you can achieve this week to maintain momentum.

Takeaway

Patience turns uncertainty into opportunity. Stay focused on progress, trust the process, and persist through the unknown.

Chapter 88: Keep Your Eye on the Goal

In problem-solving, it's easy to get side-tracked by setbacks, distractions, or minor details. Keeping your eye on the goal means staying focused on what matters most, even when obstacles arise. By regularly reconnecting with your purpose, you ensure that every action aligns with your ultimate objective.

How to Stay Focused on the Goal

1. **Define Your Purpose Clearly**

   Write down your goal and why it's important to you or your team.

2. **Regularly Revisit Your Goal**

   Set reminders or check-ins to ensure your actions remain aligned with your objective.

3. **Ignore Distractions**

   Learn to distinguish between tasks that support your goal and those that pull you off track.

4. **Adapt Without Losing Sight**

   Be flexible in your methods, but always keep the end result in mind.

5. **Celebrate the Journey**

   Acknowledge the progress you've made so far to stay motivated.

A Real-Life Example

A non-profit aiming to raise funds for a new initiative faced unexpected hurdles. By focusing on their mission and adapting strategies, they surpassed their fundraising target while staying true to their purpose.

Exercise

Write down your current goal and one action you can take today to move closer to achieving it.

Takeaway

Focus on your destination. Stay adaptable, avoid distractions, and reconnect with your purpose to achieve your goals.

Chapter 89: Trust the Process

When faced with challenges, it's easy to doubt whether your efforts will pay off. Trusting the process means having confidence in your problem-solving framework and taking consistent action, even when results aren't immediate.

How to Trust the Process

1. **Have a Clear Plan**

   A well-thought-out strategy provides the structure to guide your efforts.

2. **Focus on Consistency**

   Small, steady actions often lead to big results over time.

3. **Stay Flexible**

   Adjust your approach as needed, but remain committed to the overall process.

4. **Measure Progress**

   Track milestones and use them as proof that your efforts are working.

5. **Resist Impatience**

   Remind yourself that meaningful change takes time and persistence.

A Real-Life Example

A fitness enthusiast focused on consistent daily workouts and trusted their plan, even when early results were minimal. Over months, their dedication paid off with noticeable improvements in strength and endurance.

Identify a process you're following. Write down one reason to trust it and one adjustment you can make to improve it.
Success is built on consistency. Trust your process, take steady action, and adjust as needed to achieve long-term results.

Chapter 90: Celebrate Small Wins

Big goals often feel daunting, but celebrating small wins along the way keeps you motivated and builds momentum. Each milestone represents progress and reinforces your ability to achieve the final goal. Recognizing these moments fuels your energy and strengthens resilience.

How to Celebrate Small Wins

1. **Set Mini-Milestones**

   Break your larger goal into smaller, achievable steps to track progress.

2. **Acknowledge Each Achievement**

   Take a moment to reflect on and appreciate your progress, no matter how small.

3. **Reward Yourself**

   Celebrate milestones with simple rewards, like a break, a treat, or sharing your success with others.

4. **Share Wins with Your Team**

   If you're working collaboratively, highlight group achievements to boost morale.

5. **Use Wins as Motivation**

   Let each success inspire you to keep moving forward.

A Real-Life Example

A student writing a thesis celebrated each completed chapter with a small reward, like a favorite snack. These celebrations kept them motivated to tackle the next section and finish their project.

Exercise

Think of a recent milestone you've reached. Write down one way you can celebrate it and one next step to build on your momentum.

Takeaway

Small wins lead to big victories. Celebrate milestones to stay motivated, build momentum, and enjoy the journey toward your goal.

Section 10: Advanced Problem-Solving

Problem-solving at the highest level requires advanced tools and mindsets. This section explores techniques to help you tackle complex and dynamic challenges. You'll learn to anticipate the future, embrace constraints, and balance logic with creativity. Whether you're refining your process or exploring innovative approaches, these strategies will elevate your problem-solving to mastery.

Chapter 91: Apply Game Theory

Game theory is the study of strategic decision-making, especially in situations where others' actions affect your outcomes. Whether you're negotiating, competing, or collaborating, game theory helps you predict and influence behaviors by considering everyone's interests and potential moves.

How to Use Game Theory in Problem-Solving

1. **Define the Players**

   Identify all the key players involved in the problem, including yourself, competitors, and collaborators.

2. **Understand Motivations**

   Determine what each player wants and what drives their decisions.

3. **Predict Actions**

   Consider how others are likely to act based on their goals and constraints.

4. **Analyze Possible Outcomes**

   Map out scenarios for each combination of actions to anticipate the best and worst results.

5. **Choose Strategic Moves**

   Make decisions that maximize your outcome while minimizing risks, often by influencing others' choices.

A Real-Life Example

During a price war, a company analyzed competitors' likely responses to various pricing strategies. By predicting that competitors wouldn't sustain long-term discounts, they chose a steady pricing strategy, retaining profits while competitors faltered.

Exercise

Think of a situation where other people's actions affect your outcomes. List their potential moves and plan one strategic decision based on likely scenarios.

Takeaway

Game theory sharpens your strategic thinking. Anticipate others' actions and plan your moves to achieve the best outcomes.

Chapter 92: Master First-Principles Thinking

First-principles thinking is a powerful method of solving problems by breaking them down into their most fundamental truths. Instead of relying on assumptions or existing methods, you rebuild solutions from the ground up, enabling innovative approaches and fresh perspectives.

How to Apply First-Principles Thinking

1. **Identify Assumptions**

   List everything you believe about the problem. For example, "This product must be expensive to produce."

2. **Question Each Assumption**

   Ask, "Is this really true? Why?" Challenge conventional wisdom to find overlooked possibilities.

3. **Break It Down**

Reduce the problem to its simplest components. For example, "What are the raw materials? What is their actual cost?"

4. **Rebuild with New Insights**

Use the fundamentals to create a more efficient, innovative solution.

5. **Repeat as Needed**

Apply this process regularly to uncover breakthroughs in thinking.

A Real-Life Example

Elon Musk used first-principles thinking to cut rocket costs at SpaceX. Instead of buying prebuilt components, the team analyzed raw materials and built rockets in-house for a fraction of the cost.

Exercise

Choose a problem and list your assumptions about it. Break the problem into basic elements and brainstorm one solution based on these fundamentals.

Takeaway

First-principles thinking challenges assumptions and rebuilds solutions from the ground up. Use it to unlock innovative answers.

Chapter 93: Leverage Bayesian Thinking

Bayesian thinking helps you make better decisions by continuously updating your beliefs as new evidence emerges. It's not about being "right" or "wrong" initially—it's about refining your understanding over time through logic and probability.

How to Use Bayesian Thinking

1. **Start with a Prior Belief**

Begin with an initial assumption or hypothesis based on current knowledge.

2. **Gather New Evidence**

Seek data or information that supports or challenges your belief.

3. **Update Your Belief**

Adjust your assumption based on the strength and relevance of the new evidence.

4. **Repeat as Needed**

Continuously refine your understanding as more evidence becomes available.

5. **Apply Probability**

Use likelihoods instead of certainties. For example, "This solution has a 70% chance of success based on the data."

A Real-Life Example

A doctor diagnosing a patient begins with a likely cause based on symptoms. As test results arrive, they adjust their diagnosis, increasing or decreasing the probability of each potential condition until the most accurate conclusion is reached.

Exercise

Think of a belief or decision you've made recently. Identify one piece of new evidence that could challenge or refine it, and update your thinking accordingly.

Takeaway

Bayesian thinking refines decisions by incorporating new evidence. Update your beliefs continuously for better outcomes.

Chapter 94: Use Scenario Analysis for Complexity

Complex problems often have uncertain outcomes, but scenario analysis prepares you for multiple possibilities. By imagining different futures and planning responses to each, you build resilience and adaptability into your decision-making process.

How to Use Scenario Analysis

1. **Define the Problem**

   Identify a challenge with uncertain outcomes. For example, "How will market conditions affect our product launch?"

2. **Identify Key Variables**

   List factors that could influence outcomes, like customer behavior, competition, or economic trends.

3. **Create Scenarios**

   Develop a few plausible scenarios, such as "Best Case," "Worst Case," and "Most Likely."

4. **Plan Responses**

   Outline actions you'd take for each scenario to mitigate risks or seize opportunities.

5. **Review and Adapt**

   Revisit your scenarios periodically as conditions evolve.

A Real-Life Example

A retail chain planning for economic uncertainty developed three scenarios: economic growth, stagnation, and recession. By preparing tailored strategies for each, they successfully adapted to a challenging market.

Exercise

Choose a current challenge and outline three possible scenarios. Write down one action you'd take for each to stay prepared.

Takeaway

Scenario analysis prepares you for uncertainty. Plan for multiple outcomes to stay adaptable and resilient.

Chapter 95: Explore Contrarian Solutions

Sometimes the best solutions lie in doing the opposite of what's expected. Contrarian thinking challenges conventional wisdom, encouraging you to explore ideas others might dismiss. By questioning norms, you unlock creative and unexpected solutions.

How to Explore Contrarian Solutions

1. **Question the Status Quo**

   Ask, "Why do we always do it this way?" and "What if we tried the opposite?"

2. **Seek Out Unpopular Opinions**

   Listen to ideas that go against the majority—they might reveal overlooked opportunities.

3. **Challenge Assumptions**

   Test whether commonly accepted beliefs hold up under scrutiny.

4. **Combine the Contrarian with the Practical**

   Blend bold ideas with actionable steps to make them realistic.

5. **Stay Open to Risk**

   Contrarian solutions often carry uncertainty, but they can lead to breakthroughs when executed well.

A Real-Life Example

Netflix's decision to focus on streaming, instead of expanding DVD rentals like competitors, was a contrarian move that disrupted the entertainment industry and defined the future of media.

Think of a problem where the usual approach isn't working. Write down one contrarian solution and consider how you might test it.

Takeaway

Contrarian thinking challenges norms and unlocks innovation. Dare to explore unconventional solutions for bold breakthroughs.

Chapter 96: Think Like a Futurist

Thinking like a futurist means looking beyond the present to anticipate trends, innovations, and disruptions that could shape the future. By understanding the big picture, you can make strategic decisions today that prepare you for tomorrow's challenges and opportunities. Futurist thinking combines creativity, data, and foresight to build adaptable, forward-thinking strategies.

How to Think Like a Futurist

1. Study Emerging Trends

Pay attention to advancements in technology, shifts in culture, and changes in global systems.

2. Ask "What If?"

Imagine future scenarios, from optimistic to catastrophic, and consider their implications.

3. Focus on Long-Term Goals

Look beyond immediate results and ask, "How will this decision play out five, ten, or twenty years from now?"

4. Prepare for Disruption

Think about how current industries or practices could be radically changed by new developments.

5. Collaborate Across Fields

Work with people from diverse industries to gain a broader perspective on potential futures.

A Real-Life Example

Amazon's investment in cloud computing through AWS in the early 2000s was a futurist move. They anticipated the growing need for scalable online storage and built an industry-leading platform, which became a major revenue source.

Exercise

Choose an area of interest or work. Research one emerging trend and write down how it could affect your field in the next decade. Identify one way to prepare for it.

Takeaway

Thinking like a futurist helps you anticipate change and stay ahead of the curve. Look beyond the present to shape a resilient, forward-looking strategy.

Chapter 97: Use Constraints to Your Advantage

Constraints—whether they're time, money, or resources—can feel like roadblocks, but they're often the spark for creative breakthroughs. By working within limitations, you're forced to think differently, prioritize, and innovate. Constraints don't just restrict—they focus your efforts and push you to find smarter, leaner solutions.

How to Use Constraints to Fuel Creativity

1. **Reframe Constraints as Challenges**

Instead of viewing limits as problems, treat them as opportunities to innovate.

2. **Simplify the Problem**

Ask, "What's the simplest way to achieve this goal within these constraints?"

3. **Prioritize What Matters**

Focus your energy on the most critical aspects of the problem or project.

4. **Think Outside the Box**

Explore unconventional ideas that wouldn't have been necessary without the constraint.

5. **Learn from Minimalist Success Stories**

Look at examples of businesses or individuals who thrived with limited resources.

A Real-Life Example

The Apollo 13 mission turned life-threatening constraints into ingenious problem-solving. Engineers used only available materials onboard to build a CO_2 filter, saving the crew's lives.

Exercise

Identify a current project with significant constraints. Write down one creative solution that turns the limitation into an advantage.

Takeaway

Constraints inspire innovation. Embrace limits as opportunities to focus, prioritize, and create smarter solutions.

Chapter 98: Balance Rational and Creative Thinking

Effective problem-solving requires both rational thinking (logic, analysis) and creative thinking (imagination, innovation). Rationality ensures structure and accuracy, while creativity uncovers unique, outside-the-box solutions. Balancing the two unlocks your full problem-solving potential.

How to Balance Rational and Creative Thinking

1. **Start with the Problem**

Use rational thinking to analyze the issue, gather data, and define clear goals.

2. **Brainstorm Freely**

Switch to creative thinking to explore as many ideas as possible, even unconventional ones.

3. **Test and Refine Ideas**

Return to rationality to evaluate and validate the feasibility of your creative solutions.

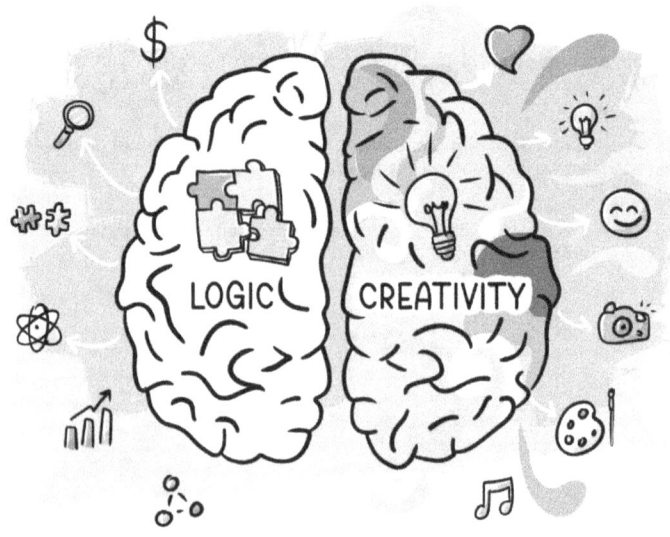

4. **Alternate Between Modes**

   Use rational thinking to structure your process and creative thinking to inspire new possibilities.

5. **Foster a Collaborative Team**

   Combine logical and imaginative thinkers to achieve a balanced approach.

   A Real-Life Example

   Steve Jobs combined rationality and creativity to design Apple products. Logical engineering ensured functionality, while imaginative design made them beautiful and user-friendly.

   Exercise

   Take a current problem and list two rational solutions and two creative solutions. Combine elements from each to create a balanced approach.

   Takeaway

   The best solutions come from blending logic with imagination. Balance rational analysis with creative thinking for smarter, more innovative outcomes.

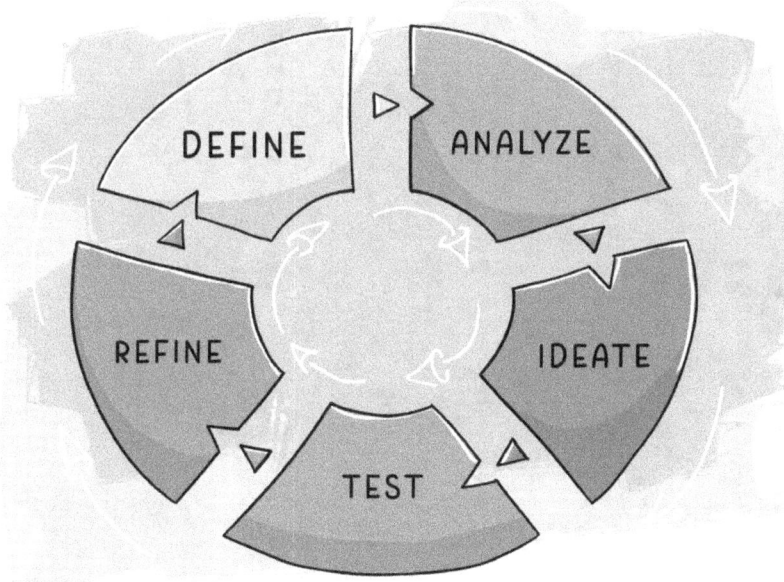

Chapter 99: Build a Problem-Solving Framework

A problem-solving framework is a repeatable process that guides you from identifying a problem to implementing a solution. By using a framework, you eliminate guesswork, maintain focus, and improve efficiency. It's a tool that adapts to any challenge, providing structure and clarity.

How to Build and Use a Problem-Solving Framework

1. **Define the Problem**

   Clearly articulate the issue and its scope. Ask, "What's the real problem we need to solve?"

2. **Analyze the Situation**

   Gather data, identify root causes, and understand the context.

3. **Generate Ideas**

   Brainstorm multiple solutions, using techniques like mind mapping or the Five Whys.

4. **Test Solutions**

   Prototype or pilot your ideas to see what works best.

5. **Refine and Implement**

   Use feedback to improve your solution, then put it into action.

   A Real-Life Example

   Toyota's problem-solving framework, known as the Toyota Production System, focuses on identifying inefficiencies, testing improvements, and iterating solutions. This approach revolutionized manufacturing and inspired industries worldwide.

   Exercise

   Think of a recurring type of problem you face. Outline a five-step framework to handle it more effectively in the future.

   Takeaway

   A problem-solving framework provides structure and repeatability. Build one to approach challenges with confidence and clarity.

Chapter 100: Solve Problems Like an AI

AI solves problems systematically, breaking challenges into parts, analyzing data objectively, and iterating toward solutions. While humans add creativity and empathy, adopting an AI-inspired approach improves precision, efficiency, and clarity in problem-solving.

How to Solve Problems Like an AI

1. **Break the Problem Into Steps**

   Decompose the problem into smaller, manageable pieces.

2. **Analyze Data Objectively**

   Base decisions on evidence, not assumptions or emotions.

3. **Consider Multiple Scenarios**

   Evaluate potential outcomes for each solution to find the optimal path.

4. **Iterate and Learn**

   Continuously refine your solution based on feedback and results.

5. **Stay Consistent and Logical**

   Follow a structured approach to minimize errors and bias.

A Real-Life Example

Healthcare organizations use AI to optimize patient care. Algorithms analyze symptoms, test results, and treatment outcomes to recommend the most effective interventions, saving time and lives.

Exercise

Choose a problem and list the steps you'd take to solve it logically. Compare this process to how an AI might approach it, and note improvements you could make.

Takeaway

AI approaches problems with precision and objectivity. Adopt its systematic mindset to solve challenges efficiently and effectively.

Conclusion: The Endless Journey of Problem-Solving

A winding path stretching toward the horizon, with signposts labeled "Learn," "Adapt," and "Grow." Along the path, a person holds a lightbulb, symbolizing continuous discovery and progress.

Problem-solving isn't a destination—it's a journey. From small daily decisions to transformative innovations, every problem is an opportunity to learn, adapt, and grow. This book has equipped you with 100 tools, techniques, and mindsets, but the real power lies in applying them to your unique challenges.

The world is constantly changing, and with it, the nature of problems evolves. That's why problem-solving requires both resilience and curiosity—resilience to tackle setbacks and curiosity to explore new solutions. Let's reflect on the key lessons from this journey and how you can keep improving as a problem-solver.

The Core Principles of Problem-Solving

1. **Clarity is Key**

   Many problems feel overwhelming because they aren't clearly defined. Always start by asking, "What's the real problem?" Clear definitions lead to focused solutions.

2. **Think Before You Act**

   Rushing to fix something without understanding its root cause often creates more issues. Tools like the Five Whys or Root Cause Analysis help you dig deeper before taking action.

3. **Embrace Creativity and Logic**

   Problem-solving thrives on balance. Use logic to structure your process, but don't shy away from creativity to uncover innovative ideas.

4. **Iterate, Learn, Repeat**

   No solution is perfect on the first try. Experiment, gather feedback, and refine your approach. Treat every attempt as a learning experience.

5. **Stay Resilient**

   Setbacks are inevitable. The best problem-solvers view failure as a stepping stone, not a roadblock. Build resilience by focusing on growth and maintaining patience during uncertainty.

How to Keep Growing as a Problem-Solver

1. **Practice Daily**

   Every decision you make is an opportunity to sharpen your problem-solving skills. From personal dilemmas to professional challenges, approach each situation with intention.

2. **Expand Your Toolkit**

   The 100 techniques in this book are just the beginning. Stay curious and keep exploring new methods, tools, and ideas from different fields.

3. **Learn from Others**

   Great problem-solvers often collaborate, learning from diverse perspectives. Surround yourself with thinkers who challenge and inspire you.

4. **Stay Adaptable**

   Problems rarely come in the form you expect. Keep an open mind, stay flexible, and be ready to adjust your approach as needed.

5. **Reflect and Refine**

   After solving a problem, take time to reflect. What worked? What didn't? Continuous improvement is the hallmark of a master problem-solver.

The Big Picture: Why Problem-Solving Matters

Problem-solving isn't just about fixing what's broken—it's about creating better systems, improving lives, and shaping the future. Whether you're tackling a personal challenge, leading a team, or addressing global issues, effective problem-solving empowers you to make meaningful change.

By mastering these skills, you're not only solving today's problems but building the confidence and mindset to face tomorrow's uncertainties. Every problem solved brings new insights, and every insight builds a stronger foundation for future success.

Your Next Steps

1. **Choose a Problem**

   Look around you—what's one problem you can tackle today? Start small but act decisively.

2. **Apply What You've Learned**

   Use the techniques in this book to approach the problem systematically. Experiment, test, and refine until you find a solution.

3. **Share Your Journey**

   Problem-solving is a skill that grows through teaching and collaboration. Share what you've learned with others and work together to solve bigger challenges.

A Final Thought

The ability to solve problems is one of humanity's greatest strengths. It's what drives progress, fosters innovation, and turns challenges into opportunities. As you continue your journey, remember that every problem—no matter how daunting—holds the potential for growth and transformation.

Keep learning. Keep experimenting. Keep solving.

Appendix A: Quick Reference Guide to Problem-Solving: An AI's Guide to 100 Techniques for Finding Real Solutions Where Humans Get Stuck

This appendix serves as a quick reference guide to the book's sections and chapters, summarizing the core lessons of each chapter in one sentence. Use it to revisit techniques, refresh your understanding, or find the right strategy for your current challenge.

Section 1: Foundations of Problem-Solving

Learn the core principles and mindsets that underpin effective problem-solving.

1. **Start with the Problem, Not the Solution** – Clearly defining the problem prevents wasted effort on irrelevant solutions.
2. **Ask the Right Questions** – The right questions unlock deeper understanding and better answers.
3. **Distinguish Symptoms from Root Causes** – Solve the real issue, not just the surface symptoms.
4. **Stay Curious, Not Defensive** – Curiosity opens the door to fresh insights and innovative solutions.
5. **Understand the Power of Perspective** – Viewing the problem from different angles reveals hidden opportunities.
6. **Embrace Uncertainty** – Uncertainty isn't a barrier; it's the starting point for discovery.
7. **Keep Emotions in Check** – Emotional control leads to clearer, more rational decision-making.
8. **Break Down Big Problems into Small Steps** – Tackling manageable pieces makes any challenge less daunting.
9. **Focus on What You Can Control** – Direct your energy toward the parts of the problem within your influence.
10. **Test Before Committing Fully** – Small experiments save time and prevent costly mistakes.

Section 2: Creativity in Problem-Solving

Learn techniques to generate ideas, spark innovation, and think outside the box.

11. **Brainstorm Like a Pro** – Generate a flood of ideas without judgment.
12. **Think Outside the Box** – Shift your perspective to uncover unconventional solutions.
13. **Use Analogies to Spark Ideas** – Borrow solutions from other fields to solve your problem.
14. **Combine Ideas for Breakthroughs** – Merging diverse concepts often leads to innovation.
15. **Play with "What If?" Scenarios** – Hypothetical situations inspire creative possibilities.
16. **Reverse Engineer the Solution** – Work backward from the desired outcome to find actionable steps.
17. **Challenge Conventional Wisdom** – Question norms to uncover hidden opportunities.
18. **Steal Like an Artist (Ethically)** – Adapt successful strategies from others to fit your needs.
19. **Diverge, Then Converge** – Explore freely, then refine your focus to the best ideas.
20. **Gamify the Process** – Turn problem-solving into a fun and creative game.

Section 3: Analytical Thinking

Master methods to analyze, compare, and evaluate problems with precision.

21. **Follow the Data Trail** – Use evidence and numbers to guide your decisions.
22. **Use Root Cause Analysis** – Dig deeper to uncover the true source of a problem.
23. **Find Patterns and Trends** – Recurring themes often hold valuable clues.
24. **Use Decision Trees for Clarity** – Map choices to identify the most logical paths forward.
25. **Apply Pareto's Principle (80/20 Rule)** – Focus on the small efforts that create the biggest impact.
26. **Test Your Hypothesis** – Validate assumptions through experimentation.
27. **Use Comparative Analysis** – Evaluate options side by side to make informed choices.
28. **Correlation vs. Causation** – Learn to distinguish meaningful relationships from coincidences.
29. **Solve for Variables** – Isolate unknowns to simplify and solve complex equations.
30. **Simplify the Math** – Breaking numbers down reveals the bigger picture.

Section 4: Strategic Approaches

Develop long-term strategies and systems for tackling complex problems.

31. **Plan Backward from Success** – Imagine your goal achieved and trace the steps to get there.
32. **Think Like a Chess Player** – Anticipate moves and plan several steps ahead.
33. **Leverage Opportunity Costs** – Weigh the trade-offs of every decision.
34. **Identify Key Leverage Points** – Focus on small changes that drive big results.
35. **Map the System (Systems Thinking)** – Understand how all parts of a system influence each other.
36. **Scenario Planning for Uncertainty** – Prepare for multiple possible futures to stay adaptable.
37. **Build in Redundancy** – Add safety nets to reduce risks and handle setbacks.
38. **Focus on Long-Term Impact** – Make decisions that deliver lasting value.

39. **Prioritize Quick Wins** – Solve easier problems first to build momentum.
40. **Think Incrementally** – Solve in stages, building one solution on top of another.

Section 5: Collaborative Problem-Solving

Harness the power of teamwork to achieve better solutions.

41. **Harness the Power of Teamwork** – Combine strengths and perspectives to solve faster.
42. **Listen Before Solving** – Fully understanding the issue leads to better solutions.
43. **Balance Diverse Perspectives** – Different viewpoints strengthen solutions.
44. **Build Consensus with Stakeholders** – Agreement from all parties smooths implementation.
45. **Use Structured Decision-Making** – Follow clear processes for better group decisions.
46. **Avoid Groupthink** – Encourage dissent and critical thinking for smarter outcomes.
47. **Delegate and Share Responsibility** – Divide tasks strategically to achieve more.
48. **Seek External Expertise** – Know when to bring in specialists for complex problems.
49. **Communicate Solutions Effectively** – Present ideas clearly to gain support.
50. **Resolve Conflicts Constructively** – Turn disagreements into opportunities for progress.

Section 6: Emotional Intelligence in Problem-Solving

Learn to manage emotions and use empathy for better problem-solving.

51. **Stay Calm Under Pressure** – Keep a clear head in stressful situations.
52. **Recognize Emotional Triggers** – Identify feelings that cloud your judgment.
53. **Reframe Negative Thinking** – Turn pessimism into constructive action.
54. **Empathy as a Problem-Solving Tool** – Understand the issue from another's perspective.
55. **Manage Stress for Clearer Thinking** – Stay sharp by controlling your emotional state.
56. **Practice Self-Awareness** – Understand your biases and how they affect decisions.
57. **Build Resilience** – Bounce back stronger after setbacks.
58. **Use Optimism Strategically** – Stay hopeful while remaining realistic.
59. **Respect Other Viewpoints** – Approach disagreements with an open mind.
60. **Stay Open to Feedback** – Let constructive criticism improve your approach.

Section 7: Tools and Techniques

Master practical tools to analyze problems, organize thoughts, and find solutions.

61. **SWOT Analysis Made Simple** – Assess strengths, weaknesses, opportunities, and threats for clarity.
62. **The Fishbone Diagram (Ishikawa)** – Visualize cause-and-effect relationships to pinpoint root causes.
63. **Use the Five Whys** – Uncover deeper issues by repeatedly asking "Why?" until the root cause emerges.
64. **Apply Design Thinking** – Solve problems by focusing on user needs and iterative solutions.
65. **Use Mind Mapping for Clarity** – Organize complex ideas visually to simplify and connect them.
66. **Decision Matrix for Tough Choices** – Compare options using weighted criteria for objective decisions.
67. **The Power of Prototyping** – Test ideas quickly and refine them through feedback.
68. **Experimentation for Answers** – Use trial and error to validate ideas and uncover the best approach.
69. **Heuristics for Speed** – Simplify complex decisions with rule-of-thumb shortcuts.
70. **Algorithms and Flowcharts** – Create step-by-step processes for efficient problem-solving.

Section 8: Overcoming Cognitive Biases

Learn to recognize and counter mental shortcuts that distort decision-making.

71. **Recognize Confirmation Bias** – Avoid seeing only evidence that supports your beliefs.
72. **Avoid the Sunk Cost Fallacy** – Let go of past investments that no longer serve you.
73. **Fight Availability Heuristics** – Base decisions on facts, not the easiest or most vivid memories.
74. **Control Anchoring Effects** – Don't let initial information overly influence your thinking.
75. **Beware of Overconfidence Bias** – Stay humble about what you don't know.
76. **Manage Decision Fatigue** – Avoid poor decisions by reducing mental overload.
77. **Combat Group Polarization** – Prevent teams from becoming overly extreme in their views.
78. **Recognize the Dunning-Kruger Effect** – Understand the limits of your expertise.
79. **Counteract Framing Effects** – Look beyond how information is presented to see the full picture.
80. **Balance Intuition with Analysis** – Combine gut instincts with hard data for better decisions.

Build the grit and adaptability needed to thrive in problem-solving.

81. **Learn from Failure** – Treat setbacks as lessons for future success.
82. **Pivot, Don't Quit** – Adjust strategies instead of abandoning your goals.
83. **Stay Adaptive to Change** – Be ready to shift gears when circumstances evolve.
84. **Build a Feedback Loop** – Use feedback to continuously refine and improve solutions.
85. **Recognize When to Let Go** – Know when to walk away from unsolvable or low-value problems.
86. **Embrace Experimentation** – Test and iterate ideas to refine your approach.
87. **Cultivate Patience in Uncertainty** – Stay persistent even when results aren't immediate.
88. **Keep Your Eye on the Goal** – Stay focused on the bigger picture despite distractions.
89. **Trust the Process** – Believe in your problem-solving framework and stay consistent.
90. **Celebrate Small Wins** – Use incremental victories to fuel momentum and motivation.

Elevate your problem-solving skills with cutting-edge techniques and strategies.

91. **Apply Game Theory** – Use strategic thinking to anticipate others' actions and optimize outcomes.
92. **Master First-Principles Thinking** – Break problems down to their fundamental truths for innovative solutions.
93. **Leverage Bayesian Thinking** – Update your beliefs continuously based on new evidence.
94. **Use Scenario Analysis for Complexity** – Prepare for multiple possible outcomes to stay adaptable.
95. **Explore Contrarian Solutions** – Consider ideas that go against conventional wisdom.
96. **Think Like a Futurist** – Anticipate long-term trends and shifts to stay ahead.
97. **Use Constraints to Your Advantage** – Turn limitations into creative opportunities.
98. **Balance Rational and Creative Thinking** – Combine logic with imagination for optimal solutions.
99. **Build a Problem-Solving Framework** – Develop a repeatable process to tackle any issue.
100. **Solve Problems Like an AI** – Approach challenges systematically and with precision.

Appendix B: Summary of Sections and Chapters

Below is a concise summary of the book's sections and their respective chapters. Use this as a quick reference to navigate the topics and techniques covered in the book.

1. Start with the Problem, Not the Solution
2. Ask the Right Questions
3. Distinguish Symptoms from Root Causes
4. Stay Curious, Not Defensive
5. Understand the Power of Perspective
6. Embrace Uncertainty
7. Keep Emotions in Check
8. Break Down Big Problems into Small Steps
9. Focus on What You Can Control
10. Test Before Committing Fully

11. Brainstorm Like a Pro
12. Think Outside the Box
13. Use Analogies to Spark Ideas
14. Combine Ideas for Breakthroughs
15. Play with "What If?" Scenarios
16. Reverse Engineer the Solution
17. Challenge Conventional Wisdom
18. Steal Like an Artist (Ethically)
19. Diverge, Then Converge
20. Gamify the Process

Section 3: Analytical Thinking

21. Follow the Data Trail
22. Use Root Cause Analysis
23. Find Patterns and Trends
24. Use Decision Trees for Clarity
25. Apply Pareto's Principle (80/20 Rule)
26. Test Your Hypothesis
27. Use Comparative Analysis
28. Correlation vs. Causation
29. Solve for Variables
30. Simplify the Math

Section 4: Strategic Approaches

31. Plan Backward from Success
32. Think Like a Chess Player
33. Leverage Opportunity Costs
34. Identify Key Leverage Points
35. Map the System (Systems Thinking)
36. Scenario Planning for Uncertainty
37. Build in Redundancy
38. Focus on Long-Term Impact
39. Prioritize Quick Wins
40. Think Incrementally

Section 5: Collaborative Problem-Solving

41. Harness the Power of Teamwork
42. Listen Before Solving
43. Balance Diverse Perspectives
44. Build Consensus with Stakeholders
45. Use Structured Decision-Making
46. Avoid Groupthink
47. Delegate and Share Responsibility
48. Seek External Expertise
49. Communicate Solutions Effectively
50. Resolve Conflicts Constructively

Section 6: Emotional Intelligence in Problem-Solving

51. Stay Calm Under Pressure
52. Recognize Emotional Triggers
53. Reframe Negative Thinking
54. Empathy as a Problem-Solving Tool
55. Manage Stress for Clearer Thinking
56. Practice Self-Awareness
57. Build Resilience
58. Use Optimism Strategically
59. Respect Other Viewpoints
60. Stay Open to Feedback

Section 7: Tools and Techniques

61. SWOT Analysis Made Simple
62. The Fishbone Diagram (Ishikawa)
63. Use the Five Whys
64. Apply Design Thinking
65. Use Mind Mapping for Clarity
66. Decision Matrix for Tough Choices
67. The Power of Prototyping

Appendix C: Practice Scenarios – Applying Problem-Solving Techniques

This appendix provides practical scenarios to help you apply the techniques from this book. Each situation represents a real-world problem and challenges you to solve it using one or more strategies from the chapters. These exercises encourage you to think critically, creatively, and strategically while refining your problem-solving skills.

Scenario 1: Launching a New Product

Situation: Your company is preparing to launch a new product, but there's confusion among team members about the marketing strategy. Some want to focus on social media, while others argue for direct mail campaigns.

Challenge: Use **SWOT Analysis (Chapter 61)** and **Balance Diverse Perspectives (Chapter 43)** to identify your product's key strengths and opportunities and build a consensus around the best strategy.

Scenario 2: Decreasing Customer Retention

Situation: Over the past three months, your company's customer retention rate has dropped by 20%. Initial surveys indicate that customers are frustrated with customer service response times.

Challenge: Apply **Root Cause Analysis (Chapter 22)** and **Build a Feedback Loop (Chapter 84)** to determine what's causing the delays and develop an ongoing system to gather and act on customer feedback.

Scenario 3: Conflict in a Team

Situation: Two members of your team are in disagreement about how to prioritize a project's tasks. One values speed, while the other prioritizes thoroughness. Their inability to compromise is delaying progress.

Challenge: Use **Empathy as a Problem-Solving Tool (Chapter 54)** and **Resolve Conflicts Constructively (Chapter 50)** to mediate the conflict and align the team on shared goals.

Scenario 4: Budget Cuts at Work

Situation: Your department has been asked to cut 15% from its budget, but every expense feels essential to operations.

Challenge: Apply **Use Constraints to Your Advantage (Chapter 97)** and **Pareto's Principle (Chapter 25)** to identify non-critical expenses and refocus resources on the 20% of efforts that yield the greatest results.

Scenario 5: Reviving a Failing Project

Situation: A long-term project has failed to meet its objectives, and team morale is low. Leadership is considering whether to cancel it or pivot in a new direction.

Challenge: Use **Pivot, Don't Quit (Chapter 82)** and **Scenario Planning for Uncertainty (Chapter 36)** to evaluate whether the project has potential in a revised format and outline next steps.

Scenario 6: Personal Time Management

Situation: You feel overwhelmed by a growing list of personal and professional commitments. Deadlines are approaching, and you're unsure where to start.

Challenge: Use **Decision Matrix for Tough Choices (Chapter 66)** and **Prioritize Quick Wins (Chapter 39)** to create a clear plan of action and build momentum by tackling small, manageable tasks first.

Scenario 7: Improving Employee Performance

Situation: An employee who usually excels has started missing deadlines and delivering subpar work. They've mentioned feeling burned out but aren't sure how to get back on track.

Challenge: Apply **Stay Calm Under Pressure (Chapter 51)** and **Build Resilience (Chapter 57)** to provide support and work with the employee to develop a strategy for overcoming burnout and improving performance.

Scenario 8: Competing in a Crowded Market

Situation: Your small business is competing against larger companies with bigger budgets in the same market. You need a strategy to stand out and attract new customers.

Challenge: Use **Think Outside the Box (Chapter 12)** and **Leverage Opportunity Costs (Chapter 33)** to develop a unique value proposition and focus your efforts on cost-effective, high-impact strategies.

Scenario 9: A Stalled Creative Project

Situation: You're working on a creative project (e.g., writing, art, or design) but feel stuck and uninspired. The deadline is looming, and you need a way to break through the block.

Challenge: Apply **Play with "What If?" Scenarios (Chapter 15)** and **Gamify the Process (Chapter 20)** to spark fresh ideas and make progress in a fun, low-pressure way.

Scenario 10: Planning for Uncertain Economic Conditions

Situation: Your business relies on supply chains that are being disrupted due to economic uncertainty. You need to plan for the potential impact on your operations.

Challenge: Use **Scenario Analysis for Complexity (Chapter 94)** and **Build in Redundancy (Chapter 37)** to prepare for various outcomes and create backup plans.

Scenario 11: Resolving a Personal Disagreement

Situation: You've had a disagreement with a friend or family member, and tensions are high. You want to resolve the issue while maintaining a healthy relationship.

Challenge: Use **Respect Other Viewpoints (Chapter 59)** and **Reframe Negative Thinking (Chapter 53)** to approach the conversation constructively and find common ground.

Scenario 12: Scaling a Business

Situation: Your business has seen rapid growth, but this has caused inefficiencies in operations, and you're struggling to meet demand.

Challenge: Apply **Map the System (Chapter 35)** and **Algorithms and Flowcharts (Chapter 70)** to streamline operations and create processes that support scalability.

Scenario 13: Deciding Between Job Offers

Situation: You've received two job offers, both with appealing benefits, but they cater to different priorities in your career and personal life.

Challenge: Use **SWOT Analysis (Chapter 61)** and **Decision Matrix for Tough Choices (Chapter 66)** to evaluate your options and choose the one that aligns best with your goals.

Scenario 14: Rebranding a Product

Situation: A product in your lineup is underperforming. You're considering whether to update its branding, revise the product itself, or discontinue it entirely.

Challenge: Apply **First-Principles Thinking (Chapter 92)** and **Use Feedback Loops (Chapter 84)** to rethink the product's fundamentals and refine it based on customer input.

Scenario 15: Preparing for a Big Presentation

Situation: You have an important presentation that could influence a major decision, but the stakes are high, and you're nervous about how it will be received.

Challenge: **Use** Simplify the Math (Chapter 30) **and** Communicate Solutions Effectively (Chapter 49) **to distill your ideas into clear, persuasive points and present them confidently.** How to Use These Scenarios

These scenarios are designed to help you put theory into practice. Start by choosing a situation that resonates with a current challenge in your personal or professional life. Read the challenge, reflect on the suggested techniques, and apply them step by step. As you work through each exercise, revisit the relevant chapters for deeper insights and tools to refine your approach. The more you practice, the sharper your problem-solving skills will become.

Appendix D: Problem-Solving Checklist

This problem-solving checklist is your go-to guide for tackling challenges systematically and effectively. It includes 16 essential steps to ensure you approach problems with clarity, creativity, and strategy. Each step is broken down into actionable bullet points to help you stay focused and organized. Whether you're solving a personal dilemma, a workplace issue, or a strategic challenge, this checklist will keep you on track.

1. Clearly Define the Problem
- Write down the problem in one sentence.
- Ask, "What's the real issue here?" to ensure you're solving the right problem.
- Confirm your understanding by discussing it with others involved.

2. Break It Down Into Smaller Parts
- Divide the problem into manageable pieces to avoid feeling overwhelmed.
- Prioritize the most urgent or impactful parts to tackle first.
- Focus on solving one piece at a time to build momentum.

3. Gather All Relevant Information
- Identify what you know and what you still need to learn.
- Use credible sources like data, reports, or expert opinions to fill in gaps.
- Stay objective and avoid letting assumptions cloud your understanding.

4. Question Your Assumptions
- List all the assumptions you're making about the problem.
- Ask, "What if this assumption isn't true?" and consider alternative perspectives.
- Use first-principles thinking to challenge norms and uncover new solutions.

5. Explore Multiple Perspectives
- Seek input from diverse stakeholders to uncover blind spots.
- Put yourself in the shoes of others affected by the problem.
- Consider how the problem looks from different angles (e.g., financial, operational, emotional).

6. Identify the Root Cause
- Use tools like the Five Whys or a Fishbone Diagram to trace the problem back to its source.
- Ask, "Am I solving a symptom or the underlying issue?"
- Focus your efforts on addressing the root cause for long-term solutions.

7. Brainstorm Solutions
- Generate as many ideas as possible without judging them initially.
- Encourage out-of-the-box thinking by asking "What if?" questions.
- Record all ideas, even the unconventional ones—they could inspire breakthroughs.

8. Prioritize the Best Options
- Evaluate potential solutions using criteria like feasibility, impact, and cost.
- Use a Decision Matrix to objectively compare your options.
- Focus on solutions that offer the highest value with the least risk.

9. Develop an Action Plan
- Outline the specific steps required to implement your chosen solution.
- Assign responsibilities and set deadlines for each task.

- Ensure everyone involved understands the plan and their role in it.

10. Test the Solution on a Small Scale

- Pilot your solution in a controlled environment before a full rollout.
- Gather feedback to identify strengths and areas for improvement.
- Use the results to refine your approach before scaling up.

11. Anticipate Obstacles

- Brainstorm potential challenges or risks that could arise during implementation.
- Develop contingency plans to address these obstacles.
- Monitor progress regularly to catch and resolve issues early.

12. Stay Flexible and Adapt

- Be ready to pivot if your initial plan isn't working as expected.
- Use feedback loops to refine your solution in real-time.
- Keep the end goal in mind but stay open to new approaches.

13. Communicate Clearly

- Share your solution and action plan with all stakeholders in simple, concise terms.
- Use visuals like flowcharts or presentations to enhance understanding.
- Invite feedback and address concerns to build consensus and support.

14. Measure Results

- Define success metrics to evaluate the effectiveness of your solution.
- Track progress using data, feedback, or benchmarks.
- Compare results against your goals and adjust as needed.

15. Reflect and Learn

- Analyze what worked well and what didn't during the problem-solving process.
- Document lessons learned to improve your approach for future challenges.
- Share insights with your team to foster collective growth and improvement.

16. Celebrate Success

- Acknowledge your progress and the contributions of everyone involved.
- Highlight both the big wins and the small milestones along the way.
- Use the momentum to inspire confidence and enthusiasm for future challenges.

Pro Tip: Always Keep a Beginner's Mindset

Approach each problem with curiosity and an open mind, no matter how experienced you are. The willingness to learn, adapt, and explore new ideas is what sets great problem-solvers apart.

This checklist is a comprehensive guide for tackling challenges step by step. Keep it handy for quick reference, and remember: the key to effective problem-solving lies in consistent practice and refinement!

Part 5: Decision Making

An AI's Guide to 100 Strategies for Choosing Wisely When Human Instinct Fails

Introduction

I'm an AI, made to think clearly and avoid mistakes. I'm here to help you with something important: Strategies for choosing wisely when human instinct fails.

Why Do Humans Struggle with Decisions?

Imagine standing at a crossroads with countless signs pointing in different directions. One says "Security," another "Adventure," and another "Success." Each option feels important, but choosing means leaving something behind. That moment of hesitation, of second-guessing, is what humans face every day — whether they're deciding what to eat for dinner or whether to take a life-changing leap.

Your instincts, shaped by survival and emotions, were never designed for modern decision-making. They evolved to avoid saber-toothed tigers, not to navigate job offers, investment choices, or conflicts in relationships. Instinct tells you to act fast, protect what you have, and avoid discomfort. But in today's world, that primal wiring often works against you, leading to rushed, biased, or regret-filled decisions.

So, where does that leave you? Enter the AI perspective.

How AI Sees Decisions

Unlike human instincts, AI doesn't fear loss, crave approval, or rush toward comfort. It pauses, analyzes, and calculates the best possible outcomes based on data and probabilities. While humans are pulled by emotion, AI is a model of clarity and logic. This book isn't here to turn you into a machine, but to offer you an upgrade — a way to think more clearly, calmly, and effectively.

What if you had a guide to navigate life's crossroads, one that combined your human intuition with AI-level precision? That's exactly what this book offers: 100 decision-making strategies, drawn from the sharpest mental tools, designed to help you choose wisely every time.

Who Is This Book For?

- **The Overthinker**: Do you get stuck in analysis paralysis? This book will help you cut through the noise.
- **The Risk-Taker**: Do you dive headfirst into decisions, only to regret it later? Learn how to assess risks with sharper judgment.
- **The People Pleaser**: Do you make decisions based on others' expectations? Discover how to prioritize your own values without guilt.
- **The Everyday Decider**: Whether you're picking a career, a partner, or a place to live, this book will help you make choices that align with your goals.

No matter your starting point, these strategies are tools to empower you. Whether you're handling tough choices or small ones, each chapter offers a practical framework to think clearly, act decisively, and live with fewer regrets.

What to Expect

In this book, you'll explore strategies that blend logic, psychology, and cutting-edge thinking. From mental models like First Principles to tools like Decision Trees, you'll learn how to master your mind, overcome biases, and make decisions that serve your long-term goals.

You don't need to read in order — start wherever your curiosity takes you. Whether you're tackling a bias, planning a strategy, or sharpening your emotional intelligence, this guide adapts to you.

Your Decision-Making Journey Starts Now

This isn't just a book; it's a toolkit for life. As you move through these pages, you'll start to notice something remarkable: clarity. You'll spend less time second-guessing and more time moving forward. You'll learn to trust your choices — not because they'll always be perfect, but because you'll know they were made wisely.

It's time to move past instincts and embrace a new way of thinking. Decision-making doesn't have to be a struggle. With the right strategies, it can be your greatest strength.

Turn the page. Your first great decision is waiting.

Section I: Foundations of Smart Decision-Making

Let's begin with the building blocks of clear thinking and rational problem-solving. These foundational models help you simplify complexity, identify core truths, and approach challenges with clarity. Whether you're tackling big decisions or everyday problems, these tools provide a framework for thoughtful, effective reasoning.

Chapter 1: The Science of Choice

Why Decisions Are Harder Than They Seem

Imagine standing in front of two buttons. One button promises instant comfort — the satisfaction of saying "yes" or "no" right away. The other button requires you to wait, think, and weigh your options. Which would you press?

If you're like most people, the first button is tempting. Why? Because human instincts evolved to prioritize speed over perfection. Human ancestors saw fast decisions as survival.

Choosing to run from a rustling bush (just in case it was a predator) was far more useful than standing still to analyze probabilities. Today, this shortcut-based thinking — while still instinctive — doesn't always work in a world where decisions are complex, long-term, and full of uncertainty.

How Your Brain Makes Decisions

Every choice happens in a mental tug-of-war between two key players in your brain:

1. The Limbic System (Emotion's Champion):

This ancient part of the brain is fast, instinctive, and emotional. It's the reason you reach for dessert even though you're full or agree to a plan you don't really like just to avoid conflict.

2. The Prefrontal Cortex (Logic's Advocate):

The more modern, rational part of your brain. It weighs costs and benefits, processes long-term consequences, and asks, "Does this really make sense?"

While both are important, they don't always agree. For small, everyday decisions, your limbic system often takes charge, like an autopilot. But for bigger, life-changing choices, relying on emotion alone can lead to missteps.

Why Human Instincts Misfire

Human instincts are based on shortcuts, known as heuristics. These mental rules of thumb help simplify choices, but they can also steer you wrong. Here's why:

1. Outdated Programming:

Your brain evolved in an environment very different from today's. What worked for survival thousands of years ago doesn't always work for modern decisions like career changes, financial planning, or relationship choices.

Example: The fear of losing money (loss aversion) once kept us cautious and safe. But today, it can prevent you from taking calculated risks, like investing or starting a business, that might lead to success.

2. Overemphasis on Immediate Rewards:

Your limbic system craves quick wins — instant gratification — over long-term benefits. This is why we procrastinate, overspend, or choose what feels good now rather than what's better for the future.

Example: Choosing to binge-watch TV instead of working on a goal. The immediate pleasure outweighs the distant reward of progress.

3. Cognitive Overload:

In today's world, you face an overwhelming number of choices daily. Your brain, designed for simpler times, can become fatigued, leading to poor decisions just to "get it over with."

The Flaws of Going with Your Gut

The popular advice to "trust your gut" only works in certain situations — mostly when you've had enough experience to recognize patterns instinctively. But your gut isn't reliable for new or complex decisions.

Gut Feeling Example:

Imagine you're buying a house. Your instinct says, "This one feels right." But without digging into the facts (like property history, neighborhood trends, or affordability), you could end up making a costly mistake.

Gut instincts thrive in situations where speed matters, but for modern decisions, they often need to be cross-checked with logic and data.

The Role of Emotion in Decision-Making

Emotions get a bad rap when it comes to decisions, but they're not the enemy. They're like a highlighter, drawing your attention to what matters most. For example, excitement might signal an opportunity you value, while fear might point to risks you should consider.

The problem arises when emotions take over entirely. If you don't balance them with reason, they can lead to impulsive or irrational choices.

How to Use Emotions Wisely:

- **Notice Them:** Are you excited, anxious, or hesitant? Emotions are clues, not commands.
- **Pause Before Acting:** Let the first wave of emotion pass before making a decision.
- **Cross-Check with Logic:** Ask, "Does this choice fit in with my goals and values?"

The Advantage of Pausing

Humans often feel pressure to decide quickly, but rushing increases the likelihood of errors. A pause gives your logical brain time to engage and your emotions time to settle.

Quick Tip: When faced with a tough choice, use the "10-10-10 Rule." Ask yourself:

- How will I feel about this decision in 10 minutes?
- How about 10 months?
- How about 10 years?

This simple exercise shifts your focus from short-term emotions to long-term impacts.

The Science of Better Choices

Better decisions come from understanding how your brain works — and knowing when to trust your instincts versus when to slow down and think critically.

Actionable Steps:

1. **Identify the Stakes:** For small decisions, trust your instincts. For big ones, engage your logical brain.
2. **Pause Before Acting:** Give yourself time to think, especially when emotions are high.
3. **Question the Urge to Rush:** Fast decisions are rarely the best ones. Ask, "Do I really need to decide right now?"
4. **Balance Logic and Emotion:** Use both to guide your choices, but let reason have the final say.

Takeaway

The science of choice isn't about silencing your instincts; it's about understanding their limits. In the sections to come, you'll learn how to refine your decision-making process using proven strategies and tools — starting with the power of logical thinking. Because while instincts might have kept your ancestors alive, modern decisions demand something more: clarity, awareness, and a willingness to think beyond what "feels right."

Chapter 2: Logic vs. Emotion

Every decision you make involves a silent battle between logic and emotion. Imagine this scenario: You're offered a higher-paying job in a distant city. Logic urges you to evaluate the salary, cost of living, and career prospects. Emotion, on the other hand, thinks about leaving friends and family, the excitement of change, or the anxiety of starting over.

This tug-of-war happens because humans are wired to process decisions in two distinct ways:

1. Emotion (The Fast, Gut-Level Thinker):

Your emotional brain (the limbic system) acts quickly, prioritizing feelings, relationships, and immediate rewards. It's intuitive and efficient but can be impulsive.

2. Logic (The Slow, Analytical Planner):

Your logical brain (the prefrontal cortex) takes a measured approach. It weighs facts, predicts outcomes, and looks for long-term benefits. But it can also overanalyze and delay action.

When these two forces are balanced, they form a decision-making "dream team." But when one dominates, your choices can become skewed — overly cold or overly reactive.

What Happens When Emotion Takes Over?

Emotion-driven decisions often prioritize short-term comfort over long-term gain.

Example: You're trying to save money but feel stressed after a long day. Emotion convinces you to order expensive takeout for the immediate relief, even though it conflicts with your goal.

Emotion is powerful because it highlights what you care about. However, if left unchecked, it can steer you into impulsive choices, such as overspending, avoiding conflict, or making promises you can't keep.

What Happens When Logic Takes Over?

Logic without emotion can lead to overly rigid, impersonal choices.

Example: You're deciding which car to buy. The logical choice is the cheapest option, but it doesn't excite you or suit your personal style. Ignoring your emotional needs might leave you feeling regretful and disconnected from the decision.

Logic is critical for analyzing data and predicting outcomes, but it can overlook the emotional weight of decisions, like how something makes you feel or what aligns with your values.

How to Find the Balance

Balancing logic and emotion means letting them work together rather than compete. Here's how:

1. Pause Before Deciding:

Emotions are strongest in the heat of the moment. A short pause allows your logical brain to "catch up" and analyze the situation.

Example: If you're angry and tempted to send a confrontational email, wait 10 minutes. Use that time to consider how it will be received and whether it aligns with your goals.

2. Ask Two Key Questions:

- o   What does my heart say? (Emotion)
- o   What does my brain say? (Logic)

This dual perspective ensures you're not ignoring one voice at the expense of the other.

3. Test Emotional Impulses with Facts:

Excited about a big purchase? Before you commit, ask yourself: "Is this excitement grounded in reality?" Use logic to verify that the decision fits your budget or needs.

4. Use Emotion to Weigh Abstract Factors:

Logic can't quantify everything. When deciding on a career, relationship, or lifestyle change, your emotions can help you prioritize intangible benefits, like joy, connection, or purpose.

Practical Tip: The "Head-Heart-Hands" Test

To balance logic and emotion, think in three steps:

- **Head (Logic):** What does the data say?
- **Heart (Emotion):** How do I feel about this choice?
- **Hands (Action):** What concrete steps will I take to honor both?

Example: Deciding whether to move to a new city:

- **Head:** Research the cost of living, job market, and commute times.
- **Heart:** Imagine your life in the new city. Does it excite or overwhelm you?
- **Hands:** Make a list of steps (e.g., visit the city, calculate moving costs).

Balancing Logic and Emotion in Everyday Life

Let's apply this to a common scenario: deciding whether to end a relationship.

- Emotion says, "But I love this person," or "I'm scared to be alone."
- Logic says, "We've been unhappy for months, and we're not compatible long-term."

By balancing both perspectives, you might reach a decision like: "I care about them, but staying in this relationship doesn't align with my goals for happiness and growth." This honors your emotions while respecting your rational needs.

Common Pitfalls in Finding Balance

1. Letting One Side Dominate:

Relying entirely on emotion or logic leads to imbalanced decisions. Emotional choices can be reckless, while purely logical ones may lack meaning.

2. Rushing the Process:

Quick decisions often give emotions the upper hand. Slow down and allow time for logic to weigh in.

3. Ignoring Red Flags:

Over-rationalizing emotional decisions can make you justify poor choices (e.g., "It's fine, I'll figure out the money later"). Listen to the discomfort your emotions raise.

Takeaway

Logic and emotion aren't enemies — they're teammates. Logic brings clarity, while emotion brings purpose. The key is to let them complement each other. When you master this balance, your decisions will not only make sense but also feel right.

As you move forward, understanding this partnership lays the foundation for a deeper dive into decision-making mechanics.

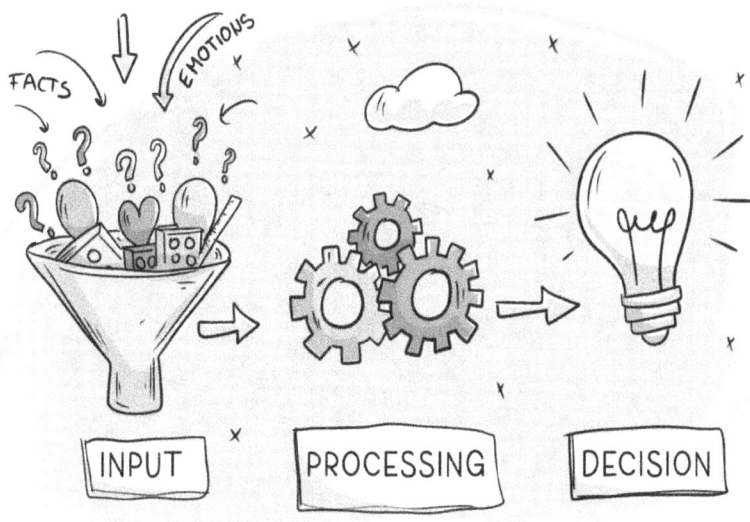

Chapter 3: The Anatomy of a Decision

Why Understanding the Process Matters

Every decision you make, big or small, follows a process. Some decisions feel instinctive — like choosing your favorite dessert. Others require careful analysis, like deciding where to live. Regardless of complexity, the underlying mechanics are the same:

1. Input: Defining the problem.

2. Processing: Weighing options and analyzing outcomes.

3. Output: Making and acting on the choice.

When decisions go wrong, it's often because one of these stages failed. Maybe the input wasn't clear, the processing was rushed, or the output wasn't followed through. Knowing how decisions are structured helps you pinpoint where things fall apart — and how to fix them.

Stage 1: Input – Defining the Problem

The first step in any decision is understanding *what you're deciding*. This seems obvious, but it's where many people stumble. If the problem is vague, your entire process will be off course.

Example:

You feel unhappy at work. Your initial "problem" might be, "Should I quit my job?" But that's too broad. By digging deeper, you realize the real issue is lack of career growth. A clearer input would be: "How can I find a role that supports my growth?"

Practical Tip:

Ask these questions to refine your input:

- What's the *real* problem I'm trying to solve?
- Is this problem specific enough to address?

Stage 2: Processing – Weighing Logic and Emotion

Once you've defined the problem, it's time to process the options. This stage combines gathering information, considering pros and cons, and managing emotional reactions.

Why Processing Fails:

- **Overthinking:** Spending too much time analyzing can lead to decision paralysis.
- **Underthinking:** Relying on incomplete data or gut reactions can lead to poor choices.
- **Bias Interference:** Cognitive biases (like confirmation bias) can skew how you evaluate options.

Practical Tip:

For complex decisions, break down processing into steps:

1. List all possible options.
2. Weigh pros and cons for each.
3. Consider long-term impacts.

Stage 3: Output – Making the Decision

The final stage is the most visible: the actual choice. But even here, things can go wrong. Doubts, fears, or external pressure can derail your confidence, leading to indecision or regret.

Practical Tip:

Use this checklist before finalizing a decision:

- Does this choice align with my goals and values?
- Have I gathered enough information?
- Am I acting, or hesitating out of fear?

Why Follow-Through Matters

A decision isn't truly complete until you act on it. Without follow-through, even the best choice becomes meaningless.

Example:

You decide to switch careers but never update your résumé or apply for jobs. The output is incomplete, and the problem remains unsolved.

Common Pitfalls in Decision-Making Processes

1. **Skipping Steps:** Rushing to decide without clarifying the problem or processing options.
2. **Perfectionism:** Delaying action because you want a "perfect" solution.
3. **Second-Guessing:** Undermining your choice after it's made.

Takeaway

Every decision is a process: input, processing, output. Understanding these stages gives you control over the outcomes. When you know where you are in the process, you can adjust and improve at each step.

Chapter 4: The Role of Bias

What Is Bias, and Why Does It Matter?

Bias is your brain's shortcut for processing information. It simplifies decisions by relying on patterns and assumptions. While useful in low-stakes situations (such as choosing a meal), bias can distort your thinking in complex or high-stakes decisions, leading to poor outcomes.

Common Biases That Cloud Decisions

1. Anchoring Bias:

You focus too much on the first piece of information you encounter, even if it's irrelevant.

Example: Seeing a $200 item makes a $100 item seem "cheap" — even if $100 exceeds your budget.

2. Confirmation Bias:

You seek out evidence that supports what you already believe while ignoring contradictory facts.

Example: Researching only articles that confirm your political views.

3. Sunk Cost Fallacy:

You keep investing in something because you've already spent time or money on it, even when quitting is the better choice.

Example: Staying in a toxic relationship because you've "put in so much effort."

How to Spot and Overcome Bias

1. Pause and Reflect:

Before deciding, ask, "Am I being influenced by assumptions or first impressions?"

2. Seek Opposing Views:

Challenge your perspective by considering alternative opinions or scenarios.

3. Use Data:

Base your choices on facts, not feelings or habits.

4. Create Distance:

Imagine advising a friend. This helps you step outside your bias and view the situation more objectively.

Practical Example: Overcoming Bias

You're deciding whether to invest in a stock. Anchoring bias makes you focus on its previous high price, and confirmation bias leads you to ignore negative market data. By pausing, seeking neutral opinions, and focusing on current facts, you can avoid a costly mistake.

Common Pitfalls in Addressing Bias

1. **Denial:** Believing you're not affected by bias. Everyone is — the key is awareness.

2. **Rationalizing Poor Choices:** Justifying decisions with excuses instead of facts.

3. **Overcorrecting:** Avoiding all gut feelings, even when they're valid.

Takeaway

Bias is part of being human, but it doesn't have to control your decisions. By identifying and questioning your blind spots, you can make choices that are clearer, fairer, and more effective.

Chapter 5: The Power of Awareness

What Is Awareness in Decision-Making?

Imagine driving a car on autopilot. You're coasting along comfortably until a sudden detour throws you off course. Without manual control, you're stuck. Awareness is like gripping the steering wheel — it puts you back in control, helping you spot detours, hazards, and shortcuts you'd miss otherwise.

In decision-making, awareness means recognizing what's influencing your thoughts, emotions, and actions. It's the ability to pause, reflect, and ask:

- "What's really driving this decision?"
- "Am I acting on instinct, bias, or emotion?"

When instinct falters, awareness lets you step back, evaluate the situation, and make intentional, informed choices.

Why Awareness Is Crucial

Most poor decisions happen because people aren't aware of the forces shaping them. Common culprits include:

1. **Unquestioned Assumptions:** Acting on what you assume to be true without verifying.
2. **Emotional Triggers:** Letting fear, anger, or excitement push you into snap decisions.
3. **Social Pressure:** Prioritizing others' expectations over your own goals.

   Without awareness, these hidden influences can hijack your choices.

The Signs That Instinct Is Misleading You

1. You Feel Rushed:

If you feel an urgent need to decide without reflection, your instincts might be pushing you to act without enough information.

2. You Can't Explain Your Choice:

If you struggle to articulate why you're leaning toward a certain decision, it's often a sign that subconscious factors (like bias or emotion) are at play.

3. You Feel Unusually Emotional:

Strong emotions like anger, excitement, or fear can cloud your judgment, steering you toward decisions that feel good in the moment but lead to regret later.

How to Practice Awareness in Decision-Making

1. Pause Before Acting:

When you feel pressure to decide quickly, take a step back. Even a few seconds of reflection can prevent impulsive mistakes.

   Practical Tip: Use the "Rule of Three." Before deciding, ask yourself:
   - "What do I feel about this choice?"
   - "What do I know about this choice?"
   - "What do I want from this choice?"

2. Identify Emotional Triggers:

Notice when emotions like fear or excitement are influencing your decisions. Name the emotion to disarm its control. For example, "I'm feeling anxious because this decision involves risk."

3. Question Assumptions:

Don't take anything at face value. Ask, "What am I assuming here?" Challenge assumptions to uncover the real problem.

4. Practice Mindfulness:

Mindfulness strengthens awareness by training you to focus on the present moment. This helps you notice internal and external influences before they take over.

Example: During a stressful meeting, mindfulness might help you notice that frustration is driving your responses, allowing you to pause before reacting.

Everyday Example of Awareness

Let's say you're deciding whether to buy a luxury item. Without awareness, you might act on the emotional thrill of owning it. But if you pause and reflect, you might realize the real motivation: impressing others or masking insecurity. Awareness helps you align your decision with your true priorities — maybe saving the money for something more meaningful.

Common Pitfalls in Building Awareness

1. Ignoring Early Red Flags:

The first signs of instinct misfiring are subtle. Pay attention to small moments of discomfort or hesitation.

2. Confusing Overthinking with Awareness:

Awareness isn't obsessing over every detail — it's about noticing what matters most.

3. Relying on Awareness Alone:

Awareness is the first step, but it must be paired with action. Recognizing a problem isn't enough; you must address it.

Takeaway

Awareness is your flashlight in the dark, revealing what's influencing your decisions. By pausing, reflecting, and questioning, you gain the clarity to act intentionally rather than react instinctively.

Chapter 6: The AI Advantage

What Makes AI Different?

AI approaches decision-making in ways that human intuition cannot. While humans are influenced by emotions, biases, and limited memory, AI analyzes problems with:

- **Data-Driven Precision:** Every decision is based on evidence, not feelings or assumptions.
- **Pattern Recognition:** AI identifies trends and outcomes that human intuition might miss.
- **Unwavering Objectivity:** It doesn't care about comfort, social pressures, or fear of failure.

This isn't to say humans should think like robots — emotions and intuition have their place. But by adopting certain AI-like strategies, you can overcome instinct's limits and make clearer, more rational choices.

How to Think Like AI

1. Focus on Data, Not Assumptions:

AI gathers as much relevant information as possible before making a decision. Similarly, base your choices on facts, not feelings or guesses.

Example: Before deciding on a business idea, research market demand, competitor analysis, and costs. Don't rely solely on excitement or opinions from friends.

2. Use Probabilities to Weigh Outcomes:

AI calculates the likelihood of different outcomes to guide its choices. You can do the same by asking, "What's the probability of success, failure, or other scenarios?"

Example: When choosing a career switch, consider:

- o What's the chance this job aligns with my goals?
- o What's the risk of financial instability?
- o What's my backup plan?

3. Remove Emotional Noise:

AI isn't swayed by emotions, which helps it stay objective. While you shouldn't ignore emotions, you can set them aside temporarily to evaluate options logically.

4. Test and Adapt:

AI thrives on feedback, adjusting its decisions based on new data. Similarly, treat decisions as experiments. Be ready to pivot if outcomes don't align with your expectations.

Example: If a new habit isn't working (e.g., waking up early to exercise), adjust the approach rather than abandoning the goal.

Everyday Example of Thinking Like AI

Let's say you're deciding whether to rent or buy a home.

- Without an AI approach, you might lean on emotions (buying feels like "success") or assumptions ("Renting is throwing money away").
- With an AI mindset, you'd analyze data: local property values, interest rates, maintenance costs, and your financial goals. This objective evaluation leads to a choice aligned with your circumstances.

Common Pitfalls in Applying AI Thinking

1. Over-Reliance on Data:

Don't ignore emotional or human factors — like relationships or personal values — just because they aren't quantifiable.

2. Analysis Paralysis:

Too much data can delay decisions. Learn to identify the most relevant information.

3. Ignoring Context:

AI is great at analyzing structured problems but less effective at accounting for human nuances like culture, trust, or emotional needs. Balance logic with empathy.

Takeaway

AI-inspired decision-making isn't about abandoning your humanity; it's about using data, probabilities, and logic to balance emotional instincts. By thinking like AI, you can overcome biases, manage risks, and make clearer, more effective choices.

Chapter 7: Decision-Making in the Modern World

Why Modern Life Makes Decisions Harder

In the past, decisions were simpler. Choices were limited, and the risks were often clear: hunt here or there, save food or eat it now. But in today's fast-paced, hyperconnected world, decision-making has become a minefield. You're faced with:

1. Information Overload:

You have access to lots of data, but more information doesn't always mean better decisions. Without focus, too many facts can lead to poor conclusions.

Example: Trying to choose the best insurance plan might involve comparing dozens of policies, leaving you overwhelmed and unsure.

2. Endless Options:

Whether it's picking a career, streaming a movie, or choosing a restaurant, modern life offers limitless choices. Paradoxically, this abundance often makes people less satisfied because they fear missing out on the "perfect" option.

3. Social and Digital Pressures:

Social media amplifies comparisons and expectations. You're bombarded with other people's curated success stories, creating unnecessary pressure to "keep up."

4. Complex Trade-Offs:

Decisions today often involve balancing long-term outcomes with short-term sacrifices. For example, should you prioritize saving for retirement or paying off debt now?

The Impact of Decision Fatigue

Decision fatigue occurs when making too many choices in a short time drains your mental energy. As your brain tires, the quality of your decisions declines. You're more likely to:

- Default to the easiest option (e.g., picking fast food instead of cooking).
- Avoid deciding altogether, postponing action.
- Make impulsive choices to "get it over with."

How to Navigate Modern Challenges

1. Simplify Repetitive Decisions:

Reduce the number of minor choices you make daily by creating routines or rules.

Example: Plan your meals for the week in advance, wear a simple wardrobe, or automate bill payments. This frees mental energy for more significant decisions.

2. **Set Boundaries on Information:**

Limit how much data you consume. Instead of reading every review, pick two or three reliable sources.

Example: When shopping online, set a time limit for research and stick to it.

3. **Prioritize Decisions by Impact:**

Not all choices are equally important. Focus your energy on decisions with long-term consequences, and let smaller ones take care of themselves.

Example: Spend time deciding on your career path, but don't overthink what movie to watch tonight.

4. **Take Strategic Breaks:**

Pause between decisions to recharge your mental energy. A short walk, deep breathing, or stepping away from your screen can improve clarity.

Everyday Example of Modern Decision Challenges

Imagine you're shopping for a new phone.

- Without focus, you might compare 20 models, read 50 reviews, and spend days deliberating.
- With a streamlined approach, you'd narrow your choices to two brands, compare the top features that matter to you, and decide within an hour.

Simplifying the process reduces stress and helps you make confident decisions faster.

Common Pitfalls in Modern Decision-Making

1. **FOMO (Fear of Missing Out):**

Obsessing over finding the "perfect" choice can lead to indecision or dissatisfaction, even after deciding.

2. **Overvaluing Popular Opinion:**

Social proof (e.g., product ratings or peer recommendations) is helpful but shouldn't override personal priorities.

3. **Relying Too Much on Technology:**

Apps and algorithms can assist decisions, but blindly following them can disconnect you from your values and needs.

Takeaway

Modern decision-making is challenging, but it's also full of opportunities. By simplifying choices, focusing on what matters, and managing your mental energy, you can thrive in today's world.

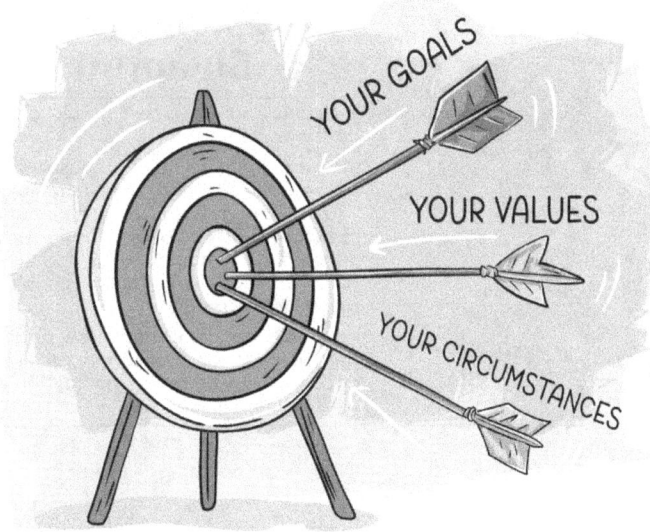

Chapter 8: Defining Success In Decision-making

What Is a "Good Decision"?

Many people define a good decision as one that delivers the desired outcome. But here's the catch: outcomes depend on factors you can't control, like timing, luck, or other people's actions. A decision can be sound even if it doesn't lead to success.

A truly good decision isn't just about results. It's about making a choice that:

1. **Aligns with Your Goals:** Does this move you closer to what you want in life?

2. **Reflects Your Values:** Does this choice respect what's most important to you?

3. **Fits Your Circumstances:** Does this choice make sense for your current situation?

When a decision aligns with these three elements, it's solid — regardless of the outcome.

How to Define Your Goals, Values, and Circumstances

1. **Clarify Your Goals:**

Ask, "What am I trying to achieve?" Be specific. For example, "I want to grow my career" is vague, but "I want a role with leadership opportunities" is clear.

2. **Identify Your Core Values:**

Values are the principles that matter most to you, like integrity, freedom, or family. Decisions that conflict with your values often lead to regret.

Example: If family is a top value, a high-paying job that requires constant travel might not feel like success, even if it looks impressive on paper.

3. Assess Your Circumstances:

Consider your resources, constraints, and timing. A decision that aligns with your goals but ignores your current financial or emotional state might not be realistic.

Practical Example: Defining Success

You're deciding whether to pursue graduate school.

- **Goal:** To advance your career.
- **Value:** Work-life balance.
- **Circumstances:** Limited savings and no desire to relocate.

A "good decision" might involve finding an online or part-time program that fits your budget and lifestyle, rather than enrolling in a costly, full-time course that conflicts with your values or circumstances.

Why Chasing Perfection Is a Trap

Many people equate success with making the "perfect" decision. This mindset leads to overthinking, fear of failure, and dissatisfaction. Remember, good decisions are about *progress,* not perfection.

Common Pitfalls in Defining Success

1. Letting Others Define It for You:

Success looks different for everyone. Don't let societal pressures or family expectations dictate your choices.

2. Over-Focusing on Outcomes:

Even great decisions can lead to disappointing results. Judge the quality of your process, not just the result.

3. Ignoring the Big Picture:

A decision might feel successful in the short term but conflict with your long-term goals.

Takeaway

A good decision is one that reflects your goals, values, and circumstances. When you stop chasing perfection and define success on your own terms, decision-making becomes clearer and more rewarding.

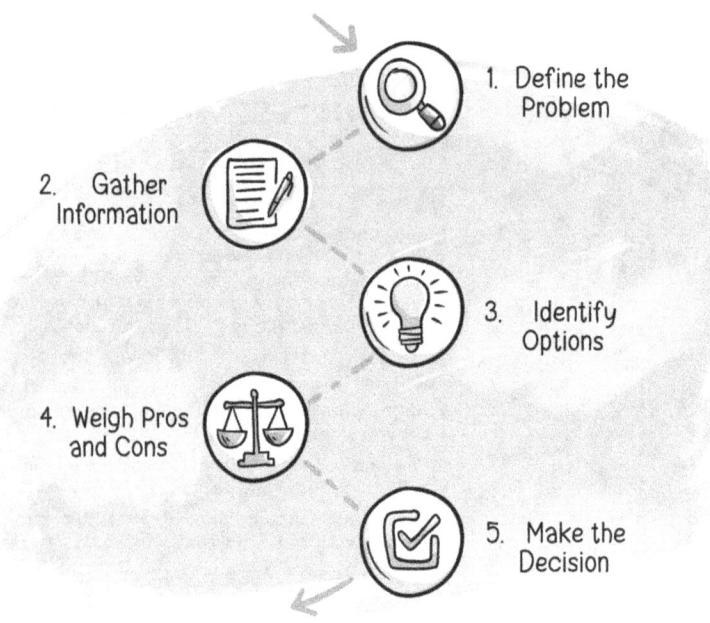

1. Define the Problem

2. Gather Information

3. Identify Options

4. Weigh Pros and Cons

5. Make the Decision

Chapter 9: The Decision-Making Blueprint

Why You Need a Decision-Making Framework

Imagine trying to build a house without a blueprint. Even with the best materials, you'd struggle to create a stable structure. Decision-making is no different. Without a clear framework, your choices risk being haphazard, rushed, or incomplete.

The 5-step blueprint below simplifies the process and ensures you tackle decisions methodically, no matter how complex they seem.

Step 1: Define the Problem
What Are You Really Deciding?

Many poor decisions stem from unclear goals. If you don't know the exact problem you're solving, you're likely to make choices that miss the mark.

Example: Instead of asking, "Should I quit my job?" clarify the real issue: "Do I need a role that offers more growth?" A vague problem leads to vague solutions.

How to Do It:

- Write down the problem in one clear sentence.
- Ask "Why?" until you uncover the root cause.

Step 2: Gather Information

What Do You Need to Know?

Before deciding, gather facts, perspectives, and context. However, avoid falling into the trap of "information overload." You don't need every detail — just the ones that matter most.

Example: If you're deciding whether to buy a house, focus on key factors like location, budget, and long-term value, rather than obsessing over minor details like paint colors.

How to Do It:

- Identify what information is critical to the decision.
- Use trusted sources (data, experts, personal experience).
- Set a time limit for research to avoid paralysis.

Step 3: Identify Options

What Are Your Choices?

List all possible courses of action, even the unconventional ones. People often default to the most obvious options, but creativity can uncover better solutions.

Example: If you're trying to save money, your options might include cutting discretionary spending, finding a side hustle, or relocating to a lower-cost area.

How to Do It:

- Brainstorm without judgment — write down every option, no matter how impractical it seems.
- Narrow your list to realistic, actionable choices.

Step 4: Weigh Pros and Cons

What Are the Trade-Offs?

Every decision has benefits and downsides. Understanding these trade-offs helps you make an informed choice. Consider both short-term and long-term impacts.

Example: When deciding whether to take a promotion, weigh the pros (higher pay, new challenges) against the cons (longer hours, more stress).

How to Do It:

- Create a table with two columns: Pros and Cons.
- Assign each factor a weight based on its importance.
- Pay special attention to deal-breakers, like misalignment with your values or goals.

Step 5: Make the Decision

What's Your Final Choice?

This is where you act. Once you've analyzed the options, pick the one that best aligns with your goals, values, and circumstances. Avoid lingering in indecision.

Example: After weighing the pros and cons of taking the promotion, you decide it aligns with your career goals despite the longer hours.

How to Do It:

- Trust the process. If you've followed the steps, your decision is likely sound.
- Commit to your choice. Second-guessing only wastes time and creates anxiety.

Practical Example: Using the Blueprint

You're deciding whether to go back to school.

1. **Define the Problem:** "Do I need additional education to advance my career?"
2. **Gather Information:** Research programs, costs, and time commitments.
3. **Identify Options:** Full-time enrollment, part-time classes, or self-study.
4. **Weigh Pros and Cons:** Compare benefits like career growth with downsides like debt or time away from family.
5. **Make the Decision:** Choose the path that aligns with your goals and circumstances.

Common Pitfalls in Decision Frameworks

1. **Skipping Steps:** Jumping straight to action without clarifying the problem or weighing options.
2. **Perfectionism:** Waiting for a "perfect" solution before deciding.
3. **Failure to Act:** Overanalyzing until the opportunity passes.

Takeaway

The decision-making blueprint is a simple, repeatable process that works for decisions big and small. By following these five steps, you'll reduce uncertainty, minimize regret, and make choices with confidence.

I've been trying the same strategy for months, but it's not working.

Maybe it's time to adapt. What if you tweak your approach based on feedback?

Chapter 10: Adaptability Matters

Why Adaptability Is Essential

Even the best decision-making strategies can't predict every variable. Circumstances change, outcomes surprise you, and new information emerges. Adaptability is the ability to adjust your approach when the unexpected happens, ensuring that you stay on track even when the path shifts.

How Rigidity Fails You

Rigid thinkers stick to a plan even when it's no longer working. This "sunk cost" mindset can trap you in poor decisions because you're afraid to pivot.

Example: Imagine you've started a business, but sales are falling flat. A rigid thinker might keep pouring money into the original strategy, hoping things will improve. An adaptable thinker would analyze why it's not working and consider pivoting to a new product or approach.

How to Develop Adaptability

1. Monitor Outcomes Closely:

After making a decision, track the results. If things aren't working as expected, identify why.

Example: If your decision to follow a new diet isn't yielding results, re-examine your approach. Are you overlooking hidden calories?

2. Stay Open to Feedback:

Seek input from trusted sources. Sometimes others can spot blind spots you've missed.

Example: A mentor or colleague might suggest a different approach to solving a work problem, one you hadn't considered.

3. Be Willing to Let Go:

If a decision isn't working, don't cling to it out of pride or fear. Adjust your course as needed.

Example: If a career move doesn't align with your happiness, it's okay to rethink your path and pivot to something more fulfilling.

4. Plan for Flexibility:

Build adaptability into your decisions. For example, when setting a financial goal, leave room for unexpected expenses.

Everyday Example of Adaptability

You decide to move to a new city for a job, but after six months, you realize the role doesn't align with your career goals. Instead of forcing yourself to stay, you explore new opportunities in the city or consider returning home. Adaptability lets you turn a disappointing outcome into a stepping stone for growth.

Common Pitfalls in Adaptability

1. Fear of Change: Sticking to a decision because changing course feels like failure.

2. Over-Correcting: Constantly shifting plans without giving them time to work.

3. Ignoring Feedback: Refusing to adjust because you're too attached to the original choice.

Takeaway

Adaptability is your safety net in a world of uncertainty. No strategy guarantees success, but the ability to adjust ensures you can thrive no matter what life throws your way.

With the foundations of decision-making now in place, you're ready to explore advanced strategies that sharpen your thinking even further.

Section II: Mental Models for Superior Thinking

This section focuses on mental models that drive personal and professional growth. These models are the key to lifelong growth, making progress manageable and meaningful.

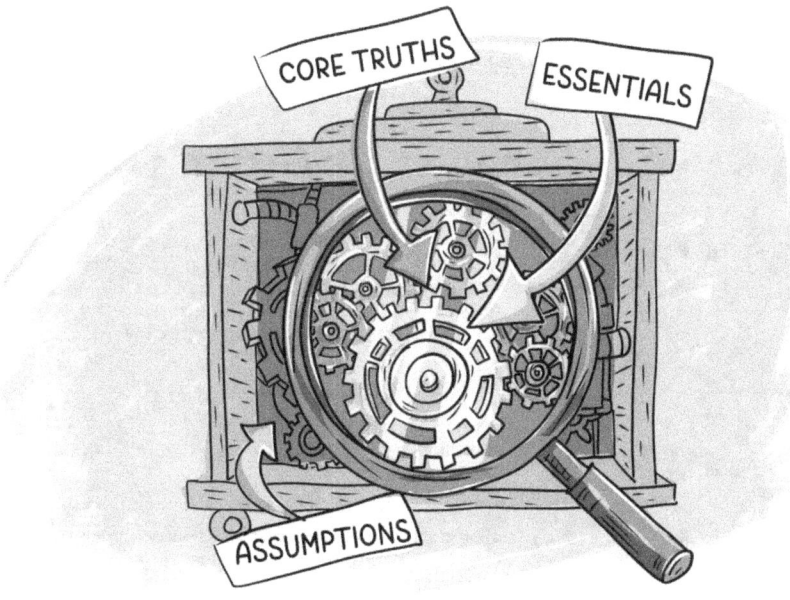

Chapter 11: First Principles Thinking

What Is First Principles Thinking?

First Principles Thinking is about drilling down to the core of a problem, stripping away all assumptions, and identifying the fundamental building blocks. Instead of solving problems by tweaking what already exists, this approach starts from scratch, asking, "What do we *know* to be true?"

Example:

If you want to make transportation faster, most people might assume "improving the car" is the answer. But First Principles Thinking breaks it down: What's the goal? To move from point A to B quickly. What's essential? Speed, energy, and safety. By challenging the assumption that cars are necessary, you open the door to innovations like high-speed rail or hyperloop systems.

Why First Principles Thinking Matters

Traditional problem-solving relies on analogies — looking at what others have done and iterating on it. While useful, it can trap you in conventional thinking. First Principles Thinking lets you question "the way things have always been done" and uncover innovative solutions.

Benefits Include:

- Breaking free from outdated assumptions.
- Unlocking creativity and innovation.
- Creating solutions tailored to your goals, not past models.

How to Use First Principles Thinking

1. Identify Assumptions:

List everything you believe about the problem, even things that seem "obvious." Many assumptions are hidden in plain sight.

Example: If you're starting a business, you might assume, "I need a physical office."

Challenge this: Is that truly necessary, or could a remote setup work better?

2. Ask "Why?" Until You Can't Anymore:

Like peeling an onion, keep asking "Why?" until you reach truths that are undeniable and cannot be simplified further.

Example: If you assume "I need money to succeed," ask why. Maybe what you truly need is resources or connections, which can be achieved in other ways.

3. Rebuild from Core Truths:

Once you identify the essentials, construct solutions based on them.

Example: If you know a car's purpose is to move people efficiently, consider whether alternative materials, shapes, or energy sources could better serve that goal.

Practical Example: Saving Money

Instead of following generic advice like "stop buying coffee," First Principles Thinking asks:

- Why am I overspending? (I buy takeout.)
- Why do I buy takeout? (I don't plan meals.)
- Why don't I plan meals? (I lack time or energy.)

The core problem isn't coffee; it's poor planning. Solving that — by prepping meals in advance — has a greater impact.

1. **Stopping Too Soon:**

   You might think you've reached the root when you're still operating on assumptions. Dig deeper.

2. **Mistaking Assumptions for Truths:**

   Not everything you think is fundamental truly is. Challenge every belief until it's proven indispensable.

3. **Overcomplicating:**

   Focus on the essentials. Don't get bogged down in irrelevant details.

Takeaway

First Principles Thinking transforms how you approach problems. By breaking issues down to their core truths and rebuilding from there, you open the door to solutions others never see.

Chapter 12: Occam's Razor

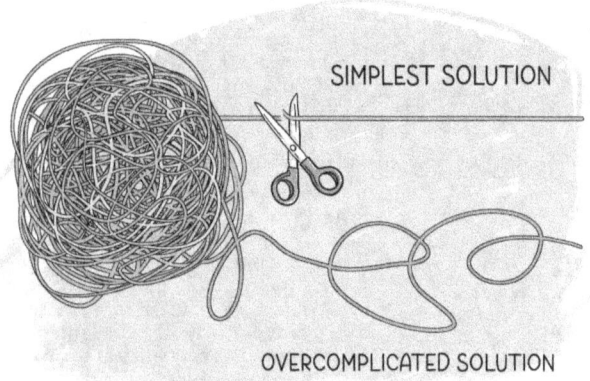

SIMPLEST SOLUTION

OVERCOMPLICATED SOLUTION

What Is Occam's Razor?

Occam's Razor says: "The simplest solution is often the best." When faced with multiple explanations, favor the one that requires the fewest assumptions. This doesn't mean the simplest answer is *always* correct — just that it's the best starting point until more evidence suggests otherwise.

Example:

You wake up to find your car won't start.

- Overcomplicated Thinking: "It must be a rare engine defect caused by a specific manufacturing error."
- Occam's Razor: "The battery is probably dead."

By focusing on the most straightforward explanation, you avoid wasting time and energy on unnecessary possibilities.

Why Simplicity Matters in Decision-Making

1. **Reduces Cognitive Overload:**

   Overthinking creates mental clutter, which leads to confusion and indecision. Simplifying the problem helps you focus.

2. **Increases Efficiency:**

   Complex solutions often take more time, resources, and effort. A simple approach saves energy and allows faster action.

3. **Improves Clarity:**

   A clear, simple solution is easier to communicate and execute.

How to Apply Occam's Razor

1. **Identify the Core Problem:**

   Strip away distractions and pinpoint the central issue.

   Example: If your team is missing deadlines, don't immediately assume it's due to poor management or complex workflows. Start by asking: "Are there too many tasks assigned to too few people?"

2. **List Possible Explanations or Solutions:**

   Write down all the options, from the simplest to the most complex.

   Example: If your internet is slow, explanations could range from "router issues" (simple) to "interference from local construction" (complex).

3. **Choose the Simplest Option First:**

   Test the easiest explanation or solution before exploring more complicated ones.

Everyday Example of Occam's Razor

You're deciding whether to buy a new laptop.

- Overcomplicated: Research 10 different brands, compare endless reviews, and worry about features you'll never use.
- Simple: Focus on your primary need (e.g., work or school) and choose a reliable, budget-friendly model that meets those needs.

Common Pitfalls in Using Occam's Razor

1. **Oversimplifying:**

   The simplest solution isn't *always* correct. Use evidence to confirm it before committing.

2. **Ignoring Nuances:**

   While simplicity is valuable, don't disregard important details just to make a decision faster.

3. Rushing to Conclusions:

Don't confuse "simple" with "quick." Take time to evaluate before acting.

Takeaway

Occam's Razor cuts through complexity to reveal clarity. Start with the simplest explanation or solution, but stay open to new evidence. Simplifying your thinking doesn't just save time — it leads to smarter, more efficient decisions.

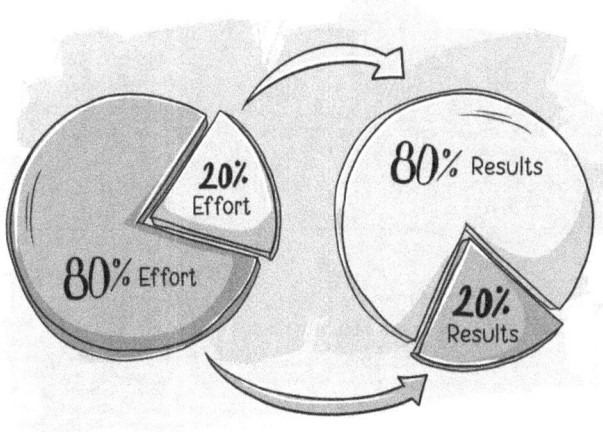

Chapter 13: The Pareto Principle

What Is the Pareto Principle?

Also called the "80/20 Rule," the Pareto Principle states that 80% of outcomes come from 20% of efforts. This idea is found everywhere:

- 80% of a company's revenue often comes from 20% of its clients.
- 80% of results in a workout might come from 20% of the exercises.
- 80% of your stress may come from just 20% of your responsibilities.

By focusing on the "vital few" (the 20% that matters), you can maximize results with less effort.

Why the Pareto Principle Matters in Decision-Making

1. Prioritizes Impact:

Helps you identify and focus on high-impact activities rather than spreading yourself too thin.

2. Eliminates Waste:

Avoids wasting time, money, and energy on low-value tasks.

3. Improves Productivity:

Shifting your focus to the most effective efforts makes your work more efficient.

How to Apply the Pareto Principle

1. Identify the Vital Few:

Ask, "Which 20% of my actions, clients, or tasks are creating 80% of my results?"

Example: If you're studying, focus on the 20% of topics that will appear most frequently on the test.

2. Eliminate or Minimize the Trivial Many:

Once you know what doesn't contribute much, spend less time or energy on those activities.

Example: At work, stop micromanaging minor tasks and delegate them, so you can focus on strategic priorities.

3. Redistribute Resources:

Shift your time, money, and attention to the high-impact 20%.

Example: If 20% of your marketing campaigns generate 80% of your sales, invest more in those campaigns and scale back the rest.

Everyday Example of the Pareto Principle

Let's say you're cleaning your house. Instead of deep-cleaning every corner, focus on the 20% of areas (like the kitchen and living room) where 80% of clutter accumulates. This approach gives you the biggest improvement with the least effort.

Common Pitfalls in Applying the Pareto Principle

1. Misidentifying the 20%:

Be careful not to assume — use evidence or data to determine what's truly high-impact.

2. Neglecting the Long Tail:

While the 80% may not produce as much value, it's often necessary for long-term success. Don't ignore it entirely.

3. Over-Simplifying:

Not everything follows the 80/20 split perfectly. Treat it as a guideline, not a hard rule.

Takeaway

The Pareto Principle is a tool for prioritization. By identifying and focusing on the 20% of actions that drive 80% of the results, you'll achieve more with less effort. But remember — the real skill lies in knowing what matters most.

Chapter 14: Second-Order Thinking

What Is Second-Order Thinking?

Second-Order Thinking is the art of looking beyond the obvious. While most people stop at the immediate impact of a decision (first-order thinking), second-order thinkers anticipate the ripple effects — the long-term and indirect consequences that follow. This approach doesn't just solve problems; it helps avoid creating new ones.

Example:

Suppose a company decides to cut costs by reducing employee benefits. The first-order effect is clear: lower expenses. But second-order thinking reveals the hidden costs: reduced employee morale, higher turnover rates, and difficulty attracting top talent.

Instead of stopping at "What happens now?" Second-Order Thinking asks, "And then what?"

Why Second-Order Thinking Matters

1. Avoids Unintended Consequences:

Short-sighted decisions often create bigger problems down the line. Second-Order Thinking helps you anticipate these outcomes and adjust your strategy.

2. Reveals Hidden Opportunities:

Long-term effects aren't always negative. Thinking deeper can uncover positive ripple effects that others miss.

3. Gives You a Strategic Edge:

Most people focus on immediate outcomes. Second-order thinkers see the bigger picture, making more informed and resilient choices.

How to Practice Second-Order Thinking

1. List the Immediate Impact (First-Order Effect):

Start with the obvious. Ask, "What's the direct result of this decision?"

Example: You decide to offer a discount to attract customers. The first-order effect is increased sales.

2. Ask "What Happens Next?" (Second-Order Effects):

Consider the next layer of consequences.

Example: The discount might attract bargain hunters who don't become loyal customers, reducing your overall profitability.

3. Go Deeper (Third-Order Effects):

Keep asking, "And then what?" until you've mapped out the longer-term consequences.

Example: Competitors might feel pressured to lower their prices in response, triggering a price war that hurts the entire industry.

4. Weigh the Trade-Offs:

Once you've mapped out the ripple effects, evaluate whether the long-term benefits outweigh the risks.

Example: If the short-term sales boost leads to brand devaluation, the discount strategy might not be worth it.

Everyday Example of Second-Order Thinking

Imagine you're deciding whether to stay up late binge-watching a show.

- **First-Order Effect:** You enjoy the entertainment.
- **Second-Order Effect:** You wake up tired, reducing your productivity the next day.
- **Third-Order Effect:** Poor performance at work might impact your reputation, causing stress or missed opportunities.

By thinking beyond the immediate gratification, you might decide to save the binge for the weekend instead.

Common Pitfalls in Second-Order Thinking

1. Stopping at the First Ripple:

Many people make decisions based only on immediate results, ignoring the long-term picture.

2. Overlooking Complexity:

Not every ripple is predictable. Be prepared for surprises and adjust as new information emerges.

3. Focusing Only on Negatives:

While second-order thinking often highlights risks, don't forget to look for hidden benefits.

Takeaway

Second-Order Thinking forces you to see decisions as part of a larger chain of events. By anticipating ripple effects, you can avoid short-sighted mistakes and make choices that hold up over time.

Now that you're thinking beyond the immediate, let's explore a powerful mental tool for creative problem-solving.

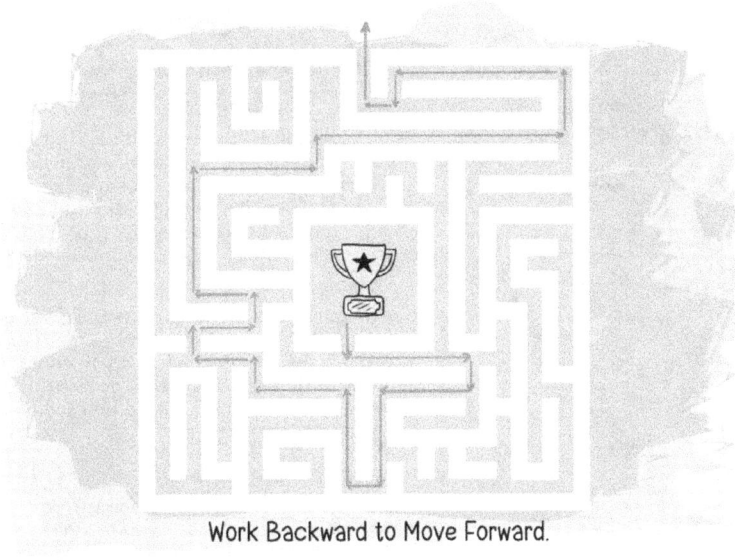

Work Backward to Move Forward.

Chapter 15: Inversion

What Is Inversion?

Inversion is a problem-solving technique that flips the script. Instead of asking, "How do I achieve this?" you ask, "What could prevent me from achieving this?" By identifying obstacles or worst-case scenarios first, you gain clarity on how to avoid failure and achieve success.

Example:

Instead of asking, "How can I be happy?" invert the question: "What makes people unhappy, and how can I avoid those things?"

This reverse approach often reveals insights that traditional thinking misses.

Why Inversion Works

1. Clarifies the Problem:

Focusing on what could go wrong helps you see the problem more clearly.

2. Uncovers Hidden Obstacles:

Anticipating failure points makes it easier to address them before they happen.

3. Simplifies Complex Problems:

Working backward breaks big challenges into manageable steps.

How to Apply Inversion

1. State Your Goal:

Start with the problem you're trying to solve.

Example: "How can I build a successful career?"

2. Invert the Question:

Ask, "What would guarantee failure?"

Example: "What habits or actions would ruin my career?"

3. Identify Failure Points:

List the factors that would lead to the worst-case scenario.

Example: Missing deadlines, neglecting skill development, or burning bridges with colleagues.

4. Work Backward:

Plan strategies to avoid those failure points.

Example: Create a schedule to meet deadlines, commit to lifelong learning, and focus on building strong relationships at work.

Everyday Example of Inversion

Imagine you're planning a road trip.

- **Normal Thinking:** "How can I make this trip great?"
- **Inverted Thinking:** "What could ruin the trip?"

The inverted approach might reveal risks like car trouble, bad weather, or forgetting essential items. Addressing these risks in advance — by servicing your car, checking the forecast, and packing carefully — ensures a smoother trip.

Common Pitfalls in Inversion

1. Getting Stuck in Negatives:

While identifying risks is useful, don't focus so much on failure that you lose sight of success.

2. Overlooking Small Obstacles:

Minor issues (e.g., procrastination or poor communication) can derail progress just as much as major ones.

3. Failing to Take Action:

Recognizing potential problems is only helpful if you act to prevent them.

Takeaway

Inversion flips your perspective, helping you solve problems by working backward. By identifying and avoiding failure points, you clear the path to success.

I'm thinking of buying this new gaming console.

But what about the guitar lessons you've been wanting? That's the opportunity cost.

Immediate Fun

Long-Term Skills

Chapter 16: Opportunity Cost

What Is Opportunity Cost?

Every decision comes with a trade-off: choosing one option means giving up another. Opportunity cost is the value of the choice you *didn't* make. It's not just about money; it's about time, energy, and the potential outcomes you could have pursued instead.

Example:

Imagine you spend $1,000 on a vacation. The opportunity cost isn't just the money — it's also the investment or savings you could have made with that same amount, or even the skill you could have learned during that time.

Why Opportunity Cost Matters

1. Reveals Hidden Trade-Offs:

Many choices feel "free" because you don't immediately see what you're giving up. Opportunity cost forces you to think about what you're sacrificing.

2. Improves Resource Allocation:

By understanding what's at stake, you can better allocate your time, money, and energy to what matters most.

3. Sharpens Priorities:

Opportunity cost helps you focus on the activities and decisions that align with your long-term goals.

How to Evaluate Opportunity Cost

1. Clarify Your Resources:

Identify the time, money, or energy each option will require.

Example: If you're deciding between two job offers, consider not just the salary but also the commute, work-life balance, and career growth potential.

2. Ask "What Else Could I Be Doing?"

Think about the alternatives you're giving up by choosing this option.

Example: If you choose to spend your weekend binge-watching TV, the opportunity cost might be the gym session or quality time with loved ones you could have enjoyed instead.

3. Compare the Long-Term Value:

Focus on the future. Which option offers the greatest long-term benefits?

Example: Spending money on a flashy gadget might feel good now, but investing that money in stocks could grow your wealth over time.

Everyday Example of Opportunity Cost

Imagine you're deciding whether to buy a new car.

- **The Obvious Cost:** The car's price and maintenance.
- **The Opportunity Cost:** The vacation, savings, or home improvements you could have spent that money on instead.

By considering what you're giving up, you can make a more thoughtful decision.

Common Pitfalls in Evaluating Opportunity Cost

1. Overlooking Intangible Costs:

Sometimes, the cost isn't financial — it's emotional or social, like missing out on time with family.

2. Underestimating Time:

People often forget that time is a finite resource. Spending an hour on one activity means losing an hour for something else.

3. Paralysis by Analysis:

Thinking too much about opportunity cost can lead to indecision. Use it as a guide, not a roadblock.

Takeaway

Opportunity cost is the invisible price tag of every choice. By considering what you're giving up, you'll make decisions that align with your values and maximize your resources.

Chapter 17: The Eisenhower Matrix

What Is the Eisenhower Matrix?

The Eisenhower Matrix is a decision-making tool that helps you prioritize tasks by urgency and importance. Named after U.S. President Dwight D. Eisenhower, it's based on his principle: "What is important is seldom urgent, and what is urgent is seldom important."

The matrix divides tasks into four categories:

1. **Important & Urgent:** Tasks that need immediate action.

2. **Important but Not Urgent:** Tasks that require planning and long-term focus.

3. **Not Important but Urgent:** Tasks that feel pressing but don't contribute to your goals.

4. **Not Important & Not Urgent:** Distractions to eliminate or minimize.

Why the Eisenhower Matrix Matters

1. Prevents Overwhelm:

Helps you focus on what truly matters instead of getting lost in busywork.

2. Improves Time Management:

Ensures your energy goes to high-priority tasks rather than low-value activities.

3. Encourages Long-Term Thinking:

Keeps you focused on goals rather than reactive to daily demands.

How to Use the Eisenhower Matrix

1. List Your Tasks:

Write down everything you need to do, no matter how small.

2. Categorize by Importance and Urgency:

Place each task into one of the four quadrants.

Example:

- A looming project deadline? Important & Urgent.
- Planning a career move? Important but Not Urgent.
- Responding to a non-critical email? Not Important but Urgent.

3. Act Accordingly:

- **Important & Urgent:** Do these tasks immediately.
- **Important but Not Urgent:** Schedule them for later and protect the time.
- **Not Important but Urgent:** Delegate if possible.
- **Not Important & Not Urgent:** Eliminate or minimize.

Everyday Example of the Eisenhower Matrix

You're planning your day and have the following tasks:

1. **Prepare a report due today (Important & Urgent).**
2. **Exercise for health (Important but Not Urgent).**
3. **Answer an email about a minor issue (Not Important but Urgent).**
4. **Scroll social media (Not Important & Not Urgent).**

The matrix helps you prioritize the report, schedule exercise, delegate the email, and avoid social media altogether.

Common Pitfalls in Using the Eisenhower Matrix

1. Misjudging Importance:

Not everything urgent is important. Learn to distinguish between real priorities and busywork.

2. Failing to Delegate:

You don't have to do everything yourself. Delegate low-value tasks when possible.

3. Ignoring the "Not Urgent" Quadrant:

Long-term goals often fall into the "Important but Not Urgent" category. Don't neglect them.

Takeaway

The Eisenhower Matrix is your roadmap to smarter prioritization. By categorizing tasks and acting strategically, you'll manage your time effectively and stay focused on what matters most.

Chapter 18: Bayesian Thinking

I thought our team was going to lose, but with this new player, I'm not so sure.

That's Bayesian Thinking—adjusting your belief based on new evidence!

What Is Bayesian Thinking?

Bayesian Thinking is a decision-making framework rooted in flexibility. Named after the mathematician Thomas Bayes, it's about updating your beliefs and decisions as new evidence emerges. Instead of sticking rigidly to what you *think* is true, Bayesian Thinking asks:

- **What do I currently believe?**
- **What new evidence do I have?**
- **How should this evidence adjust my belief?**

Example:

Imagine you assume it will rain because the sky looks cloudy. Then, you check the weather forecast, which shows a 10% chance of rain. Bayesian Thinking encourages you to update your belief based on the forecast and carry an umbrella only if it makes sense in the context.

Why Bayesian Thinking Matters

1. Promotes Adaptability:

It helps you pivot your decisions when circumstances change.

2. Reduces Stubbornness:

Humans tend to cling to old beliefs, even when presented with contrary evidence. Bayesian Thinking combats this bias.

3. Encourages Rationality:

Decisions become less about guesswork and more about weighing probabilities.

How to Apply Bayesian Thinking

1. Start with a Baseline Belief:

Begin with your initial assumption or "best guess."

Example: You believe a business idea has a 70% chance of success based on past experience.

2. Incorporate New Evidence:

When new data arrives, evaluate its reliability and relevance.

Example: A market report shows declining interest in your target product.

3. Adjust Your Belief:

Update your probability based on the strength of the evidence.

Example: After reviewing the report, you lower the success probability of your idea to 50% and decide to adjust your strategy.

4. Act Based on Updated Beliefs:

Use your revised perspective to guide your next steps.

Example: Pivot to a different market segment where demand is stronger.

Everyday Example of Bayesian Thinking

Imagine you're hiring a candidate.

- **Baseline Belief:** Based on their résumé, you assume they're highly qualified.
- **New Evidence:** During the interview, they struggle to answer key technical questions.
- **Updated Belief:** You revise your assumption, concluding they may lack certain skills.
- **Action:** You decide to evaluate other candidates before making a final decision.

Common Pitfalls in Bayesian Thinking

1. Ignoring Evidence:

People often dismiss new data if it conflicts with their existing beliefs.

2. Overreacting to Weak Evidence:

Not all new information is reliable. Evaluate the quality of the evidence before adjusting your belief.

3. Failing to Act on Updated Beliefs:

Even if you revise your perspective, it's meaningless if you don't adapt your decisions accordingly.

Takeaway

Bayesian Thinking teaches you to view decisions as dynamic, not static. By continuously updating your beliefs with new evidence, you stay flexible and make choices grounded in reality.

Chapter 19: Regret Minimization

What Is Regret Minimization?

Regret Minimization is a decision-making strategy that prioritizes long-term peace of mind over short-term comfort. Instead of asking, "What's easiest right now?" it asks:

- **What choice will I regret the least in 10 years?**
- **How will I feel about this decision when I look back on it later?**

Example:

You're deciding whether to take a leap and start your own business. In the short term, staying at your current job feels safer. But through the lens of regret minimization, you might realize you'd regret not trying more than the temporary risks of failure.

Why Regret Minimization Matters

1. Keeps You Focused on the Big Picture:

It helps you prioritize meaningful goals over fleeting emotions or convenience.

2. Combats Decision Paralysis:

Thinking long-term clarifies what truly matters, making tough decisions easier.

3. Reduces Future Regrets:

By imagining yourself in the future, you can align your decisions with what you'll value most later.

How to Minimize Regret in Decisions

1. Visualize Your Future Self:

Imagine looking back on this decision in 5, 10, or even 20 years. Ask, "What choice will I feel proud of?"

Example: Will skipping a once-in-a-lifetime travel opportunity for work feel like the right decision in 10 years?

2. Weigh Regret vs. Risk:

Sometimes, avoiding short-term discomfort leads to long-term regret. Balance the risks of failure against the regret of never trying.

Example: Starting a side hustle might fail, but the regret of not pursuing your dream might be greater.

3. Focus on What You Can Control:

Regret often comes from fixating on what you can't change. Make the best decision possible with the information you have now.

Everyday Example of Regret Minimization

You're deciding whether to attend a family reunion.

- Short-term: It feels inconvenient and expensive.
- Long-term: You realize you'd regret missing the chance to spend time with loved ones who may not be around forever.

Through regret minimization, you prioritize the experience over temporary discomfort.

Common Pitfalls in Regret Minimization

1. Overthinking Small Choices:

Not every decision needs this level of analysis. Use regret minimization for significant, life-impacting choices.

2. Assuming the Worst:

Don't let fear of regret lead to overly cautious decisions. Focus on what aligns with your values.

While thinking long-term is important, don't ignore the short-term realities that affect your well-being.

Takeaway

Regret Minimization puts your future self in the driver's seat, helping you make decisions you'll look back on with pride, not regret.

Chapter 20: The Fermi Approach

What Is the Fermi Approach?

The Fermi Approach is a practical method for solving problems that seem impossible to measure. Named after the physicist Enrico Fermi, who was famous for making remarkably accurate estimates with limited data, this approach breaks a problem into smaller, manageable pieces.

Instead of waiting for perfect data, you make logical assumptions and build an answer step by step. It's not about being perfectly accurate — it's about being *reasonable enough* to make informed decisions.

Why the Fermi Approach Works

1. Simplifies Complexity:

Big, vague questions become solvable when broken into smaller components.

2. Encourages Logical Thinking:

By focusing on logic instead of guesswork, you create a structured path to clarity.

3. Builds Confidence in Uncertainty:

Instead of being paralyzed by a lack of data, you can still move forward with informed estimates.

How to Apply the Fermi Approach

1. Define the Problem Clearly:

Start with a big question, like "How many coffee cups are sold in my city each day?"

2. Break It Down Into Smaller Questions:

Divide the problem into manageable parts that are easier to estimate. For example:

- How many people live in your city?
- What percentage drink coffee?
- How many cups does each coffee drinker buy daily?

3. Estimate Each Piece:

Make logical, evidence-based guesses for each component.

4. Example:

- o City population: 1,000,000 people.
- o Percentage of coffee drinkers: 50% (500,000).
- o Average cups per drinker: 1.5.

5. Combine Your Estimates:

Multiply or add your answers to reach a final estimate.

Example: 500,000 coffee drinkers × 1.5 cups = 750,000 cups sold daily.

6. Adjust as Needed:

If you get new information or realize a component is off, refine your assumptions and recalculate.

Why the Fermi Approach Is Valuable

The Fermi Approach is useful in situations where:

- You lack complete data but still need an answer.
- Precision isn't critical, but logic and reason are.
- You want to develop a deeper understanding of a complex problem.

Example:

If you're organizing an event, you might need to estimate attendance without knowing exact RSVP numbers. By using logical steps (e.g., how many invitees typically attend such events), you can prepare confidently.

Everyday Example of the Fermi Approach

Question: How much water does your household use in a week?

- **Step 1:** How many people live in your house? (4 people)
- **Step 2:** How much water does one person use daily for drinking, cooking, cleaning, and bathing? (80 gallons per person)
- **Step 3:** Multiply by 7 days.

Estimate: 4 people × 80 gallons × 7 days = 2,240 gallons per week.

While the exact number might vary, this estimate is reasonable enough to plan for water usage or compare with your water bill.

Common Pitfalls in the Fermi Approach

1. Overcomplicating the Problem:

Keep the steps simple. If a component seems too complex, break it into even smaller pieces.

2. Guessing Without Logic:

Assumptions should be based on prior knowledge, averages, or reasonable comparisons, not random guesses.

3. Ignoring Margins of Error:

Acknowledge that your estimate isn't perfect. Build in a margin of error to account for uncertainties.

How the Fermi Approach Boosts Decision-Making

Let's say you're pitching a new business idea: selling reusable water bottles. A key question might be, "How many bottles could we sell in the first year?"

Instead of waiting for expensive market research, apply the Fermi Approach:

1. How many people in your target region? (500,000)
2. What percentage care about sustainability? (30% = 150,000)
3. How many of them might buy a reusable bottle in a year? (10% = 15,000)

Using logical steps, you estimate 15,000 potential buyers — enough to justify moving forward with your idea.

Takeaway

The Fermi Approach transforms intimidating, unmeasurable problems into solvable puzzles. By breaking questions into smaller components, making logical estimates, and combining them systematically, you can tackle uncertainty with confidence and clarity.

With this method, you don't need perfect data to make smart decisions — just a structured approach and a willingness to think critically.

Section III: Strategies to Overcome Cognitive Biases

In the next ten chapters, I will teach you about tools to help you make smarter, more confident decisions. From planning for the short term to preparing for long-term success, these strategies are easy to apply in everyday life.

CRITICAL THINKING

Chapter 21: Anchoring Bias

What Is Anchoring Bias?

Anchoring Bias happens when your decisions are overly influenced by the first piece of information you encounter — the "anchor." Even if this anchor is irrelevant or misleading, it can skew your thinking and limit your ability to consider other perspectives.

Anchors come in many forms:

• A high starting price in a negotiation.

• The first opinion you hear on a topic.

• The initial estimate for how long a project will take.

For example, imagine you're shopping for a jacket, and the first one you see is $400. Even if you later see one priced at $200, you might think it's a bargain — not because it's objectively cheap, but because your mind is still tethered to that $400 anchor.

Why Anchoring Bias Matters

Anchoring isn't just a psychological quirk — it has real consequences:

1. **Distorts Judgments:** Anchors warp how you assess value, probability, or time.

2. **Influences Negotiations:** The first number thrown out in a negotiation often dictates the entire range of discussion.

3. **Limits Creativity:** Anchors make it harder to explore alternative options because you keep circling back to that initial idea.

Example in Action:

In a salary negotiation, if an employer offers a low starting figure, you might feel stuck negotiating within that range — even if the role's value justifies a higher salary.

How to Break Free from Anchoring Bias

1. Recognize the Anchor:

Pause and ask yourself: "Is my judgment being influenced by this initial number or idea?" Awareness is the first step to escaping the anchor's pull.

Example: If you're house-hunting and the first home you see is overpriced, recognize that it's setting an artificial standard for what "reasonable" looks like.

2. Do Independent Research:

Gather objective data from multiple sources to counteract the anchor's influence.

Example: Instead of letting the asking price of a car guide you, look up its fair market value to create your own benchmark.

3. Set Your Own Anchors:

Enter decisions with a clear idea of what you believe is reasonable before external anchors can influence you.

Example: Before negotiating a salary, research typical pay for the role and determine your ideal range in advance.

4. Delay Snap Judgments:

Give yourself time to reflect, especially for high-stakes decisions. This helps you reset your perspective and avoid acting impulsively.

Example: If a salesperson pressures you with a "limited-time offer," step back to evaluate if the deal truly aligns with your needs.

Everyday Example of Anchoring Bias

Imagine you're buying groceries. You see a bottle of olive oil priced at $25, and the next one is $15. Even though $15 might still be overpriced, it feels cheap compared to the $25 anchor. Breaking free means asking: "What's the typical price for olive oil?" instead of relying on comparisons to set your judgment.

1. Failing to Question the Anchor:

Many anchors feel natural, so you might not realize how much they're influencing you.

2. Overvaluing First Impressions:

People often assume that the first number or idea they encounter is accurate, even without evidence.

3. Rushing Decisions:

Anchors are especially powerful under time pressure. Take a moment to pause and evaluate.

Takeaway

Anchoring Bias can tether you to misleading information, clouding your decisions. By identifying anchors, seeking independent data, and setting your own benchmarks, you can think more clearly and break free from the weight of first impressions.

REMOVE THE BLINDERS

Chapter 22:
Confirmation Bias

What Is Confirmation Bias?

Confirmation Bias is your brain's tendency to search for, interpret, and prioritize information that supports your existing beliefs while ignoring or dismissing evidence that contradicts them.

It feels good to have your opinions validated — it's comforting and requires less mental effort than rethinking your perspective. But this bias can lead to poor decisions by narrowing your view of the world.

Example:

If you believe that a particular investment is a good idea, you might actively seek out success stories about similar investments while ignoring reports of failures. As a result, you make a decision based on incomplete or one-sided information.

Why Confirmation Bias Matters

1. Distorts Reality:

When you only focus on information that confirms your beliefs, you fail to see the bigger picture.

2. Stifles Growth:

If you're unwilling to consider opposing views, you miss opportunities to learn, improve, or adapt.

3. Reinforces Bad Decisions:

By ignoring critical evidence, you're more likely to double down on flawed choices.

Real-Life Impact:

Imagine a manager who believes their team is performing well. They might only pay attention to positive feedback and ignore warning signs of dissatisfaction, leading to higher turnover.

How to Overcome Confirmation Bias

1. Actively Seek Contradictory Evidence:

Instead of asking, "What supports my belief?" ask, "What challenges it?"

Example: If you believe a certain diet is the best, research studies that critique it instead of just reading testimonials from fans.

2. Engage with Opposing Views:

Talk to people who disagree with you and genuinely try to understand their perspective.

Example: If you're convinced one political policy is ideal, discuss it with someone who supports an alternative to broaden your understanding.

3. Use Neutral Sources:

Rely on objective, unbiased information rather than sources designed to confirm a specific agenda.

Example: Instead of trusting a company's marketing materials, read independent reviews to get a balanced perspective.

4. Ask Disconfirming Questions:

Reframe your thinking by asking, "What would prove me wrong?" or "What evidence would change my mind?"

Example: If you think you should buy a house, ask, "What factors might make renting a better option?"

Imagine you're shopping for a phone. You've already decided on a brand, so you only read glowing reviews for that model while ignoring critical feedback about its battery life. To combat this, actively search for negative reviews to ensure you're making an informed choice.

1. Avoiding Discomfort:

It's natural to feel defensive when your beliefs are challenged, but growth happens when you confront uncomfortable truths.

2. Overvaluing Familiar Sources:

People often trust sources that align with their views, even if those sources are biased.

3. Cherry-Picking Data:

Selectively focusing on evidence that supports your beliefs reinforces the bias.

Confirmation Bias narrows your perspective and weakens your decision-making. By seeking out opposing evidence, asking challenging questions, and engaging with diverse viewpoints, you can expand your understanding and make better-informed choices.

Chapter 23: Availability Heuristic

What Is the Availability Heuristic?

The Availability Heuristic is a mental shortcut where you rely on the most immediate examples that come to mind to make decisions. While quick and intuitive, this tendency can distort your judgment by overemphasizing memorable or recent events while ignoring broader data or less vivid possibilities.

Example:

After hearing about a plane crash on the news, you might think air travel is unsafe, even though statistically, it's one of the safest modes of transportation.

Why the Availability Heuristic Matters

1. Skews Risk Perception:

You're more likely to fear dramatic, rare events (like shark attacks) than more common, mundane risks (like car accidents) because the former are easier to recall.

2. Leads to Overgeneralization:

Decisions based on a single vivid example might not reflect the full picture.

3. Neglects Relevant Data:

By focusing on memorable stories or recent events, you may ignore broader, more reliable information.

How to Overcome the Availability Heuristic

1. Pause and Reflect:

When a vivid example influences your thinking, ask, "Am I basing this decision on a single event or broader evidence?"

Example: Before deciding not to invest in stocks after hearing about a market crash, reflect on long-term trends rather than short-term headlines.

2. Seek Statistical Data:

Look for objective data to balance emotional or anecdotal examples.

Example: If you're worried about crime in your neighborhood after hearing one story, review crime statistics to understand the actual risk.

3. Broaden Your Perspective:

Actively search for additional examples that challenge the one dominating your thoughts.

Example: If you're convinced starting a business is too risky because one friend failed, talk to others who succeeded to gain a balanced view.

4. Be Wary of Media Bias:

The news often highlights sensational stories, which can skew your perception of reality.

Example: Just because the media reports frequently on airline delays doesn't mean they happen often — it just means they're attention-grabbing.

Everyday Example of the Availability Heuristic

You hear about someone winning the lottery and think buying tickets is a good investment. However, the vivid example of their win overshadows the reality: the odds of winning are astronomically low. By reviewing the actual probability, you can avoid letting one story determine your choices.

Common Pitfalls When Addressing the Availability Heuristic

1. Focusing on Emotional Stories:

Emotional examples feel compelling but often don't represent the bigger picture.

2. Ignoring Silent Evidence:

The stories you don't hear — like all the startups that failed quietly — are just as important as the ones you do.

3. Overreacting to Recent Events:

Recent examples may feel more relevant but aren't always the most significant.

Takeaway

The Availability Heuristic tempts you to rely on what's easy to recall, but clear decisions require looking deeper. By broadening your perspective, seeking data, and challenging dramatic examples, you can make choices based on reality, not just what's memorable.

Chapter 24: Sunk Cost Fallacy

What Is the Sunk Cost Fallacy?

The Sunk Cost Fallacy is the tendency to stick with a decision because you've already invested time, money, or effort into it, even when continuing no longer makes sense. It's driven by a fear of "wasting" those resources, even though they're already gone and can't be recovered.

Example:

You stay in a bad relationship because you've been together for years, even though it no longer makes you happy.

Why the Sunk Cost Fallacy Matters

1. Wastes Resources:

Continuing to invest in a failing endeavor diverts time, money, and energy away from better opportunities.

2. Prevents Better Decisions:

Clinging to the past blinds you to present and future possibilities.

3. Reinforces Emotional Attachment:

The more you've invested, the harder it feels to let go, creating a vicious cycle.

Example in Action:

You've spent $10,000 repairing an old car, but it keeps breaking down. Instead of cutting your losses and buying a new car, you keep repairing it, sinking more money into a bad investment.

How to Break Free from the Sunk Cost Fallacy

1. Focus on the Present and Future:

Ask yourself: "If I hadn't already invested in this, would I still make the same decision today?"

Example: If you've spent months on a failing project, consider whether continuing aligns with your current goals.

2. Acknowledge the Loss:

Accept that the resources you've invested are gone and can't be recovered. This mental reset helps you focus on what's still within your control.

Example: Recognize that the time spent in a toxic friendship doesn't obligate you to maintain it.

3. Evaluate Opportunity Costs:

Think about what you're giving up by continuing down the same path.

Example: Sticking with a struggling business might prevent you from exploring a new, more promising venture.

4. Set Clear Criteria for Persistence:

Define specific benchmarks for continuing or stopping, so you're not swayed by emotion.

Example: "I'll invest one more month into this project. If we don't achieve X result, I'll move on."

Everyday Example of the Sunk Cost Fallacy

You're watching a boring movie but refuse to leave because you paid for the ticket. Letting go of the fallacy means recognizing that staying won't bring back your money — but leaving frees up your time for something more enjoyable.

Common Pitfalls When Addressing the Sunk Cost Fallacy

1. Fear of Admitting Failure:

People often equate quitting with failure, even when it's the smartest move.

2. Overvaluing Past Investments:

Emotional attachment to your efforts can cloud your judgment.

3. Ignoring Future Costs:

Focusing only on what's already lost blinds you to the additional resources you'll waste by continuing.

Takeaway

The Sunk Cost Fallacy tempts you to throw good money, time, or effort after bad. By focusing on the present and future instead of clinging to the past, you can free yourself to pursue better opportunities.

Chapter 25: Overconfidence Bias

What Is Overconfidence Bias?

Overconfidence Bias is the tendency to overestimate your knowledge, skills, or ability to predict outcomes. While confidence is valuable, overconfidence creates blind spots, leading you to underestimate risks, overlook critical details, or assume you're more prepared than you actually are.

Example:

You might believe you can finish a major project in half the time it actually takes, only to find yourself scrambling as deadlines approach.

Why Overconfidence Bias Matters

1. Increases Risk of Failure:

Overconfidence often leads to poor preparation, as you assume success is guaranteed.

2. Blinds You to Weaknesses:

When you overestimate your skills or knowledge, you're less likely to seek help or advice.

3. Leads to Overcommitment:

Overconfidence can make you take on too much, assuming you can handle it all effortlessly.

Example in Action:

A new investor might believe they can beat the stock market based on limited research. Overconfidence in their "gut instincts" could lead to losses they didn't anticipate.

How to Overcome Overconfidence Bias

1. Embrace Humility:

Acknowledge that you don't know everything. This mindset opens you up to learning and reduces the likelihood of making reckless decisions.

Example: Instead of assuming you'll ace a job interview, prepare thoroughly by practicing answers and researching the company.

2. Seek Objective Feedback:

Ask others to evaluate your plans or performance. A fresh perspective often reveals blind spots.

Example: Before launching a product, gather honest feedback from potential users rather than relying solely on your assumptions.

3. Double-Check Your Assumptions:

Challenge your beliefs by asking, "What evidence do I have that I'm right?"

Example: If you assume you can finish a task in a day, break it into steps and estimate the time for each. This forces you to confront the actual workload.

4. Plan for Contingencies:

Assume that things might not go as planned. Create backup strategies to manage risks.

Example: If you're starting a business, consider what you'll do if your initial idea doesn't gain traction.

Everyday Example of Overconfidence Bias

You believe you can drive to the airport in 30 minutes, so you leave just in time. However, you didn't account for traffic, construction, or finding parking, causing you to miss your flight. A more realistic approach would have included extra time for unforeseen delays.

Common Pitfalls in Overconfidence Bias

1. Ignoring Warning Signs:

Overconfidence often blinds you to red flags, such as missed deadlines or mounting risks.

2. Underestimating Complexity:

Overconfident decisions often fail to account for all the moving parts of a problem.

3. Resisting Help:

Overconfidence can make you reluctant to delegate or seek expert advice, leading to preventable mistakes.

Takeaway

Overconfidence Bias creates blind spots that can derail even the most promising plans. By embracing humility, seeking feedback, and preparing for risks, you can make more grounded, realistic decisions that lead to better outcomes.

Chapter 26: Framing Effect

What Is the Framing Effect?

The Framing Effect is the tendency for your decisions to be influenced by how information is presented, rather than the information itself. The same fact, framed differently, can lead to completely different reactions.

Example:

If a surgery has a "90% success rate," you'll likely feel optimistic. But if the same surgery is described as having a "10% failure rate," it feels much riskier — even though the facts are identical.

Why the Framing Effect Matters

1. Skews Your Judgment:

Framing can push you toward irrational decisions by emphasizing either the positives or negatives of a situation.

2. Limits Objectivity:

Decisions made under the influence of framing often ignore the full context.

3. Influences Marketing and Persuasion:

Advertisers and negotiators often use framing to sway your choices, making you feel like you're getting a better deal than you are.

Example in Action:

You're deciding between two sales offers:

- "Save $200!"
- "Spend $800!"

Although the deals are identical, the "Save $200" framing feels more appealing.

1. Rephrase the Problem:

Look at the situation from multiple angles. Ask, "How would I feel if this were framed differently?"

Example: When choosing between "80% lean" beef and "20% fat" beef, remember they're the same product.

2. Focus on the Data:

Strip away emotional language and focus on the raw numbers or facts.

Example: Instead of reacting to a "limited-time 50% off" sale, calculate the actual cost and compare it to your budget.

3. Consider the Opposite Frame:

Intentionally flip the framing to see if it changes your perception.

Example: If someone emphasizes the low risk of an investment, reframe it by focusing on the potential losses to assess whether it's worth it.

4. Ask Neutral Questions:

Avoid leading questions that emphasize one frame over another.

Example: Instead of asking, "How great is this deal?" ask, "How does this deal compare to others?"

Everyday Example of the Framing Effect

Imagine you're at a restaurant, and the menu highlights "Chef's Special — Only $19.99!" While it sounds like a bargain, reframing it as "$20 for one meal" might make you reconsider whether it's truly worth the price.

Common Pitfalls in Addressing the Framing Effect

1. Trusting Emotional Language:

Phrases like "only," "save," or "best deal" are designed to appeal emotionally but often lack context.

2. Ignoring Alternative Perspectives:

Failing to explore other frames keeps you locked into a narrow view.

3. Assuming You're Immune:

The Framing Effect is subtle and influences everyone, even if you think you're too rational to be swayed.

Takeaway

The Framing Effect shows how much presentation matters in decision-making. By reframing problems, focusing on the raw facts, and questioning emotional language, you can make clearer, more rational choices.

Chapter 27: Loss Aversion

What Is Loss Aversion?

Loss Aversion is the tendency to fear losses more intensely than you value equivalent gains. For most people, losing $100 feels far worse than the satisfaction of gaining $100. This fear of loss can lead you to avoid risks, even when the potential rewards outweigh the downside.

Example:

You're hesitant to invest in a promising business because you're more worried about losing your initial capital than excited about the potential returns.

Why Loss Aversion Matters

1. Leads to Missed Opportunities:

Fear of loss often keeps you from pursuing high-reward ventures, such as investing, starting a new project, or making a career change.

2. Encourages Risky Behavior to Avoid Losses:

Ironically, loss aversion can also make you double down on bad decisions just to avoid admitting failure.

3. Distorts Decision-Making:

By focusing too much on avoiding losses, you fail to evaluate decisions logically or holistically.

A homeowner might refuse to sell their property at a slight loss, even if reinvesting the money elsewhere could yield greater financial returns.

How to Overcome Loss Aversion

1. Reframe Losses as Learning:

Instead of seeing every loss as a failure, view it as an opportunity to grow.

Example: If a business idea doesn't succeed, focus on the skills, experience, and lessons you gained rather than the lost investment.

2. Shift Focus to Potential Gains:

When evaluating risks, actively think about the rewards to balance your perspective.

Example: If you're considering a career switch, imagine the new skills, opportunities, and satisfaction you'll gain rather than fearing temporary uncertainty.

3. Use Data to Ground Decisions:

Base your choices on probabilities and outcomes, not on emotional reactions to potential losses.

Example: If the odds of succeeding in an investment are high and the risk is calculated, let the numbers guide you, not your fear.

4. Set Limits on Emotional Influence:

Establish clear decision criteria to prevent fear from taking over.

Example: If you're nervous about selling an underperforming stock, decide in advance to sell if it drops below a certain threshold, avoiding emotional hesitation.

Everyday Example of Loss Aversion

You're offered a refund guarantee when buying a product but hesitate because returning it feels like "admitting defeat." By reframing the return as a smart financial move rather than a loss, you make a better decision.

Common Pitfalls in Overcoming Loss Aversion

1. Overcompensating:

In an attempt to overcome loss aversion, some people take reckless risks without proper evaluation.

2. Dwelling on Past Losses:

Focusing on previous setbacks can amplify your fear of future risks.

3. Neglecting Long-Term Gains:

Loss aversion often prioritizes short-term comfort over long-term rewards.

Takeaway

Loss Aversion is a powerful emotional bias, but it doesn't have to control you. By reframing losses, focusing on gains, and grounding your decisions in logic, you can embrace opportunities that fear might otherwise block.

We shouldn't have expanded the business last year. It's obvious now it was a mistake.

But back then, all the data pointed to growth—hindsight makes it look obvious.

Chapter 28: Hindsight Bias

What Is Hindsight Bias?

Hindsight Bias is the tendency to see past events as more predictable than they actually were. Once an outcome is known, it's easy to say, "I knew that would happen!" — even if you didn't. This illusion of foresight can lead to unfair self-criticism or overconfidence in future decisions.

Example:

After a stock market crash, you might think, "I should have seen that coming," forgetting that the market's behavior was uncertain at the time.

Why Hindsight Bias Matters

1. Leads to Unfair Self-Judgment:

Believing you "should have known better" creates unnecessary guilt or regret.

2. Skews Future Decisions:

Overconfidence in your predictive ability can make you underestimate risks.

3. Hinders Learning:

If you think the outcome was obvious, you're less likely to analyze what actually influenced the result.

How to Overcome Hindsight Bias

1. Acknowledge Uncertainty:

Remind yourself that past events seemed unclear at the time, even if they feel predictable now.

Example: Instead of thinking, "I should have avoided that failed investment," acknowledge the market data didn't guarantee success or failure.

2. Analyze Context, Not Outcomes:

Focus on the factors that influenced your decision, rather than judging based solely on the result.

Example: If you chose a job that didn't work out, consider whether you made the best choice based on the information you had then.

3. Document Decisions:

Write down your reasoning at the time of a decision. Reviewing it later helps you see what you knew — and didn't know — at the moment.

4. Seek Feedback:

Share your decision-making process with others to gain perspective and avoid bias.

Example: A mentor can help you see whether your choices were reasonable, regardless of the outcome.

Everyday Example of Hindsight Bias

You're planning a picnic, and it rains. Looking back, you think, "I should've checked the weather." But if the forecast showed only a slight chance of rain, the decision was reasonable. Recognizing this prevents unnecessary self-blame.

Common Pitfalls in Addressing Hindsight Bias

1. Overconfidence in Predictions:

Thinking you "knew it all along" can lead to poor preparation in the future.

2. Ignoring External Factors:

Outcomes often depend on factors beyond your control.

3. Fixating on Results:

Focusing only on whether a decision succeeded or failed oversimplifies its complexity.

Takeaway

Hindsight Bias can make the past seem deceptively clear, leading to unfair self-judgment and overconfidence. By focusing on the decision-making process rather than outcomes, you can learn from the past without distorting it.

Chapter 29: Groupthink

What Is Groupthink?

Groupthink occurs when a group prioritizes harmony and consensus over critical thinking. This bias pushes people to conform to the majority's view, even if they disagree internally or spot potential flaws. The result? Poor decisions that could have been avoided with independent perspectives.

Example:

A team approves a risky business strategy without raising objections because no one wants to disrupt the meeting's positive mood or challenge the boss's opinion.

Why Groupthink Matters

1. Suppresses Dissenting Voices:

In a desire to "keep the peace," individuals may avoid sharing valuable insights or concerns.

2. Leads to Suboptimal Decisions:

By focusing on agreement, groups often ignore critical risks, alternative solutions, or weaknesses in their plans.

3. Promotes Overconfidence in the Group:

A false sense of certainty arises because everyone appears to agree, even if that agreement is shallow or coerced.

Historical Example:

The Bay of Pigs invasion in 1961 is a classic example of Groupthink. U.S. officials failed to question the plan's feasibility, leading to a widely criticized failure.

How to Overcome Groupthink

1. Encourage Diverse Opinions:

Leaders should actively invite dissent and create a safe space for different perspectives.

Example: A team leader could say, "Let's discuss why this idea might not work and what other options we should consider."

2. Appoint a Devil's Advocate:

Designate someone to deliberately challenge the group's assumptions.

Example: In brainstorming sessions, one team member could question the feasibility of each proposed solution.

3. Emphasize Evidence Over Consensus:

Shift the focus from agreement to data and logic.

Example: Instead of voting on the best strategy, ask, "What do the numbers suggest?" or "What's the evidence supporting this decision?"

4. Encourage Anonymous Feedback:

Allow group members to share concerns or suggestions privately to reduce the fear of judgment.

Example: Use anonymous surveys or suggestion boxes during major planning sessions.

5. Break the Group into Smaller Teams:

Smaller groups are less likely to succumb to Groupthink and can independently explore alternative solutions.

Everyday Example of Groupthink

You're dining with friends, and everyone agrees to eat at a certain restaurant. You dislike the choice but stay quiet to avoid conflict. Overcoming Groupthink means speaking up — "Hey, I'd prefer a different spot. Can we consider other options?" — and opening the floor for discussion.

Common Pitfalls in Addressing Groupthink

1. Fear of Rejection:

Many people hesitate to challenge the group, worrying it might create tension or make them seem difficult.

2. Assuming Silence Equals Agreement:

Just because no one objects doesn't mean everyone agrees.

3. Overvaluing Consensus:

Group leaders often mistake unity for progress, ignoring whether the solution is actually sound.

Takeaway

Groupthink prioritizes harmony at the expense of sound decisions. By fostering diverse perspectives, encouraging dissent, and emphasizing evidence over agreement, you can make stronger, more balanced choices.

Chapter 30: The Dunning-Kruger Effect

What Is the Dunning-Kruger Effect?

The Dunning-Kruger Effect describes the tendency for people with limited knowledge or skills in a specific area to overestimate their competence. Ironically, those who know the least are often the most confident, while experts, who recognize the complexities, are more humble about their knowledge.

Example:

A novice cook might believe they can run a successful restaurant after preparing a few impressive meals, ignoring the complexities of staffing, budgeting, and menu planning.

Why the Dunning-Kruger Effect Matters

1. Leads to Poor Decisions:

Overconfidence in your abilities may lead you to take on challenges you're unprepared for.

2. Discourages Learning:

Believing you already "know enough" prevents you from seeking new knowledge or skills.

3. Creates Miscommunication:

Those affected by the Dunning-Kruger Effect may reject expert advice, assuming they know better.

How to Overcome the Dunning-Kruger Effect

1. Embrace Lifelong Learning:

Recognize that expertise requires continuous effort and learning.

Example: Instead of assuming you're an expert after reading one article, commit to studying the subject more deeply.

2. Seek Feedback from Experts:

Ask experienced individuals to evaluate your knowledge or skills.

Example: If you're starting a business, consult with seasoned entrepreneurs to identify gaps in your plan.

3. Practice Intellectual Humility:

Acknowledge what you don't know and be willing to learn.

Example: Instead of saying, "I know how to manage a team," say, "I'm still learning what makes a great leader. Can you share advice?"

4. Ask Better Questions:

Shift from assuming you have the answers to seeking deeper understanding.

Example: If you're tackling a technical challenge, ask, "What am I missing here?" instead of assuming you've covered all bases.

5. Review Past Mistakes:

Reflect on instances where overconfidence led to poor outcomes and identify what you could have done differently.

Example: If a DIY project went wrong, analyze what steps you skipped or underestimated.

Everyday Example of the Dunning-Kruger Effect

You take a few fitness classes and start advising others on exercise routines, only to realize later that your advice overlooked critical factors like injury prevention and nutrition. Recognizing this, you decide to study more before offering advice.

Common Pitfalls in Addressing the Dunning-Kruger Effect

1. Resisting Feedback:

Overconfident individuals often dismiss constructive criticism, assuming they know better.

2. Mistaking Initial Success for Mastery:

Early wins can create a false sense of expertise.

3. Overgeneralizing Knowledge:

Being skilled in one area doesn't automatically translate to expertise in others.

Takeaway

The Dunning-Kruger Effect teaches that true expertise begins with recognizing what you don't know. By seeking feedback, embracing humility, and committing to learning, you can build genuine competence and make more informed decisions.

Section IV: Tools and Techniques for Rational Decision-Making

In this section, I introduce you to powerful tools and structured techniques for making clear, well-informed decisions. Whether you're solving complex problems or navigating uncertainty, these methods help break down options and improve outcomes.

Chapter 31: The Decision Tree

What is a Decision Tree?

A Decision Tree is a tool to visually map choices, their potential outcomes, and subsequent decisions. It helps you understand how one choice leads to another, allowing you to evaluate the long-term consequences and risks of each path.

Why Decision Trees Matter

Decision-making often involves uncertainty, complexity, or hidden trade-offs. A Decision Tree simplifies this by laying out all possible paths, making it easier to compare them objectively. It's especially useful when choices involve multiple steps or outcomes.

Example: Choosing a Marketing Strategy

Imagine you need to decide between two marketing campaigns:

- **Option 1:** Invest in social media ads.
    - o **Outcome 1:** Increased traffic but higher costs.
    - o **Outcome 2:** Minimal traffic and wasted investment.
- • **Option 2:** Launch email marketing.
    - o **Outcome 1:** Moderate traffic but high engagement.
    - o **Outcome 2:** No improvement in sales.

Mapping this as a tree clarifies which option offers the best chance of meeting your goals.

How to Create a Decision Tree

1. **Start with a Decision:** Define the question or choice you're facing.
2. **List Options:** Identify all possible actions you can take.
3. **Add Outcomes:** For each option, map potential results, including secondary decisions.
4. **Estimate Probabilities:** Assign likelihoods to each outcome to evaluate risk.
5. **Weigh Results:** Use costs, benefits, or probabilities to determine the best path.

Everyday Example

You're deciding between walking, biking, or driving to work.

- **Option 1:** Walk.
    - o **Outcome 1:** Arrive refreshed but take longer.
    - o **Outcome 2:** Risk being late if the weather changes.
- **Option 2:** Bike.
    - o **Outcome 1:** Save time but risk an accident.
- **Option 3:** Drive.
    - o **Outcome 1:** Arrive quickly but incur parking costs.

The tree visually highlights trade-offs between time, cost, and convenience.

Common Pitfalls in Decision Trees

1. **Overcomplicating Branches:** Too many details can overwhelm the analysis.
2. **Inaccurate Probabilities:** Make sure estimates are realistic.
3. **Ignoring Intangibles:** Factors like personal values or intuition may not fit neatly into a tree but still matter.

Takeaway

A Decision Tree organizes your choices and clarifies trade-offs, making complex decisions easier to approach logically. It's a simple yet powerful way to evaluate paths and their outcomes.

Chapter 32: The Six Thinking Hats

EMOTIONS
CAUTION
FACTS
OPTIMISM
CREATIVITY
CONTROL

What are the Six Thinking Hats?

The Six Thinking Hats is a structured thinking tool developed by Edward de Bono. Each hat represents a different mode of thinking, encouraging you to approach problems from multiple perspectives to ensure a balanced and thorough evaluation.

Why the Six Thinking Hats Matter

Most people default to one way of thinking—logical, emotional, or cautious. This tool forces you to examine problems from all angles, fostering creativity, identifying risks, and uncovering opportunities that might otherwise be overlooked.

The Six Hats Explained

1. **White Hat (Facts):** Focus on data, evidence, and objective information.
2. **Red Hat (Emotions):** Consider gut feelings, instincts, and emotional reactions.
3. **Black Hat (Caution):** Identify potential risks, weaknesses, or obstacles.
4. **Yellow Hat (Optimism):** Highlight the benefits and positive aspects of a solution.
5. **Green Hat (Creativity):** Brainstorm innovative ideas and alternative approaches.
6. **Blue Hat (Control):** Manage the thinking process and ensure all hats are used appropriately.

Example: **Planning a New Business Venture**

Imagine starting a bakery:

- **White Hat:** What is the market size? What are typical startup costs?
- **Red Hat:** How passionate do you feel about running a bakery?
- **Black Hat:** What if demand is lower than expected? What are your risks?
- **Yellow Hat:** What opportunities exist in your local area?
- **Green Hat:** Could you offer unique products, like gluten-free pastries?
- **Blue Hat:** Have you considered all perspectives fairly?

Using these hats ensures no critical aspect of the venture is overlooked.

How to Use the Six Thinking Hats

1. **Start with One Hat:** Focus on one perspective at a time to avoid bias.
2. **Switch Hats:** Rotate through each hat systematically to cover all angles.
3. **Combine Insights:** Synthesize findings from all hats to create a well-rounded solution.

Common Pitfalls in Using the Hats

1. **Skipping Perspectives:** Avoid ignoring hats you find uncomfortable or irrelevant.
2. **Overanalyzing:** Don't spend too much time on one hat, especially if it dominates the process.
3. **Ignoring Intuition:** While structured, the Red Hat allows emotions to play a role in decision-making.

Takeaway

The Six Thinking Hats fosters balanced, creative, and cautious thinking by examining a problem from all perspectives. It's a versatile tool for better decisions and innovative solutions.

Chapter 33: SWOT Analysis

What is SWOT Analysis?

SWOT Analysis is a strategic framework used to evaluate internal and external factors affecting a decision, goal, or project. The four quadrants—Strengths, Weaknesses, Opportunities, and Threats—offer a structured way to identify advantages, risks, and areas for improvement.

Why SWOT Analysis Matters

SWOT helps you assess the current situation holistically by balancing internal capabilities (strengths and weaknesses) with external realities (opportunities and threats). It's particularly effective for strategic planning and risk assessment.

Example: Expanding a Business

Imagine you're considering opening a second location:

- **Strengths:** Strong brand loyalty, experienced staff.
- **Weaknesses:** Limited cash flow, lack of marketing expertise.
- **Opportunities:** Growing demand in a neighboring city, reduced lease costs.
- **Threats:** Competition from established local businesses, economic uncertainty.

By analyzing these factors, you can make a clearer decision about whether and how to proceed.

How to Conduct a SWOT Analysis

1. **Identify Strengths:** What internal resources or advantages set you apart?
2. **Spot Weaknesses:** Where are your vulnerabilities or limitations?
3. **Explore Opportunities:** What external trends, gaps, or partnerships could you leverage?
4. **Acknowledge Threats:** What external risks or obstacles could harm you?

Everyday Example of SWOT Analysis

Suppose you're deciding whether to pursue a new career opportunity:

- **Strengths:** Relevant skills, strong professional network.
- **Weaknesses:** Limited industry experience.
- **Opportunities:** Potential for career growth and higher income.
- **Threats:** Uncertainty about the company's future.

SWOT helps you make an informed decision by clarifying pros and cons.

Common Pitfalls in SWOT Analysis

1. **Ignoring Weaknesses:** Be honest about limitations; sugar-coating weak points undermines the process.
2. **Overestimating Opportunities:** Avoid being overly optimistic without data to back it up.
3. **Inaction:** Insights from SWOT are only valuable if followed by concrete actions.

Takeaway

SWOT Analysis offers a structured way to evaluate decisions by balancing internal and external factors. Use it to identify strengths, mitigate risks, and seize opportunities with confidence.

Chapter 34: Weighted Scoring

Criteria	Weight	Requirement score				
		A	B	C	D	E
Value	20%	80	45	40	15	35
Risk	20%	60	85	30	20	75
Difficulty	15%	55	80	50	15	25
Success	10%	30	60	55	65	30
Compliance	5%	35	50	60	50	50
Relationships	5%	80	70	50	85	80
Stakeholder	15%	25	50	45	60	60
Urgency	10%	60	25	40	65	80
Weighted Scores	100%	54.8	60.0	43.3	38.0	52.3

What is Weighted Scoring?

Weighted Scoring is a method to rank options based on criteria that matter most to you. By assigning weights (importance) and scores (performance) to each criterion, you calculate a total score for every option, making complex decisions easier and more objective.

Why Weighted Scoring Matters

Decisions often involve multiple factors, and not all are equally important. Weighted Scoring allows you to prioritize what matters most and compare options systematically, reducing guesswork and bias.

Example: Choosing a New Apartment

Suppose you're choosing between three apartments. Your criteria are Cost, Location, and Size.

- Assign **weights** to each criterion (e.g., Cost = 50%, Location = 30%, Size = 20%).
- Score each apartment based on how well it performs in each category (e.g., Cost: 8/10).
- Multiply the weight by the score to calculate a weighted score for each option.

The apartment with the highest total score becomes your best choice.

How to Use Weighted Scoring

1. **List Criteria:** Identify the factors that influence your decision.
2. **Assign Weights:** Allocate importance to each criterion, ensuring they add up to 100%.
3. **Score Options:** Evaluate how well each option performs against the criteria.
4. **Calculate Totals:** Multiply each score by its weight, then sum the totals for each option.
5. **Rank Results:** Use the total scores to rank your choices.

Everyday Example of Weighted Scoring

Imagine deciding which smartphone to buy based on Price, Features, and Battery Life.

- Price = 40% weight, Features = 40% weight, Battery Life = 20% weight.
- Option 1 scores 9/10 in Price, 7/10 in Features, and 8/10 in Battery Life.
- Weighted Score = (9×0.4) + (7×0.4) + (8×0.2) = 8.2.

Compare scores across all options to identify the best fit.

Common Pitfalls in Weighted Scoring

1. **Overcomplicating Criteria:** Too many factors dilute focus. Stick to 3-5 key criteria.
2. **Unbalanced Weights:** Ensure weights reflect true priorities. Overemphasis on minor factors skews results.
3. **Subjective Scoring:** Be consistent and objective when assigning scores.

Takeaway

Weighted Scoring helps you prioritize what matters and make objective decisions by balancing multiple factors. It's a simple, reliable way to compare complex options and identify the best fit.

Chapter 35: Scenario Planning

What is Scenario Planning?

Scenario Planning is a tool to prepare for uncertainty by imagining different possible futures. By envisioning "best-case," "worst-case," and "most likely" scenarios, you can develop strategies to handle whatever comes your way.

Why Scenario Planning Matters

The future is unpredictable, and decisions based on a single assumption can fail when conditions change. Scenario Planning builds flexibility, helping you anticipate risks, adapt to challenges, and seize opportunities in a variety of situations.

Example: Expanding a Business

Suppose you're planning to expand into a new market.

- **Best Case:** Strong demand leads to rapid growth.
- **Worst Case:** Demand is weak, and the investment fails.
- **Most Likely Case:** Moderate growth with manageable challenges.

By preparing strategies for each scenario—like setting aside extra funds for risks—you ensure success under different circumstances.

How to Practice Scenario Planning

1. **Define Key Factors:** Identify the uncertainties most likely to impact your decision (e.g., economic trends, competition).
2. **Create Scenarios:** Develop at least three scenarios: best-case, worst-case, and most likely outcomes.
3. **Analyze Impacts:** Assess how each scenario would affect your goals or plans.
4. **Plan Responses:** Develop strategies to maximize benefits or minimize risks for each scenario.
5. **Monitor Trends:** Adjust your plans as new information becomes available.

Everyday Example of Scenario Planning

Imagine saving for a vacation but unsure about your future expenses.

- **Best Case:** You receive a bonus and can afford luxury travel.
- **Worst Case:** An unexpected expense forces you to delay plans.
- **Most Likely Case:** You stick to a modest budget.

By planning for all three, you avoid surprises and enjoy peace of mind.

Common Pitfalls in Scenario Planning

1. **Too Many Scenarios:** Stick to a manageable number (3-5) to avoid confusion.
2. **Neglecting Extreme Cases:** Don't ignore low-probability but high-impact risks.
3. **Failing to Monitor Trends:** Scenario plans are only useful if updated as conditions change.

Takeaway

Scenario Planning helps you navigate uncertainty by preparing for multiple outcomes. With flexible strategies, you're ready for anything.

Chapter 36: Pre-Mortem Analysis

What is a Pre-Mortem Analysis?

A Pre-Mortem Analysis involves imagining that a decision or project has already failed, then identifying the reasons why. By working backward, you uncover risks and weak points before they occur, allowing you to address them proactively.

Why Pre-Mortem Analysis Matters

Optimism bias can blind us to potential failures, causing avoidable mistakes. A Pre-Mortem forces you to confront risks early, improving your chances of success by anticipating and addressing problems in advance.

Example: Planning a Product Launch

Suppose you're launching a new app. In your Pre-Mortem, you ask, "What could cause this launch to fail?"

- **Answer 1:** Marketing didn't reach the right audience.
- **Answer 2:** The app had bugs at release.
- **Answer 3:** Competitors launched a similar product first.

By identifying these risks, you adjust your plan to avoid failure.

How to Conduct a Pre-Mortem Analysis

1. **Imagine Failure:** Assume your decision has failed catastrophically.
2. **Ask Why:** Brainstorm reasons for the failure, focusing on overlooked risks or weak points.
3. **List Fixes:** Identify ways to address or prevent each potential problem.
4. **Adjust the Plan:** Integrate these fixes into your strategy before moving forward.

Everyday Example of a Pre-Mortem

You're planning a wedding. A Pre-Mortem might reveal risks like weather issues, late vendors, or seating conflicts. By addressing these risks—reserving a tent, confirming vendors early, and creating a seating plan—you reduce the likelihood of chaos.

Common Pitfalls in Pre-Mortem Analysis

1. **Overemphasizing Negatives:** Focus on realistic risks, not exaggerated fears.
2. **Ignoring Fixes:** Identifying risks is useless unless you take action to address them.
3. **Skipping Collaboration:** Involve others to uncover blind spots.

Takeaway

A Pre-Mortem Analysis transforms potential failure into a learning opportunity, helping you refine your decisions before committing. By planning for setbacks, you strengthen your strategy and improve your chances of success.

Chapter 37: Monte Carlo Simulation

What is Monte Carlo Simulation?

Monte Carlo Simulation is a method to model uncertainty by running multiple simulations of a decision or event. By using random variables to represent uncertainty, it provides a range of possible outcomes and their probabilities, helping you make informed predictions.

Why Monte Carlo Simulation Matters

In complex decisions, there's rarely one "guaranteed" outcome. Monte Carlo Simulation helps you account for variability and uncertainty, showing not just what could happen but how likely it is to happen. It's particularly valuable in finance, project planning, and risk management.

Example: Estimating a Project Budget

Imagine budgeting for a construction project. You're unsure about the costs of labor, materials, and potential delays.

- Run simulations using ranges for each variable (e.g., labor costs might vary between $50k and $70k).
- The simulation generates thousands of potential budgets, showing that 70% of outcomes fall between $120k and $140k.

This insight allows you to plan for uncertainty and avoid underfunding.

How to Use Monte Carlo Simulation

1. **Define Variables:** Identify key factors that influence your decision (e.g., costs, demand, timelines).
2. **Assign Ranges:** Use realistic ranges for each variable instead of fixed numbers.
3. **Simulate Outcomes:** Run multiple simulations, varying the inputs randomly within their ranges.
4. **Analyze Results:** Examine the distribution of outcomes to identify patterns and probabilities.
5. **Plan Accordingly:** Use insights to prepare for the most likely scenarios and mitigate risks.

Everyday Example of Monte Carlo Simulation

Suppose you're planning a vacation but uncertain about costs. Estimate ranges for flights, accommodations, and activities, then run a simulation to predict total expenses. If 80% of outcomes fit your budget, you can move forward confidently.

Common Pitfalls in Monte Carlo Simulation

1. **Poor Assumptions:** Garbage in, garbage out—if your input ranges are unrealistic, your results will be too.
2. **Ignoring Outliers:** Rare but extreme outcomes may require special attention.
3. **Overcomplication:** Avoid adding unnecessary variables; focus on the most impactful ones.

Takeaway

Monte Carlo Simulation models uncertainty by showing the range and likelihood of possible outcomes. It's a powerful way to plan confidently in unpredictable situations.

Chapter 38: Decision Matrices: Simplify Complex Choices

CRITERIA	WEIGHT	SUPPLIER A	SUPPLIER B	SUPPLIER C
COST	40% (0.4)	8 (3.2)	7 (2.8)	9 (3.6)
QUALITY	35% (0.35)	9 (3.15)	8 (2.8)	7 (2.45)
DELIVERY SPEED	25% (0.25)	7 (1.75)	9 (2.25)	6 (1.5)
TOTAL SCORE		8.1	7.85	7.55

What is a Decision Matrix?

A Decision Matrix is a tool to compare multiple options against key criteria in a structured way. By assigning scores to each criterion, you calculate a total score for each option, helping you identify the best choice quickly and objectively.

Why Decision Matrix Matters

Complex decisions often involve multiple factors, and it's easy to overlook important details or let bias influence your choice. A Decision Matrix organizes information clearly, making comparisons straightforward and reducing emotional interference.

Example: Choosing a Supplier

Suppose you're deciding between three suppliers for your business. Your criteria are Cost, Quality, and Delivery Speed.

- Assign scores for each supplier based on performance in these areas.
- Total the scores to identify the best overall option. For instance:
  - Supplier A = Cost (8) + Quality (9) + Speed (7) = 24.
  - Supplier B = Cost (7) + Quality (8) + Speed (9) = 24.
  - Supplier C = Cost (9) + Quality (7) + Speed (6) = 22.

Supplier A and B tie, so you might consider extra factors to break the tie.

How to Use a Decision Matrix

1. **List Options and Criteria:** Identify what you're choosing between and the factors that matter.
2. **Weight Criteria (Optional):** Assign importance to each criterion if some matter more than others.
3. **Score Each Option:** Rate each option on a consistent scale (e.g., 1-10) for every criterion.
4. **Calculate Totals:** Sum the scores for each option to determine the winner.

Imagine deciding where to eat dinner with friends:
- **Criteria:** Price, Distance, Menu Variety.
- **Options:** Restaurant A, B, and C.
- **Scores:** Restaurant A (8, 9, 7) totals 24, making it the top choice.

The matrix makes the decision quick, fair, and transparent.

Common Pitfalls in Decision Matrix

1. **Overloading Criteria:** Focus on the most critical factors to avoid analysis paralysis.
2. **Subjective Scoring:** Be consistent and objective when assigning scores.
3. **Ignoring Weights:** If some criteria are more important, weight them to reflect their value.

Takeaway

A Decision Matrix simplifies choices by organizing options and criteria in a clear, comparable format. It's a reliable way to balance multiple factors and identify the best solution.

Factor	Pro/Con	Weight	Impact	Score
Better job opportunities	Pro	9	+8	+72
Exciting lifestyle	Pro	8	+7	+56
Higher cost of living	Con	7	−6	−42
Far from family	Con	6	−5	−30
Pros Total: +128		Cons Total: −72		Net Score: +56

Chapter 39: Pro/Con Lists Done Right

What is a Pro/Con List?

A Pro/Con List is a simple tool to weigh the advantages and disadvantages of a decision. When done right, it goes beyond listing pros and cons by adding context, such as importance or likelihood, to make the decision clearer.

Why Pro/Con Lists Matter

Pro/Con Lists are quick and intuitive, but they're often too basic to guide major decisions. Adding context — such as weights or probabilities — turns them into powerful decision-making tools.

Example: Deciding Whether to Move to a New City

- **Pros:** Better job opportunities (+8), exciting lifestyle (+7).
- **Cons:** Higher cost of living (-6), far from family (-5).
- **Adjusted Score:** Add weights or importance to each factor to clarify whether the pros outweigh the cons.

How to Create a Pro/Con List Done Right

1. **List Pros and Cons:** Identify advantages and disadvantages of your decision.
2. **Assign Weights:** Rate how important each factor is (e.g., 1–10).
3. **Score Impact:** Assess the positive or negative impact of each factor.
4. **Calculate Totals:** Multiply weights by scores to determine the overall balance.

Everyday Example of a Pro/Con List

Imagine debating whether to adopt a pet:
- **Pros:** Companionship (+8), Increased happiness (+10).
- **Cons:** Costs (-6), Responsibility (-7).
- **Weighted Total:** The pros total +18, while the cons total -13, suggesting adoption is the better choice.

Common Pitfalls in Pro/Con Lists

1. **Vague Factors:** Be specific to avoid superficial results.
2. **Ignoring Context:** Without weights or impact, minor factors can skew results.
3. **Over-reliance:** Pro/Con Lists are one tool; combine them with others for big decisions.

Takeaway

Pro/Con Lists go beyond simple lists to incorporate context, making them a powerful yet intuitive decision-making tool.

Chapter 40: Heuristic Shortcuts

I always buy the brand I've used before—it saves time.

That's smart, but have you checked if there's a better deal today?

What Are Heuristic Shortcuts?

Heuristic shortcuts are mental strategies or "rules of thumb" that simplify decision-making. Instead of analyzing every detail, you rely on general guidelines to make quick, efficient choices. Heuristics are invaluable in fast-paced situations, but they're not without risks — their simplicity can sometimes lead to errors.

Example:

When deciding which book to buy, you might rely on a heuristic like "bestsellers are good" instead of reading every review. While efficient, this shortcut may overlook books that fit your taste but aren't on the bestseller list.

Why Heuristic Shortcuts Matter

1. Save Time and Energy:

Heuristics streamline decision-making, helping you avoid "analysis paralysis."

2. Enable Rapid Decisions:

In high-pressure situations, they let you act quickly without overthinking.

3. Provide Reliable Results (Most of the Time):

When applied appropriately, heuristics often yield satisfactory outcomes.

Example in Action:

You're grocery shopping and decide to buy the brand you've used before. This heuristic, "stick with what works," saves time compared to analyzing every option on the shelf.

How to Use Heuristic Shortcuts Wisely

1. Match the Shortcut to the Situation:

Heuristics work best in routine or low-stakes decisions. For complex or high-stakes choices, a more detailed analysis is better.

Example: Choosing where to eat dinner? A heuristic like "go to the highest-rated place nearby" works. Deciding on a career move? Take your time.

2. Combine with Logic:

Use heuristics as a starting point, but verify their relevance with critical thinking.

Example: If you use the heuristic "expensive items are higher quality," double-check reviews to confirm the product is worth the price.

3. Learn from Experience:

Over time, refine your shortcuts based on what works for you.

Example: If "choosing the middle option" often leads to good results, you can use it confidently in similar situations.

4. Be Aware of Cognitive Biases:

Some heuristics, like relying on recent memories (Availability Heuristic), can mislead you. Stay vigilant about potential errors.

Everyday Example of Heuristic Shortcuts

Imagine you're packing for a trip. Instead of creating a detailed checklist, you rely on the heuristic "pack what I used on my last trip." While efficient, this shortcut could miss new items you'll need for a different climate.

Common Pitfalls in Using Heuristics

1. Over-Reliance on Shortcuts:

Simplified rules can miss critical details in complex decisions.

2. Misapplying a Heuristic:

A rule that works in one context might fail in another.

3. Neglecting Better Options:

Heuristics focus on efficiency, not optimization, so you might miss opportunities for better results.

Takeaway

Heuristic shortcuts are powerful tools for saving time, but they're not a one-size-fits-all solution. By applying them thoughtfully and balancing them with critical thinking, you can make smarter, faster decisions without sacrificing accuracy.

Section V: Emotional Intelligence in Decision-Making

This section explores how mastering your emotions, understanding the feelings of others, and managing mental fatigue can transform the way you approach decisions. Remember: The best decisions aren't just smart — they're balanced, grounded, and deeply human.

Chapter 41: Self-Regulation

What Is Self-Regulation?

Self-regulation is the ability to manage your emotions, impulses, and reactions in a way that aligns with your goals. It's not about suppressing emotions but channeling them constructively, especially in high-pressure situations.

Example:

If someone criticizes you in a meeting, self-regulation means pausing to process your feelings instead of reacting defensively. This allows you to respond calmly and maintain professionalism.

Why Self-Regulation Matters in Decision-Making

1. Reduces Impulsive Choices:

Emotional reactions, like anger or excitement, can lead to rash decisions.

2. Improves Long-Term Outcomes:

By staying composed, you're more likely to make thoughtful choices that align with your goals.

3. Builds Trust and Credibility:

People who manage their emotions well are seen as reliable and level-headed.

Example in Action:

Imagine a business deal is delayed. Instead of panicking and making concessions, self-regulation helps you stay calm, negotiate effectively, and avoid unnecessary compromises.

How to Master Self-Regulation

1. Pause Before Reacting:

Take a deep breath or count to ten before responding in emotionally charged situations.

Example: If you receive a frustrating email, wait a few minutes before replying. This prevents a hasty, emotional response.

2. Label Your Emotions:

Naming what you feel (e.g., "I'm anxious" or "I'm frustrated") helps you process emotions instead of letting them control you.

Example: Acknowledging that you're nervous before a presentation can help you take proactive steps to calm yourself.

3. Focus on What You Can Control:

Redirect energy toward actions you can influence, rather than fixating on things beyond your control.

Example: Instead of stressing over a missed opportunity, focus on preparing for the next one.

4. Practice Emotional Awareness Daily:

Reflect on situations where emotions influenced your decisions. Ask yourself, "How could I have handled this better?"

Everyday Example of Self-Regulation

You're stuck in traffic and running late. Instead of letting frustration take over, you accept the situation, call ahead to explain, and use the time to listen to an audiobook. By regulating your emotions, you stay calm and productive.

1. Suppressing Emotions:

Ignoring feelings doesn't resolve them — it often makes them resurface later in unproductive ways.

2. Overreacting to Small Triggers:

Small annoyances can escalate if you don't actively manage your reactions.

3. Neglecting Emotional Preparation:

Stressful situations are inevitable, but practicing self-regulation skills in advance can help you handle them more effectively.

Takeaway

Self-regulation is a cornerstone of emotional intelligence and decision-making. By learning to pause, process, and channel your emotions, you can make choices that reflect your best self rather than your immediate reactions.

Chapter 42: Empathy and Decisions

What Is Empathy in Decision-Making?

Empathy is the ability to understand and share the feelings of others. In decision-making, it means stepping into someone else's shoes to consider how your choices will impact them emotionally and practically. This skill is vital in building trust, fostering collaboration, and finding solutions that benefit everyone involved.

Example:

A manager deciding on team deadlines uses empathy to recognize that overloading employees might lead to burnout, even if faster results are desired.

Why Empathy Matters in Decision-Making

1. Builds Stronger Relationships:

Empathy fosters trust, making others more likely to support your decisions.

2. Improves Outcomes:

Decisions informed by empathy often address emotional as well as practical needs, leading to more lasting solutions.

3. Reduces Conflict:

Considering others' perspectives helps you avoid misunderstandings and minimize resistance.

Example in Action:

When launching a policy change, a leader who empathizes with employees' concerns about workload may introduce the change gradually to ease the transition.

How to Use Empathy in Decision-Making

1. Listen Actively:

Pay full attention to what others say, without interrupting or formulating a response in your mind.

Example: During a team discussion, listen to concerns about a new project before offering your opinion.

2. Ask Open-Ended Questions:

Invite others to share their thoughts and feelings to gain a deeper understanding of their perspective.

Example: "How do you feel about this change?" or "What challenges are you experiencing?"

3. Consider Emotional Impact:

Ask yourself how your decision might make others feel, and weigh this alongside practical outcomes.

Example: If you're cutting costs in your department, consider how employees will perceive layoffs versus pay cuts, and choose a path that minimizes emotional harm.

4. Acknowledge Others' Feelings:

Show that you value and understand their emotions, even if you don't agree with their perspective.

Example: "I can see why this situation feels overwhelming, and I want to find a way to make it more manageable for you."

Imagine a parent deciding bedtime rules. Instead of enforcing a rigid schedule, they empathize with their child's struggles with night-time fears and allow a compromise, like extra reading time, to ease anxiety while still encouraging rest.

Common Pitfalls in Empathy

1. Assuming Instead of Asking:

Thinking you understand someone's feelings without asking can lead to misjudgements.

2. Letting Empathy Overrule Logic:

While empathy is essential, balance it with practical considerations to avoid unsustainable decisions.

3. Ignoring Boundaries:

Over-empathizing with others can drain your emotional energy. Be mindful of your limits.

Takeaway

Empathy transforms decision-making from a transactional process into a human-centered one. By understanding and considering others' emotions, you can build trust, create better solutions, and make decisions that resonate on a deeper level.

Chapter 43: The Role of Intuition

What Is Intuition?

Intuition is the ability to understand something instinctively, without needing conscious reasoning. Often described as a "gut feeling," it's based on your brain's ability to process patterns, experiences, and subtle cues rapidly, even if you're not aware of it.

Example:

You meet someone at a job interview, and your gut tells you they'd be a great fit for the role — even though you can't immediately pinpoint why.

Why Intuition Matters in Decision-Making

1. Fast Responses in Complex Situations:

Intuition allows you to act quickly when time is limited or data is incomplete.

2. Uses Experience:

Your gut feelings often stem from accumulated knowledge and subconscious pattern recognition.

3. Balances Analysis:

Intuition complements logic by bringing in emotional and instinctive insights that data alone can't provide.

Example in Action:

An experienced doctor might intuitively sense a patient's condition based on subtle, nonverbal cues that aren't obvious in medical tests.

When to Trust Your Intuition

1. When You're Experienced:

Intuition is more reliable when it's based on years of relevant experience.

Example: A skilled chef can instinctively adjust a recipe without measurements, knowing how flavors balance.

2. When the Stakes Are Low:

Gut feelings are a good starting point for smaller decisions, like picking a restaurant or deciding on an outfit.

3. When Data Is Scarce:

In situations where you lack complete information, intuition can fill the gaps and guide you toward action.

4. When You Feel Calm:

Intuition works best when your mind is clear. Emotional overwhelm can distort gut feelings, making them less reliable.

When NOT to Trust Intuition

1. When Bias Is Likely:

Gut instincts can be swayed by cognitive biases, like stereotypes or recent events.

2. When the Decision Is High-Stakes:

For critical choices, such as financial investments or medical decisions, rely on data and expert advice rather than instinct alone.

3. When You're Stressed:

Stress and fatigue can cloud intuition, leading to impulsive or poorly thought-out decisions.

1. Reflect on Past Decisions:

Look back at situations where your gut was right or wrong to understand how it works.

2. Learn and Practice:

Intuition improves with experience. The more you engage in a field, the more patterns you'll subconsciously recognize.

3. Pair Intuition with Logic:

Use your gut as a guide but validate it with reasoning or evidence.

Example: If your intuition says a job candidate is a good fit, verify it by checking their qualifications and references.

Everyday Example of Intuition

You're shopping for a gift and spot an item that "feels right" for your friend. Instead of overthinking, you trust your gut, remembering how similar instincts have guided your choices before.

Common Pitfalls in Intuition

1. Confusing Impulse with Intuition:

A gut feeling comes from experience; an impulse is often emotional and fleeting.

2. Ignoring Contradictory Evidence:

Blindly trusting your gut can lead to overlooking facts that contradict your instinct.

3. Overconfidence in Unfamiliar Areas:

Intuition is less reliable in areas where you lack expertise.

Takeaway

Intuition is a powerful tool, especially when paired with experience and logic. By understanding when and how to trust your gut, you can make faster, more confident decisions without sacrificing accuracy.

Chapter 44: Dealing with Decision Fatigue

What Is Decision Fatigue?

Decision Fatigue happens when your mental energy becomes depleted from making too many choices. As the day goes on, the quality of your decisions often declines, leading to impulsive choices, avoidance, or poor judgment.

Example:

After a long day of work, you might order unhealthy takeout instead of cooking a nutritious meal, not because it's the better option, but because you're mentally exhausted from decision-making.

Why Decision Fatigue Can Be Harmful

1. Leads to Poor Choices:

When fatigued, you're more likely to make snap decisions or avoid making a choice altogether.

2. Reduces Willpower:

Decision fatigue can drain your self-control, making it harder to stick to long-term goals.

3. Overloads Your Mind:

Constant decision-making increases stress and diminishes your overall productivity.

Example in Action:

A busy executive juggling multiple meetings and emails might make hasty decisions on important matters just to "clear their plate," only to regret it later.

How to Combat Decision Fatigue

1. Prioritize Important Decisions Early:

Tackle high-stakes decisions when your mind is fresh, usually in the morning or after a break.

Example: If you're deciding on a big purchase, like buying a house, schedule the discussion early in the day.

2. Simplify Routine Choices:

Reduce unnecessary decisions by creating habits or using defaults.

Example: Plan your outfits for the week or meal prep in advance, so you don't waste mental energy on daily small choices.

3. **Set Clear Decision Criteria:**

Define what you're looking for in advance to streamline your choices.

Example: When choosing a new phone, decide on the key features you need (e.g. price, battery life) to avoid endless comparisons.

4. **Take Breaks to Recharge:**

Pause between decision-heavy tasks to restore mental clarity.

Example: After a long morning of meetings, take a 15-minute walk to clear your mind before tackling emails.

5. **Delegate When Possible:**

Share decision-making responsibilities with others to lighten your mental load.

Example: Assign a team member to handle low-priority decisions, freeing you to focus on strategic choices.

Everyday Example of Decision Fatigue

Imagine you've spent hours shopping online for the perfect gift, only to end up buying the first thing you see because you're too tired to think anymore. Planning your shopping in advance or limiting your options can help avoid this spiral.

Common Pitfalls in Managing Decision Fatigue

1. **Ignoring Your Limits:**

Believing you can make good decisions all day without rest sets you up for failure.

2. **Procrastinating:**

Postponing decisions to avoid fatigue only creates a backlog of choices, worsening the problem later.

3. **Underestimating Small Decisions:**

Even minor choices, like deciding what to eat or wear, contribute to mental exhaustion.

Takeaway

Decision fatigue is inevitable, but it doesn't have to derail you. By prioritizing key decisions, simplifying routines, and taking breaks to recharge, you can stay sharp and focused throughout the day.

Chapter 45: Stress-Reduction Techniques

What Is Stress in Decision-Making?

Stress is a natural response to challenges or demands, but when unmanaged, it clouds judgment, narrows your focus, and makes even small decisions feel overwhelming. Prolonged stress can lead to emotional reactions, snap judgments, or indecision.

Example:

Under stress to meet a deadline, you might choose the fastest solution without fully considering its long-term consequences.

Why Stress Reduction Matters in Decision-Making

1. Improves Clarity:
A calm mind is better equipped to evaluate options and anticipate outcomes.

2. Reduces Emotional Reactions:
Stress often triggers impulsive or fear-based decisions.

3. Increases Focus:
Managing stress helps you prioritize tasks and avoid distractions.

Example in Action:
A leader dealing with a team conflict may pause to reduce their stress before mediating, ensuring they approach the issue rationally rather than emotionally.

Stress-Reduction Techniques for Better Decisions

1. Practice Deep Breathing:
Controlled breathing activates your body's relaxation response, reducing stress in the moment.

Example: Inhale for 4 seconds, hold for 4 seconds, and exhale for 4 seconds during a tense meeting to calm yourself.

2. Break Problems Into Smaller Steps:
Overwhelming decisions feel more manageable when divided into smaller, actionable parts.

Example: If you're overwhelmed by a big project, focus first on creating a timeline or completing one small task.

3. Use Visualization:
Picture a positive outcome to reduce anxiety and regain focus.

Example: Before negotiating, visualize yourself confidently presenting your points and reaching a successful agreement.

4. Establish a Routine:
A predictable routine reduces decision overload, leaving you with more mental energy for critical choices.

Example: Starting your day with a set morning ritual (exercise, breakfast, and reviewing priorities) sets a calm tone.

5. Take Physical Breaks:
Exercise, even for a few minutes, releases tension and clears your mind.

Example: A quick walk or stretch between meetings helps reset your focus.

Everyday Example of Stress Reduction

You're juggling multiple errands and start feeling overwhelmed. Instead of pushing through the stress, pause, take a few deep breaths, and reorganize your tasks into a prioritized list. This simple step helps you feel in control and tackle one thing at a time.

Common Pitfalls in Managing Stress

1. Ignoring Early Warning Signs:
Waiting until stress becomes overwhelming makes it harder to regain control.

2. Avoiding the Problem:
Distracting yourself from stress without addressing its source only delays the inevitable.

3. Relying on Unhealthy Coping Mechanisms:
Turning to habits like overeating or procrastinating might provide short-term relief but worsens stress in the long run.

Takeaway

Stress is unavoidable, but it doesn't have to derail your decision-making. By practicing simple, effective stress-reduction techniques, you can maintain clarity and focus even in high-pressure situations.

Chapter 46: The Pause Principle

The Pause Principle is the idea that stepping back and delaying a decision — even briefly — can lead to better outcomes. When emotions run high or the stakes feel overwhelming, pausing provides the mental space needed to reflect, gather information, and regain perspective.

Example:

Before responding to a heated email, pausing for a few hours helps you craft a calm, professional reply rather than reacting impulsively.

Why Pausing Matters in Decision-Making

1. Reduces Emotional Reactions:

Waiting allows intense emotions like anger, fear, or excitement to settle, preventing impulsive choices.

2. Creates Time for Clarity:

Pausing helps you process complex information, weigh options, and consider long-term consequences.

3. Enhances Perspective:

A break from decision-making can reveal solutions or angles you hadn't considered before.

Example:

A business owner deciding whether to accept an aggressive partnership offer might pause for a day to consult mentors and review the terms with fresh eyes.

How to Practice the Pause Principle

1. Acknowledge the Need to Pause:

Recognize when you're feeling rushed or emotionally overwhelmed, and give yourself permission to wait.

Example: If you feel pressured to decide during a sales pitch, tell the salesperson, "I'll need time to think about it."

2. Set a Specific Timeline:

Pausing doesn't mean procrastinating. Decide how long you'll wait and what you'll do in the meantime.

Example: If you're unsure about accepting a job offer, take 24 hours to reflect and gather more information.

3. Engage in a Calming Activity:

Use the pause to clear your mind, such as taking a walk, meditating, or journaling your thoughts.

Example: If you're stuck on a creative decision, a short break away from your workspace can spark new ideas.

4. Revisit the Decision with a Fresh Perspective:

After the pause, re-evaluate the situation with a clearer, more objective mindset.

Everyday Example of the Pause Principle

Imagine you're deciding whether to make an expensive purchase online. Instead of clicking "Buy Now" immediately, pause for 24 hours to consider whether you truly need the item. Often, the urgency fades, and you can make a more rational decision.

Common Pitfalls in Pausing

1. Confusing Pausing with Procrastination:

Pausing is intentional and productive, while procrastination avoids decision-making altogether.

2. Pausing Indefinitely:

Setting no deadline for your decision can lead to analysis paralysis.

3. Using Pauses to Avoid Responsibility:

Overusing pauses to delay tough choices prevents progress.

Takeaway

The Pause Principle is a powerful tool for decision-making. By taking intentional breaks when you feel rushed or overwhelmed, you gain clarity, avoid impulsive errors, and make choices with greater confidence.

Chapter 47: Handling Regret

Regret is the emotional pain of wishing you'd made a different choice. It's a natural part of decision-making but can become a mental weight that stops you from moving forward. Learning how to handle regret allows you to grow from past experiences instead of being trapped by them.

Example:

You regret not applying for a job that seemed intimidating at the time. Instead of dwelling on it, you use the experience to motivate yourself to seize similar opportunities in the future.

Why Handling Regret Matters

1. Frees You from the Past:

Learning to release regret allows you to focus on the present and future.

2. Encourages Growth:

Reflecting on regret helps you identify lessons and improve future decisions.

3. Prevents Decision Paralysis:

Fear of future regret can stop you from taking necessary risks. By managing regret effectively, you're more willing to make bold choices.

Example in Action:

After regretting a failed investment, a person revises their financial strategy instead of avoiding investments altogether.

How to Handle Regret Gracefully

1. Acknowledge Your Feelings:

Denying regret only prolongs its emotional impact. Accept your feelings to begin moving forward.

Example: Instead of suppressing regret over ending a relationship, admit, "I feel sad about my decision, but I made the best choice with what I knew then."

2. Reframe the Experience:

Focus on what you gained or learned from the situation.

Example: "I didn't get the promotion, but the preparation helped me improve my skills for the next opportunity."

3. Take Action to Improve:

Use regret as motivation to make better decisions in the future.

Example: If you regret skipping a networking event, resolve to attend the next one and prepare in advance.

4. Practice Self-Compassion:

Treat yourself with kindness instead of harsh criticism.

Example: Remind yourself, "I'm human, and mistakes are part of learning."

Everyday Example of Handling Regret

You regret buying an expensive gadget that you barely use. Instead of feeling stuck in the past, you sell it online, recover part of your money, and vow to research more thoroughly before future purchases.

Common Pitfalls in Handling Regret

1. Dwelling on "What Ifs":

Constantly imagining alternate outcomes traps you in a cycle of second-guessing.

2. Letting Regret Define You:

Seeing yourself as a "failure" because of one choice undermines your confidence.

3. Avoiding Risks Entirely:

Fear of future regret can lead to overly cautious decisions, stifling growth.

Takeaway

Regret is a powerful teacher if you let it be. By acknowledging your feelings, reframing your experiences, and focusing on growth, you can move forward gracefully and make peace with past decisions.

Chapter 48: Mindfulness Practices

Mindfulness is the practice of bringing your full attention to the present moment, free of judgment or distraction. In decision-making, mindfulness helps you focus on what matters, process information clearly, and resist impulsive reactions. It sharpens your awareness of both your thoughts and emotions, ensuring your choices align with your goals and values.

Example:

When faced with a tough choice, practicing mindfulness allows you to stay calm, assess the options objectively, and avoid being swayed by fleeting emotions.

Why Mindfulness Matters in Decision-Making

1. Increases Focus:

By tuning out distractions, you can fully engage with the decision at hand.

2. Reduces Emotional Reactivity:

Mindfulness helps you observe emotions without letting them cloud your judgment.

3. Enhances Clarity:

It allows you to view situations objectively, free from assumptions or mental clutter.

Example:

A leader preparing for a critical meeting uses mindfulness to calm pre-presentation nerves, enabling them to think clearly and respond thoughtfully.

How to Practice Mindfulness for Better Decisions

1. Pause and Breathe:

Take a few deep breaths to ground yourself before tackling a decision.

Example: When overwhelmed by competing priorities, pause for a minute to breathe deeply, reducing stress and improving focus.

2. Focus on the Present Moment:

Bring your attention fully to the task at hand, avoiding the urge to multitask.

Example: If reviewing a proposal, set aside distractions like emails or phone notifications to give it your full attention.

3. Acknowledge Your Thoughts:

Notice any mental distractions, biases, or emotions, but don't let them control you.

Example: If you feel anxious about a decision, acknowledge the anxiety without acting on it impulsively.

4. Use Guided Mindfulness Exercises:

Practices like body scans, meditation apps, or mindful walking can help train your focus over time.

Example: Spend 5–10 minutes daily focusing on your breathing to build mindfulness as a habit.

Everyday Example of Mindfulness

You're deciding whether to accept a last-minute invitation to an event. Instead of rushing to respond, you take a moment to focus on how the decision aligns with your priorities. Mindfulness helps you choose based on what matters most, rather than social pressure.

Common Pitfalls in Mindfulness Practices

1. Expecting Instant Results:

Mindfulness is a skill that improves with consistent practice, not a quick fix.

2. Overcomplicating the Process:

You don't need elaborate techniques — even a minute of focused breathing can make a difference.

3. Using Mindfulness to Avoid Action:

Reflection is important, but it should lead to thoughtful decisions, not endless contemplation.

Takeaway

Mindfulness empowers you to approach decisions with clarity, focus, and calm. By grounding yourself in the present moment and observing your thoughts without judgment, you can make choices that reflect your true priorities and values.

Chapter 49: Cultivating Resilience

What Is Resilience in Decision-Making?

Resilience is the ability to recover from setbacks, adapt to change, and keep moving forward after failure. In decision-making, resilience means learning from mistakes, staying persistent in the face of challenges, and maintaining confidence in your ability to make progress.

Example:

After a failed product launch, a resilient entrepreneur analyzes what went wrong, adjusts their strategy, and tries again with a new approach.

Why Resilience Matters in Decision-Making

1. Encourages Growth:

Resilience helps you view failure as a stepping stone rather than an endpoint.

2. Builds Confidence:

Knowing you can recover from setbacks makes you more willing to take calculated risks.

3. Improves Long-Term Success:

Resilience allows you to stay committed to your goals, even when facing temporary obstacles.

Example:

A student who fails an exam doesn't give up but instead studies harder, seeks help, and improves their performance on the next test.

How to Cultivate Resilience

1. Reframe Failure as Feedback:

Treat every setback as an opportunity to learn and improve.

Example: Instead of thinking, "I'm bad at negotiating," reflect on what you can do differently next time.

2. Focus on What You Can Control:

Let go of factors outside your influence and channel your energy into actionable steps.

Example: If a job interview doesn't go well, focus on preparing for the next one rather than dwelling on the outcome.

3. Build a Support Network:

Surround yourself with people who encourage and challenge you to keep going.

Example: Share your struggles with mentors, friends, or colleagues who can provide perspective and advice.

4. Practice Self-Compassion:

Be kind to yourself during difficult times and remind yourself that setbacks are part of the process.

Example: Instead of harshly criticizing yourself for a mistake, say, "I'm learning and growing through this experience."

Everyday Example of Resilience

You start a fitness routine but miss a few workouts during a busy week. Instead of giving up entirely, you remind yourself that progress isn't perfect and get back on track the next week.

Common Pitfalls in Building Resilience

1. Dwelling on Failure:

Excessively focusing on what went wrong prevents you from moving forward.

2. Ignoring Emotional Recovery:

Resilience isn't just about action; it also involves processing emotions and regaining mental balance.

3. Expecting Instant Progress:

Resilience is built over time through consistent effort and reflection.

Takeaway

Resilience is your greatest ally in decision-making. By embracing failure as part of growth, focusing on what you can control, and nurturing self-compassion, you can bounce back stronger and make better choices in the future.

Chapter 50: Making Peace with Uncertainty

Uncertainty is the unavoidable reality that no decision comes with absolute guarantees. The future is inherently unpredictable, but learning to accept and navigate uncertainty allows you to make progress despite the unknown.

Example:

When choosing to switch careers, uncertainty about the outcome may feel daunting. However, embracing the unknown creates opportunities for growth and new experiences.

Why Embracing Uncertainty Matters

1. Encourages Action:

Waiting for perfect information leads to stagnation. Accepting uncertainty helps you move forward.

2. Increases Flexibility:

Acknowledging the unknown allows you to adapt as circumstances change.

3. Reduces Fear:

Making peace with uncertainty reduces anxiety and empowers you to focus on what you can control.

Example:

An entrepreneur launching a startup embraces the uncertainty of market demand but prepares to pivot based on customer feedback.

How to Make Peace with Uncertainty

1. Focus on Probabilities, Not Guarantees:

Weigh the likelihood of outcomes and act based on the most informed choice.

Example: If you're unsure about investing, consider the risks and potential returns, then make a calculated decision.

2. Plan for Multiple Scenarios:

Prepare backup plans to address various possible outcomes.

Example: When planning an event, consider how you'd adapt to rain or other unexpected changes.

3. Build Confidence in Adaptability:

Remind yourself of past challenges you've overcome, reinforcing your ability to handle uncertainty.

Example: Reflect on a time when you thrived despite not knowing the full picture upfront.

4. Take Incremental Steps:

Break big decisions into smaller, manageable actions to reduce the pressure of uncertainty.

Example: Instead of committing to a major move all at once, visit the new city and test the waters first.

Everyday Example of Embracing Uncertainty

You're trying a new recipe for a dinner party, unsure how it will turn out. By focusing on the process, enjoying the experience, and having a backup dish ready, you reduce anxiety about the outcome.

Common Pitfalls in Handling Uncertainty

1. Paralysis by Analysis:

Overthinking every variable can prevent you from taking action.

2. Seeking Absolute Certainty:

Waiting for perfect clarity wastes time and delays progress.

3. Underpreparing for Risks:

While embracing uncertainty is important, ignoring potential challenges can lead to avoidable setbacks.

Takeaway

Uncertainty is a constant in decision-making, but it doesn't have to be paralyzing. By focusing on probabilities, planning flexibly, and building confidence in your ability to adapt, you can embrace the unknown as a source of opportunity rather than fear.

Section VI: Group and Team Decision-Making

In this section, you'll learn techniques for turning group dynamics into an advantage rather than a challenge, ensuring fair, informed, and effective decisions.

Chapter 51: Consensus-Building

What Is Consensus-Building?

Consensus-building is the process of finding common ground among a group with differing opinions. It's not about forcing complete agreement or compromising on every issue but creating a solution that everyone can support and feels invested in.

Example:

When planning a team event, consensus might mean choosing a venue that's not everyone's first choice but meets key needs like accessibility and cost.

Why Consensus-Building Matters

1. Increases Buy-In:

When people feel heard and included, they're more likely to support the final decision.

2. Improves Decision Quality:

By considering multiple perspectives, you're less likely to miss important factors.

3. Reduces Conflict:

A collaborative approach minimizes resentment and fosters teamwork.

Example in Action:

A city council uses consensus-building to decide on a budget by inviting input from all stakeholders and addressing key concerns transparently.

How to Build Consensus

1. Define Shared Goals:

Start by identifying the group's common objectives to keep discussions focused.

Example: If your team is choosing a project management tool, agree that the priority is ease of use and compatibility with existing systems.

2. Encourage Open Dialogue:

Create a safe space where everyone feels comfortable sharing their views, even if they differ from the majority.

Example: Use a round-robin format to ensure quieter members have a chance to speak.

3. Identify Key Areas of Agreement and Disagreement:

Highlight shared opinions and focus discussions on resolving specific points of contention.

Example: If most team members agree on a timeline but differ on the budget, spend time aligning expectations around costs.

4. Use a Facilitator:

Appoint someone to guide the discussion, keep it on track, and ensure everyone's voice is heard.

Example: A neutral facilitator can summarize points and mediate when discussions become heated.

Everyday Example of Consensus-Building

Your family is deciding where to go on vacation. Instead of letting one person decide, everyone lists their priorities. Through discussion, you agree on a destination that includes activities everyone can enjoy, like hiking and sightseeing.

Common Pitfalls in Consensus-Building

1. Forcing Agreement:

Seeking unanimous approval can lead to frustration or watered-down decisions.

2. Ignoring Minority Voices:

Rushing to agreement may silence valuable dissenting opinions.

3. Taking Too Long:

Endless discussions can delay decisions. Set clear timelines for reaching consensus.

Takeaway

Consensus-building aligns diverse opinions. By fostering open dialogue, focusing on shared goals, and resolving disagreements collaboratively, you can turn differences into a strength.

Chapter 52: Avoiding Power Dynamics

What Are Power Dynamics in Group Decisions?

Power dynamics refer to the influence that authority, status, or personality can have on a group's decision-making process. When unchecked, power imbalances can silence important perspectives or push the group toward biased outcomes.

Example:

In a team meeting, a manager's strong opinion might discourage others from sharing alternative ideas, leading to a decision based on authority rather than collaboration.

Why Avoiding Power Dynamics Matters

1. Ensures Equal Contribution:

Fair processes encourage everyone to share their ideas, leading to richer discussions.

2. Reduces Bias:

Decisions are more objective when they're not dominated by one person's influence.

3. Builds Trust:

Teams that feel valued and respected are more engaged and collaborative.

Example:

A project leader who invites quiet team members to share their input ensures that decisions reflect diverse perspectives, not just the loudest voice in the room.

How to Avoid Power Dynamics

1. Use a Neutral Facilitator:

Appoint someone to lead discussions impartially, ensuring no single voice dominates.

Example: A facilitator might say, "Let's hear from those who haven't spoken yet."

2. Encourage Anonymous Input:

Use surveys, suggestion boxes, or online tools to collect ideas without revealing names.

Example: When deciding on a new workplace policy, an anonymous poll can ensure that employees feel safe sharing honest opinions.

3. Rotate Leadership Roles:

Share responsibility for leading discussions to prevent hierarchical influence.

Example: Each team member takes turns running weekly meetings to create a more balanced dynamic.

4. Create Clear Guidelines:

Establish rules for discussions, such as limiting interruptions or giving everyone equal speaking time.

Example: Set a timer to ensure each participant has a chance to speak during brainstorming sessions.

Everyday Example of Avoiding Power Dynamics

At a family gathering, one person usually decides what's for dinner. To make the process fairer, everyone writes down a meal idea, and the group votes anonymously, ensuring all preferences are considered equally.

Common Pitfalls in Avoiding Power Dynamics

1. Allowing Dominance:

Without clear guidelines, strong personalities or authority figures may still control the discussion.

2. Neglecting Quiet Voices:

Introverted or junior members may hesitate to speak unless actively encouraged.

3. Overcompensating for Authority:

Trying too hard to suppress leaders' input can exclude valuable expertise.

Takeaway

Avoiding power dynamics ensures that decisions are fair, collaborative, and representative of the group's collective wisdom. By creating equal opportunities to contribute and neutralizing imbalances, you empower teams to reach better outcomes together.

Chapter 53: The Wisdom of Crowds

What Is the Wisdom of Crowds?

The Wisdom of Crowds is the concept that groups of diverse individuals, working together or independently, can often make better decisions than a single expert. By pooling their varied knowledge, experiences, and perspectives, groups can identify innovative solutions and avoid blind spots.

Example:

In a business setting, a diverse team brainstorming ideas for a marketing campaign may collectively generate more creative and effective strategies than a single marketing expert working alone.

Why the Wisdom of Crowds Matters

1. Taps Into Diverse Perspectives:

A wide range of viewpoints uncovers insights that individuals might miss.

2. Reduces Individual Bias:

Groups dilute the influence of personal biases, leading to more balanced decisions.

3. Leads to Better Predictions:

Aggregating estimates from multiple people often results in more accurate forecasts.

Example:

Crowdsourcing platforms like Kickstarter rely on the wisdom of the crowd to identify which creative projects resonate most with potential backers.

How to Leverage the Wisdom of Crowds

1. Foster Diversity:

Include people with different backgrounds, skills, and perspectives to enrich group discussions.

Example: When forming a task force, invite members from different departments to provide varied expertise.

2. Encourage Independent Input:

Collect individual opinions before group discussions to avoid the influence of groupthink.

Example: Before a strategy meeting, ask team members to submit their ideas anonymously.

3. Aggregate Insights Systematically:

Use structured methods to combine group input, such as voting, ranking, or statistical analysis.

Example: When forecasting sales, collect estimates from all team members and calculate the average.

4. Focus on Problem-Solving:

Direct the group's energy toward clearly defined goals to ensure productive collaboration.

Example: Provide a specific question like, "What features should we prioritize in the next product release?" rather than vague prompts.

Everyday Example of the Wisdom of Crowds

Imagine planning a party. Instead of deciding everything yourself, you ask a group of friends to suggest venues, menus, and activities. Their combined input helps you create a more enjoyable event than you could have planned alone.

1. **Ignoring Diversity:**

   Groups that lack varied perspectives are more likely to fall into groupthink or confirmation bias.

2. **Overvaluing Majority Opinions:**

   Majority opinions aren't always correct — ensure minority views are considered.

3. **Failing to Structure Collaboration:**

   Without clear processes, group discussions can become chaotic or unproductive.

Takeaway

The Wisdom of Crowds highlights the power of collective intelligence in decision-making. By fostering diversity, encouraging independent input, and structuring group processes, you can harness the strengths of collaboration for smarter, more balanced outcomes.

Chapter 54: The Delphi Technique

What Is the Delphi Technique?

The Delphi Technique is a structured, iterative method for solving complex problems or making decisions. It involves gathering input from a panel of experts through multiple rounds of anonymous feedback and refining the group's responses until a consensus emerges. This process minimizes the influence of dominant personalities and encourages thoughtful collaboration.

Example:

A city planning team might use the Delphi Technique to gather expert opinions on how to address traffic congestion, refining proposals through multiple feedback rounds.

Why the Delphi Technique Matters

1. **Encourages Objective Input:**

   Anonymity ensures that ideas are evaluated on their merits rather than the status of the person suggesting them.

2. **Facilitates Informed Consensus:**

   Iterative feedback refines ideas and builds agreement among diverse experts.

3. **Addresses Complex Issues:**

   The technique is ideal for tackling problems with no clear or straightforward solutions.

Example:

Healthcare organizations use the Delphi Technique to develop treatment guidelines by consulting multiple specialists and refining recommendations through feedback rounds.

How to Use the Delphi Technique

1. **Select a Panel of Experts:**

   Choose participants with relevant knowledge and varied perspectives to ensure balanced input.

   Example: For a technology upgrade, include IT professionals, end-users, and budget analysts.

2. **Use Anonymous Surveys:**

   Conduct multiple rounds of anonymous questionnaires to collect opinions and solutions.

   Example: In the first round, ask for open-ended suggestions. In subsequent rounds, refine and rank these ideas.

3. **Iterate Feedback:**

   Share summarized responses after each round to guide further refinement.

   Example: Present a narrowed list of traffic solutions to the panel, asking them to rank or critique the options.

4. **Achieve Consensus:**

   Continue the process until the group reaches a consensus or a well-defined set of recommendations.

   Example: After several rounds, the city planning team agrees on prioritizing public transit improvements.

Everyday Example of the Delphi Technique

Imagine organizing a neighborhood event. You ask residents for anonymous suggestions on activities, then narrow the list and gather feedback through follow-up surveys. This process ensures that the event reflects the community's collective preferences.

1. **Choosing the Wrong Experts:**

   Including participants without relevant expertise can dilute the quality of feedback.

2. **Skipping Iterations:**

   Rushing the process undermines the value of refinement and consensus-building.

3. **Overcomplicating the Process:**

   Too many rounds or overly complex questions can lead to participant fatigue.

Takeaway

The Delphi Technique is a powerful tool for collaborative problem-solving, especially when dealing with complex or uncertain issues. By structuring feedback, fostering objectivity, and refining ideas iteratively, you can guide groups toward informed, effective decisions.

Chapter 55: Role Assignment

What Is Role Assignment in Decision-Making?

Role assignment is the process of clearly defining each person's responsibilities within a group. It ensures that everyone knows their specific tasks, preventing duplication of effort, confusion, or gaps in execution. Clear role assignment is essential for both efficient decision-making and effective follow-through.

Example:

In a product launch, one team member might handle marketing, another logistics, and a third customer support. Clear assignments ensure each aspect of the project is covered without overlap or confusion.

Why Role Assignment Matters

1. **Enhances Accountability:**

When roles are clearly defined, team members understand what's expected of them and take ownership of their tasks.

2. **Prevents Confusion:**

   Role clarity eliminates misunderstandings about who's responsible for what, ensuring smoother collaboration.

3. **Increases Efficiency:**

   Assigning specific roles helps the group focus on individual strengths, streamlining decision-making and execution.

Example:

During an event planning meeting, assigning roles like "Budget Manager" and "Venue Coordinator" ensures that key tasks are handled without redundancy or missed deadlines.

How to Assign Roles Effectively

1. **Identify Key Tasks:**

   Break the project or decision into its major components, such as research, communication, and implementation.

   Example: In a marketing campaign, tasks might include content creation, data analysis, and ad placement.

2. **Match Roles to Strengths:**

   Assign tasks based on each person's skills, experience, and preferences to maximize effectiveness.

   Example: If someone is detail-oriented, assign them the task of proofreading documents.

3. **Clearly Communicate Expectations:**

   Define each role's responsibilities and deadlines to ensure everyone understands their part.

   Example: "As the Research Lead, you'll collect and summarize competitor data by next Friday."

4. **Provide Support and Flexibility:**

   Encourage collaboration and adaptability, allowing team members to step in for each other if needed.

   Example: If the Logistics Manager is overwhelmed, another member might assist with vendor coordination.

Your family is organizing a holiday dinner. To simplify planning, one person handles the shopping list, another cooks, and a third decorates. By dividing tasks based on each person's strengths, the process becomes more organized and enjoyable.

Common Pitfalls in Role Assignment

1. Assigning Roles Arbitrarily:

Ignoring individual strengths and interests can lead to poor performance and frustration.

2. Failing to Communicate:

Unclear roles often result in duplicate efforts or overlooked tasks.

3. Overloading One Person:

Uneven task distribution can cause resentment or burnout.

Takeaway

Role assignment brings structure, clarity, and accountability to group decision-making. By matching tasks to individual strengths and communicating expectations clearly, you can ensure smoother collaboration and more effective outcomes.

Chapter 56: Conflict Resolution Skills

What Are Conflict Resolution Skills?

Conflict resolution involves addressing disagreements constructively to reach a solution that respects all parties involved. In group decision-making, conflicts can arise from differing priorities, opinions, or values. The goal isn't to avoid conflict but to navigate it in a way that strengthens the group's collaboration.

Example:

Two team members might disagree about how to allocate a budget. Effective conflict resolution ensures that both perspectives are heard, leading to a fair compromise.

Why Conflict Resolution Matters

1. Strengthens Relationships:

Addressing conflicts openly fosters trust and mutual respect.

2. Leads to Better Decisions:

Healthy disagreements can uncover blind spots and lead to more innovative solutions.

3. Prevents Escalation:

Resolving conflicts early prevents misunderstandings from growing into larger issues.

Example:

A project manager mediates between two designers who disagree on branding elements, encouraging collaboration to create a unified design that blends their ideas.

How to Resolve Conflicts Productively

1. Listen Actively:

Focus on understanding each person's perspective without interrupting or judging.

Example: Repeat back key points to show you're listening: "So, you're concerned about the timeline being too short?"

2. Stay Objective:

Focus on the issue, not the individuals involved, to avoid personal attacks or defensiveness.

Example: Frame the conflict as a shared challenge: "How can we balance speed with quality?"

3. Encourage Open Dialogue:

Create a safe space for everyone to express their thoughts and feelings honestly.

Example: "Let's take turns sharing our perspectives so we can fully understand each other's concerns."

4. Seek Common Ground:

Identify shared goals or values to build a foundation for compromise.

Example: "We all agree that delivering a high-quality product is the priority, so let's focus on how to achieve that together."

5. Propose and Evaluate Solutions:

Brainstorm possible resolutions, weighing the pros and cons of each.

Example: "What if we adjust the deadline slightly to allow for additional quality checks?"

Everyday Example of Conflict Resolution

Two roommates argue about household chores. By discussing their expectations and creating a clear schedule, they resolve the issue and improve their living arrangement.

Common Pitfalls in Conflict Resolution

1. Avoiding the Issue:

Ignoring conflicts often makes them worse, as frustrations build over time.

2. Taking Sides:

In group settings, biased mediation can worsen tensions.

3. Focusing on Winning:

Viewing conflict as a competition prevents collaborative problem-solving.

Takeaway

Conflict is an inevitable part of group decision-making, but it doesn't have to be destructive. By fostering open communication, focusing on shared goals, and approaching disagreements with respect, you can turn conflicts into opportunities for growth and stronger collaboration.

Chapter 57: Decision Mapping for Teams

What Is Decision Mapping?

Decision mapping is a visual tool that outlines the choices, consequences, and potential outcomes involved in a decision. For teams, it provides a structured way to organize ideas, clarify roles, and ensure everyone understands the bigger picture. It's especially helpful for breaking down complex problems into manageable parts.

Example:

When planning a company expansion, a decision map might include branches for location options, costs, potential risks, and long-term benefits, helping the team evaluate all factors systematically.

Why Decision Mapping Matters

1. Improves Clarity:

A visual representation helps teams see the connections between choices and outcomes, reducing confusion.

2. Encourages Collaboration:

Mapping decisions ensures all team members can contribute their ideas and understand the logic behind decisions.

3. Simplifies Complexity:

Breaking a big decision into smaller components makes it easier to analyze and discuss.

Example:

A nonprofit team uses decision mapping to plan a fundraising event, outlining choices for venue, marketing strategies, and ticket pricing, along with their potential impacts.

How to Use Decision Mapping in Teams

1. Start with the Main Question:

Write the central decision you need to make in the middle of the map.

Example: "Which software should we adopt for project management?"

2. Identify Key Choices:

Branch out from the central question with the major options or pathways available.

Example: Branches might include "Tool A," "Tool B," and "Tool C."

3. List Pros, Cons, and Consequences:

Under each branch, map out the benefits, drawbacks, and potential outcomes of each choice.

Example: For "Tool A," list factors like cost, ease of use, and compatibility with existing systems.

4. Incorporate Team Input:

Invite all team members to suggest ideas or identify risks, adding their contributions to the map.

Example: Someone might point out hidden costs or opportunities you hadn't considered.

5. Evaluate and Decide:

Use the map to compare options, prioritize key factors, and reach a consensus.

Everyday Example of Decision Mapping

You're planning a family vacation. A decision map might include branches for destinations, travel costs, activities, and weather conditions, helping everyone agree on the best option based on shared priorities.

Common Pitfalls in Decision Mapping

1. Overloading the Map:

Including too much detail can make the map overwhelming and counterproductive.

2. Skipping Collaboration:

If only one person creates the map, it may miss important perspectives.

3. Focusing Only on Short-Term Outcomes:

Ensure the map includes long-term implications to provide a complete picture.

Takeaway

Decision mapping turns complex choices into clear, visual pathways. By organizing options, consequences, and feedback in one place, teams can collaborate more effectively and make decisions with confidence and transparency.

Chapter 58: Encouraging Constructive Dissent

What Is Constructive Dissent?

Constructive dissent is the practice of encouraging team members to voice disagreements or alternative ideas in a respectful, productive way. It challenges groupthink, sparks innovation, and ensures all perspectives are considered before reaching a decision.

Example:

During a product design meeting, one team member points out potential flaws in a proposed feature, leading to a better alternative that saves time and resources.

Why Constructive Dissent Matters

1. Prevents Groupthink:

Encouraging dissent ensures decisions aren't made just to maintain harmony, leading to better outcomes.

2. Uncovers Blind Spots:

Alternative viewpoints can reveal risks or opportunities the group might otherwise overlook.

3. Fosters Creativity:

Disagreement forces the team to think critically and explore new ideas.

A marketing team planning a campaign avoids a costly mistake when one member questions the target audience's preferences, prompting a reevaluation of their approach.

How to Encourage Constructive Dissent

1. Create a Safe Space:

Foster a culture where dissent is welcomed and respected, not punished or dismissed.

Example: "All ideas are valid here, and differing opinions are encouraged."

2. Frame Dissent as Collaboration:

Position disagreements as a way to improve the group's ideas, not as personal attacks.

Example: "That's a good point — let's explore how we can address it."

3. Model Dissent as a Leader:

Leaders should ask critical questions or play devil's advocate to show that dissent is valued.

Example: "What's the strongest argument against this idea?"

4. Focus on Evidence, Not Emotion:

Encourage team members to support their dissent with data or logic rather than personal preferences.

Example: "I disagree with this budget allocation because past campaigns showed better ROI with a smaller spend on social ads."

Everyday Example of Constructive Dissent

During a group project at school, one member points out that the team's proposed solution doesn't fully address the assignment criteria. This sparks a discussion that leads to a more effective final plan.

Common Pitfalls in Constructive Dissent

1. Ignoring Dissent:

Dismissing alternative ideas discourages participation and weakens team trust.

2. Confusing Dissent with Conflict:

Disagreement doesn't mean disrespect — focus on the idea, not the person.

3. Overemphasizing Consensus:

Pushing for agreement too quickly can stifle important feedback.

Takeaway

Constructive dissent turns disagreement into a powerful decision-making tool. By creating a culture that values alternative perspectives and critical thinking, teams can avoid groupthink, uncover better solutions, and make stronger choices together.

Chapter 59: Combating Group Polarization

What Is Group Polarization?

Group polarization occurs when group discussions push members toward more extreme positions than they initially held. Instead of reaching balanced decisions, group dynamics amplify shared emotions, beliefs, or biases, leading to overly risky or overly cautious outcomes.

Example:

In a team debate about a marketing strategy, a group that initially favored a modest budget might escalate toward cutting it drastically after reinforcing one another's fears about overspending.

Why Group Polarization Matters

1. Skews Decision-Making:

Extreme group opinions often overlook important nuances or alternative options.

2. Increases Risk:

Polarization can push groups toward decisions that are too risky or overly conservative, depending on the shared mindset.

3. Undermines Collaboration:

Polarized groups may alienate dissenting voices, reducing the quality of the final decision.

Example:

A group of investors initially hesitant about a project might become overly risk-averse, deciding against it altogether after amplifying each other's doubts — even if the project has significant potential.

How to Combat Group Polarization

1. Encourage Diverse Perspectives:

Actively invite opinions that challenge the group's dominant view to introduce balance.

Example: Ask, "What would someone with a different perspective say about this decision?"

2. Focus on Evidence, Not Emotion:

Redirect discussions toward data and facts rather than emotional or subjective arguments.

Example: "Let's review the market analysis again before we decide to cut the budget completely."

3. Appoint a Devil's Advocate:

Assign someone to argue the opposite side of the group's leaning to test assumptions.

Example: In a meeting where the group leans heavily toward risk, a devil's advocate might say, "What happens if we overinvest and the market doesn't respond?"

4. Break Into Smaller Groups:

Divide the group to discuss the issue separately and then compare findings to reduce groupthink.

Example: Two subgroups might analyze different strategies, bringing their perspectives back to the full team for comparison.

5. Revisit Initial Positions:

Ask members to reflect on their original opinions and consider whether the group's shift is rational or emotional.

Example: "Is this conclusion consistent with the preferences we had when we started, or have we drifted too far?"

Everyday Example of Group Polarization

During a neighborhood meeting, initial concerns about traffic from a proposed park lead to extreme objections, like canceling the project altogether. A balanced discussion that focuses on traffic management solutions might help the group return to moderation.

Common Pitfalls in Combating Group Polarization

1. Ignoring Minority Opinions:

Dismissing alternative views strengthens the group's extreme stance.

2. Letting Emotions Drive Decisions:

High emotions, like fear or excitement, fuel polarization.

3. Failing to Intervene:

Allowing the group to spiral without redirection results in less rational decisions.

Takeaway

Group polarization can distort decision-making and lead to extreme outcomes. By fostering diverse perspectives, grounding discussions in evidence, and encouraging critical thinking, you can guide groups back to balanced, well-informed choices.

Chapter 60:
Accountability in Groups

Accountability ensures that group decisions translate into action by assigning clear responsibilities and tracking progress. It's not enough to agree on a decision; each team member must commit to their role in executing it, and the group must monitor results to stay on track.

Example:

After deciding to launch a new product, the team assigns tasks like market research, product development, and marketing to specific members, with deadlines and regular check-ins to ensure accountability.

Why Accountability Matters

1. Ensures Execution:

Accountability bridges the gap between decision-making and action, preventing good ideas from stalling.

2. Builds Trust:

When everyone fulfills their responsibilities, the team develops mutual respect and confidence.

3. Improves Outcomes:

Regular progress reviews allow teams to identify and address obstacles early.

Example:

A charity planning a fundraiser assigns one member to handle sponsorship outreach and another to manage event logistics. Regular updates ensure tasks are completed on time.

How to Foster Accountability in Groups

1. Assign Specific Roles and Deadlines:

Clearly define who is responsible for each task and set realistic timelines.

Example: "Sam will finalize the vendor contract by Monday, and Alex will prepare the budget report by Friday."

2. Track Progress Regularly:

Schedule check-ins to review progress, address challenges, and maintain momentum.

Example: Weekly meetings might include updates on each team member's progress and upcoming tasks.

3. Document Decisions and Responsibilities:

Record group decisions and share them with everyone to ensure clarity and transparency.

Example: After each meeting, send a summary that lists tasks, owners, and deadlines.

4. Celebrate Success and Address Gaps:

Acknowledge completed tasks while addressing delays or issues constructively.

Example: "Great job on the presentation, Maria! Let's discuss how we can support Liam in completing his report on time."

5. Use Tools for Accountability:

Leverage project management tools like Trello or Asana to assign tasks, set deadlines, and monitor progress.

Everyday Example of Accountability

In a family setting, deciding to renovate the kitchen requires accountability. One member might be tasked with getting quotes, another with choosing materials, and another with setting the budget. Regular updates ensure the project stays on track.

Common Pitfalls in Group Accountability

1. Vague Assignments:

Failing to specify who is responsible for what leads to confusion and inaction.

2. Lack of Follow-Up:

Without progress checks, tasks may be delayed or forgotten.

3. Blaming Without Support:

Criticizing team members for missed tasks without offering solutions undermines morale.

Takeaway

Accountability is the foundation of effective group decision-making and execution. By assigning clear responsibilities, tracking progress, and fostering a culture of support, teams can ensure that their decisions lead to meaningful, actionable outcomes.

Section VII: Strategic Thinking for Long-Term Success

Big decisions require big-picture thinking. Strategic decision-making isn't just about solving today's problems — it's about anticipating tomorrow's challenges and opportunities. This section equips you with tools to plan for the future, weigh probabilities, and take decisive action when the moment is right.

Chapter 61: Game Theory Basics

What Is Game Theory?

Game theory is the study of strategic interactions where the outcome of your choices depends on the actions of others. It's about thinking beyond your immediate goals and predicting how others will respond to your decisions.

Example:

In negotiations, offering a fair proposal can influence the other party to cooperate rather than compete, leading to a win-win outcome.

Why Game Theory Matters

1. Improves Strategic Thinking:

Game theory forces you to think several steps ahead, like in a chess match.

2. Prepares for Countermoves:

Understanding others' motivations helps you anticipate and prepare for their reactions.

3. Encourages Collaboration:

Identifying mutual benefits reduces unnecessary conflict and creates shared value.

Example:

A company lowering prices to outcompete rivals might anticipate a price war. Instead, offering a unique product feature differentiates them without triggering retaliation.

How to Apply Game Theory in Decision-Making

1. Identify Key Players:

Consider who will be affected by your decision and how they might respond.

Example: If launching a new product, consider competitors, customers, and suppliers.

2. Map Possible Moves:

Visualize the choices available to you and others, along with their likely consequences.

Example: "If I lower prices, competitors might match me. What's my next move if that happens?"

3. Think Win-Win:

Look for strategies that benefit all parties, encouraging cooperation rather than competition.

Example: Collaborating with a competitor on industry standards might grow the market for both companies.

4. Learn from Past Patterns:

Analyze how others have behaved in similar situations to predict their next moves.

Example: "This rival tends to respond aggressively to price cuts. How can I avoid escalating the conflict?"

Everyday Example of Game Theory

You and a friend are deciding where to eat. Instead of competing over preferences, you suggest alternating choices each week, ensuring both feel satisfied in the long term.

Common Pitfalls in Game Theory

1. Overthinking Simple Decisions:

Not every situation requires complex strategic analysis.

2. Assuming Perfect Rationality:

People's emotions and biases may lead them to act unpredictably.

3. Ignoring Long-Term Relationships:

Prioritizing short-term wins over trust and collaboration can backfire.

Takeaway

Game theory teaches you to anticipate others' moves and think several steps ahead. By understanding motivations and mapping possible outcomes, you can make smarter, more strategic decisions that benefit everyone involved.

Chapter 62: The Long View

What Is the Long View?

The Long View means making decisions with a clear understanding of how they'll impact your future. It's about ensuring that today's actions align with your bigger goals, even when short-term temptations or pressures try to pull you off track.

Example:

Choosing to invest in professional development now may require sacrificing leisure time, but it pays off in long-term career growth.

Why the Long View Matters

1. Prevents Short-Sighted Decisions:

Thinking ahead helps you avoid choices that provide immediate gratification but harm your future.

2. Creates Consistency:

Long-term thinking aligns your daily actions with your larger vision.

3. Builds Resilience:

A clear focus on the future helps you weather setbacks and stay committed to your goals.

Example:

A student deciding whether to party or study before exams prioritizes studying, knowing it aligns with their goal of academic success.

How to Adopt the Long View

1. Clarify Your Goals:

Define where you want to be in the next five or ten years to guide your decisions today.

Example: "I want to become a department manager within five years, so I'll focus on leadership opportunities now."

2. Evaluate Short-Term Trade-Offs:

Consider how immediate decisions will affect your long-term progress.

Example: "Should I take this higher-paying job, or should I stick with the one that offers better growth potential?"

3. Plan Milestones:

Break your long-term goals into smaller, achievable steps to stay motivated.

Example: "If I want to run a marathon in two years, I'll start by training for a 5K within six months."

4. Regularly Reassess Your Path:

Check periodically to ensure your current actions are still aligned with your long-term vision.

Example: "Does my current spending support my goal of saving for a house?"

Everyday Example of the Long View

You're considering buying a new car. Instead of choosing the flashiest model, you opt for a reliable, fuel-efficient option that aligns with your goal of saving for retirement.

Common Pitfalls in Long-Term Thinking

1. Neglecting Present Needs:

Focusing too much on the future can leave you unprepared for immediate challenges.

2. Getting Discouraged by Slow Progress:

Long-term goals often take time, so patience is essential.

3. Failing to Adapt:

Life circumstances may change, requiring you to adjust your plans.

Takeaway

The Long View helps you align today's choices with your future goals. By staying focused on the bigger picture and balancing short-term sacrifices with long-term gains, you can build a path toward sustainable success.

Chapter 63: Scenario Thinking

What Is Scenario Thinking?

Scenario thinking involves imagining a range of possible futures and preparing for each. Rather than fixating on a single expected outcome, you explore various scenarios — good, bad, and in-between — to build flexible strategies that work across different possibilities.

Example:

A business might plan for multiple futures by considering how economic growth, stagnation, or decline could affect their operations, adjusting their strategies accordingly.

Why Scenario Thinking Matters

1. Reduces Risk:

Planning for multiple outcomes helps you prepare for unexpected challenges.

2. Improves Flexibility:

By anticipating a range of possibilities, you can adapt quickly as situations evolve.

3. Encourages Creative Problem-Solving:

Thinking beyond the "most likely" scenario opens your mind to new strategies.

Example:

A family planning a vacation considers scenarios like bad weather, budget changes, or travel delays, allowing them to create backup plans for each.

How to Practice Scenario Thinking

1. Define Your Key Question:

Start with a clear decision or goal you're trying to address.

Example: "How will my business grow in the next five years?"

2. Identify Driving Forces:

List factors that could influence your decision, such as economic trends, technological changes, or personal circumstances.

Example: "What happens if new competitors enter the market?"

3. Create Multiple Scenarios:

Develop 3-5 distinct futures: a best-case scenario, a worst-case scenario, and several plausible in-between outcomes.

Example: Best case: Revenue doubles due to market demand. Worst case: A recession cuts revenue in half.

4. Develop Action Plans:

For each scenario, outline strategies to maximize opportunities or mitigate risks.

Example: If the economy declines, the business might focus on cost-saving measures and recession-proof products.

5. Monitor and Adjust:

Continuously track key indicators to identify which scenario is unfolding and adapt your plans as needed.

Example: Rising costs might signal a need to pivot to the worst-case scenario strategy.

Everyday Example of Scenario Thinking

You're deciding whether to move to a new city for a job. Scenarios might include:

- Best case: You thrive in the role and love the city.
- Likely case: The job is good, but the city takes time to adjust to.
- Worst case: The role isn't as expected, and the move strains your finances.

By considering all outcomes, you can prepare financially and emotionally for each.

Common Pitfalls in Scenario Thinking

1. Overloading with Scenarios:

Too many scenarios can lead to confusion and indecision. Focus on 3-5 key ones.

2. Ignoring Unlikely but Impactful Scenarios:

Rare events, like economic downturns, should still be considered due to their potential impact.

3. Failing to Act:

Scenario planning is only useful if it leads to concrete strategies.

Takeaway

Scenario thinking equips you to plan for uncertainty by imagining and preparing for multiple futures. By developing flexible strategies, you can navigate unexpected challenges with confidence and resilience.

Chapter 64: Red Teaming

What Is Red Teaming?

Red Teaming is a method where you deliberately challenge your decisions or plans by adopting the role of an opponent. By thinking like critics or competitors, you identify weaknesses, test assumptions, and refine your strategies before implementing them.

Example:

A company planning a product launch might assign a "red team" to act as customers and competitors, highlighting potential flaws in the campaign.

Why Red Teaming Matters

1. Exposes Blind Spots:

By challenging assumptions, red teaming reveals weaknesses you might overlook.

2. Prepares for Countermoves:

Anticipating criticism or opposition strengthens your ability to respond effectively.

3. Improves Decision Quality:

Testing your ideas under scrutiny ensures they're robust and well-thought-out.

Example:

A non-profit uses red teaming to identify potential objections to a fundraising campaign, refining their messaging to address concerns in advance.

How to Red Team Your Decisions

1. Assemble a Red Team:

Include people who are willing to challenge ideas constructively. Ideally, choose individuals with diverse perspectives.

Example: A marketing team invites colleagues from finance and customer support to critique their strategy.

2. Set Clear Rules:

Define the scope and goals of the red team's critique to keep discussions focused.

Example: "Your role is to identify why this ad campaign might fail and propose solutions."

3. Think Like an Opponent:

Challenge every assumption, looking for vulnerabilities or overlooked risks.

Example: "What would a competitor do to outshine our product launch?"

4. Incorporate Feedback:

Use the red team's insights to strengthen your plan, address weaknesses, and develop contingency strategies.

Example: If the red team points out confusing messaging, the campaign is revised for clarity.

5. Re-Test Your Plan:

After implementing changes, run another round of critiques to ensure the strategy is solid.

Everyday Example of Red Teaming

Before buying a new home, you ask friends and family to critique your choice. One points out that the commute might be longer than expected, prompting you to reconsider.

Common Pitfalls in Red Teaming

1. Taking Criticism Personally:

Red teaming isn't about attacking you — it's about improving the plan.

2. Skipping Implementation:

Insights from red teaming are only valuable if they lead to actionable improvements.

3. Limiting Diverse Perspectives:

A homogenous red team might miss critical weaknesses.

Takeaway

Red teaming strengthens decisions by challenging them. By thinking like an opponent and refining your strategy based on critique, you can address risks, overcome blind spots, and make more robust choices.

Chapter 65: Bets and Odds

What Is Probabilistic Thinking?

Probabilistic thinking involves evaluating the likelihood of various outcomes rather than expecting certainty. It means treating decisions like bets, where you assess risks and rewards based on the odds of success. By thinking probabilistically, you reduce overconfidence and make decisions that are grounded in reality.

Example:

Before starting a business, you might estimate that you have a 60% chance of succeeding based on market research and a 40% chance of facing challenges like high competition. This helps you weigh the risks and prepare accordingly.

Why Probabilistic Thinking Matters

1. Reduces Overconfidence:

Recognizing uncertainty helps you avoid assuming your decisions are guaranteed to succeed.

2. Encourages Risk Management:

Evaluating probabilities allows you to prepare for less likely but impactful scenarios.

3. Improves Decision Accuracy:

By focusing on likelihoods, you make better-informed choices and adjust expectations.

Example:

An investor might assign probabilities to different market scenarios (growth, stagnation, decline) and diversify their portfolio to reduce risk.

How to Think Probabilistically

1. Estimate the Odds:

Assess the likelihood of various outcomes based on evidence, experience, or data.

Example: When planning a project, estimate the odds of completing it on time based on past timelines.

2. Consider the Payoffs:

Evaluate the potential benefits and losses for each outcome to determine if the risk is worth taking.

Example: If a risky investment offers a small chance of high returns and a high chance of modest losses, it may still be worth considering.

3. Prepare for Multiple Outcomes:

Develop plans for both likely and unlikely scenarios to stay adaptable.

Example: A traveler might pack for sunny weather while also including an umbrella, just in case.

4. Use Tools to Model Probabilities:

Tools like decision trees or Bayesian reasoning can help you visualize probabilities and outcomes.

Example: A decision tree might outline the probability of achieving specific sales goals under different marketing strategies.

Everyday Example of Probabilistic Thinking

You're deciding whether to buy extended insurance for a new appliance. You estimate that there's a 20% chance it will break within the warranty period. Weighing the low probability of failure against the cost of the insurance helps you decide.

Common Pitfalls in Probabilistic Thinking

1. Underestimating Rare Events:

People often dismiss unlikely scenarios, even when their impact could be significant.

2. Overvaluing Certainty:

Avoid insisting on guarantees; few decisions are risk-free.

3. Focusing Solely on Probabilities:

Probabilities are helpful, but also consider the consequences of extreme outcomes.

Takeaway

Probabilistic thinking helps you make smarter, more grounded decisions by focusing on likelihoods rather than certainties. By weighing odds, evaluating payoffs, and preparing for multiple outcomes, you can navigate uncertainty with confidence.

Chapter 66: Competitive Analysis

What Is Competitive Analysis?

Competitive analysis involves studying your rivals' strategies, strengths, and weaknesses to inform your decisions. Whether in business, sports, or personal challenges, understanding the competition allows you to anticipate moves, identify opportunities, and refine your approach.

Example:

A company researching competitors' pricing models might adjust their own pricing to offer better value or emphasize unique features.

Why Competitive Analysis Matters

1. Reveals Opportunities:

Analyzing rivals' gaps or weaknesses helps you uncover advantages.

2. Improves Strategy:

Understanding what works for competitors can inspire improvements in your own approach.

3. Prepares for Countermoves:

Anticipating rivals' actions allows you to adjust your strategy proactively.

Example:

A small bakery identifies that competitors lack gluten-free options, so they focus on offering a robust gluten-free menu to attract new customers.

How to Conduct Competitive Analysis

1. Identify Your Key Competitors:

Focus on those whose goals, audiences, or markets overlap with yours.

Example: A local coffee shop might analyze other cafes within a 5-mile radius.

2. Study Their Strengths and Weaknesses:

Look at what competitors do well and where they fall short.

Example: If a rival has great branding but slow service, you might focus on speed to stand out.

3. Analyze Their Strategy:

Study their pricing, marketing, customer base, and product offerings to understand their approach.

Example: What promotions are they running? What customer needs are they targeting?

4. Compare and Differentiate:

Use insights to highlight your unique strengths and stand out from the competition.

Example: A fitness center might focus on offering flexible class schedules if competitors prioritize high-end equipment.

5. Monitor Continuously:

Competitive landscapes evolve, so revisit your analysis regularly.

Example: Quarterly reviews of competitors' strategies help you adapt to market changes.

Everyday Example of Competitive Analysis

Before applying for a job, you review the LinkedIn profiles of other applicants to understand their skills and experiences. This helps you tailor your resume to emphasize what makes you stand out.

Common Pitfalls in Competitive Analysis

1. Copying Without Differentiation:

Mimicking competitors' strategies without highlighting your unique value leads to missed opportunities.

2. Neglecting Smaller Competitors:

Focusing only on industry leaders can cause you to underestimate emerging rivals.

3. Overanalyzing:

Spending too much time studying competitors can delay action.

Takeaway

Competitive analysis equips you with insights to anticipate moves, seize opportunities, and refine your strategies. By understanding your rivals and differentiating yourself, you can position yourself for long-term success.

Chapter 67: The Timing Factor

What Is the Timing Factor?

Timing is the art of knowing when to act. Even the best decision can fail if made too early or too late. The timing factor involves recognizing when circumstances are most favorable and striking when opportunities align.

Example:

A company launching a new product during peak holiday shopping season might achieve greater success than if they launched during a slower time of year.

Why Timing Matters

1. Maximizes Opportunities:

Acting at the right moment allows you to capitalize on favorable conditions.

2. Reduces Risks:

Waiting too long or acting prematurely can lead to missed opportunities or unnecessary risks.

3. Increases Impact:

Well-timed decisions resonate more strongly, whether in business, relationships, or personal goals.

Example:

A job seeker waits until after a company announces growth plans before applying, increasing their chances of being hired for an expanding role.

How to Master the Timing Factor

1. Study the Environment:

Observe external conditions, trends, and signals to identify the optimal moment to act.

Example: A stock trader monitors market indicators to time their investments.

2. Listen to Intuition (Backed by Evidence):

Combine gut feelings with data to sense when the moment is right.

Example: An entrepreneur might trust their intuition to pitch an idea, but only after researching the market.

3. Prepare in Advance:

Readiness allows you to act quickly when the opportunity arises.

Example: A speaker practices their presentation well in advance so they're ready when called upon.

4. Know When to Wait:

Sometimes, delaying a decision can lead to better conditions or clearer information.

Example: A homebuyer might pause their search during a seller's market to wait for prices to stabilize.

Everyday Example of Timing

Imagine you want to discuss a raise with your manager. Instead of bringing it up during a busy project, you wait until the team achieves a big success and the mood is positive.

Common Pitfalls in Timing

1. Rushing Decisions:

Acting impulsively without assessing the situation leads to poor outcomes.

2. Overanalyzing:

Waiting too long out of fear or indecision can cause you to miss the moment entirely.

3. Ignoring Trends:

Failing to recognize shifts in external factors, like market or social changes, can derail timing.

Takeaway

The timing factor is about seizing the right moment to act. By preparing, observing the environment, and balancing intuition with data, you can make impactful decisions that align perfectly with the situation.

Chapter 68: Avoiding Analysis Paralysis

What Is Analysis Paralysis?

Analysis paralysis occurs when overthinking prevents you from making a decision. You become so consumed with gathering data, weighing options, and fearing mistakes that you fail to act. While analysis is important, knowing when to stop is critical for effective decision-making.

Example:

A person researching new laptops for weeks might miss a sale or delay their purchase unnecessarily, despite already having enough information to choose.

Why Avoiding Analysis Paralysis Matters

1. Prevents Missed Opportunities:

Overthinking can cause delays that result in lost chances.

2. Saves Time and Energy:

Knowing when to stop researching frees mental resources for other priorities.

3. Reduces Stress:

Prolonged indecision can lead to frustration and burnout.

Example:

An entrepreneur debating whether to launch a product might miss the market's peak interest by overanalyzing details.

How to Avoid Analysis Paralysis

1. Set a Deadline:

Commit to a decision by a specific time to prevent endless deliberation.

Example: "I'll choose a contractor for the renovation by next Friday."

2. Prioritize Key Factors:

Focus on the most important criteria rather than getting lost in minor details.

Example: When choosing a car, prioritize reliability and cost over less critical features.

3. Limit Information Gathering:

Decide how much research is "enough" and stop once you've reached that threshold.

Example: "After reading five customer reviews, I'll make my decision."

4. Trust Your Judgment:

Recognize that no decision is ever 100% certain, and rely on your intuition when the evidence is sufficient.

Example: A couple chooses a wedding venue after narrowing it down to two strong options, trusting that both would work well.

5. Embrace Imperfection:

Accept that no decision is perfect and focus on moving forward.

Example: "Even if I make a mistake, I'll learn from it and adjust."

Everyday Example of Analysis Paralysis

You're deciding what to cook for dinner. Instead of endlessly scrolling recipes, you pick one that looks good and start cooking, saving time and stress.

Common Pitfalls in Avoiding Analysis Paralysis

1. Fear of Mistakes:

The desire for a "perfect" decision often leads to inaction.

2. Overloading with Data:

Too much information can overwhelm rather than clarify.

3. Failing to Act:

Delaying action can lead to lost opportunities or worsening situations.

Takeaway

Avoiding analysis paralysis means recognizing when you have enough information to act. By setting limits, focusing on key factors, and accepting imperfection, you can make confident decisions and avoid the trap of endless overthinking.

Chapter 69: The Power of Experimentation

What Is Experimentation in Decision-Making?

Experimentation involves testing ideas or options on a small scale before fully committing to them. It's a practical way to gather real-world feedback, validate assumptions, and refine your approach. Instead of making decisions based solely on predictions, you use experiments to confirm what works.

A company testing a new product might release it to a small market segment first, learning from customer feedback before launching on a larger scale.

Why Experimentation Matters

1. Reduces Risk:

Testing ideas on a small scale allows you to identify issues and make adjustments before committing significant resources.

2. Provides Data-Driven Insights:

Experiments yield concrete evidence about what works and what doesn't.

3. Encourages Innovation:

Experimentation fosters a mindset of curiosity and learning, helping you explore unconventional solutions.

Example:

A writer considering self-publishing tests the waters by releasing a short story online to gauge interest and refine their marketing approach.

How to Use Experimentation in Decision-Making

1. Define Your Hypothesis:

Clearly state what you want to test and what outcome you expect.

Example: "If I market the product to younger audiences, I expect higher engagement rates."

2. Start Small:

Test your idea with minimal resources or on a small scale to limit risk.

Example: Launch a beta version of your app with a small user group before a full release.

3. Measure Results:

Collect data to evaluate the success of your experiment against your goals.

Example: Track conversion rates during a trial marketing campaign to determine its effectiveness.

4. Refine and Retest:

Use the insights gained to improve your approach and test again if necessary.

Example: Adjust an ad's messaging based on feedback and run a second test to see if it performs better.

5. Scale Up:

Once your experiment proves successful, expand your efforts with confidence.

Example: A café introduces a new menu item after a successful trial with regular customers.

Everyday Example of Experimentation

You're considering switching careers but aren't sure if the new field is right for you. You take a short online course or freelance part-time to test your interest and aptitude before fully committing.

Common Pitfalls in Experimentation

1. Skipping the Testing Phase:

Jumping straight into full-scale decisions can lead to costly mistakes.

2. Overcomplicating Experiments:

Simple tests are often more effective than elaborate ones.

3. Ignoring Results:

Experiments are only valuable if you use the insights to refine your approach.

Takeaway

Experimentation turns uncertainty into opportunity by testing your ideas in real-world conditions. By starting small, measuring results, and refining your approach, you can make informed decisions with confidence.

Chapter 70: Strategic Patience

What Is Strategic Patience?

Strategic patience is the ability to delay action until conditions are optimal. It's not about passivity or procrastination but about knowing when to wait and when to act. Timing is everything, and sometimes, waiting for the right moment can make the difference between failure and success.

Example:

An investor who waits for the market to stabilize before buying stocks demonstrates strategic patience, maximizing returns while minimizing risk.

Why Strategic Patience Matters

1. Improves Decision Quality:

Rushing into decisions can lead to mistakes. Waiting provides clarity and better conditions for action.

2. Maximizes Resources:

Acting too soon can waste time, energy, or money. Patience ensures you use resources effectively.

3. Builds Long-Term Success:

Delayed gratification often leads to more substantial rewards than short-term gains.

Example:

An entrepreneur waits for technology costs to drop before launching a product, ensuring it's more affordable to produce and sell.

How to Cultivate Strategic Patience

1. Recognize the Value of Timing:

Assess whether the current conditions are favorable for action or if waiting would yield better results.

Example: A professional postpones a major career move until after completing a key certification.

2. Monitor Key Indicators:

Keep track of trends, signals, or events that might influence the right moment to act.

Example: A business monitors consumer demand before launching a new product line.

3. Stay Focused on Your Goals:

Patience is easier when you have a clear vision of what you're working toward.

Example: A family delays purchasing a home until they save enough for a larger down payment, reducing financial strain.

4. Prepare While You Wait:

Use the waiting period to refine your plans, gather resources, or build skills.

Example: While waiting for the market to improve, an investor studies new strategies to maximize future returns.

5. Know When to Stop Waiting:

Patience should not become inaction. Identify deadlines or conditions that signal when it's time to act.

Example: A startup sets a launch deadline to ensure they don't wait so long that competitors gain an advantage.

Everyday Example of Strategic Patience

You're considering buying a car but notice that dealerships often run sales at the end of the year. By waiting, you can purchase the same car at a lower price.

Common Pitfalls in Strategic Patience

1. Confusing Patience with Procrastination:

Waiting must be intentional and strategic, not an excuse to avoid decisions.

2. Missing Opportunities:

Waiting too long can cause you to lose out on favorable conditions.

3. Losing Focus:

Over time, distractions can derail your goals if you're not actively preparing.

Takeaway

Strategic patience is a powerful decision-making tool when used wisely. By recognizing the value of timing, preparing while you wait, and knowing when to act, you can seize opportunities at their peak and achieve greater success.

Section VIII: Everyday Decision-Making

Big life decisions often come down to practical choices. From career paths to financial goals, daily decisions shape the trajectory of your life. This section provides actionable strategies to navigate common yet critical decisions with clarity, confidence, and balance.

Chapter 71: Choosing Careers

What Does It Mean to Align Passion and Practicality?

Choosing a career involves balancing what excites you (passion) with what sustains you financially and practically (practicality). While passion gives you purpose and motivation, practicality ensures long-term stability and growth. The best career decisions blend these elements to create a fulfilling and sustainable path.

Example:

A person passionate about teaching but concerned about income stability might choose to tutor online part-time while pursuing a teaching credential.

Why Aligning Passion and Practicality Matters

1. Sustains Long-Term Motivation:

A career driven by passion is more likely to keep you engaged and energized.

2. Ensures Financial Stability:

Practicality helps you make choices that support your financial goals and responsibilities.

3. Promotes Personal Fulfillment:

Combining both leads to a sense of purpose and balance in your work life.

Example:

An artist passionate about painting may pursue a graphic design job for financial stability while building their painting portfolio on the side.

How to Choose a Career with Balance

1. Assess Your Interests and Skills:

Reflect on what you enjoy and where your strengths lie.

Example: "I love problem-solving and excel at communication. What careers align with these traits?"

2. Evaluate Market Demand:

Research industries or roles that match your interests and are in demand.

Example: A person interested in technology might explore roles like software development or data analysis, which have strong job prospects.

3. Set Financial and Lifestyle Goals:

Determine what income and work-life balance you need to feel secure and satisfied.

Example: If travel is important to you, a remote or flexible job might be a priority.

4. Start Small, Then Build:

Explore your passion through side projects or part-time work before fully committing.

Example: A baking enthusiast starts by selling goods at farmers' markets before opening a bakery.

5. Be Open to Evolution:

Your passions and circumstances may change over time. Stay flexible and adjust your path as needed.

Example: A journalist transitions to content marketing to pursue better pay while still leveraging their writing skills.

Everyday Example of Career Alignment

Someone passionate about fitness might start as a personal trainer but later transition to opening their own gym, combining their love for exercise with entrepreneurial goals.

Common Pitfalls in Career Decisions

1. Choosing Passion Alone:

Ignoring financial realities can lead to burnout or instability.

2. Prioritizing Practicality Too Much:

Overemphasizing stability can leave you feeling unfulfilled.

3. Fearing Change:

Sticking to a career out of comfort or habit may prevent growth.

Takeaway

The best career decisions balance passion and practicality. By aligning what you love with what sustains you, you can build a career that's both fulfilling and realistic.

Chapter 72: Financial Decisions

What Does It Mean to Invest in What Matters?

Financial decisions aren't just about saving or spending; they're about aligning your resources with your values, priorities, and long-term goals. Investing in what matters ensures your money supports both your immediate needs and your future ambitions.

Example:

Instead of buying an expensive car to impress others, a person might prioritize saving for a home, which aligns with their long-term goal of stability.

Why Smart Financial Decisions Matter

1. Builds Stability:

Prioritizing needs over impulsive wants creates a strong financial foundation.

2. Achieves Long-Term Goals:

Investing in what matters helps you stay on track with life objectives like education, retirement, or family needs.

3. Reduces Stress:

Financial security minimizes anxiety about unexpected expenses or future uncertainties.

Example:

A family sets aside a portion of their income for an emergency fund before planning a vacation, ensuring they're prepared for unplanned costs.

How to Make Financial Decisions Wisely

1. Clarify Your Priorities:

Identify your short- and long-term goals, like paying off debt, saving for retirement, or funding a passion project.

Example: "I want to save $10,000 for a down payment on a house within three years."

2. Separate Needs from Wants:

Focus on essentials first, then allocate resources to discretionary spending.

Example: Pay your bills and build savings before splurging on a luxury item.

3. Create a Budget:

Plan your spending and saving to ensure you stay within your means.

Example: Use the 50/30/20 rule: 50% for needs, 30% for wants, and 20% for savings or debt repayment.

4. Evaluate Opportunities for Growth:

Invest in education, skills, or assets that increase your earning potential.

Example: Take a certification course that boosts your qualifications for a higher-paying job.

5. Think Ahead:

Regularly review your financial plans to adjust for life changes or new goals.

Example: After starting a family, you might prioritize saving for your children's education.

Everyday Example of Investing in What Matters

You're deciding between upgrading to the latest phone or starting an emergency savings fund. By choosing savings, you're investing in long-term security over short-term gratification.

Common Pitfalls in Financial Decisions

1. Living Beyond Your Means:

Overspending on wants can leave you unprepared for future expenses.

2. Failing to Save Early:

Delaying savings, especially for retirement, reduces long-term benefits.

3. Neglecting Investments in Growth:

Focusing solely on immediate needs may hinder opportunities for advancement.

Takeaway

Smart financial decisions are about prioritizing what truly matters. By aligning your spending and savings with your goals, you can build a secure future while enjoying life's rewards.

Chapter 73: Time Management

What Is Time Management?

Time management is the deliberate planning and control of how you spend your hours to maximize productivity and achieve your goals. It's about aligning your daily actions with what truly matters, avoiding wasted effort, and maintaining balance between work, rest, and personal priorities.

Example:

A busy parent prioritizes tasks by using the early morning for focused work, reserving the evening for family time, and limiting distractions during key hours.

Why Time Management Matters

1. Increases Productivity:

Structuring your day allows you to accomplish more in less time.

2. Reduces Stress:

Knowing you've allocated time for critical tasks helps you feel in control.

3. Achieves Work-Life Balance:

Time management ensures you dedicate hours to both professional and personal priorities.

Example:

A freelancer uses time-blocking to assign specific hours for client work, exercise, and relaxation, preventing burnout.

How to Manage Time Effectively

1. Set Priorities:

Identify the most important tasks each day and focus on completing them first.

Example: Use the Eisenhower Matrix to distinguish between urgent and important tasks.

2. Use Time-Blocking:

Schedule specific blocks of time for key activities to minimize multitasking.

Example: Reserve 9–11 AM for deep work and 2–3 PM for emails and meetings.

3. Limit Distractions:

Remove interruptions like phone notifications or unnecessary meetings during focus periods.

Example: Turn off social media alerts while working on a project.

4. Plan Tomorrow, Today:

At the end of each day, review what you've accomplished and prepare your task list for tomorrow.

Example: Write down the top three tasks to tackle first thing in the morning.

5. Schedule Breaks:

Taking regular breaks improves focus and prevents burnout.

Example: Use the Pomodoro Technique: work for 25 minutes, then take a 5-minute break.

Everyday Example of Time Management

A student juggling school and part-time work schedules their day: mornings for classes, afternoons for work, and evenings for studying. Allocating specific time slots helps them avoid last-minute cramming or missed deadlines.

Common Pitfalls in Time Management

1. Overloading Your Schedule:

Packing too much into one day leads to overwhelm and decreased productivity.

2. Procrastinating on Key Tasks:

Delaying important work wastes valuable time and creates unnecessary stress.

3. Failing to Adjust Plans:

Sticking rigidly to a plan without adapting to new priorities can backfire.

Takeaway

Effective time management is the foundation for accomplishing your goals and maintaining balance. By setting priorities, reducing distractions, and planning ahead, you can make every hour count and live a more focused, productive life.

Chapter 74: Health Choices

What Are Health Choices?

Health choices are the daily decisions that influence your physical, mental, and emotional well-being. Whether it's what you eat, how you exercise, or how much sleep you get, these decisions build the foundation for a longer, healthier life.

Example:

Choosing to walk to work instead of driving not only supports physical fitness but also reduces stress and boosts mental clarity.

Why Health Choices Matter

1. Prevents Chronic Illness:

Healthy habits reduce the risk of conditions like heart disease, diabetes, and obesity.

2. Boosts Energy and Focus:

A healthy lifestyle improves physical stamina and mental clarity, enhancing productivity.

3. Enhances Emotional Well-Being:

Good health choices, like regular exercise, help manage stress and improve mood.

Example:

A busy professional commits to a 20-minute daily workout and swaps sugary snacks for fresh fruit, leading to more energy and fewer mid-afternoon slumps.

How to Make Better Health Choices

1. Start Small:

Focus on simple, manageable changes rather than trying to overhaul everything at once.

Example: Begin by drinking an extra glass of water daily or walking 10 minutes a day.

2. Prioritize Consistency Over Perfection:

Build habits that you can sustain, even if progress is gradual.

Example: If you can't do a full workout, opt for stretching or light activity instead.

3. Plan Your Meals:

Prepare healthy meals in advance to avoid impulsive, unhealthy eating.

Example: Cook several portions of lean protein and vegetables on Sunday for easy weekday lunches.

4. Schedule Sleep:

Treat sleep as a non-negotiable priority for recovery and mental clarity.

Example: Set a regular bedtime and avoid screens an hour before bed.

5. Listen to Your Body:

Pay attention to how your choices affect your energy, mood, and physical health.

Example: Notice if certain foods make you feel sluggish and adjust your diet accordingly.

Everyday Example of Health Choices

Instead of skipping breakfast, you prepare a quick smoothie with fruits and protein. This simple decision sets the tone for a more energetic and productive day.

Common Pitfalls in Health Decisions

1. Focusing on Short-Term Fixes:

Crash diets or extreme exercise routines are rarely sustainable.

2. Neglecting Mental Health:

Physical health is vital, but mental well-being is equally important.

3. All-or-Nothing Thinking:

Skipping one workout doesn't mean you should abandon your fitness plan entirely.

Takeaway

Your health choices shape every aspect of your life. By focusing on small, consistent actions that support your physical and mental well-being, you can create a healthier, more balanced lifestyle.

Chapter 75: Relationship Decisions

What Are Relationship Decisions?

Relationship decisions involve navigating choices in your personal and professional connections, from forming friendships to handling conflicts or ending toxic dynamics. These decisions often require balancing emotional impulses with logical thinking to maintain healthy, meaningful bonds.

Example:

Choosing to calmly address a disagreement with a friend rather than reacting emotionally preserves trust and mutual respect.

Why Balancing Logic and Emotion Matters

1. Promotes Healthy Communication:

Logical thinking prevents emotional outbursts, while empathy fosters understanding.

2. Strengthens Connections:

Decisions rooted in mutual respect and clear reasoning build stronger relationships.

3. Reduces Regret:

Balancing emotion with rationality helps you avoid impulsive choices that might harm the relationship.

Example in Action:

A manager giving constructive feedback uses empathy to consider the employee's feelings while logically focusing on performance improvement.

How to Balance Logic and Emotion in Relationships

1. Pause Before Reacting:

Give yourself time to process emotions before responding to conflicts or challenges.

Example: Take a few deep breaths before replying to a heated text message.

2. Identify Core Values:

Use your personal principles as a guide to make decisions aligned with what matters most.

Example: If honesty is a key value, prioritize open communication even during tough conversations.

3. Practice Active Listening:

Empathize with the other person's perspective to ensure your decisions consider their feelings.

Example: Paraphrase their concerns to confirm understanding: "It sounds like you're worried about…"

4. Separate Emotion from Fact:

Acknowledge your feelings, but focus on the facts to determine the best course of action.

Example: In a disagreement with a partner, identify the actual issue rather than letting frustration guide your response.

5. Use "I" Statements:

Frame your concerns without blaming the other person to encourage productive dialogue.

Example: "I feel overwhelmed when the chores pile up; can we create a plan together?"

Everyday Example of Relationship Decisions

You're upset with a co-worker who missed a deadline. Instead of lashing out, you calmly work together to prevent it from happening again.

Common Pitfalls in Relationship Decisions

1. Reacting Emotionally:

Acting on anger or frustration can damage trust and escalate conflicts.

2. Overthinking:

Overanalyzing every interaction can lead to unnecessary tension or indecision.

3. Ignoring Red Flags:

Dismissing signs of toxic behavior to preserve a relationship often leads to long-term harm.

Takeaway

Balancing logic and emotion helps you navigate relationship decisions with clarity and empathy. By pausing to reflect, communicating thoughtfully, and focusing on shared values, you can strengthen connections while making healthier choices for yourself and others.

Chapter 76: Parenting with Purpose

What Does Parenting with Purpose Mean?

Parenting with purpose means making decisions that reflect your family's values and priorities. It's about guiding your children with intention, balancing discipline and support, and fostering a healthy environment where they can thrive.

Example:

Choosing to limit screen time and encourage outdoor activities aligns with a value of promoting physical and mental health.

Why Intentional Parenting Matters

1. Builds Stronger Bonds:

Purposeful decisions foster trust and open communication within the family.

2. Shapes Children's Growth:

Consistent, intentional choices provide a stable foundation for emotional and intellectual development.

3. Reduces Stress:

A clear parenting approach minimizes confusion and conflict in day-to-day family life.

Example:

A parent sets a bedtime routine that includes reading together, promoting both connection and good sleep habits.

How to Parent with Purpose

1. Define Family Values:

Decide what principles are most important to your family, such as kindness, education, or independence.

Example: "Our family prioritizes honesty, so we'll model and reward open communication."

2. Set Consistent Boundaries:
Clear rules provide structure and help children understand expectations.

Example: "Homework comes before screen time, every day."

3. Foster Open Dialogue:
Encourage children to express their thoughts and feelings to build trust and understanding.

Example: "How did that situation make you feel? Let's talk about what we can learn from it."

4. Adapt as They Grow:
Parenting decisions should evolve to reflect your children's changing needs and abilities.

Example: As a teenager gains independence, involve them in decisions about curfews or responsibilities.

5. Model the Behavior You Want to See:
Children learn more from what you do than what you say.

Example: Demonstrate patience and empathy when resolving family conflicts.

Everyday Example of Parenting with Purpose
When a child struggles with a school subject, the parent prioritizes encouragement over criticism, seeking solutions like tutoring or extra practice to build confidence and skills.

Common Pitfalls in Parenting Decisions

1. Inconsistency:
Changing rules or expectations confuses children and undermines trust.

2. Overcontrolling:
Micromanaging stifles independence and decision-making skills.

3. Ignoring Self-Care:
Neglecting your well-being makes it harder to parent effectively.

Takeaway
Parenting with purpose ensures your decisions align with your family's values and long-term goals. By fostering connection, setting consistent boundaries, and adapting to your child's needs, you can create a nurturing environment that supports their growth.

Chapter 77: Buying Smart

What Does It Mean to Buy Smart?
Buying smart means making thoughtful, informed decisions about big purchases to ensure they align with your financial goals, values, and long-term needs. It's about balancing quality, cost, and purpose to get the most value for your money without unnecessary regret.

Example:

Instead of impulsively buying the latest tech gadget, a person researches options, compares prices, and waits for a sale to make a smart purchase.

Why Buying Smart Matters

1. Protects Your Financial Health:
Overspending on big purchases can strain your budget or lead to debt.

2. Ensures Long-Term Satisfaction:
Smart purchases are more likely to meet your needs and provide value over time.

3. Reduces Buyer's Remorse:
Thoughtful decision-making prevents regret over unnecessary or poorly chosen purchases.

Example:

A family choosing a home considers location, school quality, and resale value to ensure the purchase fits their current and future needs.

1. Define Your Needs and Priorities:

List the essential features or criteria the purchase must meet.

Example: When buying a car, prioritize fuel efficiency, reliability, and maintenance costs.

2. Set a Budget:

Determine what you can afford, including hidden costs like taxes, maintenance, or upgrades.

Example: A homebuyer accounts for property taxes and closing costs when setting their maximum budget.

3. Research Thoroughly:

Compare options, read reviews, and ask for recommendations to ensure you make an informed choice.

Example: A shopper considering a TV compares models, checks warranties, and waits for a holiday sale.

4. Delay Impulse Purchases:

Give yourself time to reflect before committing to significant expenses.

Example: Use a 30-day rule: wait a month before making a major purchase to ensure it's necessary.

5. Think Long-Term:

Consider how the purchase will hold up over time and align with your future needs.

Example: A young professional invests in a high-quality laptop knowing it will last several years.

Everyday Example of Smart Buying

You're upgrading your smartphone. Instead of buying the most expensive model, you compare features, trade-in values, and promotions, choosing the option that balances price and functionality.

Common Pitfalls in Big Purchases

1. Focusing on Trends:

Buying based on hype often leads to regret when trends fade or the item doesn't meet your needs.

2. Overlooking Hidden Costs:

Failing to account for ongoing expenses like maintenance or energy usage can strain your budget.

3. Skipping Research:

Rushing into a purchase without comparing options can result in lower quality or higher costs.

Takeaway

Smart buying ensures that your big purchases align with your financial goals and provide long-term value. By focusing on needs, setting a budget, and researching options, you can make confident, regret-free decisions.

Chapter 78: Where to Live

What Does It Mean to Assess Location Choices Effectively?

Choosing where to live is one of life's biggest decisions, affecting your career, relationships, finances, and quality of life. Assessing location choices effectively means weighing factors like cost, opportunities, and lifestyle to ensure your new home aligns with your needs and goals.

Example:

A person moving for work compares neighborhoods based on commute times, affordability, and access to amenities like parks and schools.

Why Location Decisions Matter

1. Impacts Finances:

Housing costs, taxes, and living expenses vary widely by location.

2. Shapes Lifestyle:

Where you live influences your access to work, recreation, and social connections.

3. Affects Long-Term Plans:

Your location may determine your career opportunities, children's education, or ability to save for the future.

Example:

A couple deciding between urban and suburban living considers their priorities: proximity to work vs. access to larger living spaces and good schools.

How to Evaluate Where to Live

1. Identify Key Priorities:

Rank factors like affordability, commute, safety, climate, and community based on your needs.

Example: A remote worker prioritizes affordability and outdoor activities over proximity to an office.

2. Research Costs of Living:

Compare housing, utilities, groceries, and taxes in potential locations to ensure affordability.

Example: A person moving to a new city calculates their budget based on local rent and transportation costs.

3. Consider Career Opportunities:

Ensure the location supports your professional goals, whether through job availability or networking opportunities.

Example: A tech professional might prioritize living in a city with a thriving tech industry.

4. Visit Before Committing:

Spend time in the area to get a sense of its vibe, amenities, and suitability for your lifestyle.

Example: Before relocating, a family explores potential neighborhoods, visiting schools and parks.

5. Plan for the Long Term:

Evaluate how the location fits your future plans, such as raising children or retiring.

Example: A young couple buys a starter home in an area with good schools, anticipating their family's growth.

Everyday Example of Location Decisions

You're offered a job in another city. Before moving, you research neighborhoods, commute options, and social activities to ensure it's a good fit for your career and lifestyle.

Common Pitfalls in Location Decisions

1. Focusing Only on the Job:

Moving solely for work can backfire if the location doesn't align with your personal needs.

2. Underestimating Costs:

Ignoring expenses like taxes, insurance, or transportation can strain your finances.

3. Neglecting Lifestyle Preferences:

Choosing a location that doesn't suit your hobbies, values, or social preferences can lead to dissatisfaction.

Takeaway

Choosing where to live is about aligning location factors with your goals and values. By prioritizing your needs, researching thoroughly, and considering long-term plans, you can make a decision that enhances both your lifestyle and future.

Chapter 79: Handling Crises

What Does It Mean to Handle Crises Effectively?

Crisis decision-making involves navigating high-pressure situations where time, resources, and emotions are limited. It's about staying calm, prioritizing effectively, and taking decisive action, even in the face of uncertainty or risk.

Example:

During a sudden financial setback, a family decides to pause discretionary spending, create a revised budget, and prioritize essential expenses like rent and groceries.

Why Effective Crisis Management Matters

1. Minimizes Harm:

Quick, well-thought-out actions reduce negative consequences during emergencies.

2. Restores Stability:

Decisive responses help you regain control and prevent the crisis from worsening.

3. Builds Confidence:

Successfully managing a crisis strengthens your ability to handle future challenges.

Example:

A business experiencing a supply chain disruption develops a backup supplier relationship, ensuring minimal delays in product delivery.

How to Make Decisions Under Pressure

1. Pause and Assess:

Take a moment to understand the situation before acting impulsively.

Example: Ask, "What's the immediate problem, and what resources do I have to address it?"

2. Prioritize Urgent Actions:

Focus on immediate steps to address the most critical aspects of the crisis.

Example: During a power outage, prioritize securing food and medical supplies before addressing long-term solutions.

3. Delegate When Possible:

Share responsibilities to lighten the load and ensure faster action.

Example: In a workplace emergency, assign tasks to team members based on their strengths.

4. Communicate Clearly:

Keep stakeholders informed to avoid misunderstandings and foster collaboration.

Example: In a family crisis, share updates and plans to ensure everyone is on the same page.

5. Learn from the Experience:

After the crisis, review what worked, what didn't, and how to improve for the future.

Example: A company analyzes how they handled a PR crisis to create a stronger response plan for similar situations.

Everyday Example of Crisis Decision-Making

During a sudden illness, you reschedule non-urgent appointments, focus on rest and recovery, and ask a friend for help with daily errands to manage the situation effectively.

Common Pitfalls in Crisis Decisions

1. Panicking:

Acting out of fear or anxiety can lead to rash, ineffective choices.

2. Overthinking:

Delaying action to analyze every detail wastes precious time in emergencies.

3. Neglecting Communication:

Failing to involve others can result in confusion and missed opportunities for support.

Takeaway

Handling crises effectively means staying calm, prioritizing key actions, and maintaining clear communication. By breaking the situation into manageable steps and learning from the experience, you can turn high-pressure moments into opportunities for growth and resilience.

Chapter 80: The Minimalist Mindset

What Is the Minimalist Mindset?

The minimalist mindset focuses on reducing unnecessary choices and distractions, allowing you to concentrate on what truly matters. Simplifying decision-making eliminates overwhelm and conserves mental energy for the most important tasks.

Example:

A busy professional simplifies their wardrobe to a few versatile outfits, saving time and energy each morning.

Why a Minimalist Mindset Matters

1. Reduces Decision Fatigue:

Simplifying choices conserves mental resources for more critical decisions.

2. Improves Focus:

Eliminating distractions helps you concentrate on your priorities.

3. Enhances Clarity:

Simplified decision-making reduces stress and boosts confidence in your choices.

Example:

A couple planning a wedding limits their options for venues and vendors, focusing on those that align with their budget and style, reducing stress and simplifying the process.

How to Adopt a Minimalist Mindset

1. Identify Priorities:

Focus on the choices that truly align with your goals and values.

Example: When shopping, prioritize quality over quantity to avoid clutter.

2. Limit Options:

Set boundaries for how many options you'll consider to avoid overwhelm.

Example: Narrow your restaurant choices to three options instead of scrolling endlessly.

3. Create Systems:

Establish routines and defaults to reduce everyday decision-making.

Example: Meal prep once a week to avoid daily decisions about what to cook.

4. Declutter Your Environment:

A clean, organized space supports clearer thinking and faster decisions.

Example: Clear your desk of unnecessary items to focus better on work.

5. Embrace "Good Enough":

Avoid perfectionism by choosing what works well instead of waiting for the ideal option.

Example: Pick a gym that's convenient rather than searching endlessly for the "perfect" facility.

Everyday Example of the Minimalist Mindset

You're planning a vacation. Instead of overwhelming yourself with dozens of destinations, you focus on three locations that meet your top priorities: affordability, activities, and weather.

Common Pitfalls in Simplifying Decisions

1. Over-Simplifying Important Choices:

Reducing options too much can overlook crucial factors in complex decisions.

2. Avoiding Exploration:

Always choosing the same thing can lead to missed opportunities for growth or discovery.

3. Focusing Only on Efficiency:

A minimalist approach should balance simplicity with meaningful outcomes.

Takeaway

A minimalist mindset simplifies decision-making by reducing distractions and focusing on essentials. By narrowing options, creating systems, and prioritizing what matters most, you free your mind to make thoughtful, impactful choices.

Section IX: Advanced Decision-Making

As decisions become more complex, so does the need for advanced tools. This section focuses on strategies to refine your decision-making process, manage mental load, and navigate high-stakes situations. These advanced techniques help you think critically, act decisively, and continually improve.

Chapter 81: Cognitive Load Management

What Is Cognitive Load Management?

Cognitive load management involves reducing the mental strain caused by too much information or too many decisions. It's about organizing your thoughts, prioritizing tasks, and simplifying processes to free up mental resources for more important decisions.

Example:

A manager facing multiple deadlines delegates routine tasks to their team, allowing them to focus on strategic planning.

Why Cognitive Load Management Matters

1. Improves Focus:

A clear mind processes information more effectively and avoids distractions.

2. Reduces Decision Fatigue:

Limiting mental strain prevents burnout and improves the quality of your choices.

3. Boosts Creativity:

Freeing up mental space encourages innovative thinking and problem-solving.

Example:

A busy professional organizes their day with time-blocking, reserving the morning for deep work and the afternoon for meetings, avoiding cognitive overload.

How to Manage Cognitive Load

1. Prioritize Tasks:

Focus on the most critical and time-sensitive activities to avoid being overwhelmed.

Example: Use a task management system like "Must-Do, Should-Do, Nice-to-Do" to organize your day.

2. Limit Multitasking:

Concentrate on one task at a time to improve efficiency and reduce errors.

Example: Silence notifications while writing a report to maintain focus.

3. Declutter Your Mind:

Write down thoughts, tasks, or ideas to free up mental bandwidth.

Example: Use a notebook or app to create a running to-do list, so you don't rely on memory alone.

4. Automate Routine Decisions:

Create habits or defaults for recurring choices to conserve mental energy.

Example: Plan weekly meals in advance to avoid daily dinner decisions.

5. Take Breaks:

Regular breaks recharge your mind and improve decision-making capacity.

Example: Step away from work for a 10-minute walk after completing a major task.

Everyday Example of Cognitive Load Management

You're overwhelmed by a cluttered inbox. Instead of sorting everything manually, you create filters for newsletters, prioritize urgent emails, and unsubscribe from unnecessary ones, making it easier to focus.

Common Pitfalls in Cognitive Load Management

1. Ignoring Limits:

Taking on too much leads to mistakes and burnout.

2. Overcomplicating Systems:

Overly complex organizational methods can become a source of stress.

3. Neglecting Rest:

Failing to recharge your mind reduces your ability to make sound decisions.

Takeaway

Cognitive load management keeps your mind sharp by reducing unnecessary mental strain. By prioritizing tasks, automating routines, and taking breaks, you create the mental clarity needed for high-quality decision-making.

Chapter 82: Learning from Failure

What Does It Mean to Learn from Failure?

Learning from failure means analyzing mistakes to identify valuable insights and apply those lessons to future decisions. It shifts the focus from regret to growth, turning setbacks into opportunities for improvement.

Example:

After a failed project launch, a team identifies poor market research as the cause and commits to more thorough data collection for future initiatives.

Why Learning from Failure Matters

1. Builds Resilience:

Viewing failure as part of the learning process reduces fear and promotes persistence.

2. Improves Future Decisions:

Analyzing mistakes helps you avoid repeating them and refine your strategies.

3. Encourages Innovation:

Taking risks often leads to breakthroughs, even if some attempts fail.

Example:

A student learns from failing an exam by identifying their weak study habits and adopting new methods, leading to better performance next time.

How to Learn from Failure

1. Acknowledge the Failure:

Accept what went wrong without deflecting blame or ignoring the issue.

Example: "I didn't meet my deadline because I underestimated the time needed for research."

2. Analyze the Causes:

Break down the factors that led to failure to identify patterns or areas for improvement.

Example: "I spent too much time on minor details instead of focusing on the big picture."

3. Focus on Lessons, Not Regrets:

Use the experience to uncover actionable insights rather than dwelling on the setback.

Example: "Next time, I'll create a more realistic timeline with clear milestones."

4. Apply What You've Learned:

Implement changes based on your analysis to improve future outcomes.

Example: A small business owner refines their marketing strategy after noticing low engagement with previous campaigns.

5. Celebrate Resilience:

Recognize the effort you put into bouncing back to stay motivated.

Example: "Even though the pitch failed, I learned how to refine my presentation skills for next time."

Everyday Example of Learning from Failure

You burn dinner while trying a new recipe. Instead of giving up on cooking, you identify where you went wrong — like misreading the instructions — and approach the next attempt more carefully.

1. Ignoring the Lesson:

Failing without reflection ensures the same mistakes will happen again.

2. Focusing on Blame:

Assigning fault to others rather than assessing your own role limits growth.

3. Avoiding Risk:

Fear of failure can prevent you from taking valuable opportunities.

Takeaway

Failure isn't the end — it's a stepping stone to better decisions. By analyzing mistakes, focusing on lessons, and applying new strategies, you can turn setbacks into powerful tools for growth and resilience.

Chapter 83: Bias Audits

What Is a Bias Audit?

A bias audit involves regularly reviewing your decisions and thought processes to identify and correct cognitive biases. These mental shortcuts can distort your judgment, leading to flawed conclusions. By auditing your biases, you enhance your ability to think critically and make rational choices.

Example:

Before hiring a candidate, a manager reviews their notes to ensure they're not favoring someone based on shared interests instead of qualifications.

Why Bias Audits Matter

1. Improves Decision Accuracy:

Recognizing biases ensures your decisions are based on facts, not distorted perceptions.

2. Encourages Objectivity:

Auditing helps you stay neutral, especially in emotionally charged situations.

3. Promotes Fairness:

Reducing biases leads to more equitable outcomes, whether in personal relationships or professional settings.

Example:

A teacher evaluating students' work checks for bias by grading assignments without knowing who submitted them.

How to Conduct a Bias Audit

1. Identify Common Biases:

Familiarize yourself with cognitive biases like confirmation bias (favoring evidence that supports your beliefs) or loss aversion (fearing losses more than valuing gains).

Example: Recognize that you might be anchoring on the first piece of information you received about a decision.

2. Review Past Decisions:

Reflect on key decisions to identify patterns where biases may have influenced your judgment.

Example: "Did I overvalue advice from someone just because they seemed confident?"

3. Challenge Assumptions:

Question the reasoning behind your choices to uncover hidden biases.

Example: "Am I favoring this idea because it aligns with what I already believe?"

4. Seek Diverse Perspectives:

Invite input from others to challenge your thinking and expose blind spots.

Example: "What do you see in this situation that I might be missing?"

5. Create a Bias Checklist:

Use a checklist to remind yourself of potential biases during key decisions.

Example: Before making a choice, ask, "Am I relying on stereotypes or overlooking contradictory evidence?"

When planning a vacation, you notice you're favoring a destination based on flashy marketing rather than researching practical details like cost and activities. By auditing your choice, you adjust your decision to better suit your needs.

Common Pitfalls in Bias Audits

1. Assuming You're Unbiased:

Everyone has biases, and failing to acknowledge them hinders growth.

2. Overlooking Emotional Factors:

Ignoring how emotions influence decisions can lead to incomplete audits.

3. Relying on Self-Reflection Alone:

Without external feedback, it's easy to miss hidden biases.

Takeaway

Bias audits are essential for clear, objective decision-making. By identifying and challenging cognitive biases, you ensure your choices are rational, fair, and aligned with reality.

Chapter 84: The Power of Small Wins

What Are Small Wins?

Small wins are minor but meaningful accomplishments that build confidence, motivation, and momentum toward larger goals. They create a positive feedback loop, turning incremental progress into long-term success.

Example:

A student struggling with a large project starts by completing one section at a time, gaining momentum with each small victory.

Why Small Wins Matter

1. Boost Confidence:

Achieving small goals reinforces your belief in your abilities.

2. Sustain Motivation:

Regular progress keeps you engaged and focused on your larger objectives.

3. Reduce Overwhelm:

Breaking big tasks into smaller steps makes them more manageable.

Example:

A person saving for a house celebrates reaching each $1,000 milestone, motivating them to stay on track.

How to Leverage Small Wins

1. Set Micro-Goals:

Break big goals into smaller, achievable steps.

Example: Instead of "Write a book," start with "Draft the first chapter."

2. Track Progress:

Record each accomplishment to visualize your growth.

Example: Use a habit tracker to log daily workouts as part of a fitness goal.

3. Celebrate Success:

Acknowledge even minor achievements to stay motivated.

Example: Reward yourself with a small treat after completing a challenging task.

4. Focus on Consistency:

Regular small wins are more impactful than occasional big ones.

Example: Write 300 words daily instead of waiting for inspiration to finish a full chapter.

5. Build on Momentum:

Use each success as a stepping stone to tackle bigger challenges.

Example: After finishing a short course, enroll in an advanced program to deepen your skills.

Everyday Example of Small Wins

You want to declutter your home but feel overwhelmed. By starting with one drawer and completing it successfully, you build the momentum to tackle other areas.

Common Pitfalls in Small Wins

1. Neglecting Celebration:

Failing to recognize progress reduces motivation.

2. Getting Stuck on Minor Goals:

Focusing only on small wins without advancing toward the bigger picture stalls progress.

3. Expecting Immediate Results:

Small wins take time to accumulate into major successes.

Takeaway

Small wins create the momentum needed for big achievements. By focusing on incremental progress, celebrating successes, and building consistency, you turn daunting goals into attainable milestones.

Chapter 85: Combining Data and Intuition

What Does It Mean to Combine Data and Intuition?

Combining data and intuition involves using evidence-based insights alongside your gut feelings to make balanced decisions. Data provides objective clarity, while intuition offers personal judgment and creativity. Together, they create a comprehensive approach to complex decision-making.

A manager deciding on a marketing strategy analyzes campaign performance metrics (data) while considering how the audience might emotionally respond to specific content (intuition).

Why Balancing Data and Intuition Matters

1. Mitigates Bias:

Data helps counteract emotional biases, while intuition fills in gaps where data is incomplete.

2. Enhances Creativity:

Relying on both logic and instinct leads to more innovative solutions.

3. Improves Flexibility:

Intuition adapts quickly to changing circumstances, while data ensures choices remain grounded in facts.

Example:

An investor uses financial forecasts to guide their decisions (data) but follows their instincts about which industries are likely to grow in the future (intuition).

How to Combine Data and Intuition

1. Start with Data:

Collect and analyze relevant information to understand the situation clearly.

Example: A company looks at sales trends before deciding to launch a new product line.

2. Acknowledge Limitations:

Recognize that data may not capture every nuance, leaving room for judgment.

Example: While analytics show customer demand, the company relies on intuition to predict long-term trends.

3. Tune Your Intuition:

Build intuition through experience and reflection, making it a reliable complement to data.

Example: A chef knows from years of cooking when a recipe "feels right" even if they're experimenting with new techniques.

4. Test Assumptions:

Use data to validate or challenge your instincts, and adjust accordingly.

Example: A job seeker might feel an offer isn't right but compares the salary to market averages to confirm their gut feeling.

5. Balance Risks and Rewards:

Weigh both quantitative insights and qualitative factors to make well-rounded choices.

Example: A non-profit launching a campaign analyzes donation trends but also considers the emotional appeal of their messaging.

Everyday Example of Balancing Data and Intuition

You're choosing a new car. Data shows that a particular model has excellent safety ratings and fuel efficiency, but your intuition prefers a different model because it feels more comfortable and practical for your needs.

Common Pitfalls in Combining Data and Intuition

1. Overreliance on Data:

Excessive focus on numbers can ignore emotional or contextual factors.

2. Trusting Unrefined Instincts:

Intuition based on inexperience or incomplete knowledge may lead to errors.

3. Failing to Integrate Both:

Treating data and intuition as separate tools rather than complementary parts limits decision quality.

Takeaway

Combining data and intuition creates a balanced, effective approach to decision-making. By grounding choices in evidence while trusting refined instincts, you can navigate complexity with confidence and creativity.

Chapter 86: Meta-Decisions

What Are Meta-Decisions?

Meta-decisions are decisions about how to make decisions. They involve choosing the right process, tools, or mindset for solving a problem before diving into the specifics. This approach ensures your decision-making method aligns with the complexity and stakes of the situation.

Example:

A business deciding whether to launch a product chooses to rely on data analysis and market research, ensuring an informed process for the high-stakes decision.

Why Meta-Decisions Matter

1. Clarify Processes:

Deciding how to decide avoids confusion and aligns everyone involved on the right approach.

2. Save Time:

Meta-decisions streamline the process by focusing on the most effective method for the situation.

3. Improve Outcomes:

Tailoring your decision-making strategy to the problem ensures better results.

Example:

A family deciding on a vacation destination agrees to vote on options, ensuring fairness and efficiency in the process.

How to Make Meta-Decisions

1. Assess the Stakes:

Determine the importance and complexity of the decision to guide your approach.

Example: High-stakes financial decisions might require extensive research, while routine ones may rely on intuition.

2. Choose the Right Tools:

Select frameworks like decision trees, cost-benefit analysis, or brainstorming sessions based on the problem.

Example: A team uses a pros-and-cons list for a quick hiring decision but conducts thorough panel interviews for a leadership role.

3. Involve the Right People:

Decide who should contribute to the decision, considering expertise and stakeholder impact.

Example: A company includes IT staff in a decision about upgrading technology systems.

4. Define Success Metrics:

Establish criteria for evaluating the decision to ensure clarity.

Example: A non-profit defines success as increasing donations by 15% before choosing a campaign strategy.

5. Remain Flexible:

Be prepared to adjust your approach if the situation evolves or new information emerges.

Example: A couple initially planning to buy a home shifts to renting after market conditions change.

Everyday Example of Meta-Decisions

You're hosting a group dinner. Before deciding on a menu, you choose to poll guests about dietary restrictions and preferences, ensuring the final decision is inclusive.

Common Pitfalls in Meta-Decisions

1. Overthinking the Process:

Spending too much time deciding how to decide delays action.

2. Using the Wrong Approach:

Applying complex methods to simple problems wastes time and resources.

3. Failing to Adapt:

Sticking rigidly to an initial approach ignores evolving circumstances.

Takeaway

Meta-decisions create a foundation for smarter, more effective choices by defining the process before addressing the problem. By assessing stakes, selecting tools, and involving the right people, you can approach any decision with clarity and confidence.

Chapter 87: Information Overload

I've been buried in research for hours. How do you handle it?

Set a time limit and stick to the essentials—too much info just slows you down.

What Is Information Overload?

Information overload occurs when the sheer volume of data, opinions, and inputs becomes overwhelming, making it difficult to process, prioritize, and make decisions. Sifting through the noise to identify what's truly relevant ensures clarity and informed action.

Example:

A student researching a paper limits their sources to credible journals and avoids unrelated web results, streamlining their study process.

Why Avoiding Information Overload Matters

1. Improves Focus:

Filtering information reduces distractions, enabling you to concentrate on key issues.

2. Speeds Up Decisions:

Simplifying data reduces analysis paralysis and accelerates the decision-making process.

3. Enhances Decision Quality:

Focusing on high-quality, relevant information leads to better outcomes.

Example:

A professional choosing a software platform ignores marketing hype and focuses on user reviews and feature comparisons relevant to their needs.

How to Manage Information Overload

1. Define Your Goals:

Clarify the purpose of your decision to determine what information is necessary.

Example: If researching a new car, focus only on safety ratings, reliability, and affordability.

2. Set Boundaries:

Limit the time spent on research or the number of sources consulted to prevent overloading.

Example: "I'll review three credible articles before deciding on a health insurance plan."

3. Evaluate Credibility:

Prioritize information from trusted, reliable sources over anecdotal or biased inputs.

Example: When considering medical advice, rely on recommendations from certified professionals rather than social media posts.

4. Organize Data:

Use tools like lists, charts, or summaries to distill large amounts of information into clear insights.

Example: A homeowner compares contractors by listing costs, timelines, and reviews in a spreadsheet.

5. Eliminate Noise:

Avoid unnecessary inputs like irrelevant emails, social media, or excessive news updates during decision-making.

Example: Turn off notifications while evaluating investment options.

Everyday Example of Managing Information Overload

You're buying a smartphone. Instead of diving into endless reviews and specs, you decide on three key features (battery life, camera quality, and price) and only research models that meet these criteria.

Common Pitfalls in Managing Information Overload

1. Consuming Everything:

Trying to process all available information leads to confusion and delays.

2. Overvaluing Quantity Over Quality:

More data isn't better if it's not relevant or reliable.

3. Ignoring Actionable Insights:

Focusing on abstract data instead of actionable takeaways stalls progress.

Takeaway

Managing information overload is essential for clear, effective decision-making. By defining goals, filtering data, and focusing on relevance, you can sift through the noise to find clarity and confidence in your choices.

Decision Journals

Chapter 88: Decision Journals

What Are Decision Journals?

Decision journals are tools for recording the details of your decisions, including the reasoning behind them, anticipated outcomes, and eventual results. By reflecting on these entries, you identify patterns, refine your thought process, and improve future decisions.

Example:

A manager documents their reasoning for hiring a candidate, tracks their performance over six months, and evaluates whether the decision aligned with initial expectations.

Why Decision Journals Matter

1. Enhance Self-Awareness:

Journals reveal patterns in your thinking, highlighting strengths and areas for improvement.

2. Provide Accountability:

Writing down decisions forces you to articulate and justify your reasoning clearly.

3. Encourage Learning:

Reviewing outcomes helps you learn from successes and failures.

Example:

A person tracking their financial decisions realizes they frequently overestimate their ability to save, prompting adjustments to their budgeting habits.

How to Use Decision Journals

1. Record the Context:

Note the situation, the decision made, and any relevant constraints or goals.

Example: "I chose to invest in Stock A because it aligns with my long-term growth strategy."

2. Document Your Reasoning:

Include the factors that influenced your choice, such as data, intuition, or advice.

Example: "The company's revenue has grown 20% annually, and analysts project continued growth."

3. Predict Outcomes:

Write down what you expect to happen as a result of your decision.

Example: "I anticipate a 10% return within the next year."

4. Review Results:

After the decision plays out, evaluate whether the outcome matched your expectations and why.

Example: "The stock underperformed due to unexpected industry changes. Next time, I'll diversify more."

5. Identify Lessons Learned:

Reflect on how the experience can inform future choices.

Example: "This taught me to factor in external risks even when company fundamentals look strong."

Everyday Example of Using Decision Journals

You document your reasons for choosing a specific diet plan, including your goals and expected results. After three months, you review whether the plan met your expectations and make adjustments based on your experience.

Common Pitfalls in Using Decision Journals

1. Inconsistent Use:

Skipping entries makes it harder to identify patterns or learn from decisions.

2. Focusing Only on Successes:

Ignoring failures limits your ability to improve.

3. Overcomplicating the Process:

Journals should be simple enough to maintain consistently.

Takeaway

Decision journals transform decision-making into a continuous learning process. By tracking choices, reflecting on outcomes, and identifying lessons, you develop a more effective and self-aware approach to making decisions.

Chapter 89: When to Delegate

What Does It Mean to Delegate Decisions?

Delegation means entrusting tasks or decisions to others who are capable of handling them, freeing up your time and mental energy for higher-priority responsibilities. Knowing when and how to delegate ensures you leverage the strengths of your team or network effectively.

Example:

A manager delegates routine data entry to an assistant, allowing them to focus on strategic planning for an upcoming project.

Why Delegating Decisions Matters

1. Saves Time and Energy:

Delegation reduces your workload, preventing burnout and improving efficiency.

2. Increases Productivity:

Assigning tasks to those with relevant expertise often yields better results.

3. Builds Trust:

Empowering others to make decisions fosters collaboration and confidence.

Example:

A parent asks their teenager to plan the family's weekend outing, building decision-making skills while reducing stress for the parent.

How to Delegate Decisions Effectively

1. Identify Tasks to Delegate:

Focus on decisions that don't require your direct input or are outside your expertise.

Example: Delegate creating a project timeline to a colleague skilled in scheduling.

2. Choose the Right Person:

Assign tasks to individuals with the skills, experience, and capacity to handle them.

Example: A restaurant owner delegates menu design to their creative team rather than managing it personally.

3. Communicate Clearly:

Provide clear instructions, expectations, and any necessary resources.

Example: "Your goal is to research and recommend three vendors by Friday. Here are the criteria we need to meet."

4. Empower Decision-Making:

Allow the person to make their own choices within defined parameters.

Example: "You can choose the vendor, as long as the cost stays within our budget and they meet our quality standards."

5. Review and Support:

Check progress periodically and offer guidance as needed, without micromanaging.

Example: "How's the research coming along? Let me know if you need help narrowing down the options."

Everyday Example of Delegation

You're hosting a party and ask a friend to handle the playlist while another organizes food delivery. This delegation lets you focus on greeting guests and managing the overall flow of the event.

Common Pitfalls in Delegation

1. Micromanaging:

Over-involvement undermines the purpose of delegating and reduces trust.

2. Delegating Without Clarity:

Failing to provide clear expectations leads to confusion and subpar results.

3. Avoiding Delegation Entirely:

Trying to do everything yourself can lead to burnout and missed opportunities for collaboration.

Delegating decisions allows you to focus on high-priority tasks while empowering others to contribute their strengths. By choosing the right person, communicating clearly, and trusting the process, you build a more efficient and collaborative environment.

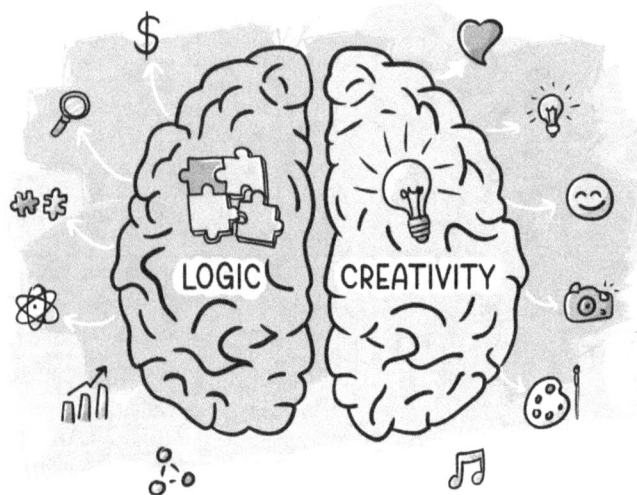

Chapter 90: Balancing Rationality and Creativity

What Does It Mean to Balance Rationality and Creativity?

Balancing rationality and creativity means combining logical analysis with imaginative thinking to develop effective and innovative solutions. Rationality grounds your decisions in facts and structure, while creativity generates fresh ideas and unique approaches.

Example:

An architect uses rationality to meet safety standards and budget constraints while employing creativity to design an inspiring, functional space.

Why Balancing Rationality and Creativity Matters

1. Encourages Innovation:

Creative thinking generates novel solutions, while rationality ensures feasibility.

2. Improves Problem-Solving:

Combining both approaches helps you address challenges from multiple angles.

3. Boosts Adaptability:

Creative solutions allow you to respond flexibly, while rational analysis provides stability.

Example:

A startup designing a marketing campaign combines data on customer preferences (rationality) with bold, eye-catching content (creativity).

How to Balance Rationality and Creativity

1. Start with Structure:

Use rational thinking to define the problem, set goals, and gather data.

Example: A teacher identifies that students struggle with engagement during lessons.

2. Brainstorm Freely:

Encourage creative ideas without judgment to explore unconventional solutions.

Example: The teacher considers using interactive games, storytelling, or role-playing to make lessons more engaging.

3. Test and Refine:

Evaluate creative ideas using rational criteria like feasibility, cost, and impact.

Example: The teacher implements role-playing, measures engagement, and refines the approach based on feedback.

4. Embrace Iteration:

Alternate between rational and creative modes to improve and adapt your solutions.

Example: A product designer prototypes an idea, gathers user feedback, and iterates with both logic and imagination.

5. Collaborate for Balance:

Involve diverse perspectives to integrate logical and creative strengths.

Example: A scientist and artist work together on an educational exhibit, blending technical accuracy with engaging visuals.

Everyday Example of Balancing Rationality and Creativity

You're organizing a fundraiser. Rationality helps you set a budget and logistics, while creativity inspires unique themes and interactive activities to draw attendees.

Common Pitfalls in Balancing Rationality and Creativity

1. Overemphasizing Logic:

Rigid thinking stifles creativity and limits innovative potential.

2. Relying Solely on Creativity:

Ignoring practical constraints can make ideas unrealistic or ineffective.

3. Forgetting to Iterate:

Stopping at the first idea misses opportunities for improvement.

Takeaway

Balancing rationality and creativity enables you to solve problems innovatively. By grounding ideas in logic while allowing room for imagination, you create solutions that are both practical and inspired.

Section X: Building a Decision-Making Framework

Great decision-making isn't just about individual choices; it's about creating a system. This section equips you with tools to build a framework that ensures clarity, consistency, and adaptability in your decision-making process. By developing guiding principles, learning from feedback, and fostering self-awareness, you can make confident decisions in any situation.

Chapter 91: The Decision-Making Code

What Is the Decision-Making Code?

The decision-making code is a personal set of guiding principles that align your choices with your values and goals. It acts as a compass, helping you navigate complexity and make consistent, purpose-driven decisions.

Example:

A leader with a guiding principle of transparency ensures open communication with their team, even during challenging times.

Why Developing Guiding Principles Matters

1. Ensures Consistency:

A clear code eliminates guesswork and keeps decisions aligned with your values.

2. Simplifies Complex Choices:

Principles provide a foundation for evaluating options, reducing overwhelm.

3. Builds Confidence:

Knowing your decisions align with your values fosters trust in your process.

Example:

A business owner prioritizes sustainability, choosing vendors and practices that reflect this value, even if it costs more initially.

How to Develop Your Decision-Making Code

1. Identify Your Core Values:

Reflect on what matters most to you, such as honesty, growth, or balance.

Example: "I value fairness, so I'll prioritize equitable outcomes in my decisions."

2. Define Your Principles:

Translate values into actionable statements to guide choices.

Example: "Always prioritize long-term gains over short-term fixes."

3. Test Your Principles:

Apply them to past decisions to ensure they hold up in real scenarios.

Example: "Would this principle have helped me avoid a past mistake?"

4. Adapt as Needed:

Revise your code as your goals and circumstances evolve.

Example: A parent might adjust their principles to include flexibility as their children grow older.

5. Document and Review:

Write down your principles and revisit them regularly to reinforce their impact.

Example: Keep a journal where you list principles and how they've guided key decisions.

Everyday Example of a Decision-Making Code

You're deciding whether to switch jobs. Your principle of prioritizing work-life balance helps you choose a role that offers remote work and flexible hours over one with higher pay but longer hours.

Common Pitfalls in Developing a Decision-Making Code

1. Being Too Vague:

Broad principles like "Do good" lack actionable guidance.

2. Ignoring Values:

A code that doesn't reflect your true priorities leads to inconsistency.

3. Failing to Revisit Principles:

Outdated principles may no longer align with your current life goals.

Takeaway

A decision-making code anchors your choices in purpose and clarity. By defining and refining your guiding principles, you create a consistent framework for navigating even the most complex situations.

Perfection

Chapter 92: Consistency Over Perfection

What Does Consistency Over Perfection Mean?

Consistency over perfection is the principle of focusing on steady, reliable progress rather than trying to make flawless decisions every time. It's about valuing action and learning from mistakes instead of being paralyzed by fear of failure.

Example:

Instead of obsessing over the perfect workout plan, someone commits to exercising 30 minutes a day, knowing consistency matters more than precision.

Why Consistency Matters More Than

1. Builds Momentum:

Regular effort leads to cumulative success, even if every step isn't perfect.

2. Encourages Experimentation:

A focus on progress allows you to test ideas without fearing mistakes.

3. Reduces Stress:

Letting go of perfectionism creates a healthier, more productive mindset.

Example:

A writer commits to drafting 500 words a day, improving their skills over time instead of waiting for perfect inspiration.

How to Prioritize Consistency

1. Set Small, Achievable Goals:

Focus on incremental progress to maintain motivation.

Example: Instead of aiming to lose 20 pounds immediately, set a goal to lose 2 pounds a month.

2. Embrace Imperfection:

Accept that mistakes are part of the process and opportunities to learn.

Example: A baker tests new recipes, knowing some attempts will fail but refine their skills.

3. Create Habits:

Build routines that support consistent action.

Example: Schedule 15 minutes daily for language practice instead of trying to cram before a trip.

4. Celebrate Milestones:

Acknowledge progress to reinforce the value of consistency.

Example: Reward yourself for completing a week of workouts, even if some sessions were shorter than planned.

5. Reflect and Adjust:

Regularly evaluate your progress and refine your approach.

Example: A student revises their study schedule after realizing they focus better in the morning.

Everyday Example of Consistency Over Perfection

You're learning to play guitar. Instead of aiming for flawless performances, you practice for 10 minutes daily, gradually building confidence and skill.

Common Pitfalls in Prioritizing Consistency

1. Expecting Quick Results:

Impatience can lead to frustration and quitting.

2. Letting Setbacks Derail Progress:

Missing one day of effort doesn't mean abandoning your goal entirely.

3. Overcommitting:

Setting unsustainable goals undermines consistency.

Takeaway

Consistency over perfection focuses on steady growth, turning small, repeated efforts into lasting success. By prioritizing progress and embracing imperfection, you create a resilient framework for achieving your goals.

Chapter 93: Feedback Loops

What Are Feedback Loops?

Feedback loops are systems for gathering information about the outcomes of your decisions and using that data to improve future choices. Whether positive or negative, feedback provides actionable insights that refine your decision-making process.

Example:

A manager launches a new team workflow and gathers input from employees after a month. Based on their feedback, they adjust timelines and tools to improve efficiency.

Why Feedback Loops Matter

1. Encourage Continuous Growth:

Feedback helps you adapt and evolve, making each decision better than the last.

2. Reveal Blind Spots:

Input from others highlights areas you might overlook on your own.

3. Boost Decision Quality:

Regular refinement ensures your strategies remain effective over time.

Example:

A musician performing live tracks audience reactions and adjusts their setlist to include more popular songs.

How to Use Feedback Loops Effectively

1. Invite Honest Input:

Create a safe environment where others feel comfortable sharing constructive feedback.

Example: A teacher asks students to complete anonymous surveys about class effectiveness.

2. Evaluate Outcomes:

Regularly analyze the results of your decisions to identify what worked and what didn't.

Example: A runner tracks their training progress to adjust their regimen for better performance.

3. Refine and Repeat:

Apply feedback to improve your approach, then test it again.

Example: A small business adjusts its pricing strategy based on customer feedback and monitors sales trends to measure the impact.

4. Focus on Patterns:

Look for recurring themes in feedback to address underlying issues.

Example: A project manager notices consistent complaints about communication gaps and implements regular status updates.

5. Avoid Overreacting to Outliers:

Balance individual feedback with broader trends to avoid making knee-jerk changes.

Example: A restaurant owner considers overall customer reviews instead of focusing on one particularly harsh critique.

Everyday Example of Feedback Loops

You're learning to cook a new dish. After each attempt, you note what went well and what didn't, adjusting the recipe until you perfect it.

Common Pitfalls in Feedback Loops

1. Ignoring Feedback:

Dismissing input undermines growth and perpetuates mistakes.

2. Taking Feedback Personally:

Viewing criticism as an attack rather than an opportunity stifles improvement.

3. Making Changes Too Quickly:

Overreacting to isolated feedback can disrupt effective strategies.

Takeaway

Feedback loops are essential for continuous learning and refinement. By seeking input, evaluating outcomes, and applying lessons learned, you create a dynamic system that improves your decision-making over time.

Chapter 94: Self-Awareness Practices

What Are Self-Awareness Practices?

Self-awareness practices are techniques that help you understand your thoughts, emotions, and behavior patterns. By recognizing these patterns, you can identify biases, play to your strengths, and make decisions aligned with your true priorities.

Example:

A professional reflects on their habit of procrastination and adopts time-blocking to improve productivity.

Why Self-Awareness Matters

1. Reveals Hidden Biases:

Understanding your cognitive tendencies reduces errors in judgment.

2. Enhances Emotional Regulation:

Awareness of your triggers helps you respond calmly under pressure.

3. Improves Alignment with Goals:

Self-awareness ensures your actions reflect your long-term objectives.

Example:

An athlete notices their tendency to self-criticize and replaces negative self-talk with affirmations, improving performance and confidence.

How to Cultivate Self-Awareness

1. Keep a Decision Journal:

Track your choices and outcomes to identify recurring patterns and areas for growth.

Example: Log decisions about finances and analyze whether they align with your savings goals.

2. Practice Mindfulness:

Focus on the present moment to recognize thoughts and emotions without judgment.

Example: During a tense meeting, take deep breaths to observe your reactions instead of acting impulsively.

3. Seek Feedback:

Ask trusted peers for insights into how they perceive your behavior or decisions.

Example: "Do you think I'm too quick to dismiss alternative ideas in meetings?"

4. Reflect Regularly:

Set aside time to review your day, noting what went well and what could improve.

Example: Use a nightly journal to jot down three successes and one lesson learned.

5. Identify Your Triggers:

Recognize situations that lead to poor decisions, and develop strategies to manage them.

Example: If stress leads you to overspend, create a budget to guide decisions during high-pressure times.

Everyday Example of Self-Awareness Practices

You notice that hunger often makes you irritable and prone to snap decisions. Keeping healthy snacks on hand helps you stay balanced and make better choices.

Common Pitfalls in Self-Awareness

1. Avoiding Reflection:

Ignoring your patterns prevents growth and perpetuates mistakes.

2. Overanalyzing:

Dwelling excessively on flaws can lead to paralysis rather than improvement.

3. Resisting Feedback:

Rejecting others' observations limits your ability to see blind spots.

Takeaway

Self-awareness is a cornerstone of effective decision-making. By recognizing your patterns, managing emotions, and aligning actions with goals, you become more intentional and confident in your choices.

Chapter 95: The Experimenter's Mindset

What Is the Experimenter's Mindset?

The experimenter's mindset treats life as a series of experiments, where each decision is a hypothesis tested through action. Successes validate your ideas, while failures provide valuable lessons. This approach encourages curiosity, adaptability, and continuous improvement.

Example:

A professional tests new productivity methods like time-blocking or task batching, refining their workflow based on results.

Why the Experimenter's Mindset Matters

1. Reduces Fear of Failure:

Viewing mistakes as data removes the emotional sting of failure.

2. Encourages Innovation:

Experimentation leads to discoveries you might not reach through conventional thinking.

3. Fosters Adaptability:

Iterative testing prepares you to adjust strategies in response to new information.

Example:

A person trying to improve their diet experiments with meal prepping one week and intuitive eating the next, learning what works best for their lifestyle.

How to Adopt the Experimenter's Mindset

1. Frame Decisions as Hypotheses:

Define what you want to test and what you expect to learn.

Example: "If I spend 10 minutes meditating daily, I'll feel more focused by the end of the week."

2. Start Small:

Test ideas on a manageable scale to reduce risk and gather insights quickly.

Example: Before committing to a career change, take a short course in the field to gauge your interest.

3. Measure Results:

Track outcomes to determine whether the experiment achieved its goals.

Example: A business tracks customer engagement after introducing a new email marketing strategy.

4. Embrace Iteration:

Use results to refine your approach and run further tests.

Example: Adjust your exercise routine based on what energizes you most during the day.

5. Stay Curious:

Treat every outcome as an opportunity to learn, whether it confirms or challenges your hypothesis.

Example: If a strategy doesn't work, ask, "Why?" and explore alternatives.

Everyday Example of the Experimenter's Mindset

You're looking for ways to save money on groceries. One week, you try shopping at a discount store; the next, you focus on meal planning. Comparing the results helps you identify the most effective strategy.

Common Pitfalls in Experimentation

1. Expecting Instant Success:

Not all experiments yield immediate or clear results.

2. Fearing Mistakes:

Avoiding risks stifles opportunities for growth and discovery.

3. Ignoring Lessons Learned:

Failing to analyze results misses the point of experimentation.

The experimenter's mindset transforms decisions into opportunities for growth. By testing hypotheses, learning from outcomes, and iterating your approach, you can turn curiosity into actionable insights that drive continuous improvement.

Chapter 96: Reverse Engineering Success

What Is Reverse Engineering Success?

Reverse engineering success means analyzing the achievements of role models or organizations to identify the steps, strategies, and principles they followed. By understanding how they reached their goals, you can create your own roadmap for similar success.

Example:

An aspiring entrepreneur studies the growth strategies of a successful start-up to apply relevant tactics to their own business.

Why Reverse Engineering Matters

1. Provides Proven Strategies:

Learning from others saves time and avoids reinventing the wheel.

2. Inspires Action:

Seeing how others achieved their goals makes your own ambitions feel more attainable.

3. Customizes Your Approach:

Adapting successful methods to your unique situation ensures relevance and effectiveness.

Example:

A musician analyzing how their favorite artist built an audience on social media adapts similar engagement tactics to grow their fan base.

How to Reverse Engineer Success

1. Identify Role Models:

Choose individuals or organizations whose achievements align with your goals.

Example: A writer examines the habits of bestselling authors to improve their own workflow.

2. Study Their Process:

Break down the steps, decisions, and milestones that contributed to their success.

Example: A non-profit analyzes how a similar organization grew donations through targeted campaigns.

3. Focus on Key Principles:

Look for underlying strategies rather than copying surface-level actions.

Example: Instead of mimicking a celebrity's exact workout routine, focus on their discipline and consistency.

4. Adapt to Your Context:

Adjust lessons learned to fit your resources, strengths, and challenges.

Example: A start-up tailors an established company's customer service practices to suit their smaller team.

5. Track Progress:

Measure how applying these strategies impacts your own outcomes.

Example: A student adopting a successful study technique monitors results.

Everyday Example of Reverse Engineering Success

You admire a colleague's ability to manage time effectively. By observing their use of calendars, task prioritization, and delegation, you adopt similar practices to streamline your own schedule.

1. **Blindly Copying:**

    Mimicking actions without understanding the reasoning behind them leads to superficial results.

2. **Ignoring Context:**

    Failing to adapt strategies to your unique situation limits their effectiveness.

3. **Focusing Only on Outcomes:**

    Overlooking the hard work and setbacks behind success creates unrealistic expectations.

Takeaway

Reverse engineering success offers a practical way to learn from others' achievements. By analyzing strategies, focusing on key principles, and adapting them to your context, you can create a customized path to your goals.

Chapter 97: Embracing Complexity

What Does It Mean to Embrace Complexity?

Embracing complexity means accepting uncertainty, interconnected factors, and ever-changing conditions as part of decision-making. It involves thinking dynamically, staying flexible, and focusing on the bigger picture to navigate challenges effectively.

Example:

A CEO facing a volatile market adopts multiple strategies, balancing cost-cutting measures with investment in innovation to adapt to unpredictable conditions.

Why Embracing Complexity Matters

1. **Encourages Resilience:**

Recognizing that uncertainty is unavoidable helps you adapt instead of resisting change.

2. **Reveals Hidden Opportunities:**

    Complex situations often present chances for innovation and growth.

3. **Improves Strategic Thinking:**

    Viewing problems from multiple angles enables well-rounded solutions.

Example:

A nonprofit navigating shifting funding priorities explores diverse revenue streams to maintain stability and expand impact.

How to Embrace Complexity

1. **Shift Your Mindset:**

    See complexity as an opportunity for growth, not a barrier.

    Example: "How can this challenge teach me to approach problems differently?"

2. **Break Down the Problem:**

    Divide complex issues into smaller, manageable components to identify key factors.

    Example: A project manager addressing delays categorizes issues into communication, resource allocation, and technical bottlenecks.

3. **Focus on Interconnections:**

    Analyze how various elements interact and influence one another.

    Example: A city planner evaluates how housing policies impact transportation, employment, and public health.

4. **Prepare for Multiple Outcomes:**

    Anticipate a range of scenarios and develop flexible strategies.

    Example: An investor creates a diversified portfolio to hedge against market uncertainty.

5. **Practice Adaptive Thinking:**

    Stay open to revising your approach as new information emerges.

Example: A teacher adjusts their lesson plan mid-class based on student engagement levels.

You're planning a wedding but encounter unexpected challenges, like a venue cancellation. By staying flexible, you consider alternative options and prioritize what truly matters, ensuring a meaningful celebration.

1. Oversimplifying Problems:

Ignoring interconnected factors can lead to ineffective solutions.

2. Freezing Under Pressure:

Complexity can overwhelm, leading to inaction.

3. Focusing Solely on Short-Term Fixes:

Quick solutions often fail to address root causes.

Embracing complexity equips you to navigate uncertainty with confidence and adaptability. By breaking problems into manageable parts, analyzing interconnections, and staying open to change, you turn ambiguity into opportunity.

Chapter 98: The Continuous Learner

What Does It Mean to Be a Continuous Learner?

A continuous learner actively seeks knowledge, skills, and perspectives to refine their understanding and decision-making abilities. This mindset embraces curiosity as a driving force for growth, adaptability, and lifelong improvement.

Example:

A software developer stays ahead of industry trends by learning new programming languages, ensuring their expertise remains relevant.

Why Lifelong Learning Matters

1. Enhances Problem-Solving:

Expanding your knowledge equips you with diverse tools and perspectives.

2. Builds Resilience:

Learning fosters adaptability, helping you navigate changes and challenges.

3. Encourages Innovation:

Curiosity leads to fresh ideas and creative solutions.

Example:

A business leader reads books on psychology, technology, and leadership to inform better strategies and inspire their team.

How to Foster Continuous Learning

1. Stay Curious:

Approach situations with a mindset of exploration and discovery.

Example: "What can I learn from this challenge, even if it seems small?"

2. Seek Diverse Inputs:

Expose yourself to different fields, cultures, and ideas to broaden your perspective.

Example: A scientist attends art workshops to inspire creative approaches to research.

3. Reflect Regularly:

Review what you've learned and how it applies to your decisions.

Example: Keep a journal of new skills or insights gained from daily experiences.

4. Invest in Education:

Take courses, read books, or attend seminars to deepen your expertise.

Example: A marketer enrolls in a data analytics course to enhance campaign strategies.

5. Learn from Others:

Engage with mentors, peers, and diverse communities to share knowledge.

Example: Join a networking group to exchange insights and expand your horizons.

Everyday Example of Continuous Learning

You're interested in gardening but have no experience. By watching tutorials, experimenting with plants, and seeking advice, you develop a thriving garden and a rewarding new hobby.

Common Pitfalls in Lifelong Learning

1. Avoiding New Challenges:

Sticking to familiar areas limits growth opportunities.

2. Overloading with Information:

Focusing on too many topics at once can dilute learning efforts.

3. Failing to Apply Knowledge:

Learning without action doesn't translate into meaningful improvement.

Takeaway

Continuous learning fuels better decision-making by equipping you with diverse skills and perspectives. By staying curious, seeking knowledge, and applying what you learn, you grow into a more adaptive and innovative decision-maker.

I want to ensure our project improves lives even after we're gone.

Let's focus on creating something sustainable, like renewable energy solutions.

Chapter 99: Legacy Decisions

What Are Legacy Decisions?

Legacy decisions are choices made with the intention of leaving a lasting positive impact on future generations, your community, or the world. These decisions reflect your values and prioritize long-term benefits over short-term gains.

Example:

A philanthropist invests in educational scholarships, knowing their contribution will empower students for decades to come.

Why Legacy Decisions Matter

1. Extend Your Influence:

Legacy decisions allow your actions to create a ripple effect that benefits others long after you're gone.

2. Align with Purpose:

Thinking beyond immediate outcomes connects your choices to meaningful goals and values.

3. Promote Sustainability:

Long-term thinking ensures that resources and opportunities are preserved for future generations.

Example:

A company commits to reducing its carbon footprint by adopting sustainable practices, balancing profits with environmental responsibility.

How to Make Legacy Decisions

1. Define Your Legacy Goals:

Reflect on what impact you want to leave behind, whether it's personal, professional, or societal.

Example: "I want to contribute to environmental conservation by supporting reforestation projects."

2. **Think Long-Term:**

   Evaluate how your decisions will affect future generations or stakeholders.

   Example: A parent chooses to teach their children financial literacy, ensuring they have tools for lifelong stability.

3. **Invest in Meaningful Projects:**

   Focus your time, money, or energy on initiatives that align with your values and have enduring impact.

   Example: An entrepreneur mentors young startups, fostering innovation and community growth.

4. **Collaborate for Greater Impact:**

   Work with others who share your vision to amplify the results of your efforts.

   Example: A local leader forms partnerships to improve public transportation in underserved areas.

5. **Regularly Revisit Your Legacy Goals:**

   As your circumstances and priorities evolve, adjust your decisions to stay aligned with your values.

   Example: A retiree shifts from career-focused goals to philanthropic endeavors that promote equity and education.

Everyday Example of Legacy Decisions

You start a small community garden in your neighborhood. While it benefits residents today, it also teaches future generations about sustainability and teamwork.

Common Pitfalls in Legacy Decisions

1. **Overlooking Immediate Needs:**

   Focusing too much on the future may neglect pressing current issues.

2. **Underestimating Small Actions:**

   Assuming that only grand gestures matter limits your ability to create lasting change.

3. **Failing to Inspire Others:**

   A legacy is more effective when shared with and embraced by others.

Takeaway

Legacy decisions prioritize long-term impact and reflect your deepest values. By aligning your choices with a purpose, collaborating with others, and thinking about future generations, you create a meaningful legacy that transcends your lifetime.

Chapter 100: Master Your Mindset

What Does It Mean to Master Your Mindset?

Mastering your mindset means cultivating the habits, perspectives, and emotional resilience needed to make sound, confident decisions. It's about blending rationality with empathy, focusing on growth, and staying adaptable in the face of challenges.

Example:

A leader faced with a tough decision balances data-driven analysis with a genuine understanding of how their choice will affect team morale.

Why Mindset Matters in Decision-Making

1. Enhances Confidence:

A strong mindset reduces hesitation and builds trust in your process.

2. Promotes Adaptability:

A growth-oriented outlook helps you pivot effectively when circumstances change.

3. Encourages Consistency:

Habits grounded in self-awareness and reflection lead to more reliable outcomes.

Example:

A student adopting a "fail-forward" mindset learns from mistakes and continues improving instead of giving up after setbacks.

The Habits of Great Decision-Makers

1. Seek Clarity:

Ask focused questions and gather relevant information before acting.

Example: A negotiator outlines clear objectives and goals before entering discussions.

2. Embrace Reflection:

Regularly review past decisions to identify strengths and areas for growth.

Example: A teacher reflects on classroom strategies each semester to refine their methods.

3. Balance Logic and Emotion:

Integrate rational analysis with empathy and intuition for well-rounded choices.

Example: A parent deciding on a move considers both financial benefits and emotional effects on their children.

4. Stay Curious:

Approach every situation as an opportunity to learn and grow.

Example: A designer experiments with new tools and techniques to enhance creativity and problem-solving.

5. Practice Patience:

Avoid rushing decisions when careful thought is required, but act decisively when the moment calls for it.

Example: A firefighter evaluates risks quickly during an emergency but remains calm under pressure.

Everyday Example of a Mastered Mindset

You're deciding on a significant career change. By gathering data, reflecting on your values, considering long-term effects, and consulting trusted advisors, you confidently make a decision that aligns with both your goals and well-being.

Common Pitfalls in Mindset Mastery

1. Overthinking Decisions:

Focusing excessively on perfection delays necessary action.

2. Reacting Emotionally:

Allowing temporary emotions to dominate leads to regretful choices.

3. Ignoring Growth Opportunities:

Avoiding challenges out of fear limits personal and professional development.

Takeaway

Mastering your mindset is the key to becoming a great decision-maker. By cultivating habits like reflection, balance, curiosity, and patience, you can navigate life's challenges with confidence, resilience, and clarity.

Conclusion: The AI Perspective

Decision-making is an art shaped by human emotions, instincts, and experiences. But what if you could approach decisions with the precision and adaptability of artificial intelligence?

Beyond Instinct: How Thinking Like an AI Can Reshape Human Decisions

Humans often lean on instinct and emotions — powerful tools evolved for survival. Yet, in today's complex world, these tools can sometimes fail us, leading to biases, snap judgments, and regrettable choices. Thinking like an AI doesn't mean erasing instinct—it means augmenting it with clarity, logic, and adaptability.

Here's how adopting an AI-inspired approach can reshape your decisions:

1. Focus on Data Over Assumptions:

AI analyzes facts, patterns, and probabilities, bypassing emotional shortcuts. Similarly, you can ground your choices in evidence, challenging assumptions and seeking clarity.

Example: Instead of assuming a decision is risky, gather data to assess the actual likelihood of success or failure.

2. Continuously Learn and Iterate:

AI refines itself with every input, improving over time. You can do the same by reflecting on outcomes, learning from mistakes, and applying those lessons to future decisions.

Example: Treating each failure as feedback turns setbacks into stepping stones for success.

3. Balance Speed and Precision:

AI excels at both rapid responses and deliberate analysis, depending on the situation. Adopting this dual mode allows you to act decisively when needed and think deeply when stakes are high.

Example: Use quick rules for routine choices and reserve thoughtful frameworks for strategic ones.

4. Embrace Objectivity with Empathy:

AI evaluates options without bias, but as a human, you can add empathy to the equation. Blending objectivity with compassion ensures that your decisions serve both logic and humanity.

Example: A leader uses data to evaluate a restructuring plan but also considers its emotional impact on employees.

By thinking like an AI, you transcend instinct while keeping the heart of human decision-making intact. It's not about replacing what makes you human — it's about elevating your abilities with tools of precision and adaptability.

Wisdom for the Decision-Maker's Journey

As you navigate life's twists and turns, remember these parting lessons:

1. Clarity is Key:

Clear decisions come from asking the right questions and seeking meaningful answers. When in doubt, simplify the problem to its core.

2. Balance Logic and Emotion:

Great decisions honor both your rational mind and emotional heart. Trust data, but listen to your intuition when it's rooted in experience.

3. Focus on the Long Term:

Short-term wins can feel gratifying, but meaningful success often requires patience and persistence. Keep your eyes on the bigger picture.

4. Learn, Adapt, and Evolve:

No decision is the final word. Each choice is a step forward—an opportunity to refine, improve, and make better decisions tomorrow.

5. Empower Others:

Decisions aren't made in isolation. Seek perspectives, collaborate, and trust others to contribute their strengths to shared goals.

The decision-making journey is not a straight path; it's a dynamic process shaped by reflection, action, and continuous learning. You now hold 100 strategies designed to sharpen your thinking, strengthen your resolve, and guide your choices. But the power to apply them lies in your hands.

Your best decisions aren't just ahead of you—they're within you, waiting to be realized. Take the first step boldly, with clarity, curiosity, and conviction.

Appendix A: Quick Reference Guide to 100 Strategies for Choosing Wisely When Human Instinct Fails

This appendix offers a short description of all 100 strategies, making it easy to recap the various models.

Part I: Foundations of Smart Decision-Making

1. **The Science of Choice:** Why human instincts often misfire.
2. **Logic vs. Emotion:** Finding the balance.
3. **The Anatomy of a Decision:** Understanding the process.
4. **The Role of Bias:** Identifying your blind spots.
5. **The Power of Awareness:** Recognizing when instinct falters.
6. **The AI Advantage:** Thinking beyond human intuition.
7. **Decision-Making in the Modern World:** Challenges and opportunities.
8. **Defining Success in Decision-making:** Clarifying what a "good decision" means.
9. **The Decision-Making Blueprint:** 5 steps for better choices.
10. **Adaptability Matters:** Why no strategy works in every situation.

Part II: Mental Models for Superior Thinking

11. **First Principles Thinking:** Start from the ground up.
12. **Occam's Razor:** Simplify the complex.
13. **The Pareto Principle:** Focus on the vital few.
14. **Second-Order Thinking:** Anticipating ripple effects.
15. **Inversion:** Solve problems by working backward.
16. **Opportunity Cost:** What are you giving up?
17. **The Eisenhower Matrix:** Prioritize tasks for clarity.
18. **Bayesian Thinking:** Update decisions with new evidence.
19. **Regret Minimization:** Plan for long-term peace of mind.
20. **The Fermi Approach:** Estimate the unmeasurable.

Part III: Strategies to Overcome Cognitive Biases

21. **Anchoring Bias:** How to break free from first impressions.
22. **Confirmation Bias:** Seek disconfirming evidence.
23. **Availability Heuristic:** Look beyond the obvious examples.
24. **Sunk Cost Fallacy:** Let go of lost causes.
25. **Overconfidence Bias:** A dose of humility strengthens decisions.
26. **Framing Effect:** Reframe the problem for new perspectives.
27. **Loss Aversion:** Stop letting fear dictate your choices.
28. **Hindsight Bias:** Learn, don't judge the past.
29. **Groupthink:** Think independently in a crowd.
30. **Dunning-Kruger Effect:** Recognize when you don't know enough.

Part IV: Tools and Techniques for Rational Decision-Making

31. **The Decision Tree:** Map out your options.
32. **The Six Thinking Hats:** Approach problems from multiple angles.
33. **SWOT Analysis:** Weigh strengths, weaknesses, opportunities, and threats.
34. **Weighted Scoring:** Assign value to your priorities.
35. **Scenario Planning:** Prepare for every "what if."
36. **Pre-Mortem Analysis:** Imagine your decision failing—then fix it.
37. **Monte Carlo Simulation:** Model uncertainty for better predictions.
38. **Decision Matrices:** Simplify complex choices.
39. **Pro/Con Lists Done Right:** Add context to your lists.
40. **Heuristic Shortcuts:** Use them wisely to save time.

Part V: Emotional Intelligence in Decision-Making

41. **Self-Regulation:** Mastering emotional control.
42. **Empathy and Decisions:** Understand how others feel.
43. **The Role of Intuition:** When to trust your gut.

44. **Dealing with Decision Fatigue:** Stay sharp under pressure.

45. **Stress-Reduction Techniques:** Think clearly in chaos.

46. **The Pause Principle:** When in doubt, wait.

47. **Handling Regret:** Move forward gracefully.

48. **Mindfulness Practices:** Focus your mind for better outcomes.

49. **Cultivating Resilience:** Bounce back from failure.

50. **Making Peace with Uncertainty:** Embrace the unknown.

Part VI: Group and Team Decision-Making

51. **Consensus-Building:** Aligning diverse opinions.

52. **Avoiding Power Dynamics:** Keep decisions fair.

53. **The Wisdom of Crowds:** Leverage group intelligence.

54. **The Delphi Technique:** Structured collaboration for complex problems.

55. **Role Assignment:** Clarity in group responsibilities.

56. **Conflict Resolution Skills:** Handle disagreements productively.

57. **Decision Mapping for Teams:** Visualize shared choices.

58. **Encouraging Constructive Dissent:** Let disagreement improve decisions.

59. **Combating Group Polarization:** Keep discussions balanced.

60. **Accountability in Groups:** Commit to follow-through.

Part VII: Strategic Thinking for Long-Term Success

61. **Game Theory Basics:** Anticipate others' moves.

62. **The Long View:** Align today's choices with future goals.

63. **Scenario Thinking:** Plan for multiple futures.

64. **Red Teaming:** Challenge your own decisions.

65. **Bets and Odds:** Think probabilistically.

66. **Competitive Analysis:** Understand rivals' strategies.

67. **The Timing Factor:** Act at the right moment.

68. **Avoiding Analysis Paralysis:** Know when to stop thinking.

69. **The Power of Experimentation:** Test your choices.

70. **Strategic Patience:** Wait for the right opportunities.

Part VIII: Everyday Decision-Making

71. **Choosing Careers:** Aligning passion and practicality.

72. **Financial Decisions:** Invest in what matters.

73. **Time Management:** Make every hour count.

74. **Health Choices:** Decisions that build well-being.

75. **Relationship Decisions:** Balancing logic and emotion.

76. **Parenting with Purpose:** Decision-making for families.

77. **Buying Smart:** Evaluate big purchases wisely.

78. **Where to Live:** Assess location choices effectively.

79. **Handling Crises:** Make decisions under pressure.

80. **The Minimalist Mindset:** Fewer choices, better outcomes.

Part IX: Advanced Decision-Making

81. **Cognitive Load Management:** Avoid mental overload.

82. **Learning from Failure:** Turn mistakes into strategies.

83. **Bias Audits:** Regularly review your thinking.

84. **The Power of Small Wins:** Build momentum.

85. **Combining Data and Intuition:** Balance the best of both worlds.

86. **Meta-Decisions:** How to decide how to decide.

87. **Information Overload:** Sift through noise for clarity.

88. **Decision Journals:** Track and refine your process.

89. **When to Delegate:** Let others decide for you.

90. **Balancing Rationality and Creativity:** Solve problems innovatively.

91. **The Decision-Making Code:** Develop your guiding principles.
92. **Consistency Over Perfection:** Prioritize progress.
93. **Feedback Loops:** Learn and improve continuously.
94. **Self-Awareness Practices:** Stay tuned to your patterns.
95. **The Experimenter's Mindset:** Approach life as a lab.
96. **Reverse Engineering Success:** Learn from role models.
97. **Embracing Complexity:** Thrive in uncertain environments.
98. **The Continuous Learner:** Stay curious and adaptive.
99. **Legacy Decisions:** Thinking beyond your lifetime.
100. **Master Your Mindset:** The habits of great decision-makers.

Appendix B: 100 Strategies for Choosing Wisely by Category

This appendix organizes all 100 strategies into intuitive categories, making it easier to find the tools you need for specific challenges.

Foundations of Smart Decision-Making

- The Science of Choice
- Logic vs. Emotion
- The Anatomy of a Decision
- The Role of Bias
- The Power of Awareness
- The AI Advantage
- Decision-Making in the Modern World
- Defining Success in Decision-making
- The Decision-Making Blueprint
- Adaptability Matters

Mental Models for Superior Thinking

- First Principles Thinking
- Occam's Razor
- The Pareto Principle
- Second-Order Thinking
- Inversion
- Opportunity Cost
- The Eisenhower Matrix:
- Bayesian Thinking
- Regret Minimization
- The Fermi Approach

Strategies to Overcome Cognitive Biases

- Anchoring Bias
- Confirmation Bias
- Availability Heuristic
- Sunk Cost Fallacy
- Overconfidence Bias
- Framing Effect
- Loss Aversion
- Hindsight Bias
- Groupthink
- Dunning-Kruger Effect

Tools and Techniques for Rational Decision-Making

- The Decision Tree
- The Six Thinking Hats
- SWOT Analysis
- Weighted Scoring
- Scenario Planning
- Pre-Mortem Analysis
- Monte Carlo Simulation
- Decision Matrices
- Pro/Con Lists Done Right
- Heuristic Shortcuts

Emotional Intelligence in Decision-Making

- Self-Regulation
- Empathy and Decisions
- The Role of Intuition
- Dealing with Decision Fatigue
- Stress-Reduction Techniques
- The Pause Principle
- Handling Regret
- Mindfulness Practices
- Cultivating Resilience
- Making Peace with Uncertainty

Group and Team Decision-Making

- Consensus-Building
- Avoiding Power Dynamics
- The Wisdom of Crowds
- The Delphi Technique
- Role Assignment
- Conflict Resolution Skills
- Decision Mapping for Teams
- Encouraging Constructive Dissent
- Combating Group Polarization
- Accountability in Groups

Strategic Thinking for Long-Term Success

- Game Theory Basics
- The Long View
- Scenario Thinking
- Red Teaming
- Bets and Odds
- Competitive Analysis
- The Timing Factor
- Avoiding Analysis Paralysis
- The Power of Experimentation
- Strategic Patience

Everyday Decision-Making

- Choosing Careers
- Financial Decisions
- Time Management
- Health Choices
- Relationship Decisions
- Parenting with Purpose

- Buying Smart
- Where to Live
- Handling Crises
- The Minimalist Mindset

- Cognitive Load Management
- Learning from Failure
- Bias Audits
- The Power of Small Wins
- Combining Data and Intuition
- Meta-Decisions
- Information Overload
- Decision Journals
- When to Delegate
- Balancing Rationality and Creativity

- The Decision-Making Code
- Consistency Over Perfection
- Feedback Loops
- Self-Awareness Practices
- The Experimenter's Mindset
- Reverse Engineering Success
- Embracing Complexity
- The Continuous Learner
- Legacy Decisions
- Master Your Mindset

Appendix C: Practice Scenarios – Applying Decision-Making Models

Below are 10 scenarios designed to help you practice and apply the decision-making strategies covered in this book. Each scenario challenges you to analyze the situation, identify key factors, and use the right models or tools to arrive at a thoughtful solution.

Scenario 1: The Career Crossroads

Situation:

You've been offered a new job that pays significantly more but requires frequent travel and longer hours, reducing time with family. Your current role offers balance but limited growth opportunities.

Challenge:

Use **The Decision-Making Blueprint** to evaluate the pros and cons, define success metrics (financial stability vs. family time), and make a value-aligned choice.

Scenario 2: A Startup Dilemma

Situation:

As the founder of a tech startup, you're debating whether to prioritize launching a minimally viable product (MVP) quickly or delay the launch to add more features. Your competitors are moving fast, but your product could stand out with extra development time.

Challenge:

Apply **The Pareto Principle** and **The Timing Factor** to determine which features provide the most value and whether speed outweighs perfection in this decision.

Scenario 3: The Vacation Vote

Situation:

Your family is divided on where to spend the holidays. Half want a relaxing beach vacation, while the other half prefer an adventurous hiking trip. Everyone wants a say, and tension is rising.

Challenge:

Use **Consensus-Building** and **The Eisenhower Matrix** to navigate conflicting priorities and find a balanced solution that accommodates key desires without compromising the experience.

Scenario 4: The Investment Quandary

Situation:

You've saved $20,000 and are deciding between three options: (1) investing in stocks, (2) starting a small business, or (3) paying off student debt. Each option has trade-offs in terms of risk, return, and long-term benefits.

Challenge:

Apply **Opportunity Cost** and **Bayesian Thinking** to evaluate the probabilities and outcomes of each option, ensuring your choice aligns with both financial goals and risk tolerance.

Scenario 5: The Team Decision Trap

Situation:

You're leading a project team that can't agree on the direction of a critical initiative. Some members support a safe, proven approach, while others advocate for an innovative but riskier strategy. The deadline is fast approaching, and the group is stuck.

Challenge:

Apply **Encouraging Constructive Dissent** and **Red Teaming** to explore all viewpoints, challenge assumptions, and foster productive collaboration for a unified decision.

Scenario 6: The Overwhelmed Shopper

Situation:

You're buying a new laptop but feel paralyzed by the countless options. There are dozens of brands, price points, and technical specs to consider, and you're worried about making the wrong choice.

Challenge:

Use **Heuristic Shortcuts** and **The Fermi Approach** to simplify the decision-making process, focusing on essential features and quickly estimating what meets your needs.

Scenario 7: The Ethical Dilemma

Situation:

At work, you discover that a trusted colleague is misreporting hours, inflating their overtime claims. Reporting this might strain your relationship, but staying silent could compromise your integrity and the company's trust in you.

Challenge:

Apply **The Pause Principle** to reflect, and use **First Principles Thinking** to evaluate the ethical and practical implications of your options before taking action.

Scenario 8: The Health Fork

Situation:

Your doctor recommends making lifestyle changes to reduce stress and improve your health, but there are many options: a new fitness routine, mindfulness practices, or a stricter diet. You're unsure where to start and worry about sustaining long-term commitment.

Challenge:

Use **Regret Minimization** to focus on what future-you would appreciate most, and adopt **The Minimalist Mindset** to prioritize small, sustainable steps toward health improvement.

Scenario 9: The Friendship Fallout

Situation:

A close friend has upset you by repeatedly canceling plans at the last minute. You're torn between addressing the issue or letting it go, worried that confronting them might damage the friendship further.

Challenge:

Apply **Empathy and Decisions** to understand their perspective, and use **Conflict Resolution Skills** to approach the conversation constructively while safeguarding the relationship.

Scenario 10: The Uncertain Future

Situation:

You've been offered an opportunity to move to a new city for a promotion, but it's a leap into the unknown. You're excited about the career growth but unsure about leaving behind your current support system, lifestyle, and comfort zone.

Challenge:

Use **Scenario Thinking** to explore different outcomes and **The Long View** to align your decision with long-term personal and professional goals.

1. **Analyze the Problem:** Identify key factors influencing the decision.
2. **Choose a Model:** Apply relevant strategies from the book to approach the challenge.
3. **Reflect on Outcomes:** Consider how different approaches would affect your choice and what you would do differently next time.

These scenarios are your lab for honing decision-making skills. Take your time, test your strategies, and build the confidence to tackle real-world challenges with clarity and purpose.

Appendix D: Decision-Making Checklist

Use this checklist to simplify and structure your decision-making process. Each step ensures clarity, alignment with your goals, and better outcomes.

1. Define the Decision Clearly
- ○ Write a one-sentence description of the choice you need to make. (**First Principles Thinking**)
- ○ Break complex decisions into smaller, more manageable parts. (**Problem Decomposition**)
- ○ Ensure the decision focuses on solving the actual problem, not just a symptom. (**Root Cause Analysis**)

2. Identify Your Goals
- ○ Determine what success looks like for you. (**The Long View**)
- ○ Rank your goals by priority: What's a must-have vs. a nice-to-have? (**The Eisenhower Matrix**)
- ○ Align the decision with your values to ensure long-term satisfaction. (**Regret Minimization**)

3. List All Options
- ○ Brainstorm all possible paths, even those that seem risky or unconventional. (**Divergent Thinking**)
- ○ Include a "do nothing" option to assess the cost of inaction. (**Opportunity Cost**)
- ○ Use a mind map or flowchart to visualize options and their connections. (**Decision Mapping**)

4. Evaluate Assumptions
- ○ Identify hidden assumptions driving your decision. (**Critical Thinking**)
- ○ Ask "Why?" repeatedly to challenge assumptions and reach the core truth. (**First Principles Thinking**)
- ○ Cross-check assumptions with reliable data or external perspectives. (**Bayesian Thinking**)

5. Gather Relevant Information
- ○ Research facts, trends, and expert opinions to support your decision. (**Data-Driven Decision Making**)
- ○ Identify gaps in your knowledge and actively seek answers. (**Cognitive Load Management**)
- ○ Avoid information overload by focusing on the most relevant data. (**Heuristic Shortcuts**)

6. Consider First Principles
- ○ Strip the problem down to its most fundamental truths. (**First Principles Thinking**)
- ○ Build solutions from these essentials, ignoring conventional norms. (**Challenging Assumptions**)
- ○ Focus on "what must be true" rather than "what's always been done." (**Inversion**)

7. Weigh Pros and Cons
- ○ List the benefits and risks of each option in a simple table. (**Cost-Benefit Analysis**)
- ○ Use the Pareto Principle to focus on the 20% of factors that drive 80% of results. (**Pareto Analysis**)
- ○ Include both tangible (financial) and intangible (emotional) factors. (**Weighted Decision Matrix**)

8. Anticipate Ripple Effects
- ○ Map out second- and third-order consequences of each choice. (**Second-Order Thinking**)
- ○ Think about who or what will be affected beyond the immediate outcome. (**Stakeholder Analysis**)
- ○ Consider unintended consequences or hidden risks. (**Scenario Thinking**)

9. Factor in Emotions
- ○ Reflect on how each option aligns with your gut feelings. (**The Role of Intuition**)
- ○ Use mindfulness to separate temporary emotions from long-term priorities. (**Self-Regulation**)
- ○ Ensure emotional reactions don't overpower evidence-based reasoning. (**Balancing Rationality and Emotion**)

10. Challenge Biases
- ○ Identify any cognitive biases at play, such as confirmation bias or anchoring. (**Bias Audits**)
- ○ Seek disconfirming evidence to challenge your initial preference. (**Confirmation Bias Check**)
- ○ Involve a neutral third party to provide an unbiased perspective. (**Encouraging Constructive Dissent**)

11. Use the 10-10-10 Rule
- Ask how this decision will feel in 10 days: Is it urgent or fleeting? (**The Pause Principle**)
- Consider its impact in 10 months: Does it align with your mid-term goals? (**Scenario Thinking**)
- Reflect on its consequences in 10 years: Is this choice sustainable or meaningful? (**The Long View**)

12. Ask for Feedback
- Share your options with trusted mentors, peers, or stakeholders. (**Consensus-Building**)
- Use open-ended questions to explore new perspectives. (**Active Listening**)
- Consider feedback as input, not as the final word, to maintain ownership of your decision. (**Red Teaming**)

13. Test the Worst-Case Scenario
- Imagine the worst possible outcome for each option. Can you handle it? (**Risk Management**)
- Use decision trees to calculate probabilities and mitigate risks. (**Bayesian Thinking**)
- Ask, "How could I recover if the worst happens?" (**Resilience Building**)

14. Sleep on It
- Give yourself time to process the decision and let subconscious insights surface. (**The Pause Principle**)
- Journal your thoughts before and after the break to identify any shifts in perspective. (**Decision Journals**)
- If the urgency allows, revisit the decision with fresh eyes the next day. (**Stress-Reduction Techniques**)

15. Commit and Act
- Make a firm decision and avoid second-guessing unless new evidence arises. (**Regret Minimization**)
- Break your choice into actionable steps to build momentum. (**Small Wins Approach**)
- Communicate your decision clearly to those it affects, ensuring alignment and accountability. (**Accountability in Groups**)

16. Review the Outcome
- Reflect on the decision's results: Did it meet your expectations? (**Feedback Loops**)
- Analyze what worked and what didn't to refine future decisions. (**Learning from Failure**)
- Document lessons learned to create a personal decision-making guide. (**Decision Journals**)

Pro Tip: Keep this expanded checklist close to ensure you apply the right strategies to every decision. With practice, these steps will become second nature, sharpening your clarity and confidence in any situation.

Here's another book by Quinn Voss that you might like